NEW ZEALAND
PLANT FINDER

Compiled by
Meg Gaddum

David Bateman

To my mother Dinks Gaddum

First published in 1997 by
David Bateman Ltd, 30 Tarndale Grove,
Albany, Auckland, New Zealand

Copyright © Meg Gaddum, 1997
Copyright © David Bateman Ltd, 1997

ISBN 1 86953 375 5

Cover photograph of *Sedum* courtesy of Bob Wishart
Cover design by Errol McLeary
Printed by Australian Print Group

Contents

Note to users from the compiler

As the compiler of this book, I have made every effort to supply the correct data. I cannot guarantee, however, that the plant names given by nurseries always correspond with the plants actually listed in this book. That responsibility rests with the nursery.

While every effort has been made to check the accuracy of the information, in a book of this size errors and omissions will, inevitably, occur and while I humbly apologise for any mistakes that may have been made and inconvenience that may have been caused, I do not accept responsibility for any concequences that may arise from such errors.

Also, the nature of the nursery industry means that I do not in any way guarantee that a nursery is still able to supply the plants listed by them in this book. To avoid disappointment, I suggest that you always:

Contact the nursery before visiting or ordering

Introduction

About the *New Zealand Plant Finder*

This book contains over 22,000 plant names and details of the nurseries that stock them. It was compiled from the catalogues and lists supplied by nurseries throughout New Zealand. Over 400 nurseries were invited by letter to submit their stock lists. The nurseries targeted were retail nurseries who sold on site and/or by mail order. Wholesale nurseries (those that do not sell direct to the public) and garden centres that do not publish a regular catalogue and do not propagate their own material are not included in this book.

My main objective was that this book should be easy to use by all gardeners. Firstly, therefore, the botanical names are adhered to except when it became clear that it would be easier for the user if a common name was used to group classes of plants together or the botanical species name is rarely used. For example, the Yen Ben lemon is listed as Citrus, lemon Yen Ben, and the crabapple floribunda is listed as Malus crabapple floribunda so that all the crabapples are grouped together. Secondly, common names are included where they were given by nurseries.

It is also hoped that the *New Zealand Plant Finder* helps to put gardeners in touch with nurserymen. It does not offer value judgements on the nurseries or the plants listed, nor intend any reflection on any nursery or plant not listed.

How to use this book

The plants are listed alphabetically with codenames of the nurseries stocking them listed beneath. If you only know the common name of the plant you want, then the Common Names Index at the back of the book may help. This index was compiled from common names supplied by nurseries.

Look up the nursery codenames in the Nursery Index, also at the back of the book, for addresses and other contact details. Suffixes to nursery codenames:

means seed
S   means scion wood
C   means cuttings

I have used the *Royal Horticultural Society Plant Finder* (UK) as a reference text for names and spelling.

If you cannot find a plant, please look through the entire Genus (plant family), as it may be listed by using a more complete name. If a plant has a reference to an updated name ("now") or to an old name ("was") then look also under that other name for more sources. Nurseries are listed under the name they used for the plant.

Some plants have no name supplied, just a brief description. If you feel you know the name of the plant, please contact the nursery listed.

(v) denotes the plant is variegated if no such indication is given by the plant name.

What if you cannot find the plant you want?

This book is compiled from an ongoing, continually updating database which is the InfoGarden plant sourcing business. If you are looking for a plant which is not listed in this book, you may like to send details, plus $2 search fee per plant, to InfoGarden, Box 2237, Gisborne. If the plant is listed in the updated database we will send you the details. If it is not listed, then its name will be entered into the database and you will be contacted as soon as a source becomes known to us.

Feedback please

It is expected that this plant finder will be updated regularly in print, so if you have any feedback about the plants, layout or nurseries please write direct to Meg Gaddum at the above box number.

Plant Directory

Abelia

Edward Goucher
BlueM, Denes

floribunda.
Denes

x grandiflora (Glossy Abelia)
BlueM, Butlr, Kayd, Morgn, Mtato, Pionr, SelGr

x grandiflora Alba
BlueM, Diack, TopTr

x grandiflora Dwarf White
Denes, Mtato

x grandiflora Francis Mason (Golden Abelia)
BlueM

schumanii
BlueM, Butlr, TopTr

Abeliophyllum

distichum
Titok

Abies

alba (European Silver Fir)
Cedar, CPete, NZtr #, WakaC, Wensl

amabilis (Red Fir)
Apple, Cedar, WakaC

balsamea (Balsam Fir)
Apple, BlueM, Cedar, CPete, WakaC

balsamea Blue -imported
WakaC

balsamea f. hudsonia (Dwarf Balsam Fir of Canada)
BlueM, Caves, CPete

balsamea Nana
Cedar

bornmuelleriana (Turkey Fir)
Cedar, CPete, WakaC

bracteata (Bristlecone Fir)
Cedar, CPete, WakaC

cephalonica (Grecian Fir)
Cedar

chensiensis var salouenensis was ernestii s.
Cedar

cilicica (Cilician Fir)
Cedar

concolor (Colorado White Fir)
Apple, BlueM, Cedar, Chedd, CPete, WakaC

concolor Candicans
WakaC

concolor var. lowiana
Cedar

delavayii var forrestii
Cedar

delavayii var. fabri
Cedar

durangensis (Durango Fir)
Cedar

durangensis var. coahuilensis (Coahuilan Fir
Cedar

equi-trojani (Trojan Fir)
Cedar

fargesii
Cedar

firma (Momi Fir)
Cedar, WakaC

fraserii (Fraser's Fir, Sthn Balsam Fir)
Apple, Cedar, CPete, WakaC

grandis (Grand Fir)
Apple, BlueM, Caves, Cedar, CPete

homolepis (Nikko Fir)
Cedar, CPete, WakaC

kawakamii (Taiwan Fir)
Cedar

koreana (Korean Fir)
Apple, BlueM, Cedar, CPete, WakaC

lasiocarpa (Subalpine Fir)
Cedar, CPete, WakaC

magnifica (Red Fir)
CPete, WakaC

nordmanniana (Caucasian Fir)
Cedar, WakaC

nordmanniana Ambrolauri
Cedar

nordmanniana x forrestii
Cedar

pindrow (West Himalayan Fir)
Cedar

pinsapo (Spanish Fir)
Apple, Caves, Cedar, CPete, WakaC, Wensl

pinsapo Glauca (Blue Spanish Fir)
BlueM, Cedar, WakaC

procera (Noble Fir)
Apple, Caves, Cedar, CPete, WakaC

procera Glauca (Blue Noble Fir)
Cedar

religiosa (Sacred Fir)
Cedar

sachalinensis (Sakhalin Fir)
Cedar, CPete, WakaC

sibirica (Siberian Fir)
Cedar, WakaC

spectabilis (Himalayan Fir)
Cedar

veitchii (Veitch Fir)
Cedar, CPete, WakaC

vejarii (Vegar Fir)
Cedar, WakaC

Abutilon

arborea
Parva

Ashford Red
Woodl

Deep Rose
Denes

x Defiance
Hackf

Golden Fleece
Denes, Hackf

x hybridum yellow form
Ormon, TopTr

x hybridum Albus
Hackf

x hybridum Keiller's Surprise
BlueM

x hybridum pink
Parva

x hybridum red form
BlueM, Ormon

x hybridum San Francisco Pink
Hackf

x hybridum white
Denes, Ormon, TopTr

Insigne
>Woodl

maroon fl
>MillH

megapotamicum
>BlueM, Ormon, Telfa, TopTr

vitifolium
>AynDa, BlueM, Denes, Dream, Nikau, Parva, Vall #

vitifolium Album
>BlueM, Denes, Nikau, Parva, Vall #

vitifolium Blue Bells
>Parva

Acacia

acuminata (Raspberry Jam Wattle)
>Matwh

baileyana (Cootamundra/Golden Wattle)
>BlueM, Burbk, Ford, Hewsn, Kayd, Matwh, Morgn, Mtato, NZtr #, Pionr, Reic #, SouWo

baileyana purpurea (Purple Leaf Wattle)
>BlueM, Burbk, Hewsn, Matwh, Morgn, NZtr #, Pionr, Reic #

binervia was A. glaucescens
>Ref

botrycephala (Sunshine Wattle)
>Reic #

brownii
>Reic #

cardiophylla (Wyalong Wattle)
>BlueM, NZtr #, Pionr

cultriformis (Knife-leaf Wattle)
>NZtr #, Reic #

cyanophylla now A. saligna.
>Ref

dealbata (Silver Wattle)
>BlueM, Chedd, Diack, Ford, Hewsn, Koan, Matai, Matwh, Morgn, Mtato, NZtr #, Pionr, SouWo, WakaC

decora (Graceful Wattle)
>Reic #

decurrens (Green Wattle,Early Black Wattle)
>Mtato, NZtr #, Pionr, Reic #

elata (Cedar Wattle)
>Matwh, NZtr #, Reic #

falciformis (Hickory Wattle)
>Matwh, NZtr #

farnesiana (Perfume Wattle)
>Reic #

fimbriata (Fringed Wattle)
>Pionr, Reic #

floribunda (Sallow/Sally Wattle, Gossamer Wattle)
>Burbk, Ford, Kayd, McKe, Morgn, Mtato, NZtr #, Pionr

glaucescens now A. binervia
>Reic #

iteaphylla (Flinders Range Wattle)
>Pionr

iteaphylla weeping form
>Reic #

longifolia (Sydney Golden Wattle)
>Ford, Matwh, McKe, Mtato, NZtr #, Pionr

mearnsii (Black Wattle)
>Ford, Matwh, Mtato, NZtr #, Pionr, SouWo

melanoxylon (Tasmanian Blackwood)
>Chedd, Diack, Ford, Hewsn, Matai, Matwh, McKe, Morgn, Mtato, NZtr #, Pionr, PuhaN, Reic #, SouWo, Terra

mollissima
>Reic #

pendula (Weeping Myall)
>TopTr

podalyriifolia (Queensland Silver Wattle)
>Reic #

pravissima (Ovens Wattle, Alpine Wattle)
>BlueM, Burbk, Diack, Ford, Hewsn, Matai, Morgn, Mtato, NZtr #, Pionr, Reic #, SouWo

pycnantha (Golden Wattle)
>NZtr #, Reic #

retinoides (Swamp Wattle, Werilda Wattle)
>Mtato

rubida (Red Stemmed Wattle)
>Matai, Mtato, NZtr #, Pionr, SouWo

saligna syn cyanophylla (Golden Wreath Wattle WA Weeping Wattle)
>Reic #

sophorae (Coastal Wattle)
>Ford, Matwh, Mtato, Pionr

suaveolens (Sweet-scented Wattle)
>NZtr #, Reic #

transluscens
>Reic #

verniciflua (Varnish Wattle
>NZtr #

verticillata Rewa (Rice's Wattle, Prickly Moses)
>BlueM

Acaena

aridula
>JoyPl

caesiiglauca (Glaucous Piripiri)
>JoyPl, Orati, Terra

fissistipula (Piripiri)
>Orati

inermis (Piripiri)
>Orati, Pgeon

inermis Purpurea (Purple Piripiri)
>CottP, Gordn, Looij, Orang, Orati, Otepo, Pgeon, Telfa, Terra, Trolh

microphylla (Scarlet Piripiri)
>CottP, Orati, Ormon, Terra

novae-zelandiae (Piripiri)
>Orati

pallida
>Terra

Acalypha

varieties (Chenille Plants)
>LakeN

godeseffiana Heterophylla
>LakeN

marginata
>Frans

wilkesiana Hoffmanii

LakeN

Acanthus

balcanicus

Parva

caroli alexandri

BayBl, JoyPl, Peak

Hollards Gold

JoyPl

mollis

Ashto, Dream, KeriP,
MaraN, MillH, Pkrau,
Reic #, Sweet, Telfa

mollis Hollards Lemon

MaraN, Telfa

mollis latifolius

Dowde

spinosissimus

MaraN

syriacus

Hackf

Acca

**sellowiana (Feijoa,
Pineapple Guava)**

Chedd, Coatv, McKe,
Pionr, Reic #, SelGr,
TreeC

sellowiana Apollo

Pionr

sellowiana Mammoth

Pionr

sellowiana Triumph

Pionr

sellowiana Unique

Chedd, Mtato

Acer

albopurparascens

Woodl

amplum (Broadleaf Maple)

Apple, Diack, PuhaN

**Autumn Blaze (x freemanii
var Jeffersred)**

Denes

**buergerianum (Trident
Maple)**

Apple, Burbk, Diack,
Peele, PuhaN, Pukho,
TopTr, Wensl

campbellii

Caves

campbellii ssp wilsonii

Caves, TopTr

**campestre (Field/Hedge
Maple)**

Apple, Peele, PuhaN,
Wensl

**capillipes (Red Snakebark
Maple)**

Apple, Chedd, Hewsn

**cappadocium
(Caucasian/Coliseum Maple**

BlueM, PuhaN

cappadocium Aureum

BlueM, Denes, TopTr

cappadocium Rubrum

Apple, Burbk, Chedd,
Denes, Diack, PuhaN,
Pukho, Wensl

**caudatifolium was A.
kawakamii,
A.morrisonense
(Taiwanese Snakebark
Maple)**

Caves, Diack

**caudatifolium Summer
Surprise**

Caves

circinatum (Vine Maple)

Apple

circinatum x palmatum

Apple

crataegifolium

TopTr

**davidii (Snakebark Maple,
Davids Maple)**

Diack, Ford

davidii George Forrest

Denes, Pukho

Esk Flamingo

Caves

fabri

Caves

freemanii Autumn Blaze

Pukho

**ginnala now A.tartaricum
ginnala**

Burbk, PuhaN

**glabrum var douglasii
(Brit.Columbian Mtn
Maple)**

Apple

griseum (Paperbark Maple

Apple, BlueM, Caves,
Chedd, Denes, Diack,
Dove, EasyB, Hackf,
MJury, Ormon, Peele,
PuhaN, Pukho, TopTr

grosseri (Grosser's Maple)

Apple, Dove, PuhaN

**grosseri hersii (Hers
Snakebark Maple)**

Chedd, Dove, YakuN

**japonicum Aconitifolium
(Fern-leaf Maple)**

Denes

**japonicum aureum now
shirasawanum a.**

Denes, Pukho

japonicum Green Cascade

Caves, Denes, Pukho

**japonicum Vitifolium
(Grape-leaf Maple)**

Denes

leucoderme

Caves

**macrophyllum (Big Leaf
Maple)**

Apple, Caves, Dove

miyabei

Caves

**monspessulanum
(Montpellier Maple)**

PuhaN

**morrisonensis now
caudatifolium**

Pukho

negundo (Box Elder)

Apple, BlueM, Burbk,
Chedd, Coatv, Diack,
Dove, Peele, Pionr,
PuhaN, TopTr, Wensl

**negundo
Argenteovariegatum now
n.Variegatum**

Burbk, Chedd, Denes

**negundo Elegans (Golden
Box Elder)**

Burbk, Denes

negundo Flamingo

Burbk, Chedd, Pukho,
TopTr

negundo Kellys Gold

Burbk, Chedd, Coatv,
MJury, Peele, Pionr,
Pukho

negundo Mexicana

MJury

negundo Violaceum

Burbk, Caves, Chedd,
Denes, Peele, Pukho

oliverianum ssp oliveri

TopTr

3

opalus (Italian Maple)

PuhaN

palmata Shaina

Pukho

palmatum (Japanese Maple)

BlueM, Burbk, Chedd, Coatv, EasyB, Mtato, Ormon, Peele, Pionr, PuhaN, Pukho, Terra, Wensl

palmatum atropurpureum

Apple, Chedd, Coatv, Denes, Hackf, Mtato, Peele, PuhaN, Terra

palmatum Beni-komachi (Beautiful Little Red Girl)

Denes, Pukho

palmatum Beni-otake

Denes, Pukho

palmatum Beni-schichihenge

Pukho

palmatum Bloodgood

Coatv, Denes, Pukho

palmatum bronze (Bronze Japanese Maple)

Apple

palmatum Burgundy Lace

Burbk, Denes, Pukho

palmatum Chishio now Shishio

Denes, Pukho

palmatum Crippsii

Coatv, Pukho

palmatum dissectum (Cutleaf Japanese Maple)

Apple, Caves, Coatv, Pionr, PuhaN

palmatum Dissectum Atropurpureum

Hackf, Pionr

palmatum Dissectum Crimson Queen

Coatv, Denes, Pukho, YakuN

palmatum Dissectum Ever Red

Denes, Pukho, SpecT

palmatum Dissectum Filigree

Denes, Pukho

palmatum Dissectum Filigree Red Lace

Pukho

palmatum Dissectum Garnet

Pukho

palmatum Dissectum Lion Heart

Pukho

palmatum Dissectum Palmatifidum (Eagle Claw Maple)

Pukho

palmatum Dissectum Red Dragon

Pukho

palmatum Dissectum Rubrifolium

Pukho

palmatum Dissectum Variegatum

Denes, Pukho

palmatum Dissectum Viridis

Denes, Pukho

palmatum Fireglow

Pukho

palmatum green (small seeds)

Apple

palmatum Kamagata

Pukho

palmatum Katsura

Denes, Pukho

palmatum Linearilobum

Peele, Pukho

palmatum Mikawa Yatsabusa

Pukho

palmatum mixed colours (large seeds)

Apple

palmatum O-kagami

Denes, Pukho

palmatum Omurayama

Pukho

palmatum Osakazuki

Denes, Pukho

palmatum Purpurea

Pukho

palmatum Red Filigree Lace

Caves

palmatum Red Pygmy

Pukho

palmatum Redwings

PuhaN

palmatum Roseomargimatum (Tricolour Maple)

Burbk, Coatv, Denes

palmatum Rubrifolium

Burbk

palmatum Sanguineum

Burbk

palmatum Seiryu

Coatv, Denes, Pukho

palmatum Senkaki (Coral Bark Maple)

Apple, Coatv, Denes, Hackf, Mtato, Pionr, PuhaN, Pukho

palmatum Sherwood Flame

Denes

palmatum Shigitatsu-sawa (Reticulatum Maple)

Pukho

palmatum Shindeshojo (Ruby Leaf Maple)

Burbk, Denes, Pukho

palmatum Shishigashira seedlings

Caves

palmatum Suminagashi

Coatv, Denes, Pukho

palmatum Trompenburg

Denes, Pukho

palmatum Ukon (Green Twig Maple)

Denes

palmatum Viridus

Burbk

pensylvanicum (Goose Foot Maple, Snake Bark Mple)

Apple, TopTr

pentaphyllum

Caves

platanoides (Norway Maple)

Apple, BlueM, Diack, EasyB, Mtato, Peele, Pionr, PuhaN

platanoides Crimson King

Hewsn, Pukho

platanoides Dissectum (Cutleaf Norway Maple)

PuhaN

platanoides Drummondii (v)

Denes, Pukho

platanoides Nigrum (Purple Norway Maple)
Apple, Chedd, Denes, Diack, Dove, Mtato, Ormon, Pionr, PuhaN, TopTr, Wensl

platanoides Palmatifidum
Dove

platanoides Schwedleri
Peele, Pukho

pseudoplatanus (Sycamore)
Apple, Chedd, Coatv, Diack, Dove, EasyB, Ford, Mtato, NZtr #, Peele, Pionr, PuhaN, Pukho

pseudoplatanus Brilliantissimum
Denes, Pukho

pseudoplatanus Eastwoodhill
Pukho

pseudoplatanus Esk Sunset
Denes, Pukho

pseudoplatanus Prinz Hanjery
Chedd, Peele, Pukho

pseudoplatanus Purpureum (Purple Sycamore)
Apple, Burbk, Coatv, Denes, Diack, EasyB, Ford, Peele, Pionr, PuhaN, Wensl

pseudoplatanus variegatum
Diack

rubrum (American Red Maple, Canadian Maple)
Apple, BlueM, Burbk, Chedd, Denes, Diack, Ford, Mtato, Peele, PuhaN, TopTr

rubrum Autumn Glory
Denes

rubrum Columnare
Pukho

rubrum October Glory
Denes

rubrum Red Sunset
TopTr

rubrum Scanlon
Denes, Peele, Pukho, TopTr

rufinerve (Grey-budded Snakebark)
Apple, Denes, Dove, Peele, Wensl

saccharinum (Silver Maple)
Apple, Chedd, Diack, Peele, PuhaN, Pukho, TopTr, Wensl

saccharum (Sugar Maple)
Apple, Caves, Chedd, Diack, Dove, Ford, MJury, Peele, Pionr, PuhaN, Pukho

saccharum ssp nigrum (Mid-west Sugar Maple)
Peele

shirasawanum aureum was japonicum a.
Denes

sikkimensis
Caves

Silver Vein
Caves

Stardust
Caves

tartaricum ssp ginnala seminowii
Hackf

tataricum ssp ginnala (Amur Maple)
Apple, Chedd, PuhaN

tegmentosum (Manchurian Snakebark Maple)
Wensl

truncatum (Shantung Maple)
Caves

truncatum mayrii (Painted Maple)
PuhaN

velutinum var. vanvolxemii
PuhaN

wilsonii (Wilsons Maple)
Denes, PuhaN, YakuN

Achillea

ageratifolia
Pgeon, TRidg

ageratifolia ssp aizoon
Marsh

ageratum was decolorans (Sweet Milfoil, Mace Yarrow, Maudlin)
CottP, Della, Marsh, Mills, Orang, Sweet

ageratum WB Child
Marsh, Pgeon

Anthea
BayBl, CottP, Marsh, Nikau, Parva, Peak, Telfa, Warwk

Apple Blossom
CoFlo, CottP, Marsh, Peak

argentea may be A.clavennae or umbellata or Tanacetum argenteum
Della, Otepo

aurea Grandiflora now A.chrysocoma G (Sweet Nancy)
CottP, Della

clavennae
MaraN

Credo
CottP, Parva, Warwk

decolorans now ageratum
CottP, Della, Mills, Orang, Sweet

Fanal
Marsh

filipendulina (Yellow Yarrow)
Marsh, Orang, Sweet, Telfa

filipendulina Cloth Of Gold
Della, King #, MaraN, Mills, Trans

filipendulina Gold Plate
CottP

filipendulina Parkers Variety
Dream

Fire King
Della

Forncett Beauty
BayBl, CottP, KeriP, MillH

Hope
BayBl, CottP, Della, KeriP, MillH, Sweet, Warwk

Lavender Lace
CottP, KeriP, Parva, Telfa

Lavender Pink
Nikau

Lemon
CoFlo

x lewisii
Nikau, Orang, Pgeon

x lewisii King Edward
MaraN

Martina
BayBl

millefolium Cerise Queen
Ashto, CottP, Della, King #, MillH, Telfa, WaiMa

millefolium Cherry Pie
Della

millefolium Creamy Yellow
Trans

millefolium Custard
Marsh

millefolium lilac pink
Trans

millefolium Pink Beauty
Marsh

millefolium Red Beacon
Della

millefolium Rose Queen
Trans

millefolium Roseum (Red Yarrow)
Orang, Sweet

millefolium Summerpastels
Ashto, MillH

millefolium white (White Yarrow)
Sweet

Moonshine
Mills

Moonwalker
Della, MillH, Sweet

nana
MaraN

nana Lemon
Telfa

Pink Lace
KeriP

ptarmica (Sneezewort)
Orang, Sweet

ptarmica Innocence (Unschuld)
BayBl, BlueM, CottP, Trans

ptarmica The Pearl
Ashto, BayBl, CoFlo, CottP, Della, King #, MillH, Mills, Nikau, Otepo, Parva, Pgeon, Telfa, Trans

rupestris
BayBl, Pgeon

Salmon Beauty
BayBl, CoFlo, CottP, Della, Marsh, Nikau, Trans

x tagatea
Pgeon

The Beacon (Fanal)
BayBl, CoFlo, CottP, MillH, Nikau, Parva, Peak, Sweet, Trans, Warwk

tomentosa (Woolly Yarrow
Ashto, Mills

tomentosa Aurea
MaraN

umbellata
Orang, Ormon, Seasd

Weser River Sandstone
BayBl, CottP, KeriP, Peak, Trans, Warwk

Achimenes

Carmencita
Reic #

Palette mixed
Reic #

Prima Donna
Reic #

Acidanthera

see Gladiolus
Ref

bicolor
DaffA

murielae
Kayd

Aciphylla

aurea (Golden Spaniard, Golden Spear Grass)
KeriP, Mtato, Orati, Parva

colensoi (Spear Grass)
Burbk, Orati

ferox
Wahpa

horrida
Terra

squarrosa (Kurikuri, Spear Grass)
NZtr #, Orati, Terra

Acis

autumnale now Leucojum a.
Ref

Ackama

rosaefolia see Caldcluvia rosifolia
Orati

Acmena

smithii   syn. Eugenia s. (Monkey Apple)
McKe, SpecT

Acnistus

australis now Dunalia a.
Ref

Aconitum

anthora
MaraN

x Arendsii
MaraN

Bressingham Spire
Telfa

carmichaelii (Monkshood)
AynDa, CoFlo, Looij, MaraN, Pgeon, Vall #

lamarkia now lycotonum neopolitanum
Vall #

napellus (Monkshood)
BayBl, CoFlo, JoyPl, MillH, Mills, Orang, Peak, Telfa, Vall #

napellus Album
Vall #

orientale now lycotonum neapolitanum
Telfa

variegated
Sweet

Acorus

calamus (Sweet Flag, Calamus root)
Burbk

calamus Variegatus
Diack, Hains, Sweet, WaiMa, WilAq, WriWa

gramineus Ogon
BayBl, Hains

gramineus Pusillus
Titok

gramineus Variegatus (Japanese Rush , Dwarf Sweet Flag)
BayBl, Diack, KeriP, MillH, Mills, Otepo, WaiMa, WilAq, WriWa

Acradenia

frankliniae
BlueM, Denes, Woodl

Acrocarpus

fraxinifolius (Pink Cedar)
Reic #

Actinidia

chinensis (Kiwifuit)
TreeC

chinensis female Hayward
Chedd

chinensis male
Chedd

kolomikta
CouCl, Denes

Actinodium

**cunninghamii
(Swamp/Albany Daisy)**
Denes, MatNu

Actinostrobus

**pyramidalis (Swan River
Cypress)**
TopTr

Adenandra

**fragrans (Rose China
Flower)**
Denes, MatNu

uniflora (China Flower)
Chedd, Denes, KeriP,
MatNu, Matth, Trans

Adenophora

confusa (Ladybell)
CoFlo

liliifolia Ladybells
Otepo

Adiantum

aethiopicum (Maidenhair)
Orati

cuneatum now raddianum
Reic #

**cuneatum Elegans
(raddianum E.)**
Reic #

**cuneatum Fragrans
(raddianum F.)**
Reic #

Fritz Luthi
Reic #

fulvum
Reic #

Gracillimum
Reic #

hispidulum (Maidenhair)
Orati

**species indoor
(Maidenhair)**
Manna

tenerum scutum
Reic #

Adonis

aestivalis
King #

amurensis
NewlR

Aeonium

arboreum
Ormon

arboreum Atropurpureum
Parva

arboreum Schwarzkopf
Ormon

Aeschynanthus

varieties
LakeN

Aesculus

**x carnea (Red Horse
Chestnut)**
Burbk, Chedd, Coatv,
Denes, Peele, Pionr

x carnea Briotti
Pionr, Pukho, TopTr

**flava was octandra
(Sweet/Yellow Buckeye)**
Caves

**hippocastanum (Horse
Chestnut)**
Apple, BlueM, Burbk,
Chedd, Coatv, Denes,
Diack, Dove, EasyB,
Ford, Hewsn, Mtato,
NZu #, Peele, Pionr,
PuhaN, Reic #, SouWo,
Sweet, Terra, TopTr,
Wensl

hippocastanum Baumanii
Mtato, Pukho

**indica (Indian Horse
Chestnut)**
Apple, Burbk, Chedd,
Diack, Dove, Ford, NZtr
#, Peele, PuhaN, Pukho,
TopTr

indica Sydney Pearce
Chedd, Pukho

x neglectus Erythroblastos
Denes, Pukho

pavia
Burbk, Denes, Mtato,
Pukho

splendens
Mtato, Pukho

Aethionema

coridifolium
MaraN

grandiflorum
Seasd

Agapanthus

Albus Roseus
Margu

Baby Blue
Burbk, Butlr, Diack,
Mills, Morgn, Mtato,
Ormon, Reic #, Seasd,
Telfa, Trans

Blue Boy
Diack, Hackf

Blue Dot
Parva

Blue Skies
Margu

campanulatus
Diack

campanulatus hybrids
Diack

comptonii
AynDa

Crystal Drop
Diack

Flore Plena
Diack

Gayles Lilac
Parva

Getty White
Butlr, Diack, Reic #

Hazy Days
Diack

Headbourne Hybrids
BlueM, Vall #

Ice Queen
MillH

inapertus
Vall #

Isis
Titok

Mid Blue
Vall #

Milky Blue
Nikau, Vall #

Mini Blue
CottP

7

natalensis
Diack

orientalis Blue
Butlr, Diack, Dove,
Margu, Morgn, Mtato,
Nikau, Pionr, Reic #,
Terra

orientalis White
Diack, Dove, Morgn,
Mtato, Nikau, Pionr,
Reic #

Peter Pan
Diack, KeriP, Pionr,
Trolh, Vall #

Purple Cloud
Diack, Margu, Taunt

Snowball
BayBl, Diack, Margu,
Ormon, Taunt

Snowdrops
Egmon, Parva, TRidg

Stormcloud
Diack, Frans, JoyPl,
Nikau, Vall #

Streamline
Ashto, BayBl, Diack,
Egmon, Frans, JoyPl,
Kayd, KeriP, Margu,
MillH, Parva, Peak,
Taunt, Trans

The Giant
Vall #

Tinkerbell (v)
BayBl, CottP, Diack,
Kayd, KeriP, Margu,
Mtato, Ormon

WavyNavy
Margu

white dwf
Trolh

White Ice
Diack, Frans, Margu,
Ormon

Agapetes

buxiifolia
BlueM

hosseana (Red Elf)
BlueM

serpens was Pentapterygium s. (Flame Heath)
BlueM, MJury

smithiana
BlueM, Woodl

Agastache

Alba
Warwk

anisata now A.foeniculum
MaraN, MillH

anisata var Alba now A. foen. Alba
Dream

Blue Spire
KeriP

brittonastrum
Peak, Warwk

cana
Wells

foeniculum was anisata (Anise Hyssop)
Della, King #, Koan #,
Looij, MaraN, Marsh,
Mills, Nikau, Orang,
Sweet, Trolh

foeniculum Alba
Della, Marsh, Orang,
Sweet

lavender blue fls
Trans

Liquorice White
MillH

mexicana (Giant Mexican Hyssop)
Dream

mexicana Champagne
Della, Dream, King #,
MillH, Warwk

nepetoides (Yellow Giant Hyssop)
Mills

rugosa (Korean Mint)
Dream

sp Giant Hyssop
Vall #

White Spike
Sweet

Agathis

australis (Kauri)
Burbk, Cedar, Chedd,
Coatv, CPete, Denes,
Gordn, Matwh, Mtato,
NZtr #, Orati, Pionr,
Terra, Wahpa

vitiensis (Fijian)
Cedar

Agathsoma

ceridifolium
Ether

Agave

americana (Century Plant)
Reic #, Wells

americana variegata
Wells

angustifolia
Reic #

attenuata
Frans, KeriP, Lsendt,
Reic #, SpecT

cerulata nelsonii
JoyPl

filifera
Reic #

filifera type green/white
MJury

palmeri
JoyPl

victoriae regina
Reic #

Ageratum

houstonium
KeriP, Nikau, Trans

Agonis

flexuosa (Willow Myrtle, Peppermint Willow)
Burbk, Chedd, Coatv,
Denes, Frans, Mtato,
Reic #, TopTr

juniperina (Juniper Myrtle
MatNu

juniperina Florists Star
Denes, Matth, Mtato

juniperina Mini Star
Butlr, Denes

Agrimonia

eupatoria (Agrimony)
Della, Mills, Orang,
Sweet

Agropyron

scabrum (Bluegrass)
Orati

Agrostemma

githgo (Corn cockle)
King #

githgo coeli rosea (Wild Corn Cockle)
King #

Ailanthus

altissima (Chinese Tree of Heaven)

Chedd, NZtr #

Ajania

pacifica

Parva, Trans

Ajuga

varieties

Roswd

lobata

Taunt

multicolour

KeriP

Pink and White Elfs

JoyPl

Pink Pewter

Warwk

pyramidalis

CottP, JoyPl, Pgeon, Pkrau

pyramidalis metallica crispa

Parva

pyramidalis Pink Elf

CottP, KeriP, MillH

reptans (Blue Bugle)

Ashto, CottP, Telfa

reptans Alba

BayBl, CottP, MaraN, MillII, Nikau, Oasis, Parva, Telfa, WaiMa, Warwk

reptans atropurpurea

KeriP, Mills, Nikau, Trans, WaiMa

reptans Braunherz

Telfa

reptans Burgundy Glow

Ashto, AynDa, CoFlo

reptans Burgundy Lace

CottP, Nikau, Sweet, Trans

reptans Catlin's Giant

BayBl, Dowde, KeriP, Parva, Peak, Telfa, Trans, Warwk

reptans Jungle Beauty

AynDa, CoFlo, CottP, Hackf, JoyPl, KeriP, MaraN, Marsh, MillH, Mills, Nikau, Oasis, Parva, Peak, Pgeon, Pkrau, Sweet, Trans, WaiMa, Warwk, Wells

reptans Multicolour

CottP, Telfa

reptans Pink Elf

MaraN, Telfa

reptans Purple Torch

BayBl, CottP, KeriP, Oasis, Parva, Peak, Warwk

reptans Purpurea

AynDa, CottP, Looij, MaraN, MillH, Pkrau, Sweet, Telfa

reptans Purpurea Alba

Looij

reptans Silver Carpet

BayBl, CottP, JoyPl, Pgeon

reptans Splash Of Gold

CottP, MillH

reptans Tricolour (Rainbow)

MaraN, Mills, Telfa

reptans Variegata

Ashto, AynDa, CottP, KeriP, Looij

Royalty

CottP, Parva, Peak

Akebia

quinata (Chocolate Vine)

BlueM, CouCl, Denes, Reic #

Alberta

magna

TopTi

Albizia

julibrissin (Persian Silk Tree, Pink Mimosa)

Burbk, Coatv, Frans, Matwh, Morgn, Mtato, NZtr #, Peele, PuhaN, Pukho, Reic #

julibrissin Red Silk

Caves, Denes, SpecT

julibrissin Rosea

Apple, Burbk, Chedd, Denes, Dove, Peele, Pionr, SpecT, TopTr, Wensl

lebbek (Woman's Tongue)

Reic #

lophantha now Paraserianthes l. (Evergreen Silk Tree, Cape Wattle, Plume Albizia)

Morgn, NZtr #, Reic #

Albuca

altissima

Parva

canadensis

AynDa, JoyPl, KeriP, MaraN, MJury

Alcea

Black Beauty

TRidg

ficifolia

Dream

officinalis   now Althea o

AynDa

rosea double mixed (Hollyhock)

Della, King #

rosea single mixed

CoFlo, King #, MillH

rosea Double Apricot

CoFlo

rosea Double Black

Parva

rosea Double Pink

Parva

rosea Double Purple

Parva

rosea Double Salmon

Parva

rosea Double White

Parva

rosea Double Yellow

Parva

rosea majorette Dwarf Majorette   mixed

AynDa, King #

rosea Single Black

CoFlo

rosea single soft lemon

Marsh

rosea var. nigra (Black Hollyhock,Mallow)

AynDa, King #, Mills

rugosa

TRidg

Alchemilla

alpina

MaraN, Pgeon

erythropoda

BayBl, Marsh, MillH, Telfa, TRidg

faeroensis

Oasis

mollis (Ladies Mantle)

Ashto, AynDa, BayBl,
CottP, Dream, Egmon,
JoyPl, Looij, MaraN,
Marsh, NewlR, Nikau,
Oasis, Orang, Otepo,
Parva, Pgeon, Pkrau,
Sweet, Telfa, Trans,
TRidg, Vall #, Warwk

mollis Auslese

Peak

vulgaris

Della, Mills

Alectryon

excelsus (Titoki)

Chedd, Coatv, Denes,
Gordn, Matwh, Mtato,
NZtr #, Orati, Pionr,
Pukho, SpecT, Terra,
Wahpa

Aliceara

Mervyn Grant

AnnM

Alisma

lanceolatum

WaiMa

parviflorum

WilAq

plantago-aquatica (Water Plantain)

Diack, WaiMa, WriWa

plantago-aquatica var.parviflorum

WaiMa

Allamanda

carthatica double fl selection

LakeN

neriifolia yellow trumpet fl

Reic #

Allium

albopilosum now A. christophii

BayBl, Oasis, Taunt

amabile

Pgeon

ampeloprasum (Elephant Garlic)

Koan #, Mills

ampeloprasum Musselburgh (Leek)

MTig #

asconicum (Shallots)

Koan #

carinatum pulchellum

DaffA, KeriP, TRidg

cepa Borettana (Italian Button Onions)

King #

cepa Lelsae Sweet Giant

King #

cepa var. proliforum (Egyptian Tree Onion)

CottP, Della, Koan #,
Marsh, Mills

cepa viriparium (Egyptian Tree Onion)

Orang

cernuum

AynDa, BayBl, TRidg

cernuum Major

Pgeon

christophii was albopilosum

BayBl, DaffA, JoyPl,
Kerer, Oasis, Peak, Telfa

cutflower sp 1.5 m, fl 100-150mm

LeFab

edible mix incl A.amp.,A sativum(purple,white &pink),A.s. Ophioscorodon (Rocambole)etc

MTig

falcifolium

Kerer, Otepo

fistulosum Welsh Onion

King #, Trolh

flavum (Small Yellow Onion)

DaffA, TRidg

flavum minus

NewlR

giganteum

Kayd

glaucum

CottP

hyalinum

DaffA

loratum

Kerer

Lucy Ball

BayBl, JoyPl, Peak

moly (Yellow Onion, Golden Garlic)

BayBl, CottP, DaffA,
JoyPl, Kayd, Kerer,
NewlR, Otepo, Telfa,
VanEe

multiplying leek

Koan #

murryanum

CottP

narcissiflorum

Della

neapolitanum (Naples Garlic)

AynDa, Dream, Kerer,
MaraN

neapolitanum Grandiflorum

Parva

odorum (Chinese Leek)

King #

oreophilum Zwanenburg

Kerer

pulchellum now carinatum p.

Telfa, TRidg, Vall #

Purplette Red Skinned Mini Onion

King #

sativum (Garlic)

Sweet

sativum Dalmatian

Koan #

schoenoprasum (Chives)

CottP, Della, Kayd, King
#, MillH, Mills, Nikau,
Orang, Trans

schubertii

Parva

siculum now Nectaroscordum s.

DaffA

sphaerocephalon (Round-headed Leek)

BayBl, CottP, DaffA,
JoyPl, MaraN, Telfa

toloumonense

Trans

tuberosum (Garlic Chives)

Della, MillH, Mills,
Nikau, Orang, Sweet,
Telfa

uniflorum

Kerer

vineale (Crow Garlic)

Dream

Welsh Onions

Orang

Allocasuarina

stricta was Casuarina s. (Coast/Drooping Sheoak)
Seasd

torulosa was Casuarina t. (Rose Sheoak)
Chedd, Pionr

Allophyllus

abyssinicus (Forest Velvet Allophyllus)
Ether

Alniphyllum

fortunei
Caves

Alnus

acuminata (Andean Alder)
Chedd, Matwh, Peele

acuminata ssp arguta
Hackf

cordata (Italian Alder)
Apple, Burbk, Chedd, Coatv, Denes, Diack, Dove, EasyB, Ford, Matai, Morgn, Mtato, NZtr #, Peele, Pionr, PuhaN, Pukho, SouWo, TopTr, WakaC, Wensl

firma (Japanese Alder)
PuhaN

formosana (Taiwan Alder)
Mtato

glutinosa (European/Black Alder)
Apple, Burbk, Chedd, Coatv, Diack, Dove, Ford, Hewsn, Matai, McKe, Morgn, Mtato, NZtr #, Peele, Pionr, PuhaN, Pukho, SouWo, WakaC

glutinosa Aurea
Caves

glutinosa Imperialis
Caves, TopTr

glutinosa Laciniata
Caves

hirsuta
Apple, Chedd

incana (Grey Alder)
Diack, Ford, Hackf, NZtr #, PuhaN

incana Pendula (Weeping Alder)
Caves, Pukho

inokumae
Apple

japonica
Apple

jorullensis (Evergreen/Mexican Alder)
Burbk, Coatv, Dove, Ford, LanSc, Matwh, McKe, Mtato, Pukho, SpecT

maximowiczii (Hokkaido Mountain Alder)
Diack

nitida (Himalayan Alder)
Apple, Matwh, Pukho, SpecT

rubra (Oregon/Red Alder)
Apple, BlueM, Burbk, Coatv, Diack, Dove, Ford, Hewsn, Mtato, NZtr #, Peele, Pionr, PuhaN, Pukho, SouWo, TopTr, WakaC, Wensl

rubra aurea (Golden Stemmed Red Alder)
Diack, Pukho

serrulata (American Smooth Alder)
Apple, TopTr

x spaethii
Apple

tenuifolia
Apple

viridis
NZtr #

Alocasia

species
Frans

Leaf (vegetable)
Koan

odora (Scented Taro, Elephants Ears)
Lsendt

Palangi (vegetable)
Koan

sanderiana (Elephants Ears)
LakeN

Aloe

aculiata
JoyPl

africana
JoyPl

arborescens
JoyPl, Lsendt, Reic #

barbadensis now A.vera
Orang

candelabrum
Reic #

chinensis
MTig, MTig #

ciliaris
JoyPl, Lsendt, Peak

davyana
Reic #

marolthii
Reic #

plicitalis
JoyPl, MJury, Ormon, Peak

saponaria
JoyPl, Lsendt

spectabilis
JoyPl, Lsendt

spinosissima
Wells

thraskii
Frans, JoyPl, Wells

vera
Manna, Mills, MTig, MTig #, Orang, Sweet

vogtsii
JoyPl

Alonsoa

mixed scarlet to peach pink
Vall #

coral red
Nikau

meridionalis
Oasis

meridionalis Mutisii
Dream

peach
Egmon, KeriP, Nikau, Vall #

pink
Trolh

scarlet red
Nikau, Trolh

warscewiczii Apricot
CottP, KeriP

white
Nikau

Alophia

platensis
TRidg

Aloysia

**triphylla was Lippia
citriodora (Lemon Verbena**
MillH, Mills, Orang,
Pgeon, Trolh

Alpinia

caerulea (Blue Ginger)
Reic #

purpurata (Red Ginger)
Reic #

speciosa now zerumbet
Reic #

zerumbet (Shell Ginger)
Frans, Lsendt

Alseuosmia

macrophylla (Toropapa)
Gordn, Orati

pusilla
Terra

Alstroemeria

Alpha
Parva

aurantiaca
Ashto, Telfa

Awakeri Cream
BayBl

Awakeri Yellow
BayBl

Bridal Pink
BayBl, Parva, Peak, Telfa

Burgundy
BayBl

carminia
JoyPl

clear pink
TRidg

Delta
Parva

Dusky Pink
Egmon, Telfa

English Pink
BayBl

Fireglow
BayBl, Egmon, Peak,
Telfa

golden yellow
Taunt

Hawera
JoyPl, MaraN

hookerii
JoyPl

magnifica
Parva, Telfa

pelegrina Alba
BayBl

pelegrina Rosea
BayBl

Pink Butterfly
Kayd, Parva

Pink Dream
Kayd

Pink Joy
Ormon

Pink Joy Butterfly
JoyPl

psittacina (Parrots Beak)
Ashto

pulchella now psittacina
BayBl, Pgeon, Trans

pulchella Mona Lisa
BayBl, JoyPl

pulchra
Telfa

red
Ormon, Taunt

Red Baron
Parva

soft pink
Taunt

Sunset
BayBl, Parva, Peak

Violet Butterfly
JoyPl

Walter Fleming
BayBl, Egmon, JoyPl,
Peak

Yvette
Parva

Alternanthera

**roseacefolia (Rubra
beetroot -aquatic)**
WaiMa

sessilis
WilAq

**Sessilis Rubra (Aquatic
Beetroot)**
WaiMa

versicolor
LakeN

Althaea

officinalis (Marshmallow)
CoFlo, Della, King #,
Marsh, Mills, Orang,
Sweet

Alyssoides

urticulata Tinkerbells
King #

Alyssum

cuneifolium
Telfa

idaeum
Pgeon

**saxatile (Gold Dust, Sweet
Alyssum)**
Looij, Telfa, TRidg

saxatile Gold Ball
Oasis

saxatile Gold King
BayBl

saxatile Sulphureum
MaraN, Warwk

sphacioticum
Telfa

Amaranthus

**caudatus Red (Love Lies
Bleeding)**
King #, Sweet

**caudatus viridus Green
(Love Lies Bleeding)**
King #, Sweet

**gangeticus Red Amaranth
(Chinese Spinach)**
King #

mixed 3 species
MTig #

Pygmy Torch
Koan #

**tricolour Illumination
(Josephs Coat, Summer
Poinsettia)**
King #

Amaryllis

mixed
Kayd

Beacon
DaffA

belladonna cream form
Trans

belladonna Major
Kayd

hybrid dk rose fl 1m
JoyPl

Amelanchier

**arborea (Downy
Serviceberry)**
Diack

12

canadensis (Shad Bush)
Apple, Chedd, Denes, Diack, Peele, Pionr, Pukho, TopTr

lamarckii (Serviceberry)
Diack, Dove, Pukho, TopTr

ovalis (European Snowy Mespilus)
Apple

Ammi

majus (Q. Anne's Lace, Bishops Flower)
Dream, King #, Vall #

visnaga (Fern-leaf Bishops Flower)
Dream, King #

Amorpha

fruticosa
Woodl

Amorphophallus

kiuisianus
Caves

rivieri (Penis Plant)
Parva

Ampelopsis

aconitifolia
CouCl

arborea
CuuCl

brevidunculata
CouCl, Denes

brevipendunculata Elegans
CouCl, Denes

brevipendunculata var maximowiczii
CouCl

megalophylla
CouCl

Amsonia

tabernaemontana
Peak, Telfa

Anacardium

occidentale (Cashew Nut)
Reic #

Anacyclus

depressus (Garden Gnome, Mt Atlas Daisy)
Ashto, BayBl, CoFlo, Otepo, Pgeon

depressus Silver Kiss
MaraN

Anagallis

arvensis ssp arvensis (Scarlet Pimpernel)
Sweet

arvensis ssp coerulea (Blue Pimpernel)
Sweet

grandiflora Blue Light
King #

linifolia Gentian -orange
Vall #

linifolia Gentian Blue
King #

monelli
Dream, Peak, TRidg

tenella Studland
Peak

Ananas

cosmosus (Smooth Stem Pineapple)
LakeN

cosmosus Variegatus
LakeN

Anaphalis

keriensis was Ghaphalium k.
Gordn

margaritacea New Snow (Siberian Eidelwess)
Ashto, King #, MillH, TRidg

margaritacea yedoensis
NewlR

nubigens now nepaulensis monocephala
Marsh

triplinervis
CoFlo

Anchusa

varieties (Forget-me-nots)
Roswd

azurea Dropmore
MaraN, MillH, Oasis

azurea Feltham Pride was italica FP
Egmon

azurea Loddon Royalist
BayBl, Mills, Pgeon

Blue Giant
Kayd

capensis (Cape Forget-me-not)
Reic #

capensis Blue Angel
Dream, King #, Vall #

capensis Dwarf mixed
King #

Androsace

carnea
Della

lactea
Pgeon

lanuginosa (Rock Jasmine)
AynDa, MaraN, Oasis, Otepo, Telfa, Trans

lanuginosa Leichtlinii
BayBl, Della, NewlR, Pgeon

rotundifolia
Pgeon

sarmentosa
Pgeon

sarmentosa Sherrif's
NewlR

sempervivoides
CottP, Oasis

vitaliana now V.primuliflora
NewlR

Anemanthele

lessoniana syn Oryzopsis l.
Diack, Hains, Matai, NZtr #, Orati, Parva, Pkrau, Wahpa

Anemone

alpina
Marsh

Beaute Parfait
JoyPl

blanda
BayBl, Kayd, KeriP

blanda Charmer
Kerer

blanda White Splendour
Kerer, VanEe

bracteata
NewlR

bracteata pleniflora
BayBl

caroliniana
AynDa

caucasica
Della

coronaria St Bridget
Altrf

coronaria The Governor
MillH

coronaris De Caen
Altrf

demissa
Pgeon

flaccida
Peak

Fuji San
KeriP, Parva

hupehensis
Ashto, JoyPl, Parva

hupehensis Hadspen Abundance
JoyPl

hupehensis var japonica Bressingham Glow
Telfa

hupehensis var japonica Prince Henry
BayBl, Telfa, Trans

x hybrida   was japonica (Japanese Windflower)
AynDa, BayBl, JoyPl, MaraN, MillH

x hybrida Deep Pink
CottP

x hybrida double pink
Mills

x hybrida Honorine Jobert
BayBl, Egmon, JoyPl, MaraN, Parva, Pgeon, Telfa, Trans

x hybrida Pamina
BayBl, Telfa

x hybrida Queen Charlotte
Parva, Telfa

x hybrida Richard Ahrens
BayBl, Oasis

x hybrida single pale pink
Peak

x hybrida single pink
Egmon, Kayd, KeriP, Mills, Nikau, Oasis, Trans

x hybrida single white
Ashto, Kayd, Mills, Nikau, Peak

x hybrida Snow Queen
Oasis

x hybrida Whirlwind
BayBl, KeriP, Parva

x hybrida White Knight
CottP, Parva

japonica now x hybrida or hupehensis
Ref

x lesseri
Dream, NewlR, Pgeon, Telfa, Vall #

x lipsiensis
Peak

magellanica
Otepo, Pgeon

nemorosa (Woodland Anemone)
Ashto, Parva, Peak, TRidg

nemorosa Alba
CottP

nemorosa Alba Plena
NewlR

nemorosa Allenii
BayBl, Peak

nemorosa Blue Bonnet
NewlR

nemorosa Bracteata
Peak, RosPl

nemorosa Robinsoniana
BayBl

nemorosa Royal Blue
BayBl

nemorosa Vestal
CottP, NewlR, RosPl

nemorosa white or blue
RosPl

palmata
TRidg

ranunculoides
NewlR, Parva, RosPl

ranunculoides Flore Plena
RosPl

rivularis
AynDa, MaraN, Nikau, Oasis, Otepo, Telfa, Vall #

seemanii
NewlR, Parva, RosPl

sp evergreen, creamygreen fl
Parva

sylvestris (Snowdrop Windflower)
AynDa, Dream, MaraN, NewlR, Oasis, Otepo, Parva, Telfa, TRidg

vitifolia now A. tomentosa
MaraN, MillH

Anemonella

thalictroides Alba
Titok

Anemonopsis

macrophylla
Taunt

Anethum

graveolens (Dill)
Della, King #, Trans, Trolh

graveolens Fernleaf (Fernleaf Dill)
King #, Sweet

graveolens Tetraploid
Della

Angelica

acutiloba (Japanese Angelica)
Marsh, Mills, Orang

archangelica (Sweet Angelica)
AynDa, CottP, Della, King #, Looij, Mills, Sweet

atropurpurea
Marsh

gigas (Gigantic Angelica)
Caves

pachycarpa (Shiny Angelica)
King #, Mills, Orang, Sweet, Vall #

Angophora

costata (Sydney Red Gum)
NZtr #, TopTr

Anigozanthos

bicolor
Reic #

Bush Twilight
KeriP

flavidus
Trans

flavidus green
Reic #

flavidus pink/red
Reic #
humilis
Reic #
manglesii red/green
Reic #
Solace
Kayd
Suffuse
Kayd
Sundown
Kayd
Sunup
Kayd
Surouge
Kayd
viridis
Matth, Reic #
Wallaby
Matth

Anisodontea

African Queen
Parva
compacta
Parva
Priscilla Pink
KeriP
scabrosa (Pink Mallow)
Reic #

Anisotome

lyallii
Parva

Annona

cherimola (Cherimoya)
MTig
cherimola Burton's Favourite
Koan, LakeN
cherimola Chaffey
Chedd
cherimola Conchalisa
Koan
cherimola Reretai
LakeN
cherimola Spanish
Koan
cherimola White
Koan

Anomalesia

splendens
DaffA

Anomatheca

fistulosa
DaffA
grandiflora
DaffA
laxa was Laperousia l.
DaffA, Irida, KeriP
laxa alba
CottP
laxa blue
DaffA
viridis
Kerer

Anopterus

glandulosus (Tasmanian Laurel)
Caves, MatNu, Vall #

Antennaria

dioica (Pussy Toes, Catsfoot)
Della, Oasis
dioica rosea
NewlR
rosea
CottP

Anthemis

varieties
Roswd
argentea
CottP
montana   now A.cretica
Pgeon
nobilis now Chamaemelum n
CottP, Della, Orang, Sweet, Telfa
nobilis Flora Plena now Chamaemelum n.F.P.
BayBl, CottP, Della, KeriP, MillH, Telfa
punctata ssp cupianiana (False Chamomile)
Ashto, CoFlo, KeriP, Marsh, Nikau, Peak, Pgeon, Seasd, Sweet, Telfa, Trans
sancti-johannis
KeriP, MaraN, MillH
tinctoria (Dyers Chamomile)
Ashto, CoFlo, Della, Mills, Nikau, Orang, Pkrau, Sweet

tinctoria E C Buxton
BayBl, CottP, KeriP, Marsh, MillH, Nikau, Peak, Pkrau, Trans, Warwk
tinctoria Grallagh Gold
Marsh, Pgeon
tinctoria Kelwayi
CoFlo, MaraN
tinctoria Kewayi Yellow
Dream
tinctoria Sauce Hollandaise
BayBl, CoFlo, Egmon, JoyPl, KeriP, Marsh, MillH, Nikau, Pkrau, Trans
tinctoria Wargrave
Marsh

Anthericum

liliago (St Bernards Lily)
MaraN

Anthocleista

grandiflora
Frans
zambesiaca
AynDa

Antholyza

ringens
DaffA

Anthriscus

cerefolium (Chervil)
Della, Orang, Sweet
cerefolium Brussels Winter
King #, Sweet
cerefolium Curled
King #
Ravens Wing (Perennial Q.Anne's Lace)
Peak, Telfa, TRidg, Vall #
sylvestris (Cow Parsley, Woodland Chervil)
King #

Anthurium

andreanum hybrids mixed (Flamingo Flowers)
LakeN
coraceum
LakeN
scherzerianum red fl selection
LakeN

15

Anthyllis

montana
Seasd

vulneraria (Kidney Vetch, Lady's Fingers)
Dream

Antirrhinum

braun-blanquetti
BayBl, Oasis, Ormon, Trans

hispanicum
Pgeon, Telfa

hispanicum roseum
BayBl, MaraN, MillH, Oasis, Peak, Warwk

majus Orchid Monarch
MillH

majus Scarlet Giant
Dream

majus ssp linkianum (Perennial Snapdragon)
Vall #

nanum White Wonder
Dream

Raspberry Ripper
BayBl, KeriP, Parva, Warwk

Aphelandra

clair snowflake
Manna

Apium

graveolens (Celeriac, Celery-rooted Turnip)
MTig #

graveolens Chinese Celery (Kunn Choi)
King #

graveolens Par-Cel
King #, Orang, Trolh

graveolens rapaceum Giant Prague (Celeriac)
King #

graveolens secalinum (Leaf Celery)
Sweet

graveolens var dulce Nutty Celery
Koan #

Aponogeton

distachyus (Water Hawthorn)
WilAq

Aptenia

cordifolia Crimson Heartleaf
Seasd

cordifolia Purple Heartleaf
Seasd

Aquilegia

mixed
KeriP, Looij, Otepo, Vall #

varieties
Roswd

akitensis
Ashto, MaraN

Almost Black
Della

alpina
Della, King #, MaraN, Nikau, Pgeon, Sweet, TopTr, Trans

alpina caucasica alba
Telfa

alpina caucasica pink
Telfa

atrata
BayBl, Dream, MaraN, Pgeon

bertolonii
MaraN, Pgeon

biedermeier
King #, NewlR

Black Barlow
BayBl

Blue Bonnet
Nikau

Blue Star
BayBl, King #, Nikau, Peak

buergeriana
Della, Parva

caerula Rot Gold
Ashto

caerulea wild form (Colorado State Flower)
BayBl

canadensis (Rock Bells)
AynDa, BayBl, Dream, King #, MaraN, Nikau, Pgeon, Trans

chrysantha
King #, Nikau, Peak, Pgeon, Warwk

chrysantha Yellow Queen
Parva

clematiflora now vulgaris stellata
MaraN, Vall #

Coral
BayBl

Crimson Star
BayBl

Crystal
BayBl

x cultorum Coral
Parva

x cultorum Crystal
Parva

x cultorum Heavenly Blue
BayBl, Parva

x cultorum Maxi
Parva

discolor
Otepo, Pgeon

Double Blue
Vall #

Double Pleat
Wells

Double Pleat blue/white
Reic #

Double Pleat pink/white
Reic #

Double Purple
Della

double red
Otepo

Double Rose
KeriP

einseleana
MaraN

Fairy Pink
Wells

Fairyland mixed
Vall #

Fantasy Lilac
Parva

Fantasy mixed
CoFlo

Fantasy Pink
Parva

Fantasy Purple
Parva

Fantasy White
Parva

Firewheel
Vall #

flabellata (Japanese Fan Columbine)
Della, Pgeon, Telfa, TopTr, Vall #

flabellata Alba
Telfa

flabellata Blue Angel
BayBl

flabellata Midget Blue
CottP, King #

flabellata Mini Star
TRidg

flabellata nana
Herew

flabellata nana alba
BayBl, Herew, Parva, Pgeon

flabellata nana alba flore plena   syn Snowflakes
Vall #

formosa
Pgeon

fragrans
Ashto, Della, Dream, Parva, Trans

grata
Dream

hirsuta
Della

hybrida Sunlight White
Dream

hybrids long spurred
Vall #

Irish Elegance
Warwk

Jills
Looij

Kristall
Peak

longissima
KeriP, Parva

McKana's strain mixed
Della, Kayd, King #, Oasis, Sweet

McKano red
Otepo

Mellow Yellow
Parva, TRidg, Vall #

moorcroftiana
MaraN

navy/white
Otepo

oxysepala
Dream

Parkers Blue
Parva

Phyll's Bonnet
Parva

pink
Telfa

Pink Bonnet
Nikau, Parva

pink(dark) & lemon
Wells

Pom-Poms Rose
Parva

Pom-Poms Violet
Parva

Pom-Poms White
Parva

Red Hobbit
BayBl, Parva

Red Star
King #, Nikau, Peak

rockii rockii
Ashto

Roman Bronze
TRidg, Vall #

saximontana
Pgeon

secundiflora
Dream

shockleyi
Vall #

Silver Edge
TRidg

skinneri
Della, MaraN, Parva, Pgeon

Snowflakes syn flabellata nana alba flore plena
Vall #

Songbird Blue Jay
Egmon

Songbird Robin
Egmon

steltata Rosea
Dream

Variegated
Della, Marsh

viridiflora
Dream, Pgeon

viridiflora Chocolate Soldier
Della, King #, MillH, Trans

vulgaris alba
Orang, Parva

vulgaris anemonaeflora
BayBl

vulgaris Cherry
Parva

vulgaris Flora Plena
BlueM, Pgeon, TRidg

vulgaris Heidi
BayBl

vulgaris Magpie
Oasis, Peak, Pgeon

vulgaris Matthew Strominger
King #

vulgaris Michael Stromminger
Dream

vulgaris mid-blue
Orang

vulgaris Nora Barlow
Ashto, BayBl, BlueM, CoFlo, Della, Dream, KeriP, King #, MaraN, Nikau, Parva, Peak, Pgeon, Sweet, TopTr, Trans, Trolh, Vall #

vulgaris pale blue
Orang

vulgaris Plena
Ashto

vulgaris rose pink
Orang

vulgaris Ruby Port
BayBl, Parva, Warwk

vulgaris Vervaeneana (v)
AynDa, King #

vulgaris Woodside (v) mixed
Vall #

vulgaris Woodside blue fl (v)
Parva

vulgaris Woodside ruby (v)
Parva

white
Della, Trolh

White Barlow
Kayd

White Star
King #, Nikau

William Guiness(vulgaris Magpie)
King #, Parva, Vall #

Yellow Queen
BayBl

Yellow Star
Telfa

Arabis

albida alba now alpina

caucasica alba
Della

albida flore plena
Ashto, BayBl

albida rosea now A.alpina

caucasica rosea
Della

alpina caucasica Snowcap
Sweet

alpina caucasica Variegata
Della, Telfa

androsacea
Della

blepharophylla
Della, Vall #

blepharophylla Spring Charm
Della, King #, Sweet

ferdinandi-coburgi
Seasd

ferdinandi-coburgii Variegata
MaraN

Aralia

cachemirica
TopTr

elegantissima
Reic #

sieboldii now Fatsia japonica
Reic #

spinosa (Devils Walking Stick)
TopTr

Araucaria

angustifolia (Candelabra Tree)
Cedar

araucana (Monkey Puzzle)
Cedar, Chedd, Coatv, CPete, Denes, Diack, Reic #, WakaC

bidwillii (Bunya-Bunya)
Cedar, Chedd

cunninghamii (Australian Hoop/Moreton Bay Pine)
Cedar, CPete

heterophylla (Norfolk Is Pine)
Burbk, Cedar, Coatv, CPete

heterophylla Hawaiian Hybrid
CPete

Araujia

sericifera (Cruel Plant -pest up north)
AynDa

sericifera variegata
CouCl

Arbutus

x andrachnoides
Denes

unedo (Killarney Strawberry Tree)
BlueM, Diack, Morgn, MTig, Ormon, Reic #, Wells

unedo f. rubra
BlueM

Archontophoenix

alexandrae (King Palm)
Frans, LakeN, Lsendt, PalmF, Reic #

cunninghamia (Bangalow/Seaforthia palm)
Burbk, Coatv, Frans, Kayd, LakeN, PalmF, Reic #, SpecT

Mt Lewis syn purpureum
Frans, PalmF, Reic #

Arctium

lappa (Burdock, Takinogawa)
King #, Mills, Sweet

Arctostaphylos

manzanita (Manzanita)
BlueM, Caves

uva-ursi (Red Bear Berry)
BlueM, NewlR

uva-ursi Woods Red (Bear Berry)
BlueM, Seasd, Woodl

Arctotis

Apricot Silk
Parva

Cherry Silk
Parva

Gold
Oasis

Areca

lutescens - chrysalidocarpus
LakeN

triandra
Reic #

Arecastrum

romanzoffianum now Syagrus r.
LakeN, Reic #

Arenaria

caespitosa aurea now Minuartia verna c. (Golden Irish Moss)
BayBl, CottP, Della, MillH

festucoides
MaraN

ledebouriana
NewlR

montana (Mountain Sandwort)
BayBl, Della, KeriP, MaraN, MillH, Telfa, Trans

recurva
NewlR

tetraquetra (Cushion Sandwort)
MillH, NewlR, Seasd

Argemone

grandiflora White Lustre
TRidg

mexicana Yellow Lustre
Vall #

munita
Otepo

single white fl, grey lv (Mexican Crepe Poppy)
Trans

white (Mexican Crepe Poppy)
Trolh

yellow (Mexican Crepe Poppy)
Trolh

Argyranthemum

Bounty
Parva

Bridesmaid Pink
 Nikau
Deep Pink
 CottP
Etoile d'Or
 KeriP, MillH, Nikau
Fuji Dawn
 Parva
Fuji Sunset
 CottP, Parva
Hot Lips
 KeriP, Nikau
Large White Single
 CottP
Lemon Souffle
 KeriP
Mrs Sanders
 CottP
pacificum
 MillH
Peace
 Nikau
Peach Cheeks
 KeriP, Parva
Pink
 CottP, Mtato
Pixies White
 Nikau
Rollisons Red
 CottP
Rose Pom Pom
 Della
Roseline
 KeriP
Sugar and Ice (Federation Daisy)
 Parva
Sugar Baby (Federation Daisy)
 Parva
Summer Angel (Federation Daisy)
 Parva
Summer Pink (Federation Daisy)
 Parva
Sunbeam
 MillH
Surprise Party (Federation Daisy)
 Parva, Wells
The Pearl
 Parva

White
 Mtato
white (more frost tolerant)
 Seasd
white double
 CottP, KeriP, MillH
white single
 KeriP
yellow double
 KeriP

Arisaema
amurense
 JoyPl, Parva, TRidg
canadensis
 MJury
candidissimum
 Parva
flavum
 MJury, Parva
praecox (Dwarf Cobra Lily
 CottP
ringens
 Parva
sikokianum
 MJury
speciosum
 MJury, Parva
tortuosum
 JoyPl, MJury, Parva
triphyllum (Jack-in-the-Pulpit)
 Parva

Arisarum
proboscideum (Mouse Plant)
 AynDa, BayBl, CottP, Della, KeriP, MaraN, NewlR, Pgeon

Aristea
africana
 JoyPl
capitata
 Ormon
ecklonii
 AynDa, Irida, KeriP, MillH, Oasis, Telfa, TRidg, Vall #
major syn. A.thyrsifolia
 Dream, Irida, JoyPl, KeriP, MaraN, TRidg, Warwk
thyrsiflorus (Blue Brilliant)
 Nikau

Aristolochia
elegans (Dutchmans Pipe)
 AynDa, Parva

Aristotelia
fruticosa (Mountain Wineberry)
 Matai, Orati
serrata (Makomako, Wineberry)
 Burbk, Gordn, Matai, Matwh, Morgn, Mtato, NZtr #, Orati, Pionr, Sweet, Terra, Wahpa

Armeria
alpina variegata
 Telfa
Bevan's Variety
 Parva
Corran Ferry
 NewlR, Oasis
maritima (Sea Thrift, Sea Pink)
 Ashto, KeriP
maritima Alba
 BayBl, CottP, Della, KeriP, MaraN, MillH, NewlR, Nikau, Trans
maritima Bloodstone
 BayBl, CottP, NewlR
maritima Coral Pink
 Trans
maritima Corsica
 BayBl, CottP, Della, Pgeon
maritima Dusseldorf Pride
 CottP
maritima lavender pink
 Nikau
maritima Lilac
 Parva
maritima Pink Balls
 CottP
maritima rosea
 Della, Pgeon
maritima Splendens
 Mills
maritima watermelon pink
 Nikau
plantaginea
 Ashto
pseudarmeria
 Ashto, KeriP

pseudarmeria Bee's hybrids mixed

MillH, Telfa

pseudarmeria Bees Ruby

CottP

tweedyi

Della

variegata

Parva

welwitschii

Della

Armoracia

rusticana was Cochlearia arm. (Horseradish)

Della, Mills

Arnica

montana (Arnica, Mountain Tobacco)

Della, MaraN, Mills, Orang, Sweet

Aronia

arbutifolia (Red Chokeberry)

Chedd

meloncarpa (Black Chokeberry)

Apple, Chedd, Dove

Artemisia

abrotanum (Southernwood, Lad's Love, Old Man)

CottP, Della, Mills, Orang, Sweet

absinthium (Wormwood)

Della, King #, MTig #, Orang, Pgeon, Sweet

absinthium Lambrook Silver

CottP, Marsh, Orang, Parva, Peak

afra (African Wormwood)

Orang

alba Canescens

Orang, Peak, Trans

annua (Sweet Wormwood, Sweet Annie)

King #, Orang

arborescens (Tree wormwood, Silver Wormwood)

Dowde, KeriP, Orang, Ormon, Seasd

californica

Orang

cana now Seriphidium c. (Silver Sagebrush)

Sweet

caucasica was pedemontana

BayBl, Oasis, Ormon

chamaemefolia

Orang

dracunculus (French Tarragon)

CottP, Della, MillH, Mills, Orang, Sweet, Trolh

dracunculus dracunculoides (Russian Tarragon)

Della, King #, Orang, Sweet

japonica

Orang

lactiflora (White Mugwort)

BayBl, Egmon, Marsh, Mills, Nikau, Orang

lactiflora Guizho

CottP, JoyPl, KeriP, Parva, Peak, Telfa, Trans, Warwk

ludoviciana (Louisiana Sage)

BayBl, Dream, MaraN, Marsh, MillH, Orang, Warwk

ludoviciana Silver Queen

BayBl, Nikau, Ormon, Trans

ludoviciana Valerie Finnis

BayBl, MaraN, Marsh, MillH, Ormon, Pgeon, Telfa, Trans, TRidg, Warwk

maritima now Seriphidium m

Orang

pedemontana now caucasica

Oasis, Ormon

pontica (Roman Wormwood)

Marsh, Mills, Orang, Seasd

Powis Castle

BayBl, CottP, Della, Dowde, Egmon, KeriP, Marsh, MillH, Ormon, Peak, Pgeon, Trans, Warwk

pycnocephala

BayBl, Trans

schmiditiana Nana (Silver Mound)

Seasd

stelleriana (Beach Wormwood)

Seasd

stelleriana Mori

Marsh, Ormon, Peak

valesiaca Guizho

MaraN

verlotorum (Chinese Mugwort)

Orang

vulgaris (Mugwort, Mother Of Herbs)

Della, Mills, Orang, Sweet

Arthropodium

candidum (Star Lily)

CottP, Hains, MaraN, Oasis, Orati, Parva, Terra

candidum Bronze

Parva

candidum purpureum

Orati

candidum Rubrum

Hains, MaraN, MillH, Trans

cirratum (Reinga Lily, Rengarenga lily)

CottP, Denes, Dream, Frans, Gordn, Hains, Looij, MaraN, Matai, Matwh, Morgn, Mtato, Nikau, NZtr #, Orati, Ormon, Pionr, Pkrau, Reic #, Seasd, Sweet, Telfa, Terra, Trans, TRidg, Vall #, Wahpa, Wells

cirratum glauca

KeriP

cirratum Parnell

KeriP, Parva

Matapouri Bay

BayBl, Brown, Denes, Diack, Kayd, KeriP, MillH, Telfa

milleflorum (Pale Vanilla Lily)

Hains

Three Kings

TopTr

Arum

agrophylum

Parva

dioscoridis Green
Kerer

dioscoridis Spectabile
Kerer

Green Goddess see Zantedeschia
Herit

italicum pictum
MillH, Taunt

maculatum (Lords and Ladies)
Kerer

Aruncus

aethusifolius
BayBl, Hackf, MaraN, Pgeon, TRidg, Vall #

dioicus was sylvester (Goat's Beard)
Ashto, BayBl, BlueM, Egmon, JoyPl, KeriP, MaraN, Marsh, Mills, Parva, TRidg, Vall #, WilAq

Arundinaria

auricoma
Hains, Manna

fortunei
Hains, Manna

gracilis
BlueM, Diack, TopTr

nitida now Fargesia n.
Manna

tricolour
Manna

viridistriata now Pleioblastus auricomus
Diack

Asarina

barclayana now Maurandya b.
AynDa, Vall #

erubescens now Lophospermum e.
CouCl, Vall #

macranthea
Telfa

procumbens (Cickabiddy)
Dream, MaraN, MillH, Pgeon, Warwk

Ascarina

lucida (Hutu)
Gordn, Orati, Pionr

Asclepias

curassavica (Bloodflower)
King #, Orang, Sweet

incarnata
MaraN, Telfa, Vall #

incarnata Ice Ballet
BayBl, MillH, WilAq

physocarpa (Swan Plant)
Kayd, Matwh, Morgn, Orang, Reic #, Sweet

tuberosa
BayBl, MaraN, Pgeon, Vall #

tuberosa Gay Butterflies
WilAq

Asimina

triloba (Custard Pawpaw/Banana, American Red Pawpaw)
Frans, Koan, Manna

Asparagus

densiflorus Sprengeri
Manna, Reic #

densiflorus Sprengeri variegated
Reic #

medeoloides
Reic #

meyerii
LakeN, Reic #

myriocladus
Reic #

plumosus nanus
Reic #

plumosus robustus
Reic #

sarmentosus
Reic #

virgatus
Manna

Asperula

azurea-setosa (Blue Woodruff)
King #

cyananchica
NewlR

odorata now Galium o.
CottP, Della, Mills, Telfa

Asphodeline

liburnica
JoyPl

lutea (Kings Spear)
Hackf, MaraN, MillH, Mills, Nikau, Ormon, Pgeon, Telfa

Asphodelus

acaulis
Parva

albus
Looij, MaraN, Pgeon

cerasiferus
MaraN, Ormon

fistolusus
KeriP, MaraN, Nikau, Ormon, Telfa, Trans

sp chive-like lvs white fl w dk eye
AynDa

Aspidistra

elatior
LakeN, Manna

Asplenium

bulbiferum (Hen & Chicken Fern, Mother Spleenwort)
Gordn, JoyPl, LakeN, Manna, Mtato, Orati, PalmF

flaccidum (Hanging Spleenwort)
Orati

flaccidum haurakiense (Coastal Spleenwort)
Orati

lyallii
Orati

nidus (Birds Nest Fern)
LakeN

oblongifolium (Shining Spleenwort)
Gordn, Orati

oblongifolium x bulbiferum
Orati

obtusatum
JoyPl

polyodon
Orati

shuttleworthianum
Orati

Waihere
JoyPl

Astartea

fasicularis
Butlr

21

het. white

    KeriP

Winter Pink (Happy Thoughts)

    Denes, MatNu

Astelia

banksii (Wharawhara, Shore Astelia)

    Hackf, Hains, Orati, Terra, Wahpa

chathamica (Silver Spear)

    BlueM, Burbk, Caves, Denes, Diack, Frans, JoyPl, KeriP, Matai, Matth, MJury, Mtato, Orati, Parva, Terra, Wahpa

cockaynei

    Orati

fragrans (Bush Lily, Kakaha)

    Dream, KeriP, Matai, Mtato, NZtr #, Orati, Terra, Wahpa

fruticans

    Diack

grandis (Swamp Astelia, Bush Flax)

    Orati, Pionr, Terra

nervosa (Mountain Astelia)

    BlueM, Gordn, KeriP, NZtr #, Orati, Otepo, Terra, Trans, Wahpa

nervosa Purple

    Diack

nervosa Red

    Matai

solandri (Kowharawhara)

    Orati, Terra

trinervia (Kauri Grass)

    Orati

Westland

    BlueM

Aster

alpinus

    CoFlo, CottP, NewlR, Oasis, Pgeon, Telfa

alpinus Albus

    MaraN, NewlR, Pgeon

alpinus Happy End

    MaraN

amellus hybrids

    Oasis

amellus Rudolph Goethe

    MaraN

Andrew

    Parva

Buxtons Blue

    CottP

Buxtons Dwarf

    BayBl

Claw / paw aster mixed

    King #

Coombe Fishacre

    BayBl

cordifolia Silver Spray

    Coult

divaricata

    Ashto

Durango

    Parva

ericoides Carrara

    CottP

ericoides Esther

    Pgeon

ericoides Monte Casino

    CottP, Coult, Kayd, Parva, Pgeon

ericoides Pink

    Coult

ericoides Tivoli

    CottP, Telfa

farreri

    BayBl

farreri Herggarten

    NewlR

flaccidus (purdomii)

    NewlR

x frikartii

    Pgeon

x frikartii Monch

    Nikau, Parva, Peak

Hella Lacy

    Parva

himalaicus

    Pgeon

Igel Rosamunde

    King #

incomparabilis

    CottP

Kylie

    BayBl, CottP, Otepo

lateriflorus Horizontalis (Calico Aster)

    BayBl, Warwk

linariifolius

    Pgeon

Little Carlow

    BayBl

lutea

    CottP

montanensis

    CottP, NewlR

Nancy

    Ashto

Nicholas

    Parva

novae-angliae mxd

    WilAq

novae-angliae Alma Potshke

    BayBl, CottP, Peak

novae-angliae Harrington's Pink

    BayBl, Parva, Warwk

novae-angliae Purple Dome

    BayBl

novae-angliae Treasure

    BayBl

novi-belgii Appleblossom

    CoFlo, CottP, KeriP, Parva

novi-belgii Ardon

    Pgeon

novi-belgii Bendon

    Pgeon

novi-belgii Blandie

    CottP

novi-belgii blue

    Orang

novi-belgii Blue Boy

    Ashto

novi-belgii Climax

    BayBl, Marsh, Parva

novi-belgii Coombe Ronald

    Marsh

novi-belgii Coombe Violet

    CottP, Marsh, Parva

novi-belgii Erica

    Marsh

novi-belgii Fellowship

    BayBl, CottP, Marsh

novi-belgii Flamingo

    BayBl

novi-belgii Glow

    Pgeon

novi-belgii Harrisons Blue

    CottP, KeriP, Marsh, MillH

novi-belgii Helen Ballard
KeriP

novi-belgii Janet McMullen
Marsh

novi-belgii Lady In Blue
Ashto, CottP, NewlR,
Pgeon

novi-belgii Little Boy Blue
Parva

**novi-belgii Little Pink
Beauty**
BayBl

novi-belgii Magnet
BayBl, CottP, Marsh

novi-belgii Marjorie
Ashto

novi-belgii Melba
Della

novi-belgii Mt Everest
Ashto

**novi-belgii New Hybrids
mixed**
AynDa, MillH

novi-belgii Patricia Ballard
Marsh

novi-belgii pink
Orang

novi-belgii Pink Lace
Ashto, BayBl, CottP,
NewlR, Nikau, Parva,
Pgeon

novi-belgii Plenty
Parva

**novi-belgii Prof Anton
Kippenberg**
BayBl, CottP, KeriP,
Parva

novi-belgii Royal Ruby
BayBl, CottP, Marsh,
Nikau, Parva, Warwk

novi-belgii Sarah Ballard
BayBl, Marsh

novi-belgii Snowball
Marsh

novi-belgii Snowlady
Parva

novi-belgii Snowsprite
Ashto, CottP, MillH,
NewlR, Parva, Pgeon

**novi-belgii Stanfords White
Swan**
Marsh

novi-belgii Victor
Ashto, BayBl

novi-belgii Water Perry
BayBl, Marsh, Parva

novi-belgii White Wings
Marsh

**novi-belgii Winston
Churchill**
Parva

Paeonia mixed
King #

pringlei Monte Cassino
BayBl

ptarmicoides
King #

purdomii
CottP

sedifolius
Pgeon

tibeticus
Pgeon

Tom Thumb
KeriP

tongolensis
MaraN

yunnanensis
CottP, KeriP, NewlR

yunnanensis Napsbury
CottP

Astilbe

mixed colours
Ashto, Diack, Kayd,
WilAn

Alba
Warwk

Amethyst
BayBl, Diack, Egmon,
Nikau, Parva, Telfa

apricot-pink & cream fls
TRidg

Betty Cuperus
Diack, Egmon, Mills,
Oasis, Pgeon, TRidg,
WaiMa

Bridal Veil
BayBl, Egmon, Peak

Cattleya
Ashto, Diack, Parva,
Telfa, TRidg, WaiMa

chinensis
Ashto, MaraN

chinensis var pumila
BayBl, NewlR, Telfa

Crimson King
Egmon, WaiMa

Deutschland
NewlR

Diamante
BayBl, CottP, Peak,
WaiMa

Elizabeth Bloom
BayBl

Erica
Ashto, Nikau, WaiMa

Fanal
BayBl, Diack, JoyPl,
Parva, Telfa, TRidg

ferdersee
Ashto

Fuschia Spangles
Parva, Telfa, WaiMa

Gertrud Brix
Diack

Granat
WaiMa

Hyacinth
BayBl, Diack, Mills,
Oasis, Parva, TRidg,
WaiMa

Irene Rottisper
BayBl, Peak

Kohl
Diack, Oasis

Liligues
Parva

Manis
BayBl, Diack, WaiMa

Mowe
BayBl, Parva, WaiMa

Professor Van der Wielen
CottP, Diack, Oasis,
Parva, TRidg, WaiMa

Rosea
BayBl

Rubens
CottP, Peak

Serenade
BayBl, Diack, Parva,
Telfa

Siegfried
BayBl, CottP, Parva

simplicifolia
Ashto, BayBl, MaraN,
TRidg

Spinell
BayBl

Sprite
BayBl, CottP, Parva, Peak

Straussenfeder
Ashto, BayBl, Diack, Parva, TRidg, WaiMa

taquetii
Ashto, BayBl, MaraN, Vall #

taquetii Hybrids
Dream, TRidg

taquetii Superba
Parva

Vesuvius
Diack, Nikau, Oasis, Peak, Pgeon, WaiMa

Weisse Gloria (White Gloria)
Diack, Nikau, Pgeon

White
Telfa

William Buchanan
BayBl

Astilboides

tabularis   was Rodgersia t.
Parva, Peak

Astrantia

carniolica
Otepo

carniolica Rubra
MaraN

involucrata
Marsh

major (Masterwort)
Ashto, BayBl, CoFlo, MaraN, Mills, Parva, TRidg, Vall #, Warwk

major alba
JoyPl, MaraN, Marsh

major Cennaman
Peak

major Joan Reid Seedlings
Marsh

major Primadonna
Pgeon

major Rose Symphony
MaraN

major Rubra
Oasis

major Ruby Cloud
Marsh

major Sunningdale variegated
Peak, Telfa

maxima
Marsh, TRidg, Vall #

Moonglow
Nikau

Asyneuma

canescens
Marsh

Atherosperma

moschatum (Black Sassafras)
BlueM, Woodl

Athrotaxus

cupressoides (Smooth Tasmanian Cedar)
Cedar

laxifolia (Tasmanian Cedar
Cedar

selaginoides (King William Pine)
Cedar

Athyrium

felix-femina
Gordn

japonicum
Gordn

Atriplex

halimus (Salt Bush)
Seasd

hortensis (Orach, Mountain/Tree Spinach)
King #, Koan #

Aucuba

japonica crotonoides (f) (Spotted Japanese Laurel)
BlueM, Chedd, Denes, Kayd, Wells

japonica Forest Green
Denes

japonica Mr Goldstrike
BlueM

japonica Picturata (m)
BlueM, Chedd

japonica Sulphurea
BlueM

japonica Variegata
Kayd

Aulax

cancellata   was A. pinifolia
Matth

cancellata female form
MatNu

Austrocedrus

chilensis (Chilean Cedar)
Cedar

Averrhoa

carambola (Starfruit)
LakeN

Azalea

see Rhododendron Azalea
Ref

Azara

integrifolia Variegata
TopTr

lanceolata
Hewsn

microphylla (Vanilla Tree, Box-lvd Azara)
BlueM, Chedd, Coatv, Denes, EasyB, Hewsn, Ormon, Woodl

microphylla Variegata
BlueM

petiolaris
TopTr

serrata
BlueM, Coatv, Denes, Ormon, Taunt, Woodl

Azolla

fairy moss (Floating Fern)
WaiMa

Azorella

trifurcata (Balm of Ecuador)
Marsh, NewlR, Pgeon, Scasd, Telfa

Babiana

ambigua
DaffA, Irida

angustifolia
AynDa, DaffA

blues/purples mixed
Altrf, Kayd

curviscapa
DaffA

dregei
DaffA

erectifolia
DaffA

falcata
DaffA

24

hybrid early fls lavenderblue
Irida

hybrid maybe stricta x pulchra
Irida

leipoldtii
DaffA

patersoniae
Irida

plicata
Irida

pulchra
Irida

pygmaea
DaffA, Irida

rubrocyanea
DaffA

spathacea
DaffA

tubulosa
AynDa

vanzijliae
DaffA, Irida

villosa
Irida

Zwanenburg Glory
DaffA

Baccharis

hallmifolia Twin Peaks (Coyote Brush)
Mtato, TopTr

Backhousia

citriodora (Sweet Verbena Tree, Lemon Scented Myrtle)
Coatv

Bacopa

amplexicaulis now caroliniana
WilAq

caroliniana (Babies Tears, Water Hyssop)
WaiMa

Snowflake now Sutera cordata S.
KeriP

Baeckea

virgata La Petite
Butlr

Baileyana

multiradiata (Desert Marigold)
King #

Baldellia

ranunculoides
WilAq

Ballota

acetabulosa
MaraN, Marsh, MillH

All Hallows Green
TopTr

nigra (Black Horehound)
Sweet

pseudodictamnus
BayBl, Peak, Trans

Balsamita

major var tomentosum now Tanacetum bal. tom.
Ref

Bambusa

albostriata
Isaac

alphonse.k.green
Isaac

arundinaceae
Isaac

dissimulator
Isaac

gigantea
Isaac

gracilis (Fairy Bamboo)
Coatv, Diack

gracillima (Chinese Clump Bamboo)
Denes

Kumasasa
Manna

m. variegata
Isaac

malengensis
Isaac

multiplex was glaucescens (Fern Leaf Bamboo)
Isaac

multiplex Alphonse Karr
Diack, Isaac, Wpuna

multiplex Fernleaf
Isaac

multiplex riviereorum
Isaac

multiplex Wong Tsai (Japanese Twisted Bamboo)
Manna

oldhami
Isaac, Wpuna

pervariabilis
Isaac

Shidatasea
Manna

textilis
Isaac

ventricosa tegens
Isaac

vulgaris striata
Isaac

Banksia

varieties
Reic #

attenuata
MatNu, Matth

baxteri (Birds Nest Banksia)
MatNu, Matth

brownii (Feather-lvd Banksia)
MatNu, Matth

coccinea (Scarlet/Albany/Waratah Banksia)
MatNu, Matth, Reic #

collina dwarf form
MatNu, Matth

ericifolia (Heath-lvd Banksia)
Denes, MatNu, Matth, Reic #

gardneri
Matth

grandis (Bull Banksia)
Denes, MatNu, Matth, Reic #

hookerana
Reic #

hookerana occidentalis (Red Swamp Banksia)
Denes

integrifolia (Coast Banksia, White honeysuckle)
Butlr, Chedd, Coatv, Denes, MatNu, Matth, Matwh, McKe, Morgn, Mtato, Pionr, Pukho, Reic #

integrifolia Prostrate
Matth

laevigata
Reic #

marginata (Silver Banksia)
MatNu, Mtato

menziesii
Reic #

occidentalis (Red Swamp Banksia, Water Bush)
MatNu, Matth, Reic #

ornata (Desert Banksia)
Matth

robur (Swamp Banksia)
MatNu, Matth

serrata (Saw Banksia, Red Honeysuckle)
Denes

speciosa (Showy Banksia)
MatNu, Matth

spinulosa
Reic #

victoriae (Woolly Orange Banksia)
Reic #

violacea (Violet Banksia)
Reic #

Baptisia

australis (Indigo -false)
AynDa, MaraN, MillH, Nikau, Peak, Sweet, TRidg

Barbarea

verna (Upland Cress, Landcress)
King #, Orang, Sweet

verna variegata (Variegated Upland Cress)
MillH, Orang

Basella

rubra (Malabar Spinach)
King #

Bauera

rubioides Alba (Tasmanian Heath)
BlueM

rubioides Double White
BlueM

rubioides Fairy Pink
MatNu

rubioides Plum Duff
MatNu

rubioides River Rose
BlueM

rubioides White (White River Dog Rose)
Denes

rubioides white selection
MatNu

Bauhinia

alba
Reic #

galpinii
Frans, Reic #

purpurea
Frans, Reic #

variegata (Orchid Tree)
Reic #

Baumea

articulata (Jointed Twig Rush)
Orati, Terra, WaiMa

juncea
Orati

rubiginosa
Orati

teretifolia (Pakihi Rush)
Terra

Beaucarnea

guatemalensis (Red Ruby Pony Tail)
Reic #

recurvata (Ponytail Palm, Elephant Foot Tree)
LakeN, Lsendt, Manna, PalmF, Reic #

stricta (Desert Pony Tail)
Reic #

Beaufortia

sparsa (Gravel Bottlebrush, Swamp Brush Myrtle)
Denes

Beaumontia

grandiflora
CouCl

Begonia

varieties
Reic #

Bernat Klein
Sherl

boliviensis Firecracker
Parva

Buttermilk
Sherl

Charleston
Sherl

Cleopatra
Manna

Cloudy Yellow
Sherl

Cocktail
Reic #

Collection American Picotee
BeauB

Collection American Rose & Ruffled
BeauB

Collection Frilled
BeauB

Collection Garden (mixed)
BeauB

Collection Pendula Mixed
BeauB

Collection Pendula Picotee
BeauB

Collection Pendula Roseform
BeauB

Collection Pendula Ruffled
BeauB

Collection Popular Standard (mixed)
BeauB

Collection Separate Colour (white, apricot, red)
BeauB

Colourvision
Reic #

Corona
Sherl

Dianna
BeauB

Elaine Tartelin
Sherl

Elephant Ear
Manna

Everest
Sherl

Excelsior
BeauB

Flamboyant red
Parva

Formula Mixed Doubles
Reic #

fuschoides
Kayd, KeriP

glabrata
  Manna
grandis var evansiana
  BayBl, Peak
Happy End mixture
  Reic #
Honey Dew
  Sherl
Illumination Light Pink
  Reic #
Jaffa
  BeauB
Jamboree
  Sherl
Jean Blair
  Sherl
Lady Munsel
  Sherl
Love-me-pink
  Reic #
Mandy
  BeauB
Mimi
  Sherl
Molten Gold
  Sherl
Orange & Yellow Picotee
  BeauB
Pearl
  BeauB
Pearly Queen
  Sherl
Percules
  Sherl
Pink & White Picotee
  BeauB
Pink Posy
  Sherl
Primrose
  Sherl
Raymond Hendrix
  Sherl
Red & White Picotee
  BeauB
Rio
  BeauB
Rosanna
  Sherl
Rose Marie
  Sherl
Royalty
  Sherl

Ruth Ward
  Sherl
Saturn
  Sherl
Seville
  Sherl
Standard Fiery Red
  BeauB
Standard Orange Ruffled
  BeauB
Standard Salmon Roseform
  BeauB
Sugar Candy
  Sherl
Sweetie
  BeauB
Tahiti
  Sherl
TB Toop
  Sherl
Venus
  BeauB
Vogue
  Sherl
Yellow Roseform
  BeauB
Yellow Sweetie
  Sherl
Zoe College
  Sherl
Zulu
  Sherl

Beilschmiedia

tarairi (Taraire)
  Chedd, Coatv, Gordn, Orati, Pionr, Terra
tawa (Tawa)
  Denes, Gordn, Mtato, Orati, Pionr, Terra, Wahpa

Belamcanda

apricot & lemon mix (Leopard Lily)
  Vall #
chinensis
  BayBl, King #, MaraN
orange red fl
  Della

Beleperone

see Justicia
  Ref

Bellevalia

pycnantha
  Kerer
romana
  KeriP
Rowan
  Vall #

Bellis

perennis
  Orang
perennis Enorma
  Orang
perennis Pomponette red & pink
  Orang
perennis Rob Roy
  NewlR

Benincasa

hispada Chinese Winter Melon (Tong Gwa, White/Wax Gourd)
  King #
hispada Fuzzy Melon (Tseet Gwa, Mao Gwa, Jointed Gourd)
  King #

Berberidopsis

becklerii
  Caves
corallina (Coral Vine)
  BlueM

Berberis

darwinii
  Denes
x stenophylla Gracilis
  BlueM
thunbergii Atropurpurea (Purple Barberry)
  SelGr, TopTr, Wells
thunbergii Atropurpurea Nana
  Looij
thunbergii Atropurpurea Superba now x ottawensis Superba
  BlueM
thunbergii Aurea
  Denes, TopTr, ZinoN
thunbergii Gold Rings
  BlueM, Denes
thunbergii Little Favourite
  BlueM, SelGr

thunbergii Pink Queen
BlueM, Denes, TopTr

thunbergii Rose Glow
BlueM, Coatv, Denes,
SelGr, TopTr

thunbergii Silver Beauty
TopTr, Wells

Bergenia

Abendglut
Parva, Taunt

Alba
Telfa

Bressingham Ruby
BayBl, Peak

Bressingham Salmon
Taunt, TRidg

Bressingham White
BayBl, Peak, Taunt

Britten
Parva

ciliata (was ligulata)
JoyPl, Marsh, Taunt,
WaiMa

cordifolia (Elephants Ear)
Ashto, BayBl, BlueM,
JoyPl, KeriP, MaraN,
Nikau, Parva, Pkrau,
Reic #, Telfa, TRidg,
WaiMa, Wells

cordifolia hybrids winter flwg
AynDa

cordifolia New Hybrids
Marsh

cordifolia Purpurea
Pgeon

cordifolia Redstart
Oasis

cordifolia Winterglut
Parva

Dwarf Pink
Ashto

ligulata
MaraN

purpurascens was delavayi
AynDa, MaraN, Parva,
Telfa

Rotblum
BayBl

sdlgs fr Ballswley, Sartok, Bizet(?dk pink)
TRidg

sdlgs fr Brahms, Britten, etc(?white)
TRidg

Silberlicht
TRidg

stracheyi
MaraN

Winterglow
BayBl

Wintermarchen
Taunt

Bergeranthus

multiceps
Seasd

Berzelia

abrotanoides
Matth

lanuginosa (Button Bush)
Denes, MatNu, Matth,
Reic #

Beta

beet Early Wonder (Red Beet)
MTig #

beet Rainbow mix (Albina Vereduna,Golden Beetroot,Chioggia)
Koan #

beet Rhubarb Chard
King #

beet silver Five Colours mixed (Rainbow Chard)
Koan #, MTig #

beet silver Fordhook Giant (Silverbeet)
MTig #

beet Tricolour
King #

beetroot Golden
King #

beetroot Little Mini Ball
King #

beetroot Red/White
King #

beetroot White Albina
King #

Betula

albo-sinensis (Red Chinese Birch)
Apple, Burbk, Chedd,
Diack, Ford, Pionr,
PuhaN

albo-sinensis septentrionalis
Caves

alleghaniensis was lutea (Yellow Birch)
Apple, Diack, Ford,
PuhaN

costata (Nth Chinese Mtn Birch)
Apple, Burbk, Caves,
Denes, Diack, Pukho

cylindrica
Caves

davurica (Nth Chinese Black Birch)
Apple

ermanii syn Grayswood Hill, B.costata (Japanese Silver Birch)
Denes, Pukho, TopTr

ermanii Coleridge strain
EasyB

glandulosa
Reic #

jacquemontii now utilis j.
Apple, BlueM, Burbk,
Caves, Denes, Dove,
Peele, PuhaN, Pukho,
Taunt, Titok

Jermyns
AynDa, Caves, Denes,
Pukho

lenta (American Cherry Birch)
Apple, Reic #

luminifera
Caves

lutea now alleghaniensis
Diack, TopTr

maximowicziana (Monarch Birch)
AynDa

nigra (River/Black Birch)
Apple, Burbk, Caves,
Chedd, Coatv, Dove,
Peele, Pionr, PuhaN,
TopTr, Wensl, YakuN

nigra Heritage
Caves

nigra Uru-Tawhai
Caves

papyrifera (Paper/Canoe Birch)

    Apple, Chedd, Coatv, Denes, Diack, Dove, Ford, Hackf, Hewsn, Morgn, Mtato, NZtr #, Peele, Pionr, PuhaN, Pukho, Reic #, TopTr

papyrifera commutata (Fraser River Birch)

    Apple, BlueM, Diack, Pukho, TopTr

papyrifera Kenaica (Alaskan Paper Birch)

    Apple, Burbk, Caves, Diack, MJury, Pukho

pendula (Silver Birch)

    Apple, BlueM, Burbk, Chedd, Coatv, Diack, Dove, EasyB, Ford, Hewsn, Matai, Morgn, Mtato, NZtr #, Ormon, Peele, Pionr, PuhaN, Pukho, Reic #, Terra, Wensl

pendula Dalecarlica now p.Laciniata (Cut leaf Birch, Swedish Birch)

    Denes, Pukho, TopTr

pendula Purple Splendour

    Burbk, Coatv, Denes, Pukho

pendula Purpurea

    Denes, Diack, Reic #

pendula Tristis

    Apple, Burbk, Denes, Mtato, Pukho

pendula Youngii (Young's Weeping Birch)

    Coatv, Denes, Diack, Hewsn, Mtato, Pionr, Pukho, TopTr

platyphylla (Manchurian Birch)

    Apple, Ford, MJury, Wensl

platyphylla japonica (Japanese White Birch)

    Apple, Burbk, Chedd, Diack, Dove, Hewsn, MJury, Mtato, Peele, TopTr, Wensl

populifolia (American Grey Birch)

    Apple, Peele, Pionr, TopTr, Wensl

pubescens (White/Downy Birch)

    PuhaN

szechuanica

    Caves, Diack

utilis (Himalayan Birch)

    Burbk, Mtato, PuhaN, YakuN

utilis Jacquemontii

    TopTr

Biarum

davisii

    Kerer

Bidens

ferulaefolia Golden Goddess

    KeriP, King #, Vall #

heterophylla

    Peak

Bifrenaria

harrisoniae

    NormP

Bignonia

rosea

    Denes

Billardiera

longiflora

    BlueM, Vall #

Billbergia

nutans (Angels Tears)

    Parva, Trans

Bixa

orellana (Lipstick Plant)

    Reic #

Blandfordia

grandiflora (NSW Christmas Bells)

    Reic #

Blechnum

brazilensis

    Gordn, JoyPl

capense

    Gordn, Morgn

chambersii

    Orati

colensoi

    Orati

discolor (Piupiu, Crown Fern)

    Gordn, JoyPl, Morgn, Mtato, Orati

fluviatile (Kiwakiwa, CreekFern)

    Gordn, JoyPl, Mtato, Orati

fraseri

    Gordn

Green Bay (Kiokio)

    Orati

minus (Swamp Kiokio)

    Orati

moorei

    Reic #

penna-marina

    Gordn, Orati

procerum

    Mtato

sp 1 (Kiokio)

    Orati

sp Kermadec Is Kiokio

    JoyPl, Orati

vulcanicum

    Orati

Bletilla

striata (Hyacinth Orchid,Japanese Ground Orchid)

    JoyPl, KeriP, MaraN, NewlR, Telfa, WilAq

striata albo-variegata

    Parva

Bloomeria

crocea aurea

    Kerer

Boehmeria

dealbata

    Orati

Boltonia

asteroides (False Starwart)

    CottP, MaraN, MillH, Pgeon, Telfa, Trans, Warwk

asteroides var latisquama

    BayBl, CoFlo, CottP, KeriP, Otepo, Trans

asteroides var latisquama Nana

    MillH

Bolusanthus

speciosus (Tree Wisteria)

    Reic #

Bomarea

multiflora
CouCl, Denes, JoyPl

sasilla
JoyPl

Bomaria

gerardiana
Ether

Borago

laxiflora now pygmaea
Dream

officinalis (Borage)
Della, King #, Koan #,
MillH, Sweet, Trans,
Trolh

officinalis Alba
King #, Sweet, Trolh

Boronia

Carousel
Denes, Wells

**crenulata (Graceful
Boronia)**
Denes, Mtato

**denticulata (Toothed
Boronia)**
MatNu, Mtato

denticulata Pink Falls
Denes

heterophylla (Red Boronia)
BlueM, Butlr, MatNu,
Matwh, Mtato, Reic #

Lipstick
Denes, MatNu

**megastigma (Brown
Boronia)**
Denes, MatNu, Mtato,
Reic #

metastigmata Heaven Scent
Denes

metastigmata Lutea
Denes

**pilosa Rose Blossom (Hairy
Boronia)**
Denes, MatNu, Matth,
Mtato

pinnata pale pink
Denes

pinnata white
MatNu, Matth

Sunset Serenade
Denes, MatNu, Mtato

thujona Pinnata
BlueM

Bougainvillea

varieties
LakeN

Hawaiian Pink
Denes

Scarlet O'Hara
Chedd, Denes

**Smarti Pants now Lord
Willingdon**
KeriP

Bouteloua

**gracilis (Mosquito Grass,
Blue Grama)**
MaraN, MillH

Bowenia

spectabilis
LakeN

Boykinia

**tellimoides now
Peltoboykinia**
Oasis

Brachychiton

**acerifolius (Illawarra
Flame Tree)**
Coatv, Denes, Frans,
Matwh, Reic #

populneus
Reic #

**rupestris (Queensland
Bottle Tree)**
Denes, Reic #

Brachyglottis

compacta
Pkrau

greyi
Butlr, Diack, Dowde,
Gordn, Matai, Morgn,
Terra

greyi Sunshine
Matai, Matwh, Orati

huntii Rautini
Terra

Leith Gold
Matai, Orati

monroi
Diack, Matai, Morgn,
Orati, Pkrau

Otari Cloud
Orati

Otari Gold
Matai

peridicoides (Raukumara)
Wells

reinoldii
Diack

repanda (Rangiora)
Gordn, NZtr #, Orati,
Sweet, Terra

repanda Purpurea
Diack, Matwh, Orati

Silver cloud
Diack, Orati, Wells

Brachyscome

Amethyst
KeriP

augustifolia
NewlR

Bright Eyes
BayBl

**iberidifolia (Swan River
Daisy)**
BayBl, Della, King #

iberidifolia Blue Star
King #

Lemon Drops
Wells

melanocarpa var pilbara
BayBl

**multifida (White Bush
Daisy, Rock Daisy)**
Ashto, BlueM, CottP,
KeriP, Matwh, Mtato,
Telfa

multifida Break-o-Day
BlueM, CottP, Kayd,
Matwh, Pgeon, Telfa,
Trans

multifida dilitata
KeriP

multifida Pink Angel
BayBl, KeriP

nivalis
NewlR, Seasd

pilliga Posie
Wells

Pink Haze
Wells

rigidula
NewlR

stolonifolia
Marsh

Strawberry Mousse
Taunt

White Ice
KeriP

Brahea

armata (Blue Palm)
Reic #

edulis (Guadalupe Palm)
Lsendt, PalmF, Reic #

Brassaia

actinphylla now Schefflera a.
Manna

Brassica

broccoli Chinese (Gai Lohn, Chinese Kale)
King #

broccoli De Cicco
Koan #, MTig #

broccoli Italian mixed
King #

broccoli Perennial (Perennial Broccoli)
MTig #

broccoli Purple Sprouting Early
King #

broccoli Raab
King #

broccoli Romanesco
MTig #

brussel sprouts Catskill (Brussel Sprouts)
MTig #

cabbage chinese flowering
King #

cabbage chinese Orange Queen
King #

cabbage chinese Pak Choi Green (Chinese Cabbage)
MTig #

cabbage chinese Tah Tsai (Rosette Pak Choi, Tatsoi)
King #

cabbage Dalmatian
Koan #

cabbage Flower of Spring
MTig #

cabbage Mustard
Koan #

cabbage oriental leaf Choho
King #

cabbage Palm Tree - Di Toscana (Black Cabbage)
King #

cabbage Red Acre
MTig #

cabbage Succession (Cabbage)
MTig #

cauliflower Green - Alverda
King #

cauliflower Orange Bouquet
King #

cauliflower Violet Sicilian
King #

collard Hi Crop
King #

kale flowering
King #

kale flowering Sunrise
King #

kale flowering Sunset
King #

kale Lacinato
Koan #

kale ornamental Red Peacock
King #

kale ornamental White Peacock
King #

kale Ragged Jack (Red Russian Kale)
King #, Koan #, MTig #

kohlrabi Early Purple Vienna (Kohlrabi, Stem Turnip)
MTig #

kohlrabi Gigante
King #

mibuna Green Spray
King #

misome
King #

mizuna (Mizuna, Jap.Greens, Chin.Lettuce)
King #, Koan #, MTig #

mizuna Tokyo Belle
King #

mustard 5 varieties
King #

mustard horned
King #

mustard Spinach Komatsuma - Okiyo
King #

mustard spinach Savannah
King #

Pak Choi Baby (Mei Quing Choi)
King #

Pak Choi Flowering
King #

Pak Choi Joi Choi
King #

Pak Choi Purple
King #

Pak Choi Tai Sai (Upright Soup Spoon Pak Choi)
King #

rutabaga Gilfeather (Swedish Turnip, Swede)
King #

Santo frilled leaf (Tokyo Bekana)
King #

Santo round leaf (Maruba Santo)
King #

senposai Oriental Green
King #

spinach 3 varieties
King #

turnip Golden Ball
Koan #

turnip Milan White
King #

turnip Red Round
King #

turnip Tokyo White Cross
King #

Breynia

nivosa Roseo Picta (Shades of Pink Plant)
LakeN

Brimeura

amethystina
Kerer

fastigiata
AynDa, Kerer

Briza

maxima (Quaking Grass)
AynDa, King #, Vall #

media (Quaking Grass, Doddering Dillies)
MaraN

minima
King #

Brodiaea

elegans
Kerer

ida maia now Dichelostemma i.m.
DaffA, JoyPl

laxa now Triteleia l.
MaraN

Queen Fabiola
JoyPl, Kayd

terrestris
Kerer

Bromeliad

hardy types
JoyPl

Broussonetia

papyrifera (Paper Mulberry)
Reic #, TopTr

Browallia

Blue Troll
Reic #

Jingle Bells mixed
Reic #

White Troll
Reic #

Brugmansia

Double White
MJury

Dwarf Yellow
MJury

Large Yellow
MJury

Pink Noel's Blush
Denes, Frans, MJury

salmon
Manna

sanguinea
Frans

species pinks,yellows,oranges
LakeN

suaveolens
Frans

versicolor
Frans

yellow
Manna

yellow through to orange red
Koan

Brunfelsia

calycina now pauciflora (Kiss-me-quick Shrub)
Reic #

calycina Eximea now pauciflora (Yesterday,Today,Tomorrow Bush)
Brown, Denes

latifolia (Yesterday,Today,Tomorrow Bush)
Denes

Brunia

albiflora
MatNu

stokoei
MatNu, Matth

Brunnera

macrophylla
MaraN, NewlR, Peak, Sweet, Warwk

Brunsvigia

josephinae
DaffA

litoralis
JoyPl

Buckinghamia

celcissima Ivory Curls
JoyPl

Buddleia

alternifolia (Fountain Butterfly Bush)
BlueM, Caves, Hewsn

colvilei
Caves

colvilei Kewensis
Denes, Hackf, TopTr

cordata
Hackf

crispa
Caves

davidii (Butterfly Bush, Summer Lilac)
Mtato

davidii Black Knight
BlueM, Hewsn

davidii Empire Blue
BlueM, Hewsn

davidii Harlequin
BlueM, TopTr

davidii Ile de France
Ormon

davidii Nanho Blue
Kayd, TopTr, Wells

davidii Petite Indigo
Denes, Diack, MillH, Mtato

davidii Pink Delight
Denes, Kayd, Ormon, Telfa, Wells

davidii Royal Red
BlueM, Diack, Pionr, Wells

davidii Variegata
Hewsn

davidii White Cloud
BlueM, Hewsn, Peele

fallowiana
Denes, Ormon, TopTr

fallowiana alba
TopTr

globosa (Orange Ball Tree)
AynDa, BlueM, Caves, Hewsn

lindleyana
Telfa

Lochinch
BlueM, Denes, Ormon

madagascariensis
Hackf

salviifolia (SA Sage Wood)
BlueM, Pionr

Spring Promise
Denes, Diack, Kayd, Taunt, TopTr

x weyerana Golden Glow
BlueM, Hewsn

Bulbine

alooides
Trans

bulbosa
Otepo

Bulbinella

angustifolia (Maori Onion)
NZtr #

floribunda
BayBl

hookeri (Maori Onion, Bog Lily)
BayBl, Mills, Nikau, Ormon, Parva, Vall #

nutans var nutans
JoyPl

setosa latifolia
Parva, Trans

Bulboschoenus

fluviatilis
Orati

Bunium

bulbocastanum (Earth Chestnut)
Mills

Buphthalmum

salicifolium (Yellow Ox-eye)
Ashto, MaraN, MillH

speciosum (Yellow Ox-eye)
CoFlo, MaraN, Telfa

Bupleurum

fruticosum
Caves, TopTr

Green Gold
King #, TRidg

Butia

capitata (Wine palm, Jelly palm)
Coatv, Frans, LakeN, Lsendt, PalmF, Reic #, SpecT

Buxus

balearica (Balearica Is Box)
Denes, Pionr

microphylla
LanSc

microphylla Compacta
BlueM

sempervirens (Box)
Ashto, AynDa, BayBl, Burbk, Chedd, Denes, Diack, Dowde, Ford, KeriP, LanSc, Looij, Morgn, Mtato, Nikau, Ormon, Pgeon, Pionr, SelGr, TopTr, TRidg, Trolh, ZinoN

sempervirens Albomarginata
Looij

sempervirens Argentea
TRidg

sempervirens Aureovariegata
Pgeon

sempervirens dwarf
TRidg

sempervirens Elegans
BlueM, Hewsn

sempervirens Gold Tip
BlueM, Dove

sempervirens Handsworthiensis
Ormon

sempervirens Marginata
Morgn, Orang, Otepo

sempervirens Silver Beauty
Ashto

sempervirens Suffruticosa (Dwarf Box)
BlueM, Denes, Morgn, Mtato, Parva, SelGr

sempervirens Suffruticosa Nana
Denes

sempervirens Variegata
Ashto, AynDa, Nikau, Orang, Ormon, Pionr, SelGr, Trans, ZinoN

wallichiana
MJury

Caesalpinia

ferra (Leopard Tree)
Frans, Reic #

gilliesii (Poinciana)
Reic #

pulcherrima (Pride Of Barbados)
Manna, Reic #

spinosa
Frans

Caladium

hortulanum hybrids mixed
LakeN

Calamagrostis

x acutiflora Karl Foerster
CottP, Peak

Calamintha

alpina now Acinos a.
KeriP, MillH, Telfa

clinopodium now Clinopodium vulgare (Wild Basil)
Dream

grandiflora (Calamint)
Della, MaraN, Marsh, Telfa

nepeta (Lesser Calamint)
Dream, MillH, Otepo, Sweet

officinalis (Calamint)
Mills, Orang

Calamus

australis
Reic #

Calandrinia

grandiflora
Pgeon

Calanthe

masuca dwarf form
Parva

Calceolaria

clear lemon fl
Vall #

falklandica
MaraN

Caldcluvia

rosaefolia was Ackama r. (Makamaka)
Coatv, Gordn, Terra

Calendula

Kablouna Gold
King #

Kablouna Orange
King #

officinalis (Pot Marigold)
Koan #, Orang, Sweet

officinalis Art Shades mixed
King #

officinalis Double
King #

officinalis Dwarf mixed
King #

officinalis prolifera (Hen & Chickens Marigold)
King #

officinalis single
King #

Touch of Red - series
King #

Calla

see Zantedeschia
Ref

Calliandra

Blushing Pixie
Denes

Pink Select
Butlr

portoricensis (Snowflake Acacia)
Denes

pulcherrima

Denes

Callicarpa

bodinieri

Caves

bodinieri var giraldii Profusion (Beauty Berry)

BlueM

dichotoma (Chinese Beauty Berry)

Denes

japonica Alba Bacca

Denes

Callistemon

varieties

Coatv, Reic #

citrinus (Crimson Bottlebrush)

Matwh, Morgn, Mtato, NZtr #, Reic #, Wells

citrinus austraflora Firebrand

Mtato

citrinus Splendens

Wells

citrinus Violet

Mtato

Kings Park Special

Butlr, Chedd

linearis

Reic #

mauve

Chedd

paludosus

Reic #

pinifolius (Green Bottlebrush)

Reic #

polandii

Reic #

Red Clusters

Butlr, Chedd, Pionr

rigidus

Reic #

rigidus Superbus

BlueM

salignus

Denes, Frans, Reic #

seiberi

Reic #

viminalis (Weeping Bottlebrush)

Burbk, Frans, Morgn, Reic #

viminalis Captain Cook

Frans, Mtato

viminalis Hanna Ray

Chedd

viminalis Little John

Burbk, Chedd

Western Glory

Kayd

Callistephus

chinensis (China Aster)

King #

Callitris

columellaris

TopTr, WakaC

columellaris var intratropica

Cedar

endlicheri syn calcarata

Cedar

glauca

TopTr

muelleri (Illawara Pine)

Cedar

oblonga (Tasmanian Cypress Pine)

Cedar

rhomboidea syn cupressiformis or tasmanica (Dune Cypress Pine)

Cedar, NZtr #

Calluna

vulgaris Andrew Proudley

BlueM

vulgaris Darkness

BlueM

vulgaris Elsie Purnell

BlueM, Looij

vulgaris Golden Feather

BlueM

vulgaris Hammondii Aurea

BlueM, Looij

vulgaris Jimmy Dyce

BlueM

vulgaris Kinlochruel

BlueM, Denes

vulgaris Radnor

BlueM, Looij

vulgaris Sister Anne

BlueM

vulgaris Spring Torch

BlueM

vulgaris Tib

BlueM

vulgaris Wickwar Flame

Denes

vulgaris Winter Red

ZinoN

Calocedrus

decurrens (Incense Cedar)

Apple, Cedar, Pionr

Calocephalus

brownii (Skeleton Bush, Ghost Bush, Silver Ghost)

Peak, Seasd

Calochortus

albus rubellus

AynDa

barbatus

DaffA

sp larger form of C.uniflorus

Kerer

uniflorus

CottP, DaffA, Herew, Kerer, NewlR

venustus

DaffA

Calodendron

capense (Cape Chestnut)

Frans

Caltha

palustris (Marsh Marigold, KingCup)

Diack, WaiMa, WilAq

palustris Flore Pleno

MaraN

palustris var alba

WaiMa

Calycanthus

chinensis now Sinocalycanthus c.

Caves

floridus (Carolina Allspice)

Apple, Caves, Denes, Dove, MJury, TopTr

occidentalis (Spice Bush)

Caves, JoyPl

Calystegia

sepium
Orati
soldanella
Orati
tuguriorum
Orati

Calytrix

**alpestris was Lhotskya a.
(Swan River/Snow Myrtle)**
Denes

Camassia

cusickii
Kayd, Telfa
esculenta now quamash
Kerer, Oasis, Telfa
leichtlinii
Telfa
**leichtlinii Alba now l. ssp
leichtlinii**
MaraN, TRidg
leichtlinii Semi Plena
TRidg
quamash
CottP, Kerer, MaraN

Camellia

Seedlings sasanqua
Chedd
Varieties
Coatv, Kayd, McKe
Adorable hybrid
CameH, Denes, Jordn
Aino Izumi hybrid
CameH
**Alfred Upton
japonica**
MJury
**Allison Leigh Woodroof
japonica**
CameH
Alpen Glow hybrid
CameH, Denes, Jordn,
MJury
Amabel Lansdell
Denes
**Amazing Graces
hybrid**
CameH
**Andrea Sebire
japonica**
CameH
Anemiflora japonica
Denes

Angel japonica
Denes, Jordn
Angel Wings hybrid
Denes
Annette Carol hybrid
CameH, Denes, Jordn
Anticipation hybrid
CameH, Denes, Jordn,
Kayd, Mtato, Nikau
Anticipation Variegated
CameH, Denes
Applause reticulata
CameH, MJury
**Apple Blossom
sasanqua**
Jordn
**Apple Blossom Sun
hybrid**
MJury
Arcadia reticulata
CameH, MJury
Ariel's Song hybrid
CameH, Jordn, SpecT
Aspasia MacArthur
Denes
**Autumn Herald
hybrid**
CameH
Avalanche
Denes
Ave Maria japonica
Denes
Baby Bear hybrid
CameH, Denes, Jordn,
MJury
**Baby Brother
hybrid**
CameH
Baby Pearl japonica
Jordn
Baby Sargent
Jordn
Baby Willow hybrid
CameH
**Ballet Dancer
japonica**
CameH, Denes, Jordn
Ballet Queen hybrid
CameH, Denes, Jordn,
Nikau
Ballet Queen Variegated
Denes, Hewsn, MJury

Barbara Clark hybrid
CameH, Denes, Jordn,
SpecT
**Beatrice Emily
sasanqua**
CameH
**Berenice Boddy
japonica**
CameH, Denes, Jordn
Bert Jones sasanqua
Denes
**Bettie Patricia
sasanqua**
CameH
**Betts Supreme
hybrid**
CameH, Denes
Betty Ridley hybrid
CameH, Denes
Betty's Beauty hybrid
CameH
**Bill Woodruff
reticulata**
CameH
Black Lace hybrid
CameH, Denes, Jordn
Black Opal hybrid
CameH, Denes
Black Tie japonica
CameH
Blast Off
Jordn
Blissful Dawn
Denes
Blondy hybrid
CameH, Denes, Jordn,
MJury
Bob Hope japonica
CameH, Denes, Hewsn,
MJury
**Bob's Tinsie
japonica**
CameH, Denes, Jordn
Bogong Snow
Denes
Bonanza sasanqua
CameH, Denes, Jordn
Bonnie Bell japonica
Jordn
Bonsai Baby sasanqua
CameH, Denes, Jordn
Botan Yuki hybrid
CameH, Jordn

brevistyla
CameH

Brian   hybrid
CameH, Denes, Matwh

Brigadoon   hybrid
Jordn

Brushfields Yellow
hybrid
CameH, Denes, Hewsn,
Jordn, Mtato

Bunny Girl   sasanqua
hybrid
CameH

Burgundy Boy   japonica
Jordn

Burgundy Gem   japonica
Denes, Jordn

Butterfly Wings
reticulata
CameH

Buttons 'N Bows
hybrid
CameH, Denes, Jordn

C M Wilson   japonica
CameH, Denes, Nikau

Cambria   reticulata
CameH

Camelot   reticulata
CameH, Denes

Cameron Cooper
reticulata
CameH, Denes

Can Can   japonica
CameH, Hewsn

Canterbury
japonica
CameH

Captain Rawes
reticulata
CameH

Carter's Sunburst
japonica
CameH, Denes

Chansonette   sasanqua
Denes

chekiangoleosa
Denes, MJury

Cherries Jubilee
Denes

China Doll
japonica
CameH, Denes, Jordn

Chinese Lanterns
Denes

Chrissie's Retic
reticulata
CameH

Christmas Daffodil
hybrid
CameH

chrysantha Hu Toyama
CameH

Chrysanthemum Petal
reticulata
CameH, Denes

Cinderella   japonica
Nikau

Cinnamon Cindy
hybrid
BayBl, CameH, Denes,
Jordn, Matwh, MJury,
Mtato

Confetti Blush
Denes

Contemplation   hybrid
CameH

Cornish Snow   hybrid
CameH, Denes, LanSc

Coronation   japonica
CameH, Jordn

Cotton Candy   sasanqua
CameH, Denes

Cover Girl   japonica
Nikau

Crimson King   sasanqua
CameH, Denes

cuspidata
CameH, Denes

Dahlohnega   hybrid
CameH, Jordn

Daintiness   hybrid
Denes

Dark Of the Moo
japonica
CameH, Denes

Dave's Weeper
hybrid
CameH

Debbie   hybrid
CameH, Denes, Hewsn,
Jordn, Mtato

Debbie's Carnation
hybrid
MJury

Debut   reticulata
MJury

Debutante   hybrid
CameH, Denes, Hewsn,
Jordn, SpecT

Dellie McCaw   japonica
Denes

Demi-Tasse   japonica
CameH, Jordn

Desire   japonica
CameH, Denes

Dixie Night   japonica
CameH, Denes, Jordn

Dolly Dyer   japonica
CameH, Denes, Jordn

Dona Herzilia de Freitas
Magalhaes hybrid
CameH, Jordn

Donation   hybrid
CameH, Chedd, Denes,
Hewsn, Matwh, Mtato

Donna's Dream
Jordn

Dorothy Culver
hybrid
CameH

Dorothy James
Denes

Dr Alvin Johnson
reticulata
MJury

Dr Clifford Parks
reticulata
CameH, Denes

Dr Emil Carroll
reticulata
CameH

Dr Lilian Hanchey
hybrid
CameH, Denes

Dr Tinsley   hybrid
Denes

Drama Girl   japonica
Chedd

Dream Baby
Denes

Dream Boat   hybrid
CameH, Denes, Hewsn,
Jordn, MJury

Dream Girl   sasanqua
hybrid
CameH

Dresden China   hybrid
CameH, Denes, MJury

Early Pearly   sasanqua
CameH, Denes

Easter Morn   japonica
Denes, Jordn, Nikau,
Wells

EG Waterhouse hybrid
BlueM, CameH, Chedd, Denes, Jordn

El Dorado hybrid
BlueM, CameH, Denes, Jordn

Elegans japonica
CameH

Elegans Champagne
japonica
CameH, Denes, Hewsn, Jordn

Elegans Splendour
japonica
CameH, Denes, Mtato

Elegans Supreme
japonica
CameH, Denes, Jordn

Elegant Beauty hybrid
CameH

Elfin Charm
Jordn

Elfin Rose sasanqua
CameH, MJury

Elizabeth Weaver
Jordn

Elsie Jury hybrid
CameH

Emma Leonard
Jordn

Exquisite sasanqua
CameH, Denes, TopTr, Wells

Extravaganza
Jordn

Fair Lass
Denes

Fairy Blush hybrid
MJury

Fairy Bouquet
Jordn

Fairy Wand hybrid
CameH, Denes, Jordn, MJury

Faith
Denes

Fiesta Grande
sasanqua
CameH

Fimbriata japonica
CameH

Fire Chief variegated
MJury

Firedance japonica
Jordn

Flame
Denes

Florence Daniel
Denes

Flower Girl sasanqua
hybrid
CameH

forrestii
Jordn

Fox's Fancy hybrid
Denes

Fragrant Boutonnlere
Denes

Fragrant Joy
hybrid
CameH, Denes

Francie L reticulata
CameH, Denes, Jordn

Francis Council
Denes, Jordn

Frank Pursel reticulata
CameH

fraterna
CameH

Freedom Bell hybrid
CameH, Denes, Jordn

Fukuzutsumi sasanqua
CameH, Jordn

Gael's Dream reticulata
CameH

Gay Baby hybrid
BayBl, CameH, Denes, Matwh, MJury

Gay Buttons hybrid
MJury

Gay Pixie hybrid
CameH, Denes, Parva

Gay Sue sasanqua
CameH, Denes, Matwh

gigantocarpa
CameH

Ginger japonica
Jordn

Glen 40 japonica
CameH, Denes

Grace Caple japonica
CameH

Grand Marshall
japonica
CameH

Grand Prix japonica
Jordn

Grand Slam japonica
CameH, Matwh

granthamiana
CameH, Denes, Woodl

Great Eastern
BlueM

Green Dolphin
Denes

grijsii
CameH, Jordn, MJury

Guest of Honour
japonica
CameH, Matwh

Guilio Nuccio
japonica
BlueM, CameH, Chedd, Denes, Hewsn, Jordn, Kayd, Matwh, Mtato, Nikau

Gwen Pike
sasanqua
CameH, Jordn

Gwen Washbourne
Denes

Gwenneth Morey
japonica
CameH, Chedd, Denes, Jordn, Matwh

Hakuhan Kujaku
japonica (Peacock Camelia)
CameH, Denes, MJury

Hall's Pride Variegated
retic.
CameH

Hana-Fuki
Denes

Harold L. Paige
reticulata
CameH, Denes, Jordn, MJury, Parva

Harriet Bisbee
japonica
CameH

Harry Cave
Caves

Hatano
Jordn

Hawaii japonica
CameH, Denes

Hi-No-Maru
Denes

High Fragrance
hybrid
CameH, Denes, Jordn, MJury, Parva

Himatsuri japonica
CameH

Hiryu sasanqua
Chedd, Denes, Hewsn

Hishi Karaito
japonica
CameH

Holly Bright hybrid
CameH, Denes, Jordn

Hopkins Pink miniature
Jordn

Howard Asper reticulata
Denes

Huia reticulata
CameH

Hulyn Smith
reticulata
CameH, MJury

Interlude sasanqua
CameH, Denes, MJury

Isaribi hybrid
Jordn

Itty Bit hybrid
CameH, Denes, Jordn,
MJury

James Lockington
japonica
CameH, Denes, Jordn

Jamie hybrid
CameH, Denes

Jan's Chance hybrid
CameH

Japanese Fantasy hybrid
CameH

Jean Claris hybrid
Denes

Jean Clere japonica
CameH

Jean May sasanqua
CameH, Denes, Jordn

Jean Pursel
reticulata
MJury

Jeannie Gwynne
sasanqua
Denes

Jennifer Susan
sasanqua
BayBl, CameH, Jordn,
Matwh

Jingle Bells
Denes

John Hunt
reticulata
CameH

John Taylor
Jordn

Jubilation hybrid
CameH, Denes

Judy Anne Morris
Denes

Julie Felix japonica
Jordn, MJury

June Buchanan
Denes

Jury's Yellow
hybrid
CameH, Denes, Jordn

Just Darling japonica
Denes, Jordn

Just Sue hybrid
CameH, Denes

K. Sawada
japonica
CameH, Denes

Kanjiro sasanqua
CameH, Jordn, Nikau

Katherine Nuccio
Denes

Kathryn Funari
japonica
CameH, Denes

Kelly McKnight
sasanqua
Jordn

Kewpie Doll japonica
Jordn

Kick Off japonica
CameH

Kitty miniature
Jordn

Kramer's Beauty
Denes

Kramer's Fluted Coral
hybrid
CameH, Jordn

Kramer's Supreme
japonica
CameH, Denes, Jordn,
Matwh

Kuro Tsubaki
japonica
CameH, Jordn

La Petite
Denes

Lady Loch japonica
CameH

Larry Piet reticulata
CameH

Lasca Beauty reticulata
CameH, Jordn

Laura Walker japonica
Denes

Laurie Bray
japonica
CameH, Denes, Nikau

Lemon Drop hybrid
CameH, Denes, Jordn

Leonora Novick
japonica
CameH, Denes, MJury,
Wells

Les Jury hybrid
CameH, Denes

Lilemac japonica
Denes

Lily Pons japonica
CameH, Denes

Lipstick
Denes, Jordn

Little Babe japonica
Denes

Little Bit Variegated
hybrid
Jordn

Little Bo-Peep
Jordn

Little Lavender hybrid
Hewsn

Little Michael hybrid
CameH, Jordn

Little Pearl sasanqua
Denes

Little Slam japonica
Jordn

Little Susie
Denes, Jordn

Liz Carter
Denes

Lois Shinault reticulata
Denes

longicarpa
Denes, Jordn

Lovelight japonica
Denes

Lovely Lady reticulata
Denes

LT Dees   hybrid
CameH

Lucinda   sasanqua
Denes, Jordn

Lulu Belle   japonica
Denes

lutchuensis
CameH, Denes, Jordn,
MJury, Woodl

lutchuensis formosan form
CameH

Magnoliaeflora
Denes

Mandy
Jordn

Mansize   japonica
CameH, Denes, Jordn,
Parva

**Margaret Davis
japonica**
CameH, Denes, Jordn,
Mtato

**Margaret Hilford
reticulata**
CameH, Denes, MJury

Margaret Waterhouse
Denes

Margarete Hertrich
Denes

Marie Young   sasanqua
Denes

Mark Alan   japonica
CameH, Denes, Hewsn

**Maroon and Gold
japonica**
CameH, Denes, Hewsn,
Jordn, Mtato, Parva

Mary Paige   japonica
CameH, Denes

**Mary Phoebe Taylor
hybrid**
BlueM, CameH, Denes,
LanSc

**Mary Wheeler
japonica**
CameH, Denes

Maui   japonica
CameH

Memento   japonica
CameH

Midnight   japonica
CameH, Denes, Jordn,
Mtato

**Midnight Lover
sasanqua**
CameH

Mignonne   sasanqua
CameH

Mimosa Jury   hybrid
CameH, Denes, Jordn,
MJury

**Mine No Yuki
sasanqua**
CameH, Denes, Hewsn,
LanSc

Mini Mint   hybrid
CameH, Denes, Jordn

Mini Pink   hybrid
Denes

**Miss Bessie Beville
hybrid**
CameH

**Miss Rebecca
reticulata**
CameH

**Miss Tiny Tot Princess
hybrid**
Denes

**Misty Moon
sasanqua**
CameH, Denes, MJury

miyagii
CameH, Denes

Modern Art   hybrid
CameH

Momento
Jordn

Momudan   hybrid
CameH

Mona Jury   hybrid
Jordn

Moshio   japonica
CameH, Denes

**Moutancha
reticulata**
CameH

Mrs D W Davis   japonica
BlueM, Jordn

Myrtifolia   japonica
CameH

**Narumigata
sasanqua**
CameH, Denes, Jordn

Navajo   sasanqua
Caves, Denes

Nicky Crisp   hybrid
CameH, Denes, Jordn,
Mtato, Parva

**Night Rider
japonica**
CameH, Caves, Denes,
Jordn, Matwh, MJury

Nokogiri-Ba   japonica
(Sawtooth Camelia)
Denes

**Nonie Haydon
hybrid**
CameH, Denes

**Nuccio's Cameo
hybrid**
CameH

**Nuccio's Carousel
japonica**
CameH, MJury

**Nuccio's Gem
japonica**
CameH, Denes, Jordn

**Nuccio's Jewel
japonica**
CameH, Denes, Kayd

**Nuccio's Pearl
japonica**
CameH, Denes, Jordn,
Mtato

**Nuccio's Pink Lace
japonica**
CameH, MJury

Nuccio's Red Velvet
Denes

Nuccio's Ruby   reticulata
Denes

Nymph   hybrid
CameH, Denes, Jordn

**Okke's Delight
sasanqua**
CameH, Denes

Ole   hybrid
Denes

oleifera
CameH

Oleifera Jaune
Denes

Olive Honnor
Denes

**Onetia Holland
japonica**
CameH, Denes, Jordn

Opal Princess
Denes

**Otome Sazanka
sasanqua**
CameH

Our Betty Variegated
hybrid
CameH, Jordn

Our Melissa hybrid
CameH, Denes, Jordn

Overture
Jordn

Pagoda
reticulata
CameH

Peach Blossom japonica
Denes, Nikau

Peacock
Nikau

Pearl Terry
reticulata
CameH

Peekaboo
hybrid
CameH

Peer Gynt sasanqua
Jordn

Peerless sasanqua
Denes

Peremier
Jordn

Persuasion hybrid
CameH

Pink Cameo hybrid
CameH

Pink Dahlia hybrid
CameH, Jordn

Pink Ruffles hybrid
CameH, Jordn

Pink Smoke hybrid
CameH, Jordn

pitardii var. pitardii
CameH

Plantation Pink
sasanqua
CameH, Denes, Hewsn,
Jordn, SelGr, TopTr

Pollyanna
Denes

polydonta
CameH, Denes

Pope John
Jordn

Pride Of California
hybrid
CameH, Denes

Prima Ballerina
Denes, Jordn

Prudence
Denes

Punkin
Denes, Jordn

Purple Gown reticulata
CameH, Denes, MJury

Purple Swirl
Denes

Queen Diana japonica
CameH, Denes, Jordn,
MJury

Queenslander sasanqua
CameH

Quintessence hybrid
CameH, Denes, Jordn,
MJury, Parva

Rainbow sasanqua
CameH

Ralph Peer sasanqua
Jordn

Raspberry Ice hybrid
CameH, Jordn

Raspberry Ripple hybrid
CameH

Red Crystal
reticulata
CameH, Denes, MJury

Red Dahlia japonica
Jordn

Red Foam
Jordn

Red Red Rose japonica
CameH, Denes, Jordn,
Kayd, Nikau

Reigyoku japonica
Jordn

Rendezvous hybrid
Hewsn, MJury

Rhonda Elizabeth hybrid
CameH

Richard Nixon hybrid
CameH

RL Wheeler japonica
Denes

Roger Hall japonica
CameH, Denes, Jordn,
MJury

Rosabelle hybrid
CameH, Denes

rosaeflora
CameH, Denes

rosaeflora Cascade
hybrid
CameH, Denes, Jordn

Rose Ann sasanqua
CameH

Rose Bouquet hybrid
CameH, MJury

Rosette sasanqua
CameH, Denes

Royal Velvet japonica
CameH, MJury

Ruby Wedding
Denes

Rudolph hybrid
CameH, Denes

salicifolia
CameH, Caves, Denes

San Dimas japonica
CameH, Denes

San Marino reticulata
CameH, MJury

Sanpei Tsubaki japonica
CameH

Saotome sasanqua
Denes

Satsuma japonica
CameH

Sawada's Dream
japonica
CameH

Scented Gem hybrid
CameH, Jordn

Scentsation hybrid
CameH

Scentuous hybrid
CameH, Denes, Jordn,
MJury

Seaspray hybrid
CameH

Setsugekka sasanqua
BayBl, CameH, Denes,
Jordn, LanSc, Matwh,
SpecT

Shikabu
Jordn

Shishi Gashira sasanqua
CameH, Denes

Show Girl
Denes

Showa No Sakae
sasanqua
CameH, Jordn, LanSc

Silver Anniverary
japonica
CameH, Denes, Jordn

Silver Chalice japonica
Denes

Silver Cloud
Jordn

Silver Dollar   sasanqua
CameH, Denes, Jordn, Matwh

Silver Tower   japonica
CameH

Silver Waves
Jordn

sinensis (Tea)
Caves, Jordn, MTig, MTig #

Sir Victor Davies
Denes

Snippet   hybrid
Denes, Jordn

Snowdrop   hybrid
CameH, Denes, Jordn

Softly   hybrid
CameH, Denes, Jordn, MJury

Something Beautiful
japonica
CameH, Denes

Souzas Pavlova
Jordn

SP Dunn   reticulata
CameH, MJury

Sparkling Burgundy
sasanqua
Denes, MJury

Spring Festival   hybrid
BayBl, CameH, Chedd, Denes, Jordn, Mtato

Spring Mist   hybrid
CameH, Denes, Jordn, Wells

Sprite   hybrid
CameH, Denes

Standard Bearer
hybrid
CameH, Jordn

Star Above Star
sasanqua
CameH, Denes

Steve Blount
Denes

Sugar Babe   hybrid
CameH, Denes

Sugar Dream   hybrid
CameH, Denes

Sundae   hybrid
CameH, Denes

Sunsong   japonica
CameH

Super Star
Denes, Jordn, MJury

Swan Lake   japonica
Denes

Sweet Dreams   japonica
CameH

Sweet Emily Kate   hybrid
CameH, Denes, Jordn, MJury, Taunt

Sweet Jane   hybrid
CameH

Sweetheart
Denes

Taishuhai   sasanqua
CameH

Takanini   japonica
CameH

Tali Queen   reticulata
CameH

Tama-No-Ura   hybrid
Denes

Tammia   japonica
Denes

Tanya   sasanqua
CameH

Taylor Maid
Denes

Temple Mist   reticulata
MJury

Terrell Weaver
reticulata
Denes, MJury

The Elf
Jordn

Thomasville Beauty
Denes

Tiffany   japonica
Denes, Hewsn

Tinsie   hybrid
Denes, Jordn

Tiny Princess   hybrid
CameH, Denes, Jordn, LanSc

Tiny Star   hybrid
CameH, Denes, Jordn, MJury, Wells

Tiptoe   hybrid
CameH, Denes, Jordn

Tom Durant   reticulata
CameH

Tom Knudsen   japonica
CameH, Denes, Jordn

Tom Thumb   hybrid
CameH, Jordn

Tomorrow Park Hill (v)
Denes

Tootsie   japonica
Jordn

transariensis
Jordn

transnokoensis
CameH, Denes, Jordn, Mtato

tsaii
CameH, Denes, Jordn, Matwh, Woodl

Tui Song   reticulata
CameH

Twilight   japonica
CameH, Denes

Twinkle Star   japonica
CameH, Denes

Un Ryu   hybrid
CameH

Valentines Day   reticulata
CameH, Denes, Mtato

vietnamensis
CameH

Ville de Nantes   japonica
Jordn

Violet Bouquet   japonica
CameH

Virginia Franco Rosea   jap.
CameH

Volcano   hybrid
CameH, Denes

Waiwhetu Beauty   hybrid
CameH

Water Lily   hybrid
CameH, Chedd, Denes, Hewsn, Jordn, Mtato, Nikau

Wedding Cake
Jordn

White Doves Benten
sasanq.
CameH

White Hibiscus   hybrid
CameH

White Nun   japonica
Jordn

Wilamina   japonica
CameH, Denes, Hewsn, Jordn, Wells

Wildfire   japonica
CameH, Denes, Hewsn, Jordn

William Hertrich reticulata
MJury

Willow Wand   reticulata
CameH

Winelight
Denes

Winsome   sasanqua
Denes, MJury

Wirlinga Gem   hybrid
CameH

Wirlinga Princess   hybrid
CameH

Woodford Harrison reticulata
Jordn

Yamato Nishiki
Jordn

Yoimachi   hybrid
CameH, Denes

Yours Truly   japonica
Denes

Yuhsienensis
Denes

Yuhsienensis compact form
CameH

Yuletide   sasanqua
CameH, Caves, Denes, Hewsn, Jordn, Matwh, Parva

yunnanense
Jordn

Zambo   hybrid
CameH, Denes, Jordn

Camissonia

bistorta Sunflakes
King #

Campanula

varieties
Roswd

alliariifolia
AynDa, BayBl, BlueM, Dream, KeriP, MaraN, Nikau, Parva, Peak, Warwk

Avalon
NewlR

barbata
BayBl, MaraN, Pgeon

Birch Hybrid
BayBl, CottP, Della

Burghaltii
AynDa, BayBl, Oasis, Trans

carpatica (Carpathian Harebell)
Looij, NewlR, Pgeon

carpatica alba
NewlR, Pgeon, Sweet

carpatica Blaue(Blue) Clips
Egmon, NewlR

carpatica blue form
Oasis

carpatica Chewton Joy
CottP, NewlR

carpatica Deep Blue
Parva

carpatica Elaine
Parva

carpatica Hannah
NewlR

carpatica Lyndel
Pgeon

carpatica Molly Pinsent
NewlR, Otepo

carpatica Weisse(White) Clips
Egmon, KeriP, Parva

cervicaria
MaraN

chamissonis   was pilosa (Blue Harebells)
Ormon, Otepo

cochlearifolia   was pusilla (Fairy Thimbles)
MaraN, NewlR, Oasis, Otepo, Parva, Pgeon, Telfa

cochleariifolia var. alba
BayBl, Della, Marsh, Parva

collina
BayBl

Diamond
NewlR

EK Toogood
NewlR, Nikau, Pgeon, Sweet

elatines var. elatinoides
MaraN

Elizabeth
BayBl, CottP, Peak, Telfa

Elizabeth May
Titok

ephesia
MaraN

fenestrellata
Parva

fragilis
Oasis, Wells

garganica
CottP, Della, MaraN, NewlR, Oasis

glomerata (Clustered Bellflower, Twelve Apostles
CoFlo, CottP, Della, Dream, KeriP, Nikau, Oasis, Sweet, Telfa

glomerata acaulis
BayBl, NewlR

glomerata alba
Ashto, BayBl, Dream, MaraN, Mills, Parva, Telfa

glomerata Alba Nana
Peak, Pgeon

glomerata dahurica
MaraN, Parva

glomerata Superba
Ashto, AynDa, BayBl, CoFlo, MillH, Parva, Pgeon, Trans, Warwk

glomerata Superba Alba
Warwk

x haylodgensis   now h.Plena
Marsh, NewlR

x haylodgensis Plena
Otepo

incurva Blue Ice
Wells

kemulariae
MaraN, NewlR

Kent Belle
BayBl

kolenatiana
MaraN

lactiflora
Ashto, BayBl, BlueM, Egmon, Looij, MaraN, MillH, Nikau, Parva, Telfa, Vall #, Warwk

lactiflora Blue Cross
BayBl

lactiflora Loddon Anna
Parva

lactiflora New Hybrids
BlueM, MaraN

lactiflora Pouffe
BayBl, Parva

lactiflora White Pouffe
BayBl

lasiocarpa
NewlR

latifolia
    BayBl, KeriP, Marsh,
    Oasis, Trans
latifolia var macrantha
(Great Bellflower)
    BlueM, Dream, Egmon,
    MaraN, Parva, Warwk
latifolia var macrantha
alba
    Parva, Warwk
latiloba
    BayBl, JoyPl, Nikau,
    Pcak
latiloba blue
    Vall #
latiloba Hidcote Amethyst
    KeriP, Parva, Peak, Trans
Maie Blythe
    NewlR, Pgeon
medium (Canterbury Bells)
    King #
medium Chelsea Pink
    King #
muralis now
portenschlagiana
    BayBl, Parva, Sweet
nitida now persicifolia
planiflora
    MaraN, NewlR
Norman Grove
    NewlR
olympica
    Pgeon
pallida
    MaraN
persicifolia (Peach-lvd
Bellflower)
    BayBl, Egmon, Hackf,
    Looij, MaraN, Marsh,
    Oasis, Pgeon, Trans,
    Wells
persicifolia alba
    AynDa, BayBl, Egmon,
    King #, MaraN, Marsh,
    Parva, Pgeon, Sweet,
    Trans, Warwk
persicifolia blue
    King #, Telfa, Warwk
persicifolia blue double
    Marsh
persicifolia Caerulea
    Parva
persicifolia China Blue
    Mills
persicifolia Fleur de Neige
    CottP, Pgeon, Trans

persicifolia Grandiflora
    Parva
persicifolia Moerheimii
    MillH
persicifolia planiflora was
nitida
    MaraN, NewlR
persicifolia planiflora alba
was nitida a.
    NewlR
persicifolia Pride Of
Exmouth
    CottP, Egmon, MaraN,
    Pgeon
persicifolia Snowdrift
    CottP
persicifolia Telham Beauty
    BayBl, CottP, Egmon,
    KeriP, Parva
persicifolia white double
    Marsh
pilosa now chamissonis
    CottP, Ormon
pilosa Superba
    Pgeon
portenschlagiana was
muralis
    Pgeon, Seasd, Sweet
poscharskyana
    CoFlo, CottP, KeriP,
    MaraN, Nikau, Pgeon,
    Trans
poscharskyana E H Frost
    BayBl, CottP, Della,
    KeriP, NewlR, Nikau,
    Oasis, Ormon, Parva,
    Pgeon, Telfa, Trans
poscharskyana Lisduggan
    BayBl, Oasis, Otepo
primulifolia
    AynDa, Dream, MaraN,
    Marsh, Trans
pulla
    Dream
x pulloides
    Otepo
punctata
    AynDa, CottP, Della,
    MillH
punctata Nana Alba
    Parva
punctata Rubra
    Oasis
punctata Rubriflora
    Marsh, Parva

pusilla Alba now
C.cochleariifolia a.
    Della
pusilla Miranda
    NewlR
pyramidalis (Chimney
Bellflower)
    BayBl, Dream, MaraN,
    Parva
pyramidalis alba
    BayBl, MaraN, Parva
raddeana
    CottP, Della, MaraN,
    NewlR, Oasis, Parva,
    Pgeon
rapunculoides (Creeping
Bellflower)
    Ashto, AynDa, CottP,
    Dream, Nikau
rhomboidalis now
rapunculoides
    MaraN
rotundifolia (Harebell)
    BayBl, CottP, MaraN,
    Marsh, Orang, Pgeon,
    Telfa
rotundifolia alaskana
    Marsh
sarmatica
    Della, MaraN
sartorii
    MaraN
x Stansfieldii
    Otepo
Stella Blue
    Reic #
Stella White
    Reic #
tachasamense
    MaraN, MillH
takesimana
    AynDa, Caves, CoFlo,
    CottP, Hackf, KeriP,
    Marsh, Oasis, Ormon,
    Otepo, Parva, Peak,
    Pgeon, Telfa, Trans
thyrsoides (Yellow
Bellflower)
    AynDa, Dream
trachelium (Bats in the
Belfry, Nettle-lvd Bellflower
    Ashto, BayBl, Dream,
    KeriP, MaraN, Pgeon,
    Warwk
trachelium alba
    Pgeon

trachelium Bernice
> BayBl, Parva, Peak

vidallii
> AynDa, Della, King #,
> Wells

White Bell
> CoFlo, Sweet

Campsis

grandiflora
> CouCl

radicans
> CouCl

**x tagliabuana Madame
Galen**
> CouCl, Denes

Canna

mixed
> Kayd

Aida
> Podgo

America
> Podgo

Anna Gretian
> Podgo

Anthony Crozy
> Podgo

Beatrix
> Podgo

C Meblin
> Podgo

Capri
> Podgo

Cerase
> Podgo

CF Cole
> Podgo

Cheerfulness
> Podgo

Chinese Choral
> Podgo

City of Portland
> Podgo

Coles Pale Superba
> Podgo

Colossal
> Podgo

Confetti
> Podgo

Cornelius Cole
> Podgo

Dr Giesler
> Podgo

Duke of Marlborough
> Podgo

**edulis now indica (Achira,
Red Canna,Arrowroot)**
> Koan, Lsendt, MTig

Elma Cole
> Podgo

Enchantress
> Podgo

Evolution
> Podgo

Felix Ragout
> Podgo

Feur Zauber
> Podgo

Fire Bird
> Podgo

Fire Flame
> Podgo

Francis Berti
> Podgo

Frau Gartenburg
> Podgo

Furst Weid
> Podgo

Gaiety
> Podgo

Garum
> Podgo

Gnom
> Podgo

Goldbird
> Podgo

Heinrich Siedal
> Podgo

Henry Cohen
> Podgo

Henry Cole
> Podgo

Hoffe
> Podgo

Hungaria
> Podgo

HW Cole
> Podgo

JB Van Der Schoot
> Podgo

Jean Krupp
> Podgo

Joseph Bischau
> Podgo

King City Gold
> Podgo

King Midas
> Podgo

La Boheme
> Podgo

La Londe
> Podgo

La Traviata
> Podgo

LG Cole
> Podgo

Lillian Cole
> Podgo

Madame Butterfly
> Podgo

Marie Nagel
> Podgo

Marjorie Cole
> Podgo

Merle Cole
> Podgo

Mignon
> Podgo

Mr A Carroll
> Podgo

Nattie Cole
> Podgo

Niagara
> Podgo

Orange King
> Podgo

Pacific Beauty
> Podgo

Parkes
> Podgo

Peach Glow
> Podgo

Perkeo
> Podgo

Pfitzers Salmon Apricot
> Podgo

Pfitzers Stadt Fellbach
> Podgo

PJ Berkman
> Podgo

Podgora
> Podgo

President
> Podgo

President Mayor
> Podgo

Pride of Holland
> Podgo

Professor Went
  Podgo
Queen Charlotte
  Podgo
Red King Humbert
  Podgo
Redhead
  Podgo
Reign of Stuttgart
  Podgo
Rosencavalier
  Podgo
Ruby Cole
  Podgo
Schwarbriche Heimut
  Podgo
Singapore Girl
  Podgo
Souv d'R Owen
  Podgo
Souv de President Garnot
  Podgo
Statue of Liberty
  Podgo
Tango Tango
  Podgo
Tellbach
  Podgo
The Gem
  Podgo
Triumph
  Podgo
Tropical Rose
  Kayd
Tropicanna
  Parva
Vera Cole
  Podgo
WC Fields
  Podgo
William Berry
  Podgo
Winters Colossal
  Podgo
Wyoming
  Podgo
Yellow Humbert
  Podgo
Zebra Cole
  Podgo

Cantua

buxifolia (Sacred Flower of the Incas, Magic Flower)
  Denes, Woodl
buxifolia alba
  JoyPl
pyrifolia
  Woodl

Capsella

bursa-pastoris (Shepherd's Purse)
  Sweet

Capsicum

annum (Pepper)
  Orang
annum Cayenne Pepper
  King #, Sweet
annum Sweet Banana syn Yellow Banana, Hungarian
  King #, MTig #
annum Yolo Wonder
  MTig #
annuum 37 varieties sweet to v.hot & ornamental
  King #
annuum 6 varieties
  Koan #
perennial hot peppers
  Koan

Cardamine

lyrata (Pennywort)
  WaiMa
pratensis (Lady's Smock, Cuckoo Flower)
  MillH, WilAq

Cardiocrinum

giganteum (Giant Lily, Himalayan Giant Lily)
  AynDa, Caves, MaraN, Mills, Peak, TRidg, Vall #

Carex

bifida
  Hackf
buchananii
  BlueM, Burbk, CottP, Diack, Ford, Gordn, Hains, KeriP, Matai, MillH, Morgn, Nikau, NZtr #, Orati, Parva, Pkrau, Terra, Wahpa, Wensl
chathamica
  Diack

comans
  Burbk, Butlr, CottP, Diack, Matai, Mtato, NZtr #, Orati, Parva, Pionr, Terra, Wells
comans bronze
  Burbk, Gordn, Hains, KeriP, Matwh, NZtr #, Pkrau, PuhaN
comans Frosted Curls
  BlueM, CottP, Della, Diack, Gordn, Hains, Kayd, KeriP, Morgn, Mtato, Nikau, NZtr #, Pkrau, Seasd, Telfa, Terra, Trans, Wahpa
comans green
  Hains, KeriP, Matwh, Wensl
conica Hime-Kan-Suge
  Hains, Otepo
coriacea (Sedge Grass)
  Matwh, NZtr #, PuhaN, Terra
dipsacea (Tahoata)
  Diack, Egmon, Hains, Orati, Terra
dissita
  Hains, KeriP, Nikau, NZtr #, Orati, Telfa
egmontia
  Diack
elingamita
  Orati
fasicularis
  Telfa
flagellifera
  Diack, Hains, KeriP, Matai, Mtato, NZtr #, Parva, Pionr, Terra, Wensl
flagellifera Bronze
  Morgn, Orati, Pkrau, Wahpa
flagellifera Green
  Orati, Pkrau
geminata
  NZtr #, Orati, Terra
glauca
  Parva
hachijoensis Evergold (Japanese Sedge Grass)
  Ashto, AynDa, BayBl, BlueM, Butlr, Diack, Gordn, Hains, KeriP, Nikau, Pionr, Seasd, Wahpa

hime-kansugi now conica H.
  Hains, Ormon

kermadecensis
  Orati

lambertiana
  Hains

lessoniana
  Orati

lucida
  BlueM, Diack, Orati

maorica
  Orati

montana (Blue Sedge Grass)
  PuhaN

morrowii
  Diack

morrowii Evergold now hachijoensis E.
  Hains, Looij, Mtato

morrowii Variegata
  Diack, Mtato

oshimensis Evergold now hachijoensis E.
  AynDa

pendula (Drooping Sedge)
  BlueM, Hains, Pkrau

petrei
  Matwh, Orati

pumila (Sand Sedge)
  Orati, Terra

remota (sedge)
  Diack, WaiMa

secta (Pukio)
  Burbk, Diack, Hains,
  KeriP, Matai, Matwh,
  Morgn, Mtato, NZtr #,
  Orati, Parva, Pkrau,
  Terra, Wahpa

secta var tenuiculmis
  Pkrau

Small Red
  Matai

solandri
  Diack, Hains, KeriP,
  Mtato, NZtr #, Telfa,
  Terra

stricta Aurea (Bowles Golden Grass)
  Hains

testacea
  AynDa, Burbk, Diack,
  Gordn, Hackf, Hains,
  Matwh, Morgn, Mtato,
  NZtr #, Orati, Ormon,
  Parva, Pionr, Pkrau,
  Seasd, Telfa, Terra,
  Wahpa

testacea Anawhata
  Orati

trifida (Tataki, Mutton Bird Sedge)
  Burbk, Diack, Gordn,
  Hains, JoyPl, Matwh,
  NZtr #, Orati, Parva,
  Pionr, Terra, Wahpa,
  WaiMa

variegated
  Oasis

virgata
  NZtr #, Orati, Terra

Carica

pentagona (Babaco)
  Koan, Lsendt

pubescens (Mountain Pawpaw)
  Koan

Carissa

grandiflora now macrocarpa (Natal Plum)
  Frans, TopTr

Carmichaelia

aligera (Nth Is Broom)
  Orati, Terra

appressa
  Terra

cunninghamii
  Hackf

grandiflora
  Matai

kirkii (Scrambling Broom)
  Orati, Terra

odorata (Maukoro, Scented Broom)
  BlueM, Orati, Ormon,
  Terra

williamsii (Large Flower Broom)
  Gordn, Orati, Ormon,
  Terra

Carpentaria

acuminata (Carpentaria Palm)
  Reic #

Carpenteria

californica (Tree Anenone)
  BlueM, Caves, Denes,
  JoyPl

californica Ladham's Variety
  TopTr

Carpinus

betulus (Hornbeam)
  Apple, Caves, Chedd,
  Dove, Ormon, Peele,
  Pionr, PuhaN, SelGr,
  TopTr

japonica (Japanese Hornbeam)
  Apple, Peele

laxiflora
  MJury, TopTr

Carpodetus

serratus (Putaputaweta, Marbleleaf)
  BlueM, Burbk, Coatv,
  Gordn, Matai, Matwh,
  Morgn, Mtato, NZtr #,
  Orati, Pionr, Pkrau,
  Terra, Wahpa

Carthamus

tinctorius Goldtuft
  King #

tinctorius Grenade mixed
  King #

Carum

carvi (Caraway)
  Della, King #, Sweet

copticum (Ajowan)
  Sweet

Carya

illinoinensis (Pecan)
  Chedd

ovata (Shagbark Hickory)
  Chedd

Caryopteris

x clandonensis (Blue Spiraea, Blue Beard)
  BayBl, BlueM, Parva

x clandonensis Dark Knight
  Parva

x clandonensis Heavenly Blue
  Denes

incana
  Egmon

Caryota

mitis
  Reic #
urens
  Reic #

Casimiroa

edulis (White Sapote)
  Chedd, Frans, LakeN, MTig
edulis Mac's Golden
  Koan
edulis Pike
  Koan

Cassia

australis
  Reic #
corymbosa John Ball (Buttercup Tree)
  Butlr, Denes, Matwh, Mtato
didymobotrya (Popcorn Bush)
  Reic #
fistula (Golden Shower Tree)
  NZtr #, Reic #
grandis (Pink Shower Tree)
  NZtr #, Reic #
javanica (Java Shower, Appleblossom Cassia)
  NZtr #, Reic #
prostrata
  Vall #
renigera (Velvet Cassia)
  Reic #
siamea
  Reic #

Cassinia

amoena
  Orati
leptophylla (Tauhinu)
  Gordn, Matai, Orati, Pkrau, Terra
leptophylla albida
  Matai
leptophylla fulvida (Golden Tauhinu/Cottonwood)
  Matai, Orati, Pkrau
leptophylla vauvilliersii (Mountain Cottonwood)
  Orati

Castanea

crenata (Japanese Chestnut)
  Chedd
crenata (906)
  Chedd
crenata Disk ll
  Chedd
crenata Mayrick King (905)
  Chedd
crenata MayrickQueen (907)
  Chedd
sativa (Sweet Chestnut, Spanish Chestnut)
  Apple, Burbk, Chedd, Diack, Dove, Ford, Pionr, PuhaN
sativa No 1002
  Chedd
sativa No 1005
  Chedd, Harri, Pionr
sativa No 1007
  Denes, Harri, Pionr
sativa No 1015
  Chedd, EasyB, Harri

Castanopsis

cuspidata Sieboldii
  TopTr

Casuarina

cunninghamiana (River Sheoak)
  Chedd, Matwh, McKe, Mtato, NZtr #, Pionr, Reic #
equisetifolia (Horse Tail Oak)
  NZtr #, Reic #
glauca (Swamp Sheoak)
  Matwh, McKe, Morgn, Mtato, NZtr #, Pionr, Reic #
littoralis (suberosa) now Allocasuarina l. (Black sheoak)
  Reic #
nana (Dwark Oak)
  Reic #
obesa (Swamp Sheoak)
  Matwh
stricta (Drooping Sheoak)
  NZtr #, Reic #
torulosa see Allocasuarina
  Chedd, Pionr, Reic #

Catalpa

bignonioides (Indian Bean Tree, Tree Bignonia)
  Chedd, TopTr
bignonioides Aurea
  Pukho
bignonioides Variegata
  TopTr
bungei
  Apple
x erubescens Purpurea was bignonioides P.
  TopTr
fargesii (Farges Catalpa)
  Burbk, PuhaN
fargesii duclouxii
  TopTr
ovata (kaempferi)
  NZtr #, TopTr
speciosa (Western/Northern Catalpa
  Chedd, Dove, Mtato, NZtr #, Peele, Pionr, PuhaN
speciosa Purpurea
  Pukho

Catananche

caerulea (Cupid's Dart, Blue Strawflower)
  BayBl, CottP, Dream, King #, MaraN, MillH, Mllls, Oasis, Pgeon, Seasd, Vall #
caerulea Alba
  BayBl, MaraN, MillH
caerulea Bicolor (White Cupids Dart)
  AynDa, CottP, King #, Mills, Oasis, Pgeon, Vall #

Catharanthus

Grape Cooler
  Reic #
Peppermint Cooler
  Reic #
roseus Little Bright Eye
  Reic #
roseus Little Linda
  Reic #

Cattleya

bicolor punctissima xself
  AnnM

forbesii
AnnM

forbesii olive green
AnnM

schofieldiana
AnnM

Cavendisha

acuminata (Colombian Heath)
Woodl

Ceanothus

Blue Carpet
Mtato

Blue Mound
BlueM, SelGr

x delileanus Gloire de Versailles
Denes, TopTr

x delileanus Henri Desfosse
TopTr

gloriosus Emily Brown
BlueM, Ford

griseus horizontalis Yankee Point (Carmel Creeper)
BlueM, Kayd, Mtato

impressus
BlueM, Morgn, ZinoN

Joyce Coulter
BlueM, Dove, ZinoN

Julia Phelps
BlueM

Mini Mound
BlueM

x pallidus Marie Simon
Denes, TopTr

papillosus var.roweanus
BlueM, Butlr, Chedd, Ford, Matwh, Mtato, Pkrau

Snow Flurries
BlueM, Denes, ZinoN

Cedrela

sinensis now Toona s. (Chinese Toon)
Chedd, KeriP, Peele, Pukho, TopTr, Wells

sinensis Flamingo now Toona s.F.
Caves, Coatv, Denes

Cedronella

canariensis was triphylla (Balm of Gilead)
CottP, Della, Mills, Orang, Sweet, Telfa

Cedrus

atlantica now a.libani (Atlas Cedar)
CPete, NZtr #, WakaC

atlantica Aurea (Golden Atlas Cedar)
BlueM, Cedar, CPete, Denes, EasyB

atlantica Cheltenham
Cedar

atlantica Fastigiata
CPete

atlantica Glauca (Blue Atlas Cedar)
BlueM, Burbk, Cedar, Coatv, CPete, Denes, EasyB, NZtr #, Pukho

atlantica Glauca Aurea
Cedar, CPete

atlantica Glauca Pendula (Weeping Blue Cedar)
BlueM, Cedar, Coatv, CPete, WakaC

brevifolia (Cyprus Cedar)
Cedar, CPete, WakaC

deodara (Himalayan Cedar, Indian Cedar)
Apple, BlueM, Burbk, Cedar, Chedd, Coatv, CPete, Diack, Dove, Ford, Mtato, NZtr #, Ormon, Pionr, PuhaN, Pukho, SouWo, TopTr, WakaC, Wensl

deodara Albospica
Caves, Cedar

deodara Aurea (Golden Himalayan Cedar)
BlueM, Cedar, CPete, Pukho

deodara Lime Glow
Cedar

deodara Mylor
Cedar, CPete

deodara Pendula
Cedar

deodara Pendula -fine lvd form
Cedar

deodara Pendula -tree form
Cedar

deodara Prostrata
Cedar, CPete

deodara Raywoods Prostrate Dwarf
Cedar, CPete

deodara Vinks Golden
Cedar, CPete

deodara Waverley Ridge
Cedar

deodara Woodendean
Cedar

libani (Cedar of Lebanon)
Cedar, CPete, WakaC

libani Compte de Dijon
CPete

libani Gold Tip
Cedar, CPete

libani Nana (Dwarf Lebanon Cedar)
BlueM, Cedar, CPete

libani Pendula
Cedar

libani Sargentii (Weeping Lebanon Cedar)
Caveo, Cedar, CPete

libani var stenacoma
Cedar

Celastrus

orbiculatus
Denes

Celmisia

hookeri
Matwh

incana (Native White Daisy
Terra

lyallii (False Spaniard)
Terra

mackaui
Parva

major (Egmont Daisy)
Terra

petiolata (Purple Stalked Daisy)
Terra

semicordata (Cotton Plant)
Matwh, Terra

sessiliflora (Mountain Cushion Daisy)
Terra

spectabilis (Cotton Daisy)
Terra

traversii
Parva

verbascifolia
Terra

viscosa
Terra

Celosia

7 varieties (Cockscomb)
King #

Celtis

africana
Ether, TopTr

australis (Mediterranean Hackberry)
PuhaN

laevigata
Apple

occidentalis (Nth American Hackberry)
Apple, Dove, Hackf, Peele, TopTr

Cenia

turbinata
Seasd

Centaurea

bella
Seasd

cineraria
KeriP

cyanus Blue Boy
King #

cyanus Florence colours
King #

cyanus Frosty mixed
King #

cyanus Polka Dot mixed
King #

cyanus Snowman
King #

dealbata (Perennial Cornflower)
AynDa, BayBl, CoFlo, CottP, Della, Dream, KeriP, MaraN, Nikau, Oasis, Parva, Pgeon, Trans, Vall #, Warwk

dealbata Steenbergii
Wells

hypoleuca John Coutts
BayBl, Peak

jankae
AynDa, KeriP, Telfa

macrocephala (Globe Centaury, Yellow Centaury/ Hardhead)
Ashto, CoFlo, Della, Dream, JoyPl, King #, MaraN, MillH, Mills, Pgeon, Telfa, Trans, Vall #, Warwk

montana (Mountain/Perennial Cornflower, Mountain Bluet)
BayBl, CoFlo, CottP, Della, Dream, MaraN, MillH, Mills, Nikau, Oasis, Orang, Parva, Peak, Pkrau, Telfa, Warwk

montana alba
BayBl, CottP, Orang, Otepo, Parva, Peak, Telfa

montana Violetta
Telfa

moschata The Bride
King #

nigra rivularis
MaraN, Trans, Warwk

ochroleuca
CottP, Parva

phrygia
CoFlo

pulcherrima
Parva

scabiosa (Greater Knapweed)
Della

simplicicaulis
NewlR, Ormon

simplicifolia
Telfa

uinflora ssp nervosa
Marsh

Centaurium

erythraea (Centaury)
MaraN, Sweet

scilloides
NewlR, Parva

Centella

asiatica (Gotu Cola, Arthritis Herb)
Orang, Sweet

uniflora
Orati

Centranthus

calyptrata Rose Cloud
King #

macrosiphon
King #

pacificum
BayBl

Rosenrot
Peak

ruber (Red/False Valerian)
Kayd, Looij, MillH, Orang

ruber Albus (White False Valerian)
AynDa, BayBl, Dream, Kayd, MaraN, MillH, Otepo, Telfa, Trans

ruber Albus Snowcloud
BlueM, CoFlo, CottP, Della, King #, Nikau, Sweet

ruber Atrococcineus
Dream

ruber Coccineus
BayBl, MaraN, Trans

ruber Pretty Betsy
BlueM

ruber Rosy Red
BayBl

Cephalanthus

occidentalis (American Button Bush)
Apple, TopTr

Cephalaria

alpina was Scabiosa a. (Alpine Scabious)
Dream, MillH

gigantea (Giant Scabiosa)
Della, Dream, Orang, Telfa, TRidg, Vall #

Cephalotaxus

fortunei (Chinese Plum Yew)
Cedar, WakaC

harringtonia Fastigiata (Japanese Plum Yew)
BlueM, Cedar, Denes

harringtonia Prostrata
Cedar

harringtonia var drupacea (Cow's Tail Pine)
Cedar, CPete, WakaC

Cerastium

Silver Carpet

BayBl

tomentosum (Snow in Summer)

Della, Looij, MillH, Seasd

tomentosum var columnae

King #

Ceratonia

siliqua (Carob)

King #, MTig, NZtr #, Reic #, Sweet

Ceratopetalum

gummiferum (NSW Christmas Tree)

Reic #

gummiferum Rubies n' Lace

Chedd, Denes, Matth

Wildfire

Wells

Ceratostigma

plumbaginoides (Dwarf Chinese Plumbago)

BlueM, Denes, Parva, Trans

willmottianum (Chinese Plumbago)

BlueM, Denes, Hackf, KeriP, Trans

Cercidiphyllum

japonicum (Katsura Tree)

Denes

Cercis

canadensis (Eastern American/Canadian Redbud)

Apple, Caves, Chedd, Dove, Peele, PuhaN, Pukho, Reic #, TopTr

canadensis Alba

Caves, Denes, Pukho

canadensis Forest Pansy (Forest Pansy)

Caves, Chedd, Coatv, Denes, Pukho

chinensis (Chinese Redbud)

Apple, Chedd, Dove, Peele, PuhaN, Reic #, TopTr

chinensis Avondale

Denes, MJury

gigantea

Apple

occidentalis

Reic #

siliquastrum (Judas Tree, European Redbud)

Apple, Burbk, Chedd, Coatv, Dove, Hewsn, NZtr #, Peele, Pionr, Pukho, Reic #

siliquastrum alba

Caves, Dove, Ormon, Peele, Reic #, Wensl

siliquastrum Bodnant

Denes, Pukho

Cerinthe

major (Honeywort, Pride of Gibraltar)

Ashto, Parva, Roswd, Seasd, Telfa, Vall #

major (mixed colours)

Orang

major Purpurascens (Honeywort)

Della, Dream, King #, MillH, Sweet

Ceropegia

linearis woodii

LakeN

Cestrum

aurantiacum

Denes

elegans (purpureum)

Denes

Hugh Redgrove

Denes

nocturnum (Night-scented Jessamine)

Denes, Reic #

violaceum was Iochroma v.

AynDa

Chaenomeles

Alba

BlueM, Pukho

Alison's Red

Pukho

Cameo

Denes, Pukho

cathayensis (Ornamental Quince)

Dove

Dr Burton

BlueM

Early Orange

Denes

Green Ice

Denes, Pukho

japonica (Japonica, Japanese Flowering Quince)

NZtr #, Reic #

japonica Green Jade

JoyPl

speciosa (Japanese Quince)

Chedd, Mtato

Sunset Gold

Pukho

x supreba Rowallane

Pukho

Yoyonisheiko

Pukho

Chaenorrhinum

glareosum

Pgeon

origanifolium

Pgeon

Chamaecyparis

Ericoides Red Star

Burbk, Butlr

formosensis (Formosan Cypress)

Cedar

funebris was Cupressus f. (Chinese Weeping Cypress)

Cedar

lawsoniana (Lawson Cypress)

Apple, BlueM, Dove, Ford, Morgn, NZtr #, PuhaN, Terra, WakaC

lawsoniana Albovariegata

Cedar, CPete

lawsoniana Alumii

Cedar

lawsoniana Anderleyensis Nana

BlueM

lawsoniana Argentea Compacta now C.l.Nana Albospica

BlueM, Cedar

lawsoniana Aurea

WakaC

lawsoniana Aurea Densa

Cedar, CPete

lawsoniana Aureovariegata

Cedar, CPete

lawsoniana Azurea
Cedar, CPete

lawsoniana Barry's Silver
(Barry's White)
Cedar, CPete

lawsoniana BD Edginton
Cedar, CPete

lawsoniana Blom
Cedar

lawsoniana Blue Gem
BlueM, Cedar, Coatv,
CPete

lawsoniana Blue Mountain
BlueM, CPete

lawsoniana Blue Weeper
Cedar

lawsoniana Brilliance
Cedar, CPete

lawsoniana Chingii
Cedar

lawsoniana Columnaris
Cedar, Coatv, Diack,
Dove

lawsoniana Columnaris
Glauca
EasyB, Ford, Hewsn,
Mtato

lawsoniana Darleyensis
BlueM

lawsoniana Dows Gem
Cedar

lawsoniana Duncanii
BlueM, Cedar, CPete

lawsoniana Dutch Gold
Cedar

lawsoniana Ellwood's Gold
BlueM, Cedar, CPete

lawsoniana Ellwood's
Pygmy
BlueM, Cedar, CPete

lawsoniana Ellwoodii
BlueM, CPete, Diack

lawsoniana Ellwoodii
Variegata
BlueM

lawsoniana Ellwoods
Ultragold
CPete

lawsoniana Erecta
Cedar

lawsoniana Erecta Aurea
Cedar, CPete

lawsoniana Fleckellwood
CPete

lawsoniana Fletcheri
(Fletcher's Cypress)
BlueM

lawsoniana forsteckensis
Cedar

lawsoniana Gillingham's
Blue
Cedar

lawsoniana Gnome
Cedar

lawsoniana Gold Splash
Cedar, CPete

lawsoniana Golden King
Cedar, CPete

lawsoniana Golden
Wonder
Cedar

lawsoniana Grayswood
Feather
BlueM, Cedar

lawsoniana Grayswood
Pillar
BlueM, Cedar, CPete,
Dove

lawsoniana Green Globe
BlueM, Cedar, CPete

lawsoniana Hughesii
BlueM, Cedar

lawsoniana Imbricata
Pendula
BlueM, Cedar

lawsoniana Jonesll
Cedar

lawsoniana Juvenilis
Stricta
BlueM, CPete, Hewsn

lawsoniana
Knowefleldensis
Cedar

lawsoniana Lane
Cedar

lawsoniana Lutea
Cedar

lawsoniana Lutea Nana
Cedar

lawsoniana Minima
BlueM

lawsoniana Minima Aurea
BlueM, Cedar, CPete

lawsoniana Minima Glauca
CPete

lawsoniana Moerheimi
Cedar

lawsoniana Nana Albospica
BlueM, Cedar

lawsoniana Nidiformis
BlueM, Cedar

lawsoniana Pembury Blue
BlueM, Cedar, CPete,
Hewsn, Matai

lawsoniana Pendula Glauca
CPete, WakaC

lawsoniana Pottenii
Cedar

lawsoniana Pygmaea
Argentea
BlueM, Cedar, CPete

lawsoniana Silver Queen
BlueM, Cedar, CPete,
Diack, EasyB, Matai

lawsoniana Smithii
Cedar

lawsoniana Snowflurry
BlueM

lawsoniana Southern Gold
Cedar, CPete

lawsoniana Spek
Cedar

lawsoniana Stewartii
BlueM, Cedar, EasyB,
Hewsn, Matai

lawsoniana Tamariscifolia
BlueM

lawsoniana Tharandtensis
Caesi
BlueM, Cedar, CPete

lawsoniana Triompf van
Boskoop
Cedar

lawsoniana versicolor
Cedar

lawsoniana Waitomo
Cedar

lawsoniana Wallis Gold
BlueM, CPete, Diack,
Hewsn

lawsoniana Westermanii
BlueM, Cedar, CPete

lawsoniana Wisselii
BlueM, Cedar

lawsoniana Yellow
Transparent
BlueM, Cedar, CPete

nootkatensis (Nootka
Cypress)
BlueM, Cedar, CPete

nootkatensis Aurea
Cedar

nootkatensis Aurea Pendula
BlueM

nootkatensis Pendula
Cedar, CPete, WakaC

obtusa (Hinoki Cypress)
BlueM

obtusa (no white flecks)
Cedar

obtusa Albospica
BlueM

obtusa Albovariegata
Cedar, CPete

obtusa Brigitt
Cedar

obtusa caespitosa
Cedar, MJury

obtusa Chabo Yadori
Cedar, CPete

obtusa Confucius
BlueM, Cedar, CPete

obtusa Contorta
Cedar

obtusa Coralliformis
Cedar

obtusa Crippsii (Golden Hinoki cypress)
Cedar, Chedd, Coatv

obtusa Crippsii Johnson's form
Cedar

obtusa Densa
Cedar

obtusa Ericifolia
Cedar

obtusa Ericoides now o.Chabo Yadori
BlueM, Cedar

obtusa Fernspray Gold
BlueM, Cedar, Chedd, Coatv, CPete

obtusa filicoides
Cedar

obtusa flabelliformis
Cedar

obtusa Golden Sprite
Cedar

obtusa Hage
Cedar, CPete

obtusa Hillock
Cedar

obtusa Juniperoides
Cedar

obtusa Juniperoides Compacta
Cedar

obtusa Kosterii
BlueM, Cedar, CPete, Matai

obtusa Lutea Nana
MJury

obtusa Lutea Nova
Cedar

obtusa Lycopodioides
Cedar

obtusa Lycopodioides Aurea
Cedar

obtusa Mariesii
Cedar, CPete

obtusa Minima
Cedar

obtusa Nana
BlueM, Butlr, Cedar, CPete, Mtato

obtusa Nana Aurea
BlueM, Cedar, CPete, Mtato

obtusa Nana Gracilis
BlueM, Cedar, CPete, Matai

obtusa Nana Lutea
BlueM, Cedar, CPete

obtusa Nana Verdonii
Cedar, CPete

obtusa Pygmaea
BlueM, Cedar, CPete

obtusa Raraflora
Cedar

obtusa Rigid Dwarf
Cedar

obtusa Sanderii see Thuja orientalis Sanderii
Cedar

obtusa Templehof
BlueM, Cedar, CPete

obtusa Tetragona Aurea
Cedar, CPete

obtusa Tonia
BlueM, Cedar, CPete

obtusa Youngii
Cedar

pisifera Boulevard
BlueM, Cedar, CPete, Diack, Hewsn, Kayd, Mtato

pisifera Compacta Variegata
Cedar, CPete

pisifera Ericoides
BlueM

pisifera Filifera
BlueM

pisifera Filifera Aurea (Gold Sawara Cypress)
Cedar, Chedd, CPete

pisifera Filifera Nana
BlueM, Cedar, CPete

pisifera Filifera Sungold
Cedar, Denes

pisifera Gold Globe
Cedar

pisifera Gold Spangle
Cedar

pisifera Golden Mop
Cedar

pisifera Iceberg
Cedar

pisifera Nana
BlueM, Cedar

pisifera Nana Aureovariegata
BlueM, Cedar

pisifera Nana Gold Globe
CPete

pisifera Nana Variegata
BlueM

pisifera Nana Variegata Sport
BlueM

pisifera Plumosa
Cedar

pisifera Plumosa Albopicta
Cedar

pisifera Plumosa Aurea
Cedar, CPete

pisifera Plumosa Aurea Nana
Cedar

pisifera Plumosa Compressa
BlueM, Cedar, CPete

pisifera Plumosa Riverlea
Cedar

pisifera Plumosa Rogersii
Cedar, CPete

pisifera Plumosa Variegata
Cedar

pisifera Snow
　BlueM, Cedar
pisifera Snow Sport
　BlueM
pisifera Squarrosa
　Cedar
pisifera Squarrosa Dumosa
　BlueM, Cedar
pisifera Squarrosa
Intermedia
　Cedar
pisifera Squarrosa
Lombarts
　Cedar, CPete
pisifera Squarrosa
Sulphurea
　Cedar, CPete
pisifera Strathmore
　Cedar
pisifera Tsukumo
　BlueM, Cedar, CPete
thyoides (Atlantic White
Cedar)
　Cedar
thyoides Andelyensis
　CPete
thyoides Andelyensis Nana
　BlueM, Cedar
thyoides Ericoides
　BlueM, Cedar
thyoides Ericoides Red
Star
　BlueM, Cedar
thyoides Glauca
　Cedar
thyoides Rubicon
　BlueM, Cedar, CPete
thyoides Variegata
　Cedar, CPete

Chamaecytisus

palmensis (Tagasaste, Tree
Lucerne)
　Chedd, Matwh, Morgn,
　Mtato, NZtr #, Pionr,
　SouWo, Terra
proliferus
　Reic #

Chamaedorea

elegans (Parlour Palm)
　Coatv, LakeN, PalmF,
　Reic #
seifrizii (Bamboo Palm)
　PalmF, Reic #

Chamaemelum

nobile (Roman Chamomile)
　AynDa, CoFlo, King #,
　MillH, Mills, Orang,
　Sweet
nobile Flore Pleno (Double
Chamomile)
　CoFlo, KeriP, Marsh,
　MillH, Orang, Otepo
nobilis Treneague (Lawn
Chamomile)
　CottP, MillH, Mills,
　Orang, Parva, Sweet,
　TRidg

Chamaerops

humilis (European Fan
Palm)
　Frans, Lsendt, SpecT

Chamelaucium

Walpole Wax
　Denes

Chaminobambusa

marmorea
　Isaac

Chasmanthe

aethiopica
　JoyPl
bicolor
　AynDa, DaffA
floribunda
　DaffA, Ether
floribunda var duckittii
　JoyPl

Cheilanthes

humilis
　Orati

Cheiranthus

see Erysimum
　Ref

Chelidonium

majus (Greater Celandine)
　Della, Mills, Orang,
　Sweet
majus lacinatum Bowles
var
　Dream

Chelone

barbata now Penstemon
barbatus
　Kayd, Otepo, Vall #

obliqua (Turtlehead)
　Della, MaraN, WilAq
obliqua alba now glabra
　MaraN, MillH

Chenopodium

ambrosiodes (Epazote,
American Wormseed,
Mexican Tea)
　King #, Mills, Orang,
　Sweet
bonus-henricus (Good King
Henry)
　Della, Sweet
quinoa Andrean Hybrid
mixed
　King #, Mills #, Sweet

Chiastophyllum

oppositifolium was
Cotyledon
　Ashto, BayBl, Oasis,
　Parva, Pgeon

Chimonanthus

praecox (Wintersweet,
Allspice)
　Apple, BlueM, Chedd,
　Denes, Dove, Hewsn,
　Peele, Pionr, PuhaN,
　Pukho, TopTr
praecox Luteus
　Denes, MJury, Pukho

Chionanthus

retusus (Chinese Fringe
Tree)
　Apple, Caves, TopTr
virginicus (American
Fringe Flower/Tree, Old
Man's Beard)
　Apple, Caves, Woodl

Chionochloa

Beddie
　Diack
bromoides (Coastal
Tussock)
　Orati
conspicua (Hunangamoho,
Plumed Tussock Grass)
　BlueM, Diack, Matwh,
　NZtr #, Orati, Parva,
　Pkrau, Telfa, Terra,
　TopTr
crassiuscula
　Pkrau

flavescens (Broad-lvd Snow Tussock)

Diack, Matai, Matwh, TopTr

flavicans (Snow Tussock, Dwarf Toetoe)

Burbk, Diack, Frans, Hains, JoyPl, KeriP, MillH, Morgn, Mtato, Orati, Parva, Telfa, Terra, Wahpa

pallins (Mid-ribbed Snow Tussock)

Terra

rigida (Narrow-lvd Snow Tussock)

NZtr #, Terra

rubra (Red Tussock)

BlueM, Diack, Frans, KeriP, Matai, Matwh, Morgn, Mtato, NZtr #, Orati, Parva, Pkrau, Telfa, Terra, Wahpa

Chionodoxa

luciliae

Kerer, Parva, RosPl, VanEe, Winga

luciliae Blue Giant

DaffA

luciliae Pink Giant now forbesii P.G.

Winga

luculiae gigantea

Kerer, Winga

luculiae gigantea Alba

NewlR

sardensis

CottP, DaffA, Kerer, NewlR, Winga

sardensis alba

DaffA

Chlidanthus

fragrans (Sea Daffodil)

Kayd

Chlorophytum

laxum

LakeN

Choisya

Aztec Pearl

Denes, Mtato, SelGr, Taunt, Telfa, TopTr, Wells

ternata (Mexican Orange Blossom)

BlueM, Burbk, Chedd, Coatv, Denes, Hewsn, Matwh, MillH, Morgn, Mtato, Nikau, Pionr, Pkrau, SelGr, Sweet, TopTr

Chordospartium

stevensonii (Weeping Broom)

Dove, Orati

Chorisia

speciosa (Floss Silk Tree)

Chedd, Denes, Frans, Manna

Christella

dentata

Gordn, Orati

Chrysalidocarpus

lucubensis

Reic #

lutescens

Reic #

Chrysanthemum

alpinum now Leucanthemopsis a.

Della

aschshatscheffii

Ashto

balsamita now Tanacetum b

CottP, Della, MillH, Mills, Sweet

balsamita tanacetoides now Tanacetum bal. ssp bal.

Della, Mills, Orang, Sweet

bush daisies see Dendranthema

*

carinatum Polar Star

Della, King #

catananche

BayBl, CottP, NewlR

cinerarifolium now Tanacetum cin.

Della, MillH, Seasd, Sweet

Cobham Gold now Leucanthemum

BayBl

coccineum Duro now Tanacetum c.D

MillH

coccineum now Tanacetum cocc.

BlueM, MaraN, Telfa

coronarium (Edible Chrysanthemum)

Orang

coronarium Shungiku Large Leaf

King #

coronarium Shungiku Small Leaf

King #

Esther Read now Leucanthemum

BayBl

hosmariense now Rhodanthemum h.

Orang, Seasd

inodorum Bridal Rose

King #

leucanthemum now Leucanthemum vulgare

CottP, Della, KeriP, Telfa

leucanthemum polaris now Leucanthemum

MillH

mawii now Rhodanthemum gayanum

Nikau, Oasis, Seasd

mawii x leucanthemum

BayBl, NewlR

mawii x sieboldii

CottP

maximum now Leucanthemum m. or x superba

CottP, Looij

pacificum now Ajania p.

Telfa

parthenium now Tanacetum p.

CottP, Della, King #, Mills, Sweet, Trolh

parthenium golden now Tanacetum p.

CottP, Della, Sweet, Telfa

tanacetoides now Tanacetum balsamita ssp b. (Costmary, Bible Leaf)

CottP

54

weyrichii now Dendranthema w.

Ashto, BayBl

Chrysocoma

coma-aurea (Golden Hair, Goldilocks)

Oasis

Chrysogonum

virginianum

CottP, Telfa

Cichorium

endiva

Koan #

endiva 6 varieties (Endive)

King #

intybus (Chicory)

Della, King #, MaraN, Marsh, Mills, Orang, Sweet

intybus 12 varieties

King #

intybus Grumolo Green

King #, Orang

intybus Verona (Red Chicory, Whitloof)

Della, King #, Mills

Cimicifuga

americana

Peak

racemosa (Black Snakeroot)

TRidg, Vall #

simplex

JoyPl

Cineraria

maritima Silver Dust now Senecio cineraria

Dowde

Cinnamomum

camphora (Camphor Tree, Camphor Laurel)

Chedd, Coatv, Denes, Pionr, Reic #, Sweet, TopTr, Wells

Cirrhopetalum

Elizabeth Ann 'Buckleberry'

NormP

Cirsium

Early Pink Beauty

Parva

Early Rose Beauty

Parva

japonicum Pink Beauty

CottP, King #, Reic #

japonicum Rose Beauty

CottP, King #, Reic #

White Puff

Parva

Cissus

antarctica

CouCl

discolor

LakeN

hypoglauca

CouCl

striata

Hackf

Cistus

albidus

Ormon

Anne Palmer

Hackf

Bennetts White

BlueM, Denes, KeriP, Matwh, MillH, Ormon, TopTr, Trans, TRidg, ZinoN

Blanche

Hackf

Brilliancy

BlueM, Butlr, Matwh, Mtato, Nikau, Ormon, Telfa, TopTr, Wells

crispus

Telfa

x cyprius Albiflorus

Ormon

x dansereaui Decumbens was x lusitanicus D.

BlueM

formosus now Halimium lasianthum

BlueM

incanus ssp creticus

Dream

incanus ssp creticus Albus (Sun Rose)

BlueM, TopTr

ladanifer (Gum Cistus)

BlueM, Denes

ladanifer Palhinhae

Marsh

laurifolius (Sun Rose)

BlueM, Dream, Seasd

x laxus

Hackf

x lusitanicus now x dansereaui (Sun Rose)

BlueM, CottP, KeriP, Ormon, Telfa

Paladin

Hackf

Pink Gem

Wells

psiliosepalus

Hackf

x pulverentus Sunset

KeriP, MillH, Mtato, Telfa

x pulverulentus

BlueM

Rainey's White

KeriP

salvifolius

Mtato, Ormon, Telfa

salviifolius Prostatus

BlueM

Silver Pink (Sun Rose)

BlueM, Diack, Mtato, Telfa, Trans

x skanbergii

BlueM, Hackf, JoyPl, Ormon, Pkrau, Trans

Snowmound

BayBl, Burbk, Hackf, KeriP, Trans

sp soft pink fl, compact 30cm

Parva

villosus now incanus

Dream, KeriP, MillH

Citrullus

lanatus Sugar Baby

MTig #

Citrus

grapefruit varieties

Coatv

grapefruit Golden Special

Chedd, Mtato, Pionr, TreeC

grapefruit Wheeney

Chedd, TreeC

lemon varieties

Coatv

lemon Lisbon
Chedd
lemon Meyer
Burbk, Chedd, LanSc,
Matwh, Mtato, Pionr,
TreeC, Wells
lemon Villa Franca
Chedd, Pionr
lemon Yen Ben
Chedd, LanSc, TreeC
Lemonade
Chedd, Diack, Mtato,
Pionr, TreeC
lime varieties
Coatv
lime Mexican
Mtato
lime Tahitian
Chedd, Pionr, TreeC
**lime West Indian Key Lime
(Lime variety)**
Frans
mandarin varieties
Coatv
mandarin Burgess Scarlet
Chedd, TreeC
mandarin Clementine
Chedd, LanSc, Mtato,
Pionr, TreeC
mandarin Encore
Chedd
mandarin Miyagawa Wase
Chedd
mandarin Murcott
Chedd
mandarin Richards Special
Chedd
mandarin Satsuma
Mtato, Pionr, TreeC
mandarin Silverhill
Chedd, Mtato, Pionr
orange Carters Navel
Chedd, Mtato
orange Harwood Late
Chedd, Mtato
orange Navel
PuhaN
orange Seville
Chedd
orange Valencia
Chedd, PuhaN
orange Washington Navel
Mtato

oranges varieties
Coatv
tangelo
Chedd
tangelo varieties
Coatv
tangelo Seminole
Pionr, TreeC
**trifoliata Italian Strain
rootstock**
Reic #
Ugli
Chedd, Mtato, TreeC

Cladastris
lutea (Yellowwood)
Denes, Dove, Peele,
Pionr, TopTr

Cladium
sinclairii
Reic #

Clarkia
**pulchella Passion for
Purple**
King #
**unguiculata (Rocky
Mountain Garland)**
King #
unguiculata Appleblossom
King #

Clausina
lansium (Wampee)
MTig

Claytonia
megarhiza nivalis
Oasis, Telfa
perfoliata (Miners Lettuce)
King #
virginica
Trans

Clematis
modern hybrids
Vall #
Abundance
YakuN
afoliata (Leafless Clematis)
CouCl, Matai, Orati
akebioides
CouCl
Allanah
Denes

**alpina (Alpine Virgin
Flower)**
BlueM
alpina Columbine
Denes, TRidg
alpina Constance
Denes
alpina Flamingo
Denes
alpina Frances Rivis
Denes, TRidg
alpina Helsingborg
Denes
alpina Pamela Jackman
Denes
alpina Ruby
TRidg
alpina White Columbine
Denes
alpina White Swan
Denes
armandii
Caves, CouCl, Denes
armandii Snowdrift
CouCl, Denes
Asao
Denes
Ascotiensis
Denes
australis
Parva
Barbara Jackman
Denes, YakuN
Bees Jubilee
Parva
Belle Of Woking
Denes, Parva, YakuN
Black Prince
Denes
Blue Lagoon
ZinoN
brachiata (Travellers Joy)
Denes
buchananiana
CouCl
x cartmanii Joe
Denes
Chariisima
Denes
chrysocoma
Ashto
chrysocoma Snowflake
YakuN

cirrhosa
CouCl, Denes, Hackf, YakuN, ZinoN

cirrhosa Freckles
CouCl, Denes, Parva, TRidg

cirrhosa var balearica (Fern-lvd Clematis)
BlueM, CouCl, Denes

Comtesse de Bouchaud
Denes, YakuN

cunninghamii
CouCl, JoyPl, Orati

Daniel Deronda
Denes

Dr Ruppel
Denes, YakuN

Duchess of Albany (texensis)
Denes

Duchess Of Edinburgh
Denes, TRidg

Duchess of Sutherland
Denes

x durandii
YakuN

Edith
Denes

Edomuraski
Denes

Elsa Spath   was Xerxes
Denes

Ernest Markham
Denes, YakuN

Etoile Rose (texensis)
Denes

Fair Rosamunde
Vall #

Fireworks
Denes

flammula
Denes, Hackf, TRidg

Floralia
Denes

florida Alba Plena
Denes

foetida (Scented Clematis)
CouCl, Herew, Orati

forsteri (Puataua)
Matai, Orati, Parva, TRidg

grata
Hackf

Gravetye Beauty (texensis)
Denes

grewiiflora
CouCl

Guiding Star
Denes

Hagley Hybrid
Denes

Henryi
Denes

heracleifolia
BayBl, Parva, TRidg

HF Young
Denes, Parva

Hills Violet
JoyPl

hookeriana
CouCl, JoyPl

Huldine
Denes, YakuN

integrifolia
BayBl, MaraN, TRidg, Vall #

Jackmanii Superba
Denes

japonica
Denes

John Huxtable
Denes

Kathleen Dunford
Denes

Lady Betty Balfour
YakuN

Lady Northcliffe
Denes

Lasurstern
Denes

Lincoln Star
Denes, TRidg, YakuN

Lord Nevill
Denes

Louise Rowe
Denes

macropetala Blue Lagoon now C.m.Maidwell Hall
YakuN

Madame La Coultre now Marie Boisselot
ZinoN

marata
Denes

Marie Boisselot
YakuN

Maureen
Denes

Mme Julia Correvon
Denes, YakuN

Mme le Coultre
Denes, TRidg

montana alba
Ashto, ZinoN

montana Broughton Star
Denes, Taunt

montana Elizabeth
BlueM, CouCl, Denes, YakuN

montana Freda
CouCl, Denes, YakuN, ZinoN

montana Jenny
Denes, Taunt

montana Marjorie
BlueM, CouCl, Denes, YakuN, ZinoN

montana Persian Fragrance
BlueM, Woodl

montana Rubens
Butlr, CouCl, Mtato, Parva

montana Snowflake
Butlr, MillH

montana Tetra Rose
BlueM, CouCl, ZinoN

montana Tetra White
BlueM, CouCl

montana Wilsonii
CouCl, Denes, ZinoN

Mrs Cholmondeley
Denes

Mrs N Thompson
Denes

Mrs Spencer Castle
Denes

napaulensis
Vall #

Nelly Moser
Denes, Vall #, YakuN

Niobe
Denes, Parva

orientalis (Orange-Peel Clematis)
CouCl, Denes, Woodl

Pagoda
Denes

paniculata (Puawhananga)
> CouCl, Gordn, Matai,
> NZtr #, Orati, Parva,
> Taunt, Wahpa

paniculata male
> Denes

Perle d'Azur
> Denes

petriei
> Orati

Pink Champagne
> Denes

Pink Fantasy
> Denes

pitcherii
> Denes

Polish Spirit (vitacella)
> Denes

Prince Charles
> Denes

Princess Of Wales
> YakuN

Proteus
> Denes

recta
> AynDa, JoyPl, MaraN,
> Parva, TRidg

recta Purpurea
> MaraN, MillH, Vall #

Richard Pennell
> Denes

Rouge Cardinal
> Denes

Royalty
> Denes

Scartho Gem
> Denes

seedlgs mixed hybrids
> NewlR

Sir Garnet Wolseley
> Denes, YakuN

Sky Blue
> YakuN

sp white w.lilac-pink edge,4 petals
> Vall #

spooneri
> CouCl

spooneri Snowflake

spoonerii Snowflake
> Denes

stans
> MaraN, Parva, Telfa

Sunset
> Denes

Sylvia Denny
> Denes

tangutica (Golden Clematis
> AynDa, CouCl, Della,
> Denes, Vall #, YakuN

terniflora
> Denes

texensis Sir Trevor Lawrence
> YakuN

The President
> Denes, Parva

tibetana
> Della, TRidg

Twilight
> Denes

Veronica's Choice
> Denes

Ville de Lyon
> Denes

Vino
> Denes

Violet Elizabeth
> Denes, TRidg

viticella
> CouCl, Denes

viticella Purpurea Plena Elegans
> Denes

Vyvyan Pennell
> Denes, YakuN

Wada's Primrose
> Denes, TRidg

Will Goodwin
> Denes, Vall #

Yellow Queen now Moonlight
> Denes

Cleome

deep purple
> Trolh

Helen Campbell (White Cleome)
> King #

pink
> Trolh

spinosa mixed now hassleriana (Spider Flower)
> King #, Koan #

white dwf
> Trolh

Clethra

alnifolia (Sweetpepper Bush)
> Dove, Pukho

alnifolia Rosea
> Denes

arborea (Lily of the Valley Tree)
> Denes

arborea Flore Pleno
> BlueM

delavayi
> Denes

fargesii
> Caves

mexicana
> Caves, MJury

Cleyera

fortunei variegata now japonica Fortunei was Eurya j.v.
> MJury

Clianthus

formosus (Sturts Desert Pea)
> Reic #

puniceus (Kaka Beak,Parrot Beak, Lobster Claw)
> AynDa, BlueM, Chedd,
> Gordn, Matai, Matwh,
> Morgn, Mtato, Orati,
> Terra, Wahpa

puniceus albus (White Kakabeak)
> AynDa, BlueM, Gordn,
> Hackf, Matwh, Morgn,
> NZtr #, Orati, Reic #

puniceus Kaka King
> Matwh

puniceus Maximus
> BlueM

puniceus pink
> Matwh, Reic #

puniceus Red Cardinal (Red Kaka Beak)
> Coatv

puniceus Roseus (Red Kaka Beak)
> NZtr #, Pionr

puniceus White Heron
> Coatv

Clinopodium

vulgare was Calamintha cl. (Wild Basil)
Sweet

Clivia

gardenii
Parva
miniata (Kaffir Lily)
BayBl
miniata Aurea
Parva

Clytostoma

callistegioides (Painted Trumpet)
CouCl, Denes, JoyPl

Cnicus

benedictus (Blessed Thistle)
Orang, Sweet

Cobaea

scandens (Cup & Saucer Vine)
Sweet

Coccoloba

uvifera Sea Grape
LakeN

Cochlearia

armoracia now Armoracia rusticana
Mills, Orang, Sweet, Trolh
officinalis (Scurvy Grass)
Sweet

Codiaeum

hybrids mixed (Crotons)
LakeN
megalocarpus (Croton)
Ether

Codonopsis

clematidea
AynDa, BayBl, MaraN, Reic #
dicentrifolia
MaraN
mollis
MaraN
ovata
Della, MaraN, Pgeon
pilosula
AynDa, CouCl, MaraN
tangshen
MaraN

tubulosa
MaraN
viridis
MaraN, MillH

Coelogyne

massangeana
AnnM

Coix

lacryma-jobi (Job's Tears)
Orang, Sweet

Colchicum

mixed
Kerer
aggripinum
DaffA, Kerer
autumnale
Kerer
minor alba now autumnalea
NewlR
speciosum (Autumn Crocus)
BayBl, JoyPl
speciosum Album
BayBl, Parva
speciosum Atrorubens
JoyPl
The Giant
CottP, DaffA, Kayd, Kerer

Colensoa

physalioides
Orati

Coleonema

album (Breath of Heaven)
MatNu
compactum
Butlr
pulchrum rubrum (Pink Diosma, Confetti Bush)
MatNu, Matwh, Wells
Sunset Gold
BlueM, Hewsn, MatNu, Matwh, Mtato

Coleus

canina now Plectranthus ornatus
Sweet
hybrids (now Solenostemon or Plectranthus)
LakeN

Collinsia

heterophylla (Chinese Houses)
King #

Collospermum

hastatum (Kahakaha, Perching Lily)
Orati, Terra
microspermum
Orati

Colocasia

esculenta (Green Taro, Big Elepht ears)
Frans, Lsendt, WilAq
esculenta Black (Black Taro)
Frans, LakeN, Manna
esculenta Fontanesii (Black Stemmed Taro)
Caves, Lsendt, WilAq

Colquhounia

coccinea
Hackf

Columnea

species
LakeN

Commelina

coelestis (Sleeping Beauty)
AynDa, Della, Kayd, KeriP, King #, Orang, Pgeon, Telfa, TRidg, Vall #
dianthifolia Minor
Vall #

Consolida

ajacis 6 varieties (Larkspurs)
King #
regalis Blue Cloud
King #

Convallaria

majalis (Lily of The Valley)
Ashto, BayBl, CottP, Della, Kayd, MaraN, Mills, Parva, Pgeon, Telfa, TRidg
majalis var rosea
CottP, Della, NewlR, Parva

Convolvulus

varieties
Roswd

Blue Lake
Denes

cantabricus
TRidg

cneorum (Silver Bush)
BayBl, Denes, KeriP,
Mtato, Ormon, Sweet,
Telfa, Trans

Cretian Sunset
Peak

**mauritanicus now
sabatius**
BayBl, CottP, Denes,
KeriP, NewlR, Nikau,
Ormon, Pgeon, Sweet,
Telfa, Trans, Trolh

Red Ensign
King #

Rose Ensign
King #

Royal Ensign
Della, King #

**sabatius was mauritanicus
(Ground Morning Glory)**
MaraN, Mtato, Oasis

White Ensign
King #

Cooperia
pendunculata (Rusty Stars)
CottP

Coprosma
**acerosa (Sand Dune
Coprosma)**
Butlr, Frans, Hackf,
Looij, Matai, Matwh,
Morgn, Mtato, Orati,
Pkrau, Terra

**acerosa brunnea (Brown
Stemmed Coprosma)**
Orati, Terra

acerosa Hawera
Frans, Matai

acerosa hybrid
Orati

arborea (Mamangi)
Orati

areolata
Orati

australis (Kanono)
Mtato

Beatsons Bronze
Orati

Beatsons Brown
Gordn

Beatsons Gold
BlueM, Butlr, Chedd,
Gordn, Hewsn, Matai,
Matwh, Mtato, Orati,
Pkrau, SelGr, Wahpa

Black Beauty
Matai

Brunette
Wahpa

**brunnea (Fruiting
Coprosma)**
BlueM, Gordn, Pionr

brunnea x kirkii
Gordn

Chatham Is Hybrid
Butlr

cheesemanii
Orati

Chocolate Soldier
Hewsn, Matai

Clearwater Gold
Pkrau

Coppershine
BlueM, Ford, Matai,
Mtato, Wahpa

crassifolia
Orati

Cutie
Wahpa

depressa
Matai

foetidissima (Stinkwood)
Matai

Glistener
Butlr, Orati

grandifolia (Kanono)
Gordn, NZtr #, Orati,
Terra, Wahpa

Greensleeves
BlueM, Hewsn, Mtato,
Orati, Pkrau

Hawera
Orati

Katie reyolds
Orati

kirkii
BlueM, CottP, Diack,
Ford, Gordn, Hewsn,
McKe, Morgn, Mtato,
Orati, Pionr, Terra,
Wahpa

kirkii Goldstream
Matai, Orati, Wahpa

kirkii kirkii
Ormon

kirkii Taiko
Gordn, Looij, Matwh,
Orati

kirkii variegata
BlueM, Butlr, Ford,
Gordn, Hewsn, Matai,
Mtato, Orati, Pionr, Terra

Kiwi Gold
Butlr, Ford, Gordn,
Hewsn, Matwh, Mtato

Lawrie Metcalf
Pkrau

linearifolia
Orati

Lobster
Matai, Wahpa

lucida (Shining Karamu)
Chedd, Gordn, NZtr #,
Orati, Terra, Wahpa

macrocarpa
Orati

Middlemore
Orati

neglecta
Orati

Ngaere
Wahpa

parvifolia
Orati

Pride
Butlr, Matai, Matwh,
Mtato, Orati, Wahpa

propinqua (Mingimingi)
Matai, Orati, Pionr,
Pkrau, SouWo, Terra,
Wahpa, Wensl

propinqua Greyii
Orati

prostrata
Frans, Gordn, Matwh,
McKe, Mtato, Orati,
Terra

repens (Taupata)
Matwh, Morgn, Mtato,
NZtr #, Orati, Pionr, Reic
#, Seasd, Terra

repens Bronze
Orati

repens Marble Queen
Butlr, Hewsn, Kayd,
Matwh, Orati

repens Painters palette
Chedd, Gordn, Matwh,
Mtato, Orati

repens Picturata
Mtato, Orati

repens Pink Splendour
Chedd, Gordn, Orati,
Wahpa

repens prostrate form
Frans, Orati

repens Silver Queen
Butlr, Gordn, Orati

repens variegata
Orati

repens Yvonne
Butlr, Matwh, Orati,
Wahpa

rhamnoides
Gordn, Orati

rigida
Orati, Terra

robusta (Karamu)
Ford, Gordn, Matai,
Matwh, Morgn, Mtato,
NZtr #, Orati, Pionr,
SouWo, Sweet, Terra,
Wahpa

robusta Gordons Gold
BlueM

robusta Williamsii Variegata
BlueM

Rod Syme
Mtato

rotundifolia
Mtato

Roys Red
Mtato, Wahpa

rubra
Matai

rugosa (Wrinkled Coprosma)
BlueM, Diack, Matai,
Orati

rugosa Clearwater Gold
BlueM, Matai

rugosa Prostrata
Matai

spathulata
Gordn, Orati

Taupata Gold
Wells

tenuicaulis
Orati

tenuifolia
Matai

Thompsons Hybrid
Butlr

Tuffet
Wahpa

variegata
Gordn

virescens
Caves, Orati, Wahpa

waima
Orati

Walter Brockie
BlueM

williamsii
Gordn

Cordia

abyssinica
Diher

Cordyline

australis (Cabbage Tree, Ti Kouka)
Apple, BlueM, Burbk,
Chedd, Coatv, Diack,
Dove, EasyB, Ford,
Gordn, Matai, Matwh,
Morgn, Mtato, NZtr #,
Orati, Ormon, Pionr,
Pkrau, Pukho, Reic #,
Sweet, Terra, Wahpa,
Wells, Wensl

australis Albertii
Denes, Orati

australis Purpurea Group
Burbk, Dove, Gordn,
Manna, Matai, Matwh,
Morgn, Mtato, NZtr #,
Orati, Pionr, Reic #,
Wahpa

banksii (Ti-ngahere, Forest Cabbage Tree)
Burbk, Dove, Matwh,
Mtato, NZtr #, Orati,
Pionr, Terra, Wensl

banksii purpurea
Pionr

bauerii
Coatv, Frans

Green Goddess
Coatv, Matwh, Mtato,
Orati

hybrid wide leaf red/green (tropical)
Manna

indivisa (Toi, Mountain Cabbage Tree)
BlueM, Denes, Manna,
Matai, NZtr #, Orati,
Pionr, Pkrau, Terra,
Wahpa

kaspar
Orati

nigra
Frans

pumilio (Dwarf Cabbage Tree)
Gordn, Matai, Orati

Purple Tower
Coatv, EasyB, Matwh,
Mtato, Orati

stricta
Frans, Reic #

terminalis now fruticosa
LakeN

terminalis amabilis
Frans

terminalis green wild form
Frans

terminalis hybrids :yellow,bronze,red,black, pink
LakeN, Reic #

terminalis Tricolour (Dragon Tree)
Manna

Coreopsis

Baby Gold
Pgeon

basalis Golden Crown
King #

grandiflora (Tickseed)
Looij, Orang

grandiflora Badengold
MillH

grandiflora Domino
BayBl

grandiflora Early Sunrise
DayBl, CoFlo, CottP,
Della, KeriP, King #,
Mills, Nikau, Oasis,
Pgeon, Telfa

grandiflora Sunburst
Marsh

lanceolata Sterntaler
Pgeon

rosea American Dream
CottP, KeriP, MillH,
Parva, Telfa

SP Nova
Telfa

Sunray
BayBl, Kayd

tinctoria (Dyer's Coreopsis)
King #, Orang, Sweet

tinctoria Sunny Boy

CottP, MillH

verticillata

BayBl, MaraN, MillH, NewlR, Nikau

verticillata Moonbeam

BayBl, CoFlo, CottP, Della, Egmon, Hackf, JoyPl, Nikau, Pkrau, Telfa, Trans, Warwk

verticillata Rosea

Trans

verticillata Zagreb

BayBl, Parva

Coriandrum

sativum (Coriander, Cilantro)

Della, King #, Koan #, Sweet, Trans, Trolh

Coriaria

angustissima (Dense Tutu)

NZtr #

arborea (Tutu)

NZtr #, Orati, Terra

Cornus

varieties

Coatv

alba (Redbarked Dogwood)

Caves, Dove, Pkrau, TopTr

alba Elegantissima (v)

BlueM, Denes, Diack, Dove, Pukho

alba Sibirica (Westonbirt, Siberian Dogwood)

BlueM, Chedd, Denes, TopTr

alba Spaethii (v)

BlueM, Pukho, TopTr

alternifolia (Pagoda Dogwood)

Chedd, Denes

alternifolia Argentea (v)

Caves

amomum

Caves, Denes, Dove, EasyB

canadensis

MaraN, TopTr

capitata (Himalayan Strawberry tree)

BlueM, Chedd, Coatv, Denes, Diack, Dove, Ford, Matwh, Morgn, Pukho, Reic #

controversa (Wedding Cake/Table Dogwood)

Burbk, Caves, Chedd, Denes, EasyB, MJury, Mtato, Pionr, Pukho

controversa Variegata

Caves

Eddies White Wonder

Denes, Mtato, Peele, Pionr, Pukho, TopTr

florida (Flowering Dogwood)

Apple, Chedd, Dove, Hewsn, Mtato, Peele, TopTr

florida Cherokee Chief

Denes, Peele, Pionr, Pukho

florida Cherokee Daybreak

Chedd, Denes, Pukho

florida Cherokee Princess

Denes, Pukho

florida Cherokee Sunset

Chedd, Denes, Pukho

florida Cloud 9

Chedd, Denes, Peele, Pukho

florida Pendula

Denes, Pukho

florida Rainbow (v)

Chedd, Denes

florida rubra

Diack

florida Spring Song

Denes

florida Stokes Pink

Denes, Pukho

kousa (Japanese Dogwood)

Chedd, Dove

kousa angustata (Evergreen Japanese Dogwood)

Chedd

kousa chinensis (Chinese Dogwood)

Apple, Burbk, Caves, Denes, Ford, Peele, Pkrau, PuhaN, Pukho, TopTr

kousa chinensis National

Denes

kousa chinensis Southern Cross

Denes, Pukho

macrophylla

Caves

mas (Cornelian Cherry)

Apple, Chedd, Diack, Dove, Peele, PuhaN

mas Aurea (v)

Denes, Pukho

nuttalli (Pacific/Mountain Dogwood)

Caves, Chedd, Denes, Ford, TopTr

officinalis

Apple, Denes

pumila

Peak, TopTr

sanguinea (European Dogwood)

Chedd, Dove

stolonifera

Apple

stolonifera Flaviramea

BlueM, Caves, Diack, Pkrau, TopTr

stolonifera Kelseyi (Red Osier Dogwood)

BlueM, Denes, TopTr

Corokia

buddleioides (Korokio taranga)

Gordn, Matai, Matwh, Orati, SelGr, Terra, Wahpa

cheesemanii

Gordn, Orati

cotoneaster (Korokio, Wirenetting Bush)

Chedd, Gordn, Matwh, Mtato, NZtr #, Orati, Pkrau, Terra, Wahpa

cotoneaster Little Prince

Matai, Mtato, Orati

cotoneaster Prostrate

Matai

hubbeloides

BlueM

macrocarpa (Whakataka, Hokotaka, Chatham Is Korokio)

Ford, Matai, Mtato, Orati, Terra, Wahpa

Sun Flash

Gordn

x virgata

Ford, Matai, Morgn, Ormon

x virgata Bronze Erecta

Orati

x virgata Bronze King

Diack, Hewsn, Kayd,
Mtato, Orati, Pionr,
Wahpa, ZinoN

x virgata Bronze Knight

Matai, SelGr

x virgata Bronze Lady

BlueM

virgata Emerald and Jade
(Emerald Gem, Green
Jade)

Orati, Wells

virgata Frosted Chocolate

BlueM, Kayd, Matai,
Matwh, Mtato, Orati,
Wahpa, Wells

virgata Geenty's Green

Mtato, Orati, Pionr, Wells

x virgata Red Wonder

BlueM, Diack, Hewsn,
Orati, Pkrau, Wensl,
ZinoN

x virgata Sunsplash

BlueM, Hewsn, Matai,
Mtato, Orati, Pionr,
Wahpa

x virgata Yellow Wonder

BlueM, Diack, Hewsn,
Orati, Wensl

Coronilla

valentina ssp glauca
Variegata (Daffodil Bush)

BlueM

varia

MaraN, Parva

varia Penngift
(Crownvetch)

Della, King #

Correa

alba

Mtato

backhouseana

BlueM

Dusky Bells

Mtato

flexulosa

BlueM

x h. Tomato Red

BlueM

mannii

Denes

pulchella

Denes

pulchella Minor

BlueM

pulchella New Pink

Denes

reflexa alba

BlueM

Cortaderia

fulvida (Mtn Toetoe,
Kakaho)

BlueM, JoyPl, Morgn,
Mtato, Orati, Terra,
Wahpa

richardii (S.Is Toetoe)

Matai, Morgn, NZtr #,
Terra

selloana (Pampas)

Diack, Ford, Mtato, Pionr

selloana Gold Band (v)

BlueM, Gordn, Hains,
Matai, Pionr

splendens (Toetoe)

Orati, Terra

Toe Toe Miniature

Ford

toetoe (Coastal N.Is Toetoe)

Dove, Hewsn, Matwh,
Morgn, Mtato, NZtr #,
Orati, Pionr, Terra, Wensl

tubaria (Pitt Is Toetoe)

JoyPl

Cortusa

matthioli

AynDa, Pgeon

matthioli Alba

Pgeon

Corydalis

cheilanthifolia

AynDa, Nikau, Parva,
Trans, TRidg

flexuosa

CoFlo, Mills, Oasis,
Otepo, Pgeon, Trans

flexuosa Blue Panda

Parva, Telfa

flexuosa China Blue

Parva, Peak, Warwk

flexuosa Heavenly Blue

KeriP, Nikau, Taunt,
Telfa, TRidg

flexuosa Pere David

BayBl, JoyPl, Nikau,
Parva, Peak

flexuosa Purple Leaf

Peak

lutea

Nikau, Parva

ochroleuca

Parva

ophiocarpa

AynDa, Dream, Nikau

sempervirens

Vall #

sempervirens alba

Dream

sempervirens Rock
Harlequin

AynDa, KeriP, King #,
Nikau

solida

NewlR

Corylopsis

pauciflora

Caves

sinensis Spring Purple

Denes, Pukho

spicata (Spiked Winter
Hazel)

Caves, Denes, Peele

willmottiae now sinensis s.
(Willmotts Winter Hazel)

Caves, Dove, Pukho,
TopTr

Corylus

avellana (Hazelnut)

Apple, Diack, Dove,
Ford, Hewsn, PuhaN

avellana doublegrafted:
Alexandra,Barcelona

Harri

avellana 1102

Chedd

avellana Alexandra

Chedd, Harri, Pionr

avellana Appleby

WHazl

avellana Barcelona

Harri, Pionr, WHazl

avellana Butler

Chedd, Harri, WHazl

avellana Campanica

WHazl

avellana Contorta
(Corkscrew Hazel, Harry
Lauder's Walking Stick)

Denes, Pukho, TopTr

avellana Ennis

Harri, WHazl

avellana Heterophylla
Apple

avellana Keen's Late
WHazl

avellana Merveille de Bolwiller
Chedd, Denes, Diack, Harri, WHazl

avellana MT.12-23
WHazl

avellana MT.18-114
WHazl

avellana Noccione
Chedd, WHazl

avellana Nottingham(Wispit, White Skinned Filbert)
Chedd, WHazl

avellana Oregon Barcelona
Chedd

avellana Plowright
WHazl

avellana San Giovanni
WHazl

avellana Tonda Di Giffoni
WHazl

avellana Tonda Gentile Delle Langhe
WHazl

avellana Tondo Romano
Chedd, WHazl

avellana Webb's Prize Nut
WHazl

avellana Whiteheart (Whatnot)
Chedd, Denes, Harri, WHazl

colurna (Turkish Filbert, Tree Hazel)
Apple, Caves, Denes, Peele, TopTr

maxima Purpurea (Purple-lvd Hazel)
Denes, Pionr, Pukho

Corynocarpus

laevigata (Karaka, NZ Laurel)
Butlr, Coatv, Denes, Gordn, Manna, Matwh, Morgn, Mtato, NZtr #, Orati, Pionr, Reic #, Terra

laevigata variegated cream or yellow
Manna

Cosmidium

burridgeanum Brunette
King #

Cosmos

atrosanguineus Chocolate Cosmos
Hackf, Nikau

bipinnatus 9 varieties
King #

bipinnatus Early Wonder
Reic #

bipinnatus Sensation mixed
Reic #

peucedanifolius (Candy Cosmos)
Parva

sulphurus Bright Lights mixed
King #

Cotinus

coggygria (Smoke Bush, Venetian Sumach)
Apple, BlueM, Chedd, Denes, Dove, Peele, Pionr, PuhaN, Pukho

coggygria Foliis Purpureis
Peele

coggygria Purpureus
BlueM, Chedd, Dove, PuhaN

coggygria Royal Purple
BlueM, Denes, Pukho

coggygria Velvet Cloak
Taunt

Grace
BlueM, TopTr

Cotoneaster

affinis
Diack

conspicuus
Diack

dammeri Skogholm
Mtato

decumbens
Looij

frigidus
Chedd

frigidus Cornubia
EasyB

horizontalis
Butlr

horizontalis Superba
BlueM

microphyllus (Rockspray Cotoneaster)
BlueM, Denes, Ford, Frans, Ormon

nitens
Apple, Diack, Dove, Ormon, TopTr

Red Fan
BlueM, Ford

Royal Beauty
BlueM, Ford

Cotula

coronopifolia (Soldiers Buttons, Yellow Buttons, Brass Buttons)
Orati, WaiMa

major
MillH

serrulata now Leptinella s.
Seasd

squalida now Leptinella sq.
CottP

squalida Platts Black
CottP, Otepo, Seasd

Cotyledon

orbiculata glauca
Ormon

simplicifolia now Chiastophyllum oppositifolium
Ashto

Crambe

cordifolia
MaraN

cordifolia Snowstorm
Dream

maritima
MaraN, Seasd

Craspedia

globosa (Billy Buttons)
King #

Crassula

arborescens
Frans

fascularis
Wells

sarcocaulis
BayBl, Della, Seasd

sarcocaulis alba
Della, Seasd

sedifolia
  Seasd

Crataegus

x grignonensis
  Caves

laevigata Masekii
  Denes, Pukho

laevigata Plena was oxycantha P.
  Denes

laevigata Punicea
  Pukho

oxycantha Pauls Scarlet now laevigata PS (Crimson Hawthorn)
  Pukho

Crepis

Blush Pink
  Nikau

incana
  Della

rubra
  Dream, King #

rubra var alba Snow White
  Dream, King #, Nikau

Crinodendron

hookerianum (Chilean Lantern Tree)
  BlueM

Crinum

bulbispermum
  DaffA, JoyPl, Parva

campanulatum
  JoyPl

moorei
  DaffA, JoyPl

moorei variegata
  JoyPl

x powellii
  Trans

Crocosmia

golden yellow (x crocosmiifolia)
  Irida

Lady Hamilton (x croscosmiiflora)
  BayBl

Lucifer
  BayBl, Parva

masoniorum (Montbretia)
  Ashto

orange red Bressingham hybrid
  Irida

Solfaterre (x croscosmiiflora)
  BayBl, Parva

Star of the East
  BayBl, Parva

Crocus

mixed
  Kayd

asturicus now serotinus salzmanni form
  RosPl

aureus now flavus
  NewlR

banaticus
  Kerer

biflorus Pulchricolor
  Kerer

biflorus Weldenii Fairy
  Kerer

chrysanthus varieties 10 mixed
  RosPl

chrysanthus Blue Pearl
  DaffA, VanEe

chrysanthus Blue Pearl/Blue Peter mixd
  Kerer

chrysanthus Constellation
  DaffA

chrysanthus Cream Beauty
  Kerer, VanEe

chrysanthus EA Bowles
  DaffA

chrysanthus EP Bowles
  DaffA

chrysanthus Goldilocks
  DaffA, Kerer

chrysanthus Gypsy Girl
  DaffA, Kerer

chrysanthus Harlequin
  DaffA

chrysanthus Jean D'Arc
  DaffA, VanEe

chrysanthus Ladykiller
  DaffA

chrysanthus Princess Beatrix
  DaffA

chrysanthus Purity
  Kerer, VanEe

chrysanthus Snow Bunting
  Winga

chrysanthus Sunkist
  VanEe

chrysanthus White Triumphator
  DaffA

chrysanthus Zwanenburg Bronze
  DaffA, VanEe

Cinderella
  VanEe

clusii see serotinus clusii
  RosPl

corsicus
  Kerer

dalmaticus
  Kerer

dutch hybrids (white,blue,yellow)
  RosPl

etruscus
  Kerer

etruscus Zwanenburg
  Kerer

Firefly
  VanEe

flavus was aureus
  Kerer

goulimyi
  Kerer

hadriaticus
  Kerer

hadriaticus chrysobelonicus now hadriaticus
  Kerer

imperatii ssp suaveolens
  Kerer

korolkowii
  Kerer

kotschyanus
  Kerer, RosPl

kotschyanus ssp kotschyanus albus
  Kerer

kotschyanus Suwarowianus
  Kerer

kotschyanus var leucopharynx
  Kerer

laevigatus
  Kerer

laevigatus Fontenayi
NewlR

longiflorus / medius mixd
Kerer

x luteus Golden Yellow was
Mammoth Y, GM, Dutch Y
VanEe

malyi
Kerer

Mammoth Yellow now x
luteus Golden Y.
VanEe

medius
Kerer

minimus
Kerer

niveus
Kerer

nudiflorus
Kerer

ochroleucus
Kerer

oxonian
RosPl

pestalozzae albus
Kerer

pestalozzae mixed blue &
white
Kerer

Prince Claus
VanEe

pulchellus
Kerer

pulchellus albus
Kerer

pulchellus Zephyr
Kerer

sativus (Saffron Crocus)
Parva, Winga

sativus cashmirianus
Parva

serotinus ssp clusii
Kerer, RosPl

serotinus ssp salzmannii
was asturicus
DaffA, JoyPl, Kerer,
RosPl

sieberi atticus
Kerer

sieberi sieberi
Kerer

sieberi sublimis Tricolor
Kerer

sieheanus
Kerer

speciosus
Kerer, NewlR

speciosus Cassiope
Kerer

speciosus Oxonian
DaffA, Kerer

tommasinianus
Kerer, RosPl

tommasinianus albus
Kerer

vallicola
Kerer

veluchensis
Kerer

vernus Graceus
Kerer

vernus Grand Maitre
VanEe

vernus Harlem Gem
Kerer

vernus Joan Of Arc
Winga

vernus lge deep purple
NewlR

vernus lge purple
NewlR

vernus Pickwick
Kerer, Winga

vernus Purple Giant
Winga

vernus Queen Of The Blues
Winga

vernus scepusiensis
Kerer

vernus siculus
Kerer

vernus ssp albiflorus
Kerer

vitellinus
Kerer

Zwanenburg Glory
Parva

Crowea

exalata Bindelong Compact
MatNu, Matth

exalata White Star
MatNu, Matth

Festival
MatNu

Cryptandra

scortechinii (Buckthorn)
Denes, MatNu, Matth

Cryptomeria

japonica (Sugi/Japanese
Cedar)
Burbk, Chedd, CPete,
Dove, Ford, McKe,
Mtato, NZtr #, Ormon,
Pionr, PuhaN, SouWo,
TopTr

japonica Antique Gold
Butlr, Cedar, CPete

japonica araucarioides
BlueM, Cedar

japonica Atawhai
Cedar

japonica Bandai-Sugi
Cedar, CPete

japonica Beaumonts
Cedar

japonica Compacta Nana
Cedar

japonica Compressa
Cedar, CPete, MJury

japonica Cristata
Cedar

japonica Dacrydioides see
C.j.araucarioides
Cedar

japonica Egmont
Cedar

japonica Elegans (Plume
Cedar)
BlueM, Burbk, Cedar,
CPete, Ford, Hewsn,
SelGr

japonica Elegans Aurea
BlueM, Burbk, Cedar,
CPete, Pionr

japonica Elegans
Compacta
BlueM, Cedar, Ford

japonica Elegans Nana
BlueM, Cedar, CPete

japonica Elegans Plumosa
BlueM

japonica Globosa
CPete

japonica Globosa Nana
BlueM, Cedar, CPete

japonica Haggo
Cedar

japonica Jindai-Sugi
BlueM, Cedar

japonica knaptonensis
Cedar

japonica Littleworth Dwarf
Cedar, CPete

japonica lobbii
Cedar

japonica Monstrosa
BlueM

japonica monstrosa nana
Cedar

japonica Sekkan Sugi
Cedar, CPete

japonica spiralis (Granny's Ringlets)
BlueM, Cedar

japonica Spiraliter Falcater
Cedar

japonica Tensan
Cedar, CPete

japonica Vilmoriniana
BlueM, Butlr, Cedar, CPete

Cryptotaenia

japonica (Mitsuba)
King #, MTig #

Ctenanthe

species
Frans

Cucumis

cucumber Armenian Yard Long
King #

cucumber Dekah
Koan #

cucumber Fanfare Hybrid
King #

cucumber French Cornichorn
MTig #

cucumber Lemon
King #

cucumber oriental Soo Yoh
King #

cucumber Perfection
MTig #

cucumber Port Albert
Koan #

melon musk Sweet Granite
MTig #

melon Pie Melon
Koan #

melon rock Honey Dew
MTig #

melon rock Sunrise
King #

melon rock Sweet n'Early
King #

melon tropical Passport
King #

Cucurbita

ficifolia (Chilacayote, Perennial Squash)
MTig #

pumpkin Atlantic Giant
King #

pumpkin Austrian Hull-less
Koan #

pumpkin Bill Skinners (american heirloom)
Koan #

pumpkin Buttercup(non-hybrid form)
Koan #

pumpkin Chuck's Winter (american heirloom)
Koan #

pumpkin Jack Be Little
King #

pumpkin Kumi-kumi
King #, Koan #

pumpkin maxima Baby Blue
MTig #

pumpkin moschata Butternut
MTig #

pumpkin Prize Winner
King #

squash 7 varieties
King #

summer squash Little Gem
MTig #

vegetable gourd Sweet Dumpling
King #

Cuminum

cyminum (Cumin)
King #, Sweet

Cunninghamia

konishii
Cedar

lanceolata (Chinese Coffin Tree, Chinese Fir)
BlueM, Burbk, Butlr, Cedar, Coatv, CPete, Denes, Matwh, NZtr #, Pionr, PuhaN, WakaC

lanceolata from Nth Vietnam
Cedar

lanceolata Glauca
Cedar, CPete

Cunonia

capensis (Butterknife Bush)
Denes, Reic #, Wells

Cupaniopsis

anarcardioides (Tuckeroo)
Frans

Cuphea

bianca
KeriP

hyssopifolia Rob's Mauve
Kayd, KeriP, Pgeon

hyssopifolia Ruby
KeriP

hyssopifolia White Whisper
KeriP, Pgeon

ignea (Cigar/Firecracker Plant)
KeriP

ignea alba
KeriP

llavea Tiny Mice
Parva

macropetala (Cigar Plant)
Hackf

Mad Hatter
KeriP

Midget
KeriP

viscosissima mixed
Vall #

Cupressocyparis

arilosa
Cedar

leylandii (Leyland Cypress)
Coatv, WakaC

leylandii Castlewellan Gold
BlueM, Butlr, Cedar, Chedd, CPete, Diack, Ford, Hewsn, Matai, Mtato, Pionr, SouWo, Wensl

**leylandii Ferndown was
Stapehill 21**

Cedar, Diack, Matai

leylandii Green Spire

BlueM, Matai

leylandii Haggerston Grey

Ford, Matai, SouWo

leylandii Leigton's Green

BlueM, Butlr, Cedar,
Chedd, CPete, Diack,
Dove, Ford, Hewsn,
Matai, Matwh, Mtato,
Pionr, SelGr, SouWo,
TopTr, Wensl

leylandii Mellow yellow

Cedar, Mtato, Pionr

leylandii Naylors Blue

BlueM, Cedar, Ford,
Matai, Mtato, SouWo,
TopTr

leylandii Robinsons Gold

BlueM, Butlr, Diack,
Dove, Hewsn, Matai

leylandii Rua

BlueM, Cedar

leylandii Silver Dust (v)

Cedar

leylandii Stapehill

BlueM, Matai

leylandii Stardust

BlueM

leylandii Superl

Cedar

notabilis

Cedar

ovensii

BlueM, Cedar, Ford,
Matai, McKe, WakaC

Cupressus

arizonica (Arizona Cypress

Chedd, Diack, Dove,
Ford, Matai, Morgn,
Mtato, NZtr #, Pionr,
SouWo, Wensl

arizonica arizonica

Cedar

**arizonica arizonica Arctic
(Smooth Arizona Cypress)**

BlueM, Cedar, CPete

**arizonica arizonica Arctic
fine foliage**

Cedar

**arizonica glabra Blue
Beauty**

Cedar

arizonica glabra Blue Ice

BlueM, Cedar, Coatv,
CPete, Diack, Matai,
Mtato

**arizonica glabra Blue
Pyramid**

Cedar

**arizonica glabra Blue
Streak**

Cedar

**arizonica glabra Gold
Pyramid**

Cedar

**arizonica glabra Silver
Smoke**

Cedar

arizonica revealiana

Cedar

arizonica stephensonii

Cedar

assamica

Cedar

bakerii

Cedar

**cashmeriana (Kashmir
Cypress)**

BlueM, Cedar, CPete

cashmeriana Fernside

Cedar

chengiana (Cheng Cypress)

Cedar

dargeelingensis

Cedar

**duclouxiana (Chinese
Cypress)**

Cedar

**forbesii var Baja
californica**

Cedar

**forbesii var Baja californica
cv Azul**

Cedar

**funebris now
Chamaecyparis f. (Chinese
Weeping Cypress)**

Cedar, Diack

**goveniana var pygmaea
(Mendocina Cypress)**

Cedar

**guadalupensis (Guadalupe
Cypress)**

Cedar

**guadalupensis var forbesii
syn C.forbesii**

Cedar

Lemon Spire

BlueM

**lusitanica
(Mexican/Bentham Cypress**

Apple, Cedar, Chedd,
Dove, Ford, Matai,
Matwh, McKe, Morgn,
Mtato, NZtr #, Pionr,
PuhaN, SouWo, Terra,
WakaC

lusitanica selected clones

WakaC

**lusitanica var benthamii
Mangamahoe**

Cedar

**macnabiana (MacNab's
Cypress)**

Cedar, WakaC

macnabiana glauca

Cedar

macrocarpa (Longwoods)

Pionr

**macrocarpa (Monterey
Cypress)**

Apple, BlueM, Chedd,
Diack, Dove, Ford,
Matai, Matwh, Morgn,
Mtato, NZtr #, PuhaN,
SelGr, SouWo, Terra,
WakaC, Wensl

macrocarpa Aurea

CPete

macrocarpa Aurea Saligna

Caves, Cedar, CPete

macrocarpa Brunneana

Cedar

macrocarpa Fine Gold

Burbk, Cedar, Coatv,
CPete, Matai, Mtato,
Pionr, Pukho

macrocarpa Gold Crest

Cedar, CPete

macrocarpa Gold Pillar

BlueM, Cedar, CPete,
Diack, Matai

macrocarpa Gold Spread

Cedar

**macrocarpa Greenstead
Magnificent**

BlueM, Cedar, CPete

**macrocarpa horizontalis
Aurea**

Cedar, Pionr

**macrocarpa Lambertiana
aurea see C.m.horizontalis
aurea**

Cedar

macrocarpa selected clones
WakaC

macrocarpa Sunshine
Cedar, Pionr

macrocarpa var Kukupa
Apple, Matai, SouWo, WakaC

pseudohimalaico
Cedar

sargentii (Sargent Cypress)
Cedar

sempervirens (Mediterranean Cypress)
NZtr #, Ormon, WakaC

sempervirens Gracilis
BlueM, Cedar, Chedd, Coatv, CPete, Denes, Diack, Mtato, Pionr

sempervirens Horizontalis
WakaC

sempervirens Pendula
Cedar

sempervirens stricta (Italian Pencil/Upright Cypress)
Apple, Burbk, Cedar, Chedd, Dove, Ford, Morgn, Pionr

sempervirens Swanes Golden
BlueM, Burbk, Cedar, CPete, Denes

sempervirens Swanes Variegata
Cedar

sempervirens Totem
BlueM, Cedar, Coatv, Denes, TopTr

torulosa (Himalayan/Bhutan Cypress)
Cedar, Diack, Ford, LanSc, Matai, Mtato, Pionr, WakaC

torulosa Aurea
Cedar, CPete

torulosa Battley's
Cedar

torulosa Fernside
Cedar

torulosa glauca
Cedar

X850-329
Ford, Matai

Curcuma

roscoeana (Siam Lily)
LakeN, Parva

Cussonia

paniculata (Mountain Cabbage Tree)
Reic #

spicata (Common Cabbage Tree)
Reic #

Cyananthus

lobatus
Vall #

Cyathea

australis (Rough/Hard Tree Fern)
Gordn, JoyPl

cooperi (Cicatrice Tree Fern)
Coatv, JoyPl

cunninghamia tropical
Manna

dealbata (Silver Fern)
Coatv, Gordn, Manna, Morgn, Orati, Terra

kermadecensis
Orati

medullaris (Black Mamaku, Black Ponga)
Coatv, Gordn, Mtato, Orati, Terra

milnei
Orati

smithii (Whe)
Coatv, Gordn, Morgn, Mtato, Orati, Pionr, Terra

Cycas

species
Reic #

revoluta (Sago Palm)
MJury, PalmF

revoluta female
LakeN

revoluta male
LakeN

Cyclamen

africanum
DaffA, Parva, TRidg

africanum A form
DaffA, Parva

balearicum
DaffA

cilicium
DaffA, TRidg

coum
NewlR, Ormon, Parva, TRidg

coum album
DaffA

coum Carmine
BayBl, DaffA

coum caucasicum
MJury

coum kusnetiovii
DaffA

coum Pink
BayBl, DaffA

coum Roseum
Pgeon

creticum
DaffA

cyprium
DaffA

graecum
BayBl, DaffA, JoyPl, MJury, Parva

hederifolium
Ashto, BayBl, DaffA, Della, Ormon, Parva, RosPl, Winga

hederifolium album
DaffA, Ormon, Parva

hederifolium Apollo
JoyPl

hederifolium Bowles Apollo
DaffA, Parva

hederifolium Perlenteppich
TRidg

hederifolium pink
MJury

hederifolium white
MJury

intaminatum
BayBl, DaffA, Parva, TRidg

libanoticum
BayBl, DaffA, TRidg

mirabile
DaffA

orbiculatum now coum
DaffA

persicum
DaffA, JoyPl

persicum Mirabelle
DaffA

pseudibericum
DaffA, Parva

purpurascens
DaffA

repandum
DaffA, MJury

repandum Album
DaffA

rohlfsianum
Parva

Cyclosorus

interruptus
Orati

Cydonia

oblonga (Quince)
Chedd, TopTr, TreeC

oblonga Smyrna
Denes, Harri, Pionr

oblonga Van Dieman
Pionr

Cymbalaria

muralis was Linaria (Kenilworth Ivy, Ivy-lvd Toad Flax)
CottP

muralis Rosea
Wells

Cymbidium

many hybrids
NormP

Cymbopogon

citratus (Lemongrass)
Koan, MTig, MTig #, Orang, Sweet, Trolh

Cynara

cardunculus (Cardoon)
AynDa, CoFlo, Della, Dream, JoyPl, King #, MaraN, Mills, Nikau, Orang, Peak, Roswd, Seasd, TopTr, TRidg, Trolh

cardunculus scolymus (Globe Artichoke)
Della, Mills, Orang, Pgeon, Trans, Vall #

cardunculus scolymus Green Globe Improved
King #, Trolh

cardunculus scolymus Purple de Jesi
King #, Trans

cardunculus scolymus Purple Romanesco
King #, Trans

cardunculus White Ivory
King #

Cynoglossum

amabile (Chinese Forget-me-not)
KeriP, Koan #, Marsh, Vall #

amabile Album
King #

amabile Avalanche
Vall #

amabile Firmament
King #, Nikau

amabile Mystery Rose
Dream, King #

amabile pink
Vall #

glochidiatum
MaraN, Marsh

nervosum
MaraN

nervosum Blue
Telfa

officinale (Hounds Tongue)
Sweet

officinale blue
Orang

officinale pink
Orang

Slate Blue
Marsh

Cyperus

alternifolius now involucratus (Umbrella Grass)
Hains, Reic #, WaiMa

alternifolius Nanus
Reic #

alternifolius Nanus Compactus
WaiMa

haspan (Dwarf Papyrus)
Hains, WaiMa, WilAq

minima
WaiMa

papyrus (Egyptian Papyrus)
Hains, Reic #

ustutalus
Hains, NZtr #, Orati

Cyphomandra

betacea Golden
MTig #

betacea Orange (wild)
Koan

betacea Red
Koan, MTig #, Reic #

betacea varieties (Tamarillo)
TreeC

cajanumensis (Casana)
Koan, MTig

Cypripedium

japonicum
Titok

Cyrilla

racemiflora
Woodl

Cyrtanthus

elatus was Vallota speciosa (Scarborough Lily
AynDa, DaffA

elatus Delicatus was Vallota
DaffA

elatus pink
Kayd

elatus red
Kayd

mackenii
MJury, Trans

mackenii hybrids mixed
DaffA

obrienii
BayBl, Kayd

Red Prince
DaffA, JoyPl

sanguineus
JoyPl

Venus
Altrf

Cyrtomium

falcatum Rochefordianum
Reic #

fortunei
Reic #

Cytisus

battandieri (Pineapple/Morocco Broom)
Caves, Ether, Seasd

Burkwoodii (Red Broom)
  BlueM
Lena
  Denes
x praecox
  Denes
**x praecox Warminster
(Warminster Broom)**
  BlueM, Vall #
scoparius Cornish Cream
  Denes

Daboecia

**cantabrica (Irish Heath, St
Daboec's Heath)**
  BlueM, Butlr
cantabrica alba
  BayBl, Butlr
cantabrica Cupido
  BayBl
cantabrica Pragerae
  BlueM
**cantabrica William
Buchanan now x scotia
WB.**
  BayBl, BlueM

Dacrycarpus

**dacrydioides (White Pine,
Kahikatea)**
  Apple, Durbk, Butlr,
  Cedar, Chedd, Coatv,
  Gordn, Matai, Matwh,
  Mtato, NZtr #, Orati,
  Pionr, Terra, Wahpa
**imbricatus var robusta
syn Podocarpus i. &
P.papuanus**
  Cedar

Dacrydium

**bidwillii see Halocarpus
b.**
  Cedar
**biforme see Halocarpus
bif.**
  Cedar, Denes
**colensoi see Lagarostrobus
c.**
  Cedar
**cupressinum (Rimu, Red
Pine)**
  BlueM, Cedar, Chedd,
  Coatv, CPete, Gordn,
  Hewsn, Matai, Matwh,
  Mtato, Orati, Pionr,
  Terra, Wahpa

**franklinii see
Lagarostrobus f**
  BlueM, Cedar
**intermedius see
Lepidothamnus I**
  Cedar
kirkii see Halocarpus k.
  Cedar
**laxifolium now
Lepidothamnus l.**
  Cedar, Hackf
**laxifolium Blue Gem now
Lepidothamnus l.B.G.**
  Cedar
**laxifolium Green Cascade
now Lepidothamnus l.x
intermedius G.C.**
  Cedar

Dactylorhiza

foliosa
  JoyPl
maculata (Ground Orchid)
  MJury

Dahlia

A La Mode
  Otara
Ace of Hearts
  Kayd, LeFab
Adorable You
  Otara
Adriana
  Otara
Affirmed
  Otara
Akita
  Otara
Akito No Hikari
  Otara
Alabaster Queen
  Otara
Alden Ballet Girl
  Otara
Alden Festival
  Otara
Alden Princess
  Otara
Alden Snowlodge
  Otara
Alfred C
  Otara
Alice Chalifoux
  Otara

All Triumph
  Otara
Alloway Barbara
  Otara
Alloway Candy
  Otara
Alloway cottage
  Otara
Alloway Norine
  Otara
Almand's Climax
  Otara, Sherl
Almands Supreme
  Sherl
Aloha
  Otara, Sherl
Alpen Beauty
  Otara
Alpen Blaze
  Otara
Alpen Cardinal
  Otara
Alpen Charm
  Otara
Alpen Cheer
  Otara
Alpen Cherub
  Otara
Alpen Dylan
  Otara
Alpen Marie
  Otara
Alpen Marjory
  Otara
Alpen Rhicky
  Otara
Alpen Star
  Otara
Alstergrusz
  LeFab
Altami Apollo
  Sherl
Altami Classic
  Sherl
Altamic Cosmic
  Otara
Alva's Supreme
  Otara
Alwyn Trimper
  Otara
Ambition
  Otara, Sherl

Amelia's Surprise
  Otara
Amgard Delicate
  Sherl
Amorangi Coconut Ice
  Otara
Amorangi Pearl
  Otara
Amy K
  Otara
Angora
  Otara
Annie Dahl
  Parva
Apache
  Otara, Sherl
Apollo
  Sherl
Appleblossom
  Otara
Apricot Frills
  Otara
Apricot Honeymoon Dress
  Otara
April Dawn
  Sherl
Arabian Knight
  Otara
Arabian Night
  LeFab, Otara
Araluen Fire
  Otara
Arnhem
  Otara
Arthur Lashlie
  Otara
Arthur's Delight
  Otara, Sherl
Astrid
  Otara
Athalie
  Otara
Auckland Botanic
  Otara
Aumonium Chandler
  Otara
Autumn Fire
  Otara
Awaikoe
  Otara
Baby Apricot
  Otara

Baby Burgundy
  Otara
Baby Red
  Otara
Baby White
  Otara, Parva
Ballego's Glory
  Otara
Ballerina
  Otara
Banker
  Otara
Barbara Banker
  Otara
Barbara Elaine
  Otara
Barbarossa
  Kayd, LeFab
Barbarry Banker
  Otara
Barbarry Bells
  Otara
Barbarry Bonafide
  Otara
Barbarry Carousel
  Otara
Barbarry Climax
  Otara
Barbarry Dress
  Otara
Barbarry Flush
  Otara
Barbarry Gayity
  Otara
Barbarry Gem
  Otara
Barbarry Glamour
  Otara
Barbarry Lavender
  Otara
Barbarry Olympic
  Otara
Barbarry Oracle
  Sherl
Barbarry Pinky
  Otara, Sherl
Barbarry Rhapsody
  Otara
Barbarry Riviera
  Otara
Barbarry Salmon
  Otara

Barbarry Sportsman
  Otara
Barbarry Standard
  Otara
Barbarry Stockton
  Otara
Barbarry Symbol
  Otara
Baret Joy
  Sherl
Bas W Kehl
  LeFab
Bassingbourne Beauty
  Otara
Beauty of Heemstede
  Otara
Bellboy
  Otara
Ben Huston
  Otara
Bergers Record
  Otara
Berlineer Kleen
  Otara
Berwick Wood
  Otara
Beth Serafin
  Otara
Betty Bowen
  Otara
Betty West
  Otara
Bevlah Ruth
  Otara
Biddenham Cherry
  Otara
Bill Homberg
  Sherl
Billy
  Sherl
Bingo
  Otara
Bishop of Llandaff
  Otara, Parva, Peak
Black Beauty
  Otara
Black Monarch
  Otara
Black Narcissus
  Otara
Blackbird
  Otara

Blackie
  Otara
Bloom's Amy
  Otara
Bloom's Centennial
  Otara
Bloom's Graham
  Otara, Sherl
Blooms Bronze Rays
  Otara
Blossom
  LeFab
Bob Fitzjohn
  Otara
Bokay
  Otara
Bonadventure
  Otara, Sherl
Bonne Esperance
  Kayd, LeFab, MaraN,
  Otara
Bowen
  Otara
Bracken Ballerina
  Otara
Bravo
  Otara
Brendon James
  Otara
Brides Bouquet
  Kayd, LeFab
Bright Star
  Otara
Brighton Joy
  Otara
Brilliant Eye
  Otara
Brio
  Otara
Brookside Cheri
  Otara
Brookside Snowball
  Otara
Buffie G
  Otara
Butterfly
  Otara
By Golly
  Otara
Camano Choice
  Otara
Camano CLoud
  Otara

Camano Firestorm
  Otara
Camano Melon
  Otara
Camano Shadows
  Otara
Camano Velvet
  Otara
Camelia
  Otara
Camelot Rose
  Otara
Cameo
  Otara
Cameo Peach
  Otara
Cameo Supreme
  Otara
Canby Centennial
  Otara
Candy Keene
  Otara, Sherl
Canyon Park
  Sherl
Carola
  LeFab
Carolina Moon
  Sherl
Cascade Spellbound
  Otara
Catch Phrase
  Otara
Celebrity
  Otara
Cendrillon
  Otara
Cha Cha
  Otara
Charles H
  Otara
Charlie Two
  Sherl
Charmant
  LeFab
Chas Ondries
  Otara
Cherie Dahl
  Parva
Cherry Drop
  Otara
Cherubino
  Otara

Cheyenne
  Otara, Sherl
Chickadee
  Otara
Chilson's Pride
  Otara
Chiltern Fantastic
  Otara
Chiltern Herald
  Sherl
Christina
  Kayd
Christine Hammett
  Otara
Christmas Carol
  Otara, Sherl
Christopher Nickerson
  Otara
Christopher Taylor
  Otara
Cindy Dahl
  Parva
Cindy Lou
  Otara
Claire de Lune
  Otara
Clarion
  Otara
Classic A 1
  Otara
Cliff Rushton
  Otara
Clints Climax
  Otara, Sherl
Cloverdale
  Otara
Clown
  Otara
coccinea
  Otara
Coconut Ice
  Otara
Colour Spectacle
  Kayd, LeFab, Otara
Comet
  Otara
Como Perfection
  Otara
Como Polly
  Otara
Connie Bartlam
  Otara

Conquest Joy
Otara

Conversation Piece
Parva

Copper Queen
Otara

Cora Collins
Otara

Coral Dawn
Otara

Coral Flame
Otara

Coral Jupiter
Sherl

Coralie
Otara

Cordyline Fuzz
Otara

Corey Leigh
Otara

Cote Fleurie
Otara

Cotton Candy
Otara

Cotton Tail
Otara

Crazy Legs
Otara

Cream Beauty
Otara, Sherl

Cream Kerkade
Otara

Cream Linda
Otara

Creamy
Otara

Creme of Delight
Otara

Creve Coeur
Otara

Crichton Honey
Otara

Crossfield Ebony
Otara

Croydon Supreme
Otara

Cryfield Keene
Sherl

Crystal Anne
Otara, Sherl

Cynthia Louise
Otara, Sherl

Czar Willo
Otara

D D Alison Claire
Otara

D D Bee
Otara

D D Cutie
Otara

D D Donna Marie
Otara

D D Laura May
Otara

D D Marshmallow
Otara

D D Parfait
Otara

D D Pedro
Otara

D D Vanilla Ice
Otara

Daisy Williams
Otara

Daleko Adonis
Otara

Daleko Jupiter
Otara, Sherl

Daleko Venus
Otara

Dana Iris
Otara

Daniel Edward's
Otara

Danum Arctic
Sherl

Dauntless
Otara

Dave Thompson
Otara

David's Choice
Otara

Dawn
Otara

Deanna
Otara

Debra Ann Craven
Otara

Decoy
Otara

Deep South
Sherl

Deepest Yellow
Otara

Deirdre
Otara

Del Huston
Otara

Delectus
Otara

Dell Sweetman
Otara

Denise Willo
Otara

Dentelle de Velours
Otara

Desiree
Otara

Deutschland
Kayd, LeFab, Otara

dissecta
Parva

Dommie
Otara

Don's Delight
Otara

Donny C
Otara

Doria
Otara

Doris Duke
Kayd, LeFab

Dot's Own
Otara

Downham Royal
Otara, Sherl

Dr John Granger
Otara

Drummer Boy
Otara, Sherl

Duet
Kayd, LeFab, Otara

Durlingo Jewel
Otara

Dusky Lilac
Otara

Dusky Maid
Otara

Dutch Baby
Otara

Eastern Echo
Otara

Eastwood Delight
Otara

Eastwood Moonlight
Sherl

Ebbw Vale Festival	**Ferncliff Rebel**	**Formby Perfection**
Otara, Sherl	Otara	Otara, Sherl
Ebony Witch	**Ferncliffe Illusion**	**Formby Queen**
Otara	Otara	Otara
Edinburgh	**Fernhill Champion**	**Formby Satellite**
Otara, Sherl	Otara	Otara
Efsee Beauty	**Fete d' Orange**	**Formby Supreme**
Otara	Otara	Otara
Eldon Wilson	**Fidalgo Beauty**	**Forrestal**
Otara	Otara	LeFab
Elizabeth Chiffley	**Fidalgo Julie**	**Frank Holmes**
Otara	Otara	Otara
Elizabeth Snowden	**Fidalgo Lisa**	**Frank Lovell**
Otara	Otara	Otara
Elma Elizabeth	**Fidalgo Snowball**	**Franz Kafka**
Otara, Sherl	Otara	Kayd, LeFab, Otara
Elmbrook Rebel	**Fidelgo Blackie**	**Fred Sheard**
Otara	Otara	Otara
Elnor Fiesta	**Fidelgo Lisa**	**Freestyle**
Otara	Otara	Otara, Sherl
Elnor Robyn	**Fidelgo Magic**	**Frolie**
Otara	Otara	Otara
Elsie Huston	**Figurine**	**Frosted Lavender**
Otara	Otara, Sherl	Otara
Elsie Huston dwf	**Fiona Stewart**	**Furka**
Otara	Otara	LeFab
Envy	**Fire Bird**	**Fury**
Otara	LeFab	Otara
Erik The Red	**Fire Dot**	**Gail Lane**
Otara	Otara	Otara
Erin Ann	**Fire Magic**	**Garden Festival**
Otara, Sherl	Otara	Otara
Eugenia Huston	**Fire Mountain**	**Gargantuam**
Otara	Otara	Otara
Eveline	**Fireball**	**Gartnerin**
LeFab, Otara	Otara	Kayd, LeFab
Evelyn Foster	**Firecracker**	**Gateshead Festival**
Otara	Otara	Otara, Sherl
Evening Lady	**First Love**	**Gazami**
Otara	Otara	Kayd, LeFab
Evening Mist	**Flame On**	**Geraldine Dawn**
Otara	Otara	Kayd, LeFab
Ever So Nice	**Fleck**	**Geraldine Downs**
Otara	Otara	Otara
Everlyn	**Flutterby**	**Gerrie Hoek**
Otara	Otara	Otara
Fan Dancer	**Forbes**	**Ginette**
Otara, Sherl	Otara	Otara
Fashion Monger	**Formby Chief**	**Ginger Willo**
Sherl	Otara	Otara
Fern Irene	**Formby Hill**	**Gingernut**
Otara, Sherl	Otara	Otara

Gitts Respect
Otara
Glen Valley Cathy
Otara
Glen Valley Petra
Otara
Glenbank Joy
Otara
Glenbank Opal
Otara
Glenbank Top Stuff
Otara
Glenmark
Otara
Glory
Otara
Glory of Noordwijk
Otara
Go Gay
Otara
Gold Ball
Otara
Gold coast
Otara
Gold Fire
Otara
Golden Cloud
Otara
Golden Emblem
Kayd, LeFab, Otara
Golden Impact
Otara, Sherl
Golden Nicky
Otara
Goldilocks
Otara
Good Earth
Otara
Gordon Huston
Otara
Gordon Lockwood
Otara
Goya's Venus
Otara
Grace Candy
Otara
Grand Willo
Otara
Grenidor Pastelle
Otara, Sherl
Gretchen
Otara

Guest of Honour
Otara
Guinea
Otara
Hamari Accord
Otara
Hamari Girl
Kayd, LeFab, Otara,
Sherl
Hamari Gold
Otara, Sherl
Hamari Katarina
Kayd, LeFab
Hamari Sunset
Otara
Hamilton Lillian
Otara, Sherl
Happy Days
Kayd
Happy Tune
Otara
Hayley Jane
Otara, Sherl
Heather Marie
Otara
Heatwave
Otara
Helma
LeFab
Helvetia
Otara
Herbert Smith
Kayd, LeFab, Otara
Higgo Affair
Otara
High Mark
Otara
High Society
Otara, Sherl
Highnoon
Otara
Hillcrest Blaze
Otara
Hillcrest Desire
Otara
Hillcrest Heights
Otara
Hillcrest Hilton
Sherl
Hillcrest Royal
Otara
Hillcrest Trueform
Sherl

Hillview Petone
Otara
Holland Festival
Otara
Holly Huston
Otara
Honka
Otara
Hot Number
Otara
Hot Stuff
Otara
Iama No Kogayake
Otara
Ice Frills
Otara
Idaho Red
Otara
imperialis (Tree Dahlia)
AynDa, BayBl, Otara,
Parva
imperialis Alba
Parva
Inglebrook Jill
Otara
Inglebrook Leanne
Otara
Iris
Otara
Ironstem
Otara
Island Dawn
Otara
Isobel Cox
Otara
Ivory Palaces
Otara
Jackaroo
Otara
Jacques Bocquart
Otara
Janet
Otara
Janome
Otara
Jean Enerson
Otara
Jeanne Gervais
Otara
Jeffers
Otara
Jennie
Otara

Jescot Julie
Otara

Jessica
Otara

Jessie G
Otara

Jewel K
Otara

Jim Branigan
Otara

Joan Beecham
Otara, Sherl

Joanne Heron
Otara

Johann
Otara

John Prior
Otara

Julia Pendly
Otara

Just Peachy
Otara

Just So
Otara

Juuchin
Otara

Juul's Star
Otara

Kaiwera Gold
Otara, Sherl

Kapiti Suzanne
Otara

Kapiti Vera
Otara

Karenglen
Otara

Kari Blue
Otara

Kari Lanky
Otara

Kari Quill
Otara

Karingal
Otara

Kasasagi
Otara

Kath Whitmore
Otara

Kathleen's Alliance
Otara

Kathryns Cupid
Otara

Katie Dahl
Parva

Katinka
Otara

Katrina Houston
Otara

Kazusa Kajazu
Otara

Kea Gem
Sherl

Kea Ginger
Sherl

Kea Jewel
Sherl

Kea Kiss
Sherl

Kea Pearl
Sherl

Kea Ruby
Sherl

Keewatin Gold
Otara

Keewatin Pioneer
Otara

Keewatin Sunsprite
Sherl

Keith H
Otara

Keiths Choice
Otara

Kellie Ann
Otara, Sherl

Kelly Ann
Otara

Ken's Flame
Otara

Ken's Gold
Otara

Kenmore Candice
Otara

Kennemerland
LeFab

Kenora Amethyst
Otara

Kenora Canada
Otara, Sherl

Kenora Challenger
Otara, Sherl

Kenora Clyde
Otara, Sherl

Kenora Fireball
Otara

Kenora Lisa
Otara, Sherl

Kenora Macob B
Otara

Kenora Macop
Sherl

Kenora Moonbeam
Otara

Kenora Ontario
Otara

Kenora Passion
Otara

Kenora Sunburst
Otara

Kenora Superb
Otara, Sherl

Kenora Tonya
Otara, Sherl

Kenora Valentine
Otara

Kenora Wildfire
Otara, Sherl

Keukenhof
LeFab

Kidd's Climax
Otara

Kiwi Brother
Otara

Kiwi Gloria
Sherl

KK Ipana
Otara

KK Mini
Otara

KK Taretta
Otara

KK Wistful
Otara

Klara
Otara

Knockout
Otara

Ko Bune
Otara

Kojoh Binjin
Otara

Koko Puff
Otara

Komeet
Otara

Kompliment
Otara

Koppertone
Otara
Krinjens Jubileum
Otara
Kyle Huston
Otara
Kym Willo
Otara
L'Ancreese
Otara
La Tosca
LeFab
Lady Linda
Kayd, LeFab
Langverwacht
Otara
Laredo
Otara
Lauren Michele
Otara
Laurence Fisher
Otara
Lavender Athalie
Sherl
Lavender Blue
Otara
Lavender Frills
Otara
Lavender Queen
Otara
Lawrence Welk
Otara
Le Vonne Splinter
Otara
LeFeber's Favourite
LeFab
Lemon Blush
Otara
Lemon Elegans
Otara, Sherl
Lemon Honey
Otara
Lena Lila
Otara
Leutwitchen
Otara
Lewie Lewie
Otara
Leycett
Sherl
Lilac Shadow
Kayd, LeFab

Lime Light
Otara
Linda Mary
Otara
Linton's Blue
Otara
Lions International
Otara
Lisa
Otara
Lismore Peggy
Otara
Little Cutie
Sherl
Little Laura
Otara
Little Matthew
Otara
Little Sally
Otara
Little Scottie
Otara
Little Show Off
Otara
Little Snowdrop
Otara
Little Tiger
Otara
Little William
Kayd, LeFab
Lollipop
Otara
Long Island Lil
Otara
Longwood Dainty mini
Otara
Longwood Sparkle
Otara
Look Again
Otara
Lotto
Otara, Sherl
Lucia Ann
Otara
Lucky Devil
Otara
Lucky Dip
Sherl
Ludwig Helfert
Otara
Lula Pattie
Otara

Lynette
Otara, Sherl
Madeline Ann
Otara
Mafolie
Otara
Magic Moment
Otara, Sherl
Magnificat
Kayd, LeFab, Otara
Majestic Athalie
Otara, Sherl
Majestic Kerkrade
Otara
Maltby Fanfare
Otara
Maltby Gem
Otara
Maltby Vanilla
Otara
Mana-Kau
Sherl
Mardi Gras
Otara
Margaret Ann
Otara
Margaret Duross
Sherl
Marie Schnugg
Otara
Marilyn Thompson
Otara
Mark Hardwick
Sherl
Mark Lockwood
Otara
Mark Willo
Otara
Marla Lu
Otara
Marlene Joy
Sherl
Marlow
Otara
Marmalade
Otara
Mars
Otara
Marshall
Otara
Martin's Red
Otara

Martin's Yellow	**Midnight Sun**	**Mr Ralph**
Otara	Otara	Otara
Mary Eveline	**Mildura Gem**	**Mrs Black**
Otara	Otara	Otara
Mary Evelyn	**Mini Red**	**Murray Petite**
Otara, Sherl	Otara	Otara, Sherl
Mary Hammett	**Minley Carol**	**Music Hall**
Otara	Otara	Otara
Mary Hodges	**Minley Linda**	**Mussette dwf**
Otara	Otara	Otara
Mary Jenny	**Minley Sharon**	**My Fair Lady**
Otara	LeFab	Otara
Mary Jo	**Mioss Joanne**	**My Fritz**
Otara	Otara	Otara
Mary Lee McNall	**Miriam**	**My Love**
Otara	LeFab	Otara
Mary Morris	**Miss A**	**My Pride**
Otara	Otara	Otara, Sherl
Mary Munns	**Miss Joan**	**My VAlentine**
Otara	Otara	Otara
Mary Pitt	**Miss Piggy**	**Myra Doc**
Otara	Otara	Otara
Master Michell	**Mistell Delight**	**Nagel's Solidite**
Otara	Otara	Otara
Matchmaker	**Mitsie dwf**	**Nargold**
Otara	Otara	Otara
Matilda Huston	**Moana**	**Narooma Princess**
Otara	LeFab	Otara
Matterhorn	**Mom's Special**	**Nationwide**
Otara	Otara	Otara
Maxman	**Mon J Doulman**	**Nattie Night Life**
Otara	Otara	Otara
Meadowlea	**Monk Marc**	**Neal Gillson**
Otara	Otara	Sherl
Melissa M	**Monkstown Diane**	**Neon City**
Otara	Otara	Otara
Melissa Murchenburg	**Monrovia**	**Neon Splendour**
Otara	Otara	Otara
merckii alba	**Montressor**	**Nepos**
Otara	Otara	Otara, Sherl
Merio	**Moor Place**	**Nescio**
Otara	Otara	Otara
Mersey Charm	**Moray Susan**	**Neva Ray**
Otara, Sherl	Otara	Otara
Michael J	**Morley Lady**	**New Baby**
Otara	Otara	Otara
Midnight	**Morling**	**New Church**
Otara	Otara	Otara
Midnight Dancer	**Mr Joy**	**New Creation**
Otara	Otara	Sherl
Midnight Magic	**Mr Larry**	**Newby**
Sherl	Otara	Otara

Nicaro
Otara
Nicky K
Otara
Nicola Higgo
Otara
Night Dream
Otara, Sherl
Night Editor
Otara
Nina Chester
Otara, Sherl
Nina Esther
Otara
Nivea
LeFab
Nonette
Otara
Northland's Primrose
Otara
Olympic Torch
Otara
Onesta
LeFab
Ophir Mother of Pearl
Otara
Optic Illusion
Otara
Orange Comet
Otara
Orange Cushion
Otara
Orange Jewel
Otara
Orange Pennant
Otara, Sherl
Orchid Lace
Otara
Orchid Princess
LeFab
Oreti Bimbo
Otara
Oreti Chance
Otara
Oreti Choice
Otara
Oreti Fiesta
Otara
Oreti Fifi
Otara
Oreti Kirsty
Otara

Oreti Margo
Otara
Oreti Nene
Otara
Oreti Trudy
Otara
Orfeo
Otara
Ornamental Rays
Otara
Our Anniversary
Otara
Pacific Caroline
Otara
Pagoda
Otara
Paisley gem
Otara
Pamela
Otara
Papageno
Otara
Pari Taha Sunrise
Otara
Park Princess
LeFab, Otara
Paroa Gillian
Otara
Paroa Glow
Otara
Parson's Glory
Otara
Passion
Otara
Pat Feary
Otara
Patches
Otara
Patty
LeFab
Peach Cupid
Otara
Peaches-n-Cream
Otara
Pennsford Marion
Otara
Persian Monarch
Otara, Sherl
Petite Grace
Otara
Petite Michel
Otara

Phoenix
Otara, Sherl
Phylis Farmer
Otara
Pianella
Kayd, LeFab
Pineapple Lollipop
Otara
Pinehaven
Otara
Pineholt Princess
Otara, Sherl
Pink Duke
Otara
Pink Jupiter
Otara, Sherl
Pink Leycett
Sherl
Pink Lotus
Otara
Pink Parfait
Otara
Pink Pastelle
Sherl
Pink Sensation
Otara
Pink Shirley Alliance
Otara
Pink Worton Anne
Otara
Poly Peachum
Otara
Polyand
Otara
Poppet
Otara
Porcelain
Otara
Pot Black
Otara
Precocious
Otara
Preference
Kayd, LeFab
Prestige
Otara
Pride of Place
Otara
Primrose Diane
Otara, Sherl
Prince Valiant
Otara

Priscilla	**Reg Keene**	**Rotterdam**
Otara	Sherl	Otara
Pristine	**Regal Kerkrade**	**Royal Ivory**
Otara	Otara	Sherl
Procyon	**Regency Princess**	**Royal Wedding**
Otara	Otara	Otara
Prom Queen	**Renee**	**Royston Jaffa**
Otara	Kayd, LeFab	Otara
Purbeck Lydia	**Rev P Holian**	**Ruby Myra**
Otara	Sherl	Otara
Purple Gem	**Ringo**	**Ruby Wedding**
Otara	Otara	Otara
Purple Joy	**Ringold**	**rudis**
Otara	Sherl	Parva
Purple Splash	**Rip City**	**Ruskin Ballerina**
Otara	Otara	Otara
Pyjama Game	**Risca Miner**	**Ruskin Belle**
Otara	Otara	Otara
Quantum Leap	**Rising Moon**	**Ruskin Diane**
Otara	Otara	Otara
Quel Diable	**River Road**	**Ruskin Dynasty**
Otara	Otara	Otara
Quiet Riot	**Robann Red Snowball**	**Ruskin Gypsy**
Otara	Otara	Otara
Rachel	**Robann Royal**	**Rustig**
Kayd, LeFab	Otara	Otara
Radfo	**Robert**	**Rusty Hope**
Otara, Sherl	Otara	Otara
Raewyn Leslie	**Robin Hood**	**Ruth Elaine**
Otara	Otara	Otara
Raggedy Anne	**Roilyn**	**Ruthie G**
Otara	Otara	Otara, Sherl
Raisers Pride	**Rose Cupid**	**Ryedale Prince**
Otara	Otara	Sherl
Raz-Ma-Taz	**Rose Fletcher**	**Ryedale Rebecca**
Otara	Otara	Sherl
Rebecca Lyn	**Rose Jupiter**	**Salmon Derby**
Otara	Sherl	Otara
Red Admiral	**Rose Pine**	**Salmon Keene**
Otara	Otara	Otara, Sherl
Red Alert	**Rose Preference**	**Sam Hearst**
Otara	Otara	Otara
Red Dawn	**Rose Toscano**	**Sam Huston**
Otara	Otara	Otara
Red Pygmy	**Rose Townsley**	**Sarah G**
Otara	Otara	Otara
Red Sensation	**Rosemary**	**Sarah Jane**
Otara	Otara	Otara
Red Velvet	**Rosemary Grieve**	**Scarabella**
Otara, Sherl	Otara	Otara
Reg Kappler	**Rosemary Webb**	**Scarborough Brilliant**
Otara	Otara	Otara

Scarlet Beauty
Otara

Skipley Sunset
Otara

Suffolk Bride
Otara

Scarlet Kokarade
Otara

Skipper Rock
Otara

Sugar Cane
Otara

Schweitzers Kokarade
Otara, Sherl

Sky Rocket
Otara

Summers End
Otara

Scottish Relation
Otara

Skywalker
Otara

Sunburst
Otara

Scottish Rhapsody
Otara

Small World
Otara

Sunny Boy
LeFab, Otara

Scura
Otara

Smokey Gal
Otara

Sunspot
Otara

Seimen Doorenbosh
Otara

Smoots
Otara

Sunstruck
Otara

Senzoe Ursula
Otara

Snip
Otara

Sure Thing
Otara

September Morn
Otara

Snoho Barbara
Otara

Suzette
Otara

Seuin
Otara

Snoho Blizzard
Otara

Suzie Dahl
Parva

Shadow Cat
Otara

Snow Ball
Otara

Swan Vale
Otara, Sherl

Sharowean Pride
Otara

Snow Fairy
Otara

Swan's Glory
Otara

Sharron Ann
Otara

Snowstorm
Otara

Swan's Gold Medal
Otara

Sheila Mooney
Otara

Song of Olympia
Sherl

Swan's Sunset
Otara

Sherwood Standard
Otara, Sherl

Sonja Henie
Sherl

Sweet Sixteen
Otara

Sherwood Sunrise
Otara

Sourire de Crozon
Otara

Sweetheart
LeFab

Shirley Alliance
Otara, Sherl

Sparkler
Otara

Sympathy
Sherl

Shirley Pride
Otara

Spencer
Sherl

Tabimakura
Otara

Shitamach Otime
Otara

Spices Hybrid
Otara

Taiheiyo
Otara

Show & Tell
Otara

Staci Erin
Otara

Tammy Lyn
Otara

Siedlers Stolze
Otara

Stanza
Otara

Tanjoh
Otara

Signature
Otara

Stars Favourite
Otara

Tara Brian
Otara, Sherl

Simplicity
Sherl

Stars Lady
Otara

Tara Honeymoon
Otara

Skipley Fair Lady
Otara

Stellyvonne
Otara

Tara Pink
Otara

Skipley Spot
Otara

Sterling Silver
Otara

Taratahi Lilac
Otara

Skipley Sunrise
Otara

Strawberry Puff
Otara

Taratahi Sprite
Otara

Tartan
Otara

Tasagore
Otara

Teddy
Otara

Teddy Dahl
Parva

tenuicaulis (Mexican Tree Dahlia)
Hackf, Parva, TopTr

Thistle
Otara

Thomas Edison
Otara

Tickerdy Boo
Otara

Tiger Bey
Otara

Tiki Gold
Otara

Tiptoe
Otara

Tom Yono
Otara

Tommy Doc
Otara, Sherl

Tonya
Otara

Top Choice
Kayd, LeFab, Otara

Topmix Violetta
Otara

Tranquility
Otara

Trengrove Jill
Otara

Trengrove Summer
Otara

Trudy Louise
Otara

Tu Tu
Otara

Tui Christine
Otara

Tui Daniel
Otara

Tui Gem
Otara

Tui Orange
Otara, Sherl

Tui Red
Otara

Tui Ulva
Otara

Tula Rosa
Otara

Twilight Time
Otara

Twinkle Toes
Otara

Twinks
Otara

Two Tone
Otara

Tycoon
Otara

Valentine
Otara

Valeta
Otara

Valla's Abigail
Otara, Sherl

Valla's Luke
Otara

Valla's Red
Otara

Vanessa
LeFab, Otara

Vantage
Otara, Sherl

Veere
Otara

Velvet Night
Otara

Vera May
Otara

Versa
Otara

Vigor
Otara

Vulcan
LeFab

Wallsend Jubilee
Otara

Walt Snowden
Otara

Wanda's Capella
Otara

Wanda's Moonlight
Sherl

Waterproof
Otara

Wee Ripper
Otara

Wendy's Place
Otara

Western Girl
Otara

White Alva's
Otara

White Fawn
Otara

White Kerkrade
Otara

White Linda
Kayd, LeFab, Otara, Sherl

White Moonlight
Otara

White Nettie
Otara

White Rustig
Otara

White Star
Otara

White Swallow
Otara

Wicky Woo
Otara

Wildwood Glory
Otara, Sherl

Wildwood Marie
Otara

William John Newbery (WJN)
Otara

William R
Otara

Willo's Fleck
Otara

Willo's Scarlet
Otara

Willo's Violet
Otara

Wilma Moore
Sherl

Wine & Roses
Otara

Winnie
LeFab

Wisk
Otara

Wittem
LeFab

Wonten
Otara

Wootten Impact
Otara

Wootton Carol
Otara

Wootton Cupid
Otara

Worton Ann
Sherl

Worton Blue Streak
Otara, Sherl

Yellow Bird
Otara

Yellow Frills
Otara, Sherl

Yellow Gem
Otara

Yellow Happiness
Otara

Yellow Pine
Otara

Yes Sir
Otara

Yuukyu
Otara

Yvonne
Kayd, LeFab, Otara

Zany
Otara, Sherl

Zeke
Otara

Ziepuppie
Otara

Zorro
Otara, Sherl

Dais

cotonifolia (Pompon Tree)
Denes, Ether

Daphne

acutiloba
Hackf

bholua (Himalayan Daphne)
Caves, Denes, Hackf,
JoyPl, Pukho, Taunt,
TopTr, Wells, Woodl

bholua Jacqueline Postill
Denes

x burkwoodii
Denes, MJury

x burkwoodii Somerset
Pukho

x burkwoodii Variegata
Denes

cneorum Eximia
Denes

cneorum Major
Denes

cneorum Major Variegata
Denes

cneorum Variegata
BlueM

genkwa (Chinese Daphne)
Caves, Denes, Pukho,
TopTr

longilobata (Himalayan Daphne)
Apple, Dove

mezereum (Winter Daphne
BlueM, Denes, Pukho

mezereum alba
NewlR

x napolitana
Denes

odora alba was leucanthe
Denes

odora Aureomarginata
Kayd

odora Grace Stewart
MJury

odora leucanthe now o.alba (Upright Daphne)
Denes

odora rubra
Denes

tangutica
BlueM, NewlR

Daphniphyllum

himalense macropodum
Caves

Darmera

peltata (was Peltiphylum p.)
BayBl, KeriP, Peak,
WaiMa

Datura

inoxia
Mills

inoxia ssp quinquecuspidata
KeriP, MaraN

meteloides now inoxia
Mills

see Brugmansia
Ref

Daubentonia

**tripetii syn Sesbania t.
(Scarlet Wisteria Tree)**
Reic #

Daucus

carota (Wild Carrot)
Della, King #, Sweet

carota var sativus (Carrot)
MTig #

Davallia

fejeenis (Rabbits Foot Fern
LakeN

tasmanii
Orati

Davidia

involucrata (Dove/Handkerchief/Ghost Tree)
Caves, MJury, Peele,
Pukho

involucrata var vilmoriniana
Denes, Hackf, Pionr

Decaisnea

fargesii (Blue Sausage Bush)
Apple, Caves, Denes,
Dove

Decumaria

sinensis
CouCl

Delonix

regia (Royal Flamboyant, Royal Poinciana, Peacock Flower)
LakeN, NZtr #, Reic #

Delosperma

cooperi
Seasd

Delphinium

belladonna Dark Blue
Dowde

belladonna Light Blue
Dowde

belladonna White
Dowde

Beverley Hills
KeriP, Mills

Beverley Hills salmon
Mills

Beverley Hills Scarlet
Mills

Beverley Hills yellow
Mills

Blue Sensation
BayBl, Nikau, Parva, Peak

brunonianum
NewlR

cardinale
BlueM, MaraN, MillH, Nikau

Casa Blanca
BayBl

chinensis
Trans

chinensis Blue Butterfly
BayBl, Dream, NewlR

chinensis Gentian Blue
Dowde

chinensis Sky Blue
Dowde

chinensis White
Dowde

Clear Springs mix
Dowde

Cliveden Beauty
BayBl

x cultorum Blue Fountains mixed
AynDa, King #

dark blues
CottP, Parva

Dreaming Spires mixed
KeriP

dwarf white
Warwk

elatum Giant Round Table Series
AynDa, King #

elatum mixed
Pgeon

F2hybrid NMD blues
Dowde

F2hybrid NMD mix
Dowde

F2hybrid NMD pinks
Dowde

Faust
Parva

Fountains mixed
Kayd, KeriP, Marsh, Mills

Fountains Dark Blue
Egmon, Kayd, Pgeon

Fountains Dwarf White
CoFlo

Fountains Lavender
Egmon, Kayd

Fountains Lilac Pink
Egmon

Fountains Regal Blue
CoFlo, Kayd

Fountains Sky Blue
CoFlo, Egmon, Kayd

grandiflorum
Parva

grandiflorum Blue Butterfly
Pgeon

light blues
Parva, Trans

lilac (white eye)
Wells

Lilac Rose
Warwk

mauves
Parva

new century F2 Green Expectations
Dowde

new century F2 Ivory Towers
Dowde

new century F2 Moody Blues
Dowde

new century F2 Rosy Futures
Dowde

new century F2 Ultra Violets
Dowde

new millenium Alicia
Dowde

new millenium blues
Dowde

new millenium Celia
Dowde

new millenium cream
Dowde

new millenium Dora Blanco
Dowde

new millenium Juanita
Dowde

new millenium lightblues
Dowde

new millenium mauves
Dowde

new millenium pinks
Dowde

new millenium Sara
Dowde

nudicaule
BayBl, BlueM, MaraN, Parva

Oxford Blue
Mills

pacific giant mixed
Kayd, Nikau

pacific giant Astolat
Dowde, Egmon, Peak, Pgeon, Warwk

pacific giant Black Knight
Dowde, Egmon, Mills, Warwk

pacific giant Blue Bird
Ashto, Dowde, Peak, Warwk

pacific giant Blue Jay
Ashto, Dowde, Mills

pacific giant Camelaird
Dowde, Dream, Mills

pacific giant Connecticut Yankees
Ashto

pacific giant Galahad
Dowde, Dream, Egmon, Mills, Peak

pacific giant Guinevere
Peak

pacific giant King Arthur
Dowde, Peak, Pgeon

pacific giant light blue
Kayd

pacific giant Percival
Dowde

pacific giant pink & lilac
Kayd

pacific giant pure white
Kayd

pacific giant Royal Purple
Kayd

pacific giant Scarlet Butterfly
Peak

pacific giant Summer Skies
  Ashto, Egmon, Mills
Pink Sensation
  BayBl, Parva, Peak
pinks
  Parva
requienii
  Dream, Nikau, TRidg,
  Vall #
Skyline
  Parva
Southern Noblemen mixed
  Vall #
speciosum
  Della
tatsienense
  MaraN, NewlR
ventricosa
  Ashto
violets
  Parva
whites
  Parva
zalil
  Parva

Dendranthema

Adrienne Mechen
  Coult
Allouise 25b
  Coult
Amber Shantung 25b
  Coult
Amigo
  Coult
Ann Ladygo
  Coult
Anzac
  Coult
Apricot Charm
  Coult
Apricot Courtier 24a
  Coult
Apricot Lilac Charm
  Coult
Apricot Rynoon
  Coult
Autumn Delight
  Coult
Autumn Fantasy
  Coult
Baby Tears
  Coult

Blush Pennine Gambol 29a
  Coult
Brian Pullom 23
  Coult
Bridesmaid
  Coult
Brighton 25b
  Coult
Bronze Fairy
  Coult
Bronze Pinnochio
  Coult
Bronze Shantung 25b
  Coult
Bronze Wessex Charm 29d
  Coult
Bronze William Florentine 5
  Coult
Bullfinch
  Coult
Bunty
  Coult
Cassino 94
  Coult
Champagne Shantung 25b
  Coult
Charlotte's Pink
  Coult
Chempak Rose 24b
  Coult
Cloverlea Companion
  Coult
Cloverlea Herald
  Coult
Cloverlea Star
  Coult
Coppernut
  Coult
Coral Rynoon
  Coult
Cottontail
  Coult
Courtier 24a
  Coult
Cream Impala
  Coult
Cream John Hughes 3b
  Coult
Cream Pennine Serene 29d
  Coult
Cream Shantung 25b
  Coult

Crimson Yvonne Arnaud 24b
  Coult
Crystal Falls
  CottP, Parva
Dancing Sunlight
  Coult
Dorothy Mechen
  Coult
Dorothy Mechen Reward
  Coult
Dorothy Mechen Sunburst
  Coult
Edith Mechen
  Coult
El Tora
  Coult
Elworthy 24b
  Coult
Enbee Wedding 29d
  Coult
Enchantment
  Coult
Equinox
  Coult
Ethel Zwager 25b
  Coult
Fairy
  Coult
Flora
  Coult
Florida
  Coult
Fred Reynor
  Coult
Garden Bronze
  Parva
Garden Cream
  Parva
Garden Red
  Parva
Garden White
  Parva
George Griffiths 24b
  Coult
Gillette 25b
  Coult
Gillia Fitton 3b
  Coult
Gladys Homer24b
  Coult
Goblin
  Wells

Golden Chalice
Coult
Golden Maria
Coult
Golden Treasure
Coult
Goldtone
Coult
Grace Lovell 25
Coult
Green Boy
Coult
Green Satin 5a
Coult
Hatsune
Parva
Hazel Hanmer 3b
Coult
Hazel McIntosh 5b
Coult
Helen Brandt 12a
Coult
Hesketh Crystal 5b
Coult
Hesketh Rose 3b
Coult
Honeysuckle Time 5
Coult
Ice Box 25
Coult
Impala
Coult
Irene Arnold 24b
Coult
Isla Mechen
Coult
Jim McKegg 4b
Coult
John Hughes 3b
Coult
Julie Miles
Coult
Kelvin Mandarin 12b
Coult
Kelvin Victory 12b
Coult
Kupie
Coult
Lark Rise 4b
Coult
Lasting Memories 5b
Coult

Lavender Button
Coult
Lemon Baby Tears
Coult
Lemon Lace
Coult
Lemon Pinnochio
Coult
Lemon Rynoon
Coult
Len's Girl 4b
Coult
Lilac Charm
Coult
Lynmall's Choice 23b
Coult
Madam E Rogers 5b
Coult
Magic Bronze
Parva
Magic Candy
CottP, Parva
Magic Dawn
Parva
Magic Garden
Parva
Magic Sunset
Parva
Mairehau Cameo
Coult
Mairehau Dainty
Coult
Mairehau Glow
Coult
Mairehau Maid
Coult
Mairehau Sunset
Coult
Mairehau Sunshine
Coult
Mancetta Cavalier 4b
Coult
Maria
Coult
Marion 29c
Coult
Marlene Jones 25b
Coult
Mavis
Coult
Mini Mauve
Parva

Mitzi
Coult
Morning Star
Coult
Mt Fuji
Coult
Muriel
Coult
Music 23
Coult
Newgo
Coult
Nightingale
Coult
Nova Gold 3b
Coult
Ogmore Vale
Coult
Orange Bunty
Coult
Orange Pennine Wine 29c
Coult
Orange Shantung 25b
Coult
Pat Marsden 4
Coult
Patricia Grace
Coult
Patricia Millar 4b
Coult
Pavilion 25a
Coult
Pennine Air 29d
Coult
Pennine Canary 19
Coult
Pennine Crystal
Coult
Pennine Cupid 19c
Coult
Pennine Gambol 29a
Coult
Pennine Jade 29d
Coult
Pennine Marvel 29
Coult
Pennine Mist 29c
Coult
Pennine Oriel 29a
Coult
Pennine Prince 29c
Coult

Pennine Punch 29d
Coult
Pennine Rose 29b
Coult
Pennine Serene 29d
Coult
Pennine Silk 29c
Coult
Pennine Silver 29c
Coult
Pennine Wine 29c
Coult
Pink Gin
Coult
Pink Poolys 5a
Coult
Pink Shantung 25b
Coult
Pink Statesman
CottP
Pink Tivoli 12d
Coult
Pink West Bromwich 14a
Coult
Pinnochio
Coult
Pontardulais 3b
Coult
Poolys 5a
Coult
Pretty Penny
Coult
Primrose John Hughes 3b
Coult
Primrose Margaret 19c
Coult
Primrose Pennine Oriel 29a
Coult
Primrose Pennine Wine 29c
Coult
Primrose Tone Maid 29a
Coult
Primrose West Bromwich
14a
Coult
Purple Fairy
Coult
Purple Pennine Wine 29c
Coult
Red Fairy
Coult
Red Regalia 24b
Coult

Redbreast
Coult
Refour
Coult
Regalia 24b
Coult
Ringdove
Coult
Robert Earnshaw 3b
Coult
Roblush
Coult
Rolass
Coult
Roscene
Coult
Rose Compie 29c
Coult
Rose Enbee Wedding 29d
Coult
Rose Wessex Charm 29d
Coult
Rybrite
Coult
Rynoon
Coult
Rysong
Coult
Salmon Allouise 25b
Coult
Salmon Fairy
Coult
Salmon Maria
Coult
Salmon Pennine Rose 29b
Coult
Salmon Pennine Wine 29c
Coult
Salmon Shantung 25b
Coult
Scarlet Yvonne Arnaud
24b
Coult
Sea Urchin
Coult
Senkyo Emaki
Coult
Shamrock
Coult
Shantung 25b
Coult
Shantung Queen 24b
Coult

Sheffield Centenary 3b
Coult
Small Wonder
Coult
Smokey Cloverlea
Coult
Snowden 5
Coult
Stockton 3b
Coult
Summer Joy 24
Coult
Sunflash
Coult
Susan Pullom 25
Coult
Tang
Coult
Tone Dragon 29a
Coult
Tone Maid 29a
Coult
Tone Sail 29a
Coult
Trinklet
Coult
Vera Smith 3b
Coult
Wessex Charm 29d
Coult
Wessex Cream 29d
Coult
Wessex Glow 29a
Coult
Wessex Melody 29d
Coult
Wessex Prince 29d
Coult
Wessex Royal 29d
Coult
Wessex Shell 29d
Coult
West Bromwich 14a
Coult
Weston Candy
Coult
weyrichii   was
Chrysanthemum w.
Ashto, Pgeon
Whirlaway
Coult
White Allouise 25b
Coult

White Charm
Coult

White Classic Perfection
Coult

White Margaret 19c
Coult

White Poolys 5a
Coult

William Florentine 5b
Coult

Windermere 24a
Coult

Yellow Allouise 25b
Coult

Yellow Courtier 24a
Coult

Yellow Dorothy Mechen
Coult

Yellow Hammer
Coult

Yellow Impala
Coult

Yellow John Hughes 3b
Coult

Yellow Kupie
Coult

Yellow Mitzi
Coult

Yellow Nightingale
Coult

Yellow Pennine Marvel 29
Coult

Yellow Pennine Oriel
Coult

Yellow Pinnochio
Coult

Yellow Refour
Coult

Yellow Shantung 24b
Coult

Yellow Snowden 5
Coult

Yellow Tennis
Coult

Yukari
CottP, Parva

Yvonne Arnaud 24b
Coult

Dendrobium

Aussie Cascade x striolatum (Australian Pencil Orchid)
AnnM

Cheryl Diane
AnnM

chrysanthum
AnnM

Iris Jones
AnnM

Jane Leaney
AnnM

kinglanum
NormP, Parva

Margaret Honore
AnnM

pierardii
AnnM

Pink Snow
AnnM

Susan x gracilicaule
AnnM

Tracey Wray
AnnM

Dendrocalamus

brandisii
Isaac

hamiltonii
Isaac

hookeri
Isaac

latiflorus
Isaac

strictus
Isaac

Deparia

petersenii
Orati

Deschampsia

caespitosa (Tufted Hair Grass)
MaraN, MillH

Golden Dew
Hains, Telfa

Desfontainia

spinosa
BlueM, Denes, JoyPl

Desmoschoenus

spiralis (Pingao, Golden Sand Sedge)
Morgn, NZtr #, Orati, Seasd, Terra

Deutzia

Apple Blossom
BlueM, Pgeon, Trans, Woodl

calycosa
Caves

compacta Lavender Time
BlueM, Denes, TopTr

compacta pink
Caves, Wells

compacta white
Caves

coreana (Korean Deutzia)
Caves

crenata
Caves

crenata Double
Caves

Dorothy Hamilton
BlueM, Denes

x elegantissima Rosealind
BlueM, Denes, Pgeon

gracilis (Wedding Bells)
BlueM, Denes

x hybrida Joconde
Denes, MJury, Ormon

x hybrida Magicien
Ashto, BayBl, BlueM, Denes

x hybrida Mont Rose
Denes

x hybrida Pink Pompon
BlueM

Nikko
BayBl, BlueM, CottP, Denes, Ormon, Pgeon, Trans

x rosea
Ormon

x rosea Carminea
BlueM, Denes

scabra Candidissima
Ashto, BlueM, Denes, Dove

scabra Pride of Rochester
Denes

Deyeuxia

billardierii
Orati

Dianella

intermedia (Turutu)
Gordn, Hackf, Orati, Ormon, Terra

intermedia Variegata
Orati

nigra (Turutu, Blueberry)
Hains, Matwh, NZtr #, Wahpa

tasmanica
BlueM

Dianthus

varieties
Roswd

A Painted Beauty
Nikau

Alba
Telfa

Alice
BayBl, Nikau

alpinus
Della

amurensis
MillH

amurensis Siberian Blue
MaraN

andrewskiana
NewlR

Apricot Nectar
CottP, Parva, Telfa

arenarius
AynDa, Della, King #, NewlR, Pgeon

Ariel
BayBl, CottP, NewlR

Aristo spray carnation
Kayd

arvenensis
CottP, NewlR, Otepo

Aurora
NewlR

Barbados spray carnation
Kayd

barbatus mixed (Sweet William)
Sweet

barbatus blood red/scarlet
Hackf, King #

barbatus Harlequin
King #

barbatus Indian Carpet mixed
King #

barbatus single tall mixed
King #

barbatus single tall White
King #

barbatus Sooty
Parva, TRidg

Bat's Double Red
Della, NewlR

Becky Robinson
Parva, Telfa

Belle
Parva, Pgeon

Betty Morton
NewlR

Black and White Minstrels
AynDa, King #, Parva, Telfa

Bombardier
Looij, NewlR

Bovey Belle
BayBl, CottP

brevicaulis
NewlR

Bright News
NewlR

Brilliancy
Ashto

Brook's Cottage Cerise Pink
Nikau

Brooks Cottage
NewlR

caryophyllus hot pink w maroon centre (Clove Pink)
Orang

caryophyllus mixed, double fls (Clove Pink)
Della

caryophyllus Trailing mixed
King #

caryophyllus white (Clove Pink)
Orang

caryophyllus white w maroon edge (Clove Pink)
Orang

Cerise Queen
NewlR

Checkout
Parva

Cheddar pink
Ashto

Cherry Ripe
NewlR

Clara Pandy
Parva

Cloud Nine
Parva

Counterpart
Egmon, NewlR, Nikau

Country Fair Carnation
KeriP

Crossover
Parva

Crushed Velvet
CottP, NewlR

Dads Favourite
BayBl, Mills, Parva, Pgeon

Danielle-Marie
Parva

deltoides
Seasd, Telfa

deltoides alba
Trans

deltoides pink
Telfa

Devon Castle
NewlR

Devon Glow
BayBl

Devon Maid
BayBl, CottP

Devon Pride
BayBl

Doris
CottP, KeriP, Nikau, Parva, Seasd

Doris Majestic
BayBl

Doris Supreme
BayBl, CottP, Parva

Dorothy
NewlR

Double North
CottP, Nikau, Parva

Dusty Cortina spray carnation
Kayd

Earl of Essex
CottP, Della, MillH, Parva

Edith
NewlR

Edna
NewlR

x erinaceus
   NewlR
Ernest Ballard
   CottP
Essex Witch
   Parva
Far Cry
   Nikau, Parva
Far North
   Nikau, Parva
Far Out
   Nikau, Parva
First Favourite
   NewlR
First Love
   Ashto
Flair
   NewlR
Freckles
   BayBl, NewlR
freynii
   CottP, NewlR
Fury
   Parva
gracilis var simulans
   NewlR
Green Magic spray carnation
   Kayd
Grenadier
   NewlR
Haytor White
   BayBl
Her Majesty
   Parva
Hidcote
   BayBl
Highland Fraser
   NewlR
Houndspool Ruby
   BayBl, CottP, Parva
hybridus Rainbow Loveliness
   King #, Otepo
Ian
   CottP
Inchmery
   BayBl, KeriP, NewlR, Parva
Inshriach Dazzler
   NewlR
Irish Lace
   BayBl, CottP, Telfa

ISE Pink
   Parva
ISE Red
   Parva
japonicus
   Marsh
Joyce
   NewlR
Kathryn
   BayBl, CottP, Otepo, Trans
Kiwi Frills
   Trans
Kiwi Lace
   Della, NewlR
Kiwi Magic
   Parva
knappii (yellow)
   MaraN, Marsh, Pgeon
Kortina Chanel spray carnation
   Kayd
La Bourboule
   CottP, Della, NewlR, Otepo
La Bourboule Albus
   BayBl
La Bourboule Pink
   CottP
Lara spray carnation
   Kayd
Laura
   CottP, KeriP, NewlR
Lavender/pink lge
   Nikau
Letitia Wyatt
   BayBl, Egmon, Parva
Lion Rock
   DayBl, Della, NewlR
Little Boy Blue
   Parva
Little Jewel
   Seasd
Little Jock
   Ashto, NewlR
Lively Lady
   NewlR
lumnitzeri
   NewlR
Magic Charms
   Ashto
Marcon White
   Egmon

Mars
   NewlR, Pgeon, Trans
Marshwood White
   Marsh
Mary
   BayBl, Otepo, Pgeon, Trans
Monica Wyatt
   BayBl
Mrs Clark
   CottP
Mrs Sinkins
   BayBl, Parva, Peak
Mt Pleasant
   NewlR
Muggins
   Nikau
Naomi spray carnation
   Kayd
Neat and Tidy
   Nikau
neglectus
   Della, MaraN
nitidus
   NewlR
Nyewoods Cream
   CottP, NewlR, Otepo
Nyewoods Pink
   BayBl, NewlR
Oakington Hybrid
   NewlR
Old Fragrant Plum Pink
   Nikau
Orchid
   CottP, Della, NewlR
Otaki Pinks
   Coult
pavonius
   Della
Pikes Pink
   BayBl, NewlR
pindicola now haematocalyx p.
   NewlR
Pink Champagne
   NewlR
Pink Jewels
   NewlR
Pink Scented
   Telfa
Pinky
   NewlR

Pixie
NewlR

plumarius Karlick
NewlR

Pretty
BayBl, NewlR, Pgeon,
Telfa

Princess Mixed
Ashto

pulmarius mixed (Cottage Pinks, Old Lace Pinks)
CoFlo, King #

Ragdoll
Ashto

Red Velvet
Trans

Ripples
BayBl, NewlR

Robin Redbreast
NewlR

Rosy Glow
NewlR

Royal Red Cortina spray carnation
Kayd

Royal Velvet
Parva

Roysii
NewlR

Satin Doll
NewlR

Scottish Delight
Pgeon

sequieri
MillH

Shot Silk
Pgeon

Sidneys Pink
Della, NewlR

Snowbank
Parva

sp cream
Trans

sp cyclamen shade marked darker
NewlR

sp dbl deep rose(wine centre)
NewlR

sp double wine
Pgeon

sp single mulberry pink
Marsh

sp white semi-double
Nikau

sp white single fls
KeriP, MillH

Spot On
Parva, Trans

Spotti
Parva

Spring Bouquet
Wells

Summer Wine
NewlR

superbus
WaiMa

superbus White Feathers
MillH

Susan
CottP

Sweet Memories
Parva

Target
CottP, NewlR

Terrace Beauty
NewlR

Tiny Tim alba
Otepo

Valda Wyatt
BayBl, CottP, Parva,
Trans

vesicolor
Parva

Waithman Beauty
Della, NewlR

West Diamond spray carnation
Kayd

West Pearl spray carnation
Kayd

Westflame spray carnation
Kayd

Westmoon spray carnation
Kayd

Whatfield Wisp
CottP, Peak

White Ladies
BayBl, Peak

Diascia

varieties
Roswd

Apricot
KeriP

barbarae
Ashto, CottP, Marsh,
Nikau, Pgeon

barbarae Salmon Twinspur
Dream

Blackthorn Apricot
Parva, Peak

cordata (Twinspur)
MaraN, Oasis, Pgeon

cordata Apricot
Pgeon

fetcaniensis
AynDa, BayBl, Oasis,
Warwk

integerrima
Marsh, Trans

integerrima Ivory Angel
BayBl, CottP, Parva

Joyce's Choice
CottP, Della, Nikau

Lilac Belle
BayBl, CottP, Nikau,
Oasis, Parva, Peak,
Telfa, Warwk

Lilac Mist
Nikau, Trans

Pink Cherub
BayBl, Parva

Pink Queen
Wells

rigescens
Ashto, AynDa, BayBl,
BlueM, CoFlo, CottP,
Della, Hackf, MaraN,
MillH, Nikau, Oasis,
Pgeon, Sweet, Trans

Ruby Field
AynDa, BayBl, CottP,
Della, Nikau, Pgeon

Salmon Supreme
BayBl, CottP, Egmon,
Nikau, Parva, Pkrau,
Trans

Sri
CottP, Della

stachyoides
Nikau, Telfa, Warwk

Strawberry Sundae
Parva

vigilis
CoFlo, CottP, Della,
Marsh, MillH

Wooton Birches
Nikau, Peak

Dicentra

Bountiful
MaraN, Pgeon

culcullaria
Kerer, NewlR

eximea alba syn e.Snowdrift
Ashto, BayBl, Marsh, MillH, Telfa

eximea Pink
Ashto

formosa
CoFlo, Della, Telfa, TRidg

formosa Margery Fish
Parva

formosa oregana
Parva

Langtrees
BayBl, MaraN, Parva, Peak, Telfa

Langtrees Alba
TRidg

scandens
AynDa, Hackf, MaraN, Telfa, TRidg, Vall #

spectabilis (Lady's Locket)
BlueM, CoFlo, MaraN, Parva

spectabilis Alba
Parva, TRidg

spectabilis Gold Heart
Peak

spectabilis White Heart
MaraN

Dichelostemma

congesta
Kerer

ida-maia was Brodiaea i.m. (Californian Firecracker)
Kerer

multiflorum
Kerer

volubile
Kerer

Dichondra

repens
Orati

Dichorisandra

thyrsiflora (Blue Ginger)
LakeN

Dichroa

febrifuga
BayBl, Caves, Hackf

versicolor
Caves, Denes, TopTr, Woodl

Dicksonia

antarctica (Tasmanian/Soft Tree Fern)
Gordn

fibrosa (Wheki Ponga)
Coatv, Gordn, Orati, Terra

lanata
Orati

squarrossa (Wheki, Rough Tree Fern)
Coatv, Gordn, Morgn, Mtato, Orati, Pionr, Terra

Dictamnus

albus
MaraN

albus Albiflorus
MaraN

Dictyosperma

album
Reic #

Didiscus

coerulea (Blue Lace Flower
King #

coerulea White Madonna
King #

rosea (Pink Lace Flower)
King #

Dieffenbachia

species
LakeN

Dierama

Fairy Bells
KeriP

nana
Telfa, TRidg

pendulum (Angel's Fishing Rod)
Ashto, AynDa, BayBl, BlueM

pendulum Blackbird
Parva

pendulum Blush Pink
Parva

pendulum Bright Pink
Parva

pendulum Dark Red
Parva

pendulum White
Ashto, Parva

pulcherrimum (Angel's Fishing Rod, Lady's Wand)
AynDa, Diack, Hackf, MaraN, MillH, Mills, Ormon, Pgeon, Trans, TRidg, Vall #

pulcherrimum alba
Peak, Pgeon, Vall #

sp small form
Backw

Diervilla

x splendens (Bush honeysuckle)
TopTr

Dietes

bicolor
Frans, Hackf, Herit, JoyPl, Pgeon, Reic #

butcheriana
Reic #

grandiflora (Wild Iris, Fortnightly Iris)
AynDa, Frans, JoyPl, Ormon, Parva, Reic #, Trans, TRidg

iridiflora
JoyPl

iridioides
Parva, Reic #

moraea
Vall #

pavonia
Herit

robinsoniana (Lord Howe Wedding Lily)
JoyPl

Digitalis

alba
CottP

ambigua now grandiflora
Ashto, BayBl, MaraN, Nikau, Parva

Apricot
CoFlo, Della, Parva, Trans

dubia
Parva

ferruginea (Rusty Foxglove
MaraN, Mills, TRidg,
Vall #

ferruginea Gigantea
BayBl

floribunda sulphur yellow fl
AynDa

gloxiniaeflora Foxy mixed
AynDa, Della, King #

grandiflora was ambigua
MillH, Mills, Otepo,
Peak, Pgeon

grandiflora Carillon
BayBl, King #

hectorii
Ashto

heywoodii now purpurea h.
Peak

John Innes Tetra
CoFlo, King #, Nikau

laevigata
Ashto, Dream, MaraN,
Mills

lanata (Woolly/Grecian Foxglove)
CoFlo, Dream, MaraN,
Mills

lanata x grandiflora John Innes Tetra
AynDa

lutea (Yellow Foxglove)
BayBl, Dream, MaraN,
Pgeon, Roswd, TRidg,
Warwk

x mertonensis
BayBl, KeriP, MaraN,
Mills, Oasis, Parva,
Peak, Pgeon, Trans,
TRidg, Vall #

x mertonensis Strawberry Merton
CoFlo, CottP, Della,
King #

micrantha
AynDa

obscura
BayBl, Dream, MaraN,
Parva, Telfa

parviflora
AynDa, CoFlo, MaraN,
Marsh

pink & white w heavily spotted throats tall
Orang

purpurea Alba
Dream, King #, MaraN,
MillH, Parva, Trans

purpurea albiflora
BayBl

purpurea Apricot
Pgeon

purpurea Apricot Beauty
Egmon

purpurea heywoodii
Dream

purpurea Sutton's Apricot
BayBl, Dream, King #

thapsi
Marsh

viridiflora
Parva, Roswd

white tall
Egmon, Orang

Dimorphotheca

see Osteospermum
Ref

Dimorpotheca

Buttercup
Della

spectabilis
Della

Dioon

species
Reic #

Dioscorea

discolor
CouCl

Diosma

ericoides (Breath of Heaven)
Denes, Mtato, Wells

Diospyros

digyna (Black Sapote)
Koan

kaki varieties (Persimmon)
Reic #, TreeC

kaki Fuju
Chedd

kaki Yoko
Chedd

virginiana (American Persimmon)
Apple, Dove, PuhaN

Dipelta

white pink fl w orange throat
Caves

Dipidax

triquetra now Onixotis t.
AynDa, Parva

Diplarrhena

moraea
AynDa, Telfa

Diplazium

australe
Orati

dilatata
JoyPl

Dipsacus

fullonum (Teasel (true hooked))
Della

Disa

uniflora
Backw

veitchii
Backw

Discaria

toumatou (Matagouri)
Terra

Diselma

archeri
BlueM, Cedar

Disphyma

australe (Horokaka, Native Iceplant)
Orati, Seasd, Terra

clavellatum (Jellybeans)
Seasd

Disporum

flavens
BayBl, TRidg

sessile Variegatum
BayBl, Peak, TRidg

smilacinum Daisetugo
Titok

Dissotis

canescens (Wild Lasiandra)
AynDa

princeps
AynDa

Distictis

buccinatoria was
Phaedranthus b. (Mexican
Blood Flower)
CouCl, Denes

Dodecatheon

meadia (Shooting Star)
MaraN, NewlR, Pgeon,
TRidg
pulchellum Red Wings
CottP, NewlR

Dodonaea

**viscosa (AkeAke, Hop
Bush)**
Burbk, Butlr, Chedd,
Coatv, Gordn, Kayd,
Matai, Matwh, Morgn,
Mtato, NEti #, Orati,
Pionr, Reic #, SouWo,
Terra, Wahpa
viscosa Purpurea
Chedd, Diack, Gordn,
Kayd, Matai, Matwh,
Morgn, Mtato, NZtr #,
Orati, Ormon, Pionr,
Reic #, SouWo, Terra,
Wahpa, Wensl

Dombeya

elegans
Frans
goetzenii
Ether
Pink Clouds
Woodl

Dombrowskya

tenella
Pgeon

Doodia

aspera
Orati
media
Orati
milnei
Orati
mollis
Orati

Dorichium

hirsutum
Hackf

Doronicum

**caucasicum Magnificum
now orientale M.**
MaraN

columnae (Leopards Bane)
Marsh
**orientale Magnificum
(Leopards bane)**
Ashto
plantagineum Magnificum
Della

Doryanthes

palmeri
JoyPl

Dorycnium

hirsutum now Lotus
Seasd
pentaphyllum now Lotus
Vall #

Douglasia

**vitaliana now Vitaliana or
Androsace**
NewlR

Dovyalis

caffra (Kei Apple)
Ether, Frans
**hebecarpa (Ceylon
Gooseberry)**
Frans

Doxantha

**unguis-cati now
Macfadyena**
CouCl, Denes

Draba

aizoides
Della
athoa
Della
bryoides imbricata
NewlR
dedeanna
Della
hispanica
Della
kotschyii
Della
lasiocarpa
Della, Pgeon
magellanica
Pgeon

Dracaena

draco (Dragon Tree)
Denes, Frans, JoyPl,
KeriP, LakeN, Manna,
PalmF, Reic #, SpecT,
Wells
**fragrans Deremensis
Bausei**
LakeN
**fragrans Deremensis Janet
Craig (v)**
LakeN
**fragrans Deremensis
Warneckei**
LakeN
**fragrans Massangeana (v)
(Golden Corn Plant)**
LakeN, PalmF
fragrans Victoriae
LakeN
godseffiana Florida Beauty
LakeN
godseffiana Gold Dust
LakeN
marginata
PalmF
marginata alba
Manna
marginata Marginata
LakeN
**marginata tricolour
(Rainbow Tree)**
LakeN, PalmF
species also see Pleomele
LakeN

Dracocephalum

grandiflorum
BayBl
**moldavicum (Blue
Dragonhead, Moldavian
Balm)**
King #, Sweet
sp clear blue fl compact
Dream

Dracophyllum

latifolia (Neinei)
JoyPl, MJury
**recurvum (Curved Leaf
Grass)**
Terra

Dracunculus

vulgaris
Kerer

Dregea

sinensis
CouCl

Drepanostachyum

falcatum
Isaac

falconeri
Isaac

Drimys

aromatica now lancelolata
BlueM, Denes

winterii (Winter's Bark)
BlueM, Denes

Drosanthemum

floribundum (Lavender Trails)
Seasd

Dryandra

formosa (Showy Dryandra)
Denes, MatNu, Matth, Reic #

nobilis
Reic #

polycephala
Reic #

speciosa
Reic #

Dryas

octopetala (Mountain Avens)
MaraN, NewlR, Pgeon

Dryopteris

dilatata
Gordn, JoyPl

erythrosora (Autumn Fern)
Denes, Gordn

koiozmannia
JoyPl

montana
JoyPl

odtophorum
Gordn, JoyPl

x remota
Gordn

varia
JoyPl

wallichiana
Gordn, JoyPl

Duchesnea

indica (Indian Strawberry)
Oasis

Dymondia

margaretae was Gazania Buttons
Seasd, Telfa, Trans

Dysoxylum

spectabile (Kohe Kohe)
Gordn, Matwh, Mtato, Orati, Sweet, Terra

Eccremocarpus

scaber (Chilean Glory Flower)
Marsh

scaber mixed
King #

Echeveria

Chocolate Leaf
Parva

Chocolate Prince
Peak

setosa Oliver
Peak

Echinacea

angustifolia
Marsh, Parva

Beacon Purpurea syn.Rudbeckia magnum purp
KeriP

Brilliant Star
CottP

Magnus
Peak

newmanii
MillH

pallida
BayBl, MaraN, Marsh, Parva

Pearl White
Kayd

purpurea (Coneflower , Rudbeckia)
Ashto, AynDa, CoFlo, CottP, Dream, Egmon, JoyPl, King #, Looij, MillH, Mills, Oasis, Orang, Peak, Pgeon, Reic #, Sweet, Trans

purpurea Bravado
Dream

purpurea Leuchstern
Marsh

purpurea Magnus
BayBl, MaraN, Parva, Vall #

purpurea White Lustre
Dream

purpurea White Swan
BayBl, CottP, Della, Egmon, King #, MaraN, Mills, Orang, Parva, Peak, Pgeon, Sweet, Telfa, Trans

Echinochloa

frumentacea Japanese (Japanese Millet)
MTig #

Echinodorus

magdalenensis (Dwarf Amazon Sword Plant)
WaiMa

paniculatus (Amazon Sword Plant)
WaiMa

tenellus
WaiMa

Echinops

bannaticus Blue Chip
BlueM

bannaticus Blue Globe
Vall #

bannaticus Blue Glow
MaraN, Marsh, MillH

cream w blue flrs 2m
Marsh

ritro (Globe Thistle)
BayBl, KeriP, King #, MaraN, Telfa, Trans

sphaerocephalus
MaraN

Echium

Bee Plant
Vall #

candicans was fatuosum (Pride Of Madeira)
BayBl, Denes, Dream, Kayd, MaraN, MillH, MJury, Parva, Seasd, Trolh, Wells

handiensis
MJury

pininana (Pride of Teneriffe)
BayBl, CottP, Denes, Dream, Kayd, MaraN, MJury, Parva, Seasd, Trolh, Wells

simplex
MJury

vulgare Bedder Mixture
Dream, King #

vulgare Blue Bedder
Dream, King #, Trolh

vulgare Light Blue
Dream

webbii
Ormon

wildpretii (Taginaste Roja, Pink Echium)
Dream, MJury, Seasd

wildpretii x pininiana hybrids
Dream

Edgeworthia

papyrifera Grandiflora
Denes, MJury

Elaeagnus

angustifolia (Russian Olive)
Ford, PuhaN, TopTr

x ebbingei
BlueM, SelGr, TopTr

x ebbingei Gilt Edge (v)
BlueM

x ebbingei Limelight (v)
BlueM, Butlr

No 3
ZinoN

pungens Maculata (v)
BlueM, Butlr, Denes

pungens Variegata
BlueM, Ford, ZinoN

Elaeocarpus

dentatus (Hinau)
Denes, Gordn, Mtato, Pionr, Terra

hookerianus (Pokaka)
Gordn, Matai, Mtato, Orati

Elatostema

rugosum (Parataniwha, NZ Begonia)
Gordn, Orati, Trans, Wahpa

Elegia

capensis
Caves, Denes, Diack, Ether, JoyPl, MatNu, Matth, Peak, Wells

Eleocharis

acicularis (Hair Grass)
Diack, WaiMa

acuta (Sharp Spike Sedge)
Diack, Orati, WaiMa, WilAq

dulcis (Chinese Water Chestnut)
Diack, Koan

sphacelata (Bamboo Spike Sedge, Tall Spike Rush)
Orati, Terra, WaiMa

Elingamita

johnsonii
JoyPl, Orati

Elodea

canadensis (Oxygen Weed)
Mills, WaiMa

Elsholtzia

stauntonii
MaraN

Elymus

magellanicus
Peak

Embothrium

coccineum (Fire Bush)
Hackf

coccineum Lanceolatum
BlueM

coccineum Lanceolatum Inca Flame
Denes

coccineum Longifolium (Chilean Fire Bush)
Denes

Encyclia

cochliata
AnnM

Endymion

non-scriptus now Hyacinthoides n.s.
MaraN

non-scriptus Pink Form now Hyacinthoides
MaraN

Enkianthus

campanulatus (Red Vein Bell Flower)
BlueM, Chedd, JoyPl, TRidg, Woodl

campanulatus Rubrum
Denes

chinensis
Caves

Ensete

ventricosum (Abyssinian ornamental bananas)
Frans, Lsendt

ventricosum Maurelli (Red Ornamental Banana)
LakeN, SpecT

Entelea

arborescens (Whau)
Chedd, Coatv, Gordn, NZtr #, Orati, Reic #, Terra

Eomecon

chionantha
BayBl, MillH

Epacris

impressa (Common Heath)
Butlr

pauciflora (Tamingi)
Seasd

White Candles
BlueM

Epicat

Rene Marques
AnnM

Epidendrum

pseudepepidendrum x Cat. harrisoniae
AnnM

Epilobium

glabellum
Peak

obcordatum
MaraN

parviflorum (Willow Herb)
Sweet

Epimedium

acuminatum (RL575)
Titok

davidii
Titok

grandiflorum
MaraN

grandiflorum Rose Queen
Hackf

leptorrhizum
Titok

x rubrum
Pgeon, TRidg

x versicolor Sulphureum
BayBl, Hackf, Otepo, Parva, Peak, Pgeon

x youngianum Niveum
BayBl, Hackf, Pgeon

Epipremnum

pinnatum
LakeN

Equisetum

arvense (Horsetail)
Sweet

Eragrostis

trichodes
Peak

Eranthis

hyemalis
NewlR

yellow
Altrf

Eremophila

maculata Red (Spotted Emu-bush)
Denes

Erica

arborea (Tree Heath)
BlueM

Aurora (Hybrid Cape Heath)
MatNu, Matth

australis Mr Robert
BlueM

australis Riverslea
BlueM

bauera (Bridal Heath)
Reic #

bauera Pink Maiden
Denes, MatNu, Matth

blandiflora
Backw

caffra (Kaffir Heath)
Reic #

carnea Ada Collins
BlueM

carnea Eileen Porter
BlueM

carnea Myretoun
Hewsn

carnea Myretoun Ruby
BlueM

carnea Sherwoodii
Looij

carnea Springwood White
BlueM, Denes, Hewsn, Looij

carnea Winter Beauty
Looij

cerinthoides Can Can
Kayd, Matth

cerinthoides Candy Ice
Matth

cerinthoides Pink
Denes

cerinthoides Pink Can Can
Wells

cerinthoides Pink Hairy Heath
MatNu

cerinthoides Red Hairy Heath
MatNu

cinerea Golden Drop
BlueM

cinerea Golden Hue
BlueM, Looij

cinerea Pink Spangles
BlueM

cinerea Spicata
BlueM

coccinea
Reic #

colorans White Delight
Denes, MatNu, Matth

conica compact
MatNu

daphniflora
MatNu

x darleyensis (Darley Dale Heath, Winter Heather)
Chedd, Hewsn

x darleyensis AT Johnson
BlueM

x darleyensis Bealey Pink
BlueM

x darleyensis Darley Dale
BlueM

x darleyensis Furzey
Hewsn

x darleyensis Furzey (Cherry Stevens)
BlueM

x darleyensis Jack H Brummage
BlueM, Looij

x darleyensis JW Porter
BlueM

x darleyensis Mary Helen
Looij

x darleyensis Silver Beads
Hewsn

daviesii
Denes

diaphana
Reic #

discolor
Reic #

erigena Alba (Irish Heath)
BlueM

erigena Golden Lady
BlueM, Hewsn

erigena Irish Salmon
BlueM

erigena Nana
BlueM, Hewsn

erigena Smokey MAuve
BlueM

erigena WT Rackcliff
BlueM, Hewsn

fastigata
Backw

formosa
Backw, Reic #

gibbosa
Reic #

glandulosa
Reic #

Gwavas
Hewsn

hirtiflora (Hairy-flowered Heath)
Reic #

hybrida
MatNu

hybrida Dawn
BlueM

imbricata
Reic #

laeta
Reic #

lateralis
Reic #

Lavender Mist
  MatNu
longifolia
  Reic #
Lyonesse
  Hewsn
macowanii
  MatNu
mammosa red
  Reic #
mauritanica Spring Charm
  MatNu
melanthera
  MatNu, Matth
melanthera Ruby Shepherd
  MatNu
Mrs Maxwell
  Hewsn
nana
  Backw
oatesii hybrid Winter Fire
  Matth
patersonia
  Reic #
persoluta (Pink Garland Heath)
  MatNu
perspicua
  Backw
perspicua Pink Tubes
  Denes, MatNu
peziza Velvet Bells
  MatNu
propinqua
  Reic #
Purple Beauty
  Hewsn
quadrangularis
  Reic #
Riverslea
  MatNu
Rosslare
  Hewsn
sessiliflora
  Denes, MatNu, Reic #
speciosa
  Reic #
subdivaricata Autumn Snow
  Denes, MatNu, Matth
swynnertonii
  Denes

taxifolia
  Reic #
terminalis
  Hewsn
tetralix Alba Mollis (Cross-lvd Heath)
  BlueM, Hewsn
vagans Alba (Cornish Heath)
  BlueM, Looij
vagans Fiddlestone
  BlueM
vagans Saint Keverne
  BlueM
ventricosa Globosa (Wax Heath)
  Denes, MatNu, Matth
versicolor
  Reic #
verticillata
  Reic #
viridescens
  Reic #
walkeria
  Denes
Winter charm
  MatNu, Matth, Wells
Winter Fire
  MatNu
Wittunga Satin
  MatNu

Erigeron
alpinus (Alpine Fleabane)
  Della
compositus
  MaraN
compositus Rocky
  MillH
glaucus
  Nikau, Pgeon, Seasd, Telfa
karvinskianus was mucronatus (Fleabane, Seaside daisy,Midsummer Aster)
  BayBl, Looij, Sweet, Trolh
karvinskianus Profusion
  Della, MillH
leiomerus
  Della, NewlR
mucronatus now E.karvinskianum
  BayBl, Nikau

multiradiatus
  Seasd
Pink Jewel
  CoFlo, CottP, KeriP, Telfa
pulchellus
  CottP
Rosa Triumph (Pink Triumph)
  Burbk
Rowsham
  BayBl, CottP
speciosus Best Blue
  Ashto
trifidus now compositus discoideus
  Della

Erinus
alpinus (Fairy Foxglove)
  MaraN, NewlR
alpinus albus
  MaraN, Telfa
alpinus Dr Hahnle
  BayBl, MaraN

Eriobotrya
japonica (Loquat)
  MTig, Reic #, TreeC
japonica Bright Helen
  TopTr

Eriocephalus
africanus
  Ormon

Eriogonum
fasciculatum (Californian Buckwheat)
  MillH
umbellatum
  Pgeon

Eriophyllum
lanatum
  Oasis
lanatum Pointe
  MillH

Eriostemon
myoporoides Profusion
  Butlr, Denes, MatNu, Mtato
myoporoides Stardust
  MatNu

Erodium

alba
  CottP
manescaui
  MillH, Pgeon
reichardii alba (Storksbill)
  Parva
reichardii Roseum
  MaraN, Parva, Pgeon
tricolor
  Pgeon
trifolium
  MaraN

Eruca

sativa (Rocket, Roquette, Arugula)
  King #, Koan #, Mills, MTig #, Sweet
sylvatica Italian Wild Rustic
  King #

Eryngium

varieties
  Roswd
agavifolium
  MillH, Mills, Telfa
alpinum (Sea Holly)
  Della, MaraN, Pgeon, Wells
alpinum Blue Star
  Dream, Marsh, Parva
alpinum Superbum
  King #
amethystinum
  MaraN, Peak
bierbersteinianum
  MaraN
bourgatii
  MaraN
giganteum (Miss Wilmott's Ghost)
  MaraN, TRidg
maritinum (Sea Holly)
  Marsh, Oasis
pandanifolium
  TRidg
planum (Sea Holly)
  Ashto, AynDa, BayBl, CottP, Della, Dream, Kayd, King #, MaraN, Mills, Orang, Ormon, Pgeon, Seasd, Telfa, Trans
planum Bluecap
  JoyPl, Parva

proteiflorum (Sea Holly)
  AynDa, Dream
spinalba
  MaraN
x tripartitum
  TRidg
variifolium
  TRidg
x zabelii Violetta
  Telfa

Erysimum

alpinum Sulphur
  NewlR
Apricot
  Parva
Bowles Mauve
  Egmon, MaraN, Nikau, Seasd
bright yellow dwarf
  Nikau
cheiri Aurora
  Dream
cheiri brick red
  Orang
cheiri Covent Garden
  Dream
cheiri Primrose Dame
  Dream
cheiri purple orange
  Orang
Constant Cheer
  BayBl, CottP, Marsh, Nikau, Oasis, Parva
Gypsy Girl (v)
  Della, MillH
Harpur Crewe
  Hackf, MaraN, MillH
Iron Ore
  BayBl, Nikau, Parva
Joy Gold
  BayBl, Egmon, Nikau, Oasis, Orang, Trans
Jubilee Gold
  BayBl
Julian Orchard
  BayBl
x Kewense
  Parva
Lemon Yellow
  Parva
linifolium Variegatum
  MaraN

Mauve Mist
  BayBl, MillH, Parva, Trans
Moonlight
  MillH, Parva
Orange Flame
  BayBl, Marsh
pulchellum
  Telfa
pulchellum Orange
  Telfa
pumilum
  Della
purple/bronze
  Oasis
Rufus
  MaraN
scoparium
  Marsh
Variegata
  Marsh

Erythrina

crista-galli (Cockspur/Brazilian Coral Tree)
  Reic #
humeana (Dwarf Coral Tree)
  JoyPl
indica picta (Variegated Coral Tree)
  LakeN

Erythronium

species mixed
  RosPl
californicum
  JoyPl, Kerer, RosPl
californicum White Beauty
  Kayd, Kerer, NewlR, Nikau, RosPl, TRidg
citrinum
  Kerer, RosPl
dens-canis
  Kerer, NewlR
dens-canis roseum
  RosPl
hendersonii
  RosPl
hendersonii lavender form
  Kerer
hendersonii pale form
  Kerer

hendersonii x oregonum hybrids
    MJury

oregonum cream form
    Kerer

oregonum pink form
    Kerer

Pagoda
    Kayd, NewlR, Peak

revolutum
    JoyPl

revolutum Johnsonii
    Kerer, RosPl, Taunt

revolutum pale pink
    TRidg

revolutum Pink Beauty
    RosPl

revolutum Rose Beauty
    RosPl

tuolumnense (Yellow Trout Lily)
    BayBl, CottP, Kerer, MaraN, NewlR, RosPl, TRidg

Escallonia

Alice
    BlueM, Ormon, Pionr, TopTr

Apple Blossom
    Ashto, BlueM, Butlr, CottP, Denes, Diack, Kayd, Morgn, Mtato, Ormon, Pionr, Seasd, SelGr, TopTr, ZinoN

Donard Seedling
    BlueM

Field's Scarlet
    Kayd, Morgn, Mtato, Pionr, SelGr

Fielders White
    SelGr

hybrid   pink/white fls
    TopTr

leucantha
    Caves

macrantha
    SelGr

Red Dwarf
    CottP

Red Elf
    Ashto, BlueM, Hewsn, TopTr

rubra
    Pionr

White
    Diack, Mtato

Yellow Sunset (yellow lvs)
    Woodl

Eschscholtzia

mixed
    Trolh

caespitosa Sundew (Dwarf Californian Poppy)
    King #

californica Apricot Chiffon
    CottP, Dream, King #

californica Carmine King
    CottP, King #

californica cream form
    TRidg

californica Dalli
    Dream

californica Golden West
    King #

californica Ivory Castle
    CottP, Dream, King #

californica Milkmaid
    King #

californica Milky White
    Dream

californica Orange (Californian State Flower)
    King #

californica pink & cream mixed
    Vall #

californica pink form
    TRidg

californica Purple Gleam
    Dream, King #

californica Rose Bush
    King #

californica Rose Chiffon
    King #

californica Thai Silk
    Dream

californica White
    King #

pink ex Hollards Gardens
    Vall #

Eucalyptus

varieties
    Reic #

acaciaformis (Wattle Leafed Peppermint)
    GMill

acmenioides
    Reic #

agglomerata (Blue-lvd Stringybark)
    GMill

aggregata (Black Gum)
    GMill, Reic #

alpina (Grampian/Ak Gum
    NZtr #

amplifolia (Cabbage Gum)
    GMill

amygdalina (Black Peppermint)
    GMill, Mtato, Reic #

andrewsii (New England Blackbutt)
    GMill

apiculata (Narrow-lvd Mallee Ash)
    GMill

approximans (Barren Mountain Mallee)
    GMill

archeri (Alpine Cider Gum)
    Diack, GMill

aromaphloia (Scent Bark)
    GMill

badjensis (Big Badja Gum)
    GMill

baeuerlenii (Baeuerlens Gum)
    GMill

barberi (Barbers Gum)
    GMill

benthamii (Camden White Gum)
    GMill

bicostata (Southern Blue Gum)
    GMill

blakeleyi (Blakely's Red Gum)
    GMill

blaxlandii (Blaxland Stringybark)
    GMill

botryoides (Southern Mahogany/ Mahogany Gum, Bangalay)
    Hewsn, Matwh, McKe, Morgn, Mtato, NZtr #, Pionr, PuhaN, Reic #

brookeriana (Brookers Gum)
    GMill, Morgn

caesia (Weeping Gum)
Reic #

calignosa (Broad-lvd Stringybark)
GMill

camaldulensis (Red River Gum)
Burbk, Hewsn, Matwh, NZtr #, Reic #

cameronii (Diehard Stringybark)
GMill

camphora (Mountain Swamp Gum)
GMill

cephalocarpa (Mealy Stringybark)
GMill

cinerea (Silver Dollar Gum, Argyle Apple)
BlueM, Chedd, Diack, GMill, Matwh, Morgn, Mtato, NZtr #, Reic #

citriodora (Lemon scented Gum)
Chedd, Matwh, Mtato, NZtr #, Pionr, Reic #, Sweet

cladocalyx (Sugar Gum)
NZtr #

coccifera (Snow Gum, Tasmanian Snow Gum)
Ford, GMill, NZtr #, SouWo

conica (Fuzzy Box)
GMill

cordata (Heart-lvd Silver Gum)
Diack, Ford, GMill, Matai, Matwh, Morgn, Mtato, NZtr #, Pionr, SouWo, Wensl

cosmophylla (Cup Gum)
GMill

crebra (Narrow-lvd Ironbark)
GMill

crenulata (Victorian Silver/Buxton Silver Gum)
Diack, GMill, NZtr #

cypellocarpa (Mountain Grey Gum)
GMill

dalrympleana (Mountain Gum)
GMill, NZtr #, SouWo

dealbata (Tumbledown Red Gum)
GMill

deanei (Round-lvd Gum)
GMill

delegatensis (Alpine Ash Gum)
Ford, GMill, Matai, Matwh, Morgn, Mtato, NZtr #, Pionr, Reic #, SouWo, WakaC, Wensl

dendromorpha (Budawang Ash)
GMill, Matwh, WakaC

diversicolor (Karri Gum)
Matwh, NZtr #, Pionr

dives (Broad-lvd Peppermint)
GMill, Matwh

dunnii (Dunns White Gum)
GMill

elata (River Peppermint)
GMill

eugenoides (Thin-lvd Stringybark)
GMill

fastigata (Brown Barrel Gum)
Chedd, Ford, GMill, Matai, Matwh, Morgn, Mtato, NZtr #, Pionr, SouWo, WakaC

fibrosa (Broad-lvd Red Ironbark)
GMill

ficifolia (Red Flowering Gum)
Burbk, Chedd, Matwh, McKe, Morgn, Mtato, NZtr #, Pionr, Reic #

ficifolia Orange Glow
Chedd, Denes

fraxinoides (White Ash Gum)
Ford, GMill, Hewsn, Matwh, Morgn, Mtato, NZtr #, Pionr, SouWo, WakaC

glaucescens (Tingiringi Gum)
GMill

globoidea (White Stringybark)
Matwh, Mtato, NZtr #, Pionr

globulus (Tasman Blue Gum)
GMill, Matwh, NZtr #, Pionr

gomphoecphala (Tuart)
NZtr #

goniocalyx (Long-lvd Box)
GMill

grandis (Rose Gum)
Reic #

gregsoniana (Wolgan Snow Gum)
GMill, Matai

gunnii (Cider Gum (blue form))
Diack, Ford, GMill, Matai, Matwh, Morgn, NZtr #, Pionr, Reic #, SouWo, Wensl

haemastoma (Scribby Gum)
NZtr #

johnstonii (Yellow Gum)
BlueM, GMill, Morgn, NZtr #

kartzoffiana (Araluen Gum)
GMill

kitsoniana (Bog Gum)
GMill

kybeanensis (Kybean Mallee Ash)
GMill

laevopinea (Silvertop Stringybark)
GMill

largiflorens (Black Box)
GMill

leucoxylon (Winter flowering Gum, Yellow Gum)
Chedd, GMill, Matwh, McKe, Morgn, NZtr #, Reic #

leucoxylon Rosea
Ford, Matai, Matwh, Mtato, NZtr #, Pionr, Reic #

lingustrina (Privet-lvd Stringybark)
GMill

macarthurii (Cambden Woollybutt)
GMill, NZtr #

macrocarpa (Rose of the West)
NZtr #

macrolyncha (Red Stringybark)
GMill

maculata (Spotted Gum)
GMill, Matwh, NZtr #, Reic #

maidenii (Maidens Gum)
GMill

mannifera (Brittle Gum)
GMill

mannifera several spp
GMill

marginata (Jarrah)
NZtr #

mckieana (McKies Stringybark)
GMill

melliodora (Yellow Box)
GMill, Matwh, McKe, Morgn, Mtato, NZtr #

michaeliana (Hillgrove Gum)
GMill

microcorys (Tallowwood)
Matwh, NZtr #

mitchelliana (Mt Buffalo Sally)
GMill

moorei (Narrow Leaved Sally)
GMill, Matai

morrisbyi (Morrisby's Gum)
GMill

muellerana (Yellow Stringybark)
Chedd, Matwh, Mtato, NZtr #, Pionr

neglecta (Omeo Gum)
GMill

nicholii (Narrowlvd Black Peppermint Gum)
BlueM, Burbk, Chedd, Diack, Ford, GMill, Matai, Matwh, McKe, Morgn, Mtato, NZtr #, Pionr, Reic #, SouWo

nicholii (red stemmed hybrid)
Burbk

niphophila see pauciflora n.
Reic #

nitens (Shining Gum, Silver Top Gum)
Apple, BlueM, Chedd, Diack, Dove, Ford, GMill, Hewsn, Matai, Matwh, Morgn, Mtato, NZtr #, Pionr, PuhaN, Reic #, SouWo, Terra, WakaC, Wensl

nitida (Smithton Peppermint)
GMill

notabilis (Blue Mountains Mahogany)
GMill

nova-anglica (New England Peppermint)
GMill

obliqua (Messmate Stringybark)
Ford, GMill, Matai, Matwh, Morgn, NZtr #, SouWo

oblonga (Narrow-lvd Stringybark)
GMill

obtusiflora (Port Jackson Mallee)
GMill

occidentalis (Swamp Yate)
Matwh

olsenii (Wolia Gum)
GMill

ovata (Swamp Gum)
Chedd, Ford, GMill, Hewsn, Matai, Matwh, Morgn, Mtato, NEu #, Pionr, Reic #, SouWo, WakaC, Wensl

ovata grandiflora
Mtato, Pionr

paliformis (Wadbilliga Ash
GMill

paniculata (Grey Ironbark)
NZtr #

parvifolia (Small leaved Gum)
GMill, Matai, Matwh

pauciflora (Snow Gum)
Matwh, Mtato, NZtr #, Pionr

pauciflora niphophila (Snow Gum)
BlueM, Ford, GMill, Matai, NZtr #, Wensl

pauciflora var debeuzevillei (Jounama Snow Gum)
GMill

pauciflora var pauciflora (Snow Gum)
GMill

perriniana (Spinning Gum)
GMill, Matwh

pilularis (Black Butt Gum)
Matwh, NZtr #, Pionr

piperita (Sydney Peppermint)
GMill

polyanthemos (Red Box)
GMill

pulchella (White Peppermint)
Ford, GMill, Matai, Mtato, NZtr #, Pionr

pulverulenta (Silver lvd Mountain Gum, Powdered Gum)
GMill, NZtr #, Reic #, TopTr

quadrangulata (White Topped Box)
GMill

radiata (Narrow-lvd Peppermint)
GMill

regnans (Mountain Ash)
Diack, Ford, GMill, Matai, Matwh, Morgn, Mtato, NZtr #, Pionr, PuhaN, SouWo, WakaC

risdonii (Risdon Peppermint)
GMill, Reic #

rodwayii (Swamp Peppermint)
Diack, Ford, GMill, Matai, Matwh, Morgn, NZtr #, SouWo, Wensl

rossii (Scribbly Gum)
GMill

rubida (Candle Bark)
GMill

rupicola (Cliff Mallee Ash)
GMill

saligna (Sydney Blue Gum)
Matwh, McKe, Morgn, NZtr #, Pionr, Reic #

salubris (Gimlet)
NZtr #

scoparia (Wallangara White Gum)
GMill, NZtr #

sideroxylon (Mugga Ironbark)

Matwh, Morgn, NZtr #

sideroxylon Rosea (Red Flwrd Ironbark)

McKe, NZtr #, Pionr

sieberi (Silvertop Ash)

Matwh

smithii (Gully Gum)

GMill

spathulata (Swamp Mallet)

Matwh

stellulata (Black Sally)

GMill, SouWo

stenostoma (Jillaga Ash)

GMill

stricta (Blue Mountains Mallee Ash)

GMill

sturgissiana (Ettrema Mallee)

GMill

subcrenulata (Mountain Yellow Gum)

Ford, GMill

tenuiramis (Silver Peppermint)

GMill, Matai, Morgn

torquata (Coral Gum)

Reic #

triflora (Pigeon House Ash)

GMill

urnigera (Urn Gum)

GMill

viminalis (White/Mana Gum)

Ford, GMill, Matai, Matwh, Morgn, Mtato, NZtr #, Reic #, SouWo, WakaC

viridis

Reic #

wilcoxii

GMill

yarraensis (Yarra Gum)

GMill

youmanii (Youmans Stringybark)

GMill, Reic #

Eucomis

comosa (Pineapple Lily)

Ormon

pole evansii

AynDa

sp Pineapple flower

Dream

zambesiaca

Parva

Eucommia

ulmoides

Apple

Eucryphia

cordata

JoyPl

cordifolia

BlueM, Caves, Denes, JoyPl, TopTr, Woodl

x hillieri Winton

BlueM

x intermedia

BlueM, TopTr, Woodl

lucida (Leatherwood)

BlueM, TopTr, Woodl

lucida Leatherwood Cream (v)

BlueM

lucida Pink Cloud

BlueM

milliganii

BlueM

moorei (Pinkwood)

BlueM, Denes

x nymansay

BlueM, JoyPl, Taunt

x nymansensis Nymansay

Denes

Eugenia

australis now Syzgium a. (LillyPilly, Australian Rose Apple)

Frans, MTig

luehmanii

Frans

smithii syn. Acmena s. (LillyPilly, Monkey Apple)

Denes, Mtato, Pukho, SpecT

ugni now Ugni molinae

Ref

uniflora (Menemene)

LakeN

ventenati (Weeping Lillypilly)

Coatv, LanSc

Euonymus

alatus (Burning bush)

Peele, PuhaN

europaeus f. albus (White Spindle)

BlueM, Denes

europaeus Red Cascade

BlueM, Denes, TopTr

fortunei Emerald 'n Gold (v)

BlueM, Hewsn, Ormon

fortunei Emerald Gaiety

Butlr

fortunei Emerald Gem

Mtato, Ormon

hamiltonia maackia (White fruited Spindle)

Dove

japonicus Albomarginatus (Silver Jap.Laurel)

BlueM

japonicus Albus (White Spindle)

Denes

japonicus Aurea (v) was j. Aureopicto

Butlr, Hewsn

japonicus Aureomarginatus (Golden Jap.L.)

Burbk

japonicus Ovatus Aureus (v) (Dwarf Golden J.L.)

BlueM

japonicus variegatum (Variegated Japanese Laurel)

Denes, Ford

Silver Queen

Ormon

Eupatorium

cannabinum (Agrimony Hemp, Hemp Agrimony)

Della, Dream, Marsh, Pgeon, Sweet, WaiMa

cannabinum Flore Pleno

BayBl, CottP, Telfa

coelestinum

Egmon

megalophyllum

Woodl

perfoliatium (Boneset)

Marsh, Sweet

purpureum (Joe Pye Weed)

BayBl, CoFlo, Della,
MaraN, Marsh, Orang,
Pgeon, Telfa

**purpureum maculatum
Atropurpureum (Joe Pye
Weed)**

MaraN, MillH

ruginosa (White Snakeroot)

Orang

rugosum

MaraN, Marsh

triplinerve

TRidg

Euphorbia

amydaloides

Marsh

amygdaloides Purpurea

BayBl, Caves, Hackf,
Oasis, Peak, Pgeon

amygdaloides Rubra

MaraN, Marsh, Telfa,
Warwk

amygdaloides var robbiae

Marsh, Ormon, Parva

characias

BayBl, JoyPl, MaraN,
Marsh, Ormon, Parva

characias ssp wulfenii

BayBl, Dream, Hackf,
JoyPl, MaraN, Marsh,
MillH, Ormon, Parva,
ZinoN

cognata C&Mc 607

MaraN, Marsh

cognata C&Mc 724

Marsh

corallata

Marsh, Parva, TRidg

cornigera

Marsh, Peak

**cyparissias (Cypress
Spurge)**

AynDa, Ormon

cyparissias Fens Ruby

BayBl, Peak

dulcis Chameleon

BayBl, Hackf, Marsh,
Ormon, Parva, Peak,
TopTr

**epithymoides now
polychroma**

Pgeon

epithymoides Purpurea

Pgeon

fulgens

LakeN

glauca

Hackf, JoyPl, Orati,
Ormon, Peak, Seasd,
TopTr

Gold Foam (?E.brittingeri)

TRidg

griffithii

Marsh

griffithii Dixter

BayBl, Peak

griffithii Fireglow

Ashto, KeriP, MaraN,
Marsh, MillH, Parva,
Warwk

**heterophylla (Mexican Fire
Plant, Annual Poinsettia)**

King #, LakeN

hibernica rubra

Nikau

Humpty Dumpty

Peak

hyberna (Irish Spurge)

Ormon

Jade Dragon

BayBl, Hackf, Parva,
Peak

**marginata syn variegata
(Snow on the Mountain)**

King #

x martinii

Hackf, Ormon

mellifera

Caves, Hackf, JoyPl,
MaraN, Marsh, Ormon,
Parva, Peak, Vall #

myrsinites (Blue Spurge)

BayBl, Hackf, KeriP,
MaraN, Marsh, MillH.
Ormon, Parva, Peak

nicaeensis

MaraN

oneclada

LakeN

palustris

Dream, Marsh, WilAq

palustris Zauberflote

Ashto

pithyusa

BayBl, Parva, Peak

**polychroma (Cushion
Spurge)**

BayBl, Egmon, Hackf,
KeriP, King #, MaraN,
Marsh, Otepo, Parva,
Peak, Telfa, TRidg,
Warwk

polychroma Major

Marsh

**polychroma Purpurea now
p.Candy**

Marsh, MillH, Peak

**pulcherrima plenissima (a
Poinsettia)**

LakeN

rigida was biglandulosa

Hackf, TopTr

schillingii

Hackf, Marsh, Ormon

seguierana

MaraN, Marsh, Ormon

sikkimensis

Telfa

spinosa

Marsh

splendens

LakeN

trigona

LakeN

trigona red

LakeN

Euptelea

**plelosperma was
franchetti**

Caves

Eurya

jingjungensis

Woodl

Euryops

acreaus

Hackf

Glitters

Butlr

**pectinatus (Grey Haired
Euryops)**

CottP, Diack, Kayd,
KeriP, Mtato, Seasd

Sunshine

Mtato, Telfa

tenuissimus (Paris Daisy)

Butlr

Eutaxia

obovata
Denes

Evodia

gongshanensis
Woodl

Evolvulus

Blue Sapphire
KeriP, Mtato

Exochorda

giraldii var wilsonii (Pearl Bush)
Caves, Dove

x macrantha The Bride
Denes, Hackf, Mtato

racemosa (Pearl Bush)
Apple

Fagopyrum

esculentum (Buckwheat)
King #, Sweet

Fagus

sylvatica (European Beech)
Apple, BlueM, Chedd, Coatv, Diack, Dove, EasyB, Mtato, NZtr #, Peele, PuhaN, Pukho, SelGr, TopTr, Wensl

sylvatica Ansorgei
Caves

sylvatica Aurea Pendula
Caves

sylvatica Cockleshell
Caves

sylvatica Dawyck
Caves

sylvatica Dawyck Gold
Caves, Pukho

sylvatica Dawyck Purple
Caves, Pukho

sylvatica laciniata (Fern-lvd Beech)
Caves, Denes, Pukho

sylvatica Pendula
Caves, Denes, Pukho

sylvatica Purple Fountain
Caves

sylvatica Purpurea (Copper Beech)
Apple, Burbk, Chedd, Coatv, Denes, Diack, Dove, EasyB, Hewsn, Mtato, Ormon, Peele, Pionr, PuhaN

sylvatica Purpurea Pendula
Denes, Pukho

sylvatica Riversii (Rivers Copper beech)
Caves, Coatv, MJury, Pionr, Pukho, TopTr

sylvatica Rohanii
Caves, Denes

sylvatica Roseomarginata
Caves

sylvatica Swat Magret
Caves

sylvatica Tricolour
Denes, Pukho

sylvatica Zlatia (Golden Beech)
Caves, Denes, Pukho, TopTr

Farfugium

tussaligineum Argentium (v) was Ligularia
MJury, Peak

tussaligineum Aureomaculatum (v)
BayBl, WaiMa

Fatsia

japonica was Aralia sieboldii (Japanese Aralia)
Butlr, Frans, Kayd, Manna, Mtato, Wells

Felicia

amelloides (Blue Marguerite)
KeriP, Otepo, Pgeon, Seasd

amelloides alba Felicity
CottP, KeriP, Nikau, Seasd

amelloides Pink Star
CottP, KeriP, Nikau, Pgeon, Seasd, Telfa

amelloides Santa Anita
CottP, KeriP, Pgeon

amelloides Santa Anita Variegata
Pgeon

amelloides variegata
CottP, Otepo, Seasd

angustifolia variegata
Butlr

bergeriana Cubscout (Annual Kingfisher Daisy)
King #

fruticosa
Morgn

gracilis
CottP, MillH, Pgeon

heterophylla The Blues
King #

heterophylla The Rose
King #

Kingfisher Blue
Vall #

petiolata (Pink Felicia)
AynDa

Spreading Lilac
Oasis

Ferraria

crispa was undulata
DaffA, JoyPl, Kerer

divaricata
DaffA

Ferula

communis
MaraN

Festuca

glauca (Blue Fescue, Kentucky Blue Grass)
BlueM, Diack, Looij, MaraN, Matai, Pkrau, Seasd, Telfa, TRidg

multinodus
Hains, Telfa

novae zelandiae (Hard Tussock)
Hains, Matai

ovina coxii (Chatham Is Blue Grass)
CottP, Hains, KeriP, Matai, Orati, Parva, Seasd, Telfa, Terra, Wahpa

sp blue grass
KeriP

Ficus

benghalensis
Reic #

benjamina (Weeping Fig)
LakeN, Manna, Reic #

benjamina Lady Di
LakeN, Manna

benjamina Starlight (v)
PalmF

benjamina Variegata
LakeN

Burgundy
    PalmF
carica Adriatic
    Koan C
carica Black
    Koan C
carica Black Beauty
    Pionr
carica Brown Turkey
    Chedd, Denes, Harri,
    Mtanu, TopTr
carica Brunswick
    Chedd, Harri
carica Cheddar Valley
    Chedd
carica Forage Paddock
    Koan C
carica French Sugar
    Koan C
carica Hyndmans
    Koan C
carica Kaeo
    Koan C
carica Malta
    Harri
carica Matapouri
    Mtanu
carica Mrs Williams
    Frans, Harri
elastica decora (Rubber Plant)
    LakeN, Reic #
elastica decora Black Knight
    LakeN, Manna
elastica decora Shrijvereana
    Manna
lyrata
    LakeN
macrophylla (Moreton Bay Fig)
    Reic #
obliqua
    Reic #
pumila Frosty
    LakeN, Parva
pumila Minima (Creeping Fig)
    Denes
pumila Minima Variegata
    Denes
religiosa
    Reic #

roxburghii
    LakeN
rubiginosa
    Manna

Filicium
decipiens
    Ether

Filipendula
Double Cream
    Diack, Peak
hexapetala   now vulgaris
    Ashto, BayBl, MaraN,
    Nikau, Telfa
kamtschatica pink form
    JoyPl
kamtschatica white fl
    JoyPl
palmata Nana was digitata N. (Dwarf Chinese Lace Flower)
    Ashto, CottP, Della,
    Diack, MaraN, Peak,
    Telfa
palmata Rubra
    BayBl, Peak
rubra (Queen of the Prairie, Chinese lace Flower)
    Ashto, Diack, Egmon,
    Kayd, Mills, Nikau,
    Telfa, WaiMa, WilAq
ulmaria (Meadowsweet, Queen of the Meadows)
    CoFlo, Della, Diack,
    JoyPl, King #, MaraN,
    Mills, Oasis, Orang,
    Sweet, Telfa, WaiMa,
    WilAq
ulmaria Aurea
    BayBl, Diack, Peak
ulmaria Flore Pleno (Double Meadowsweet)
    Ashto, BayBl, CottP
ulmaria Rubra
    CoFlo, MaraN
vulgaris was hexapetala (Dropwort)
    Diack, Egmon, Sweet,
    Telfa, WaiMa

Firmiana
platanifolia (Parasol Tree)
    Caves

Fitzroya
cupressoides
    Cedar

Foeniculum
vulgare Purpureum (Bronze Fennel)
    AynDa, CottP, Della,
    Dream, King #, MillH,
    Orang, Sweet
vulgare var dulce (Florence Fennel)
    Della, Koan #, Orang
vulgare var dulce Zefa Fino
    King #, Sweet
vulgare var dulce Zefa-Tardo
    Della, King #

Fokienia
hodginsii
    BlueM, Cedar

Forsythia
Beatrix Farrand
    Chedd
x intermedia Karl Sax
    Denes
x intermedia Lynwood Gold
    Pukho
x intermedia Minigold
    BlueM
x intermedia Minigold Fiesta
    BlueM
x intermedia Spectabilis
    BlueM, Pukho
x intermedia Spring Glory
    Denes
viridissima Bronxensis
    BayBl

Fortunella
margarita (Kumquat)
    Chedd, LanSc, TreeC

Fothergilla
gardenii
    Denes, Taunt
gardenii Autumn
    BayBl
gardenii Blue Mist
    BayBl, Caves, Denes,
    JoyPl, Taunt
major
    Caves

Fragaria
x ananassa Variegata
    Marsh

107

strawberry Aiko
　　TreeC

strawberry Captain Cook (heirloom)
　　Koan #

strawberry Pajaro
　　TreeC

strawberry Red Gauntlet
　　Kayd, TreeC

strawberry Tioga
　　Kayd

vesca golden (Alpine Strawberry)
　　CottP, Della, Mills, Orang, Sweet

vesca scarlet (Alpine)
　　CottP, Della, Mills, Orang, Sweet

vesca creeping (Alpine)
　　Orang, Telfa

Francoa

appeniculata
　　Pgeon

ramosa (Maidens Wreath, Bridal Wreath)
　　Ashto, Kayd, MaraN, Mills, Oasis, Peak, Pgeon, Telfa, Trans, Vall #

ramosa pink form
　　Nikau, Trans

ramosa Alba
　　MaraN, Nikau

sonchifolia (Bridal Wreath)
　　Della, MillH, Oasis, Pgeon, Sweet, Vall #

sp white fl w pink strip
　　CottP

Frankenia

laevis (Sea Heath)
　　Seasd

thymifolia
　　Looij

Franklinia

alatamaha
　　Caves, JoyPl

Fraxinus

americana (American/White Ash)
　　Apple, Chedd, Diack, Ford, Mtato, NZtr #, Ormon, Peele, PuhaN, Reic #

angustifolia was oxycarpa (Narrow-lvd Ash)
　　Apple, Chedd, Dove, Peele, PuhaN, TopTr

angustifolia syrica (Syrian Ash)
　　Apple, TopTr

chinensis (Chinese Ash)
　　PuhaN

excelsior (European Ash)
　　Apple, Burbk, Chedd, Diack, Dove, EasyB, Ford, Hewsn, Mtato, NZtr #, Peele, Pionr, PuhaN, Reic #, WakaC, Wensl

excelsior Aurea (Golden Ash)
　　Apple, Chedd, Dove, Hewsn, Mtato, Pionr, Wensl

excelsior Aurea Pendula (Weeping Golden Ash)
　　Burbk, Chedd, Dove, Pukho

excelsior Green Glow
　　Denes, Pukho

excelsior Hamner
　　Pukho

excelsior Jaspidea (Golden Ash)
　　TopTr

latifolia (Oregon Ash)
　　Apple, Peele

mariesii
　　MJury

ornus (Flowering Ash, Manna Ash)
　　Apple, Chedd, Diack, Dove, EasyB, Ford, NZtr #, Peele, Pionr, PuhaN, Pukho, Reic #, TopTr

oxycarpa now angustifolia (Desert Ash)
　　Morgn, PuhaN, Reic #

oxycarpa Raywood now angustifolia Raywood (Claret Ash)
　　Burbk, Chedd, Coatv, Denes, Dove, EasyB, Hewsn, Mtato, Peele, Pionr, PuhaN, Pukho, SpecT

pennsylvanica (Green/Red Ash)
　　Apple, Chedd, PuhaN, Reic #, TopTr

pennsylvanica var lanceolata
　　Diack, MJury, Peele

pennsylvanica Variegata
　　Pukho, TopTr

retusa integra
　　Caves

sieboldiana
　　Woodl

spaethiana (Spaths Ash)
　　Apple, PuhaN

velutina (Arizona Ash, Velvet Ash)
　　Apple, Dove, Peele, PuhaN, Reic #, TopTr

Freesia

mixed
　　Altrf, Kayd

Athene
　　LeFab

Bloemfontein
　　LeFab

blues
　　Altrf

burtonii
　　CottP, DaffA

Corona
　　DaffA

Fanfare
　　DaffA

Golden Crown
　　LeFab

Golden Melody
　　DaffA

Helvetia
　　DaffA

Kayak
　　LeFab

Mosella
　　LeFab

Olde Worlde Freesias
　　DaffA, Kayd

Orient
　　LeFab

pink
　　Altrf, LeFab

Red Diamond
　　DaffA

Romany
　　DaffA

Sailor
　　LeFab

Striped Queen
LeFab

white
Altrf

White Wings
LeFab

yellow
Altrf

Yvonne
LeFab

Fremontia

californica
Denes

Freycinetia

banksii
Orati

Fritillaria

acmopetala
DaffA, Kerer, Otepo, Parva, RosPl, Winga

affinis
Kerer, TRidg

affinis dark form
Kerer

alfredae ssp glaucoviridis
Kerer

assyriaca
BayBl, DaffA, Parva

biflora (Mission Bells)
Kerer

camschatsensis (Black Sarana, Black Fritillary)
DaffA, Kerer, RosPl, Winga

davisii
Kerer

graeca ssp thessala
Kerer

grayana was roderickii
Kerer

imperialis (Crown Imperial
JoyPl, Parva

imperialis golden yellow
Winga

imperialis orange
Winga

lanceolata now affinis
RosPl

lusitanica
Kerer

lutea now collina
JoyPl

meleagris (Snakeshead Fritillary)
Kayd, Kerer, Mills, Otepo, RosPl, Taunt, Winga

meleagris alba
BayBl, DaffA, Kerer, Parva, RosPl

meleagris Purple King
DaffA

meleagris purpurea
Kerer

messanensis
DaffA, Kerer, Marsh, Parva, Winga

michailovskyi
ReRul

pontica
BayBl, DaffA, JoyPl, Kayd, Kerer, Otepo, RosPl, Taunt, Winga

pyrenaica
Kerer, RosPl

recurva
DaffA

rubra now imperialis Rubra
JoyPl

tubiformis
Kerer

uva-vulpis
Kerer, Otepo

verticillata
DaffA, Kerer, Parva

Fuchsia

Abbe Farge
AmFu

Ada Perry
Corom

Adeline Laurie
AmFu, Corom

Alaska
AmFu, Corom, Mason, Shadi

Alberta Logue
AmFu, Corom

Alice Hoffman
AmFu

Alison Ewart
AmFu, Corom

Alison Ryle
AmFu, Corom

Ambassador
AmFu

American Snowball
Mason

Amphion
Mason

Amy Lyle
AmFu, Mason

Angel Rippon
Mason

Angela Leslie
AmFu, Mason

Angels Dream
AmFu, Corom

Angels Flight
Corom, Mason

Annabell
AmFu, Corom, Mason

Apricot Slice
AmFu

arborescens (Tree Fuschia)
AmFu

Arcady
AmFu, Mason

Archie Owen
AmFu, Corom

Arlendon
Mason

Army Nurse
AmFu, Corom, Mason

Arthur Cope
Corom

Athela
AmFu

Atlantis
Mason

Aunt Juliana
Corom

Aunty Jinks
AmFu, Corom

Australia Fair
AmFu, Corom

Autumn Orange
AmFu, Corom

Ave Maria
Corom

Azalea
Mason

Baby Pink
Corom

Bali Hi
Corom

Ballet Girl
Mason

Barbara
Mason

Baron Von Kettler
Mason

Bashful Lady
AmFu, Corom, Shadi

Beacon
AmFu

Beacon Rosa
AmFu

Beauty Of Bath
Mason

Bee Keesey
Corom

Bella Rosella
Corom

Belsay Beauty
Mason

Belvoir Beauty
Mason

Berliner Kind
Mason

Bernadette
Corom

Beryl
AmFu, Corom, Shadi

Beryl's Choice
AmFu

Beth Robley
AmFu, Corom

Betty Mason
Mason

Bi-Centennial
AmFu, Corom, Mason, Shadi

Billy Green
Mason

Bishop's Bells
Mason

Bittersweet
Corom

Black Prince
AmFu, Corom, Mason

Blanche Regina
Corom

Blessed Event
Corom

Blue Boy
AmFu, Corom

Blue Bush
Mason

Blue Danube
Mason

Blue Eyes
Corom

Blue Frills
AmFu

Blue Haze
AmFu

Blue Lagoon
Mason

Blue Moon
Mason

Blue Satin
AmFu, Corom

Blue Sleigh Bells
AmFu, Corom, Mason

Blue Smoke
Corom

Blue Veil
Corom

Blue Waves
Mason

Blush Of Dawn
AmFu, Corom

Bobby Redwings
AmFu, Corom

Bobby Shaftoe
Corom

boliviana
Mason

boliviana alba
AmFu

boliviana Mrs Marriot
AmFu

Bon Accord
AmFu, Corom, Mason

Bon Bon
AmFu, Corom, Mason

Bonanza
Corom

Border Queen
AmFu, Corom, Mason

Boudoir
Mason

Bouffant
Mason

Bountiful
Corom

Bow Bells
Mason

Brenda
AmFu, Corom

Briar Carter
Mason

Bridal Veil
AmFu

Brigadoon
AmFu

British Jubilee
AmFu

Brutus
AmFu, Mason

Buddha
Mason

Burning Bush
Corom, Mason

Buttercup
AmFu, Corom

Buttons & Bows
Mason

Caesar
Mason

Callaly Pink
Mason

Cameo
AmFu, Mason

Cameron Ryle
AmFu, Corom

Capri
AmFu, Corom

Capricorn
AmFu, Corom, Shadi

Captain Cook
AmFu, Corom

Carmel Blue
AmFu, Corom, Mason

Carmen Maria
AmFu, Corom

Caroline
Corom, Mason

Cascade
AmFu, Mason

Catalina
Corom

Catherine
AmFu

Cecile
AmFu

Celia Smedley
AmFu, Corom, Mason

Chang
AmFu, Mason

Charming
Mason

Checkerboard
AmFu, Mason

Cheers
AmFu

Chillerton Beauty
AmFu

China Doll
AmFu

China Lantern
AmFu

China Rose
AmFu, Corom

Christine Gatske
AmFu, Mason

Christmas Elf
AmFu

Cinnamon
AmFu

Citation
AmFu, Mason

City of Adelaide
AmFu, Corom

City of Pacifica
Corom

City of Pacifica No 1
AmFu

City of Pacifica No 2
AmFu

Clair Carter
Mason

Clare Evans
Corom, Mason

Cliffs Hardy
Mason

Cloth of Gold
Kayd

Cloverdale Jewel
AmFu, Kayd

Cloverdale Pearl
AmFu, Mason

Cloverdale Star
Mason

Collingwood
Corom

Colonial Dame
Corom

Colourful Lady
Corom

Come Dancing
Corom

Comet
AmFu, Corom, Mason

Commander In Chief
AmFu

Conspicua
AmFu, Corom, Mason

Constellation
AmFu, Mason

Continental
AmFu, Corom

Coquet Bell
Mason

Coquet Dale
Corom

Cornflower
AmFu

corymbiflora
AmFu

Cotton Candy
AmFu, Corom, Shadi

Countess of Aberdeen
AmFu

Court Jester
Corom

Crackerjack
AmFu

Creampuff
AmFu

Crusader
AmFu, Corom

Curtain Call
AmFu, Corom, Kayd

Curvaceous Lady
Corom

Cyndy Robyn
Corom

Daisy Bell
Mason

Dame Elizabeth
AmFu

Dancing Flame
AmFu, Corom

Danny Boy
AmFu

Dark Eyes
AmFu, Corom

Dark Secret
AmFu, Corom

Dawn
AmFu

Dawn Mist
Corom

Deaconess
AmFu, Mason

Debutante
Kayd

Deep Purple
AmFu, Corom

Delightful Lady
AmFu, Corom

Delvina
AmFu, Mason

denticulata
AmFu, Corom

Derby Imp
AmFu, Mason

Diablo
AmFu, Corom, Mason

Diana Wills
Mason

Dimples
AmFu

Display
AmFu, Corom, Kayd, Mason

Dollar Princess
AmFu

Double Delight
Corom

Drama Girl
AmFu, Corom, Shadi

Du Barry
AmFu

Dusky Beauty
Corom

Dusky Rose
AmFu

Duyfken
AmFu

Easter Bonnet
Mason

Ed Largarde
AmFu, Corom

Egmont Blue
AmFu, Corom

Egmont Trail
Corom

Eleanor Leytham
AmFu

Electra
AmFu, Corom

Elegant Lady
Corom

Elkhorn
AmFu, Mason

Elsa
Mason

Elsie Mitchell
AmFu, Corom

Enchanted
AmFu

Enid Carter
AmFu, Corom, Mason

Ernestine
AmFu, Corom, Shadi

Esme
Mason

Ethel Kempster
AmFu, Corom

Eusebia
AmFu, Corom, Shadi

excorticata (Kotukutuku, Tree Fuchsia)
Gordn, Matai, Matwh, NZtr #, Orati, Sweet, Terra, Wahpa

Falling Star
AmFu, Corom, Mason

Fan Tan
Corom

Fanfare
AmFu, Mason

Fantasy
AmFu, Corom

Fascination
AmFu

Fascination Smith
Mason

Festival
Corom

Fey
AmFu, Corom

Fifi
AmFu, Corom

Fire Mountain
AmFu

Fire Of The East
AmFu

First Love
AmFu

Flame
Corom

Flirtation Waltz
AmFu, Corom, Mason

Flocon de Neige
Mason

Florentina
Corom

Fluorescent
Corom

Fly by Night
Corom

Flying Cloud
AmFu, Corom, Mason

Foolke
AmFu

Forget-me-not
Mason

Fort Bragg
AmFu, Corom

Fountains Abbey
AmFu

Frank Unsworth
Corom

Frosted Amethyst
Corom

Frosted Flame
AmFu, Corom

Frosty Jack
AmFu, Corom

Fur Elise
Corom

Garden News
Corom, Mason

Garden Week
AmFu

Gartenmeister Bonstedt
AmFu, KeriP, Mason

Gay Anne
Mason

Gay Fandango
Corom

Gay Parasol
AmFu, Corom

Genii
Mason

Giant Falls
AmFu, Mason

Glenby
AmFu, Corom, Mason

Glowing Lilac
AmFu, Corom

Golden Anniversary
AmFu, Corom

Golden Marinka
AmFu

Golden Swingtime
AmFu, Corom

Golden Treasure
AmFu

Goody Goody
AmFu, Corom

Gov 'Pat' Brown
Mason

GreenFingers
Corom

Grey Lady
Corom

Gypsy Girl
AmFu

Gypsy Queen
Corom

Halleys comet
AmFu, Corom

Hampshire Blue
AmFu

Hampshire Treasure
AmFu

Happy Wedding Day
AmFu, Shadi

Harbour Bridge
AmFu

Harriet
Mason

Harry Gray
AmFu, Kayd

Haute Cuisine
AmFu

Hawaiian Night
AmFu, Corom

Hazel
AmFu, Corom

Heart Throb
AmFu, Mason

Heidi Ann
AmFu, Corom, Mason

Heiress
Mason

Henri Poincare
Corom

Heron
Mason

Heston Blue
Corom

HG Brown
Mason

Hidcote Beauty
AmFu, Corom, Mason

High Peak
Mason

Hollys Beauty
Corom

Hula Girl
AmFu

Imakiwi
Corom

Imperial Fantasy
AmFu

Indian Maid
AmFu, Corom, Kayd, Mason

Italiana
Corom

Jack Shahan
Mason

Jack Stanway
AmFu

Jay Jay
Corom

Joy Patmore
AmFu, Corom

Jubie Lyn
AmFu, Corom

Jules Delonges
AmFu, Corom, Kayd

Julie Dietrich
Corom

Julie Horton
AmFu, Corom, Mason, Shadi

June Revell
Mason

Ken Jennings
AmFu

Keystone
AmFu

Kiwi
Corom

Kontiki
Corom

Koralie Kwintet
AmFu

Kwintet
Corom

L'Arlesienne
AmFu

La Campanella
AmFu, Corom, Kayd, Mason

La Neige
AmFu, Corom

La Rosita
AmFu, Corom, Mason

Lace Petticoat
Corom, Shadi

Lady Beth
AmFu, Corom

Lady In Gray
AmFu, Corom

Lady Kathleen Spence
Corom, Kayd

Lady Thumb
AmFu, Mason

Lakewood
Mason

Larkspur
AmFu, Corom

Laurie
Corom, Mason

Lavender Falls
AmFu, Corom

Lavender Kate
Mason

Lechlade Tinkerbell
AmFu

Leigh Carter
Mason

Lena
AmFu, Corom, Mason, Shadi

Leonora
AmFu, Corom, Mason

Lilac Lustre
AmFu, Corom

Lilac Princess
Mason

Lillibet
Corom, Kayd

Lillydale
AmFu, Corom

Lindisfarne
AmFu, Corom

Lisa
AmFu, Corom, Shadi

Little Wonder
AmFu

Lord Byron
AmFu

Loren Adele
Corom, Mason

Lotty Hobby
AmFu, Oasis

Louis Emmershaw
AmFu, Corom

Love Knot
AmFu

Lovely Blue
AmFu, Corom

Lunar Night
AmFu, Corom

Luscious
Corom

Luscombes Choice
AmFu, Corom, Kayd

Lyes Unique
AmFu, Mason

Machu Picchu
AmFu, Corom

magellanica
AmFu

magellanica Alba
AmFu

magellanica Gracilis Variegata
AmFu, Mason

magellanica Tricolour
KeriP

magellanica var pink
MillH

Maharajah
Mason

Maidens Blush
Corom

Major Heaphy
Mason

Mancunian
AmFu, Corom

Mandarin
AmFu, Corom

Marcus Graham
AmFu, Corom

Margaret
AmFu

Margaret Roe
AmFu

Marin Belle
Mason

Marinka
AmFu, Corom, Kayd, Mason

Marlene Gilbee
Corom

Martyn Smedley
Corom, Mason

Mary
AmFu

Mauve Beauty
AmFu, Mason

Maytime
Corom

Meadowlark
Corom

Medallion
Corom

Merle Evans
Mason
Merle Hodges
Mason
microphylla
Mason
microphylla ssp hidalgensis
AmFu
Mieke Muersing
Corom
Millionaire
AmFu, Corom
Mission Bells
AmFu, Mason
Misty Lady
Corom
Molesworth
Mason
Montrose Village
Corom
Moonlight
Corom
Moonmist
AmFu, Corom
Moonraker
AmFu, Mason
More Applause
AmFu, Corom, Shadi
Morning Light
AmFu, Corom
Moth Blue
Corom, Mason
Mrs Lovell Swisher
Mason
Mrs Marshall
AmFu, Corom
Mrs Popple
Mason
Muriel
AmFu
Nancy
Mason
Nancy Lou
AmFu, Corom, Kayd, Mason
Naomi Adams
AmFu
Native Dancer
Mason
Nell Gwynn
Mason
Nettalo
AmFu, Corom

Nicola
AmFu
Nicolette
AmFu
Normandy Belle
Corom
Northern Queen
AmFu
Northumbrian Belle
Mason
Northway
AmFu, Mason
Orange Crush
AmFu, Corom
Orange Dream
Corom
Orange Mirage
Mason
Oregon Trail
Corom
Oriental Flame
AmFu
Other Fellow
AmFu, Corom
Ovation
AmFu
Pacific Queen
Mason
Pacquesa
AmFu
Painted Desert
AmFu, Corom, Shadi
Papa Bluess
Corom, Mason
Papa Cameo
Mason
Party Frock
AmFu, Mason
Pelleas et Melisande
Corom
Peloria
Mason
Peppermint Stick
AmFu, Corom, Mason
Periwinkle
AmFu
Perry Park
Mason
perscandens
Orati
Phenomenal
AmFu

Phyllis
AmFu, Corom
Pinch Me
AmFu, Corom, Mason
Pink Bon Accord
Mason
Pink Cloud
Mason
Pink Darling
AmFu, Corom
Pink Galore
AmFu, Corom, Mason, Shadi
Pink Jade
AmFu, Mason
Pink Lady Beth
AmFu, Mason, Shadi
Pink Marshmallow
AmFu, Corom, Shadi
Pink Quartet
AmFu, Corom
Pink Rain
AmFu
Pink Shower
Corom
Pink Sky
AmFu, Corom
Pink Surprise
Corom
Pinwheel
Corom
Pixie
AmFu
Polestar
Corom, Kayd
Preference
Corom
Prelude America
Corom
President Leo Boullemier
AmFu
President Margaret Slater
AmFu, Mason
President McLister
Corom
President Moir
Corom
Preston Guild
AmFu, Corom
Prince of Peace
Mason

procumbens
(Shore/Creeping Fuchsia)
  AmFu, BayBl, CottP,
  Gordn, KeriP, Mason,
  Mills, Oasis, Orati,
  Ormon, Otepo, Terra,
  Trans

procumbens Variegata
  Orati

procumbens x exorticata
  BlueM

Prosperity
  Corom, Mason

Pumila
  AmFu, BayBl

Purple Heart
  AmFu, Corom, Kayd,
  Mason

Purple Rain
  AmFu, Corom

Pussycat
  Corom

Quaser
  Corom

Queen Of Derby
  Mason

Query
  AmFu

R.A.F.
  AmFu, Corom, Mason

Raspberry
  AmFu

Ravensbarrow
  AmFu

Red Ace
  AmFu

Red Embers
  AmFu, Corom

Red Glory
  AmFu

Red Jacket
  AmFu, Corom, Mason

Red Rain
  AmFu

Red Shadows
  Corom, Shadi

Red Spider
  Mason

Reflexa
  AmFu

Regal Lady
  AmFu, Corom

regia var regis
  Mason

Riccartonii was
magellanica R.
  AmFu

Ridestar
  Mason

Robert Sharpe
  Corom

Romance
  AmFu, Corom

Ronald Lockerbie
  Corom

Rose of Denmark
  Corom

Rosetta
  AmFu

Rough Silk
  AmFu, Corom, Mason

Roy Walker
  Corom

Royal Jester
  Corom

Royal Robe
  AmFu, Corom

Royal Velvet
  AmFu

Royal Zenith
  Corom

Ruffles
  AmFu, Corom, Kayd

Sally
  Mason

Salmon Glow
  AmFu, Mason

San Diego
  AmFu, Corom, Mason

San Leandro
  AmFu, Mason

sanctae-rosae
  AmFu

Sapphire
  AmFu

Sarah Jane
  Mason

Satellite
  Corom

Scarlet O'Hara
  AmFu, Corom

Sensation
  Corom

sessifolia
  AmFu

Seventeen
  Corom

Seventh Heaven
  Corom

Shady Lady
  AmFu, Corom

Shangri-La
  AmFu

Shelley Lyn
  AmFu

Sheryl Ann
  AmFu, Corom, Shadi

Shower of Stars
  AmFu

Silver Blue
  AmFu, Corom, Mason

Silver Dawn
  Corom

Siobhan
  Mason

Sister Esther
  Mason

Sleepy
  Mason

Sleigh Bells
  AmFu, Corom, Mason

Snow Drift
  Corom

Snow Fire
  AmFu, Corom, Mason,
  Shadi

Snowburner
  AmFu, Corom

Snowcap
  AmFu, Corom

Soldier Of Fortune
  Mason

Son of Thumb
  AmFu

Sophisticated Lady
  AmFu, Corom, Mason

Southgate
  AmFu, Corom, Shadi

Southseas
  Corom

Sparks
  AmFu

Stanley Cash
  AmFu, Corom

Steeley
  AmFu, Corom

Strawberry Delight
  Corom

Strawberry Festival
  AmFu

Strawberry Sundae
Corom
String Of Pearls
AmFu, Corom, Mason
Sunburst
AmFu
Sundial
AmFu, Corom
Sunray
AmFu
Sunset
Mason
Super British
Corom
Susie Olcese
Corom, Mason, Shadi
Swanley Gem
Mason
Sweetheart
Mason
Swingtime
AmFu, Corom, Kayd, Shadi
Tangerine
AmFu, Corom
Tasman Sea
AmFu, Corom
Ted Sweetman
Corom
Television
AmFu, Corom
Temptation
AmFu, Mason
Tennesee Waltz
AmFu, Corom, Mason
Texas Longhorn
Corom
Thalia
AmFu, Mason
The Rival
AmFu, Corom, Shadi
Thomasina
AmFu
thymifolia
AmFu
Tiffany
AmFu
Ting A Ling
AmFu, Corom, Mason
Tinkerbell
Corom
Titanic
AmFu, Corom

Tom Thumb
AmFu, Corom, Mason
Torch
AmFu, Corom
Tosca
AmFu, Corom
Tower of London
AmFu
Tracey Carter
Mason
Tradewinds
Corom
Trisha
AmFu, Corom, Mason
Tropicana
AmFu, Corom
Troubador
Corom, Mason
Tuonela
AmFu, Corom, Kayd
TW Ashby
Corom, Mason
TW Ashby variegated
Mason
Twinkling Star
Corom
U.F.O.
Corom
Vagabond
AmFu
Vanessa Jackson
AmFu
variegata tricolour
Mason
venusta
AmFu
Versicolor now magellanica V.
KeriP
Victorian
AmFu, Corom
Violacea
Corom, Mason
Violet Basset-Burr
Corom
Virginia Lund
AmFu
Viva Ireland
Corom, Mason
Vivian Harris
Mason
Vogue
AmFu, Corom

Voodess
AmFu
Voodoo
AmFu, Corom, Mason, Shadi
Waitakere City
AmFu, Corom, Shadi
Waltzing Matilda
AmFu
Walz Toorts
Corom
Wave of Life
Mason
Waveney Queen
AmFu
Wedgewood
AmFu, Corom, Kayd
Whirlaway
Corom
White King
AmFu, Corom, Mason
White Lady Beth
AmFu, Corom
White Phenomenal
Corom
Wildfire
Mason
Wilson's Pearls
AmFu
Wingroves Mammoth
Corom
Winston Churchill
AmFu, Corom, Mason, Shadi
Wisteria Blue
Corom
Wood Nook
AmFu, Corom
Yuletide
Mason
Ziegfield Girl
AmFu, Corom
Zulu Chief
AmFu, Mason

Gaevina
avellana
Chedd

Gahnia
lacera
Orati
setifolia (Mapere)
Orati

Gaillardia

aristata (Blanket Flower)
Della, King #

aristata Indian Yellow
Warwk

Bremen
BayBl

Burgunder
BayBl, Marsh

Burgundy
CottP, Oasis, Peak,
Telfa, Warwk

Kobold syn Goblin
BayBl, BlueM, Sweet,
Trans

**pulchella (Wild Gaillardia,
Blanket Flower, Fire
Wheels)**
King #

Tokajer
BayBl

Galanthus

Atkinsii
DaffA

**corcyrensis now G.reginae-
olgae vernalis**
DaffA

double
SoBul

elwesii
DaffA, SoBul

flora plena
DaffA

Magnet
DaffA

nivalis (Snowdrop, English)
BayBl, DaffA, MaraN,
NewlR, Parva, SoBul

nivalis Viridapicis
MJury

plicatus
Lilyf

S Arnott
MJury

Galaxia

ovata
DaffA, Irida

Galega

bicolor
CoFlo, Vall #

x harlandii
Mills

officinalis (Goats Rue)
Della, Sweet

officionalis Alba
CoFlo, Mills, Vall #

Galium

**odoratum was Asperula o.
(Sweet Woodruff)**
CottP, Della, Mills,
Orang, Sweet

verum (Lady's Bedstraw)
Della, MillH, Mills,
Orang, Sweet

Galtonia

candicans (Cape Hyacinth)
AynDa, Kayd, KeriP,
MaraN, MillH, Mills,
Telfa, TRidg, Vall #

candicans Moonbeam
Parva

princeps
AynDa, MaraN, MJury,
Taunt, TRidg

**viridiflora (Summer
Hyacinth)**
Dream, Parva, TRidg

Gardenia

augusta Professor Pucci
KeriP

**augusta Radicans was
jasminoides r.**
Denes, Wells

jasminoides now augusta
Chedd

**jasminoides Tahiti now
augusta T.**
LakeN

Garrya

**elliptica (Catkin Bush,
Silver Tassel)**
BlueM, Denes, Diack,
JoyPl, KeriP

elliptica James Roof
BlueM, Denes

Gaultheria

antipoda (Snowberry)
NZtr #

mucronata Alba
BlueM

**mucronata Bell's Seedling
was Pernettya B.s.**
BlueM, Denes, Hewsn

shallon dwarf form
YakuN

Gaura

**lindheimeri (Butterfly
Plant)**
BayBl, CoFlo, CottP,
Dream, Egmon, Kayd,
KeriP, MaraN, MillH,
Mills, Nikau, Pgeon,
Trans, Wells

lindheimeri Corrie's Gold
BayBl, CottP, Telfa

lindheimeri The Bride
KeriP

**lindheimeri Whirling
Butterflies**
AynDa, BayBl, CottP,
KeriP, Parva, Peak,
Telfa, Warwk

Gazania

**Buttons see Dymondia
margaretae**
Seasd

Double Bronze
Parva

Double Lemon
Parva

Green Ice
CottP, Peak

Gwens Pink
CottP

Mulberry Cream
Parva

rigens Lemon Cream
Seasd

rigens var leucolaena
Seasd

splendens mixed
Della, King #

variegata
Seasd

Geissorhiza

aspera
DaffA, Irida, JoyPl

bracteata
DaffA

inflexa
DaffA

monantha
DaffA, Irida

radians
AynDa, DaffA, Irida

splendidissima
DaffA

tulbaghensis
Irida

Gelsemium

sempervirens (Carolina Jessamine)
CouCl, Denes

sempervirens Flore Pleno
CouCl

Geniostoma

ligustrifolium
Gordn

rupestre (Hangehange)
Orati

Genista

aetnensis (Mt Etna Broom)
Denes, TopTr

ardoinii
NewlR

lydia (Balkan's Golden Broom)
BayBl, BlueM

monosperma now Retama m. (Bridal Veil Broom)
BayBl, Caves, Denes, TRidg, Vall #

pilosa Procumbens
NewlR

tinctoria (Dyers Broom)
Mills, Sweet

tinctoria Flore Pleno
Ormon

Gentiana

acaulis
Ashto, NewlR, Oasis, Otepo, Parva, Pgeon, Telfa

asclepiadea (Willow Gentian)
MaraN, NewlR, Pgeon, Telfa, Vall #

Blue Velvet
NewlR

cachemirica
NewlR

Christine Jean
BayBl, Otepo

clusii
NewlR

cruciata
Parva, Pgeon

dahurica
Parva, Pgeon

decumbens
Parva

dinarica hyb No 1
NewlR

Drakes Alba
CottP, Telfa

Drakes Strain blue
TRidg

x hexafarreri
Otepo

kurroo
Parva

linearis
WaiMa

lutea
MaraN, Parva, TRidg

x macaulayi Kingfisher
Marsh

makinoi
Parva

makinoi Royal Blue
Parva

paradoxa Blue Herald
Parva

pneumonanthe (Marsh Gentian, Calathian Violet)
NewlR, WaiMa

septemfida
MaraN, Parva, Pgeon, Vall #

sikokiana
Parva

x stevenagensis
Marsh, Otepo

straminea
Otepo

tianschanica
Parva

tibetica
Parva

triflora
BlueM

Geonoma

undata (Red Crown Shaft Palm)
Lsendt

Geranium

varieties
Roswd

albanum
MaraN

aristatum
MaraN

bohemicum Orchid Blue
MaraN, Reic #

x cantabrigiense (Cambridge Cranesbill)
Mills

x cantabrigiense Biokovo
BayBl, CottP, Otepo, Peak, Trans

x cantabrigiense Cambridge
BayBl, CottP, Peak, StMar, Trans

x cantabrigiense Saint Ola
BayBl, CottP, Trans

cinereum Ballerina
BayBl, Egmon, MaraN, Marsh, Parva, Pgeon

cinereum Lawrence Flatman
BayBl

cinereum var subcaulescns
BayBl, Pgeon

clarkei Kashmir Purple
Marsh

clarkei Kashmir White
BayBl, Hackf, Mills, Peak, Taunt, Telfa, Trans, Warwk

Criss Canning
Parva

dalmaticum
Della, NewlR, Otepo

delavayi
StMar

endressii
BayBl, CottP, MaraN, Marsh, NewlR, Otepo, Pgeon

endressii var pale pink fl
Orang

endressii Wargrave Pink (French Cranesbill)
CoFlo, MillH, Oasis, Ormon, Parva, Trans, TRidg

eriostemon
MaraN

farreri
Pgeon

Gerard Druce
Pgeon, Telfa

himalayense
BayBl, Pkrau, StMar, Trans, Warwk

himalayense Plenum
  Parva
ibericum (Meadow Cranesbill)
  BayBl, CoFlo, Parva
incanum (Silver Geranium)
  BayBl, CottP, Dream, KeriP, Nikau, Pgeon, Telfa, Trans, Vall #
incanum white
  Vall #
Ingwersen's Variety
  CottP
Johnson's Blue
  BayBl, CoFlo, Egmon, Mills, Otepo, Parva, Peak, Taunt, Telfa, Vall #
macrorrhizum
  CottP, Marsh, Oasis, Orang, Otepo, Pgeon, Pkrau, StMar, Trans
macrorrhizum Album
  BayBl, CottP, Peak, Trans
macrorrhizum Bevan's Variety
  BayBl
macrorrhizum Czakor
  Marsh
maculatum (American Cranesbill)
  Sweet
maderense
  BayBl, Dream, Seasd, Vall #
x magnificum
  Peak
Mrs Mac
  MaraN
nepaulense var thunbergii
  MaraN
nodosum
  Marsh, Taunt
orthipodium
  BayBl
x oxonianum AT Johnson
  Nikau, Telfa
x oxonianum Claridge Druce
  MaraN, Marsh, Nikau, StMar, Vall #
x oxonianum Hollywood
  BayBl
x oxonianum Pearl Boland
  BayBl, CoFlo, CottP, Marsh, Nikau, Peak, Telfa

x oxonianum Sherwood
  BayBl
x oxonianum Winscombe
  BayBl, Peak, StMar
palmatum
  MaraN
phaeum (Mourning Widow
  CottP, Della, MaraN, Orang, Peak, Pkrau, Roswd, Telfa, Trans, TRidg
phaeum Alba
  Telfa
phaeum Album
  CottP, Peak
phaeum x phaeum
  Silvlai
platypetalum
  Parva
pratense (Meadow Cranesbill)
  AynDa, CoFlo, Dream, KeriP, Looij, MaraN, Marsh, Mills, Orang, Pgeon, Pkrau, Telfa, Trans, Vall #
pratense Album
  Dream, MaraN, Telfa, Trans, Vall #
pratense f.albiflorum
  StMar
pratense Mrs Kendall Clark
  StMar, TRidg
pratense Silver Queen
  Dream
pratense Striatum
  Vall #
psilostemon
  Hackf
purpureum (Little Robin Cranesbill)
  Mills
pyrenaicum
  Dream, MaraN
pyrenaicum Album
  Dream
renardii
  Otepo, Parva, Pgeon
x riversleaianum Mavis Simpson
  BayBl, Warwk

x riversleaianum Russell Pritchard
  BayBl, CottP, Egmon, Parva, Trans
robustum
  KeriP, MaraN, Trans
Rosenlight
  BayBl
rubescens
  Dream
sanguineum (Bloody Cranesbill)
  CottP, Della, MaraN, MillI, Telfa
sanguineum Album
  CottP, MaraN, Parva, Peak, Trans, Warwk
sanguineum New Hampshire Purple
  Parva
sanguineum Striatum
  StMar
sanguineum striatum splendens
  Parva
sanguineum var lancastrense
  NewlR, Parva, Pgeon, Trans
sessiflorum
  Orati
sessiflorum novae-zelandiae nigricans
  MaraN, Orati, Otepo
sinense
  Vall #
sp climbing, pinkypurple fl
  Vall #
sp small white fl, multibranch stems
  Vall #
Splish Splash
  Reic #
striatum
  Vall #
subcaulescens
  NewlR, Parva
subcaulescens Splendens
  CottP
sylvaticum (Wood Cranesbill)
  MaraN, MillH
sylvaticum Album
  MaraN, Otepo, StMar

traversii (Chatham Is Geranium)

BayBl, Hackf, JoyPl, KeriP, Orati, Otepo, Pkrau, Terra

traversii elegans

Pgeon

tuberosum

Seasd

versicolor

StMar

wallichianum Buxton's Blue

MaraN, MillH, Parva, Pgeon, Trans

Gerbera

mixed mini pot

Kayd

Geum

Borisii

BayBl, CottP, Oasis, Pgeon, Telfa

bulgaricum

NewlR

chiloense was G. coccineum

BlueM, Marsh

Lady Stratheden

BlueM, Kayd, MaraN, Nikau, Oasis, Pgeon, Reic #, Telfa, Trans

Lemon Drops

CottP, Nikau, Peak, Warwk

Lionel Cox

CottP, Peak, Warwk

macrophyllum (Yellow Avens)

MillH

montanum

Marsh, Pgeon

Mrs J Bradshaw

AynDa, BayBl, BlueM, CottP, Dream, Kayd, MaraN, MillH, Mills, Nikau, Oasis, Peak, Reic #, Sweet, Trans, Warwk

rivale (Water Avens)

CottP, Della, MillH, Mills, Pgeon, Trans, WilAq

rivale Leonards variety

BayBl, Nikau, Oasis

sibericum

BayBl, CottP, NewlR, Pgeon

sibericum Pink

Telfa

sp fully dbl orange fl

NewlR

sp single golden yellow

Nikau

urbanum (Herb Bennet, Avens)

Della, Mills, Orang, Sweet

Gigantachloa

apus

Isaac

Gilia

capitata (Queen Anne's Thimbles)

King #

leptantha (Gabriels Trumpet)

King #

tricolour Birds Eye

King #

Gingidia

montana (Maori Anise, Koheriki, Native Angelica)

Mills, Orati

Gingko

biloba (Maidenhair Tree)

Apple, Burbk, Caves, Cedar, Chedd, Coatv, CPete, Denes, Diack, EasyB, Mtato, NZtr #, Ormon, Peele, Pionr, PuhaN, Pukho, Reic #, TopTr, WakaC

biloba Autumn Gold

Cedar, Coatv, Denes, Mtato, Pionr, Pukho, TopTr

biloba Fairmont (m)

Denes, Pukho

biloba Fastigiata

Cedar

biloba grafted (m or f)

Chedd

biloba Jade Butterflies

Denes

biloba Redfearns Variegata

Pukho

biloba Saratoga

Cedar, Denes, Pukho

Gladiolus

mixed

Altrf, Kayd

alatus

DaffA, Nikau

Amanda Mahy

BayBl

Anglia   mini

Kayd

angustus

Kerer

Applause

Kayd

aureus

DaffA

byzantinus

Kerer

callianthus was Acidanthera bicolour

Ref

cardinalis

DaffA

carinatus   mixed col

AynDa, DaffA

carmineus

DaffA, JoyPl

carmineus x cardinals

JoyPl

carneus

DaffA, Kerer

Charming Beauty

Altrf

colvillea albus

Kerer

colvillei (syn. nanus)

TRidg

colvillei Blossom

MaraN

Desire

Peak

Eurovision

Kayd

Fidelio

Kayd

Friendship

Kayd

Halley

Altrf

Hunting Song

Kayd

Impressive

Kerer

maculatus

DaffA

Mirella
Altrf

nanus mixed (Painted Ladies)
Kayd

Nova Lux
Kayd

ochroleuca
Parva

Oscar
Kayd

palustris
WaiMa

papilio
Ormon, Otepo

papilio Wine form
Parva

Peter Pears
Kayd

Piccolo   mini
Kayd

priorii was Homoglossum p
DaffA

psittacinus (Winter-flowering Gladioli)
Ashto, Kayd

purpureoauratus
DaffA, Nikau, Telfa

Red Bantam
KeriP

Robinetta
BayBl, CottP

scullyi
DaffA

Snow Castle   mini
Kayd

sp was Homoglossum watsonium
DaffA

sp creamy lemon fl, small form
Vall #

Spic and Span
Kayd

tenellus
MaraN

The Bride
Altrf, BayBl, JoyPl, Kerer, Nikau, Peak

tristis
BayBl, DaffA, Herew, JoyPl, Kerer, NewlR, Taunt, Trans, TRidg

tristis var concolor
DaffA

undulatus
Kerer

usyiae
DaffA

White Friendship
Kayd

Glaucium

corniculatum (Red Horned Poppy)
MillH

flavum (Yellow Horned Poppy)
AynDa, MaraN

Glausina

lansium (Wampi)
Manna

Glechoma

hederacea (Ground Ivy)
CottP, MillH, Mills, Orang, Pgeon, Sweet, Telfa

hederacea variegata (Variegated Ground Ivy)
CottP, Mills, Seasd

Gleditsia

japonica
Pukho

sinensis
Dove, TopTr

triacanthos (Honey Locust)
Chedd, Mtato, NZtr #, Pionr, Reic #

triacanthos Emerald Cascade
Burbk, Chedd, Coatv, EasyB, Mtato, Pukho

triacanthos f. inermis (Thornless Honey Locust)
Apple, Diack, Dove, Hewsn, McKe, Mtato, NZtr #, Peele, Pionr, PuhaN, Pukho, Reic #

triacanthos f. inermis Limelight
Pukho

triacanthos female
Chedd

triacanthos male
Chedd

triacanthos Ruby Lace
Burbk, Chedd, Coatv, Denes, Mtato, Peele, Pukho, TopTr

triacanthos Skyline
Denes, Peele, Pukho

triacanthos Sunburst
Burbk, Chedd, Coatv, Denes, Hewsn, Mtato, Peele, Pionr, Pukho, TopTr

Globba

marantiana
AynDa

Globularia

bellidifolia now meridionalis
NewlR, Otepo

cordifolia
MaraN, NewlR, Pgeon

meridionalis was bellidifolia
Telfa

nudicaulis
MaraN

Glochidion

ferdinandi
Frans

Gloriosa

superba
Parva

superba red form
MJury

superba Rothschildiana
BayBl, Kayd, Parva

Yukie
Kayd

Glycyrrhiza

glabra (Liquorice)
MTig #, Sweet

Glyptostrobus

pencilis was lineatus (Canton Water Pine, Chinese Swamp Cypress)
Caves, Cedar, MJury, Woodl

Gnaphalium

keriense now Anaphalis k.
Gordn

Godetia

**amoena (Wild Godetia,
Farewell to Spring)**
    King #
amoena Sybil Sherwood
    King #
bottae Lilac Blossom
    King #
tenella Blue Magic
    King #

Gomesia

crispa
    AnnM

Gomphrena

10 varieties
    King #

Goniolimon

**dumosum Woodcreek now
G.t.angustifolium
Woodcreek**
    Della, King #
**tartaricum (Tartarian
Statice)**
    Oasis, Pgeon
tartaricum Blue Smoke
    Della
tartaricum White Smoke
    CottP, Della, King #

Gordonia

**axillaris (Fried Egg Tree,
Crepe Camellia)**
    Burbk, Coatv, Denes,
    SpecT
**sp maybe yunnanensis
GWC 280**
    Woodl
yunnanensis
    Caves

Gratiola

officinalis
    MaraN, MillH, Telfa

Grevillea

Apricot Glow
    MatNu
Audrey
    BlueM
b. Bushfire
    MatNu
banksia alba
    Reic #
banksia forsteri
    Reic #

Bonnie Prince Charlie
    Denes, MatNu, Matth
brachystylis Bush Fire
    Matth
Bronze Rambler
    Butlr, MatNu, Matth
Canterbury Gold
    BlueM
Claret
    Denes
Clearview David
    BlueM, MatNu, Mtato
Cream & Green
    BlueM, Denes, MatNu,
    Mtato
decora
    Reic #
dryandri
    Reic #
fasciculata
    MatNu, Matth
Gaudichaudii
    Denes, MatNu, Matth
glabrata (Smooth Grevillea
    Coatv, Denes, MatNu,
    Matth
lanigera (Woolly Grevillea)
    BlueM
lanigera Mt Tamboritha
    BlueM, MatNu, Matth,
    Wells
leucopteris
    Reic #
Lutea
    Denes
Olympic Flame
    MatNu
Pink Pixie
    MatNu, Matwh, Wells
Pink Star
    Matth
polybotrya
    Reic #
Poorinda Elegance
    Denes, MatNu, Matth
Poorinda Peter
    MatNu
Poorinda Rondeau
    MatNu
prostrata Aurea
    MatNu, Matth
pteridifolia
    Reic #

Red Cloud
    BlueM, Denes, MatNu,
    Matth
Red Cluster
    MatNu
Red Dragon
    MatNu
Rhondeau
    BlueM
Robin Gordon
    Chedd, Kayd
**Robin Hood (Scarlet
Toothbrush Grevillea)**
    MatNu, Matth, Wells
robusta (Silky Oak)
    Burbk, Coatv, Denes,
    MatNu, Matth, Matwh,
    NZtr #, Pionr, Reic #
rosmarinifolia Jenkinsii
    ZinoN
Scarlet Sprite
    BlueM, Butlr, MatNu
Summerleas
    BlueM
Superb
    Matth
Tickled Pink
    MatNu
Tranquility
    Kayd, Wells
Victor Harbour
    MatNu, Wells
Victoria
    BlueM, ZinoN
White Wings
    Butlr, Denes, Kayd
wickhamii
    Reic #
Wimpara Gem
    Seasd

Grewia

**occidentalis Mauve Star
(Lavender Star Flower)**
    Butlr

Greyia

**radlkoferi
(Transvaal/Natal
Bottlebrush)**
    Ether, TopTr

Grindelia

**robusta (Grindelia,
Gumplant)**
    Della, Orang

Griselina

littoralis (Broad leaf, Kapuka, Papauma)
Apple, BlueM, Burbk, Butlr, Chedd, Coatv, Diack, EasyB, Ford, Gordn, Hewsn, Matai, Matwh, Morgn, Mtato, NZtr #, Orati, Ormon, Pionr, Pkrau, SouWo, Terra, Wahpa, Wensl

littoralis Broadway Mint
SelGr

littoralis Dixon's Cream (v)
BlueM

littoralis Green Jewel (v)
Orati

littoralis Variegata (Variegated Broad leaf)
Butlr, Chedd, Diack, Gordn, Hewsn, Matai, Mtato, Pionr, Wahpa

lucida (Puka, Akapuka Broadleaf)
Burbk, Chedd, Coatv, Mtato, Orati, Terra

Grossularia

uva-crispa Invicta now Ribes u-c.I.
Chedd

Gunnera

varieties
Titok

arenaria (Sand Gunnera)
Orati, WaiMa

arenaria x monoica
WaiMa

cordata
Titok

dentata
Orati, WaiMa

flavida
Orati, WaiMa

hamiltonii
CottP, Hackf, MaraN, Orati, WaiMa

manicata
Denes, Diack, Frans, Kayd, MaraN

monoica
Orati

prorepens
MaraN, MillH, Oasis, Orati, Parva, Vall #, WaiMa

tinctoria was chilensis (Chilean Giant Rhubarb)
BlueM, JoyPl, Pkrau, WaiMa

Gymnocladus

dioica (Kentucky Coffee Tree)
Apple, Denes, Diack, Dove, Pukho, TopTr, YakuN

Gynandriris

setifolia
AynDa, DaffA

sisyrinchium
NewlR

Gynura

aurantiaca (Velvet Plant)
LakeN

Gypsophila

Bridal Veil
Coult

cerastioides
Ashto, BayBl, Della, NewlR, Pgeon

elegans
Della, King #

elegans Deep Rose
King #

pacifica
Ashto, MillH

pacifica Pacifica Pink
AynDa, CoFlo, Della, King #, Reic #

paniculata (Baby's Breath)
Ashto, King #, Reic #

paniculata Bristol Fairy
BlueM, Coult, Egmon, Pgeon

paniculata double white
AynDa, CoFlo, Della, King #, MillH

paniculata Festival Pink
Parva

paniculata Festival White
Parva

paniculata Flamingo
BlueM

paniculata Perfecta
Ashto, BlueM, Coult, Kayd, Peak, Pgeon

paniculata Pink Star
Ashto, BayBl, BlueM, Egmon, Pgeon

paniculata Snowflake
Reic #

perfoliata
Dream

repens alba (Rock Gypsophila)
BayBl, Della, Kayd, Pgeon, Reic #

repens Letchworth Rose
KeriP, NewlR

repens Monstrosa
CottP

repens Pink Beauty
BayBl, Parva, Peak

repens Rosea
BayBl, BlueM, CottP, Della, Loolj, MaraN, Pgeon, Reic #

repens Rosy Veil
BayBl, NewlR

Haberlea

fernandi-coburgi
Parva

rhodopensis
Parva

Habranthus

robustus
MaraN, Parva, TRidg

texanus
NewlR

tubispathis was andersonii
AynDa, CottP, DaffA

Hacquetia

epipactis
Marsh, NewlR

Haemanthus

albiflos
DaffA

coccineus (Blood Lily, Elephants Ears)
DaffA, JoyPl, Parva

katherinae now Scadoxus multiflorus katherinae
MJury

Hagenia

abyssinica
Caves, Ether

Hakea

laurina (Pincushion Hakea, Sea Urchin)

Denes, MatNu, Matth, Reic #

salicifolia Gold Medal (Willow-lvd Hakea)

Denes, MatNu, Matth

Hakonechloa

macra

TRidg

macra Alboaurea was macra variegata

BayBl, Denes, Diack, Kayd, NewlR, Nikau, Peak, Telfa

macra Aureola

Hains, TRidg

Halesia

carolina now tetraptera (Silverbell/Snowdrop Tree)

Apple, Caves, Chedd, Denes, Peele, TopTr, YakuN

monticola (Mountain Silverbell)

Caves, Dove, Peele, TopTr, YakuN

Halimiocistus

sahucii

Parva

Halimium

atriplicifolium

TopTr

lasianthum was Cistus formosus

Butlr

Halleria

lucida (Tree Fuchsia)

TopTr

Hallogurus

erecta Wellington Bronze (Toatoa)

Dream

Halocarpus

bidwillii was Dacrydium b. (Bog Pine)

Cedar, Gordn, Orati

biformis was Dacrydium biforme (Yellow Pine)

Cedar, Mtato, Orati

kirkii was Dacrydium k.

Cedar

Haloragis

bronze type

Dowde

depressa

BayBl

erecta

Burbk, Orati

Hamamelis

x intermedia

Apple, Diack, Hackf

x intermedia Arnold Promise

Chedd, Denes, Pukho

x intermedia Diane

Pukho

x intermedia Jelena

Denes, Pukho

x intermedia Pallida

Pukho

x intermedia Primavera

Denes

japonica (Japanese Witchazel)

Reic #

mollis (Chinese Witchhazel

Apple, Chedd, Peele, PuhaN, Pukho, Reic #

mollis Goldcrest

Pukho

virginiana (American Witchhazel)

Apple, Dove, PuhaN, Reic #

Haploppapus

coronopifolius now glutinosus

BayBl, Telfa

Hardenbergia

comptoniana (WA Coral Pea)

CouCl, Reic #

monophylla Alba

Denes

monophylla Rosea (Pink Coral Pea)

Denes

violacea

AynDa, Burbk, Denes, Reic #, Vall #

violacea Alba

CouCl, Mtato

violacea Happy Wanderer

CouCl, Denes, Mtato

violacea Rosea

CouCl

Harpephyllum

caffrum (Kaffir Plum)

Chedd, Ether, Frans, Reic #

Harpullia

pendula

Reic #

Hebe

albicans

BlueM, Diack, Dove, Dowde, Hackf, KeriP, Matai, Orati, Otepo, Pionr, Pkrau, TopTr, Trans, Wahpa

alpina

Hewsn

Amy

Marsh, Orati

x andersonii

Pkrau

annulata

BlueM, Pkrau

anomala

Mason, Mtato, Pkrau, Wahpa

armstrongii

Gordn, Matai

Autumn Glory

BlueM, Pkrau

Azurea

Orati

barkeri

Matai

Barnettii

Hackf

x bishopiana

Gordn, Kayd, Matwh, Orati, Wells

Blue Gem

Matwh, Mtato, Orati

Bold Knob Ridge

Wells

bollonsoi

Orati

Boulder Lake

Diack, Mtato

brachysiphon

Orati

buchananii

BlueM, Otepo, Pkrau

124

buchananii Minor
  BlueM, Matai
buchananii Sir George Fenwick
  NewlR
buxifolia
  Pkrau
buxifolia Aurea
  Hewsn
Carnea
  Dowde, Orati
Champagne
  Gordn, Matwh, Mtato
chathamica
  Orati
Christensenii
  BlueM, Hewsn, Matai, Pkrau
colensoi Glauca now Leonard Cockayne
  BlueM
cupressoides
  Hewsn, Matai, Morgn, Orati, Otepo, Pkrau
cupressoides Nana
  BlueM, Pkrau, Seasd
decumbens
  BlueM, Mason, Matai, Orati, Otepo, Pkrau
dieffenbachii
  MillH, Orati
diosmifolia
  Butlr, Gordn, Hackf, Mason, Orati, Pionr, Wahpa
diosmifolia mauve
  Burbk, Dove, Nikau
diosmifolia Wairua Beauty
  Matwh, Mtato
divaricata
  Terra
Dobbies Delight
  Orati
elliptica (Kokomuka)
  Diack, Ford, Gordn, Matai, Mtato, NZtr #, Orati, Terra
elliptica prostrata
  Orati, Terra
Emerald Green
  BlueM, Mason, Matai, MillH, Mtato, Pkrau, SelGr, Wahpa
Eveline was Pink Payne
  Orati, Wahpa

evenosa
  Gordn, Matai, Otepo, Pkrau, Terra, Wahpa
x franciscana
  BlueM
x franciscana Blue Gem
  Gordn
x franciscana Variegata
  BlueM
gautheriana Blue Brill (Veronica Brill Blue)
  CottP
glaucophylla
  Orati
Golden Esk
  Gordn, Matai
Great Orme
  Pkrau
Hartii
  Mason, Orati, Pkrau
Headfortii
  Orati
hectorii
  BlueM, Marsh, Matai, Pkrau
hortensis Spring Monarch
  Parva
hulkeana now Heliohebe h.
  Matai, Matwh, NZtr #, Orati, Ormon, Otepo, Seasd, Sweet, Terra
Icing Sugar
  CottP, Diack, Dove, Kayd, KeriP, Matai, Matwh, Mtato, Pionr, Trans, Wahpa
Inspiration
  Gordn, Hewsn, KeriP, Matwh, Morgn, Mtato, Orati, Pionr, Terra, Wahpa
Invermay (ex Graham Patterson)
  Hackf
James Stirling
  BlueM, Butlr, Mason, Matai, Orati, Pkrau, Terra, Wahpa
Karo Golden Esk
  Mason
La Seduisante
  Orati, TopTr, Wells
laingii
  Mtato, Orati

Lavender Lace
  Dove, Gordn, Mason, Matai, Morgn, Nikau, Orati, Wahpa
Lavender Lass
  Butlr, CottP
Lavender Spray
  Orati
lewisii
  Orati
macrantha
  BlueM, Matai, Pkrau, Wahpa
macrocarpa
  Orati, Otepo
macrocarpa var brevifolia
  Orati
macrocarpa var latisepala
  Orati, Woodl
Mary Antoinette
  Butlr, Gordn, Mason, Pionr, Wahpa
McEwanii now Macewanii
  Dowde, Gordn, Hewsn, Matai, Orati, Pkrau
Mrs Winder
  Gordn
Northern Star
  Gordn
obtusata
  Matai, Mtato, Orati
odora
  BlueM, Gordn, Mtato, Orati, Pionr, Pkrau, SelGr, Terra, Wahpa
odora Anomala
  BlueM, Matai, Terra
odora pink
  Dowde
odora Prostrata
  BlueM, Gordn, Orati, Pkrau, Terra
odora White
  Butlr
Oratia Beauty
  Butlr, Diack, Gordn, KeriP, Mason, Matwh, Mtato, Orati, Pionr, Pkrau, Trans, Wahpa
Oratia Gala
  Orati
Otari Delight
  Butlr, Dove, Mtato, Nikau, Wahpa

Pagei

Mason, Orati, Pkrau

parviflora (Koromiko-taranga)

Ford, Frans, Gordn, Matai, Mtato, Orati, Terra

pauciramosa

Matai, Pkrau

pimeleoides

Dove, Hackf, Mason, Terra, Wahpa

pimeleoides Glaucocaerulea

BlueM

pinguifolia

BlueM, Ford, Matai, Pkrau

pinguifolia Sutherlandii

Mtato

Pink Goddess

Nikau

Pink Payne   now Eveline

Diack, Matai

Pride

Gordn

Quicksilver

Matai, Matwh, Orati, Taunt, Wahpa

raoulii

Matai, Orati

recurva

Dove, Gordn, Mtato, Pkrau, Terra

salicifolia (Koromiko)

Ford, Matai, NZtr #, Pkrau, SouWo, Sweet

Snowcap

Wells

sp trailing, blue/gr lvs, grey/blue fls

Otepo

speciosa (Napuka, Titirangi)

Butlr, Diack, Ford, Gordn, KeriP, Mason, Matai, Matwh, Mtato, NZtr #, Orati, Terra, Wahpa

speciosa blue form

Nikau, Wells

speciosa Dobbies Delight

Orati, Wells

speciosa hybrid purple fl/lf backs

Trans

speciosa magenta

Dove, Nikau

speciosa Pink

Orati

stricta (Koromiko)

Ford, Gordn, Morgn, Mtato, Orati, Terra, Wahpa

stricta Wairoa

Wells

subalpina

Diack, Dove, Hackf, Mtato

sutherlandii Gold

Dove, Wahpa

tetragona

Matai

topiaria

BlueM, Butlr, CottP, Hackf, Hewsn, Mason, Matai, Matwh, Orati, Otepo, Pkrau, SelGr

townsonii

Gordn, Matwh, Mtato, Orati, Terra, Wahpa

traversii

Mtato

venustula

Orati, Terra

vernicosa

Mtato, Pkrau, Wahpa

Waikiki

Orati

Wairau Beauty

Wells

Waireka

Dove, Matwh, Orati, Wahpa

Winter Gold

BlueM

Wiri varieties

Kayd, Morgn

Wiri Blush

Diack

Wiri Charm

BlueM, Burbk, Diack, Dove, Mason, Mtato, Nikau, Orati, Wahpa, Wells

Wiri Cloud

BlueM, Burbk, Butlr, Chedd, Diack, Dowde, Gordn, KeriP, Mason, Matwh, Mtato, Orati, Pkrau, SelGr, Wahpa, Wells

Wiri Dawn

Diack, Dove, Gordn, Mason, Orati, Trans, Wells

Wiri Gem

Butlr, Dove, Gordn, Mason, Matwh, Orati, Wahpa

Wiri Grace

Butlr, Chedd, Orati

Wiri Image

BlueM, Butlr, Chedd, Diack, Gordn, KeriP, Mason, Mtato, Orati, Wahpa

Wiri Joan

Wahpa

Wiri Joy

Diack, Gordn, Mason, Matwh, Mtato, Wahpa, Wells

Wiri Mist

Burbk, Diack, Gordn, Matwh, Mtato, Orati, TopTr, Trans, Wahpa, Wells

Wiri Prince

CottP, Diack, Dove, Gordn, Wahpa

Wiri Spears

Diack, Gordn

Wiri Splash

Burbk, Diack, Dove, Gordn, KeriP, Mason, Matwh, Nikau, Orati, Wahpa, Wells

Wiri Vision

BlueM, Gordn, Matwh, Wells

Hedera

varieties

BlueM

canariensis (Canary Is Ivy)

BlueM, Looij, Mtato

canariensis Variegata

Mtato

colchica Dentata

BlueM

helix Glacier (v)

Mtato

helix Golden Mantle

Parva

helix Kalibri (v)

Parva

helix Pin Oak (Pin Oak Ivy

Looij, YakuN

helix Trident
Parva

Hedycarya

arborea (Pigeonwood, Porokaiwhiri)
Gordn, Mtato, NZtr #, Orati, Pionr, Reic #, Terra

Hedychium

Candycane
Frans

coronarium (White Ginger)
Frans

greenei (Red Ginger)
Frans, Lsendt

spicatum
MaraN

Hedyotis

caerulea
Telfa

Hedysarum

coronarium (French Honeysuckle)
AynDa

Heimia

salicifolia
AynDa

Helenium

autamnale Walstrand
CottP, Marsh

Butterpat
CottP, MillH, Telfa, Warwk

Coppelia
Telfa

Moerheim Beauty
BayBl

Helianthemum

hybrids mixed
Dream, Seasd

varieties
Roswd

alpestre
NewlR

Annabel
CottP, KeriP, Marsh, Sweet

appenninum
BayBl

Ben Alder
CottP, Pgeon, Sweet

Ben Hope
Pgeon

Cerise Queen
BayBl, KeriP

Chelsea Gem
CottP, KeriP, Pgeon, Warwk

Chocolate Blotch
KeriP, MillH

Copper Pin
KeriP

Crushed Strawberry
KeriP

dble yellow
Nikau

Helianthemum Orange
CottP, Della

Highdown
CottP, Peak, Warwk

Mrs Earle was Fireball
CottP, NewlR

nummularium obscurum was ovatum
Pgeon

Parnell's Apricot
KeriP

Prima Donna
KeriP, NewlR

Rose of Leewood
CottP, KeriP, MillH

Snow Queen
CottP, KeriP, MillH, Warwk

Sulphur Queen
Pgeon

Sunset
Burbk

Wisley Lemon
KeriP

Wisley Pink
CottP, KeriP, Looij, Nikau, Peak, Pgeon

Wisley Primrose
Peak, Pgeon, Trans, Warwk

Wisley White
CottP, KeriP, Marsh, Peak

Helianthus

annuus Autumn Beauty
King #

annuus dwf
Trolh

annuus Evening Sun
King #, Koan #

annuus Floristan
King #

annuus Giant Sungold
King #

annuus Giganteus
King #, Orang

annuus Hallo
King #

annuus Henry Wilde
King #

annuus Holiday
King #

annuus Music Box
King #

annuus Orange Sun
King #

annuus Pacino
King #

annuus Russian Giant
Koan #, Trolh

annuus Sonja
King #

annuus Sunbeam
King #

annuus Sunspot
King #

annuus tall red
Trolh

annuus Teddy Bear
King #

annuus Valentine
King #

annuus Velvet Queen
King #

Autumn Glory
Sweet

debilis syn cucumerfolius
King #

debilis Ice Cream
King #

debilis Italian White (heirloom)
King #

debilis Piccolo
King #

First Light
Parva

Loddon Gold
BayBl, MillH, Telfa

Low Down
Parva

Table Mountain

Parva

tuberosus (Jerusalem Artichoke)

Koan #, Mills, MTig

Helichrysum

angustifolium now I.italicum

BayBl, BlueM, Della, Looij, MillH, Mills, Orang, Seasd, Sweet, Trolh

argyrophyllum (Golden Guinea Everlasting)

KeriP, Looij, Nikau, Seasd, Sweet, Trans

baxterii

BayBl, KeriP

bellidioides

Orati

bracteatum now Bracteantha (Strawflower, Golden Everlasting)

King #

dimorphis

Matai

Elmswood

Seasd

glomeratum now aggregatum

Orati

Graham Patterson

BayBl, BlueM, Oasis

italicum serotinum (Curry Plant)

Ormon

petiolare

Dowde, KeriP, MillH, Nikau, Oasis, Peak, Seasd

petiolare Limelight

Dowde, KeriP, Nikau, Peak

petiolare Roundabout (v)

BayBl, CottP, KeriP, Trans

retortum

MatNu

Silver Cushion

Parva, Seasd

stoechas White Barn

Marsh

Heliconia

psittacorum (Golden Torch Flwg Ginger)

LakeN

Helictotrichon

sempervirens (Blue Oat Grass)

BlueM, Denes, Diack, KeriP, MaraN, Pkrau, Seasd, TopTr

sempervirens glauca (Blue Oat Grass)

Hains

Heliohebe

hulkeana was Hebe h. (NZ Lilac Hebe, Marlborough Lilac)

Ref

Heliophila

species

Vall #

longifolia Blue Bird

King #

Heliopsis

Flora Plena

Kayd

scabra Golden Plume

CottP

scabra Summer Sun (Sunflower (perennial))

Ashto, King #, Mills

Heliotropium

arborescens (Cherry Pie)

Trans

aureum

Trans

Helleborus

argutifolius was corsicus

AynDa, BayBl, JoyPl, Marsh, Otepo, Parva, Pgeon, Trans, Vall #

corsicus now argutifolius

Ashto, Denes, Egmon, Pkrau, Telfa, TRidg

cyclophyilus / odorus mixed

TRidg

foetidus (Christmas Rose)

Ashto, BayBl, CoFlo, KeriP, Nikau, Ormon, Otepo, Parva, Pkrau, TRidg

foetidus Green Ice

Parva

foetidus Italian form

JoyPl

foetidus Wester Flisk

BayBl, JoyPl, MillH

fragrant sp

Parva

lividus

TRidg

lividus corsicus now argutifolius

Trans

lutea

Sweet

niger (Christmas Rose)

Reic #

niger Maximus

TRidg

niger White Magic

Ashto, BayBl, Denes, Nikau, Parva

odorus (Fragrant Hellebore)

Denes

orientalis (Lenten Rose)

Ashto, CoFlo, Egmon, MaraN, Mills, Otepo, Pgeon, Pkrau

orientalis BrightRose Pink (Apex Strain)

Parva

orientalis Dusky Rose

BayBl

orientalis Dusky Wine (Apex Strain)

Parva

orientalis guttatus

BayBl

orientalis Hatch's Strain (Joy Hybrids)

BayBl, JoyPl, Parva

orientalis hybrids

AynDa, Denes, Nikau, Titok, TRidg, Vall #

orientalis Maroon

Peak

orientalis Pale Pink (Apex Strain)

Parva

orientalis Pukehou hybrids

Nikau

orientalis Pure White (Apex Strain)

Parva

orientalis rose form

Ormon

orientalis Rose Pink (Apex Strain)
Parva
orientalis sdlg black red
Nikau
orientalis sdlg deep purple
Hackf
orientalis sdlg dk plum
TRidg
orientalis sdlg tall white
TRidg
orientalis sdlg white
Hackf, JoyPl, TRidg
orientalis Starburst
BayBl
orientalis Sunrise
BayBl
orientalis Winter Moon
BayBl
purpurascens
Vall #
Santa Cruz
Ormon
x sternii
Hackf, MJury

Helxine

soleirolii see Soleirolia
soleirolii (Babies Tears)
Ref

Hemerocallis

varieties
WaiMa
Absolute Zero
Herit
Adah (mini)
Herit
Aggie Sellars
Parva, SumG
Aisha
Herit
Alcazar
BayBl, Kopua, Puket
Alec Cullen
Herit
Allegretto
Puket
Amadeus
BayBl, Herit
Amazing Grace
Ormon, Parva, Puket
Amber Glow
Puket, SumG

Amy Stewart
SumG
Angel Tears (mini)
SumG
Angie Loveland
Herit
Ann Blocher
SumG
Anna Antartica
Herit
Annie Golightly
SumG
Antique Lace
Herit
Aphrodite
BayBl
Apollodorus
Herit, SumG
Apparition
Kopua
Apple Annie
Puket, SumG
Apple Tart
Herit, SumG
Apricot Delight
BayBl, Parva, Puket
Apricot Wax
Herit
Archduke
Puket
Arpeggio
Herit
Artist
Herit
Artist Etching
HostG
Asian Pheasant
Puket, SumG
Astolat
SumG
Atlanta Heart's Desire
Herit
Azrael
Herit, Puket
Aztec Beauty
BayBl, Puket
Aztec Chalice
SumG
Baby Betsy (mini)
SumG
Baby Darling (mini)
BayBl, Puket, SumG

Babylon Sister (mini)
Herit
Baghdad
Puket
Baja
SumG
Balaringar Bunny (mini)
Herit
Balaringar Cha Cha
Herit
Balaringar Creation
Herit
Balaringar Grace
Herit
Balaringar Lordship (mini)
Herit
Balaringar Promise
Herit
Balaringar Scallywag (mini)
Herit
Ballet Belle
Puket
Balls Of Red
Herit
Bambino (mini)
Puket
Barbara Mitchell
Herit
Barbary Corsair
Parva
Bashful Belle (mini)
Herit
Beauty Of Esther
Herit
Beauty to Behold
Herit, Taunt
Becky Lynn
Kopua, Puket
Bed Of Roses
Ormon
Bells Appealing
Herit, Puket
Beloved Ballerina
Herit
Ben Arthur Davies
SumG
Benchmark
SumG
Bertie Ferris (mini)
BayBl, Herit, Parva, Puket

129

Best Of Friends
Kopua, SumG

Bette Davis Eyes
BayBl, Herit, Puket

Betty Woods
Herit

Beyond Today
Herit

Big Bird
Puket

Big Rex
Herit

Binnorie
Kopua

Bishops Crest
BayBl, Kopua

Bitsy (mini)
Herit

Black Is Beautiful
Puket

Black Plush
SumG

Blake Allen
Herit

Blazing Flame
Herit

Blessed Assurance
Kopua, Puket

Blond Is Beautiful
Herit, SumG

Blue Happiness
Kopua

Blushing Maiden (mini)
Herit

Blushing Parfait
Herit

Blythe Belle (mini)
BayBl, Egmon, Herit,
Puket

Bookmark
Herit

Botticelli
BayBl, Parva

Bouquet of Ruffles
BayBl, Herit, Puket

Bowl Of Roses
HostG

Brand New Lover
Herit

Brandenburg
Herit

Brave
Herit

Breakfast At Tiffanys
Herit

Brilliant Forecast
Herit

Brocade
Puket

Brocaded Gown
BayBl, Herit

Bronze Adonis
Herit

Bugs Ear (mini)
Herit

Bulls Eye Baby (mini)
Herit

Burlesque
Kopua, Puket, SumG

Burning Desire
Kopua, SumG

Burnt Almond
BayBl, Puket

Buttered Popcorn
Taunt

Butterfly Ballet (mini)
Herit, SumG

Butterfly Charm (mini)
Herit

Butterpat (mini)
BayBl

Butterscotch Ruffles (mini)
Herit

Button Box (mini)
Herit

By Myself
Puket, SumG

Byzantine Emperor
SumG

Cabbage Flower
Herit, Kopua, Puket

Cade Stewart
SumG

Café Society
Herit

Cajun Gambler
Herit

California Sunshine
SumG

Caliph's Robes
SumG

Call Girl
Herit

Camden Charm (mini)
Herit

Camden Gold Dollar (mini)
Herit

Cantique
Herit

Canton Harbour
Herit

Cape Cod
BayBl

Caprician Fiesta
Taunt

Caramel Lace
Herit

Carlotta
Herit

Carmen Marie
SumG

Caroli-colossal
SumG

Carrara Marble
Herit

Cat's Cradle
SumG

Catherine Woodberry
SumG

Cavatina
SumG

Cavern
Herit

Caviar
Herit

Cedar Waxwing
HostG

Cee Tee
SumG

Cellini Gold
Herit

Celtic Sunrise
BayBl, SumG

Cenla Crepe Myrtle
SumG

Chardonnay
Herit

Charles Johnston
Herit, SumG

Charlie Brown (mini)
Herit

Charlotte Rhame
Puket

Charlyene Owen
Herit

Chartwell
BayBl, Herit, Kopua,
Puket, SumG

Chateau Blanc
BayBl, SumG

Chemistry
BayBl, Parva

Cherry Chapeau
Herit

Cherry Festival
SumG

Cherry Kiss
Herit

Cherry Smoke
Kopua, Puket, SumG

Cheryl Guidry (mini)
Herit

Chestnut Lane
BayBl, Puket

Chicago
Herit

Chicago Antique Tapestry
HostG

Chicago Apache
BayBl

Chicago Arnies Choice
HostG

Chicago Cattleya
HostG

Chicago Firecracker
SumG

Chicago Knobby
Puket

Chicago Peach
SumG

Chicago Petticoats
BayBl

Chicago Picotee Pride
BayBl

Chicago Picotee Promise
Herit

Chicago Picotee Queen
SumG

Chicago Rosy
SumG

Chicago Royal Heritage
BayBl

Chicago Ruby
SumG

Chicago Star
SumG

Children's Festival (mini)
SumG

Childscraft (mini)
SumG

China Crystal
Herit

China Lake
Herit

Chinese Autumn
BayBl, Kopua, Puket

Chinese New Year
Herit

Chinese Pavilion
Kopua, Parva, Puket,
Taunt

Chinese Watercolour
Kopua, SumG

Chorus Line
Taunt

Chosen One
BayBl, Parva, Puket

Christmas Is
Herit, Puket

Chum (mini)
SumG

Cinders
SumG

Cinnamon Sweets
Herit

Circles (mini)
Kopua, Puket

Clarence Simon
Puket

Classic Caper
SumG

Claudine
Herit

Cleda Jones
Herit

Clemenceaux
Herit

Colour Me Mellow
Herit

Comanche Eyes
Herit

Condilla
Herit, SumG

Conrad Pate
SumG

Cool Jazz
Herit

Coppelia
BayBl

Coral Dawn
Herit

Coral Moon
Herit

Corky (mini)
BayBl

Cosmic Caper
Herit

Country Melody
HostG

Court Magician
Herit

Courtly Love
Herit

Crimson Icon (mini)
Herit, Puket, SumG

Crimson Shadow
HostG

Crystal Cupid (mini)
Herit, SumG

Cuivre River
Herit

Cupid's Cup (mini)
Herit

Cupid's Dart (mini)
Kopua, Puket, SumG

Cupid's Gold (mini)
Herit

Curls (mini)
BayBl, Puket

Czar's Treasure
Puket, SumG

Dacquiri
SumG

Daily Bread (mini)
BayBl, Herit

Daily Dollar (mini)
Herit

Dainty Dreamer (mini)
Herit

Dallas Star
Taunt

Dance Ballerina Dance
Herit

Dancing Beauty
BayBl, Puket

Dancing Shiva
Herit, Kopua, Puket

Dark Elf (mini)
Herit

Darrell
Herit

Decatur Dictator
SumG

Dee Dee Mac
Herit
Delicate Treasure
Herit
Delicately Yours
SumG
Delicato (mini)
Herit
Delia Mae
Herit
Demerie Doll (mini)
Herit
Devonshire
Herit
Dinah Rose
Herit
Dinkum Aussie
BayBl, Puket, SumG
Disneyland
SumG
Dodge City
SumG
Dominic
Herit
Dorothy Marie
Herit
Double Blueberry Pie
Herit
Double Cameo (mini)
BayBl, Puket, SumG
Double Cutie (mini)
BayBl, Puket, SumG
Double Pink Treasure
Herit
Double Spotlight
Herit
Double Super Duper
Herit
Double Supreme
Herit
Double Wonder
Herit
Douglas Dale
BayBl
Douglas Potter
SumG
Downing Street
SumG
Dream Awhile
Herit
Duke Of Durham
Herit, Puket, SumG

Dwarf King (mini)
Puket, SumG
Earth Angel
Herit
Easter Sunday
SumG
Ed Kirchoff
Herit
Ed Murray
BayBl, Kopua, Puket, SumG
Edie (mini)
Herit
Eenie Allegro (mini)
BayBl, Egmon
Eenie Weenie (mini)
BayBl
Ego Trip
Herit
Egyptian Ibis
Herit
Egyptian Lotus
Puket, SumG
Eighteen Karat
Puket
El Rosario
Herit
Electric
Herit
Elegant One
Herit
Elf Caps (mini)
Herit
Elfin Escapade (mini)
Herit
Elfin Imp (mini)
Herit
Elfin Stella (mini)
Parva
Elizabeth Ann Hudson
BayBl, Herit, Kopua, Puket, SumG
Elles
Herit
Emerald Crown
Puket, SumG
Enchanted Empress
Herit
Enchanters Spell (mini)
Herit
Enon
BayBl

Etosha
Herit
Euphoria
Herit
Evening Bell
Herit, Puket
Evening Frolic
Herit
Ever So Ruffled
Herit
Eves Eden
Herit
Exotic Echo (mini)
Herit
Exotic Elf (mini)
Herit
Fabulous Prize
Puket
Fair Rose
Herit
Fairest Love
Herit
Fairy Charm (mini)
HostG
Fairy Frosting (mini)
Herit
Fairytale Pink
Herit, HostG, SumG
Fashion Drama
Herit
Fashion Plate
Puket
Father Fidalis
Herit
Femme Fatale
Herit
Femme Osage
Herit
Fiesta Fling
Herit
Fifth Symphony
Puket
Fine China
Herit
Fire Music
Herit
Fire Power
Herit
Flames Of Fortune
BayBl, Herit, Puket
Flasher
SumG

Flavia
Kopua
Flirty Edna
Herit
Florence Bird
Herit
Flower Fiesta (mini)
Herit
Flower Pavilion
Herit
Forsyth Cream Puff
Taunt
Forsythe Lemon Drop (mini)
SumG
fragrans
Parva
Frank Gladney
Herit, SumG
French Porcelain
BayBl, Kopua, Puket
Frosted Creme
Herit
Full Harvest Moon
SumG
fulva double orange
Mills
fulva Kwanso Variegata
Titok
Gallent's Folly (mini)
Herit
Garden Goddess
Herit
Garden Puppet (mini)
Herit
Garnet Robe
Puket
Gaucho
Herit
Gay Cravat
BayBl, Puket, SumG
General Beauregarde
Puket
Gift Of Love
SumG
Gingerbread Man
Kopua, Puket
Gingham Maid
Herit
Giselle (mini)
Herit
Gleber's Top Cream
Puket

Glitter
Puket, SumG, Taunt
Glittering Lights
BayBl, Parva, Puket, SumG
Global Affair
Puket
Goddess
Herit
Golden Calypso
Herit
Golden Chimes (mini)
BayBl, Parva, SumG, Telfa
Golden Frills
Puket
Golden Scroll
Herit, SumG
Golden Thimble (mini)
Puket, SumG
Golden Tycoon
HostG
Goolagong
Herit
Graceful Eye
SumG
Grammie's List
HostG
Grand Palais
Herit
Grand Ways
SumG
Grape Velvet (mini)
BayBl
Great Connections
Herit
Green Eyes Wink
HostG
Green Flutter (mini)
BayBl, Parva, Puket, Taunt
Gretchen (mini)
BayBl, Puket
Guardian Angel (mini)
SumG
Gypsy Cranberry (mini)
Herit
Gypsy Spell
Puket, SumG
Haidee
SumG
Happy Reward
Puket

Harmony (mini)
BayBl, Puket
Harvest Hue
Herit
Hazel Monette
Puket, SumG
Heady Wine
BayBl, Puket
Heart's Glee (mini)
Herit
Hermitage Newton
Herit
Highland Cranberry
Herit
Holly Dew (mini)
Herit
Home Style
Herit
Homer Howard Glidden (mini)
Herit
Homeward Bound
Herit
Honour Born
Puket, SumG
Hope Diamond
BayBl
Hostess
Herit
Hot Ember
Herit
Hot Wire
Herit
Hudson Valley
SumG
Hurricane Sky
Herit
Hymn
Herit
Hyperon
Puket
Ice Carnival
Puket, Telfa
Ice Castles (mini)
Herit
Ice Cool
Puket
Icy Lemon
Herit
Ida Wimberly Munson
BayBl, Kopua, Puket
In Springtime
BayBl, Telfa

Inamorata
 SumG
Inca Gold
 Puket
Indian Paintbrush
 HostG
Indiana Goldmine
 SumG
Indonesia
 Herit
Inner Peace
 Herit
Inner View
 SumG
Inspired World
 Herit
Iridescent Jewel
 Herit
Irish Elf (mini)
 Herit
Island Sand Dollar
 HostG
Island Vespers
 Herit
Ivory Pearl
 Herit
Jack Brannon
 Puket, SumG
Jacob
 SumG
Jade Lady
 Herit
Jade Star
 Herit
Jakarta
 Puket
James Marsh
 Herit, SumG
Janet Gayle
 Herit, Puket
Jason Salter (mini)
 Herit
Jean Wootton
 Herit
Jeff
 Herit
Jen Melon
 Taunt
Jerome
 Herit, Puket, SumG
Jeune Tom (mini)
 Herit

Jewelite
 Herit
Jewelled Sunbeam (mini)
 Herit
Jim McGinnis (mini)
 Herit
Joan Senior
 BayBl
Jock Randall
 Puket
Johnny Barbour
 SumG
Jolly Hearts
 Puket
Jomico
 Puket, SumG
Joshua's Joy
 SumG
Jovial
 Herit
Joyful Occasion
 BayBl
Judith
 Taunt
Judy Koltz
 Puket
Julius Lynn
 Herit
Jumbo Red
 Kopua, Puket, SumG
June Williams
 Kopua, Puket
Kallister
 Herit
Karen Sue
 SumG
Kate Carpenter
 Herit
Katerina
 Puket, SumG
Kecia
 Herit
Kelly's Girl
 Herit, SumG
Kempion
 Herit
Ken Hensen
 Kopua
Kenneth Johnson
 Herit
Kensington Manor
 Herit

Kent's Favourite Two
 Herit
Kenya
 Herit
Kewpie Doll (mini)
 BayBl, Kopua, Puket
Kindly Light
 SumG
King Cotton
 SumG
King Lalomi
 Kopua
Kings Throne
 BayBl, Kopua, Puket,
 SumG
Kissing Cousins
 Herit
Knick Knack (mini)
 Herit
Knightsbridge
 BayBl, Puket, SumG
Koala Dance
 Puket
Kokich
 Puket, SumG
Kosciusko
 Herit
Kristen Monroe
 Herit
Kwanso
 Telfa
La Chamante
 SumG
La Favourita (mini)
 BayBl, Puket
La Reve
 Herit
La Scala
 Herit
Lacy Dawn
 Herit
Lady Bright Eyes
 Herit
Lady Grace
 Herit
Lady Limelight (mini)
 Herit
Lady Louise
 SumG
Lady Margaret (mini)
 Puket

Lady Mischief (mini)
BayBl, Kopua, Puket, SumG

Lagniappe
Herit

Lake Norman Double
Herit

Lake Norman Sunset
Herit

Laura Pooh (mini)
Herit

Lauren Leah
Herit

Lavender Falcon
Puket, SumG

Lavender Illusion
SumG

Lavender Organdy
Kopua, Puket, SumG

Leeba Orange Crush
SumG

Lemon Jade
Herit

Lemon Piper
Herit

Lemonade Supreme
Herit

Lenox
Herit

Leprechauns Lace (mini)
Herit

Lester John
Herit

Light Shine
Herit

Lilac Snow
BayBl, SumG

Lillian Fry (mini)
Herit

Lilliputian Knight (mini)
Herit

Lilting Lady (mini)
Herit

Limoges Porcelain
Herit

Limon (mini)
SumG

Little Beige Magic
HostG

Little Big Man (mini)
Herit

Little Brandy
Herit

Little Business (mini)
BayBl, Herit, Kopua, Parva, Puket

Little Cadet (mini)
Herit

Little Celina (mini)
BayBl, Herit, Kopua, Puket, SumG

Little Cherub (mini)
Kopua, Puket, SumG

Little Christine (mini)
Herit

Little Darling (mini)
Herit

Little Deeke
Herit, SumG

Little Fat Dazzler (mini)
BayBl, Herit, Puket

Little Favourite (mini)
Puket

Little Fellow (mini)
BayBl, Kopua, Puket, SumG

Little Grapette (mini)
BayBl, Herit, Parva, Puket

Little Gypsy Eyes (mini)
BayBl

Little Gypsy Vagabond (mini)
BayBl, Herit, Kopua, Puket, SumG

Little Infant Baby (mini)
BayBl

Little Jazz (mini)
Herit

Little Joy (mini)
Herit, SumG

Little Katie
Herit

Little Lamb (mini)
Herit

Little Lila (mini)
Herit

Little Love (mini)
Herit, SumG

Little Monica (mini)
SumG

Little Much (mini)
Herit

Little Mutt (mini)
BayBl, Parva, Puket, Telfa

Little Pandora (mini)
Herit

Little Papoose (mini)
Herit

Little Pumpkin Face
HostG

Little Rainbow (mini)
Herit, Puket, SumG

Little Red Warbler (mini)
Herit

Little Show Off (mini)
SumG

Little Toddler (mini)
BayBl, Herit

Little Wart (mini)
Herit, Kopua, Nikau, Parva, Puket, SumG

Little Zinger (mini)
BayBl, Herit, Puket, SumG

Littlest Angel (mini)
BayBl, Herit, Kopua, Puket, SumG

Littlest Clown (mini)
BayBl, Puket, SumG

Loisteen Kirkman
Puket

Lolabelle (mini)
Herit

Look Away
BayBl, Kopua, Puket, Taunt

Look Once Again
Herit

Lorraine Kilgour
Herit, Kopua, Puket

Louise Manelis (mini)
BayBl

Lucille Lenington
Herit

Lullaby Baby (mini)
Herit, Puket, Taunt

Lunar Sea
Herit

Lustrous Jade
Herit

Luxury Lace
Puket

Lyric Opera
Herit

MacMillan Memorial
Herit

Magic Mama
Herit

Magic Masquerade (mini)
Herit

Mambo Maid (mini)
Herit

Manchurian Apricot
Herit

Marble Faun
Herit

Mariachi
SumG

Marie Munro
Puket

Mariska
Herit, SumG

Martha Adams
Herit

Mary Helen
Herit

Mary Kate
Herit

Mary Todd
SumG

Mary Tudor
Herit

Master Plan
Herit

Matahari (mini)
Herit

Mauna Loa
Herit, SumG

May Melody
SumG

May Unger
SumG

Mayan Gold
HostG

Mayan Poppy
Herit

Meadow Sprite (mini)
Herit

Memories
Puket

Merinda Honeybunch
Herit

Merry Minx (mini)
Herit

Midnight Magic
Herit, Kopua, SumG

Mighty Mogul
SumG

Mighty Shogun
Herit

Mildred Suzanne
Herit

Milk Maid
Kopua, Puket

Ming Porcelain
BayBl, Herit, Kopua,
Puket, SumG, Taunt

Ming Temple
Herit

Ming Treasure
Herit

Mini Pearl (mini)
BayBl, Puket

Mini Stella (mini)
BayBl

Misha
Herit

Misty Penny
Herit

Mockingbird Thrill
Herit

Mojave Desert
Herit

Mokan Moon
SumG

Moment Of Ecstasy
Herit

Monica Marie
Herit

Monrovia Gem
Herit, SumG

Monsignor
Herit

Montage
Herit

Moon Goddess
Kopua, Ormon, Parva,
Puket

Moon Twilight
Herit

Moonlight Mist (mini)
BayBl, Herit

Mormon
Puket, SumG

Morning Cheerfulness
Herit

Morning Delight
BayBl, Puket

Moroccan Summer
Herit

Mosel (mini)
BayBl, Herit, Puket

Most Noble
Herit

Mumbo Jumbo
SumG

**Munchkin Moonbeam
(mini)**
Herit

My Belle
Herit, SumG

My Eye Elsie
Herit

My Mom Blanch
Herit

Mykonos
Herit

Mysterious
Herit

Nagasaki
Herit

Nashville
Puket

Navajo Blanket
Puket

Nebo
Herit

Nebula
Herit

Neddie
Puket, SumG

Needlepoint
Herit

Nell Crandall
SumG

Nell Keown
Herit

Never Get Away
Herit

Night Queen
Herit

Night Raider
Herit

Night Town
Herit

Night Wings
Herit

Nile Crane
Herit, Puket, SumG

Nile Plum
Herit

No Idea
Herit

Nuance
Herit

Ocean Rain
  Herit
Old Tangiers
  Herit
Olive Baily Langdon
  BayBl, Herit, Kopua,
  Parva, Puket
Olive Monette
  Kopua
Ono (mini)
  SumG
Opal Rosa
  Puket
Optical Delight
  Herit
Orange Layer Cake
  Herit
Orange Prelude
  Puket
Orange Tex
  Kopua, Puket
Orchard Sprite
  Herit
Oriental Ruby
  Kopua, Puket
Oriental Silk
  Kopua
Oriental Topaz
  Kopua, Puket
Osago Maiden
  Kopua, Puket
Outrageous
  Herit
Pagoda Goddess
  Herit
Palace Guard
  Herit, SumG
Palace Lantern
  Herit
Pam Sims
  Herit
Panache
  Herit
Panchen Lama
  Herit
Pandoras Box (mini)
  HostG, Puket, SumG
Pantaloons
  Herit
Paper Butterfly
  Herit
Paper Dragon
  Herit

Pardon Me (mini)
  BayBl
Paris Lace (mini)
  Herit
Party Queen
  SumG
Pas de Deux
  Herit
Pass Me Not
  BayBl, Kopua, SumG
Passionate Prize
  Herit
Pastel Accent (mini)
  Herit
Pastel Classic
  Herit
Patchwork Puzzle (mini)
  Herit
Peach Fairy (mini)
  SumG
Pearl Chiffon (mini)
  Herit
Pearl Hammond
  Herit
Pedro
  SumG
Peek-A-Boo Eyes
  Parva, Puket
Penefold
  Puket, SumG
Perfect Lemonade
  Herit, SumG
Persian Plum
  Kopua, Puket
Persian Rose
  Kopua, Puket, SumG
Petite Ballet (mini)
  Herit
Petite Palace Rose
  HostG
Phoenician Pearls
  Puket, SumG
Phoenician Ruffles
  Herit
Piccolo (mini)
  Puket
Pink Caprice
  Herit
Pink Chapeau
  Herit
Pink Cherry
  SumG

Pink Corduroy
  BayBl
Pink Duet
  BayBl, Puket
Pink Frost
  Puket
Pink Jubilation
  Herit
Pink Lavender Appeal
  BayBl
Pink Salute
  Herit
Pink Tangerine
  HostG
Pippins Magic
  Herit
Pixie Parasol (mini)
  BayBl, Puket
Pixie Pipestone (mini)
  Herit
Play Boy
  Puket
Pocket Of Dreams
  Herit
Pojo (mini)
  BayBl, Herit
Polka Time
  Puket
Pony Ride
  Puket, SumG
Ponytail Pink
  HostG
Porcelain Prince
  Herit
Prairie Blue Eyes
  BayBl, Puket, SumG
Prairie Moonlight
  SumG
Prairie Sunburst
  HostG
Praise Of Wisdom
  Herit
Precious Princess
  Herit
Prima Ballerina
  Puket
Prince Redbird (mini)
  Herit
Princess Ellen
  Herit
Prom Date
  Herit

Protocol
Herit

Puppet Show
Herit, SumG

Purple Glory
Kopua, Puket

Purple Magic
Herit

Purple Pinwheel (mini)
Herit

Purple Rain (mini)
BayBl, Puket

Purple Romance
Herit

Pyewacket (mini)
SumG

Quaker Bonnet
Herit

Queen Empress
Herit

Queen Lily
Herit

Queen's Castle
SumG

Queen's Gift
Herit

Quick Results
Herit

Quick Silver (mini)
Herit

RA Hansen
Herit

Rachel My Love
Herit

Radiant Ruffles
Herit

Raging Tiger
Herit

Raptures
Herit

Rare Gift
Kopua

Raspberry Wine
Puket

Rebecca Sue Memorial
Herit

Red Fancy
Herit

Red Pinnochio
HostG

Red Reward
HostG

Red Rhapsody
Herit

Red Roo
Herit

Red Rum
Herit

Red Volunteer
SumG

Regal Tapestry
BayBl, Puket

Retro (mini)
SumG

Ricky Rose
Herit

Right On
Herit

Riley Baron
SumG

Rily Brown
Puket

Ring Of Change
Herit

Riptide
Herit

Robbie Salter (mini)
Herit

Robes Of Psyche
Herit

Root Beer
HostG

Rose Amethyst
Herit

Rose Cherub
Kopua

Rose Emily
BayBl, Herit, Taunt

Rose Frilly Dilly
Herit

Rose Island
Herit

Rose Petite (mini)
Herit

Rose Puff
Herit

Rose Ruffling
Herit, Puket, SumG

Rose Swan
SumG

Rose Tapestry
SumG

Rose Tattoo
Herit

Rosella Sheridan
Herit, Puket, SumG

Rosemont Firebrandt
Puket

Rouged Talisman
SumG

Round Table
BayBl, Herit

Royal Diamond
Herit

Royal Eventide
Herit

Royal Fanfare (mini)
Herit

Royal Heiress
Herit

Royal Heritage
Herit, Kopua, Puket,
SumG

Royal Legacy
Herit, SumG

Royal Mountie
HostG

Royal Palace Guard
HostG

Royal Palace Prince
HostG

Royal Rage
SumG

Royal Saracen
BayBl, Herit

Royal Trumpeter
Herit

Ruby Throat
Puket

Ruffled Apricot
BayBl, HostG, Puket,
SumG, Taunt

Ruffled Dazzler
BayBl, Kopua, Puket

Ruffled Feathers
Herit

Ruffled Magic
BayBl

Ruffled Shawl
Herit, Kopua

Ruffles Elegante
BayBl, Herit

Russian Rhapsody
BayBl, Kopua, Parva,
Puket

Ruthie (mini)
BayBl, SumG

Sabbath
Herit

Sabie
BayBl, Kopua, SumG

Sachet Of Lemon
Herit

Sadie Lou
Herit

Salvation Show (mini)
Herit, SumG

Samurai Silk
Kopua, SumG

Sandalett
Herit

Sanford House
Herit

Sari
Kopua, Puket, SumG

Sariah
Herit

Sarsaparilla
BayBl, SumG

Satin Glass
SumG

Satin Siren
Herit

Saucy Rogue (mini)
Herit

Sausalito Dawn
Herit

Scarlet Orbit
Herit, SumG

Scarlet Pansy
Herit

Scotsboro
BayBl, Puket, SumG

Scruples (mini)
Herit

Searching Love
Herit

Sebastion
BayBl, Puket, SumG

Second Glance
Herit

Secret Garden
Herit

Seduction
Herit

Seductor
Herit

Seductress
SumG

Seeing Red (mini)
Puket, SumG

Serenity Morgan
Herit

Seventh Symphony
BayBl, Parva, Puket, Taunt

Shaded Eyes
Herit

Shadowed Pink
SumG

Shady Lady
SumG

Shaman
Herit

Shanghai Breeze
Herit

Shaolin Priest
Herit

Sharks Tooth
Herit

Sheik of Araby
Herit

Sheila's Wedding
Herit

Shockwave
Herit, SumG

Show Off
Puket, SumG

Siam
Herit

Sight Delight
Herit

Siloam Baby Talk (mini)
BayBl, Herit, Puket

Siloam Bertie Ferris (mini)
Herit

Siloam Bo-Peep (mini)
BayBl, Herit, Parva, Puket

Siloam Button Box (mini)
Herit

Siloam Bye Lo (mini)
Herit

Siloam Cinderella (mini)
Herit

Siloam Doodlebug (mini)
Herit

Siloam Double Classic
Herit

Siloam Dreambay (mini)
Herit

Siloam Fairy Tale (mini)
BayBl, Herit, Puket

Siloam Jim Cooper (mini)
Herit

Siloam June Bug (mini)
Puket

Siloam Ladybug (mini)
Herit

Siloam Little Girl (mini)
BayBl, Herit, Puket, SumG

Siloam Merle Kent (mini)
Herit

Siloam Pocket Size (mini)
Herit

Siloam Powder Pink (mini)
Herit

Siloam Prissy (mini)
Herit

Siloam Queen's Toy (mini)
Herit

Siloam Red Cherry (mini)
Herit

Siloam Red Ruby (mini)
Herit, Taunt

Siloam Red Toy (mini)
Herit, SumG

Siloam Ribbon Candy
Taunt

Siloam Robbie Bush (mini)
Herit

Siloam Rose Queen (mini)
Herit

Siloam Show Girl (mini)
Herit

Siloam Sugar Time (mini)
Herit

Siloam Tiny Mite (mini)
Herit

Siloam Tom Thumb (mini)
Herit

Siloam Tommy Tucker
(mini)
Herit

Siloam Ury Winniford
(mini)
Herit

Siloam Valentine (mini)
Herit

Siloam Virginia Henson
(mini)
BayBl, Herit

Silver Ice
Herit, SumG
Silver Potentate
Puket
Silver Sprite
Herit
Silver Veil
Herit
Silver Wine
BayBl, SumG
Simply Pretty
BayBl, Herit
Sir Blackstem (mini)
Herit
Sir Galahad
BayBl, Puket
Sir Prize
Herit
Sister Marie
Herit
Sister McDuffie
Herit
Ski Chalet
BayBl, Nikau
Ski Jump
Puket
Sky Kissed
Herit
Slade Brown
Herit
Snappy Yellow
HostG
Snow Bride
Herit
Snow Elf (mini)
Herit
Snow Orchid
SumG
Snowborn
Herit
Snowdrift
Herit
Snowed In
Herit
Snowfrost Pink
Herit
So Excited
Herit
So Fine
Herit
So Lovely
SumG

Soglio
Puket, SumG
Solano Bull's Eye
Herit, SumG
Sombrero Way
HostG
Song Of Praise
SumG
Song of Spring
Puket
Sorcerer's Apprentice
Herit
Sorcerer's Song (mini)
Herit
Southern Prize
Herit
Southern Sunset
Herit
Spanish Masquerade
Herit
Special Angel
Puket, SumG
Special Favour
SumG
Special Flavour
Puket
Spring Ballerina
Herit
Spring Sunrise
Herit
Springtime Bouquet
Herit
Squeaky (mini)
BayBl, Kopua
Stella d'Oro (mini)
BayBl, Herit, Parva, Puket
Stop Sign
Herit
Stoplight
SumG
Stroke Of Midnight
Herit
Stronghold
Herit
Strutters Ball
Herit
Study In Scarlet
BayBl, Herit
Sugar Candy
SumG

Sugar Cookie (mini)
BayBl, Herit, Puket, SumG
Summer Echoes (mini)
Herit
Summer Song
Puket, SumG
Sun King
Herit
Sun Lord
Herit
Sunday Gloves
Taunt
Sunset Loa
Herit
Sunset Strut
Herit
Super Doll (mini)
Herit
Superlative
Herit
Sure Thing
Herit
Svengali
Herit
Sweet Pea (mini)
Herit
Sweet Shalimar
Herit
Symphony of Spring
BayBl, Puket, SumG
Tang Porcelain
Herit
Tango Girl
Herit
Tapestry Of Dreams (mini)
Herit
Taylor Made
Parva, Puket, SumG
Teahouse Tapestry
Herit
Techny Spider
HostG
Temple Of Heaven
Herit
Tender Love
SumG, Taunt
Terra
Herit, Puket
Test Print
Herit

Thai Ballet
Puket, SumG

Thais
Herit

Thebes
Herit

Thessally
Puket, SumG

Thumbelina (mini)
Puket, SumG

Thy True Love
SumG

Tidal Wave
Herit

Tiffany Gold
Herit

Time Lord
Herit

Timeless Fire
Herit

Tiny (mini)
Puket

Tiny Pumpkin (mini)
BayBl, Herit, Kopua,
Puket, SumG

Tiny Temptress (mini)
Herit

Tiny Tiki (mini)
Puket, SumG

Tiny Trumpeter (mini)
Herit

Tom Collins (mini)
Herit

Tomato Surprise
Herit, SumG

Tonia Gay
Herit

Tony Kissing
Herit

Tootsie (mini)
Herit

Tootsie Rose (mini)
BayBl, Herit, Puket,
SumG

Touched by Midas
BayBl, Herit, Puket,
SumG

Tour De Force
Herit

Toy Troubadour (mini)
Herit

Trappist Monk
Herit

Treasured Bouquet
SumG

Treasured Memories
Puket, SumG

Trend Setter
Herit

Trogon
Herit

Tropic Sunset
Herit

Tropical Sherbert (mini)
Herit

Tropical Toy (mini)
Herit

Trumpet (mini)
Herit

Tuff Stuff
Puket

Twilight Swan
Herit, SumG

Twin Classic
Herit

Twin Dragons
Herit

Twinkle Bright (mini)
Herit

Undulata
Herit

Unforgettable
SumG

Unique Purple
SumG

Vanity Case
Herit

Velvet Shadows (mini)
BayBl, Puket

Vendette
Herit

Venetian Splendour
Herit

Vera Bigloe
Herit

Victoria Elizabeth Barnes
Puket, SumG

Victoria Therese
SumG

Victorian Violet (mini)
Herit

Vilja
Puket

Vino Di Notte
Herit

Vintage Bordeaux
BayBl, Herit, Puket

Violet Jade
Puket, SumG

Viracocha
Herit

Vohann
Herit, SumG

Voo Doo Doll (mini)
Puket, SumG

Wally Nance III
Puket

Walnut Creek
SumG

Waltz Melody (mini)
Herit

Warpaint
Herit

Wee Chalice (mini)
Herit

Wee Willie Mullis (mini)
Puket, SumG

Welcome Mat
HostG

Westfield
Puket, SumG

White Temptation
Taunt

White Tie Affair
Herit

Whooperee
Herit

Whopper Flopper
Herit

Whopper Stopper
Herit

Wicked Lady
Herit

Wicked Witch
Herit

Wide, Wide World
SumG

Wilbur Harding
SumG

Wild Enchantress (mini)
Herit, Puket, SumG

William Milo Spalding
Herit

Willy Rua (mini)
Herit, Puket

Wind Frills
SumG

Windy Pink
Herit
Wine Bubbles
HostG
Wings Of Faith
Herit
Winnie The Pooh (mini)
SumG
Witch Dame (mini)
Herit
Wynn
Herit
Yardmaster
Taunt
Yasmin
Puket
Yazoo Souffle
BayBl, Herit
Yellow Kitten
Herit
Yellow Lollipop (mini)
Herit
Yellow Petticoats
Puket
You Devil
Herit
Zella
BayBl, Puket, SumG
Zemboanga
Herit
Zinfandel
Herit
Zorba
Puket, SumG
Zulu
Herit

Hepatica
angulosa now transilvanica
NewlR
sp deep pink form
NewlR
triloba (now nobilis) pale pink form
NewlR

Heptacodium
jasminoides (Seven Son Flower of Zhejiang)
Caves, TopTr

Heracleum
Bereklaun Herkuleskrut
Telfa

Herbertia
drummondii
DaffA
lahue
Irida, Kerer
platensis
Irida

Hermodactylus
tuberosus (Mourning Widow/Snakeshead Iris)
BayBl, DaffA, Kerer

Herniaria
glabra (Rupture Wort)
Della, MillH, Orang, Sweet

Hesperaloe
parviflora (Red Yucca)
Reic #

Hesperantha
bachmannii
DaffA
baurii
DaffA, JoyPl, KeriP, MaraN, TRidg
buhrii now H.cuculata rubra
Irida
erecta
DaffA, Irida, MaraN
latifolia
Irida, Parva
pauciflora
DaffA
vaginata
DaffA
vaginata stanfordiae
DaffA

Hesperis
lutea now Sisymbrium luteum
TRidg
matrionalis (Sweet Rocket)
AynDa, KeriP, King #, MaraN, Nikau, Sweet
matronalis alba
Della, Dream, KeriP, MaraN
matronalis var purple-violet
MillH
matronalis var white
MillH

steveniana
Dream

Hesperoxiphion
peruvianum
Parva

Heterocentron
elegans was Schizocentron, Heeria (Spanish Shawl)
KeriP, Trans

Heteropterys
angustifolia
Caves

Heuchera
americana
Della, NewlR, Pgeon
americana Green Spice
Parva
Amethyst
Hackf, Peak
Amethyst Mist
Parva
Apple Blossom
Parva
Bressingham Bronze
Egmon, Hackf, Peak
Bressingham Hybrids
Ashto, AynDa, BlueM, Butlr, KeriP, Oasis, Trans
Chocolate Ruffles
Parva
Cream
Pgeon
cylindrica
MaraN
cylindrica Greenfinch
MillH
cylindrica Sky Rocket
Pgeon
Green Ivory
CottP, Ormon, Peak, Telfa
hallii
Otepo
hispida (Satin Leaf)
BayBl, MaraN, Telfa
micrantha
Ormon, Pgeon
Mint Julep
Parva
Oakington Jewell
Peak

Palace Purple
BayBl, MaraN, Oasis, Orang, Telfa, TRidg

Pewter Veil
Egmon, Parva

Plum Pudding
Parva

Red Spangles
Pgeon

rubra
CottP

Ruby Ruffles
Parva

Ruby Veil
Parva

sanguinea (Coral Bells)
BayBl, CottP, MaraN, Mills, NewlR, Orang, Pkrau

sanguinea Frosty
Parva

sanguinea Hybrids
BlueM

sanguinea Pink Fairy
Pgeon

sanguinea Splendens
BayBl

Scintillation
Parva

Snow Storm
BayBl, Parva

Strawberry Swirl
Parva

Velvet Night
Parva

White Spires
Peak

Heucherella

alba Bridget Bloom
CottP

alba Rosalie
Parva

Pink Frost
BayBl, Peak

Snow White
BayBl, CottP, Peak

Hibbertia

empetrifolia
BlueM

obtusifolia (Grey Guinea Flower)
MatNu

scandens (Snake Vine, Guinea Gold Vine)
CouCl, Denes, Reic #

tiny lvs,bright yellow flwrs
MaraN

Hibiscus

hybrids
Frans

coccineus
AynDa

diversifolius (North Cape Hibiscus)
Matwh, Orati, Terra

diversifolius Prostrata
Orati

esculentus 2 varieties (Okra)
King #

huegelii now Alogyne h.
Denes, Vall #

moscheutos (Swamp Rose Mallow)
WaiMa

paramutabilis
Reic #

rosa sinensi cooperii
LakeN

schizopetalus
Frans, LakeN

syriacus (Rose of Sharon, Syrian Rose)
Reic #

syriacus alba
Reic #, TopTr

syriacus Flying Flag
Denes, Mtato

syriacus Heidi
Denes, Mtato

syriacus Lady Stanley
Denes

syriacus Snowdrift
Denes, Mtato

tiliaceus
Frans

trionum (Puarangi)
Burbk, Gordn, Matwh, Mills, Orati, Roswd, Seasd, Terra, Trans, Vall #

Wilder's White
Frans

Hieracium

aurantiacum now Pilosella a. (Hawkweed)
Mills

Hierochloe

redolens (Holy Grass)
Orati

Hippeastrum

mixed white to deep rose
Reic #

aulicum
MJury

bifidum now Rhodophialia b.
JoyPl, MJury

Histiopteris

incisa (Water Fern)
Orati

Hoheria

angustifolia (Narrow-lvd Lacebark)
Diack, Matai, NZtr #, Orati, SouWo, Terra

glabrata (Deciduous Lacebark)
Orati, Terra, Wahpa

lyallii (Mountain Lacebark)
Denes, Matai, Terra

populnea (Houhere, Lacebark)
BlueM, Chedd, Coatv, Denes, Diack, Gordn, Matai, Matwh, Morgn, Mtato, NZtr #, Orati, Pionr, Pukho, SouWo, Terra, Wahpa

populnea alba variegata (White variegated Lacebark)
Chedd, Coatv, Denes, Orati, Pionr, Pukho, Wahpa, Wells

populnea Purpurea
Orati

populnea variegata (Yellow/green variegated Lacebark)
Coatv, Mtato, Orati, Pionr, Wahpa, Wells, Wensl

sexstylosa (Graceful Lacebark)
BlueM, Denes, Matwh, Mtato, NZtr #, Orati, Terra, Wahpa

Holboellia

latifolia
   CouCl

Holcus

mollis Variegatus
   Telfa

Holmskioldia

**sanguinea Aurea
(Chinaman's Cap)**
   LakeN

Homoglossum

huttonii
   Irida

priorii   now Gladiolus p.
   DaffA

watsonium   now Gladiolus
   DaffA

Homolanthus

polyandrus
   Orati

Horminum

pyrenaicum
   MaraN, Telfa

Hosta

mixed
   Kayd, Looij, Parva,
   WilAq

mixed decorative lvd
   Vall #

Abiqua Drinking Gourd
   HostG

Abiqua Recluse
   HostG

albomarginata
   BayBl

albopicta
   BayBl, Vall #

Allen P McConnell
   BayBl, Taunt

Antioch
   HostG, Taunt

Aphrodite
   Peak

Arctic Circle
   HostG

Aspen Gold
   HostG, Parva

August Moon
   BayBl, Diack, Hackf,
   HostG, JoyPl, KeriP,
   MJury, Taunt, TRidg,
   Woodl

Aureomarginata
   BayBl, Pgeon, TRidg,
   WaiMa

Big Daddy
   Denes, HostG, Parva,
   Peak, Taunt, TRidg

Blue Angel
   Hackf, HostG, Parva,
   Taunt

Blue Arrow
   HostG, Titok

Blue Boy
   HostG, MJury, Peak,
   Pkrau, Taunt

Blue Cadet
   BayBl, HostG, Parva,
   Taunt

Blue Dimple
   Parva

Blue Moon
   HostG, Parva, Taunt

Blue Seer
   HostG, Parva, Taunt,
   Titok

Blue Skies
   HostG, Taunt, TRidg

Blue Umbrella
   KeriP

Blue Veil
   Taunt

Blue Wedgewood
   Hackf, HostG, Parva,
   Taunt, Titok

Bright Lights
   HostG

Brim Cup
   HostG, MJury, Titok

Candy Hearts
   HostG, Taunt

Capitata
   Taunt

Carole
   BayBl

Celebration
   BayBl, HostG, Taunt,
   TRidg

Chinese Sunrise
   HostG

Christmas Tree
   HostG

Classic Delight
   Taunt

coerulea
   HostG, Taunt

Color Glory
   HostG

Cream Edge
   HostG, MJury, Taunt

crispula
   Taunt

Crowned Imperial
   HostG

Daybreak
   HostG

decorata
   HostG

elata
   MaraN

Ellerbroek
   HostG

Emerald Skies
   Taunt, TRidg

Excitation
   HostG

Fall Bouquet
   HostG

Feather Boa
   Taunt

Flora Dora
   Taunt

fluctans variegata (Sagae)
   Taunt

fortunei
   BayBl, BlueM, Diack,
   MaraN, Trans, WaiMa

**fortunei Albomarginata
(Silver Crown)**
   HostG

**fortunei Obscura-
marginata**
   HostG

fortunei var albopicta
   BlueM, HostG, Taunt

fortunei var aurea
   HostG, Taunt

**fortunei var
aureomarginata**
   HostG, JoyPl, NewlR,
   Taunt

fortunei var rugosa
   Taunt

fortunei Viridis
   HostG

Fragrant Blue
   MJury, Titok

Fragrant Bouquet
   HostG, MJury, Parva,
   Taunt

Fragrant Gold
HostG

Francee
HostG, Parva, Peak, Taunt

Francis Williams
HostG, Taunt, Vall #

Fringe Benefit
HostG, Taunt

Frosted Jade
HostG

Gay Blade
HostG

Gingko Craig
BayBl, HostG, Peak, Taunt

glauca
Denes, WaiMa

Gold Edger
BayBl, HostG, Parva, Taunt

Gold Regal
HostG, Parva, Taunt, Titok

Gold Standard
HostG, KeriP, Taunt, TRidg

Golden Medallion
HostG, Parva, Taunt

Golden Prayers
Taunt

Golden Scepter
HostG

Golden Tiara
Ashto, BayBl, Hackf, HostG, MJury, Parva, Taunt, TRidg, WaiMa

Goldrush
Denes, MJury, Taunt

Good as Gold
Taunt

gracilipes
MJury

gracilis
Ashto

gracillima
TRidg

Grand Master
HostG

Grand Tiara
MJury, Parva, Titok

Great Expectations
HostG, MJury, Parva, Taunt, Titok

Green Fountain
HostG, Taunt, TRidg

Green Standard
BayBl, Woodl

Grey Pie Crust sdlgs
TRidg

Ground Master
HostG

Hadspen Blue
HostG, Parva, Taunt, TRidg

Halcyon
JoyPl, Peak, Taunt, Woodl

helonoides f.albopicta now rohdeifolia
MJury, Taunt

Honeybells
BayBl, Diack, HostG, Pgeon, Taunt

hybrid seedlings
AynDa

Hydon Sunset
Parva

Inniswood
HostG, MJury, Parva, Titok

Invincible
BayBl, HostG, Parva, TRidg

Jade Cascade
BayBl, Peak

June
HostG

JW Mathews
Titok

Kabitan now sieboldii kabitan
Hackf, HostG, MJury, Taunt, TRidg

Kei (Butler) sieboldii
Taunt

kikutii
HostG

kikutii caput-avis
Taunt

King Tut
HostG

Krossa Regal
Denes, HostG, Parva, Taunt, TRidg

lancifolia
BayBl, Diack, Hackf, HostG, Parva, Taunt, TRidg

Lemon Lime
BayBl, HostG, Taunt

Little Aurora
HostG, TRidg

Love Pat
HostG, Parva, Taunt

Maya Yellow
HostG

Midas Touch
Taunt

Minima
Taunt

minor
MaraN, Pgeon, WaiMa

Montana Aurea Marginata
MJury, Taunt

Nagaeto
BayBl, HostG, JoyPl, Taunt, Woodl

North Hills
HostG, Taunt

On Stage
HostG, Titok

Patriot
HostG, MJury

Pearl Lake
HostG, Taunt

Piedmont Gold
HostG, TRidg

plantaginea
BlueM, Hackf, HostG, KeriP, Taunt, TRidg

plantaginea Aphrodite
Parva

plantaginea Grandiflora (The Scented Hosta)
Parva

Purple Profusion
Taunt

Rascal
HostG

Regal Splendour
MJury, Parva, Titok

Royal Quilt
HostG

Royal Standard
BlueM, HostG, Taunt, TopTr

Rudolphs #1
HostG

Ruffles
BayBl, Denes, JoyPl, KeriP, MJury, Taunt, Woodl

Saishu Jima
   HostG, Taunt
Samurai
   Denes, HostG, Taunt,
   TRidg
Sea Sprite
   HostG, TRidg
Shade Fanfare
   BayBl, HostG, Parva,
   Taunt, TRidg
Shade Master
   HostG
Shining Tot
   Taunt
sieboldiana
   Ashto, BayBl, BlueM,
   Peak, Pgeon, Pkrau,
   Taunt, Vall #, Warwk,
   Woodl
**sieboldiana aurea
marginata**
   MJury, Taunt
sieboldiana Elegans
   HostG, Pkrau, Taunt,
   Telfa, TRidg
sieboldiana Elegans Glauca
   Pkrau
sieboldii
   Kayd, MaraN
Snowcap
   Parva
Snowden
   Parva
So Sweet
   HostG, MJury, Parva,
   TRidg
Sparkling Burgundy
   Taunt
Sugar And Cream
   HostG
Sum and Substance
   HostG, Parva, Taunt,
   Titok, TRidg
Summer Fragrance
   HostG, Parva
Sun Power
   HostG, Taunt, TRidg
Sweet Susan
   Taunt
tardiflora
   HostG, Taunt, TRidg
**Thomas Hogg now undulata
albomarginata**
   Ashto, Hackf, Oasis,
   Pgeon, Taunt, WaiMa

Thumbnail
   Taunt
tokudama
   Taunt, TRidg, Vall #
tokudama flavocircinalis
   Denes, HostG, MJury,
   Taunt
Treasure Trove
   Denes, HostG, Taunt,
   TRidg
undulata
   BayBl, Pgeon, Pkrau
undulata medio-variegata
   NewlR
**undulata var albomarginata
(Thomas Hogg)**
   BlueM, Diack, Hackf,
   HostG, Oasis, Pgeon,
   Taunt, TRidg
undulata var erromena
   Ashto, HostG, Pkrau,
   Taunt, TRidg
undulata var univitata
   Hackf, HostG, MaraN,
   Taunt
undulata variegata
   MJury, Pkrau, Taunt,
   TRidg
Vanilla Cream
   HostG, Taunt
variegata var variegata
   WaiMa
ventricosa
   BayBl, Diack, Hackf,
   HostG, MaraN, Taunt,
   TopTr, Trans
ventricosa Medio Picta
   Trans
venusta
   BayBl, CottP, HostG,
   KeriP, MaraN, Marsh,
   NewlR, Taunt, Woodl
Vera Verde
   Ashto, HostG, Taunt,
   TRidg
Viettes Yellow Edge
   Taunt
Wide Brim
   BayBl, Denes, HostG,
   MJury, Parva, Taunt,
   TRidg
Wogon Gold
   Parva
Yellow River
   HostG

Zounds
   Peak, Taunt

Houstonia
caerulea
   BayBl, CottP
caerulea alba
   BayBl

Houttuynia
cordata Chameleon (v)
   KeriP

Hovenia
**dulcis (Japanese Raisin
Tree)**
   Chedd, Dove, Frans,
   MJury, Reic #

Howea
**belmoreana (Kentia, Sentry
Palm)**
   PalmF
**fosteriana (Kentia/Thatch
Palm)**
   Coatv, Frans, LakeN,
   Lsendt, PalmF, Reic #,
   SpecT

Hoya
bella
   LakeN
carnosa
   LakeN
**carnosa compacta moan
loa (Indian Rope)**
   LakeN
carnosa variegata
   LakeN
linearis
   LakeN
multiflora Shooting Star
   LakeN
nicholsonae
   LakeN
pauciflora
   LakeN
polyneura (Fish Tail Hoya)
   LakeN

Humulus
lupulus (Hops)
   CottP, Della, Mills,
   Orang
lupulus Aureus
   CouCl, TopTr

Hutchinsia

alpina now Thaspli
alpinum
NewlR

Hyacinthella

leucophaea (Pale
Hyacinthella)
Kerer

Hyacinthoides

hispanica was Scilla
campanulata (Spanish
Bluebell)
Brown

hispanica blue, white &
pink
DaffA, NewlR

hispanica Rose Queen
Kerer

non scripta was Scilla n.s.
& Endymion
(Common/English Bluebell)
Kerer, SoBul

Hyacinthus

mixed
Altrf, Kayd, VanEe

amethystinus now Brimeura
a.
MaraN

orientalis Arendsen White
Altrf

orientalis Blue Magic
Altrf, VanEe

orientalis Carnegie
VanEe

orientalis Dr Lieber
Altrf

orientalis Lady Derby Pink
Altrf

orientalis Ostara
VanEe

orientalis Princess
Margaret
VanEe

Hydrangea

Agnes Pavell
Pukho, Woodl

anomala
Caves, Woodl

anomala petiolaris
(Climbing Hydrangea)
BlueM, Caves, CouCl,
JoyPl, Taunt, TRidg

arborea cinerea (ssp
discolor)
Denes

arborescens Annabelle
BlueM, Caves, CottP,
Denes, JoyPl, Kayd,
Taunt, TopTr, Woodl

aspera (Star Hydrangea)
JoyPl

aspera ssp robusta
TopTr

aspera villosa
TopTr

Blue Deckle
BayBl, Woodl

Blue Diamond
Parva

Blue Lacecap variegated
Mtato

Bridal Bouquet
Kayd, Wells

Bridget Blue
Denes

Brilliant
BlueM, Mtato

chinensis
Caves, Woodl

Fasan
Denes

Freudenstein
Parva

heteromalla
Caves

immaculata
CottP, Woodl

indo-chinensis
Caves, Hackf

japonica macrosepela
TopTr

macrophylla Alpengluhen
(Alpen Glow)
Denes, Pukho

macrophylla Ayesha
BayBl, Hackf, Kayd,
Parva, Wells

macrophylla Blaumeise
(Blue Meise)
Denes, Parva, Pukho

macrophylla Blue Prince
CottP, Denes, Woodl

macrophylla Blue Wave
BayBl, BlueM, CottP,
Denes, Hackf, Kayd,
Pukho, TRidg, Wells

macrophylla Bodensee
Denes, Pukho

macrophylla Generale
Vicomtesse de Vibraye
Woodl

macrophylla Geoffrey
Chadbund
CottP, Denes, Mtato,
Pukho, TopTr

macrophylla Heinrich
Seidel
BlueM, Pukho

macrophylla Holstein
Denes, Pukho, Woodl

macrophylla Lanarth
White
BlueM, CottP, TopTr

macrophylla Libelle
CottP, Denes, Parva,
Pukho, Trans

macrophylla Maculata
BayBl

macrophylla Maculata
Variegata
BayBl, Denes

macrophylla Masja
Wells

macrophylla Mathilda
Gutges
CottP, Denes

macrophylla nigra
BayBl, Caves, Hackf

macrophylla Parzifal
Woodl

macrophylla Pia
BayBl, BlueM

macrophylla Quadricolour
Taunt

macrophylla Sensation
Pukho

macrophylla Silver Slipper
(Ayesha)
CottP

macrophylla Todi
BlueM, Mtato

macrophylla Tosca
BayBl, BlueM, Mtato,
TRidg

macrophylla Tricolor
BlueM

macrophylla White Swan
Kayd, Wells

macrophylla White Wave
CottP, Pukho, TopTr,
TRidg

Madam Bardsee
CottP

maritima Seafoam
Woodl

microphylla coerulea
CottP

Mrs Kumiko
BayBl, Parva, Wells

Mrs Neal
Woodl

Muche
CottP, Denes

Nightingale (Nachtigall)
BayBl, JoyPl, Woodl

nigrens
TopTr

paniculata (Japanese Hydrangea)
Caves, CottP, Denes, JoyPl, Peele, Taunt

paniculata Grandiflora (PeeGee Hydrangea)
BayBl, Caves, CottP, Denes, Hackf, JoyPl, Parva, Pukho, TopTr

paniculata Grandiflora Viridus
Denes

paniculata Kyushu
BayBl, BlueM, Caves, Taunt, TopTr, Woodl

paniculata Praecox
Woodl

paniculata Tardiva
Denes

petiolaris now annomala petiolaris
BlueM, Denes, JoyPl, Taunt, Woodl

Piamina
CottP

Preziosa
BlueM, CottP, Denes, Hackf, Mtato, Pukho, Taunt, TopTr, Woodl, YakuN

quercifolia (Oak Leafed Hydrangea)
Ashto, BlueM, Caves, CottP, Denes, Hackf, Pukho, TopTr

quercifolia Snow Flake
Woodl

quercifolia Snow Queen
CottP, Denes, JoyPl, Kayd, Parva, Pukho, Taunt, Wells

robusta
BlueM, Woodl

sargentii
Hackf

scandens
Caves

seemanii
Hackf, TopTr

serrata Grayswood
BayBl, Caves, CottP, Pukho, TopTr, Trans, Woodl

serratifolia (Climbing Hydrangea)
CouCl

unnamed (like Dichroa)
Caves

villosa
Caves, CottP, Denes, Hackf, JoyPl, Kayd, Woodl

Zaunkonig
CottP, Denes

Hydriastele

douglasiana
Reic #

Hydrocotyle

asiatica now Centella a.
Sweet

bonariensis (Giant Pennywort)
WilAq

elongata
Orati

leucocephala (Pennywort)
Diack

moschata
Orati

Snowflake
Orati

Hydrosme

rivieri (Voodoo Plant)
LakeN

Hygrophila

augustifolia (Blue Hygrophila)
Diack, WaiMa, WilAq

corymbosa (Temple Plant)
WaiMa, WilAq

difformis (Water Wisteria)
Diack, WaiMa, WilAq

polysperma
WaiMa

polysperma variegata
WaiMa

roseafolia (Red Hygrophila
WaiMa

Hymenanthera

obovata now Melicytus o.
BlueM, Diack

Hymenocallis

calathina
BayBl, Kayd

Hymenosporum

flavum (Australian Frangipani)
Chedd, Coatv, Denes, Reic #, SpecT, TopTr

Gold Nugget
Frans

Hyophorbe

verschaffeltia
Reic #

Hypericum

balearicum
KeriP

calycinum (Aaron's Beard, Creeping St J W)
BlueM

cerastioides (Prostrate Goldflower)
BayBl, BlueM, Pgeon

Golden Globe
Parva

Hidcote Gold
BlueM

kelleri
BayBl, Pgeon

leschenaultii
BlueM

x moserianum Tricolor (v)
BlueM

olympicum (St Johns Wort)
CottP

olympicum Citrinum
BayBl, BlueM

orientale
Pgeon

perforatum (St Johns Wort
Della, Mills, Sweet

polyphyllum now olympicum
Looij

Sungold now kouytchense
Mtato, Ormon

tetrapterum
Diack, WaiMa

Xanadu
BayBl

yakusimense
Otepo

Hypocalymma

cordifolium Golden Veil
MatNu, Wells

Hypoestes

Confetti series
Reic #

Hypoxis

stellata
CottP

stellata alba
BayBl, CottP

villosa
NewlR

Hyssopus

officinalis (Hyssop)
CoFlo, Della, King #, Marsh, MillH, Mills, Orang, Sweet

officinalis albus
Marsh, Sweet

officinalis roseus
CoFlo, Marsh, Mills, Sweet, TRidg

Iberis

amara (Hyacinth Flowered Iberis)
King #

gibraltarica
MaraN

sempervirens (Candytuft)
BayBl, Della, MaraN, Oasis, Pgeon, Seasd, Telfa

sempervirens Little Gem
Marsh, Otepo

sempervirens Snowflake
King #, MillH

umbellata Dwarf Fairy mixed
King #

umbellata Flash mixed
King #

umbellata White Flash
King #

Idesia

polycarpa (Chinese Wonder Tree)
Burbk, Chedd, Coatv, Dove, Peele, PuhaN, Reic #, YakuN

polycarpa female
Denes

polycarpa male
Denes

Ilex

x altaclerensis Golden King (v) (Golden Holly)
BlueM, Dove

x altaclerensis Hendersonii
BlueM, Denes

x altaclerensis Lawsoniana (v)
BlueM

aquifolium (English Holly)
BlueM, Chedd, Denes, NZtr #, SelGr

aquifolium Angustifolia
BlueM, TRidg

aquifolium Bacciflava was Fructu Luteo (Yellowfruited Holly)
BlueM

aquifolium Crispa Aureopicta
BlueM

aquifolium Flavescens (Moonlight Holly)
BlueM

aquifolium Handsworth New Silver (v)
BlueM, TopTr

aquifolium JC van Tol (v)
BlueM, TopTr

aquifolium Madame Briot (v)
BlueM, Chedd

aquifolium Silver Milkboy (v)
BlueM, Denes

aquifolium Silver Milkmaid (v)
Chedd

cornuta (Chinese Holly)
LanSc

cornuta Rotunda
Ormon

crenata Convexa
BlueM, SelGr, TopTr

crenata Golden Gem
BlueM

crenata Helleri
TRidg

crenata Mariesii
BlueM

dimorphophylla
Caves, Hackf

insignis now kingiana
Woodl

x meserveae Blue Angel
Woodl

x meserveae Blue Prince
Woodl

perado
Woodl

perado platyphylla (Canary Is Holly)
Denes

Illicium

anisatum (Star Anise)
TopTr, Woodl, YakuN

floridanum
MJury

henryi
MJury

majus
Woodl

Impatiens

Deco F1 Hybrids
Reic #

New Guinea Hybrids mixed
Manna

Imperata

cylindrica Rubra was Red Baron (Japanese Blood Grass)
KeriP, Peak

Incarvillea

arguta
Telfa

delavayi (Hardy Gloxinia, Chinese Trumpet Flower)
AynDa, Della, MaraN, Marsh, Oasis, Pgeon, Telfa, Vall #

delavayi alba
Parva, Warwk

sinensis Cheron
Dream

Indigofera

australis (Australian/False Indigo)
NZtr #, Reic #

decora (Chinese Indigo)
Denes, Mtato, NewlR, Telfa, Trans

tinctoria (Indigo)
Sweet

Inga

edulis
Frans

Inga Bean
Koan

Inula

ensifolia
CoFlo, MaraN, MillH

ensifolia Compacta
Pgeon

helenium (Elecampagne)
Della, Dream, MaraN, Mills, MTig #, Orang, Sweet

hookeri
Pgeon, Telfa

magnifica
CoFlo, KeriP, MaraN, Mills, Nikau, Vall #, Warwk

orientalis was I.glandulosa
MaraN, Oasis, Sweet

racemosa
MaraN

royleana
MaraN

sp dwarf
Orang

Iochroma

cyanea
Frans

fuschioides
AynDa

violacea   now Cestrum v.
AynDa

Ipheion

dialystemon
DaffA

Rolf Fiedler
DaffA

sellowianun
DaffA, JoyPl

uniflorum (Spring Star Flower)
CottP, MaraN, NewlR, VanEe

uniflorum album
BayBl, DaffA

uniflorum Froyle Mill
DaffA, JoyPl, Kerer, Parva

uniflorum whitefl w blue stripe
CottP, JoyPl

uniflorum Wisley Blue
DaffA, JoyPl, Kayd, Telfa

Ipomoea

alba (White Moonflower, Annual)
AynDa, King #

aquatica (Water Spinach)
King #

aquatica Bamboo Leaves
King #

cairica   was palmata
CouCl, Orati

imperialis
AynDa

imperialis Purple
King #

imperialis Smile brown/white
King #

imperialis Smile series
King #

imperialis White
King #

noctiflora (Small Purple Moonflower)
King #

palmata now cairica
CouCl

purpurea mixed (Morning Glory -heirloom)
King #

tricolour (Morning Glory)
King #

Ipomopsis

rubra (Standing Cypress, Skyrocket, Texas Plume)
King #

Iresine

herbstii (Blood Leaf)
KeriP, LakeN

herbstii Aureoreticulata
KeriP

herbstii lindenii formosa
LakeN

Iris

varieties
Roswd

attica
NewlR

bucharica
BayBl, DaffA, Kayd, Kerer

bucharica Moon Nymph
KeriP

bulleyana
WaiMa

chrysographes
Della, NewlR, Otepo, RosPl, TRidg, WaiMa

chrysographes Black form
Ashto

chrysographes sdlg fr dk red form
TRidg

confusa Martin Rix
Peak

cristata
Ashto, BayBl, NewlR, Otepo, RosPl, Telfa

cristata alba
NewlR, Telfa

danfordiae
Altrf, DaffA, Kerer

delavayi
RosPl

delavayi hybrids
Otepo

douglasiana
Hackf, Otepo, TRidg

douglasiana dwarf form
BayBl, NewlR, Otepo

douglasiana hyb mixed
Otepo

douglasiana hyb white
Otepo

douglasiana hyb yellow
Otepo

evansia (possibly wattii)
Richm

foetidissima variegata
Diack, Otepo

forrestii
Ashto, AynDa, Della,
NewlR, TRidg

Gerald Darby (hybrid)
BayBl

**germanica var florentina
(Orris Root)**
Sweet

**Gordon (bakeriana x
Cantab)**
DaffA

gracilipes
BayBl, Marsh, NewlR,
Otepo, Telfa

gracilipes alba
Della

gracilipes mauve
Della

graminea
BayBl, NewlR, Otepo,
Telfa, TRidg

histrioides George
DaffA

histrioides Major
Kerer

**Holden Clough -
pseudacorus**
Puket, WaiMa

hyacinthus
NewlR

innominata
BayBl, KeriP, Otepo,
Telfa

innominata bronze
TRidg

innominata Burgundy
Nikau

innominata Cream
Egmon

innominata Dark Purple
Nikau

**innominata
Gold&Mahogany**
Nikau

innominata Lavender
Pgeon

**innominata Lavender
Butterfly**
NewlR

innominata Lemon
Nikau, TRidg

innominata Lilac
Nikau

innominata mauve
Telfa

innominata mixed incl pink
TRidg

**innominata Pacific Coast
Hybrid**
NewlR

innominata pale blue
TRidg

innominata plum&gold
NewlR

innominata pure white
NewlR

innominata Purple
Egmon

innominata yellow
Telfa

japonica
BayBl, Herit, Wells

japonica variegata
Ashto, BayBl, Herit,
Otepo

juncea
Kerer

**kaempferi   now ensata
mixed**
Ashto

**Katherine Hodgkin
(histrioides Major x
winogradowii)**
DaffA

kerneriana
NewlR

lactea
Otepo, TRidg

laevigata
WaiMa, WilAq

laevigata Alba
Ranch

laevigata Jester's Motley
Herit

laevigata maroon
Telfa

laevigata Regal
Ranch

**laevigata Rose Queen
(laev.x ensata) now ensata
RQ**
WaiMa, WilAq

latifolia (English Iris)
Kerer

lutescens   was chamaeiris
NewlR

magnifica
Kerer, TRidg

mellita
Della, NewlR

milesii
AynDa, KeriP, Mills

milesii (C&Mc357)
MaraN

minuto-aurea
BayBl, NewlR, Otepo

nepalensis
MaraN

Nobody's Child
Otepo

notha
TRidg

orientalis   was ochroleuca
Mills

pallida (Orris Root)
Mills

pallida argentea variegata
Otepo

pallida Variegata
MaraN, MillH

prismatica
Otepo

**pseudacorus (Yellow Flag
Iris)**
Herit, Richm, Waihi,
WaiMa, WriWa

pseudacorus Alba
Taunt

pseudacorus Flora Plena
WaiMa

**pseudacorus hybrid Holden
Clough**
Puket

**pseudacorus hybrid Roy
Davidson**
Herit, Puket, Ranch

pseudacorus hybrids
WilAq

**pseudacorus Sulphur
Queen (Bastardii)**
WaiMa, WilAq

pseudacorus Variegatus
WriWa

pumila attica   now I.attica
NewlR

reticulata
DaffA, Parva

reticulata Cantab
  Kerer
reticulata Clairette
  Kerer
reticulata Edward
  Parva
reticulata Harmony
  DaffA, Kerer, VanEe
reticulata Hercules
  DaffA
reticulata Jeannine
  DaffA
reticulata Joyce
  Altrf, DaffA, Parva
reticulata JS Dijt
  DaffA, Kerer
reticulata Kath Hodgkin
  Kerer
reticulata Natascha
  DaffA
reticulata Pauline
  DaffA
reticulata Purple Gem
  DaffA
reticulata Royal Blue
  DaffA
reticulata Springtime
  DaffA, Kerer
reticulata Violet Beauty
  Kerer
reticulata Wentworth
  DaffA
Roy Davidson -
pseudacorus
  Puket
setosa
  Pgeon, TRidg, WilAq
setosa Alaskan Form
  BayBl
setosa canadensis
  Herew, Marsh
setosa Himalayan Form
  Peak
setosa Kirigamine
  BayBl
setosa variegata
  JoyPl
setosa x (larger)
  RosPl
sibirica :separate list later
  Ref

sindpers (sindjarensis x persica)
  DaffA, Kerer
sintenisii
  Otepo
spuria notha
  MaraN
spuria ssp musselmanica
  Pgeon
stylosa now inguicularis
  Parva, Trans
stylosa White
  Parva
tectorum
  NewlR, Otepo, Pgeon
tectorum Alba
  Otepo
tenax
  Otepo, TRidg
tenax Alba
  TRidg
tristus
  Della
unguicularis was stylosa
  Ashto, Hackf, MaraN, Trans
versicolor (Blue Flag Iris)
  Richm, WilAq, WriWa
virginica
  BayBl, Herit, Ranch, WilAq
winogradowii
  DaffA, Kerer

Iris Bearded

varieties (Dwarf)
  Herew
Aachen Elf (Mini Tall)
  RosPl
Abridged Version (Mini Tall)
  RosPl
Academy Awards (Tall)
  Puket
Acclamation (Tall)
  Richm
Admiralty (Tall)
  Puket
Adobe Rose (Tall)
  Puket
Afaire Affluence (Tall)
  Herit
Affinity (Intermediate)
  Herit

After Hours (Tall)
  Puket
Afternoon Delight (Tall)
  Herit
Alice Goodman (Tall)
  Herit
All Aglow (Tall)
  Kopua
All Right (Intermediate)
  Herit
All That Jazz (Tall)
  Herit
Allez Rouge (Intermediate)
  RosPl
Alluring (Tall)
  Herit
Almaden (Tall)
  Herit
Alpine Journey (Tall)
  Herit
Alpine Lake (Mini Dwarf)
  RosPl
Altruist (Tall)
  Herit
Am I Blue (Border)
  Herit, Puket, RosPl
Amazon Princess (Dwarf)
  BayBl, Kopua, Richm
Amber Snow (Tall)
  Herit
America's Cup (Tall)
  Herit
American Beauty (Tall)
  Puket
American Sweetheart (Tall)
  Herit
Amethyst Flame (Tall)
  Richm
Amigos Guitar (Tall)
  Richm
And Royal (Tall)
  Herit
Andi (Intermediate)
  RosPl
Angel Music (Dwarf)
  Richm
Angelico (Mini Tall)
  Richm
Angels Kiss (Dwarf)
  Richm, RosPl

Anjaya (Dwarf)
Herit
Ann Elizabeth (Dwarf)
Kopua, RosPl
Ann Shaver (Tall)
Herit, Puket
Anna (Dwarf)
BayBl
Anna Belle Babson (Tall)
Herit
Annie's Dress (Dwarf)
Herit
Anoka Angel (Dwarf)
RosPl
Antique Satin (Dwarf)
RosPl
Apollo's Touch (Intermed)
Herit
Apollodorus (Tall)
Herit
Apple Blossom Pink (Int)
Kopua, Richm, RosPl
Approval (Tall)
Herit
Apricot
Mills
Apricot (dwarf)
Ashto
Apricot Drift (Border)
RosPl
April Accent (Mini Dwf)
Kopua
April Ballet (Dwarf)
Seasd
April Elation (Dwarf)
Herit
April Flirt (Mini Dwarf)
RosPl
April Fog (Intermediate)
Herit, Richm
April Frost (Mini Dwarf)
RosPl
April Rose (Mini Dwarf)
RosPl
Arabi Treasure
(Intermediate)
Ashto, Richm
Arctic Mist
(Intermediate)
Richm
Ardor (Tall)
Herit

Arohanui (Tall)
Kopua
Art Form (Tall)
Herit
Art Gallery
(Intermediate)
Herit
Ashanti (Dwarf)
Herit
Ask Alma (Intermediate)
Herit, RosPl
Atonement (Tall)
Herit
Aurean (Intermediate)
Herit
Auric (Tall)
Herit
Autograph (Tall)
Herit
Autumn Heiress (Tall)
Richm
Avanelle (Intermediate)
Herit, Puket, RosPl
Az Ap (Intermediate)
Herit, Richm, RosPl
Aztec Burst (Tall)
Herit
Aztec Princess (Dwarf)
Puket
Aztec Star (Dwarf)
Kopua, RosPl
Aztec Sun (Tall)
Herit
Azure Angel (Tall)
Herit
Azure Apogee (Tall)
Richm
Azure Echo
(Intermediate)
Kopua, Richm
Azure Lustre (Tall)
Herit
Azurite (Tall)
Puket
Babbling Brook (Tall)
Richm
Babe (Mini Dwarf)
Richm
Baby Kid (Mini Dwarf)
RosPl
Baby Pink (Mini Dwarf)
RosPl

Baby Tears (Dwarf)
Kopua, RosPl
Baby Tiger (Mini Dwarf)
RosPl
Baghdad Boy (Dwarf)
Herit
Bahloo (Tall)
Herit
Ballerina Blue (Tall)
Herit
Banbury Ruffles (Dwarf)
BayBl, Kopua, NewlR,
Richm, RosPl
Barn Stormer (Dwarf)
Kopua, NewlR, Puket,
Richm, RosPl
Dashful Bride (Tall)
Herit
Batik (Border)
Richm
Battle Shout
(Intermediate)
RosPl
Bay Ruffles (Dwarf)
Herit
Bayberry Candle (Tall)
Kopua, Puket
Be A Devil (Tall)
Herit
Beach Girl (Tall)
Herit
Beacon Dream (Tall)
Herit
Beau (Dwarf)
Kopua, Richm, RosPl
Beauty Mark (Dwarf)
RosPl, Seasd
Beauty Spot (Mini
Dwarf)
KeriP, RosPl
Bedazzled (Dwarf)
BayBl, Kopua
Bee Wings (Mini Dwarf)
RosPl
Beebop (Intermediate)
Kopua, Richm
Beguine (Tall)
Herit
Behold A Lady (Tall)
Herit
Belle Plaine (Dwarf)
RosPl

Bengal Tiger   (Tall)
Herit

Bernice Row   (Tall)
Herit

Berry Flush   (Tall)
Herit

Berry Parfait
(Intermediate)
Kopua, Puket, Richm

Berry Sherbert   (Tall)
Herit

Berta B   (Tall)
Kopua

Bettina   (Mini Tall)
Richm, RosPl

Betty Emons   (Mini
Dwarf)
RosPl

Betty Simon   (Tall)
Kopua

Betty Wood   (Dwarf)
Richm

Beverley Sills   (Tall)
Herit, Puket, Richm

Beyond   (Tall)
Herit

Bibery   (Dwarf)
Richm

Billowing Sails   (Tall)
Richm

Bimini   (Intermediate)
Herit

Bink   (Mini Dwarf)
RosPl

Binnie   (Intermediate)
Kopua, RosPl

Bird Dancer
(Intermediate)
Richm

Bisbee   (Dwarf)
Herit

Bit O' Paradise   (Border)
RosPl

Bit Of Sky   (Dwarf)
Richm

Black Dragon   (Tall)
Herit

Black Fantasy   (Tall)
Herit

Black Flag   (Tall)
Richm

Black Forest   (Border)
RosPl

Black Hawk   (Border)
Richm, RosPl

Black Hills Gold   (Tall)
Herit

Black Lady   (Mini Tall)
RosPl

Black Star   (Dwarf)
Herit

Black Swan   (Tall)
Puket, Richm

Black Watch
(Intermediate)
Kopua, Richm, RosPl

Blackberry Brandy
(Interm)
Herit

Blackout   (Tall)
Herit

Blended Blue   (Mini
Dwarf)
RosPl

Blending Moods   (Tall)
Herit

Blenheim Royal   (Tall)
Herit

Bloodstone   (Dwarf)
RosPl

Blue Aristocrat   (Tall)
Herit

Blue Ballet   (Tall)
Herit

Blue Beret   (Mini Dwarf)
NewlR, Richm

Blue Birds Song (Intermed)
Kopua, Puket, Richm

Blue Calico
(Intermediate)
Herit

Blue Canary   (Mini
Dwarf)
Richm

Blue Chip Pink   (Tall)
Herit

Blue Chrome   (Dwarf)
RosPl

Blue Denim   (Dwarf)
NewlR

Blue Dimples   (Mini
Dwarf)
RosPl

Blue Doll   (Dwarf)
RosPl

Blue Eyed Blonde
(Intermed)
Herit

Blue Frost   (Mini Dwarf)
RosPl

Blue Glory
(Intermediate)
Herit

Blue Gloss   (Tall)
Herit

Blue Moss   (Dwarf)
RosPl

Blue Mountains   (Tall)
Richm

Blue Neon   (Dwarf)
Herit, RosPl

Blue Pools   (Dwarf)
Kopua, Ormon, RosPl

Blue Puff   (Dwarf)
Puket, Richm, RosPl

Blue Secret   (Dwarf)
Richm

Blue Staccato   (Tall)
Herit, Richm

Blue Trinket   (Dwarf)
RosPl

Blue Twinkle   (Mini Tall)
RosPl

Blue Vision
(Intermediate)
Kopua, Richm, RosPl

Blue Wind   (Mini Dwarf)
RosPl

Bluebird In Flight
(Intermed)
Herit

Bluebird Wine   (Tall)
Herit

Blueline   (Dwarf)
Herit

Blues Brother   (Tall)
Herit, Puket

Blues Singer   (Tall)
Herit

Bluetween   (Mini Dwarf)
RosPl

Bodacious   (Tall)
Herit

Bodderlecker   (Dwarf)
RosPl

Bogota   (Tall)
Herit

Bonnie Lassie (Intermediate)
Richm

Bonus (Intermediate)
Kopua, RosPl

Bonus Mama (Tall)
Herit

Boo (Dwarf)
BayBl, Kopua, Puket

Boogie Man (Tall)
Herit

Bordello (Tall)
Herit, Kopua

Border Bandit (Intermediate)
Herit

Border Joy (Intermediate)
RosPl

Border Pearl (Intermediate)
RosPl

Born Royal (Mini Dwarf)
RosPl

Boss Tweed (Tall)
Herit

Bountiful Harvest (Tall)
Herit

Boy Friend (Tall)
Herit

Buy O Boy (Intermediate)
Herit

Boy Scout (Border)
Richm

Brandy (Tall)
Herit

Brass Accent (Tall)
Richm

Brass Button (Mini Dwarf)
RosPl

Brass Rings (Dwarf)
Kopua, Puket, Richm

Brassie Lass (Intermediate)
Richm

Brave Viking (Tall)
Puket

Bravita (Dwarf)
RosPl

Break The Ice (Tall)
Herit

Breakers (Tall)
Herit, Puket

Breezes (Tall)
Herit

Bricky (Mini Dwarf)
RosPl

Bridal Fashion (Tall)
Herit

Brides Halo (Tall)
Kopua

Brides Pearls (Border)
Puket, Richm

Brief Encounter (Border)
Puket, Richm

Bright Baby (Mini Dwarf)
Richm

Bright Dawn (Dwarf)
Kopua, RosPl

Bright Delight (Dwarf)
Richm

Bright Herald (Tall)
Kopua

Bright Ruffles (Intermediate)
Richm

Bright Spot (Mini Dwarf)
NewlR, RosPl

Bright Vision (Dwarf)
Herit, RosPl

Bright Yellow (Intermediate)
Ashto

Brighten Up (Intermediate)
Herit

Brimstone (Tall)
Herit

Brindisi (Tall)
Kopua, Richm

British Blue (Dwarf)
RosPl

Broad Grin (Dwarf)
Herit, Kopua, RosPl

Bronze Babe (Dwarf)
RosPl

Brother Carl (Tall)
Herit

Brown Doll (Intermediate)
Kopua, Richm

Brown Imp (Mini Dwarf)
RosPl

Brown Lasso (Border)
Herit, Kopua, Richm, RosPl

Brown Spectacle (Dwarf)
RosPl

Bubble Up (Tall)
Herit

Bubbly Blue (Intermediate)
Herit

Bubbly Mood (Tall)
Herit

Buddha Song (Mini Dwarf)
RosPl

Bunnica (Intermediate)
Herit

Bunny Hop (Dwarf)
Herit

Burgundy Brown (Tall)
Kopua, Puket, Richm

Burgundy Bubbles (Tall)
Herit

Burgundy Cherry (Tall)
Puket

Burst (Tall)
Herit

Busy Bee (Mini Dwarf)
Richm

Busy Child (Mini Dwarf)
RosPl

Butter Ball (Dwarf)
RosPl

Butter Girl (Border)
RosPl

Butter Pecan (Intermediate)
Richm

Buttercup Bower (Tall)
Kopua

Buttercup Brite (Mini Dwarf)
RosPl

Buttercup Charm (Mini Dwf)
Richm, RosPl

Butterfly Boy (Intermediate)
RosPl

Butterscotch Frills (Intermed)
Richm

By Night (Tall)
Puket

155

Byword   (Dwarf)
NewlR, Richm, RosPl

Cabaret Royale   (Tall)
Herit

Cable Car   (Tall)
Herit, Puket

Caesura   (Dwarf)
RosPl

Café Society   (Tall)
Herit

**Calico Cat
(Intermediate)**
Herit

Caliente   (Tall)
Puket, Richm

**California Style
(Intermediate)**
Herit

**Calling Card
(Intermediate)**
Herit

Camelot Rose   (Tall)
Kopua, Puket

Cameo Wine   (Tall)
Herit, Puket

**Canary Baby   (Mini
Dwarf)**
RosPl

Canary Isle   (Dwarf)
Richm

Candy Apple   (Dwarf)
Kopua, Richm, RosPl

Candylane   (Mini Tall)
RosPl

Capricorn Cooler   (Tall)
Herit

Captains Joy   (Tall)
Richm

Caption   (Tall)
Herit

Car Hop   (Dwarf)
RosPl

Caracas   (Tall)
Herit

Caramel Candy   (Dwarf)
Kopua, Richm

Caribbean Dream   (Tall)
Herit

Carnaby   (Tall)
Kopua, Richm

Carol Lee   (Mini Tall)
RosPl

**Caroline Charmer
(Intermed)**
RosPl

Carolyn Rose   (Mini Tall)
Richm, RosPl

Carouselle Belle   (Dwarf)
Richm

**Carouselle Princess
(Dwarf)**
Richm

Carriage Trade   (Tall)
Herit

Carrot Curls   (Dwarf)
RosPl

Carved Cameo   (Tall)
Herit

**Cascade Blue
(Intermediate)**
RosPl

Cascade Pass   (Tall)
Herit

Cascadian Skies   (Tall)
Herit

Casey Jill   (Dwarf)
RosPl

Cat Nap   (Intermediate)
Herit

**Catalumya
(Intermediate)**
Herit

Catalyst   (Tall)
Herit, Richm

Catani   (Dwarf)
RosPl

Cayenne Capers   (Tall)
Kopua, Puket

Cayenne Pepper   (Tall)
Herit

Cedar Crest   (Tall)
Puket

Celestial Ballet   (Tall)
Herit

Celtic Prince   (Tall)
Herit

Centre Court   (Tall)
Herit

Centricity   (Dwarf)
RosPl

Chalkmark   (Dwarf)
RosPl

Chambray   (Mini Tall)
Richm

**Champagne Elegance
(Tall)**
Herit, Kopua, Richm

Champagne Taste   (Tall)
Herit

Change Of Pace   (Tall)
Herit

Chanted   (Dwarf)
Herit

Chapter   (Intermediate)
Herit

Charmaine   (Tall)
Richm

Charmed Circle   (Tall)
Herit

Charro   (Tall)
Richm

**Chatterbox
(Intermediate)**
RosPl

Cheerful One   (Tall)
Herit

Cheers   (Intermediate)
Kopua, Richm, RosPl

**Cherie Amour
(Intermediate)**
RosPl

Cherry   (Intermediate)
Herit

Cherry Cola   (Dwarf)
RosPl

Cherry Doll   (Dwarf)
Herit

Cherry Float   (Dwarf)
Kopua, RosPl

Cherry Garden   (Dwarf)
NewlR, Richm, RosPl

**Cherry Halo   (Mini
Dwarf)**
RosPl

**Cherry Lavender
(Dwarf)**
Kopua, NewlR, Richm,
RosPl

Cherry Pop   (Dwarf)
Ashto, Kopua, Richm

Cherry Spot   (Dwarf)
NewlR

Cherry Tart   (Dwarf)
BayBl, RosPl

Cherrywood   (Dwarf)
RosPl

Cherub Tears   (Dwarf)
RosPl

Chian Wine (Mini Tall)
Kopua, RosPl
Chickee (Mini Tall)
RosPl
Chico Maid (Tall)
Herit
Chinese Empress (Tall)
Herit
Chocolate Fish (Dwarf)
Parva
Chocolate Royale (Tall)
Herit, Puket
Chocolate Vanilla (Tall)
Herit
Chosen One (Tall)
Herit
Christa (Tall)
Herit
Christianne (Tall)
Kopua, Richm
Christmas Angel (Tall)
Puket
Chromeling (Mini Dwarf)
RosPl
Chubby Cheeks (Dwarf)
Herit, Richm
Chuckles (Tall)
Herit, Richm
Churchill Downs (Tall)
Herit
Cimarron Rose (Dwarf)
Herit
Cimmaron Strip (Tall)
Kopua
Cinnaman Gold (Border)
Richm
Circlette (Dwarf)
Kopua, Puket, Richm,
RosPl
Citron Creme (Tall)
Richm
Classic Look (Tall)
Herit
Classic Treasure
(Intermed)
Herit
Classy Babe (Dwarf)
Herit
Clique (Intermediate)
Kopua, Richm, RosPl
Close Your Eyes (Tall)
Herit

Cloud Capers (Tall)
Kopua
Cloud Fire (Tall)
Herit
Cloudburst (Tall)
Herit
Clouded Dreams (Tall)
Herit
Cloudless Sunrise (Tall)
Richm
Clouds Adrift (Tall)
Herit
Coal Bucket (Dwarf)
Puket
Coffee Capri (Tall)
Kopua, Puket
Coffee Klatch (Tall)
Herit
Colette (Tall)
Herit
Collage (Tall)
Herit
Colortart (Tall)
Herit
Colour Page (Tall)
Herit
Columbia Blue (Tall)
Richm
Combo (Dwarf)
Kopua, RosPl
Comfy Cozy (Dwarf)
RosPl
Comma (Dwarf)
Herit
Commencement (Mini
Dwarf)
RosPl
Como Surprise (Tall)
Kopua
Con Brio (Intermediate)
Ashto, Kopua, Richm,
RosPl
Conch Call (Tall)
Herit
Concord Torch (Dwarf)
RosPl
Confederate Soldier (Int.)
Kopua, RosPl
Confession (Tall)
Herit
Congo Wine (Dwarf)
RosPl

Congratulations (Tall)
Herit
Conjuration (Tall)
Herit
Consummation (Mini
Tall)
RosPl
Contempo (Tall)
Richm
Convention (Tall)
Kopua, Richm
Cool Satin (Dwarf)
Herit
Cool Stepper
(Intermediate)
Herit
Copper Capers (Tall)
Richm
Copper Glaze
(Intermediate)
Herit
Cora Band (Tall)
Kopua, Puket
Coral Chalice (Tall)
Puket
Coral Joy (Tall)
Richm
Corn Harvest (Tall)
Herit
Cotton Blossom (Dwarf)
RosPl
Cotton Tail (Mini
Dwarf)
Richm
Country Deejay
(Intermed.)
RosPl
Country Manor (Tall)
Richm
Court Magician (Dwarf)
BayBl
Crackles (Intermediate)
Herit, Puket
Craftsman (Tall)
Kopua, Richm
Crafty Lady
(Intermediate)
Herit
Cranberry Crush (Tall)
Herit
Cranberry Ice (Tall)
Kopua, Puket

Cream Cake (Dwarf)
Herit, Richm

Cream Frills (Intermediate)
Richm

Cream Tart (Mini Dwarf)
RosPl

Creative Stitchery (Tall)
Herit

Creme d'Or (Tall)
Herit, Kopua, Puket

Creme Lady (Mini Tall)
RosPl

Crimson Snow (Tall)
Herit

Crimson Velvet (Dwarf)
RosPl

Crispy (Mini Dwarf)
RosPl

Critic (Tall)
Herit

Crownette (Dwarf)
Herit

Crushed Velvet (Tall)
Herit

Crystal Bright (Dwarf)
Kopua, Parva, Richm, RosPl, Seasd

Crystal Glitters (Tall)
Herit

Crystalyn (Tall)
Herit

Cuban Cutie (Dwarf)
Herit, RosPl

Cumquat (Intermediate)
Kopua, RosPl

Cup And Saucer (Mini Dwarf)
RosPl

Cup Cake (Mini Dwarf)
RosPl

Cup Race (Tall)
Richm

Cupid's Arrow (Tall)
Herit

Cups of Cream (Dwarf)
RosPl

Curacao (Intermediate)
Herit

Curio (Mini Dwarf)
RosPl

Curtsey (Mini Dwarf)
Richm

Cycles (Tall)
Herit, Puket

Dache Model (Dwarf)
RosPl

Dainty Belle (Mini Dwarf)
RosPl

Dainty Terry (Dwarf)
Richm

Dainty Toddler (Dwarf)
RosPl

Daiquiri (Intermediate)
Herit

Dance Man (Tall)
Herit

Dance Master (Tall)
Herit

Dancers Veil (Tall)
Kopua

Dancin' (Intermediate)
RosPl

Dancing Beauty (Tall)
Kopua, Richm

Dancing Bee (Dwarf)
Richm

Dancing Eyes (Dwarf)
NewlR, Richm

Dancing Fairy (Border)
Puket

Dandelion (Intermediate)
Richm

Dare Devil (Tall)
Herit

Dark Blizzard (Intermediate)
Herit

Dark Eden (Intermediate)
Kopua, Richm

Dark Fairy (Dwarf)
Richm

Dark Note Dewberry (Mini Dwarf)
RosPl

Dark Opal (Dwarf)
Puket

Dark Side (Tall)
Herit, Puket

Dark Star (Dwarf)
RosPl

Dark Vader (Dwarf)
BayBl, Herit, RosPl

Date Bait (Tall)
Herit

Dawn Sky (Tall)
Herit

Dazzling Blue (Dwarf)
RosPl

Dazzling Gold (Tall)
Herit

Dear Love (Dwarf)
NewlR, Richm, Seasd

Deep Lavender (Dwarf)
Kopua

Deet (Dwarf)
RosPl

Deft Touch (Tall)
Herit

Delicate Air (Dwarf)
Kopua, Richm

Delicate Pink (Dwarf)
Herit, RosPl

Deloris Clark (Tall)
Herit

Demon (Dwarf)
Richm, RosPl

Desert Echo (Tall)
Herit

Desert Lark (Tall)
Herit

Designer Gown (Tall)
Herit

Devil's Riot (Tall)
Herit

Dialogue (Tall)
Kopua, Richm

Diana Mite (Mini Tall)
RosPl

Dilly Dilly (Intermediate)
RosPl

Dinger (Intermediate)
Kopua, Puket

Disco Jewel (Intermediate)
Herit

Distant Fire (Tall)
Herit

Ditto (Mini Dwarf)
Puket, RosPl

Divine Duchess (Tall)
Herit

Dixie Pixie (Dwarf)
RosPl

Do-Si-Do (Dwarf)
RosPl

Doll Pretty
(Intermediate)
RosPl

Doll Ribbons (Mini Tall)
RosPl

Dot (Dwarf)
Herit

Dot & Dash (Tall)
Puket

Dottie Joy (Mini Tall)
RosPl

Double Lament (Dwarf)
BayBl, Richm, RosPl

Doublemint (Tall)
Herit

Dove Wings (Dwarf)
Richm, RosPl

Dragon Baby (Dwarf)
Kopua, RosPl

Dragon Slayer (Dwarf)
RosPl

Drake's Bay (Tall)
Herit

Dream Star (Dwarf)
RosPl

Dreamchild (Dwarf)
NewlR

Dreams Adrift (Dwarf)
RosPl

Dresden Candleglow (Int.)
RosPl

Dresden Green (Tall)
Herit

Drummer Boy
(Intermediate)
RosPl

Duke Of Earl (Tall)
Herit

Dunaverty (Tall)
Richm

Dunlin (Mini Dwarf)
RosPl

Dunngarees (Tall)
Herit

Duranus (Tall)
Herit

Dusky Bluebeard
(Dwarf)
Richm

Dusky Challenger (Tall)
Herit, Puket

Dusky Gold
(Intermediate)
Richm

Dusky Jewel (Tall)
Herit

Dutch Chocolate (Tall)
Kopua, Puket, Richm

Eagles Flight (Tall)
Herit, Kopua, Richm

Earl Of Essex (Tall)
Herit

Early Edition
(Intermediate)
Kopua, Richm

Early Wish (Tall)
Herit

Earthling (Border)
Richm

Easy Strolling (Dwarf)
Richm, RosPl

Ebony Concerto (Dwarf)
RosPl

Echo One (Tall)
Puket

Eden (Tall)
Puket

Edith Wolford (Tall)
Herit, Richm

Edna's Wish (Tall)
Herit

Egret Snow (Mini Dwarf)
RosPl

Eidolia (Tall)
Herit

Electric Dreams (Dwarf)
Herit

Electrique (Tall)
Herit

Elegant Blue (Tall)
Herit, Puket

Elfin Duet (Dwarf)
Kopua, Ormon, Puket,
Richm

Ellen Q (Border)
Kopua, Richm

Elsedina (Intermediate)
Herit, Richm

Elva Wilson
(Intermediate)
RosPl

Elvis Presley (Tall)
Herit, Puket

Embroidery (Border)
RosPl

Emma Cook (Tall)
Kopua

Emmanuel (Tall)
Herit

Encanto (Dwarf)
Richm, RosPl

Endless Love (Tall)
Herit

English Charm (Tall)
Herit

Epic (Tall)
Richm

Erect (Intermediate)
Herit

Erin Lad (Dwarf)
RosPl

Erin May (Dwarf)
Puket

Erleen Richeson (Tall)
Richm

Ermine Robe (Tall)
Kopua, Richm

Esmerelda (Tall)
Herit

Esoteric (Dwarf)
Herit

Esther Faye (Tall)
Richm

Eternal Prince (Tall)
Herit

Eurythmic (Tall)
Herit, Puket, Richm

Evening Event (Dwarf)
RosPl

Evening Frolic (Tall)
Herit

Evening Gown (Tall)
Herit

Evensong (Dwarf)
Richm

Ever & Ever (Tall)
Richm

Ever After (Tall)
Herit

Ever Sweet (Mini Tall)
Puket, Richm

Everybody's Dream
(Tall)
Herit

Everything Plus (Tall)
Herit

ex June,smokey lilac w
yellow bd (Dwarf)
NewlR

Excellency (Tall)
Herit

Excite Me (Tall)
Herit

Exhilaration (Tall)
Herit

Exotic Dancer (Tall)
Herit

Exotic Melody (Tall)
Herit

Extravagant (Tall)
Herit, Richm

Eye Bright (Dwarf)
BayBl

Eye Magic (Border)
Herit, Puket

Eye Opener (Dwarf)
RosPl

Eyelash (Dwarf)
RosPl

Fair Dinkum (Tall)
Herit, Puket

Fairy Cheeks
(Intermediate)
Kopua, Richm, RosPl

Fairy Dell (Mini Dwarf)
RosPl

Fairy Fern (Dwarf)
Kopua, NewlR, Puket,
Richm

Fairy Footsteps (Dwarf)
Herit, Puket, Richm

Fairy Goblin (Mini
Dwarf)
Richm

Fairy Jewels (Border)
RosPl

Fairy Time
(Intermediate)
RosPl

Fame (Tall)
Herit

Fantastic Blue
(Intermediate)
RosPl

Fantasy Isle (Dwarf)
Kopua, RosPl

Fantasy World
(Intermediate)
Kopua, RosPl

Faraway Places (Tall)
Herit

Fashion Lady (Mini
Dwarf)
RosPl

Faux Pas (Intermediate)
Herit

Favourite Song
(Intermed.)
RosPl

Feedback (Tall)
Herit

Feminine Charm (Tall)
Kopua

Feminine Wiles (Tall)
Herit

Feminist (Tall)
Herit

Fervid (Tall)
Herit

Festive Skirt (Tall)
Puket

Fi-Fi (Dwarf)
Puket

Fiddle Faddle
(Intermediate)
Herit

Fiesta Time (Tall)
Herit

Fiftieth Anniversary
(Dwarf)
RosPl

Fine China (Tall)
Herit

Fingerprint (Dwarf)
Kopua

Fiorellino (Mini Dwarf)
RosPl

Fire Flush (Intermediate)
Richm

Fire Island (Dwarf)
Herit

Fire Pit (Tall)
Puket

Fireside Glow (Tall)
Herit

First Movement (Tall)
Herit

First Step (Dwarf)
RosPl

Fission (Tall)
Herit

Flame Kiss (Tall)
Kopua, Puket

Flaming Victory (Tall)
Herit

Flamingo Blues (Tall)
Richm

Flare Up (Tall)
Puket

Flasher (Intermediate)
Kopua, RosPl

Flashpoint (Tall)
Herit

Flirty Eyes (Dwarf)
Richm, RosPl

Flirty Mary (Dwarf)
RosPl

Flivver (Intermediate)
Herit

Float (Tall)
Herit

Floral Act (Tall)
Herit, Puket

Flourish (Intermediate)
Kopua, Richm, RosPl

Flower Show (Tall)
Herit

Fluted Haven (Tall)
Kopua, Richm

Fly With Me (Tall)
Herit

Foaming Seas (Tall)
Richm

Foggy Dew (Tall)
Kopua, Richm

Folklore (Border)
RosPl

Foolish Fancy (Tall)
Herit

Foolish Pleasure (Tall)
Herit

Footlights (Mini Dwarf)
RosPl

Footnote (Dwarf)
RosPl

For Tirah (Tall)
Herit

Forbidden (Tall)
Herit

Forest Glade (Dwarf)
NewlR, RosPl

Forest Light (Mini
Dwarf)
Richm

Fort Bragg   (Tall)
Herit

Fortunata   (Tall)
Herit

Fortune Cookie   (Dwarf)
RosPl

Fortune Seeker   (Dwarf)
BayBl

Forty Winks   (Dwarf)
Richm

Foundation Van Gogh
(Tall)
Herit

Fragrant Lilac   (Tall)
Richm

Fragrant Too   (Dwarf)
RosPl

Fred Clausen   (Dwarf)
RosPl

Free Flight
(Intermediate)
Kopua, RosPl

French Gown   (Tall)
Herit

French Silk
(Intermediate)
Herit

Frenso Calypso   (Tall)
Puket

Fresh Face   (Dwarf)
RosPl

Fresno Fiesta   (Tall)
Richm

Friday's Child   (Dwarf)
RosPl

Frivolity   (Tall)
Kopua, Richm

Frolic Time
(Intermediate)
Richm

From The
Heart(Intermediate)
Herit

Frost And Flame   (Tall)
Kopua

Frosted Angel   (Dwarf)
Richm

Frosted Cups
(Intermediate)
Richm

Frosted Ice   (Dwarf)
RosPl

Frosted Olives   (Dwarf)
RosPl

Frosted Sapphire   (Tall)
Richm

Frosted Velvet   (Mini
Tall)
Herit, RosPl

Frosty Snowball   (Tall)
Herit

Fujis Mantle   (Tall)
Kopua

Full Moon Rising   (Tall)
Herit

Full Tide   (Tall)
Herit, Puket

G'day Mate   (Tall)
Herit

Gaily Clad   (Tall)
Kopua, Richm

Gallant Rogue   (Tall)
Herit

Garnet Gleam   (Mini
Dwarf)
RosPl

Garnet Ruffles   (Tall)
Puket

Gauguin   (Tall)
Herit

Gay Comedian   (Dwarf)
RosPl

Gay Jewel   (Mini Dwarf)
RosPl

Gay Katy   (Dwarf)
Kopua, NewlR, RosPl

Gay Lights   (Tall)
Puket, Richm

Gay Mystique   (Tall)
Herit

Gay Parasol   (Tall)
Kopua

Gay Sunshine   (Mini
Dwarf)
RosPl

Gay Wings
(Intermediate)
Kopua, RosPl

Gental Rain   (Tall)
Herit

Gentle Air   (Dwarf)
RosPl

Gentle Jasmine   (Dwarf)
RosPl

Gentle Sky   (Dwarf)
RosPl

Gentle Smile   (Dwarf)
RosPl

Georgia Girl   (Tall)
Puket

Gift Of Dreams   (Tall)
Herit

Gigglepot   (Dwarf)
RosPl

Gigolette   (Dwarf)
Herit

Gimlet   (Dwarf)
RosPl

Ginger Swirl   (Tall)
Herit

Ginger Tart   (Dwarf)
NewlR

Gingerbread Man
(Dwarf)
BayBl, Kopua, NewlR,
Parva, Richm, RosPl

Gizmo   (Mini Dwarf)
RosPl

Glee Club   (Intermediate)
RosPl

Glimmer   (Intermediate)
Kopua

Glistening Circle   (Tall)
Puket

Glistening Glen   (Dwarf)
Richm

Glistening Icicle   (Tall)
Herit

Glory Story   (Tall)
Herit

Glow Gleam   (Mini
Dwarf)
RosPl

God's Handiwork   (Tall)
Herit

Goddess   (Tall)
Herit, Richm

Godsend   (Tall)
Herit

Going My Way   (Tall)
Herit, Kopua

Gold Country   (Tall)
Herit, Richm

Gold Fever   (Dwarf)
RosPl

Gold Galore   (Tall)
Herit

Gold Reprise (Tall)
Herit

Golden Accents (Tall)
Puket

Golden Blaze (Dwarf)
Richm

Golden Dewdrops
(Dwarf)
RosPl

Golden Muffin
(Intermediate)
RosPl

Golden Plunder (Tall)
Kopua

Golden Ruby (Dwarf)
Richm

Golden Starlet (Dwarf)
Kopua, Puket, Richm

Good and
True(Intermediate)
RosPl

Good Earth (Tall)
Herit

Good Hope (Tall)
Richm

Good Morning America
(Tall)
Herit

Good Show (Tall)
Herit

Goody Goody (Dwarf)
RosPl

Grace Note (Dwarf)
RosPl

Graceful Gold (Tall)
Herit

Granada Gold (Tall)
Puket

Grand Praise (Tall)
Herit

Grand Prix (Tall)
Herit

Granpa's Girl (Mini
Tall)
RosPl

Green And Gifted (Tall)
Herit

Green Meteor (Dwarf)
RosPl

Green Petals (Mini
Dwarf)
RosPl

Green Quest (Tall)
Kopua

Green Spot (Dwarf)
Ashto, RosPl

Grey Pearls (Mini Dwarf)
RosPl

Guest of Honour (Dwarf)
RosPl

Gung Ho (Dwarf)
RosPl

Gypsy Eyes (Dwarf)
RosPl

Gypsy Flirt (Dwarf)
RosPl

Gypsy Jump
(Intermediate)
RosPl

Gypsy Wings (Border)
RosPl

Gyro (Tall)
Herit

Hafnium (Dwarf)
Herit, RosPl

Hagers Helmet (Intermed.)
RosPl

Haidie (Intermediate)
Richm

Half Moon Bay (Dwarf)
RosPl

Hallowed Thought (Tall)
Herit

Hamberger Nacht
(Dwarf)
RosPl

Hampton Horizon (Tall)
Herit

Handshake (Tall)
Herit

Happening (Dwarf)
Kopua, RosPl

Happy Child
(Intermediate)
RosPl

Happy Land (Mini
Dwarf)
RosPl

Happy Mood
(Intermediate)
Richm

Harlow Gold
(Intermediate)
Herit, RosPl

Harvest Festival (Dwarf)
RosPl

Harvest Of Memories
(Tall)
Herit

He Man (Tall)
Herit

Heather Blush (Tall)
Herit

Heather Cloud (Tall)
Herit

Heaven Helped (Tall)
Herit

Heavenly Lark (Tall)
Herit

Heavenly Music (Dwarf)
RosPl

Hee Haw (Dwarf)
RosPl

Helen Proctor
(Intermediate)
Richm, RosPl

Helga's Hat
(Intermediate)
Herit

Hell Cat (Intermediate)
Herit, Puket

Hello Darkness (Tall)
Herit

Hello Hobo (Tall)
Herit

Helter Skelter (Dwarf)
Kopua, RosPl

Hermosa Rose (Dwarf)
RosPl

Hester (Dwarf)
RosPl

Hi Honey (Dwarf)
Herit

Hi Sailor (Dwarf)
Herit, RosPl

Higgledy Piggledy
(Intermed)
Herit

High Life (Tall)
Richm

High Waters (Tall)
Herit

Highland Haze (Tall)
Herit

Highland Lassie (Dwarf)
Richm

Hills District   (Tall)
Herit
Hilo Shores   (Tall)
Puket
Hindenburg   (Tall)
Herit, Puket
Hissy Fit   (Intermediate)
Herit
Holiday Flame
(Intermediate)
Richm, RosPl
Holiday Lover   (Tall)
Herit
Hollywood Blonde   (Tall)
Herit
Holy Hight   (Tall)
Herit, Puket
Homeport   (Dwarf)
Herit
Honey Behold   (Dwarf)
Herit
Honey Berry
(Intermediate)
RosPl
Honey Crunch   (Tall)
Herit
Honey Dip   (Dwarf)
RosPl
Honey Glazed
(Intermediate)
Herit, Kopua, Richm
Honey Pot   (Dwarf)
Richm
Honey Wind   (Dwarf)
Herit
Honeymoon Suite   (Tall)
Herit
Honkytonk Blues   (Tall)
Herit
Honorabile   (Mini Tall)
RosPl
Hooligan   (Dwarf)
RosPl
Hooray   (Dwarf)
Richm
Hot Fudge
(Intermediate)
Herit, Puket, Richm
Hot Gossip   (Tall)
Herit
Hot Streak   (Tall)
Herit

Hot Wheels
(Intermediate)
Herit
Houdini   (Tall)
Herit
Huddle   (Dwarf)
Herit
Hug a Bunch
(Intermediate)
Herit, RosPl
Hush Puppy   (Dwarf)
Puket
Ice Chip   (Dwarf)
Richm
Ice Sculpture   (Tall)
Herit
Iced Lemonade   (Dwarf)
Puket
Ida Mary Pattison
(Intermed)
RosPl
Imagine Me   (Tall)
Herit
Imbri   (Dwarf)
Kopua, RosPl
Impish   (Dwarf)
Herit
Impulse   (Intermediate)
Herit
In Tempo   (Tall)
Kopua
In Town   (Tall)
Herit, Puket, Richm
Inca Queen   (Tall)
Herit
Incantation   (Tall)
Herit
Incentive   (Tall)
Herit
Indian Doll
(Intermediate)
Kopua, Richm, RosPl
Indian Fire
(Intermediate)
Richm
Indian Pow Wow
(Dwarf)
RosPl
Indian Territory   (Tall)
Puket
Indigo Crown   (Dwarf)
RosPl

Indigo Princess   (Tall)
Herit
Inflamed   (Dwarf)
Herit
Inga Ivey   (Tall)
Herit
Ingleside   (Tall)
Richm
Ingrid   (Intermediate)
RosPl
Inner Circle
(Intermediate)
Herit
Inscription   (Dwarf)
Richm, RosPl
Instant Pleasure   (Tall)
Herit
Intimate   (Dwarf)
RosPl
Intrepid   (Tall)
Herit
Intuition   (Tall)
Herit
Iolani   (Border)
RosPl
Irenes Love   (Border)
Puket
Iris Irene   (Tall)
Herit
Irish Doll   (Mini Dwarf)
RosPl
Irish Temper   (Dwarf)
RosPl
Irish Trick   (Dwarf)
Puket
Island Girl   (Tall)
Herit
Ivory and Ink   (Mini
Dwarf)
RosPl
Ivory Touch
(Intermediate)
RosPl
Jack Norrick   (Dwarf)
RosPl
Jack Riley   (Dwarf)
RosPl
Jacqui J   (Intermediate)
Richm
Jade Mist   (Dwarf)
Herit, RosPl

Jakarta (Tall)
Jakarta (Tall)
 Kopua
Jana White (Mini Tall)
 RosPl
Janie Meek (Tall)
 Herit
Jared (Dwarf)
 RosPl
Jasper Gem (Mini Dwarf)
 Richm, RosPl
Jaunty Jerry (Border)
 Richm
Jaywalker (Dwarf)
 RosPl
Jazz Echo (Tall)
 Herit
Jazzamatazz (Dwarf)
 BayBl, Herit, Kopua, Puket, Richm
Jedi Knight (Tall)
 Herit
Jennie Grace (Dwarf)
 RosPl
Jesse Lee (Dwarf)
 Herit
Jesse's Song (Tall)
 Herit
Jewel Of Spring (Tall)
 Herit
Jiansada (Dwarf)
 Herit
Jill Welch (Mini Tall)
 RosPl
Jitterbug (Tall)
 Herit
Jo Jo (Mini Dwarf)
 RosPl
Joan McClemens (Tall)
 Herit, Richm
Joan Moritz (Dwarf)
 Herit
Joette (Mini Tall)
 Richm
John (Intermediate)
 Herit
Johnny (Dwarf)
 RosPl
Jolly Elf (Intermediate)
 Kopua
Jolly Fellow (Dwarf)
 Kopua, Richm

Jolly Jim (Mini Tall)
 RosPl
Jolt (Tall)
 Herit
Joyce McBride (Dwarf)
 RosPl
Joyce Terry (Tall)
 Herit, Kopua
Joyful (Dwarf)
 RosPl
Joyous Melody (Tall)
 Herit
Jubie (Mini Tall)
 RosPl
June Prom (Intermediate)
 Ashto, Richm, RosPl
June Rose (Intermediate)
 Herit, RosPl
June Sunset (Tall)
 Herit
Jungle Shadows (Border)
 RosPl
Jungle Warrior (Dwarf)
 Herit
Juris Prudence (Tall)
 Herit
Just Delicious (Tall)
 Herit
Just Magic (Tall)
 Herit
Just So (Dwarf)
 Richm
Kabaka (Tall)
 Herit, Puket
Kadaicha (Intermediate)
 Herit
Kah-nee-ta (Tall)
 Herit
Kandi Moon (Dwarf)
 Herit
Karaminka (Tall)
 Herit
Karen Olding (Intermediate)
 Kopua, Richm
Ken Ware (Tall)
 Herit
Kentucky Bluegrass (Dwarf)
 NewlR, RosPl

Kentucky Skies (Tall)
 Herit
Kermit (Intermediate)
 Herit
Kilt Lilt (Tall)
 Richm
Kingly Dignity (Tall)
 Richm
Kinsella (Dwarf)
 RosPl
Kiowa Moon (Intermediate)
 RosPl
Kirsch (Border)
 RosPl
Kirsten Marie (Dwarf)
 RosPl
Kiss Of Gold (Tall)
 Herit
Kissimee (Mini Dwarf)
 RosPl
Kissing Circle (Tall)
 Herit
Kiwi Capers (Dwarf)
 Herit
Kiwi Dream (Dwarf)
 RosPl
Kiwi Slices (Dwarf)
 Herit, Richm
Kix (Dwarf)
 Richm
Knick-Knack (Mini Dwarf)
 NewlR, Richm
Knight Templar (Tall)
 Herit
Knighted (Tall)
 Herit, Richm
Knock Out (Dwarf)
 Richm
Knotty Pine (Dwarf)
 Kopua, NewlR, Puket, Richm
Kondalilla (Tall)
 Richm
Krugerand (Tall)
 Puket
La Fortune (Tall)
 Herit
Laced Lemonade (Dwarf)
 Richm

Lacy (Intermediate)
Herit

Lady Day (Intermediate)
Herit

Lady Friend (Tall)
Herit, Kopua, Puket

Lady In Red (Dwarf)
RosPl

Lady of Charm (Mini Tall)
RosPl

Lake Moonspun (Tall)
Herit, Richm

Land Of Lakes (Tall)
Herit, Puket

Larkabout (Tall)
Herit

Larry Gaulter (Tall)
Herit

Latin Hideaway (Tall)
Herit

Latin Lark (Tall)
Herit, Puket

Latin Lover (Tall)
Richm

Latin Rock (Tall)
Herit, Richm

Launching Pad (Tall)
Kopua, Richm

Laureen (Tall)
Kopua

Laurie (Tall)
Kopua, Richm

Lavender Dawn (Mini Dwarf)
RosPl

Lavender Lass (Dwarf)
Richm

Lavender Sparkle (Tall)
Richm

Le Fleur (Tall)
Herit

Le Flirt (Dwarf)
Herit, Puket

Learn (Dwarf)
Herit

Ledas Lover (Tall)
Herit, Puket

Legato (Tall)
Herit

Lemon And Spice (Tall)
Herit

Lemon Custard (Tall)
Herit

Lemon Fever (Tall)
Herit

Lemon Flare (Mini Dwarf)
Kopua, Richm

Lemon Flirt (Mini Tall)
RosPl

Lemon Flurry (Intermediate)
Kopua, Richm

Lemon Frills (Tall)
RosPl

Lemon Lark (Dwarf)
RosPl

Lemon Lyric (Tall)
Herit

Lemon Mist (Tall)
Herit, Puket, Richm

Lemon Pop (Intermediate)
Herit

Lemon Puff (Dwarf)
Richm, RosPl

Lemon Rings (Dwarf)
Herit, RosPl

Lemon Tart (Border)
Kopua

Lenna M (Dwarf)
Kopua, Richm, RosPl

Lenora Pearl (Intermediate)
Herit

Leora Kate (Tall)
Kopua, Richm

Lesson (Dwarf)
Herit

Liaison (Tall)
Herit

Lianne (Dwarf)
Richm

Libation (Mini Dwarf)
Kopua, RosPl

Licorice Stick (Tall)
Puket, Richm

Life Of Riley (Tall)
Herit

Light Beam (Tall)
Herit, Puket

Light Cavalry (Intermediate)
RosPl

Like A Charm (Intermediate)
Herit

Like A Melody (Border)
RosPl

Lil Red Devil (Dwarf)
Kopua, Richm

Lilac and Lavender (Dwarf)
RosPl

Lilac Haze (Tall)
Richm

Lilac Lilt (Intermediate)
Kopua, Richm

Lilac Lustre (Tall)
Herit, Richm

Lilac Mist (Tall)
Richm

Lilac Thrill (Tall)
Puket

Lilac Wine (Tall)
Kopua, Richm

Lilaclil (Dwarf)
RosPl

Lilli Brown Tone (Dwarf)
Richm

Lillipinkput (Intermediate)
RosPl

Lillypilly Wine (Tall)
Herit

Lilting Melody (Tall)
Puket

Lima Colada (Dwarf)
RosPl

Lime Fizz (Tall)
Richm

Lime Lighter (Tall)
Herit

Lime Ripples (Intermediate)
Richm, RosPl

Limerick (Tall)
Richm

Lipstick Lies (Tall)
Herit

Liqueur Creme (Tall)
Herit

Little Bow Knot (Intermed.)
Kopua, Richm

Little Buccaneer (Dwarf)
BayBl, Kopua, NewlR, Puket, Richm, RosPl

Little Champ (Mini Dwarf)
RosPl

Little Chestnut (Dwarf)
Kopua, Richm, RosPl

Little Christopher (Dwarf)
RosPl

Little Demon (Dwarf)
Seasd

Little Dittie (Dwarf)
RosPl

Little Dogie (Dwarf)
RosPl

Little Dream (Dwarf)
RosPl

Little Episode (Dwarf)
Richm, RosPl

Little Grackles (Dwarf)
NewlR

Little Imp (Mini Dwarf)
Richm, RosPl

Little Louie (Dwarf)
Herit

Little Lucy (Mini Dwarf)
Richm

Little May Dancer (Mini Dwf)
RosPl

Little Miss Muffet (Dwarf)
RosPl

Little Much (Tall)
Herit

Little Pansy (Dwarf)
RosPl

Little Paul (Mini Tall)
RosPl

Little Pickle (Dwarf)
Kopua

Little Redskin (Mini Dwarf)
Kopua, RosPl

Little Saint (Intermediate)
RosPl

Little Snow Lemon (Intermed)
RosPl

Little Sunbeam (Mini Dwarf)
Kopua, Richm, RosPl

Little Witch (Dwarf)
NewlR

Live Jazz (Dwarf)
BayBl, Herit, RosPl

Lively Rose (Mini Tall)
RosPl

Locket (Mini Dwarf)
RosPl

Lollipop (Dwarf)
RosPl

London Lord (Tall)
Herit

Loop The Loop (Tall)
Richm

Los Banos (Tall)
Herit

Louden Charmer (Tall)
Kopua

Love and Desire (Tall)
Herit

Love Poem (Tall)
Herit

Love The Sun (Tall)
Herit

Lover Boy (Intermediate)
Kopua, RosPl

Lovers Lane (Tall)
Herit

Loving Touch (Intermediate)
Richm

Low Rider (Intermediate)
RosPl

Loyal Devotion (Tall)
Herit

Loyalist (Tall)
Herit

Lucky Charm (Mini Tall)
RosPl

Lucy Emmons (Dwarf)
RosPl

Lullaby of Spring (Tall)
Herit

Lunar Fire (Tall)
Kopua, Richm

Luscious One (Dwarf)
RosPl

Lysandra (Tall)
Herit

Macey (Intermediate)
RosPl

Macho Hombre (Tall)
Herit

Magenta Magic (Dwarf)
RosPl

Magharee (Tall)
Herit

Magic Dot (Dwarf)
RosPl

Magic Flute (Mini Dwarf)
RosPl

Magic Hope (Tall)
Herit

Magician's Apprentice (Tall)
Herit

Magnifique (Tall)
Richm

Maharishi (Tall)
Herit

Mahogany Rush (Tall)
Herit

Mahogany Snow (Dwarf)
RosPl

Maid Of Orange (Intermed.)
Herit

Maiden Lane (Intermediate)
RosPl

Majestic Interlude (Tall)
Herit

Majorette (Tall)
Richm

Making Eyes (Dwarf)
Herit, Kopua, Puket, Richm

Malaguena (Tall)
Herit

Malaysia (Tall)
Puket

Mama Big Bucks (Dwarf)
RosPl

Mama's Pet (Mini Dwarf)
RosPl

Mandolin (Tall)
Richm

Manhattan Blues (Dwarf)
BayBl

Manuscript (Tall)
Herit
Many Thanks (Tall)
Herit
Manzanita (Border)
RosPl
Marauder (Tall)
Herit
Marie Pinel (Tall)
Puket
Marie's Delight (Dwarf)
RosPl
Marinka (Dwarf)
Richm
Mark (Mini Dwarf)
RosPl
Marmalade (Tall)
Herit
Marmalade Skies (Border)
Herit, RosPl
Marocain (Mini Dwarf)
RosPl
Maroon Caper (Intermediate)
RosPl
Marquee (Tall)
Herit
Marriage Vows (Tall)
Herit, Richm
Marscay (Dwarf)
Herit
Marsh Imp (Mini Dwarf)
RosPl
Mary (Mini Dwarf)
RosPl
Mary Frances (Tall)
Herit, Richm
Mary Schnarr (Dwarf)
RosPl
Matinata (Tall)
Richm
Maui Moonlight (Intermed.)
Herit, RosPl
May Melody (Tall)
Kopua, Richm
Maya Mama (Dwarf)
RosPl
Maya Marvel (Mini Dwarf)
RosPl

Meadow Lark (Border)
Kopua
Meagan Elizabeth (Tall)
Herit
Medieval (Tall)
Herit
Megglethrop (Intermediate)
Herit
Melon Honey (Dwarf)
Kopua, NewIR, Richm, RosPl
Memo (Intermediate)
Herit
Memorandum (Tall)
Herit
Memphis Blues (Tall)
Herit
Merry Life (Intermediate)
Herit
Mexicali (Border)
RosPl
Michael Paul (Dwarf)
Herit, RosPl
Michiana (Mini Dwarf)
Kopua, RosPl
Midas Flush (Intermediate)
Herit, Puket
Midnight Express (Tall)
Herit
Midnight Fire (Tall)
Richm
Midnight Madness (Dwarf)
RosPl
Mighty Mite (Dwarf)
Puket
Minx (Dwarf)
RosPl
Mirror Mirror (Tall)
Puket
Miss Jeanie (Tall)
Herit
Miss Jenny (Dwarf)
RosPl
Miss Right (Intermediate)
RosPl
Miss Tootsie (Tall)
Herit
Mist-o-Pink (Mini Dwarf)
RosPl

Mister Roberts (Dwarf)
Herit, RosPl
Mists Of Avalon (Tall)
Herit
Mittagong (Tall)
Puket, Richm
Mixed Doubles (Tall)
Herit
Mixture (Tall)
Herit
Modern Music (Tall)
Herit
Modern Times (Tall)
Herit
Molten Embers (Tall)
Kopua, Richm
Moment (Dwarf)
BayBl, Puket
Momentum (Tall)
Herit
Monkey (Dwarf)
RosPl
Montevideo (Tall)
Herit
Moocha (Dwarf)
Herit
Moody Blues (Tall)
Herit
Moomba (Tall)
Herit
Moon Dawn (Dwarf)
Herit
Moon Day (Dwarf)
Richm
Moon Shade (Border)
RosPl
Moon Spinner (Dwarf)
Richm
Moon Sundae (Dwarf)
Richm
Moon Tike (Intermediate)
Richm
Moon's Delight (Tall)
Herit
Moondrops (Mini Dwarf)
RosPl
Moonfly (Intermediate)
Herit
Moonlight Lady (Tall)
Herit
Morning dew (Dwarf)
RosPl

Morroco (Tall)
Richm

Moss Bay (Intermediate)
RosPl

Mostest (Intermediate)
Herit

Mountain Red
(Intermediate)
Kopua, RosPl, Seasd

Mountain Violet (Tall)
Herit

Move On (Tall)
Herit

Muchas Gracias (Tall)
Herit

Mulberry Punch (Tall)
Herit

Mulled Wine (Tall)
Herit, Puket

Munchkin (Mini Dwarf)
RosPl

Mushroom Rings (Tall)
Puket

Music Box (Dwarf)
RosPl

Music Lady (Dwarf)
BayBl, Kopua, Parva,
Richm

Music Lover (Tall)
Herit

Music Maestro (Tall)
Herit

My Sheba (Dwarf)
Herit

My Vagabond (Tall)
Herit

My Valentine (Tall)
Herit

Myra (Dwarf)
NewlR

Mystic Lace (Tall)
Herit

Mystic Rites (Tall)
Herit

Mystic Waters (Tall)
Herit

Mystique (Tall)
Herit

Nancy Alane (Dwarf)
Herit

Natural Beauty (Tall)
Herit

Nautical Flag
(Intermediate)
Herit

Navajo Blanket (Tall)
Richm

Navajo Jewel (Tall)
Herit

Navy Chant (Tall)
Herit

Navy Doll (Dwarf)
RosPl, Seasd

Navy Waves (Tall)
Herit

Nectar (Intermediate)
Herit, Puket, RosPl

Neil Diamond (Tall)
Herit

Neutron Dance (Tall)
Herit, Puket

New Idea (Mini Tɛll)
Kopua, RosPl

New Kid (Intermediate)
Herit

New Tune (Tall)
Herit

New Vintage
(Intermediate)
Richm, RosPl

Newly Rich (Tall)
Richm

Newlywed (Tall)
Herit

Night Affair (Tall)
Puket

Night Edition (Tall)
Herit

Night Owl (Tall)
Puket, Richm

Night Ruler (Tall)
Herit, Richm

Night Shift
(Intermediate)
Herit

Nike (Tall)
Kopua, Richm

Nimble Toes (Dwarf)
Herit, Puket

Nivea (Tall)
Herit

Noble House (Tall)
Herit

Nordic Seas (Tall)
Herit

Notable (Tall)
Herit

Notorious (Tall)
Herit

Novella (Border)
RosPl

O' Cool (Intermediate)
Herit

O' What (Dwarf)
Puket

Oba Oba (Tall)
Herit

Obligato (Intermediate)
Herit, RosPl

Ocean Pacific (Tall)
Herit

Odessy (Tall)
Richm

Of Course
(Intermediate)
Kopua, Richm, RosPl

Oh Jay (Dwarf)
Herit, RosPl

Okarito (Tall)
Richm

Oklahoma Bandit
(Intermed.)
Richm, RosPl

Oktoberfest (Tall)
Herit

Old Master (Tall)
Kopua, Richm

Oliver (Dwarf)
Richm

Olymparico (Tall)
Herit

Olympiad (Tall)
Herit

Olympic Torch (Tall)
Richm

Omen (Dwarf)
Richm

On Edge (Tall)
Herit

On Fire (Dwarf)
BayBl, RosPl

On Wings (Intermediate)
Herit

Only Foolin
(Intermediate)
Herit

Opal Imp (Mini Tall)
RosPl

Open Country (Tall)
Kopua, Richm
Open Sky (Dwarf)
Richm, RosPl
Opportunity (Tall)
Herit
Oracle (Border)
Kopua, Richm
Orange Bantam (Dwarf)
RosPl
Orange Flirt (Tall)
Herit
Orange Glint (Mini Dwarf)
RosPl
Orange Petals (Intermediate)
Herit
Orange Slices (Tall)
Richm
Orange Star (Tall)
Richm
Orange Tiger (Dwarf)
Herit
Orangerie (Tall)
Herit
Orchard Girl (Tall)
Herit, Richm
Orchid Brocade (Tall)
Kopua
Orchid Raye (Dwarf)
Richm, RosPl
Orchid Wings (Tall)
Kopua
Orchidarium (Tall)
Herit, Puket
Oriental Alabaster (Tall)
Herit, Puket
Oriental Baby (Dwarf)
NewlR
Oriental Blush (Dwarf)
RosPl
Over Easy (Dwarf)
Herit
Overtone (Intermediate)
Kopua, Richm
Ozark Evening (Mini Tall)
RosPl
Ozark Sky (Mini Tall)
RosPl
Pac Man (Dwarf)
RosPl

Pacer (Intermediate)
Herit
Pacfic Peach (Tall)
Herit
Pacific Gambler (Tall)
Herit
Pacific Grove (Tall)
Herit
Pacific Mist (Tall)
Herit
Pacific Overtures (Tall)
Herit
Pacific Shores (Tall)
Richm
Pacific Tide (Tall)
Herit
Pagan (Tall)
Kopua
Pagan Dance (Tall)
Herit
Painted Blue (Tall)
Herit
Pal Sam (Dwarf)
Herit, Puket, RosPl
Palace Gossip (Tall)
Herit, Puket
Pale Cloud (Intermediate)
Richm, RosPl
Pale Star (Dwarf)
Herit
pallida Variegata (Tall)
Herit
Paprika Fonos (Tall)
Herit
Paradise (Tall)
Herit
Paris Kiss (Tall)
Puket
Parquet (Tall)
Herit
Parturient (Mini Tall)
RosPl
Pass The Wine (Tall)
Herit
Pastel Dawn (Mini Dwarf)
RosPl
Pastel Delight (Dwarf)
RosPl
Patsy Joe (Mini Dwarf)
Kopua, NewlR, Puket

Pattacake (Dwarf)
Herit
Paul (Dwarf)
RosPl
Peace And Harmony (Tall)
Herit
Peach Bavarian (Dwarf)
RosPl
Peach Bisque (Tall)
Herit
Peach Eyes (Dwarf)
Herit, Puket
Peach Float (Tall)
Herit
Peach Spot (Tall)
Richm
Peach Sundae (Tall)
Herit
Peach Tree (Tall)
Herit
Peachy Face (Intermediate)
RosPl
Pearls Of Wisdom (Tall)
Herit
Peccadillo (Intermediate)
Herit
Pemcaw (Tall)
Herit
Penguin Paradise (Tall)
Herit
Penny Anne (Tall)
Herit
Penny Ante (Dwarf)
Kopua, Richm, RosPl
Penny Candy (Mini Dwarf)
RosPl
Pepper Rim (Intermediate)
Kopua, Richm
Peppermint Crush (Tall)
Kopua, Richm
Perfect Couple (Tall)
Herit
Perky Plic (Intermediate)
RosPl
Persian Berry (Tall)
Puket
Pet Set (Dwarf)
RosPl

Petite Pink   (Dwarf)
RosPl

Petite Polka   (Mini Dwarf)
BayBl, Richm

Petkin   (Intermediate)
Kopua, Puket, Richm

Pharoah's Daughter (Intermediate)
RosPl

Philanderer   (Intermediate)
Herit

Physique   (Tall)
Herit

Picasso   (Tall)
Herit

Picayune   (Border)
RosPl

Piety   (Tall)
Richm

Pigeon   (Dwarf)
Herit

Pink Belle   (Tall)
Herit

Pink Bubbles   (Border)
Herit, Puket, Richm, RosPl

Pink Chimes   (Tall)
RosPl

Pink Confetti   (Tall)
Richm

Pink Cushion   (Dwarf)
RosPl

Pink Fancy (Intermediate)
RosPl

Pink Froth   (Tall)
Herit

Pink Gala   (Tall)
Herit

Pink Kewpie   (Border)
RosPl

Pink Kitten (Intermediate)
RosPl

Pink Midget   (Dwarf)
RosPl

Pink Panther   (Dwarf)
RosPl

Pink Prevue   (Dwarf)
Herit

Pink Reverie (Intermediate)
Richm, RosPl

Pink Splash (Intermediate)
RosPl

Pink Swan   (Tall)
Herit

Pioneer Spirit (Intermediate)
RosPl

Piper's Tune (Intermediate)
RosPl

Pipes Of Pan   (Tall)
Kopua, Puket, Richm

Pipestone   (Dwarf)
Herit

Pirates Moon   (Tall)
Herit

Pixie Pinafore   (Dwarf)
Kopua, Richm

Pixie Skies   (Intermediate)
Richm

Planned Treasure   (Tall)
Herit

Platinum Gold   (Dwarf)
Kopua

Playgirl   (Tall)
Herit

Pleated Gown   (Tall)
Kopua, Richm

Pledge Allegiance   (Tall)
Herit

Plic Sand   (Mini Dwarf)
RosPl

Plictissima   (Border)
RosPl

Plum Gleam   (Tall)
Richm

Plum-Plum   (Dwarf)
Kopua, Richm, RosPl

Poet   (Tall)
Herit

Poetic   (Tall)
Herit

Poetic Art   (Intermediate)
RosPl

Pogo Doll   (Intermediate)
Richm

Point In Time   (Tall)
Herit

Polar Seas   (Tall)
Herit

Polished Amber   (Tall)
Herit

Polka Time   (Tall)
Richm

Pompeii Lady   (Tall)
Herit

Pony   (Intermediate)
RosPl

Poppet   (Dwarf)
NewlR

Porta Villa   (Tall)
Herit, Richm

Portrait Of Amy   (Tall)
Herit

Portrait Of Larrie   (Tall)
Herit

Posh   (Intermediate)
Herit, Kopua, Puket

Pot Luck   (Intermediate)
RosPl

Power Surge   (Tall)
Herit

Prairie Clover   (Tall)
Kopua

Praise The Lord   (Tall)
Richm

Praline   (Tall)
Herit

Prancer   (Dwarf)
Kopua, RosPl

Pray For Peace   (Tall)
Herit

Precious Moments   (Tall)
Herit

Preface   (Tall)
Herit

Preferred Stock   (Tall)
Herit

Prejudice   (Tall)
Herit, Richm

Presence   (Tall)
Herit

Pretty Face   (Dwarf)
Puket, Richm

Pretty Field   (Tall)
Kopua, Richm

Pretty In Pink   (Tall)
Herit

Prince   (Dwarf)
RosPl

Prince Charming   (Tall)
Herit

Prince Indigo   (Tall)
Puket, Richm

170

Private Dancer   (Tall)
Herit
Privileged Character
(Dwarf)
Herit
Prize Drawing   (Tall)
Herit
Prodigy   (Mini Dwarf)
RosPl
Proud Tradition   (Tall)
Herit
Pulse Rate   (Dwarf)
RosPl
Pumpin' Iron   (Dwarf)
Herit
Fun   (Intermediate)
Herit
Puppet Baby   (Mini
Dwarf)
RosPl
Puppett   (Dwarf)
Richm
Puppy Love   (Mini Tall)
RosPl
Pure Allure   (Dwarf)
Herit
Purple Gown   (Dwarf)
KeriP, Parva, Seasd
Pushy   (Dwarf)
Herit
Pussytoes   (Mini Dwarf)
RosPl
Quark   (Dwarf)
Herit
Queen In Calico   (Tall)
Herit
Queen's Baby   (Mini
Tall)
RosPl
Quiet Lagoon   (Dwarf)
RosPl
Quilting Party   (Dwarf)
RosPl
Quintessence   (Tall)
Herit
Quip   (Mini Dwarf)
RosPl
Radiant Apogee   (Tall)
Richm
Radiant Energy   (Tall)
Herit
Radiant Gem   (Dwarf)
RosPl

Radiant Gem   (Tall)
Kopua, Richm
Rain Dance   (Dwarf)
Herit, Richm, RosPl
Rainbow Serenade
(Dwarf)
Kopua, RosPl
Rancho Grande   (Tall)
Herit, Puket
Rancho Rose   (Tall)
Richm
Ranee's Palace   (Tall)
Herit
Rapture In Blue   (Tall)
Herit
Rare Edition
(Intermediate)
RosPl
Rare Treat   (Tall)
Herit
Raspberry Acres
(Intermed.)
Kopua, Puket, Richm,
RosPl
Raspberry Fudge   (Tall)
Herit
Raspberry Halo   (Dwarf)
RosPl
Raspberry Jam   (Dwarf)
Herit
Ravens Roost   (Tall)
Richm
Real Coquette   (Dwarf)
RosPl
Real Delight   (Tall)
Kopua
Real Jazzy   (Mini Tall)
RosPl
Rebel Yell
(Intermediate)
Herit
Recital   (Border)
Richm
Recollections   (Dwarf)
RosPl
Recurring Ruffles   (Tall)
Herit
Red Atlast   (Dwarf)
RosPl
Red Damask   (Mini Tall)
RosPl
Red Deb   (Mini Dwarf)
RosPl

Red Gem   (Dwarf)
NewlR
Red Heart   (Dwarf)
Kopua, Puket, Richm,
RosPl
Red Lion   (Tall)
Herit
Red Pixie   (Mini Dwarf)
RosPl
Red Princess   (Dwarf)
RosPl
Red Reward   (Tall)
Herit
Red Sentry   (Mini Dwarf)
RosPl
Red Sheen   (Mini Dwarf)
RosPl
Red Tempest
(Intermediate)
RosPl
Red Zinger
(Intermediate)
Herit, RosPl
Regal Affair   (Tall)
Herit
Regalaire   (Tall)
Puket, Richm
Regards   (Dwarf)
Kopua, Richm, RosPl
Rembrandt Magic   (Tall)
Herit
Respond   (Tall)
Herit
Return To Elegance
(Tall)
Herit
Revolution   (Tall)
Herit
Revved Up
(Intermediate)
Herit, RosPl
Rhinemaidens
(Intermediate)
Herit
Rhyme   (Dwarf)
RosPl
Ribands   (Tall)
Herit
Ribbon Round   (Tall)
Kopua
Rich Again   (Tall)
Kopua, Richm
Ride The Wind   (Tall)
Herit

Righteous   (Intermediate)
RosPl

Rinky Dink
(Intermediate)
Herit

Ripe Raspberry   (Dwarf)
RosPl

Ripple Chip   (Dwarf)
Herit, RosPl

Ripplette   (Dwarf)
Herit

Rippling Snow
(Intermediate)
RosPl

Rita   (Dwarf)
RosPl

Ritz   (Dwarf)
Richm

Riverboat Blues   (Tall)
Herit, Richm

Road Song   (Tall)
Herit

Rocket Flame
(Intermediate)
Kopua, Richm

Rocket Master   (Tall)
Herit

Rocket Red   (Tall)
Herit

Role Model   (Tall)
Herit

Roman Song   (Tall)
Herit

Romantic Mood   (Tall)
Herit

Romanticist   (Tall)
Herit

Romp   (Intermediate)
Herit

Ron   (Tall)
Richm

Rondetta   (Tall)
Herit

Rondo   (Tall)
Herit

Rosarita   (Tall)
Herit

Rose Garden
(Intermediate)
RosPl

Rose Harmony   (Intermed.)
Richm, RosPl

Rosemary's Dream (Mini
Tall)
Herit, RosPl

Rosette Wine   (Tall)
Herit

Rosy Lulu   (Dwarf)
Herit

Round Table   (Tall)
Herit

Roustabout   (Dwarf)
BayBl, Kopua

Royal Celebrity   (Tall)
Herit

Royal Crusader   (Tall)
Herit

Royal Elegance   (Tall)
Herit

Royal Heritage   (Tall)
Richm

Royal Honey   (Tall)
Herit

Royal Premiere   (Tall)
Herit

Royal Tapestry   (Tall)
Richm

Royal Touch   (Tall)
Puket, Richm

Royal Trumpeter   (Tall)
Kopua, Richm

Rubistar   (Tall)
Herit

Ruby Chimes
(Intermediate)
Richm

Ruby Contrast   (Dwarf)
Richm, RosPl

Ruby Rose
(Intermediate)
Richm

Ruby Wilson
(Intermediate)
Herit

Ruckus   (Dwarf)
RosPl

Ruffled Cherub   (Border)
RosPl

Ruffles Supreme   (Tall)
Puket

Runaway   (Intermediate)
RosPl

Rustic Cedar   (Tall)
Herit, Kopua

Rustler   (Tall)
Herit

Sable Night   (Tall)
Puket

Sae Patrol
(Intermediate)
RosPl

Saffron Flame   (Tall)
Herit

Saint Teresa
(Intermediate)
RosPl

Saletta   (Dwarf)
RosPl

Saltwood   (Mini Dwarf)
Richm

Samurai Silk   (Tall)
Herit

San Jose   (Tall)
Herit

Sand Boy   (Tall)
Puket

Sand Princess   (Mini Tall)
RosPl

Sandy Rose   (Tall)
Herit

Santiago   (Tall)
Herit

Sappharine   (Tall)
Richm

Sapphire Gem   (Dwarf)
Kopua, Richm

Sapphire Hills   (Tall)
Richm

Sapphire Jewel   (Dwarf)
BayBl, Kopua, NewlR,
RosPl

Sarah Taylor   (Dwarf)
Kopua, Richm

Sarfraz   (Tall)
Herit

Sass With Class   (Dwarf)
Herit

Satin Blue   (Mini Tall)
RosPl

Satin Knight   (Tall)
Herit

Satin Lustre   (Dwarf)
Kopua, Richm

Satin Satan   (Tall)
Herit

Satin Siren   (Tall)
Herit

Scandia Delight (Tall)
Herit

Scat (Dwarf)
Herit

Scented Bubbles (Tall)
Herit

Scented Nutmeg (Tall)
Herit

Schortmans (Tall)
Puket

Scot Cream (Dwarf)
Puket, Richm

Scotch Blend (Tall)
Puket

Scribe (Dwarf)
Kopua, RosPl, Seasd

Sculptress (Tall)
Herit

Sea Haven (Tall)
Herit

Sea Of Joy (Tall)
Herit, Richm

Sea Patrol (Intermediate)
Richm

Sea Urchin (Dwarf)
RosPl

Seadancer (Dwarf)
RosPl

Secret Idea
(Intermediate)
Kopua, RosPl

Secret Melody (Tall)
Herit, Richm

Sensuous Doll (Dwarf)
RosPl

Serene Sea (Tall)
Herit

Serenity Prayer (Dwarf)
Herit, RosPl

Shah's Court (Tall)
Puket

Shampoo (Intermediate)
Kopua

Shamrock Fan (Mini
Dwarf)
RosPl

Shandy (Border)
RosPl

Shannon (Border)
RosPl

Sheer Class (Dwarf)
Herit

Sheila's Beauty (Intermed.)
Herit

Shenanigans
(Intermediate)
Herit

Shepherd's Delight (Tall)
Puket

Sherlock (Dwarf)
Herit

Shine On Wine (Tall)
Herit

Shiralee (Tall)
Herit

Shoot Out (Tall)
Herit

Shooting Sparks
(Intermed.)
Herit

Shopper's Holiday (Tall)
Herit

Show Me (Border)
RosPl

Show Me Yellow (Dwarf)
Herit

Shugar (Intermediate)
Herit, Puket

Shy Violet (Dwarf)
Herit

Sierra Grande (Tall)
Herit

Sighs And Whispers
(Tall)
Herit

Silent Strings
(Intermediate)
Herit, RosPl

Silhouette (Tall)
Herit

Silk Petals (Dwarf)
RosPl

Silk Sari (Tall)
Herit

Silkirim (Tall)
Puket

Silkwood (Tall)
Herit

Silver Cove (Tall)
Herit

Silverado (Tall)
Herit

Simply Majestic (Tall)
Herit

Simply Pretty (Tall)
Herit

Sing Again
(Intermediate)
Richm

Singing Angel (Dwarf)
RosPl

Sinister (Tall)
Herit

Six Pack (Tall)
Puket

Sixpence (Dwarf)
RosPl

Skating Party (Tall)
Herit

Skeeter (Dwarf)
Richm

Skier's Delight (Tall)
Herit, Richm

Sky & Snow (Dwarf)
Richm

Sky Blue (Dwarf)
KeriP, Parva

Sky Capers (Mini Dwarf)
RosPl

Sky Drops (Dwarf)
Puket

Sky Echo (Tall)
Herit, Puket

Sky Hooks (Tall)
Herit

Sky Search (Tall)
Puket

Sky Watch (Tall)
Richm

Skye (Tall)
Herit

Skylab (Tall)
Herit

Slap Bang (Dwarf)
Herit

Sleepy Time (Mini
Dwarf)
RosPl

Slim Jim (Mini Tall)
RosPl

Small Flash (Dwarf)
Herit

Small Gem (Mini Dwarf)
RosPl

Small Ritual (Dwarf)
Herit

Smart Aleck (Tall)
Herit

Smoke Rings (Tall)
Richm

Smoky Imp (Dwarf)
Herit

Smoky Pieces (Dwarf)
Herit

Snappie (Intermediate)
RosPl

Sneak Preview (Tall)
Herit

Sniffs'n'Sneezes (Dwarf)
RosPl

Snow Cherries
(Intermediate)
Kopua, Richm, RosPl

Snow Cream (Tall)
Herit

Snow d'Or (Tall)
Herit

Snow Girl (Mini Dwarf)
RosPl

Snow Gnome
(Intermediate)
RosPl

Snow Line (Tall)
Richm

Snow Pixie (Dwarf)
RosPl

Snow Summit (Tall)
Herit

Snowbrook (Tall)
Herit

SnuggleBug (Dwarf)
BayBl

Soap Opera (Tall)
Herit

Social Event (Tall)
Herit

Social Register (Tall)
Herit, Kopua

Soft Caress (Tall)
Herit

Softly Spoken
(Intermediate)
Herit

Solano (Tall)
Herit, Puket, Richm

Solid State (Tall)
Richm

Something Special
(Intermed.)
Herit

Song Of Norway (Tall)
Herit

Soprano (Tall)
Puket

Sorority Sister (Tall)
Herit

Sostenique (Tall)
Herit

Sounder (Border)
RosPl

Southern Autumn (Tall)
Puket

Space Odyssey (Tall)
Herit

Space Psalms
(Intermediate)
Herit

Space Viking (Tall)
Herit

Spanish Coins (Mini
Tall)
RosPl

Spanish Empire (Dwarf)
Herit

Spanish Gift (Tall)
Richm

Spanish Leather (Tall)
Herit, Kopua, Puket

Sparkling Fountain (Tall)
Herit

Sparky (Mini Dwarf)
RosPl

Spatzel (Tall)
Herit, Puket

Speakeasy (Tall)
Herit

Spiced Custard (Tall)
Herit

Spin Off (Tall)
Herit

Spirit Raiser (Tall)
Puket

Split Decision (Dwarf)
Herit

Spot Pattern (Mini
Dwarf)
RosPl

Spreckles (Tall)
Puket, Richm

Spring Bells (Dwarf)
RosPl

Spring Bonnet
(Intermed.)
Kopua, Richm, RosPl

Spring Butterfly (Dwarf)
RosPl

Spring Cheddar
(Intermed.)
RosPl

Spring Child (Tall)
Herit

Spring Dancer
(Intermediate)
Herit, RosPl

Spring Fairy (Dwarf)
Richm

Spring Harmony (Mini
Tall)
RosPl

Spring Image (Tall)
Herit

Spring Laughter (Dwarf)
Richm, RosPl

Spring Mist (Dwarf)
NewlR

Spring Night
(Intermediate)
RosPl

Spring Tidings (Tall)
Herit

Spring Wine
(Intermediate)
RosPl

St Osyth (Border)
Richm

Standing Ovation (Tall)
Herit

Star Crest (Tall)
Herit

Star Dancer (Dwarf)
Herit

Star Flight (Dwarf)
Richm

Star Frost Pink (Tall)
Richm

Star Search (Dwarf)
Herit

Star Wars (Tall)
Herit

Stardate (Dwarf)
Herit

Stardust Memories (Tall)
Herit
Starfrost Pink (Tall)
Herit
Starlight Waltz (Dwarf)
Herit
Starmaster (Tall)
Herit
Starstruck (Tall)
Herit
Status Seeker (Tall)
Herit
Stellar Lights (Tall)
Herit
Stepping Little (Border)
RosPl
Stepping Out (Tall)
Kopua, Puket, Richm
Sterling Mistress (Tall)
Herit
Sterling Silver (Tall)
Puket
Sterling Stitch (Tall)
Herit
Stockholm (Dwarf)
Richm
Stolen Dreams (Tall)
Herit
Stormy Eyes (Dwarf)
RosPl
Stormy Night (Tall)
Herit
Stormy Seas (Tall)
Puket
Storyline (Tall)
Herit
Strange Child (Dwarf)
Kopua, RosPl
Stratagem (Tall)
Herit
Straw Hat (Dwarf)
Herit
Strawberry Love
(Intermed.)
Herit
Street Walker (Tall)
Herit
Striped Pants
(Intermediate)
Herit, RosPl
Strum (Intermediate)
Herit

Stylelite (Tall)
Herit
Success Story (Tall)
Herit, Puket
Sugar (Intermediate)
RosPl
Sultry Mood (Tall)
Herit
Summer Nights (Dwarf)
RosPl
Summer Olympics (Tall)
Herit
Sun And Sand (Tall)
Herit
Sun Dappled (Tall)
Richm
Sun Doll (Dwarf)
Richm, RosPl
Sundown Red
(Intermediate)
Kopua, Puket
Sunkist Frills (Tall)
Herit
Sunlit Coral (Tall)
Herit
Sunny and Warm (Tall)
Herit
Sunny Dawn
(Intermediate)
Herit
Sunny Flavour
(Intermediate)
RosPl
Sunray Reflections (Tall)
Puket
Sunrising (Intermediate)
Kopua, RosPl
Sunshine Boy
(Intermediate)
Herit
Sunshine Buttercup
(Dwarf)
NewlR
Sunshine Lace (Tall)
Herit
Super Dancer (Tall)
Herit
Superman (Tall)
Herit
Superstition (Tall)
Herit, Puket
Supreme Sultan (Tall)
Herit

Surf Lady (Tall)
Herit
Surf Rider (Tall)
Kopua
Surfie Girl (Tall)
Herit
Swagman (Dwarf)
Herit
Swain (Tall)
Herit
Swazi Princess (Tall)
Herit, Richm
Sweet Adela (Tall)
Herit
Sweet Musette (Tall)
Herit
Sweet Reflection (Tall)
Herit
Sweetie (Intermediate)
RosPl
Sweetwater (Tall)
Herit
Swizzle (Border)
Kopua, Puket, Telfa
Syllable (Dwarf)
Herit
Sylvans Stream (Tall)
Kopua
Symmetry (Tall)
Herit
Symphony (Tall)
Kopua
Syncopation (Tall)
Herit
Taffeta Bow (Tall)
Herit, Richm
Tahola (Tall)
Kopua
Taj Regis (Tall)
Herit
Taja (Dwarf)
Herit
Talk Magic
(Intermediate)
Herit
Tan Tingo
(Intermediate)
RosPl
Tangerine Tangent
(Dwarf)
Herit
Taste Of Honey (Tall)
Richm

Tatiana (Tall)
    Herit
Tchin Tchin
(Intermediate)
    Herit
Tease (Dwarf)
    RosPl
Tebby Dare (Dwarf)
    NewlR, RosPl
Tell Fibs (Dwarf)
    BayBl, Herit
Temple Gold (Tall)
    Kopua
Temptone (Tall)
    Herit
Ten Speed (Dwarf)
    RosPl
Tender Tears (Dwarf)
    Herit
Tender Thrills (Tall)
    Herit
Tender Years
(Intermediate)
    RosPl
Tennessee Woman (Tall)
    Herit
Tennison Ridge (Tall)
    Herit
Terra Bella (Tall)
    Herit
Test Pattern (Tall)
    Herit
That Scentsation (Tall)
    Herit
That's Amore (Tall)
    Herit
That's It (Dwarf)
    RosPl
Theatre (Tall)
    Herit, Puket
Theda Clark
(Intermediate)
    Herit, Richm
Think Big (Tall)
    Herit
Thornbird (Tall)
    Herit, Richm
Three Cherries (Mini
Dwarf)
    RosPl
Three Smokes
(Intermediate)
    Kopua, Richm, RosPl

Thriller (Tall)
    Herit
Throb (Tall)
    Herit
Thunder Echo (Tall)
    Herit
Tic Tac (Mini Dwarf)
    RosPl
Tiche (Dwarf)
    Richm
Tichie (Mini Dwarf)
    RosPl
Tidbit (Mini Tall)
    RosPl
Tide Crest (Tall)
    Herit
Tide's In (Tall)
    Herit
Tidepool (Dwarf)
    RosPl
Tiffany Time (Tall)
    Herit
Tiger Beau (Dwarf)
    Herit
Tiger Shark (Tall)
    Herit
Time For Love (Tall)
    Herit
Time of Grapes (Dwarf)
    RosPl
Timepiece (Tall)
    Herit
Timescape (Tall)
    Herit
Tinkerbell (Dwarf)
    Kopua, NewlR, RosPl
Tintinara (Tall)
    Herit
Tipperary (Tall)
    Richm
Tipsy Maid
(Intermediate)
    Herit
Titan's Glory (Tall)
    Herit
Toasted Almond (Tall)
    Herit
Tobacco Land (Tall)
    Herit
Tom-Tom (Tall)
    Puket
Toneen (Mini Tall)
    RosPl

Tonya (Dwarf)
    Puket, Richm, RosPl
Topaz Jewel (Tall)
    Herit
Tortuga (Dwarf)
    RosPl
Total Recall (Tall)
    Herit
Touch Of Bronze (Tall)
    Puket
Touche (Tall)
    Kopua
Town Clown (Tall)
    Herit
Town Gossip (Tall)
    Herit
Toy Clown (Dwarf)
    Herit
Tranquil Sunshine (Tall)
    Herit, Richm
Transcribe (Dwarf)
    Herit
Treasured Love (Tall)
    Herit
Tres Jolie (Dwarf)
    Richm
Tricks (Dwarf)
    Herit
Trill (Tall)
    Richm
Triple Little (Border)
    RosPl
Triplet (Intermediate)
    Herit, Puket
Trivia (Intermediate)
    Herit
Troll (Dwarf)
    NewlR, RosPl
Tropical Fruit (Tall)
    Herit
Tulare (Border)
    Richm
Tumbago (Dwarf)
    RosPl
Turtledove
(Intermediate)
    RosPl
Tuxedo (Tall)
    Kopua, Richm
Twice Delightful (Tall)
    Herit
Twilight Blaze (Tall)
    Herit

Twilight Harmony (Tall)
Kopua

Twinkling Lights (Dwarf)
NewlR

Twinkling Star (Mini Dwarf)
RosPl

Twist Of Fate (Tall)
Herit

Twist of Lemon (Mini Dwarf)
RosPl

Tyke (Mini Tall)
RosPl

Tyrolienne (Intermediate)
Herit

Under A Cloud (Tall)
Herit

Unforgettable Fire (Tall)
Herit

Valiant Warrior (Mini Tall)
RosPl

Vamp (Intermediate)
Kopua, Richm

Van Gogh (Tall)
Herit

Vanity (Tall)
Herit, Puket, Richm

Vanity's Child (Tall)
Herit

Varga Girl (Tall)
Herit

Vasqua (Intermediate)
Herit

Vaudeville (Tall)
Puket

Velvet Bouquet (Mini Tall)
RosPl

Velvet Robe (Tall)
Richm

Velvet Toy (Mini Dwarf)
RosPl

Velvet Vista (Tall)
Herit

Velvetine (Dwarf)
Puket

Veneer (Tall)
Herit

Venus Rising (Tall)
Herit

Veri-Gay (Mini Dwarf)
RosPl

Verismo (Tall)
Herit

Verivogue (Tall)
Herit

Vibrant Spring (Intermediate)
RosPl

Vibration (Tall)
Herit

Victoria Falls (Tall)
Herit, Puket, Richm

Victorian Frills (Tall)
Herit

Victorian Lace (Tall)
Herit

Victorious Voyager (Tall)
Herit

Vigilante (Tall)
Herit

Villa Shimmer (Tall)
Herit

Villa Splendour (Tall)
Herit

Vilma V (Dwarf)
NewlR

Violet Gem (Mini Dwarf)
Kopua, Richm, RosPl

Violet Lass (Dwarf)
Herit

Vision In Pink (Tall)
Herit

Vivien (Tall)
Herit

Voila (Intermediate)
Kopua, Richm

Voodoo Doll (Intermediate)
Richm

Wake Up (Dwarf)
RosPl

Wake Up Call (Tall)
Herit

Walking On Sunshine (Dwarf)
BayBl

Wan Li (Tall)
Richm

Wanderer (Dwarf)
Herit

Warrior King (Tall)
Herit, Puket

Watch Night (Tall)
Herit

Watercolour (Dwarf)
Kopua, Richm, RosPl

Way Out West (Tall)
Herit

Webelos (Dwarf)
RosPl

Wedding Band (Tall)
Herit

Wedding Vow (Tall)
Herit

Wee Fragrance (Dwarf)
RosPl

Wee Moonlight (Mini Dwarf)
RosPl

Wee Reggie (Mini Dwarf)
Richm

Wee Ruffles (Dwarf)
RosPl

Welcome Aboard (Tall)
Herit

Well Suited (Dwarf)
Herit

Westar (Dwarf)
Puket, RosPl

Westbay (Border)
RosPl

What Magic (Tall)
Herit

Wheels (Dwarf)
RosPl

Whim (Dwarf)
Richm

Whin Hill (Tall)
Richm

Whispering (Tall)
Herit

White Chapeau (Intermed.)
Herit

White Elephant (Tall)
Herit

White Gem (Dwarf)
RosPl

White Lightning (Tall)
Herit, Kopua

White Persian (Dwarf)
RosPl

Whoop Em Up (Intermed.)
Herit, Richm, RosPl

Why Not   (Intermediate)
RosPl

Wide Horizon   (Tall)
Herit

Widget   (Mini Tall)
RosPl

Wild Jasmine   (Tall)
Herit

Wild Vision   (Tall)
Herit

Wilma Greenlee   (Dwarf)
RosPl

Wind Rose   (Dwarf)
Herit, Puket

Windsong West   (Tall)
Herit

Windsurfer   (Tall)
Herit

Wine Light   (Dwarf)
Herit

Winemaster   (Tall)
Herit

Wings Of Dream   (Tall)
Herit

Wings Of Gold   (Tall)
Herit

Winifred Ross   (Tall)
Herit

Winners Circle   (Tall)
Kopua

Winning Note   (Tall)
Herit

Winter Watch   (Tall)
Herit

Winterland   (Tall)
Herit

Wish Waltz   (Tall)
Herit

Wishful Thought (Dwarf)
RosPl

Wisteria Sachet (Intermediate)
Richm

Witch's Wand   (Tall)
Herit

Witches Sabbath   (Tall)
Herit

Witching   (Tall)
Herit

Wizard Of Id   (Dwarf)
Herit

Words And Music   (Tall)
Herit

Wych Way   (Tall)
Herit

Wyuna Evening (Intermediate)
Richm

Yaquina Blue   (Tall)
Herit

yellow   (Dwarf)
Ashto, Ormon

Yellow Doll (Intermediate)
RosPl

You're Special   (Tall)
Herit

Yukon Fever   (Tall)
Herit

Zambesi   (Tall)
Richm

Zapped   (Tall)
Herit, Puket, Richm

Zinc Pink   (Intermediate)
Herit

Zing Me   (Intermediate)
Herit

Zinger   (Intermediate)
Herit

Zipper   (Dwarf)
NewlR

Zounds   (Dwarf)
Herit

Zua   (Intermediate)
RosPl

Zula   (Mini Tall)
RosPl

Iris Dutch

mixed
Altrf, Kayd, VanEe

Apollo
Altrf

Blue Diamond
Altrf

Blue Elegance
Altrf

Blue Magic
Altrf, VanEe

Blue Ocean
Altrf

Blue Sail
Altrf

Blue Star
Altrf

Casablanca
Altrf

Crown Jewel
VanEe

Deep River
Altrf

Golden Beauty
Altrf

Golden Giant
Altrf

Harry Hylkema
Altrf

Hildergarde
Altrf

Paris
Altrf

Prof Blaauw
Altrf

Purple Rain
Altrf

Purple Sensation
Altrf

Sapphire Beauty
Altrf

Saturnus
Altrf

Symphony
VanEe

Telstar
Altrf, VanEe

White Bridge
Altrf, VanEe

Iris ensata

mixed
Kayd

varieties (was I.kaempferi)
Ashto, JoyPl

Abundant Display
Otara

Acclaim
BayBl, Diack, Mills, Otara, Telfa, WaiMa

Active Ayr
Herit

Asagira
Otara

Banners on Parade
BayBl

Beyond The Horizon
Otara

Botan Sakura
BayBl, Diack, Egmon,
Mills, Nikau, Otara,
Puket, WaiMa

Caprician Butterfly
Herit

Casprician Chimes
Herit

Centre Of Attention
Herit

Cobra Dance
Diack, WaiMa

Dark Enchantment
Otara

Dawn Ballet
Diack

Distant Echo
Puket

Dramatic Moment
Otara

Enchanted Lake
Mills

Enchanting Melody
Puket

Enchantment
Otara

Evening Episode
Otara

Flirtation
BayBl, Parva, Puket

Frilled Enchantment
Herit

Frostbound
Otara

Galatea
Diack, Otara, WaiMa

Garden Caprice
Otara

Geisha Mischief
Otara

Geisha Obi
Herit

Geisha Parasol
BayBl

Glitter and Glamour
Otara

Good Omen
Herit, Otara

Hagaroma
BayBl

Happy Awakening
Otara

Happy Faun
Otara

Hatsu Kagami
Herit

Hidenishiki
Otara

High Cascades
Otara

Horogun
Otara

Hue & Cry
Otara

Iapetus
Otara

Ike No Sazanami
Otara

Imperial Violet
Otara

Inspiration
Parva

Itogasumi
Puket

Ivory Glow
Otara

Janet Hutchinson
Herit

Kalamazoo
Herit

Knight In Armour
Otara

Kumi
Herit

Kyoto
Puket

Lady Fayre
Otara, Puket

Lady in Waiting
Egmon, Otara, WaiMa

Ling
Otara

Mammoth Marvel
Diack

maroon
Parva

mauve
Nikau

Midsummer Revelry
Parva, WaiMa

Miss Coquette
Herit

Mist Falls
Otara

Mist O' Morn
Otara

Miyako Nishiki
Otara

Numazu
Otara

Ocean Mist
Otara

Onigishima
Parva, Puket

Oriental Glamour
Puket

Pastel Princess
Otara

Peacock Dance
Herit

Pink Frost
Otara

Popular Acclaim
Otara

Prairie Chief
Otara

Prairie Coquette
Herit

Prairie Edge
Otara

Prairie Fantasy
Herit

Prairie Frost
Otara

Prairie Glory
Herit

Prairie Noble
Herit

Prairie Royalty
Otara

Prairie Sweetbriar
Otara

Prairie Twilight
Herit

Prairie Valor
Otara

Prairie Velvet
Otara

Prairie Wonder
Otara

Purity
Diack, WaiMa

Red Titian
WaiMa

Reign Of Glory
Diack, Mills, Otara,
Parva, Puket

Ringonotama
Otara, Puket

Rose Fantasy
Otara, Parva, Telfa,
WaiMa

Rose Queen(x laevigata)
BayBl, Nikau, Otara,
Parva, Peak, Puket,
WaiMa, Warwk, WilAq

Royal Crown
Herit

Royal Sapphire
Diack

Royal Venetian
Puket

Sea Titan
Otara

Sei Shonagon
Otara

Sheer Fascination
Otara

Shikinjo
BayBl, Otara, WaiMa

Shinkai No Iro
Otara

Shinonome
Herit

Siren Song
Otara

Snow Queen (white RoseQ)
Parva

Sorcerer's Triumph
Otara

Star at Midnight
BayBl

Summer Storm
BayBl, Diack, Herit,
Mills, Parva, Telfa,
WaiMa

Sunnybank
BayBl, Otara

Taga Sode
Herit

Tamatsushima
Herit

Temple Maiden
Herit

Tender Trap
Herit

Tori No Dai
Otara, WaiMa

Tuisho
Diack

Valiant Prince
BayBl

Variegata
BayBl

white
Nikau

Wine Ruffles
Otara

Winged Chariot
Otara

Winged Sprite
Otara

Worlds Delight
Otara, Parva, Telfa

Worley Pink
BayBl

Yachiyo No Sata
WaiMa

Yasaboshi
Herit

Yoshing-no-gata
Otara, Puket

Yusho
Herit

Iris louisiana

hybrids mixed colours
AynDa, WilAq

unnamed seedlings
WilAq

Acacia Rhumba
Herit

Alabaster Moon
Herit

All Agaze
Herit, Otara, Puket

Alluvial Gold
Herit

Alouette
Herit

Ann Chowding
Otara, Puket, WaiMa

Apollo's Song
Herit

Artworld
Herit, Ranch, Richm,
WaiMa

Ashley Michelle
Herit, Otara

Aunt Shirley
Otara

Bajazzo
Ranch

Barbare
Herit

Barossa
Herit, Otara

Bayou Comus
Ranch

Bellevue's Michelle
Herit

Berenice
Herit

Betty Blockbuster
Herit

Blue Shield
Ranch, WaiMa

Bluebonnet Sue
Herit

Bob Ward
Otara, Puket

Bold Pretender
Herit

Bourbon Street
Ranch

Bowie
Herit

Brookvale Nocturne
Herit, Ranch

Brookvale Overture
Ranch

Bryan Bay
Puket

Bubblegum Ballerina
Herit

Bushfire Moon
Herit

Byron Bay
Herit

C'est Chic
Herit, Puket

C'est Le Mote
Herit

C'est Si Bon
Herit, WaiMa

Cajun Cookery
Herit

Cajun Love
Puket

Cammeray
Herit, Puket

Charles Michelle
Otara, Ranch, WaiMa

Charlies Tress
Herit

Charlotte's Tutu
Herit

Chateau Michelle
Ranch

Clara Goula
Herit

Classical Note
Herit

Clyde Redmond
Herit, Ranch

Commandment
Herit

Concours Elegance
Herit

Coorabelle
Herit

Cosi Fan Tutti
Herit

Crisp Lime
Herit

Cuban Rumba
Herit

Cuisine
Puket, Ranch

Currency
Herit

Dancing Vogue
Herit

Danza
Herit, Ranch

Dawn Planet
Herit

Dazzling Star
Herit, Richm

Delta Bell
Ranch

Delta Dawn
Ranch

Delta Dove
Herit, Ranch

Delta Downs
Herit

Delta Honey
Herit

Desert Jewel
Herit

Designer's Dream
Herit

Dixie Deb
Otara

Dural Bluebird
Herit

Dural Charm
Herit

Dural Dreamtime
Herit

Dural Fantasy
Herit

Dural White Butterfly
Herit, Ranch, Richm

Edith Fear
Herit

Elusive Butterfly
Ranch

Emigre
Herit

Entree
Otara, Puket, Ranch

Eolian
Herit, WaiMa

Europa
Herit

Everett Caradine
Ranch

Exquisite Lady
Herit

Extraordinaire
Herit

FAC McCulla
Puket

Fait Accompli
Herit

Far And Away
Herit

Fat Tuesday
Herit

Festivals Acadian
Herit

Festive Fever
Herit

Fine Warrior
Herit

First Favourite
Herit

Flight Of Fancy
WaiMa

Flight Of Fantasy
Herit, Otara, Ranch, Richm

Francis Elizabeth
Ranch

Francois
Herit

Freedom Ride
Herit

Full Eclipse
WaiMa

Fulvala
Otara

Gabriel's Love
Herit

Gaia
Herit

Gate Crasher
Herit

Geisha Eyes
Herit

Genial Giant
Herit

Gentleman
Ranch

Gerry Marsteller
Herit, Puket

Gertie Butler
Herit

Gladiators Gift
Herit

Glittering Prize
Herit

Glowlight
Herit, Otara, Puket, Ranch

Going South
Herit

Good Vibes
Herit

Green Elf
Herit

Guessing Game
Herit

Gulf Shores
Herit

Heather Pryor
Herit

Heavenly Glow
Herit

Helen Naish
Herit, Puket, Ranch, WaiMa

Heliostat
Herit

High Pitch
Herit

Honey Star
Herit, Ranch

Honoured Guest
Herit

Hurricane Party
Herit

Icarus
Herit

Ice Angel
Herit

Ice Magic
Herit

Impassioned
Herit

Imperial Magician
Herit

It's Cool
Herit

Jack Attack
Herit

Jazz Ballet
Herit, Ranch, WaiMa

Jeri
Herit

Jet Ace
Ranch

Joel Fletcher
Herit

Johns Lucifer
Herit, WaiMa

Josephine Shanks
Herit

Joy Flight
Herit

Kay Nelson
Herit

King Kong
Herit

Kitti D
Herit

Knights Treasure
Herit

Koorawatha
Herit, Puket, Ranch,
WaiMa

Kristin
Ranch

La Perouse
Ranch

La Stupenda
Herit

Laser Show
Herit

Lavender Ruffles
Herit, Otara, Puket

Limited Edition
Herit

Little Nutkin
Herit

Louisiana Derby
Herit, Richm

Lucille Holley
Herit

Lucy Payens
Herit

Lydia's Love
Herit

Malibu Magic
Herit

Marble Cake
Herit

Margaret Hunter
Herit

Margaret Lee
Herit

Marie Dolores
Herit

Marie's Choice
Herit

Martha Mistric Clary
Herit

Midnight Drama
Herit

Mighty Rich
Herit

Milk Maid
Puket, Ranch

Mississippi Gambler
Otara, Ranch

Monument
Herit

Mrs Ira Nelson
Herit, Otara, Ranch

Mrs Mac
Ranch

Myra Arney
Ranch

Natural Wonder
Herit

Never Say
Herit

New Dimensions
WaiMa

News Brief
Ranch, WaiMa

Noble Planet
Herit

Obvious Heir
Herit

Oklahoma Kitty
Herit

Old South
Herit, Puket, Ranch

Our Parris
Herit, Ranch, WaiMa

Over There
Herit

Pamela Hart
Herit

Parade Music
Herit

Patient Reward
Herit, Ranch

Paul Payens
Herit

Perfect Match
Herit, Ranch

Piece de Resistance
Herit

Pink Poetry
Herit

Pintharuka
Herit

Plantation Beau
Ranch

Popsie
Herit

Poseidon's Pool
Herit

Praline Festival
Herit

Price Redmond
Ranch

Princess Sharma
Herit

Pristine Priss
Herit

Professor Barbara
Puket

Professor Ellis
Herit

Professor Ike
Herit, Otara, Puket,
Ranch, WaiMa

Professor Jim
Herit

Professor Marta Marie
Otara, Puket

Professor Paul
Herit

Purple Pallas
Herit

Quiet Harbour
Herit

Rachael's Request
Herit

Ragin' Cajun
Herit

Reputation
Herit

Rich Tradition
Herit

Royal Embrace
Ranch

Rue Royale
Puket, Ranch

Ruth Sloan
Herit

Satchmo
Herit

Screen Gem
Herit, Richm

Sea Consul
Herit

Sea Knight
Herit

Sea Lord
Herit

Sea Wasp
Richm

Shrimp Creole
Ranch

Shy Royal
Herit

Sidney Conger
WaiMa

Silencio
Herit

Sinfonietta
Herit, Otara, Puket,
Ranch, WaiMa

So Loyal
Herit

Soft Laughter
Herit, Otara

Sorbet
Herit

Southern Drawl
Herit

Southerner
Ranch

Spanish Ballet
Herit

Stage Shy
Herit

Stella Pelissot
Herit

Stop The Nation
Herit

Swamp Flame
Herit

Tahitian Night
Herit

Time Keeper
Herit

Top Notch
Richm

Top Start
Herit

Tranquil Spirit
Herit, Richm

Twirling Ballerina
Herit

Uptight
Ranch, WaiMa

Valera
Puket, WaiMa

Vermilion Treasure
Herit

Violet Ray
Ranch

Virginia Plauche
Herit

Wake Up Susie
Herit

Watch For It
Herit

Watch Out
Herit, Ranch

Waverly Pink
Herit

Well Dressed
Herit

White Umbrella
Herit

Wild Prospect
Herit

Wine And Dine
Herit

Wine Country
Herit

Iris sibirica

Alba
Telfa, Warwk

Alter Ego
Herit

Ann Dasch
BayBl, Herit

Anniversary
BayBl

Aqua Whispers
Otara

Arabian Princess
BayBl

Augery
BayBl, Peak

Ausable River
BayBl, Herit

Blue Pennant
Otara

blue violet shades
AynDa, KeriP, Mills,
Nikau, Pkrau

Butter And Sugar
BayBl, Herit, Parva

Caesars Blue
Vall #

Caesars Brother
Otara, Peak, Puket,
WaiMa

Caesars Robe
WaiMa

Carrie Lee
BayBl

Castle Grace
BayBl, Oasis, Parva,
Puket, TRidg

Chrystal Charm
Puket

clear blue, 1m stems
TRidg

Cleve Dodge
Herit

Contrast In Styles
Otara

Coolabah
BayBl, Herit, Otara

Cream Chantilly
BayBl, Parva

Dancing Nanou
Herit

dark blue
Warwk

dark blue w yellow blaze
Ashto

Dark Circle
BayBl

Dear Delight
Herit

Deep Purple
Mills, Pgeon, WilAq

Dream Holiday
Otara

Dreaming Green
BayBl

dwarf form
WaiMa

Ester CDM
Otara

Ewen
Puket

Flight of Butterflies
Otara

Fourfold White
Herit

Frosted Cranberry
Otara

Frosty Rim
BayBl, Herit, Otara

Grand Junction
Parva, WaiMa

Gulls Wing
Otara

Halcyon Seas
Herit

Harpswell Happiness
BayBl, Parva

Harpswell Haze
BayBl, Herit

Helicopter
Otara

High Standards
Otara

Hubbard
BayBl, Parva

I'm Just Blue
BayBl, Herit

Illini Charm
Otara, Puket

Indy
Otara

Jewel of Happiness
BayBl

Jewelled Crown
Otara

King of Kings
Otara

Lady of Quality
Otara

Lady Vanessa
Otara

Liberty Hills
Otara

Lights Of Paris
Herit

Lime Heart
BayBl

Little Tricolour
BayBl

Maggie Smith
BayBl, Herit

Marilyn Holmes
Herit, Otara

Moon Moth
BayBl, Puket, TRidg

Music Royal
Herit

My Love
Otara

Nana
WaiMa

Navy Brass
BayBl, Herit

Night Breeze
Herit

On And On
Herit

Orville Fay
BayBl, Herit, Parva, WaiMa

Otepopo Honey
Otepo

Other Worlds
Herit

Peg Edwards
Otara

Percheron
Otara

Pink Haze
Herit, Otara

Pink Sparkle
BayBl, Herit, Otara, Parva

Pirate Prince
Herit, Otara

Purple
Telfa

Reprise
Otara

Rikugi-Sakura
Otara

Roanke's Choice
BayBl, Otara

Romano
Puket

Rose Queen
Diack, WaiMa

Ruby Wine
Oasis

Ruffled Velvet
Otara

Sally Kerlin
BayBl

Sanquinea
Puket

Savoir Faire
Herit

Sea Horse
Peak

Sea Shadows
Peak, Pgeon

Shirley Pope
BayBl

Silver Edge
BayBl, Peak

Sky Mirror
Otara

Sparkling Rose
Parva, Puket

Star Glitter
Herit

Star Steps
Parva

Steve
WaiMa

Teal Velvet
BayBl

Teal Wood
BayBl, Puket

Temper Tantrum
Herit

Towanda Red Flare
Puket

Turquoise Cup
BayBl

Tycoon
Parva

Vasari
Parva, WaiMa

Vi Luihn
BayBl, Herit

white
TRidg

White Magnificence
Herit
White Swirl
BayBl, Herit
Wine Wings
Puket, WaiMa
Wing On Wing
Herit, Otara
Wizardry
Otara

Iris Spanish

mixed
VanEe
Canary Bird
VanEe
Delfts Blue
VanEe
Enchantress
VanEe
Fredrica
VanEe
Gypsy Queen
VanEe
Solfaterre
VanEe
Wilhelmina
VanEe

Iris spuria

Adobe Sunset
Herit
Amber Ripples
Herit
Blue Lassie
Herit
Bronzing
Herit
Butter Chocolate
Herit
Butter Paddle
Herit
Chestnut Chime
Herit
Cinnamon Roll
Herit
Cinnamon Stick
Herit
Dress Circle
Herit
Eleanor Hill
Herit
Follow Through
Herit

Forty Carats
Herit
Full Sun
Herit
Gilded Chalice
Herit
Happy Choice
Herit
Heart To Heart
Herit
Highline Amethyst
Herit
Highline Lavender
Herit
Janice Chesnick
Herit
Medallion
Herit
Minneopa
Herit
Missouri Gal
Herit
New Harmony
Herit
Redwood Supreme
Herit
Satin Wood
Herit
Social Circle
Herit
Son Of Sun
Herit
Spiced Tea
Herit
Struttin'
Herit
Terra Nova
Herit
Tiger Blues
Herit

Isatis

tinctoria (Woad)
Della, King #, Orang,
Sweet

Isoplexis

canariensis (Spanish Foxglove)
TRidg

Isopogon

anemonifolius (Coneflowers, Drumsticks)
Matth

dawsonii
Matth

Isotoma

axillaris now Solenopsis a.
AynDa
fluviatilis now Solenopsis f.
Gordn, Orati

Itea

ilicifolia (Hollyleaf Sweetspire)
Hackf
sinensis
Caves
virginica
Woodl

Ixerba

brexioides (Tawari)
Gordn, Orati, Terra

Ixia

mixed
Kayd
Amethystina
Kerer
bellendenii
DaffA
Bluebird
Kerer
Candy Stripes mixed
Altrf
capillaris
DaffA
conferta
DaffA
Crateroides
Kerer
curta
DaffA, JoyPl
dubia
Irida
Elvira
DaffA, Parva
Hogarth
Kerer
Hubert
Kerer
maculata
CottP, DaffA, Irida,
JoyPl, Kerer, TRidg
monadelpha
Irida

paniculata

DaffA, Irida, Kerer, Parva

polystachya

CottP, DaffA, Irida, JoyPl, Kerer

Rosetta

CottP

Venus

Kerer

viridiflora

BayBl, DaffA, Irida, JoyPl, Kerer, KeriP, MaraN, Oasis, Taunt, TRidg

Ixiolirion

pallasii now tartaricum

VanEe

Jaboticaba - Myricari

cauliflora

Frans

Jacaranda

mimosifolia

Burbk, Chedd, Coatv, Denes, Frans, LakeN, Matwh, NZtr #, Reic #, SpecT, TopTr

Jacobinea

pauciflora now Justicia rissini

Butlr, Denes, Mtato

Jasione

heldreichii

MaraN

humilis now J.crispa amethystina

Oasis

laevis was J.perennis (Sheeps Bit, Sheeps Scabious)

CottP, MaraN, Marsh, Nikau, Oasis, Pgeon, Telfa

laevis Blue Light

MillH, TRidg

montana Light

Dream

sp tight blue ball fl

AynDa

Jasminum

angulare

CouCl

azoricum (Azores Jasmine)

BlueM, CouCl, Denes, Mtato

beesianum

BlueM, CouCl

humile

BlueM

mesnyi (Primrose Jasmine)

BlueM

nudiflorum (Winter Jasmine)

BlueM, Denes, Dove

officinale

CouCl

officinale Aureovariegatum now o. Aureum

BlueM, CouCl

officinale Variegatum now o.Argenteovariegatum

BlueM, CouCl

parkeri (Dwarf Jasmine)

BlueM, Parva

polyanthum (Spring/Chinese Jasmine)

BlueM, ZinoN

polyanthum Perfume Princess

CouCl

rex

CouCl

sambac

CouCl

x stephanense (Chinese Jasmine)

BlueM, Denes

x stephanense Rose Spray

CouCl

Jovellana

sinclairii (Native Calceolaria)

BayBl, KeriP, Orati, Wahpa

violacea

BayBl

Juglans

ailanthifolia (Japanese Walnut)

Diack, PuhaN, TopTr

cinerea (Butternut)

Apple, Peele

hindsii (Hinds Walnut)

Apple

hindsii x regia (Hybrid Walnut)

Peele

neotropica (Andean Black Walnut)

Koan, Lsendt

nigra (Black Walnut)

Apple, Chedd, Coatv, Diack, Harri, Mtato, NZtr #, Pionr, PuhaN, Pukho

regia (Walnut)

Chedd, Diack, Hewsn, PuhaN, Terra, Wensl

regia varieties grafted

Coatv

regia AH/1335

Harri

regia BL/300

Chedd

regia Franquette

Chedd

regia H/1199/4

Chedd, Harri

regia H/1199/4 (nigra rootstk)

Harri

regia Late leafing G26

Chedd

regia Roadside 12

Chedd

regia Roadside 6

Chedd

regia seedlings East coast

Chedd

regia seedlings Christchurch

Chedd

regia seedlings Hawkes Bay

Chedd

regia seedlings Waikato

Chedd

regia Serr

Chedd

regia Tree crops IC/152

Chedd

regia Vina

Chedd, Harri

regia Waikato Wonder

Pionr

regia Wilsons W. type Wigg

Chedd

regia Wilsons Wonder
  Pionr
regia Wilsons Wonder
(nigra rootstk)
  Harri

Juncus

effusus (Common/Soft rush
  WaiMa
effusus Spiralis (Corkscrew
Rush)
  BayBl, KeriP
ensifolius
  WaiMa
filiformis syn spiralis
  Diack
inflexus syn glaucus (Hard
Rush)
  Diack, WaiMa
maritimis (Sea Rush)
  NZtr #
sarophorus (Rush)
  NZtr #

Juniperus

ashei
  Cedar, WakaC
bermudiana (Bermuda
Juniper)
  Cedar
bermudiana blue cultivar
  Cedar
californica
  Cedar
chinensis (Chinese Juniper)
  Cedar
chinensis Albovariegata
  CPete
chinensis Aurea (Golden
Chinese Juniper)
  Cedar, CPete
chinensis Aureo Variegata
  BlueM
chinensis Blaauw (Blaauw's
Juniper)
  Cedar, CPete
chinensis Blue Alps
  Cedar, CPete, Mtato
chinensis Blue Point
  BlueM, Cedar
chinensis Columnaris
Glauca
  Cedar

chinensis Densa Spartan
now c.Spartan
  BlueM
chinensis Expansa
Aureospicata was J.
davurica E.A.
  Cedar, CPete
chinensis Expansa
Variegata
  Cedar
chinensis Hetzii was J x
media Hetzii
  Cedar, Matal
chinensis Japonica
  BlueM
chinensis Kaizuka
(Hollywood Juniper)
  BlueM, Cedar, Coatv,
  CPete
chinensis Kaizuka Glauca
  Coatv
chinensis Kaizuka
Variegata
  Cedar, CPete
chinensis Keteleeri
  Cedar
chinensis Kuriwao Gold
  BlueM, Cedar
chinensis Mountbatten
  Cedar
chinensis Parsonsii was J.
davurica Expansa
  Cedar
chinensis Plumosa
Albovariegata was J.x
media P.A.
  Cedar
chinensis Plumosa Aurea
  Cedar, Chedd, CPete
chinensis Plumosa
Aureovariegata
  Cedar, CPete
chinensis Pyramidalis
  Cedar, CPete
chinensis Robusta Green
  BlueM, Cedar
chinensis San Jose
  BlueM, Cedar
chinensis Silver Shower
  CPete
chinensis Spartan
  Cedar, CPete
chinensis Stricta
  BlueM

chinensis Sunbeam
  BlueM
chinensis Variegata
  BlueM, Cedar
communis (Common
Juniper)
  Cedar
communis Compressa
(Noah's Ark Juniper)
  BlueM, Cedar, CPete,
  Diack, TopTr
communis Depressa
  BlueM
communis Depressa Aurea
  BlueM, Cedar, CPete
communis Depressed Star
  BlueM, Cedar, CPete,
  Matai
communis Gold Cone
  BlueM, Cedar, CPete
communis Hibernica (Irish
Juniper)
  Cedar, CPete
communis Hornibrookii
  BlueM, Cedar
communis McKays Weeper
  Cedar
communis Repanda
  BlueM, Cedar, CPete,
  McKe
communis Silver Lining
  BlueM, Cedar, CPete
communis Suecica Nana
  Cedar
conferta (Sand Juniper,
Shore Juniper)
  BlueM, Cedar, Hewsn,
  McKe, Mtato
conferta Blue Pacific
  Butlr, Cedar
conferta Emerald Ruffles
  Cedar
conferta Emerald Sea
  Cedar
conferta Horridus
  Cedar
davurica Expansa now J.
chinensis Parsonii
  Cedar
davurica Expansa
Aureospicata now J. chin.
E.A.
  BlueM, Cedar

davurica Expansa
Variegata now J. chin.
E.V.
BlueM, Cedar

deppeana var. Conspicua
(Alligator Juniper)
Cedar, CPete

flaccida (Mexican Weeping
Juniper)
Cedar

gaussenii
Cedar

horizontalis Bar Harbour
(Blue Carpet Juniper)
Cedar, Chedd, CPete

horizontalis Blue Chip
BlueM, Cedar, CPete

horizontalis Blue Horizon
Cedar

horizontalis Douglasii
Cedar

horizontalis Emerald
Spreader
Cedar, CPete

horizontalis Hughes
BlueM, Cedar

horizontalis Jade Spreader
BlueM, Cedar

horizontalis Marcella
Cedar

horizontalis Plumosa
(Andorra Juniper)
Cedar, CPete, Hewsn,
Mtato

horizontalis Prince Of
Wales
Cedar

horizontalis Turquoise
Spreader
Cedar

horizontalis Webberii
Cedar

horizontalis Wiltonii (lton
Carpet Juniper)
BlueM, Cedar

x media Aorangi Gold
Cedar, CPete, Mtato

x media Blaauw now
chinensis B
BlueM

x media Blue Cloud now
virginiana B.C.
BlueM, CPete

x media Dandelight
Cedar, CPete

x media Gold Coast (Gold
Coast Juniper)
BlueM, Cedar, CPete,
Dove

x media Hetzii now
J.chinensis H.
BlueM, Cedar

x media Milky Way
Cedar

x media Mint Julep
Cedar

x media Pfitzeriana (Pfitzer
Juniper)
Cedar

x media Pfitzeriana Aurea
Cedar, Matai

x media Pfitzeriana
Compacta
Cedar

x media Pfitzeriana Glauca
Cedar, CPete, Dove,
Hewsn

x media Phitz Blue
BlueM

x media Plumosa
Albovariegata see J
chinensis
Cedar

x media Plumosa Aurea see
chinensis
BlueM, Cedar

x media Plumosa
Aureovariegata see
chinensis
Cedar

x media Silver Spreader
BlueM

x media Spence Silver
BlueM

x media Sulphur Spray
BlueM, Cedar, CPete

x media Winter Gold
Cedar

monosperma
(Cherrystone/One Stone
Juniper)
Cedar

occidentalis (Western
Juniper)
Cedar, WakaC

osteosperma syn
J.utahensis (Utah Juniper)
Cedar

oxycedrus
WakaC

pinchotii
Cedar

pingii Glassell was
squamata G.
BlueM

pingii Glassell was J.
squamata G.
Cedar

pingii Pygmaea was J.
squam. P.
Cedar, CPete, Kayd

pingii Wilsonii was J.
Squam. W.
Cedar

procera
Ether

procumbens (Japanese
Garden Juniper)
BlueM, Cedar

procumbens Nana
BlueM, Cedar, CPete

recurva Audrey
BlueM, CPete

recurva Ron
BlueM

recurva var coxii (Coffin
Juniper)
BlueM, Cedar

recurva var coxii -dwarf
form
Cedar

repanda
Looij

rigida (Needle Juniper)
Cedar, CPete

sabina Arcadia
Cedar

sabina Blue Danube
Cedar

sabina Broadmoor
Cedar

sabina Erecta (Dutch Savin
Juniper)
BlueM, Cedar

sabina Tamariscifolia
BlueM, Cedar, CPete,
Hewsn

sargentii Glauca
BlueM, Cedar

scopulorum (Rocky Mountain Juniper)
   Cedar, WakaC

scopulorum Blue Heaven
   Cedar

scopulorum Blue Sabre
   Cedar

scopulorum Colorado Green (or Cologreen)
   BlueM, Cedar

scopulorum Dew Drop
   BlueM, Cedar

scopulorum Erecta Glauca
   Cedar

scopulorum Frosty Morning
   Cedar

scopulorum Gray Gleam
   BlueM, Cedar, CPete, Denes

scopulorum Hilborn's Silver Globe
   Cedar

scopulorum Moffettii
   BlueM, Cedar

scopulorum Moonglow
   BlueM, Cedar

scopulorum Pathfinder
   Cedar, CPete

scopulorum Sky Rocket
   Chedd, Kayd

scopulorum Springbank
   Cedar

scopulorum Table Top
   BlueM

scopulorum Table Top Blue
   Cedar

scopulorum Tolleson's Weeping
   BlueM

scopulorum Welchii
   Cedar

squamata Blue Carpet
   BlueM, Cedar, CPete

squamata Blue Star
   BlueM, Cedar, Chedd, CPete

squamata Glassell now pingii G
   BlueM

squamata Gold Flash
   Cedar, CPete

squamata Holger
   Cedar, CPete, Kayd

squamata Meyeri
   BlueM, Cedar, CPete

squamata Meyeri x recurva var coxii
   Cedar

squamata Pymaea see J. pingii P.
   BlueM, Cedar

squamata Spence Silver
   Cedar

squamata var fargesii
   Cedar

squamata Wilsonii see J. pingii W.
   BlueM, Cedar

taxifolia
   Looij

taxifolia var formosanum
   CPete

taxifolia var lutchuensis
   BlueM, Cedar, CPete

thurifera (Spanish Juniper)
   Cedar

utahensis syn J.osteosperma (Spanish Juniper)
   Cedar

virginiana (Eastern Red Cedar)
   Cedar, Ford, Matwh, PuhaN

virginiana Blue Cloud was J.x media B.C.
   Cedar

virginiana Burkii
   Cedar

virginiana Frosty Morn
   CPete

virginiana Glauca
   Cedar

virginiana Grey Owl
   Cedar

virginiana Hillii
   BlueM, Cedar

virginiana Silver Spreader
   Cedar

virginiana Skyrocket
   BlueM, Cedar, CPete

virginiana Canaertii
   BlueM

wallichiana (Black/Wallich Juniper)
   Cedar

Justicia

brandegeeana was Beleperone guttata (Shrimp Plant)
   Trans

brandegeeana lutea now b.Yellow Queen
   Woodl

carnea was Jacobinea c. (Brazilian Plume Flower, Flamingo Plant)
   Denes, Trans

carnea pink (compact)
   Trans

pauciflora red form now rizzinii
   LakeN

pauciflora yellow form now rizzinii
   LakeN

rizzinii red tipped w yellow (Paradise Plant)
   Butlr, Denes, Mtato, Nikau

Kadsura

japonica
   CouCl, MJury

japonica Variegata
   MJury

Kaempferia

rotunda (Resurrection Lily)
   Parva

Kalanchoe

blossfeldiana
   Trans

Fiery Blossom
   Reic #

Melody mixture
   Reic #

Tetra Vulcan
   Reic #

Yellow Tom Thumb
   Reic #

Kalmia

latifolia Bullseye
   Denes

latifolia Carousel
   BlueM, YakuN

latifolia Elf
Denes
latifolia Nipmuck
BlueM, YakuN
latifolia Ostbo Red
Denes, YakuN
latifolia rubra
Reic #
latifolia Stillwood
Denes
latifolia white selection
Reic #

Kennedia

beckxiana (scarlet)
Denes, Reic #
coccinea
Reic #
macrophylla
Reic #
nigricans (Black Coral Pea)
CouCl, Denes, Reic #
prostrata
Reic #
retrorsa
CouCl
rubicunda (Dusky Coral Pea)
CouCl, Reic #
stirlingii
CouCl

Kerria

japonica (Japanese Rose, Jew's Mallow)
BlueM, Reic #
japonica Pleniflora (Bachelor's Button)
BlueM
japonica Variegata now j.Picta
BlueM

Keteleeria

davidiana
Cedar
evelyniana
Cedar, CPete

Khaya

nyasica
Ether

Kirengeshoma

palmata
AynDa, Parva, TRidg, Vall #
palmata koreana
Titok

Knautia

arvensis (Field Scabiosa)
Marsh, Oasis
macedonica was Scabiosa rumelica
BayBl, CottP, KeriP, MaraN, Marsh, Oasis, Parva, Telfa, Trans

Knightia

excelsa (Rewarewa, NZ honeysuckle)
Chedd, Coatv, Gordn, MatNu, Matth, Matwh, Mtato, Orati, Pionr, Reic #, Terra, Wahpa

Kniphofia

burchellii
Seasd
burnt orange fl
Vall #
caulescens
Caves
citrina
JoyPl
Dwarf Scarlet
BayBl, Peak
Ernest Mitchell
BayBl
gracilis
Ormon
Green Gold
Ormon
Lemon
Peak
Lemon Poker
Nikau
Lime Poker
Nikau
linearifolia
JoyPl
Little Maid
BayBl, Ormon
Maid Of Orleans
Parva, Telfa
Peach
Peak
Pink choice
Peak

praecox
JoyPl
Primrose Beauty
Peak
red
Diack, Ormon
ritualis
JoyPl
rooperi
Caves, JoyPl
Royal Castle
Kayd
splendida
JoyPl
Stately
BayBl, Peak
triangularis
Hackf, Parva
uvaria
Parva
Winter Cheer
BayBl

Kochia

trichophylla (Burning Bush, Summer Cypress, Mock Cypress)
King #

Koelreuteria

paniculata (Golden Rain Tree, Pride Of India, Varnish Tree)
Apple, Burbk, Chedd, Denes, Dove, Hewsn, NZtr #, Ormon, Pionr, PuhaN, Pukho, Reic #, TopTr, YakuN

Kolkwitzia

amabilis (Beauty Bush)
Dove, Reic #, TRidg
amabilis Pink Beauty
TopTr
amabilis Pink Cloud
BlueM, Denes, Woodl

Kunzea

baxteri
Denes
ericoides (Kanuka, White Tea Tree)
Chedd, Gordn, Matai, Morgn, Mtato, NZtr #, Orati, Ormon, Pkrau, SouWo, Terra, Wahpa, Wensl

190

ericoides microflorum
Matai, Terra

Kompacta
Orati

Laburnocytisus

Adamii
Dove, Pukho

Laburnum

alpinum (Scotch Laburnum)
EasyB

anagyroides (Laburnum, Golden Chain Tree)
Apple, Chedd, Diack, Dove, NZtr #, Pionr, Reic #

anagyroides Pendulum
Caves

x watereri Vossii (Golden Chain Tree)
Burbk, Mtato, Pionr, Pukho, Reic #

Laccospadix

australasica (Atherton Palm)
Frans, PalmF, Reic #

calyptrocalyx
Reic #

Lachenalia

aloides
DaffA

aloides Pearsonii
Altrf, DaffA, Kerer

aloides var aurea
DaffA

arbuthnotiae
MJury

bulbifera
DaffA

carnosa
JoyPl

contaminata
AynDa, DaffA, JoyPl, MaraN, MJury, TRidg

glaucina
MJury

juncifolia
DaffA, JoyPl, Parva

mathewsii
Parva

mediana
DaffA, JoyPl

mutabilis
DaffA, JoyPl, MJury

orchiodes var glaucina
DaffA, JoyPl, Parva

orthopetala
DaffA

pallida
JoyPl, MJury, Parva

purpureo-coerulea
DaffA

pustulata
DaffA, MJury, Parva

quadricolour
DaffA, JoyPl

reflexa
JoyPl

scarlet bloom
JoyPl

tricolor now aloides
DaffA

viridiflora
JoyPl, Parva

Lactuca

sativa Black Seeded Simpson
King #

sativa Deers Tongue
King #

sativa Diamond Gemm
King #

sativa Fancy red
Trolh

sativa Grand Rapids TBR
King #

sativa Green Ice
King #

sativa Green Salad Bowl
King #

sativa Little Gem
King #

sativa Lollo Biondo
King #

sativa Lollo Rosso
King #

sativa Lovina
King #

sativa Merveille des Quatre Saisons
King #

sativa Oak Leaf
King #

sativa Paris White Cos
King #

sativa Prize Head
King #

sativa Red Cos - Rosalita
King #, Koan #

sativa Red Fire
King #

sativa Red Sails
King #

sativa Red Salad Bowl
King #

sativa Rossimo
King #

sativa Rouge d'Hiver
King #

sativa Royal Oak Leaf
King #

sativa Sangria (Red Butterhead)
King #

sativa Simpson Elite
King #

sativa Tango
King #

sativa Winter
Koan #

Laganaria

gourd Maori traditional
Koan #

Lagarostrobos

colensoi was Dacrydium c. (Westland Pine)
Cedar

franklinii was Dacrydium f (Huon Pine)
BlueM, Cedar, CPete

Lagerstroemia

varieties
Coatv

chekiangensis
Caves

fauerii
Caves

indica Andre des Martis
Caves

indica Eavesii
Caves

indica Jeanne des Martis
Caves

indica Kimono
Caves

indica Little Chief
  Denes, Pgeon
indica Mon Brazillac
  Caves
indica Saint Emilion
  Caves
indica Soir d'Ete
  Caves
indica Souvenir d'Hubert Puard
  Caves
indica Yang Tse
  Caves
limii
  Caves
subcostata (White Crepe Myrtle)
  Caves

Lagunaria
patersonii (Norfolk Is Hibiscus)
  Burbk, Coatv, Denes, Matwh, McKe, Mtato, Pionr, Reic #, TopTr

Lamium
album
  Della
galeobdolon Hermann's Pride
  BayBl, MaraN, Nikau
galeobdolon Variegatum
  CottP
James Compton
  CottP, Peak
maculatum
  Pgeon
maculatum Beacon Silver
  CottP, Della, MaraN, MillH
maculatum Chequers
  BayBl
maculatum Pink Pewter
  BayBl, Marsh
maculatum roseum
  NewlR, Nikau, Pgeon, Telfa
maculatum White Nancy
  BayBl, Marsh, Nikau, Otepo, Pgeon, Trans
Pink Pixie
  Ashto, Trans

Lampranthus

cerise
  KeriP
Coconut Ice
  BayBl, KeriP, Pgeon
cream
  Seasd
cream w gold centre
  KeriP
crimson
  Seasd
Crimson Glory
  BayBl, Pgeon
deep burgundy red
  Seasd
gold
  KeriP
mauve
  KeriP, Seasd
Melody
  Pgeon
Mini Star
  Pgeon
Minstral
  Pgeon
orange
  KeriP, Seasd
peach
  KeriP
pink
  KeriP, Seasd
Pink Maiden
  Pgeon
Purple Passion
  KeriP
red
  KeriP
salmon pink
  KeriP
Shepherds Dawn
  BayBl, Pgeon
Spring Glow
  Pgeon
Sunshine
  BayBl, Pgeon
Tango
  BayBl
Trailing pink
  KeriP
Volkyrie
  Seasd
white
  KeriP, Seasd

white w yellow centre
  Seasd
yellow
  Seasd

Lantana
Lavender Swirl
  KeriP
montevidensis
  Butlr, KeriP, Looij
montevidensis Sundancer
  KeriP
montevidensis White Lightning
  KeriP

Lapageria
alba
  BlueM, CouCl, Denes, Taunt, TRidg
rosea (Chilean Bellflower)
  Ashto, BayBl, BlueM, Caves, CouCl, Denes, Hewsn, JoyPl, MJury, Taunt
rosea x alba
  Taunt

Lapeirousia
cruenta now Anomatheca laxa
  MaraN, Vall #
divarica
  DaffA
laxa now Anomatheca l.
  JoyPl, KeriP
laxa alba now Anomatheca
  CottP
rhodesiana
  DaffA
viridis
  DaffA

Lardizabala
biternata
  CouCl

Larix
decidua (European/Common Larch)
  Apple, BlueM, Chedd, CPete, Diack, Dove, Ford, Hewsn, Matai, Morgn, Mtato, NZtr #, Pionr, PuhaN, Terra, WakaC, Wensl
decidua Pendula
  CPete

kaempferi (Japanese Larch

Apple, BlueM, Cedar,
Chedd, Denes, Diack,
Dove, EasyB, Ford,
Mtato, NZtr #, Peele,
PuhaN, TopTr, WakaC,
Wensl

laricina

Apple

Laserpitium

pale/rosy pink fl, blue/green lvs

Vall #

siler

MaraN

Lastreopsis

glabella

Orati

hispida

Orati

microsora

Gordn, Orati

Lathyrus

athoa

KeriP

belinensis

Parva

fremontii

Della

latifolius Pink Pearl

CoFlo, Parva, Telfa, Vall #

latifolius Red Pearl

King #

latifolius Rose Pearl

BayBl, MaraN

latifolius White Pearl

BayBl, King #, Parva,
Pgeon, Roswd, Vall #

nervosus (Lord Anson's Blue Pea)

MaraN, Parva

odoratus Continental mixed

King #

odoratus Knee Hi mixed

King #

odoratus Perfume Delight mixed

King #

odoratus Royal Family colours

King #

odoratus Supersnoop

King #

palustris

Diack

Pink Cupid

Parva

pubescens (Argentine Pea)

MaraN, Parva, Roswd

pubescens deep blue

Vall #

pubescens soft blue

Vall #

Red Cupid

Parva

rotundifolius (Persian Everlasting Pea)

Della

sp pink or white seedlings

AynDa

The Pearl

Telfa

vernus orobus

Vall #

Laurelia

novae zelandiae (Puketia)

Gordn, Matwh, Mtato,
Orati, Pionr, Terra,
Wahpa

Laurentia

Blue Star

Reic #

Laurus

nobilis (Bay Tree)

Apple, BlueM, Chedd,
Coatv, Denes, Diack,
Dove, LanSc, McKe,
Mtato, MTig, MTig #,
Orang, Ormon, SelGr,
Sweet, Trolh

Lavandula

varieties

Roswd

x allardii (Mitchum lavender)

BlueM, CottP, KeriP,
Looij, Nikau, Orang,
Sweet, Trolh

x allardii African Pride

Ploug

x allardii Aust

Ploug

x allardii Fiona

Ploug

angustifolia syn spica (English)

AynDa, Diack, King #,
Nikau, Orang, Pgeon,
Sweet

angustifolia 338/9

Ploug

angustifolia Alba

BayBl, BlueM, Egmon,
Otepo, Parva, Pgeon,
Pionr, Ploug, SelGr

angustifolia Andreas

Denes, Trolh, Wells

angustifolia Avice Hill (Hoopers #10)

Ploug

angustifolia Baby Blue

Ploug

angustifolia Betty's Blue

Ploug

angustifolia Blue Cushion

Ploug

angustifolia Blue Mountain

BlueM, Marsh, Peak,
Ploug

angustifolia Bosistos

Ploug

angustifolia Bowels

Ploug

angustifolia Budakalaszi

Ploug

angustifolia Buena Vista

Ploug

angustifolia Burpee

Ploug

angustifolia Cedar Blue

Ploug

angustifolia Colour Purple

Parva

angustifolia Delphensis

Ploug

angustifolia Dwarf Munstead

Della, Orang, Sweet

angustifolia Fiona English

Ploug

angustifolia Folgate Blue

Looij, Marsh, Parva,
Ploug

angustifolia Foveaux Storm

Marsh, Ploug

angustifolia Fragrant Memories

Ploug

angustifolia Frosty Gem
MillH

angustifolia Gray Lady
BlueM, Marsh, Ploug

angustifolia Helen
Batchelor
Ploug

angustifolia Hidcote
BayBl, Hackf, Looij,
Marsh, Morgn, Mtato,
Orang, Pgeon, SelGr,
Sweet

angustifolia Hidcote Blue
Ashto, Egmon, King #,
Ploug, Reic #, Wells

angustifolia Hidcote Giant
Ploug

angustifolia Hidcote Pink
King #, Marsh, Ploug

angustifolia Imperial Gem
BayBl, Ploug, Trolh

angustifolia Irene Doyle
Ploug

angustifolia Jean Davis
Ploug

angustifolia Lady
Ploug

angustifolia Lavender Lady
King #, Nikau, Orang

angustifolia Lavenite Petite
Ploug

angustifolia Loddon Blue
Ploug

angustifolia London Pink
Ploug

angustifolia Lullaby Blue
Ploug

angustifolia Lullaby Pink
Ploug

angustifolia M1 ex
Landcare
Ploug

angustifolia M4 ex
Landcare
Ploug

angustifolia Matha
Roderick
Ploug

angustifolia Mausen Dwarf
Marsh, Ploug

angustifolia Melissa
Ploug

angustifolia Mitcham(dk
blue)
Ploug

angustifolia Munstead
AynDa, BlueM, Burbk,
Diack, King #, Marsh,
Morgn, Mtato, Pgeon,
Ploug, Reic #, SelGr,
Telfa

angustifolia Munstead
Wallers
Ploug

angustifolia Nana Alba
Ploug

angustifolia Nana
Atropurpurea
Marsh, Ploug

angustifolia Nana Spica
Ploug

angustifolia O Kamara Saki
(Purple Hills)
Ploug

angustifolia Pacific Blue
King #, Ploug, Trolh

angustifolia Pacific Pink
Ploug

angustifolia Perenacia
Ploug

angustifolia Princess Blue
Ploug

angustifolia Rosea
Ashto, BayBl, CottP,
Hackf, King #, Marsh,
Mtato, Nikau, Otepo,
Parva, Pgeon, Ploug,
SelGr

angustifolia Royal Purple
Ploug

angustifolia Royal Velvet
Ploug

angustifolia Sachet
Ploug

angustifolia Seal's 7 Oaks
Ploug

angustifolia Sharon
Roberts
Ploug

angustifolia The Colour
Purple
Ploug

angustifolia Trolla.
Trolh

angustifolia Tuckers
Purple
Ploug

angustifolia Twickle Purple
BayBl, King #, Marsh,
Parva

angustifolia var
angustifolia
Ploug

angustifolia Winton
Hackf, Marsh

angustifolia Wyckoff
Ploug

Brenna
Telfa

canariensis (Canary Island
Lavender)
CottP, Dream, Orang,
Ploug, Trolh

dentata
BayBl, BlueM, CottP,
Della, Dream, Egmon,
KeriP, King #, Matwh,
Mills, Morgn, Mtato,
Nikau, Ormon, Pionr,
Ploug, SelGr, Sweet,
Trolh

dentata v. candicans
Ploug, Trolh

dentata var lambikens
Ploug

dentata var linda ligon
Ploug

dentata var monet
Ploug

dentata var Ploughmans
Blue
Ploug

Goodwins
Ploug

x heterophylla
Ploug

Imperial Gem
Trolh

x intermedia Abrailii
Ploug

x intermedia Alba
Ploug, Trolh

x intermedia Arabian Night
(Super or Impress Purple)
BayBl, Dream, KeriP,
Looij, Ploug

x intermedia Bogong
Ashto, BayBl, BlueM,
KeriP, Looij, Marsh,
Mills, Ploug

x intermedia Bridestowe 1
Ploug

x intermedia Bridestowe 2

Ploug

x intermedia Chaix

Ploug

x intermedia Dilly Dilly now
Grosso

BayBl, Looij, Parva,
Ploug, SelGr, Sweet,
Trolh

x intermedia Dutch Alba

Ploug

x intermedia Dutch Vera

Ploug

x intermedia Fred Boutin

Ploug

x intermedia Grappenhall

Marsh, Ploug

x intermedia Grey Hedger

Ashto, CottP, Looij,
Marsh, Orang, Ploug,
SelGr

x intermedia Grey Lady

Looij, Pgeon, Ploug

x intermedia Grosso

Dream, KeriP, Orang,
Ploug, Trolh, Wells

x intermedia Impress Purple

KeriP, Trolh

x intermedia Miss
Donnington

Ploug

x intermedia Nicoleii

Ploug

x intermedia Old English

Ploug

x intermedia Scottish
Cottage

Looij, Ploug

x intermedia Seal

BayBl, CottP, Looij,
Marsh, Ploug, Trolh

x intermedia Super

Ploug, SelGr, Trolh

x intermedia Sussex

Ploug

x intermedia Tasmanian (ex
Landcare)

Ploug

x intermedia Wilson Giant

BlueM, Ploug

x intermedia Yuulong

Ploug

lanata (Woolly Lavender)

Mills, Ormon, Ploug

latifolia (Spike Lavender)

BlueM, Marsh, Orang

latifolia LC8

Ploug

latifolia spiek

Ploug

multifida

Hackf, King #, Ploug,
Trolh

multifida var maroccana

Ploug

pinnata

Ploug, Trolh

pinnata var Sidonie

Denes, Parva

Richard Grey

Ploug

Rosea

BayBl, Looij

Sawyer

Ploug

Silver Frost

Ploug

spica   syn angustifolia

Ref

stoechas (French Lavender

BayBl, BlueM, Butlr,
CottP, Della, Marsh,
Mills, Morgn, Mtato,
Orang, Pgeon, Ploug,
SelGr, Sweet, Telfa,
Trolh

stoechas Alba

CottP, KeriP, Parva,
Ploug, Trolh

stoechas Andrea

Ploug

stoechas Atlas

Ploug

stoechas Avonview

Ashto, KeriP, King #,
MillH, Mtato, Ploug,
Trans, Trolh

stoechas Blueberry

Ploug, Trolh

stoechas Butterfly

KeriP, King #, Orang,
Ploug

stoechas Clare de Lune

Ploug

stoechas Delata

Ploug

stoechas Evelyn Cadzow

BayBl, Burbk, KeriP,
King #, Ploug, Trolh

stoechas Fairy Wings

Ploug

stoechas Helmsdale

CottP, Egmon, KeriP,
King #, Looij, Marsh,
MillH, Mtato, Nikau,
Orang, Otepo, Pgeon,
Ploug, Sweet, Telfa,
Trans, Trolh, Wells

stoechas Keripurple

KeriP

stoechas Leucantha

BlueM, Ploug

stoechas Major

BayBl, KeriP, King #,
Marsh, Nikau, Parva,
Ploug, Trans, Trolh

stoechas Marshwood

Ashto, BayBl, CottP,
Denes, Diack, Dream,
KeriP, King #, Looij,
MillH, Mtato, Nikau,
Orang, Pgeon, Ploug,
Sweet, Telfa, Trans,
Trolh

stoechas Merle

King #, Ploug, Trolh,
Woodl

stoechas Papillon

KeriP, Parva, Ploug

stoechas pedunculata

BayBl, KeriP, Mtato,
Orang, Pionr, Ploug,
SelGr, Sweet, Telfa

stoechas pedunculata James
Compton

BayBl, Denes, Hackf,
Marsh, Parva, Pgeon,
Ploug

stoechas pedunculata
Marsh

King #

stoechas pedunculata x
Marshwood

Ploug

stoechas pedunculata x
Viridis

King #, Ploug

stoechas Pippa

BayBl, KeriP, King #,
Mtato, Orang, Ploug

stoechas Pippa Alba

Trolh

stoechas Pippa White

Parva, Ploug

stoechas Plum
Ashto, KeriP, Looij,
Ploug, Trolh

stoechas Pukehou
Ashto, BayBl, Denes,
KeriP, King #, Nikau,
Parva, Peak, Ploug, Sweet

stoechas Purple
Ploug, Trans, Trolh

stoechas Purple Crown
Ploug

stoechas Purple Trolls
Trolh

stoechas Quasti
Parva

stoechas Raycroft
Ploug

stoechas Silver Wings
Ploug

stoechas Sommerset Mist
KeriP, Ploug, Trolh

stoechas ssp caesia
Ploug

stoechas ssp lucitanica
Ploug

stoechas ssp luisieri.
KeriP, King #, Trolh

stoechas ssp luisierii(portugal)
Ploug

stoechas ssp luisierii(spain)
Ploug

stoechas ssp sampiana
Ashto, KeriP, King #,
Ploug

stoechas Stokes Wine
LanSc, Looij

stoechas Sugar Plum
KeriP, Ploug, Telfa,
Trans, Trolh

stoechas White
Ploug, Trolh

stoechas Willowbridge Calico
Parva, Ploug

stoechas Willowbridge Snow
KeriP, Parva, Ploug

stoechas Willowbridge White
Denes, Ploug

stoechas Wine
Denes, Mtato, Orang,
Ploug

stoechas Wine Red
Dream, KeriP

viridis (Green Lavender)
BayBl, CottP, KeriP,
King #, Looij, MaraN,
MillH, Orang, Otepo,
Ploug, SelGr, Sweet,
Trans, Trolh

Wandula Willowbridge
Sweet

Lavatera

varieties
Roswd

assurgentiflora
AynDa, Vall #

Barnsley
CottP, Kayd, KeriP,
MillH, Oasis, Orang,
Parva, Pgeon, Sweet,
Telfa, Trans, Warwk

Burgundy Wine
Warwk

cachemiriana
Marsh

Candy Floss
Parva, Warwk

maritima was bicolor
BayBl, Denes, Oasis,
Parva, Sweet

olbia Rosea
Della, Orang, Pgeon

Pink Beauty
Vall #

Rosea
KeriP, Warwk

thuringiaca
MaraN

thuringiaca Ice Cool
Parva

trimensis Mont Blanc
King #, Reic #

trimensis Ruby Regis
King #, Reic #

trimensis Silvercup
King #, Reic #

white
Trolh

Lawsonia

alba (Henna)
Reic #

inermis (Henna)
Sweet

Ledebouria

cooperi was adlamii
Telfa

Leea

coccinea rubra
LakeN

Lemna

minor (Duckweed)
WaiMa

Leonotis

**leonurus (now ocymifolia)
(Lions Ear, Lions Tail)**
Kayd, KeriP

leonurus alba (Wild Dagga)
KeriP, MillH

**leonurus var albiflora
(White Lions Tail)**
JoyPl

Leontopodium

alpinum (Edelweiss)
BayBl, Della, NewlR,
Parva

alpinum Mignon
Marsh

Leonurus

cardiaca (Motherwort)
Della, Dream, MaraN,
Orang, Sweet

sibericus (Siberian Motherwort)
Dream, Mills, Sweet

Lepidium

oleraceum (Cook's Scurvy Grass)
Orati, Terra

sativum (Moss Curled Cress)
King #

Lepidothamnus

**intermedius was
Dacrydium i. (Yellow
Silver Pine)**
Cedar, Orati

**laxifolius was Dacrydium
l. (Pygmy Pine,Mountain
Rimu)**
Cedar, Hackf, Orati

**laxifolius Blue Gem was
Dacrydium l.B.G.**
Cedar, CPete

laxifolius x intermedius
Green Cascade   was
dacrydium
  Cedar

Leptinella

dioica
  Gordn, Orati

dioica large leaf form
  Orati

minor
  Orati

nana
  Orati

pusilla   was perpusilla
  Orati

pyrethrifolia
  Pgeon, Seasd

rotundata
  Orati, Otepo

serrulata   was Cotula s.
  CottP

squallida   was Cotula
sq.
  Orati, Pgeon

Leptocarpus

similis (Oioi, Jointed
Wirerush)
  Diack, NZtr #, Orati,
  WaiMa

Leptospermum

citratum   now petersonii
(Lemon Tea tree)
  Pkrau, Reic #

Copper Glow
  Durbk, Reic #

ericoides   now Kunzea e.
  Pionr, Sweet

flavescens Pacific Beauty
now polygalifolium ..
  MatNu

flavescens Pink Beauty
  Denes

Green Ice (Tasmanian
Manuka)
  BlueM

horizontalis
  Wells

humifusum   now rupestre
  BlueM

laevigatum (Coastal Tea
Tree)
  Reic #, Seasd

lanigerum   was pubescens
  Diack

nitidum Copper sheen
(Shiny Tea Tree)
  Butlr, Chedd, Coatv,
  Mtato, Pukho, Wells

petersenii   was citratum
  Denes, Pkrau

polygalifolium Montanum
  Matth

pubescens   now
L.lanigerum
  Diack

Rawara
  Orati

rotundiflorum
  Denes, Reic #

rupestre
  Reic #

scoparium (Manuka,
Kahikatoa, Tea Tree)
  Chedd, Ford, Matai,
  Matwh, Morgn, Mtato,
  NZtr #, Orati, Pionr,
  Pkrau, Sweet, Terra,
  Wahpa

scoparium Big Red
  Wensl

scoparium Blossom
  Chedd, Gordn, Matwh,
  Orati

scoparium Champagne
  Wahpa

scoparium Cherry Brandy
  Mtato

scoparium Coral Candy
  Matai

scoparium Crimson Glory
  BlueM, Chedd, Matai,
  Mtato, Orati

scoparium Jubilee
  Gordn, Kayd, Wahpa

scoparium Keatleyii
  Mtato, Orati

scoparium Martinii
  Orati, Wensl

scoparium Nanum
Elizabeth Jane
  BlueM

scoparium Nanum Huia
  BlueM, Burbk

scoparium Nanum Kea
  BlueM, Gordn, Orati

scoparium Nanum Kiwi
  BlueM, Orati, Wahpa,
  Wensl

scoparium Nanum Kotuku
  BlueM

scoparium Nanum Ruru
  BlueM

scoparium Nanum Tui
  BlueM

scoparium Pink Cascade
  BlueM, Matai, Mtato,
  Orati

scoparium Pink
Champagne
  BlueM

scoparium Pink Falls
  BlueM

scoparium Pink Splendour
  Mtato

scoparium Red Damask
  BlueM, Matai, Mtato

scoparium Red Ensign
  Chedd, Orati

scoparium Red Falls
  BlueM, Matai, Mtato,
  Orati

scoparium Rose Glory
  Wahpa

scoparium roseum
  Reic #

scoparium Rosy Morn
  Orati

scoparium Wairere
  BlueM, Orati

scoparium Wairere Falls
  Matwh

scoparium Winter Cheer
  Orati

scoparium Wiri Joan
  Chedd, Gordn

scoparium Wiri Kerry
  Matwh

scoparium Wiri Linda
  Gordn, Matwh

scoparium Wiri Shelly
  Matwh

squarrosum
  Reic #

Leschenaultia

biloba (Blue Leschenaultia)
  MatNu, Reic #

floribunda
  Reic #

Starburst
Wells

Sunrise
Denes, MatNu

Ultra Violet
Denes, Wells

Lespedeza

bicolor (Chinese Bush Clover)
Dove, Reic #, Vall #

Leucadendron

argenteum (Silver Tree)
Chedd, Denes, MatNu, Matth, Reic #

Bell's Sunrise
MatNu, Matth

Bell's Supreme
Denes, MatNu, Matth

Bright Eye
MatNu

Brook's Red
MatNu, Matth

Cherry Glow
Denes

Cloudbank Ginny
Denes, MatNu, Matth

comosum
MatNu

discolor
Reic #

discolor Firecracker
MatNu, Matth

eucalyptifolium
Reic #

floridum
Reic #

Harvest
Denes, MatNu, Matth

Inca Gold
Denes, MatNu, Matth, Wells

incisum
Denes, MatNu, Matth

Julie
MatNu, Matth

laureolum
Denes, Reic #

laureolum Rewa Gold
Denes, MatNu, Matth

laxum
MatNu, Matth

macowanii
Reic #

Maui Sunset
Denes, MatNu, Matth

Mrs Stanley
Wells

Pisa
Denes, Matth

procerum Cherry Glow
MatNu, Matth

radiatum
Matth

Red Devil
Wells

Red Gem
MatNu, Matth

rubrum
Reic #

Safari Sunset
Chedd, Denes, MatNu, Matth, Mtato

Safari Sunshine
MatNu, Matth

salignum
Reic #

salignum Early Yellow
Wells

salignum Fire Glow
MatNu

salignum Fireglow
MatNu, Matth

salignum Late Yellow
Denes, MatNu

salignum Mrs Stanley
Denes, MatNu, Matth

salignum Red Carpet
MatNu, Matth, Wells

salignum Yellow Devil
Denes, MatNu, Matth

stellare
Reic #

stelligerum red form
MatNu, Matth

strobilinum Waterlily
Denes, MatNu, Wells

Superstar
MatNu, Matth, Matwh, Wells

thymifolium
MatNu, Matth, Seasd

Wilsons Wonder
Denes, MatNu, Wells

xanthoconus Patea Gold
MatNu, Matth

Leucanthemopsis

alpina syn Chrysanth. a.
Ref

Leucanthemum

gayanum now Rhodanthemum g.
CottP

hosmariense now Rhodanthemum h.
BayBl, Oasis, Ormon, Pgeon, Trans

mawii now Rhodanthemum gayanum
Otepo

maximum also see L x superbum (Shasta Daisy)
Della, Trans

x superbum Alaska
Ashto, King #, Marsh

x superbum Cobham Gold
CottP

x superbum double white
Nikau

x superbum Double Yellow
Mtato

x superbum Esther Read
Egmon, KeriP, Pgeon

x superbum Exhibition
Pgeon

x superbum lge shaggy white
Nikau

x superbum nanum Silver Princess
Ashto

x superbum Phyllis Smith
Marsh

x superbum Polaris
Kayd, MillH

x superbum Silver Princess
Marsh

x superbum Snow Lady dwf
Seasd

x superbum Wirrel Supreme
Ashto, Marsh, Mills

vulgare was Chrysanthemum leuc.
CottP

Leucocoryne

alba

  DaffA, Parva

coquimbensis

  DaffA, Parva

purpurea

  DaffA, Parva

Leucojum

aestivum Gravetye Giant (Spring Snowflake)

  MJury

autumnale   was Acis a. (Autumn Snowflake)

  AynDa, CottP, DaffA, Irida, JoyPl, Kerer NewlR, Pgeon, RosPl

sp Snowflake

  SoBul

vernum var. carpathicum

  MaraN

Leucopogon

fasciculatus (Mingimingi)

  Orati

parviflorus

  Orati

Leucospermum

Caroline

  MatNu, Matth

cordifolium Harry Chittick

  Matth

Firefly

  MatNu, Matth

Goldie

  MatNu, Matth

No 3

  Denes, MatNu, Matth

.prostratum Groundfire

  MatNu, Matth

Red Sunset

  MatNu

Scarlet Ribbons

  MatNu, Matth

Sunrise

  Denes, MatNu, Matth

Tango

  MatNu, Matth

tottum Champagne

  Denes, MatNu, Matth

tottum hybrid Fantasy

  MatNu, Matth

Veldfire

  MatNu, Matth

Leucothoe

fontanesiana   now walteri (Lily of the Valley Shrub)

  BlueM

fontanesiana Rainbow

  BlueM, Burbk, Denes

Levisticum

officinale (Lovage, Maggi Herb)

  King #, Mills, MTig #, Orang, Sweet

Lewisia

cotyledon

  Ashto, MaraN

cotyledon Hybrids

  Parva, TRidg

nevadensis

  NewlR

Lhotskya

alpestris   now Calytrix a.

  Denes

ericoides   now Calytrix

  MatNu

Liatris

varieties

  Roswd

aspera

  MaraN

pychnostachya (Kansas Gayfeather, Prairie Blazing Star)

  CoFlo, Dream, MillH, Oasis

scariosa Gracious

  CoFlo

spicata was callilepsis (Spike Gay Feather, Button Snakewort, Gayfeather)

  Della, KeriP, King #, Looij, MaraN, Marsh, Mills, Pgeon, Pkrau, Sweet, Trans, WaiMa

spicata Alba

  CottP, MaraN, Pgeon, WaiMa

spicata Florist White

  Dream

spicata Florists Violet

  BayBl, Dream

spicata Goblin

  BayBl, CottP, Dream

spicata Kobold

  Parva, Telfa

spicata White

  Parva

Libertia

caerulescens

  BayBl, MaraN, MillH

formosa

  BlueM, Diack, JoyPl, Nikau, Ormon, Peak, Vall #, Warwk

grandiflora (Mikoikoi)

  Ashto, Burbk, Denes, Diack, Gordn, Hains, MaraN, Matwh, MillH, Mtato, Orati, Ormon, Otepo, Telfa, Terra, Trans, TRidg, Wahpa

grandiflora Sth Is form

  Telfa

ixioides (Tukauki)

  Diack, Gordn, Looij, Matwh, NZtr #, Orati, Pionr, Reic #, Telfa, Terra, Trans, Wahpa

ixioides creeping

  Orati

ixioides Tricolour

  Gordn

peregrinans

  Butlr, Diack, Gordn, Hains, KeriP, Matai, Mtato, NZtr #, Oasis, Orati, Ormon, Pionr, Seasd, Telfa, Terra, Trans

Libocedrus

bidwillii (Kaikawaka, Pahautea, Mountain Cedar)

  Cedar, Matai, Mtato, Orati, Terra

plumosa (Kawaka, Plume Incense Cedar)

  BlueM, Burbk, Cedar, Chedd, CPete, Gordn, Orati, Pionr, Terra

Licuala

grandis

  Reic #

ramsayi

  Reic #

spinosa

  Reic #

Ligularia

Cream Variegated

  Denes

dentata

  Della, Pgeon, Telfa, WaiMa

dentata Desdemona
> BayBl, Diack, JoyPl,
> Peak, Pkrau, Vall #,
> WaiMa, WilAq

dentata Dunkellaubig
> WaiMa

japonica
> Marsh

przewalskii
> Dream, Marsh, Oasis,
> Telfa, WaiMa, WilAq

sibirica
> Marsh

**sp tangerine perfumed fl,
green lf**
> Vall #

stenocephala
> Peak

stenocephala hybrids
> Marsh

tangutica now Sinacalia t.
> Marsh

**tussilaginea aurea
maculata now Farfugium
t.**
> BayBl, TRidg

veitchiana
> WaiMa

Ligustrum

**japonicum Rotundifolium
(Japanese Privet)**
> BlueM, Ormon, Woodl

ovalifolium (Privet)
> SelGr

**ovalifolium Aureum was
Aureomarginatum**
> BlueM, Diack, Hewsn

Lilaeopsis

novae-zelandiae
> WaiMa

Lilium

varieties
> Kayd, SoBul

asiatic mixed
> Kayd, Liman

asiatic Alaska
> LiliB

asiatic Ambassador
> LiliB

asiatic Ambrosia
> Lilyf

asiatic Antartica
> Lilyf

asiatic Apeldoorn
> BayBl, Eyrew, Kayd,
> LiliB

asiatic Aphrodite
> LiliB

asiatic Apollo
> LiliB

asiatic Astronaut
> LiliB, Lilyf

asiatic Avignon
> Eyrew

asiatic Bangalore
> LiliB

asiatic Beatrix
> LiliB

asiatic Beige Beauty
> LiliB, Lilyf

asiatic Black Watch
> Lilyf

asiatic Bonnie
> Lilyf

asiatic Chetoka
> Lilyf

asiatic Chianti
> Eyrew, LiliB, Lilyf

asiatic Chicago
> Eyrew

asiatic Coda
> Lilyf

asiatic Compass
> LiliB

asiatic Connecticut Beauty
> Lilyf

asiatic Connecticut King
> Eyrew, Lilyf

asiatic Connecticut Star
> LiliB

asiatic Cordelia
> LiliB

asiatic Corina
> Eyrew, LiliB

asiatic Corsica
> Lilyf

asiatic Country Dawn
> Lilyf

asiatic Cream Puff
> Lilyf

asiatic Crete
> Lilyf

asiatic Daphne
> Lilyf

asiatic Dawn Star
> Lilyf

asiatic Diplomat
> LiliB

asiatic Doeskin
> Lilyf

asiatic Dream Away
> LiliB

asiatic Echo
> LiliB

asiatic Escapade
> Eyrew

asiatic Flamboyant
> Lilyf

asiatic Golden Melody
> BayBl, Eyrew, Kayd,
> LiliB

asiatic Goldina
> Eyrew

asiatic Grand Cru
> LiliB, Lilyf

asiatic Grand Paradiso
> BayBl, Eyrew, Kayd,
> LiliB, Lilyf, Parva

asiatic Guardsman
> LiliB

asiatic Hartford
> Lilyf

asiatic Heart Throb
> TRidg

asiatic Honey Wind
> LiliB, Lilyf

asiatic Indian Brave
> Lilyf

asiatic Jamie
> Lilyf

asiatic Jet Fire
> Lilyf

asiatic Karrissa
> Lilyf

asiatic LaToya
> LiliB

**asiatic Lavender Lady
Rosemary**
> TRidg

asiatic Lucca
> LiliB

asiatic Make Up
> LiliB

asiatic Malta
> Lilyf

asiatic Maori Chief
> Lilyf

asiatic Maria Callas
> Lilyf

asiatic Marseille
Lilyf, Parva

asiatic Martha Ann
LiliB, Lilyf

asiatic Matterhorn
LiliB, Lilyf

asiatic Maureen
Lilyf

asiatic Menton
BayBl, Eyrew, Kayd,
LiliB, Lilyf

asiatic Mercedes
LiliB

asiatic Milano
BayBl, Eyrew, Kayd,
LiliB, Lilyf

asiatic Mirage
LiliB, Lilyf

asiatic Miss Alice
LiliB

asiatic Mona (Monaco)
BayBl, Eyrew, Kayd,
LiliB

asiatic Monte Rosa
Kayd, LiliB, Lilyf

asiatic Montreaux
BayBl, Eyrew, Kayd,
LiliB, Lilyf, Parva

asiatic Nepal
Eyrew, Kayd, LiliB, Lilyf

asiatic Nerone
LiliB

asiatic Nova x Miss Alice
Marsh

asiatic Nove Cento
LiliB

asiatic Orange Pixie
LiliB

asiatic Orange Sherbert
Lilyf

asiatic Out of Toyland
Lilyf

asiatic Peaceful
Lilyf

asiatic Peach Melba
Lilyf

asiatic Peaches and Cream
LiliB, Lilyf

asiatic Peacock Creation
LiliB

asiatic Pollyanna
Eyrew, LiliB, Lilyf, Parva

asiatic Prominence
LiliB, Lilyf

asiatic Pronto
LiliB

asiatic Pumpkin Sweet
Lilyf

asiatic Red Carpet
Lilyf

asiatic Red King
Lilyf

asiatic Roma
Eyrew, Kayd, LiliB, Lilyf

asiatic Sancerre
Lilyf

asiatic Sandras Joy
Lilyf

asiatic Sarah Aimee
Lilyf

asiatic Sargent Kelly
Lilyf

asiatic Sargent Pepper
Lilyf

asiatic Sirocco
Lilyf

asiatic Somers Jewel
Lilyf

asiatic Somers Pride
Lilyf

asiatic Sonne Tiger
LiliB

asiatic Sorbet
Lilyf

asiatic Southern Star
TRidg

asiatic Stardom
Lilyf

asiatic Steadfast
LiliB

asiatic Sulphur Song
Lilyf

asiatic Summer Sun
Lilyf

asiatic Sunray
LiliB

asiatic Sunshine
TRidg

asiatic Taptoe
LiliB

asiatic Theyer
Lilyf

asiatic Tiger Babies
Lilyf

asiatic Tikal
Lilyf

asiatic Tiny Tim
Lilyf

asiatic Tirreno
LiliB

asiatic Toscane
BayBl, Eyrew, Kayd,
LiliB, Lilyf

asiatic Toyland
Lilyf

asiatic Trade Winds
LiliB, Lilyf

asiatic Vanilla Ice
Lilyf

asiatic Ventroux
LiliB, Lilyf

asiatic Vinon
LiliB

asiatic Vivaldi
LiliB

asiatic Windsong
Lilyf

asiatic Yellow x Ayres
Rock
Marsh

asiatic Yolanda
Lilyf

aurelian First Love
Lilyf

aurelian Sentinel Strain
Lilyf

Bellingham Hybrids
Lilyf

Crows Hybrid
Marsh

formosanum
AynDa, KeriP, Orang,
Ormon, TRidg

formosanum Little Snow
White
TRidg

formosanum var pricei
sdlgs
TRidg

henryi Citrinum
Lilyf

LA hybrid Donau
BayBl

LA hybrid Dynamico
BayBl

LA hybrid Fantasy
BayBl

LA hybrid Highness
BayBl

LA hybrid Moneymaker
TRidg

LA hybrid Royal Fantasy
LiliB

LA hybrid Royal series, white/cream
Liman

LA hybrid Royal Victory
Lilyf

LA hybrid Showbiz
BayBl

leichtlinii
TRidg

longiflorum (Christmas Lily)
Ashto, KeriP, Liman, Telfa, TRidg

longiflorum Avita
Lilyf

longiflorum Casa Rosa
BayBl, Eyrew, TRidg

longiflorum Copper King
Eyrew, LiliB

longiflorum Gelria
Eyrew

longiflorum Lorina
BayBl, LiliB

longiflorum Pink Trumpet Gp
Lilyf

longiflorum Snow Queen
Eyrew, Kayd, Lilyf

longiflorum Virginia
BayBl

longiflorum White American
Lilyf

longiflorum White Perfection Strain
Lilyf

mackliniae
NewlR, TRidg

martagon (Turk's Cap Lily
Marsh, TRidg

oriental/auratum mixed
Kayd

oriental/auratum Acapulco
Eyrew, LiliB, Liman, Parva

oriental/auratum Alma Ata
Eyrew, LiliB, Liman

oriental/auratum Arena
Lilyf, Parva

oriental/auratum Barbaresco
Liman

oriental/auratum Belvedere
Lilyf

oriental/auratum Bergamo
LiliB

oriental/auratum Berlin
Eyrew, LiliB, Liman

oriental/auratum Black Beauty
TRidg

oriental/auratum Casa Blanca
Eyrew, Kayd, LiliB, Lilyf, Liman, TRidg

oriental/auratum Cascade
Eyrew, Liman

oriental/auratum Cathy
Parva

oriental/auratum Cologne
Parva

oriental/auratum Con Amore
LiliB, Liman

oriental/auratum Dame Blanche
Liman

oriental/auratum Dawnette
Lilyf

oriental/auratum Egypt
LiliB, Parva

oriental/auratum Flossie
MJury

oriental/auratum Golden Harvest
MJury

oriental/auratum Hit Parade
LiliB, Liman

oriental/auratum Kyoto
LiliB, Liman

oriental/auratum Le Reve (Joy)
Eyrew, LiliB, Liman, Parva

oriental/auratum Marco Polo
Eyrew, LiliB, Liman, Parva

oriental/auratum Mero Star
Liman

oriental/auratum Milady
MJury

oriental/auratum Mona Lisa
LiliB

oriental/auratum Montana
Lilyf

oriental/auratum Muscadet
Lilyf

oriental/auratum Nippon
Lilyf

oriental/auratum Noblesse
Liman

oriental/auratum Olympic Star
Eyrew

oriental/auratum Pasa Doble
Liman

oriental/auratum Passage
Liman

oriental/auratum Perugia
Liman

oriental/auratum Pesaro
Liman

oriental/auratum Pompei
LiliB

oriental/auratum Princess Gracia
Eyrew, Kayd, LiliB, Parva

oriental/auratum Red Devil
MJury

oriental/auratum Red Shades
Marsh

oriental/auratum Romance
Liman

oriental/auratum Satan's Breath
MJury

oriental/auratum Stargazer
Kayd, LiliB, Liman

oriental/auratum Summer Charm
MJury

oriental/auratum White Heron
MJury

oriental/auratum White Special
Parva

oriental/auratum white w red stripe
TRidg

oriental/auratum Widor
  LiliB
philippinense
  Vall #
pyrenaicum (Yellow Turk's Cap Lily)
  TRidg
Rangitoto hyb
  Marsh
regale (Regal Lily, Christmas Lily)
  Eyrew, Kayd, LiliB, Lilyf, Mills, Trans
Sweetheart
  TRidg
tigrinum Plenescens
  Mills
wallicheanum
  Ashto, Herew
Yellow Trumpets
  Marsh

Limnanthes
douglasii (Meadowfoam, Fried Eggs)
  King #, Orang, Sweet

Limonium
bellidifolium
  MaraN
caspium Misty Blue
  BayBl
cosyrense
  Pgeon
Forever Series
  King #
gmelinii
  CoFlo, Della, King #, MaraN, Pgeon
gougetianum
  Pgeon
latifolium (Sea Lavender)
  BayBl, BlueM, CoFlo, KeriP, King #, Pgeon
Pacific Series
  King #
perezii (Blue Smoke Statice)
  BayBl, KeriP, King #, Nikau, Trans
Petite Bouquet Series
  King #
sinense Cirrus
  MillH
sinuatum colours
  King #

tataricum now Goniolimon t (Tartarian Statice)
  Oasis, Pgeon

Linanthus
grandiflorus (Mountain Phlox)
  King #

Linaria
All Yellow
  Telfa, Vall #
Antique Silver
  BayBl
dalmatica (Toad Flax)
  Dream, MillH
genistifolia ssp dalmatica
  Marsh
maroccana Fairy Bouquet
  King #
maroccana Northern Lights
  King #
purpurea
  MillH, Mills
purpurea Alba
  Dream, TRidg
purpurea Canon Went
  BayBl, Dream, Mills, Pgeon
supina nevadensis
  Pgeon
triornithophora (Three Birds Flying)
  Dream, MaraN, Oasis, Vall #
vulgaris (Toadflax)
  Della, Sweet, Vall #

Lindera
erythrocarpa
  TopTr

Lindheimera
texana Sunny Boy
  King #

Linospadix
apetiolata
  Reic #
minor
  Reic #
monostachya (Walking Stick Palm)
  Coatv

Linum

flavum
  MaraN
flavum Compactum
  Oasis
grandiflora rubrum (Scarletflowered Flax)
  King #
grandiflorum Bright Eyes
  Dream, King #
Innocence
  BayBl
monogynum (NZ Linen,Rauhuia)
  Gordn, Orati, Vall #
narbonnense
  MaraN, MillH, Vall #
perenne (Irish Flax)
  Della, Dream, Nikau, Otepo, Trans
perenne Album
  Della, MaraN
perenne Blue Sapphire
  BayBl
perenne Diamant
  BayBl, CottP
perenne Himmelszelt
  Marsh
perenne Nanum Diamond
  King #
perenne Nanum Saphyr
  Oasis
perenne Sky Blue
  King #, Pgeon
ultratissimum (Common Flax)
  Dream, King #

Lippia
citriodora now Aloysia triphylla
  BayBl, CottP, MillH, Pgeon, Sweet
nodiflora now Phylla n.
  Della, Pgeon, Seasd, Wells

Liquidambar
formosana (Chinese Sweet Gum)
  Reic #, TopTr
styraciflua (Sweet Gum)
  Apple, Burbk, Chedd, Coatv, Diack, Dove, Ford, Hewsn, Morgn, Mtato, NZtr #, Peele, Pionr, PuhaN, Reic #, Terra, TopTr, Wensl

styraciflua Aurora
Pukho

styraciflua Burgundy
Denes, EasyB, Pukho

styraciflua festeri
Peele, TopTr

styraciflua Golden Treasure
Pukho, TopTr

styraciflua Gumball
Denes

styraciflua Lane Roberts
Denes, Pukho, TopTr

styraciflua Palo Alto
EasyB, Pukho, TopTr

styraciflua Richared
Denes, Pukho

styraciflua Richmond
Pionr

styraciflua rotundiloba
TopTr

styraciflua Vera
Denes

styraciflua Worplesdon
Denes, EasyB, Mtato, Peele, Pionr, Pukho, TopTr

Liriodendron

tulipifera (Tulip Tree, Yellow Poplar)
Apple, Burbk, Chedd, Coatv, Denes, Diack, Dove, EasyB, MJury, Mtato, Ormon, Peele, Pionr, PuhaN, Pukho, SpecT, TopTr, Wensl

tulipifera Arnold
Caves, Mtato, Pukho

tulipifera Aureomarginatum
Chedd, Denes, Peele, Pionr, Pukho

tulipifera Gold
Caves

Liriope

Moonlight
Denes

muscari was Ophiopogon (Turf Lily)
BayBl, Hackf, Pgeon, Seasd

muscari Big Blue
Denes, Parva

muscari golden variegated
JoyPl

muscari Variegata
BayBl

spicata
Otepo, Pgeon

Lisianthus

blue
Kayd

pink
Kayd

Lithocarpus

edulis
Caves

Lithodora

diffusa
Pgeon

diffusa Grace Ward
BlueM, Marsh, Nikau

diffusa Heavenly Blue
BayBl, Trans

Irish Crystals
BayBl, Pgeon, Wells

Lithospermum

Blue Carpet
Telfa

Heavenly Blue see Lithodora
Ref

officinalis (Gromwell)
Sweet

Litsea

calicaris (Mangeao)
Orati, Terra

Littonia

modesta
Kayd, MJury

Livistona

australis (Australian Cabbage Tree/Fan palm)
Coatv, Frans, Lsendt, NZtr #, PalmF, Reic #, SpecT

chinensis (Chinese Fan Palm)
Frans, LakeN, Lsendt, PalmF, Reic #

decipiens
Frans, Reic #

drudei
Frans

muelleri
Reic #

rotundifolia
Reic #

Lobelia

varieties
Roswd

anceps
Orati

Burgundy Joy
JoyPl

cardinalis (Cardinal Flower)
AynDa, BayBl, Oasis, WaiMa, WilAq

Cinnabar Rose
BayBl, BlueM, CottP, MaraN, Parva, Peak, Reic #, Telfa

Complexion
TRidg

Compliment
BlueM, Diack, MaraN, WaiMa

Compliment Blue
Egmon, Parva

Compliment Scarlet
BayBl, CottP, Peak, Telfa

Dark Crusader
BayBl, CottP, Parva

erinus compacta Riviera (3 colours)
King #

erinus Kathleen Mallard
CottP, Parva, Peak

erinus pendula Colour Cascade series
King #

erinus pendula Fountain (4 colours)
King #

erinus pendula Regatta series
King #

Fan
MaraN, MillH

Fan Deep Red
BayBl, Nikau

Fan Orchid Rose
Reic #

Fan Red
Pgeon, Reic #

Flamingo
BayBl, MaraN, Oasis

fulgens (Cardinal Flower)
CottP, Mills

x gerardii
WilAq

x gerardii Vedrariensis
AynDa, BayBl, CottP, KeriP, MaraN, Mills, Oasis, Telfa, Vall #, WaiMa, Warwk

gibberoa
Caves

x hybrida - soft pink
Trans

inflata
Sweet

laxiflora
AynDa, BayBl

linnaeioides
Orati

Minstrel
MillH

Pink Flamingo
Mills, Vall #, Wells

Queen Victoria
BlueM, KeriP, MaraN, Nikau, Pgeon, WaiMa

Russian Princess
BayBl, CottP, Oasis

sessilifolia
MaraN, WaiMa

sessilifolia var. Alba
MaraN

siphilitica
AynDa, BayBl, Dream, KeriP, MaraN, MillH, Mills, Nikau, Pgeon, Trans, Vall #, WaiMa, WilAq

siphilitica alba
AynDa, BayBl, Dream, Egmon, MaraN, MillH, Parva, Peak, WaiMa, WilAq

siphilitica Blue Auslese
WaiMa

x speciosa
Diack

x speciosa Cerise
Peak

Tim Rees   see Pratia ang. T.R.
Ref

tupa
Dream, MaraN

valida
AynDa

Lobularia

maritinum Creamery
King #

maritinum Pastel Carpet mixed
King #

maritinum Snowcloth Improved
King #

maritinum Snowdrift
King #

Lomaria

see Blechnum
Ref

Lomatia

ferruginea
Matth, Woodl

Lonas

inodora
King #

Lonicera

x americana
CouCl

x brownii Dropmore Scarlet
BlueM, CouCl

caprifolium
CouCl

etrusca
CouCl

fragrantissima (Winter-flwg Honeysuckle)
Chedd, Denes, Hackf, KeriP, MillH, Pukho

giraldii
CouCl

heckrotti Firecracker
CouCl

heckrotti Gold Flame
BlueM, CouCl

henryi
BlueM

hildebrandtiana
Woodl

involucrata ledebourii
TopTr

japonica Aureoreticulata
Ashto, CouCl, Mills

japonica Halliana
BlueM, CouCl

japonica var. repens
BlueM, CouCl, ZinoN

korolkowii
MillH, Pukho, Taunt, TopTr

nitida (Box Honeysuckle)
BlueM, Diack, Morgn, Pionr, SelGr, TopTr

nitida aurea (Gold Box Honeysuckle)
Denes, Diack, KeriP, Looij, Mtato, Pionr, SelGr

nitida Fertilis
BlueM

periclymenum Graham Thomas
Denes

periclymenum pink/cream/white fl
Mills

periclymenum Serotina
CouCl

periclymenum Winchester
BlueM, CouCl, Denes, YakuN

periclymenum yellow/cream fl
Mills

pileata
TopTr

x purpusii
TopTr

x purpusii Winter Beauty
Denes

sempervirens sulphurea
BlueM

splendida
CouCl

x tellmanniana
BlueM, CouCl, Woodl

x tellmanniana Yellow Clusters
Denes

Lophomyrtus

species
Morgn

bullata (Ramarama)
Burbk, Gordn, Matai, Orati, Terra, Wahpa

Gloriosa
Wahpa, Wells

Indian Chief
Butlr, Kayd, Mtato, Wahpa, Wensl

Kathryn
BlueM, Butlr, Chedd,
Gordn, Hewsn, Kayd,
Matai, Matwh, Mtato,
Orati, Pionr, Wahpa,
Wensl

Krinkly
Wahpa

Lilliput
BlueM

Litte Star
Mtato, Orati

Lyndale
BlueM

Matai Bay
Orati, Wells

Multicolour
Kayd, Pionr, Wahpa,
Wells

obcordata (Rohutu)
Matai, Matwh, Orati,
SouWo, Terra

Pink Dainty
Gordn, Matai

Pink Diamond
Wahpa

Pixie
BlueM, Wahpa

purpurea
Hewsn

x ralphii Variegata
BlueM, Butlr, Matai

Red Dragon
Matai, Mtato

Redwing
Kayd

traversii
Matai

Wild Cherry
BlueM

Lophospermum

**erubescens was Asarina
e.,Maurandya e. (Creeping
Gloxinia)**
CouCl, MaraN

Lophostemon

**confertus was Tristania
conferta
(Queensland/Brush Box)**
Coatv, McKe, SpecT

Loropetalum

chinense (Fringe Flower)
Denes

Lotus

see also Dorycnium
Ref

**see Tetragonolobus,
Dorycnium**
Ref

waterlily see Nymphaea
Ref

Loxostylis

alata
Ether

Loxsoma

cunninghamii
Orati

Luculia

**grandifolia (Bhutan/White
Luculia)**
Denes

**gratissima Early Dawn
(Himalayan/Pink Luculia)**
Chedd, Denes, MJury

gratissima rosea
Reic #

pinceana Fragrant Cloud
Denes, Kayd, Wells

pinceana Fragrant Pearl
MJury

Lucuma

obovata syn Pouteria
Frans

sp green skin,orange flesh
Koan

Ludwigia

repens
WaiMa

Luffa

**acutangula (Chinese Okra,
Cee Gwa)**
King #

**aegyptica (Luffa, Vegetable
Sponge)**
King #, Sweet

Luma

**apiculata was Myrtus
luma, M.apiculata
(Cinnamon Myrtle)**
Caves, Chedd, TopTr

apiculata Glanleam Gold
BlueM

Lunaria

annua Purple
King #, Vall #

annua Sissinghurst White
King #

annua white (Honesty)
Orang

**annua variegata   white or
mauve fls**
AynDa

annua variegata, purple fl
Orang, Vall #

annua variegata, white fl
Orang, Vall #

Lupinus

arboreus
Reic #

Band Of Nobles
Mills

Chandelier
MillH

**dwarf
mixed(pink,blue,white)**
Vall #

Gallery dwf mixed
Mills

Israel
Trans

nanus Pixie Delight
King #

Nobel Maiden White
Oasis

**polyphyllus   Russell strain
mixed**
Pgeon

**polyphyllus Minarette
Dwarf mxd**
Oasis

polyphyllus Russell White
King #

sp silver lv dk blue fls
JoyPl

Sunrise
Reic #

texensis (Texas Lupin)
King #

Luzula

nivea
Pkrau

sp small
Orati

sylvatica Marginata
Pkrau

sylvestris
JoyPl

ulophylla (NZ Woodrush)
Della, Diack

Lycaste

cruenta
AnnM

Lychnis

alpina
Ashto, Della, MaraN

x arkwrightii
BlueM

x arkwrightii Vesuvius
MaraN

chalcedonia (Maltese Cross, Jerusalem Cross)
Ashto, BayBl, Della, KeriP, King #, Looij, Oasis, Orang, Pgeon, Reic #, Vall #

chalcedonia Alba
CottP, KeriP, Marsh, Otepo, Vall #

chalcedonia Morgenrot
Warwk

chalcedonia Raurei
Warwk

coronaria (Rose Campion)
Della, Looij, Oasis, Pgeon

coronaria Abbotswood Rose
BlueM, Orang

coronaria Alba
Ashto, BayBl, CottP, Dream, KeriP, Orang, Peak, Pgeon, Seasd, Trans, Vall #

coronaria Angel's Blush
Della, King #, MillH, Wells

coronaria Atrosanguinea
King #, Vall #

coronaria New Hybrids
King #

coronaria Oculata
AynDa, Vall #

flos cuculi (Ragged Robin, Cuckoo Flower)
CoFlo, Della, Dream, KeriP, MillH, Nikau, WilAq

flos cuculi alba
KeriP, MillH

flos cuculi albiflora
Dream

flos-jovis (Flower of Jove, Campion)
Della, MaraN, Oasis, Orang, Trans

flos-jovis Peggy
BayBl

miqueliana
Della, Oasis

Molten Lava
Ashto, Kayd

sieboldii
Della

viscaria
BlueM, Oasis

viscaria alba
BayBl, Pgeon, Trans

viscaria Flore Pleno
Parva

viscaria Plena
BayBl

viscaria Splendens
Telfa

viscaria Splendens Plena
BayBl, Parva, Pgeon, Trans

wilfordii
Della

yunnanensis
Della, MaraN

Lycopersicon

tomato 21 heirloom varieties
King #

tomato 7 standard varieties
King #

tomato 9 varieties incl. heirlooms
Koan #

tomato Heirloom mixed
King #, MTig #

Lycopus

europaeus (Gypsywort)
Della

Lycoris

aurea
DaffA, JoyPl

radiata
JoyPl

Lyonia

ovalifolia
Caves

Lysimachia

atropurpurea
WaiMa

ciliata atropurpurea
Parva

ciliata Firecracker
BayBl, Marsh, Parva, Peak

ciliata Purpurea
BayBl, CoFlo, CottP, KeriP, Telfa, TopTr, Trans

clethroides (Gooseneck, Chinese Loosestrife)
BayBl, CottP, MaraN, Mills, Nikau, Otepo, Parva, Peak, Pgeon, Telfa, Trans, TRidg, Warwk, WilAq

clethroides Lady Jane
Diack, Dream, WaiMa

ephemerum (White Loosestrife)
AynDa, MillH, Mills, Parva, Peak, Pgeon, Telfa, Trans, Warwk

Gold Clusters
MillH

Gold Star
Telfa

lichiangensis
Dream, TRidg

nummularia (Creeping Jenny, Moneywort, Herb Twopence)
AynDa, CottP, Diack, MaraN, Mills, Orang, Sweet, WaiMa

nummularia Aurea (Golden Creeping Jenny, Gold Moneywort)
CottP, Della, Telfa, Trans, WaiMa, WilAq

punctata (Yellow Loosestrife)
Ashto, AynDa, BayBl, CoFlo, Della, KeriP, Marsh, Oasis, WaiMa

punctata Alexander's
Parva

vulgaris (Yellow Loosestrife)
MaraN, Mills, Orang, Sweet

Lythrum

hybrids mixed
Vall #

salicaria (Purple Loosestrife)
AynDa, Della, Dream, MaraN, Marsh, MillH, Mills, Nikau, Orang, Pgeon, Sweet, WaiMa

salicaria Blush
BayBl

salicaria Firecandle
BayBl

salicaria Lady Sackville
Diack, WaiMa

salicaria Mordens Pink
Kayd

salicaria Rakel
BlueM

salicaria Red Beauties
WaiMa

salicaria Robert
Telfa

salicaria Rosy Gem
Diack, MillH, WaiMa

virgatum Rose Queen
BayBl, CottP, Looij, Telfa, Trans, Vall #, WaiMa

virgatum The Rocket
BayBl, Telfa

Maackia

amurensis (Amur Maackia)
Apple, Diack, Dove, PuhaN

Macadamia

x tetraphylla seedlings
Chedd, MTig

x tetraphylla Beaumont
Chedd, Frans

x tetraphylla GT1
Frans

x tetraphylla GT201
Chedd

x tetraphylla Nelmac I
Chedd

x tetraphylla Own choice
Chedd

x tetraphylla Renown
Koan

Macfadyena

unguis-cati was Doxantha u.c. (Cat Claw Vine)
CouCl, Denes

Machaerina

sinclairii
Orati, Terra

Mackaya

bella was asystacia
Trans

Macleaya

cordata (Plume Poppy)
Parva, Trans, TRidg

microcarpa
Pgeon, Vall #

Macropiper

excelsum (Kawakawa, Pepper Tree)
Gordn, NZtr #, Orati, Pionr, Reic #, Sweet, Terra, Wahpa

melchior (3 Kings Kawakawa)
Orati

psittacorum
Orati

Macrozamia

species
Reic #

communis (NSW Cycad)
MJury, PalmF

spiralis
LakeN

Magnolia

Albatross
Caves

amoena (Beautiful Magnolia)
Caves

Ann
MJury, Pukho

Apollo
Denes, MJury, Pukho

ashei
Caves

Athene
MJury, Pukho

Atlas
MJury, Pukho

Betty
Mtato

biondii (Chinese Willow Leaf Magnolia)
Caves

x brooklynensis Woodsman
Denes, Pukho

Caerhays Belle
Denes, Pukho

campbellii (Pink Tulip Tree)
Apple, Burbk, Caves, Chedd, Denes, McKe

campbellii Charles Raffill
Caves, Denes, Pukho

campbellii Darjeeling
Caves, Denes, Pukho

campbellii mollicomata Lanarth
Caves, Denes, Pukho

campbellii Strybing White
Caves, Denes, Pukho

cylindrica
Denes

dawsoniana Chyverton Red
Denes, Pukho

Deborah
Denes

delavayii
Caves, MJury

denudata (Yulan Magnolia)
Caves, Denes, Pionr, Pukho

denudata Forrests Pink
Pukho

Early Rose
Denes

Elizabeth American Hybrid
Caves, Denes, MJury, Pukho

Evamaria American Hybrid
MJury

Galaxy
Denes, Pukho

grandiflora (Evergreen/Laurel Magnolia)
Burbk, Chedd, Coatv, LanSc, Pukho

grandiflora Ferruginea
Burbk, Coatv, Denes, EasyB, MJury, Mtato, SpecT

grandiflora Goliath
MJury

grandiflora Little Gem
  BlueM, Caves, Chedd,
  Coatv, Denes, LanSc,
  MJury, Wells

grandiflora Majestic Beauty
  Caves, Denes

grandiflora Mammoth
  Denes

grandiflora Nannetensis
  Caves

grandiflora Russet
  Coatv, SpecT

grandiflora Samuel Sommer
  Denes, MJury

grandiflora St Mary
  Coatv, Denes

grandiflora Timeless
  Denes

Heaven Scent
  Denes, MJury

hypoleuca
  Caves

Iolanthe
  Burbk, Denes, MJury,
  Mtato, Pionr, Pukho

Jersey Belle
  Caves

Kew's Surprise
  Caves

kewensis Wada's Memory
  Pukho

Koban Dori   American Hybrid
  MJury

kobus (Kobus Magnolia)
  Burbk, Coatv, Dove,
  McKe, Ormon, Peele,
  PuhaN

liliflora (Lily Magnolia)
  Burbk, Coatv

liliflora Nigra
  Denes, MJury, Pukho

x loebneri Leonard Messel
  BlueM, Denes, MJury,
  Mtato, Pukho

x loebneri Merrill
  BlueM, MJury, Pukho

Lotus
  MJury

macrophylla (Big Leaf Magnolia)
  Caves, Peele

Manchu Fan
  Denes, Pukho

Mark Jury
  MJury, Pukho

Milky Way
  Burbk, Denes, MJury,
  Pukho

New Purple Caerhays
  Caves, Denes, Pukho

Paul Cook
  Denes, Pukho

Peppermint Stick
  MJury

Pinkie
  MJury, Pukho

Purple Eye
  Pukho

Purple Globe
  Denes

Rouged Alabaster
  Denes, Pukho

Royal Crown
  Denes

salicifolia
  Caves, Denes

sargentiana
  Caves

sargentiana robusta (Caerhays)
  Caves, Pukho

sargentiana robusta (Chyverton dark form)
  Caves

Sayonara
  Caves, Denes, Pukho

Serene
  Denes, MJury, Pukho

sieboldii (Oyama Magnolia)
  Apple, Caves, Chedd,
  Coatv, Denes, Dove,
  MJury, Ormon

x soulangeana (Purple Saucer /Tulip Magnolia)
  Apple, Burbk, Chedd,
  Coatv, Dove, EasyB,
  Hewsn, Peele, PuhaN

x soulangeana Alexandrina
  BlueM

x soulangeana Burgundy
  Pukho

x soulangeana Lennei
  Denes

x soulangeana Lennei Alba
  Denes

x soulangeana Rustica Rubra
  Burbk, Mtato, Peele,
  Pionr

x soulangeana San Jose
  Burbk, Coatv, Denes

x soulangeana Star Wars
  Pionr

Spectrum
  Coatv, Pukho

sprengeri diva
  Caves, Denes

sprengeri diva Burncoose
  Caves

sprengeri diva Copeland Court
  Caves

sprengeri diva Diva
  Caves

Spring Snow
  Caves

Star Wars
  BlueM, Coatv, Denes,
  MJury, Peele, Pukho

stellata (Star Magnolia)
  Apple, BlueM, Burbk,
  Chedd, Coatv, Denes,
  Dove, EasyB, Mtato,
  Ormon, Peele, Taunt

stellata King Rose
  Denes, Pukho

stellata Rosea
  Caves, Pionr

stellata Royal Star
  Mtato

stellata standards
  Caves

stellata Waterlily
  Caves, Coatv, Pukho

Sun Dance
  Denes

Susan
  Denes, MJury, Mtato

Sweetheart
  Caves, Denes

Tina Durio
  Pukho

Tod Gresham
  Denes

tripetala
  Caves

virginiana (Sweet Bay)
  Caves, Denes

Vulcan
Caves, Denes, MJury,
Pukho, SpecT

x wiesneri (watsonii)
MJury

wilsonii
Caves

Yellow Bird American
Hybrid
Denes, MJury, Pukho

Yellow Fever American
Hybrid
Coatv, MJury, Pukho

Magtenus
boana
Pionr

Mahonia
acanthifolia
Caves

heterophylla
Denes

lomariifolia (Chinese Holly
Grape)
BlueM, Butlr, Chedd,
Denes, Hackf, Hewsn,
Woodl

mairei
Caves

Maianthemum
bifolium
MaraN

Malaviscus
arboreus (Wax Mallow)
Denes

Malcomia
maritima (Virginia Stock)
King #

Malope
trifida Pink Queen
King #

trifida White Queen
King #

Vulcan
Vall #

Malus
crabapple Elise Rathke
TopTr

crabapple florentina
TopTr

crabapple sieboldii Snow
Charm
TopTr

crabapple Ballerina
Denes, Pukho, TopTr

crabapple Barbara Ann
Denes, Peele, Pukho

crabapple Blue Mountain
Pukho

crabapple coronaria
Charlottae
Denes, Diack, TopTr

crabapple Echtermeyer
wpg
Denes, Dove, Peele,
Pukho

crabapple floribunda
(Japanese Crabapple)
Burbk, Denes, Mtato,
Peele, Pionr, Pukho,
TopTr, TreeC

crabapple Golden Hornet
Pukho, TopTr, TreeC

crabapple Gorgeous
Burbk, Chedd, Denes,
Peele, Pukho, TreeC

crabapple hupehensis
TopTr

crabapple ioensis plena
(Betchels Crab)
Chedd, Coatv, Denes,
Mtato, Peele, Pionr,
Pukho, SpecT, TopTr

crabapple Jack Humm
Chedd, Dove, Hewsn,
Mtato, Peele, TopTr

crabapple Jack Humm
Dwarf
Denes, Pukho

crabapple Kaitoke
wpg
Burbk, Denes, Mtato,
Peele, Pionr, Pukho

crabapple Maypole
columnar
TopTr

crabapple niedzwetzkyana
Chedd

crabapple Profusion
Burbk, Chedd, Denes,
Peele, Pukho, TopTr,
TreeC

crabapple Red Jade
Burbk, Chedd, Denes,
Hewsn, Peele, Pionr,
Pukho

crabapple robusta
Pukho, TopTr

crabapple Roland Young
MJury

crabapple Snowbright
Pukho

crabapple Sovereign
Peele

crabapple spectabilis
Pukho

crabapple Strathmore
Pukho

crabapple toringoides
Apple

crabapple transitoria
Apple

crabapple trilobata
Denes, Pukho

crabapple tschonoskii
Denes, Mtato, Pukho,
TopTr

crabapple Van Eseltine
Chedd, Denes, Peele

crabapple Wanden Glory
wpg
Pionr

crabapple Wrights Scarlet
Peele, Pukho, TreeC

crabapple yunnanensis
TopTr

domestica rootstock
793(dwarfing)
Koan

domestica rootstock M9
(free draining soil,lge tree)
Koan

domestica rootstock
Northern Spy(heavy wet
soils,lge tree)
Koan

domestica dualgrafted
varieties
Coatv

domestica dualgrafted:
Braebn.,Sturmr
Diack

domestica dualgrafted:
G.Smith,CoxO.
Diack

domestica dualgrafted:
G.Smith,Gala
Diack

domestica dualgrafted:
G.Smith,Spledr

Diack

domestica triplegrafted
varieties

Coatv

domestica triplegrafted:
Braebn.,CoxO.,Sturmr.

Diack

domestica triplegrafted:
Braebn.,Spledr.,G.Smith

Diack

domestica triplegrafted:
G.Smith,CoxO.,Gala

Diack

domestica Adam's
Pearmain (EM9 rootstk-
dwarf)

Harri

domestica Akane

TreeC

domestica All Red
Gravenstein

TreeC

domestica Aorangi

Diack

domestica Ballarat

Chedd

domestica Ballerina

TreeC

domestica ballerina Bolero

Harri

domestica ballerina
Maypole

Harri

domestica ballerina Polka

Harri

domestica ballerina Waltz

Harri

domestica Beacon (EM9
rootstk-dwarf)

Harri

domestica Bella Scarletta

TopTr

domestica Bella Scarletta
(EM9 rootstk-dwarf)

Harri

domestica Benoni

Koan S

domestica Benoni (Nth Spy
rootstk)

Mtanu

domestica Braeburn

Chedd, Coatv, Diack,
Pionr, TreeC

domestica Braeburn on
mm106
rootstock(semidwarf)

Diack

domestica Captain Kidd

Koan S

domestica Captain Kidd
(em9 rootstk)

Harri

domestica Captain Kidd
(mm106 rootstk)

Harri

domestica Captain Kidd
(Nth Spy rootstk)

Mtanu

domestica Cheddar Valley
(cider)

Chedd

domestica Cox's Orange

Chedd, Diack, Pionr,
TreeC

domestica Cox's Orange
(semidwarf)

Diack

domestica Dayton

TreeC

domestica Devonshire
Quarendon

Koan S

domestica Discovery

Koan S, TreeC

domestica Discovery
(rootstk dwarf)

Harri

domestica Early
Strawberry

Koan S

domestica Egremont
Russet

Koan S

domestica Egremont Russet
(rootstk-dwarf)

Harri

domestica Fiesta

Diack, TreeC

domestica Five Crowns
(Nth Spy rootstk)

Mtanu

domestica Freyberg

Koan S

domestica Freyberg
(rootstk-dwarf)

Harri

domestica Fuji

Chedd, Coatv, TreeC

domestica Gala

Coatv

domestica George Neal

TopTr

domestica Giant Geniton
(Nth Spy rootstk)

Mtanu

domestica Golden Delicious

Chedd, Pionr, TreeC

domestica Golden Russett
(Nth Spy rootstk)

Mtanu

domestica Granny Smith

Chedd, Koan S, TreeC

domestica Granny Smith
on mm106
rootstock(semidwarf)

Harri

domestica Granny Smith
(em9 rootstk)

Harri

domestica Gravenstein

Chedd

domestica Gravenstein (Nth
Spy rootstk)

Mtanu

domestica Hames Red

Koan S

domestica Irish Peach

Koan S

domestica John Standish

TopTr

domestica John Standish
(EM9 rootstk-dwarf)

Harri

domestica Jona Gold

Diack

domestica Laxton's
Fortune

Koan S

domestica Liberty

TreeC

domestica Lobo

Koan S

domestica Lobo (rootstk-
dwarf)

Harri

domestica Lord Wolseley
(Nth Spy rootstk)

Mtanu

domestica Mayflower

Koan S

domestica Merton Russet

Koan S

domestica Merton
Worcester
Koan S
domestica Misen
Jaromerska Cervana
TopTr
domestica Monroe Special
(Nth Spy rootstk)
Mtanu
domestica Niggerjack
Koan S
domestica Nonnetit
Bastard
Diack
domestica Northern Spy
Koan S
domestica Northern Spy
(Nthn Spy rootstk)
Mtanu
domestica Ohinemuri
Koan S
domestica Peasgood
Nonsuch
Koan S, Mtanu
domestica Peasgood
Nonsuch (Nth Spy rootstk)
Mtanu
domestica Peasgood
Nonsuch (rootstk-dwarf)
Harri
domestica Priam (Nth Spy
rootstk)
Mtanu
domestica Priam (rootstk-
dwarf)
Harri
domestica Prima
Diack, Pukho, TreeC
domestica Prima (Nth Spy
rootstk)
Mtanu
domestica Prima (rootstk-
dwarf)
Harri
domestica Priscilla
Diack, TopTr
domestica Priscilla (em9
rootstk)
Harri
domestica Priscilla (mm106
rootstk)
Harri
domestica Red Delicious
Chedd, Pionr

domestica Red Gravenstein
Koan S
domestica Red Melba (EM9
rootstk-dwarf)
Harri
domestica Red Spy (Nth
Spy rootstk)
Mtanu
domestica Rennette de
France
Chedd
domestica Royal Gala
Chedd, Coatv, Pionr,
TreeC
domestica Royal Gala on
mm106
rootstock(semidwarf)
Harri
domestica Scarlet
Pimpernel (Nth Spy
rootstk)
Mtanu
domestica Scarlett
Pimpernel
Koan S
domestica Sir Prize
Diack, TreeC
domestica Sir Prize (em9
rootstk)
Harri
domestica Sir Prize (mm106
rootstk)
Harri
domestica Sir Prize (Nth
Spy rootstk)
Mtanu
domestica Splendour
Chedd, TreeC
domestica Stayman
Winesap (Nth Spy rootstk)
Mtanu
domestica Sturmer
Chedd
domestica Sunset
Koan S
domestica Takapuna
Russett (Nth Spy rootstk)
Mtanu
domestica Triphook Special
(Nth Spy rootstk)
Mtanu
domestica Tydeman's Late
Koan S

domestica Tydeman's Late
(Nth Spy rootstk)
Mtanu
domestica Tydemans Late
Orange (rootstk-dwarf)
Diack, Harri
domestica Vaile Early
Koan S
domestica Vaile Early
(Nthn Spy rootstk)
Mtanu
domestica Welcome (Nthn
Spy rootstk)
Mtanu
domestica Willie Sharp
Koan S
domestica Wilson's Own
Koan S
domestica Worcester
Pearmain
Koan S

Malva

alcea var. fastigiata
MaraN, MillH
moschata (Musk Mallow)
KeriP, MaraN, Orang,
Vall #
moschata alba
Della, Dream, King #,
MaraN, Nikau, Pgeon,
Sweet, Telfa
moschata rosea
AynDa, Della, King #,
Nikau, Oasis
sylvestris (Common
Mallow)
Sweet
sylvestris mauritiana
Dream, King #
sylvestris Primley Blue
Hackf, Marsh
sylvestris Zebrina
CoFlo, Della, King #,
Sweet, Vall #
verticillata (Curled Mallow
King #

Malvastrum

Apricot Delight
Telfa
lateritium (False Mallow)
CottP, Seasd

Malvaviscus

brevipedunculata
LakeN

Mandevilla

x amoena Alice du Pont
Denes

laxa was suaveolens (Chilean Jasmine)
CouCl

sp scented white fl
Wells

suaveolens now M.laxa
BlueM, Denes, Reic #

Manglietia

628
Caves

695
Caves

insignis
Caves

insignis GWC228
Woodl

vuyuanensis
Caves

Maranta

arundinacea (Arrowroot)
Sweet

Marattia

fraxinea
PalmF

salicina (King Fern)
Coatv, Orati, Terra

Margyricarpus

pinnatus (Pearl Berry)
Seasd

Marjorana

hortensis now Origanum m.
MillH

Markhamia

lutea
Ether

Marrubium

vulgare (Horehound)
Della, King #, Orang, Sweet

Marsilea

mutica
WilAq

quadrifolia (Nardoo Plant, Water Clover)
WaiMa

Matricaria

chamomilla now recutita (German Chamomile)
King #, Koan #, MTig #, Orang, Sweet

Matteuccia

struthiopteris (Ostrich Fern)
TRidg

Matthiola

bicornis (Night Scented Stock)
King #

bright green lvs,white dbl fl
MaraN

incana Cinderella mixed (Stock)
King #

incana Cinderella Silver Blue
King #

incana Double Appleblossom
King #

incana Legacy mixed
King #

incana Trysomic 7 week mixed
King #

Maurandya

barclayana was Asarina b. (Twining Snapdragon)
AynDa, Denes, MaraN

erubescens now Lophospermum e.
MaraN

scandens
Dream, Hackf, Vall #

sp purple fl, climber
Trolh

Maytenus

boaria (Mayten Tree, Chilean Mayten)
Apple, Denes, Matai, Mtato, TopTr

Mazus

affinis pumilio
Orati

albaflorus japonicus
BayBl

novae zelandiae
CottP

Omaio
JoyPl

radicans (Swamp Musk)
CottP, Della, MillH, Mills, Orati, Pgeon, Telfa

reptans
BayBl, CottP

reptans alba
CottP

reptans Snow Carpet
Telfa

aurculosus
MaraN

Meconopsis

x beamishii
TRidg

betonicifolia was baileyi (Himalayan Poppy)
Ashto, AynDa, BayBl, BlueM, CoFlo, Della, MaraN, Parva, Peak, TRidg, Vall #

betonicifolia alba
Parva, Peak, TRidg

cambrica (Welsh Poppy)
AynDa, MaraN, Marsh, Peak, Vall #

cambrica aurantica
MaraN, Vall #

cambrica Rubra
MaraN

dhwojii
TRidg

grandis
Della, Parva, Reic #, TRidg

grandis alba
TRidg

horridula
TRidg

napaulensis (Satin Poppy)
Della, Parva

napaulensis Blue
Parva

napaulensis Silver Leaf
Parva, TRidg

nepaulensis sdlg golden form
TRidg

regia
Ashto, MaraN

regia bicolor
Marsh, TRidg

superba
TRidg

villosa
Della, TRidg

Medicago

sativa (Alfalfa)
Sweet

Medinilla

magnifica
JoyPl

Megacarpaea

polyandra
TRidg

Melaleuca

alternifolia
Reic #

armillaris (Bracelet Honey Myrtle)
Frans

decussata
Reic #

elliptica
Reic #

ericifolia nana
Reic #

hyperificolia
Reic #

incana Velvet Cushion
Denes

lateritia (Robin Redbreast Bush)
Reic #

leucadendron (Swamp Paperbark)
Frans, JoyPl

linarifolia (Snow in Summer)
Frans

nodosa
Reic #

styphelioides
Frans

thymifolia
Reic #

viridiflora Red
Reic #

viridiflora Red Cloud
Reic #

Melandrium

rubrum now Silene (Red Campion)
AynDa

Melasphaerula

graminea now ramosa
DaffA, MaraN

Melastoma

polyanthum
Frans

Melia

azederach (Bead tree, Indian Lilac, Umbrella Tree)
Burbk, Chedd, Coatv, Denes, Mtato, NZtr #, Peele, Pionr, PuhaN, Pukho, Reic #, SpecT

Melicope

simplex (Poataniwha)
Mtato, Orati

ternata (Wharangi)
Coatv, Gordn, Matwh, Mtato, NZtr #, Orati, Pionr, Reic #, Terra

Melicytus

chathamicus
Gordn

crassifolius (Thick-lvd Porcupine Plant)
Terra

lanceolatus (Willow-lvd Mahoe, Mahoewao)
Gordn, NZtr #, Orati

macrophyllus (Large-lvd Mahoe)
Gordn, Orati

micranthus
Orati

novae-zelandiae
Orati

obovatus
Diack, Orati, SelGr

ramiflorus (Mahoe, Whiteywood)
Gordn, Matwh, Morgn, Mtato, NZtr #, Orati, Pionr, Reic #, Terra, Wahpa

Melilotus

officinalis (Melilot)
Sweet

Melissa

altissima (Wild Lemon/Turkish/Bush Balm)
Mills, Orang, Sweet

officinalis (Lemon Balm)
CottP, Della, King #, MillH, Mills, Orang, Sweet, Trans

officinalis Aurea (v)
Nikau

officinalis variegata now M.o.Aurea
Della, Orang, Sweet

Mentha

aquatica (Water Mint)
Diack, WaiMa, WriWa

arvensis peper (Japanese Menthol Mint)
Della

citrata (Orange/Bergamot/Eau de Cologne Mint)
CottP, Della, MillH, Mills, Orang, Sweet

cordifolia (Winter Mint)
Della, Trans

cunninghamii (Native Mint
Orang, Orati

x gentilis now x gracilis
CottP, Della

x gracilis Variegata (Ginger Mint)
Marsh, Mills, Orang

x piperita (Peppermint)
Della, King #, Mills, Nikau, Orang, Sweet

x piperita citrata Basil (Basil Mint)
Mills

x piperita citriata
Parva

x piperita nigra (Black Peppermint)
Della, Sweet

pulegium (Pennyroyal)
CottP, Della, Mills, Orang, Sweet, Trolh

pulegium Alba
Della, Orang

pulegium decumbens
Della

requienii (Corsican/Jewel Mint)
> AynDa, CottP, Della, Diack, Marsh, Mills, Orang, Parva, Sweet, TRidg

rotundifolia now suaveolens
> CottP, Della, MillH, Sweet, Trans

rust resist Wintermint
> CottP

x smithiana (Rustfree Spearmint)
> Sweet

x smithiana Rubra (Rustfree Mint)
> Orang

spicata (Common Mint /Spearmint (rust resist))
> CottP, Della, Mills, Orang, Sweet

suaveolens (Apple Mint)
> CottP, Della, MillH, Orang, Sweet, Trans, Trolh

suaveolens variegata (Variegated Apple /Pineapple/Ginger Mint)
> Della, Mills, Orang, Sweet

sylvestris viridis (Spearmint)
> King #, MillH, Nikau

Merendera

montana
> Kerer

sobolifera
> Kerer

Mertensia

virginica now pulmonarioides (Virginian Cowslip)
> Parva

Meryta

Cream Edge
> Denes

sinclairii (Puka)
> Chedd, Coatv, Denes, Gordn, Orati, Pionr, Reic #, SpecT, Terra, Wells

sinclairii Moonlight (v)
> Denes, Orati

Mesclun

oriental mixed greens
> King #, Koan #

premixed salad greens
> King #

Mesembryanthemum

criniflorum (Livingstone Daisy)
> King #

microcephalis
> BayBl

see Lampranthus
> Ref

Mespilus

germanica (Medlar)
> Reic #, TopIf

Metasequoia

glyptostroboides (Dawn Redwood)
> BlueM, Butlr, Cedar, Chedd, Coatv, CPete, NZtr #, Peele, Pionr, Pukho

glyptostroboides Sheridan Spire
> Cedar, Denes, MJury, Pukho

Metrosideros

Bartlettii
> Denes, Orati

Butterscotch
> Gordn

carmineus (Akakura, Carmine Rata)
> Denes, Gordn, Orati

carmineus Adult
> Orati, Parva

colensoi (Rata)
> Orati

diffusa (Rata)
> Gordn, Orati

excelsus (Pohutukawa)
> Burbk, Chedd, Coatv, Gordn, Matwh, Morgn, Mtato, NZtr #, Orati, Pionr, Pukho, Reic #, SpecT, Terra

excelsus Aureus
> Gordn, NZtr #, Reic #

excelsus Lighthouse
> SpecT

excelsus Moon Maiden
> Pukho

excelsus Parnell
> Frans, Orati, SpecT

excelsus Pink Lady
> Pukho

excelsus Scarlet Pimpernel
> Denes, Orati

excelsus Spring Fire
> Chedd, Frans, Kayd, Matth

excelsus variegatus (Variegated Pohutukawa)
> Orati

Frosty (Kermadec hyb)
> Mtato

fulgens (Rata, Aka)
> Orati

kermadecensis (Kermadec Is Pohutukawa)
> Gordn, Morgn

kermadecensis Platt's Form
> Pukho

kermadecensis Variegatus
> Butlr, Denes, Gordn, Mtato, Pukho

Lewis Nicholls (Kermadec Pohutukawa)
> Orati

Maungapiko (excelsus x umbellata)
> Orati, Pukho

Mistral (excelsus x robusta)
> Orati, Pukho, Woodl

perforata (Rata)
> Orati

queenslandicus
> JoyPl

Radiant (Kermadec hyb)
> Mtato

Red & Gold (Kermadec hyb)
> Gordn, Mtato

Red Haze (Pohutukawa)
> Orati

robusta (Northern Rata)
> Burbk, Chedd, Denes, NZtr #, Orati, Pukho, Terra, Wahpa

umbellatus (Southern Rata)
> Hewsn, Mtato, NZtr #, Orati, Terra, TopTr

villosus Tahiti
> Chedd, Denes, Frans, JoyPl, Matth, Matwh, Wells

Meum

athamanticum
MaraN, MillH

Mianthemum

bifolium
CottP

yakushima
Titok

Michauxia

campanuloides
AynDa

tchihatchewii
Dream, Pgeon

Michelia

alba
MJury

Bubbles
Caves, Coatv, Denes,
MJury

champaca
Denes

doltsopa
Coatv, Pukho

doltsopa Rusty
Caves

doltsopa Silver Cloud
Caves, Denes, LanSc,
MJury, Pukho

figo (Port Wine Magnolia)
Chedd, Coatv, Denes,
Frans, Pukho

foggii
Pukho

gracipes
Caves

lanuginosa (M.velutina)
Caves, Denes

maudiae
Caves, Denes

Mixed Up Miss
Caves, MJury

sinensis
Reic #

skinneriana
Denes

Touch of Pink
Caves, Denes, Pukho

yunnanensis
Chedd, Denes, Pukho,
TopTr, Woodl

yunnanensis Stellata
Woodl

yunnanensis Velvet and Cream
Caves, MJury

Micranthus

alopecuroides
DaffA

Microbiota

decussata
BlueM, Cedar, CPete

Microcachrys

tetragona
Cedar

Microlaena

avenacea (Bush Rice Grass
NZtr #, Terra

stipoides
Orati

Microlepia

hirta
Reic #

sp tropical
Manna

Micromeria

**thymifolia was rupestris
(Thyme-lvd Savoury)**
Marsh

varia
NewlR

Mida

salicifolia (False Maire)
Orati

Milium

**effusum Aureum (Bowles
Golden Grass)**
BayBl, Della, KeriP,
MaraN, Peak, Vall #

Millettia

reticulata
CouCl

Mimetes

cucullatus was lyrigera
MatNu

Mimosa

pudica (Sensitive Plant)
AynDa, King #, Reic #

Mimulus

Andean Nymph
CottP, Della, Nikau,
Sweet, WaiMa, Warwk

cardinalis
BayBl, MaraN, Vall #,
WaiMa

Choice Tumbler mixed
Nikau

cupreus
Diack, WaiMa

cupreus Red Emperor
MaraN, Oasis

**guttatus (Monkey Musk
common lge)**
AynDa, Diack, WaiMa

Highland Red
Diack, WaiMa

lewisii
MaraN

luteus
WaiMa, WilAq

Malibu
Marsh

Malibu Ivory
Nikau

**ringens (Allegheny Monkey
Flower)**
BayBl, Diack, MaraN,
MillH, WaiMa, WilAq

Mirabilis

**jalapa (Marvel of Peru,
Four O'clock Plant)**
Della, King #, Reic #,
Trolh

Miscanthus

japonica variegata
Hains

sinensis
BlueM, Diack, TopTr,
WaiMa

sinensis Gracillimus
Pkrau

sinensis Morninglight (v)
BayBl

sinensis Variegatus
BlueM, Peak, TopTr

sinensis Zebrinus (v)
AynDa

Mitraria

coccinea
BlueM, CouCl, Hackf,
Marsh

Molinia

caerulea
Diack, WaiMa

caerulea Variegata
BayBl, JoyPl, Marsh

Moltkia

petraea
Oasis

Moluccella

laevis (Bells of Ireland)
King #

Momordica

charantia (Bitter Melon, Foo Gwa, Balsam Pear)
King #

Monarda

Aquarius
BayBl, CottP, Marsh

Beauty of Cobham
BayBl, CottP, Parva, Peak, Telfa, Trans, Warwk

bradburyana
AynDa, KeriP, MaraN, Marsh, Nikau

bright pink
Nikau

Cambridge Scarlet
CottP, Della, MaraN, Marsh, Mills, Nikau, Peak, Pgeon, Telfa, WaiMa, Warwk

citriodora (Lemon Bergamot)
Della, King #, Sweet

Croftway Pink
BayBl, Della, Looij, Marsh, Mills, Trans, WaiMa

didyma Alba
MaraN, Peak, Telfa

didyma dark purple
Sweet

didyma hybrids mixed
Ashto, MillH, Orang, Sweet

didyma Panorama mixed (Horse Mint)
Reic #

Fire Beacon
BayBl, CottP, Della

Fishes syn Pisces
Marsh

fistulosa (Wild Bergamot)
Marsh, Pgeon, Sweet

fistulosa var menthifolia
Marsh

Gold Medal
WaiMa

Gold Melissa
WaiMa

hybrida Lambada
Dream

Libra
BayBl

light blue
Telfa

Lila
Sweet

Mahogany
BayBl, CoFlo, CottP, Della, KeriP, Marsh, MillH, Mills, Nikau, Parva, Peak, Sweet, Telfa, Trans

Margaret Rose
Telfa, WaiMa

Marshwood Rose
Marsh

Mauve
Della

menthifolia
Dream

Panorama
Dream, WaiMa

pink
Telfa

Pisces syn Fishes
BayBl, CottP, Della, Egmon, KeriP, Peak, Sweet, Trans, Warwk

Prairie Fire
CottP

Prairie Glow
BayBl, CottP, Della, KeriP, Marsh, Mills, Pgeon, Sweet, Telfa

Prairie Night
AynDa, BayBl, CoFlo, Egmon, KeriP, Marsh, Mills, Otepo, Trans, WaiMa

punctata
BayBl, Dream, MaraN

purple
Warwk

Purple King
WaiMa

Red   red form of M.Prairie Night
AynDa, Sweet

Rote Tone
WaiMa

Scorpio / Scorpion
CottP, Marsh, MillH, Parva, Peak

Selected Pink
Marsh

Snowmaiden
CottP, MillH

Squaw
BayBl, Marsh, Sweet, Telfa

violaceae
WaiMa

White
Della

White Maiden
Marsh

Monardella

odoratissima
MaraN

Monopsis

lutea (Yellow Lobelia)
AynDa

Monstera

deliciosa (Fruit Salad Plant
Kayd, LakeN, Manna, Reic #

obliqua
LakeN

Moraea

aristata (Peacock Iris)
BayBl, Brown, DaffA, Irida, JoyPl, Kerer, Ormon, Parva

bellendenii
DaffA, Kerer

fugax
Irida

gigandra
JoyPl

loubseri
BayBl, DaffA, JoyPl

neopavonia
DaffA

papilionacea
Kerer

polystachya
MJury, Parva

ramosissima
DaffA, Parva

sp pale brown fl,yellow centre
TRidg

spathulata
Della

stricta
Kerer

tricolor
DaffA

tricuspidata
DaffA, JoyPl

tripetala
DaffA, JoyPl, Kerer, MJury

tulbaghensis
AynDa

unguiculata
DaffA

vegeta
Irida, Kerer

villosa
AynDa, BayBl, DaffA, JoyPl, Kerer, MJury, Parva

Morina

longifolia (Whorl Flower)
Della, Dream, MaraN, Oasis, Pgeon, Telfa

Morisia

monanthos was hypogaea
Otepo, Seasd

Morus

alba (White Mulberry)
Apple, Burbk, Chedd, Denes, Dove, Peele, PuhaN, Reic #, TopTr, Wensl

alba Pendula (Weeping White Mulberry)
Denes, Pukho, TopTr

alba tartarica (Russian Mulberry)
Reic #

Black English
Harri

nigra (Black Mulberry)
Chedd, Denes, Diack, Frans, Matwh, Peele, Reic #, Sweet, TopTr, Wells

rubra
Frans, Mtanu, Reic #

Muehlenbeckia

astonii
Hackf, Orati, Terra, Woodl

australis (Bush Pohuehue)
NZtr #, Orati

axillaris (Creeping Pohuehue/Wire Vine)
Orati

complexa (Pohuehue)
JoyPl, Matai, Orati, Terra

ephedroides
Orati

Murraya

exotica now paniculata
Reic #

paniculata (Orange Jessamine)
Frans

Musa

abyssinian see Ensete
Manna

Australian Ladyfinger
Frans

Cavendish
Frans

cavendish Williamsii
Manna

ensete Maurellii see Ensete (Purple Abyssnn Banana)
Koan, LakeN

ethiopian see Ensete
Manna

Kaiatea Lady Finger (Banana)
MTig

Ladyfinger
Koan

Misi Luki (Banana)
Frans, Lsendt

Mon Mari (Banana)
Koan, LakeN

Norfolk Island Dwarf Cavendish (Banana)
MTig

Patasina (Banana)
MTig

S.H.3481 Gold Finger (Banana)
LakeN

sapientum (Banana)
Lsendt

velutina (ornamental)
Frans

Muscari

armeniacum (Armenian Grape Hyacinth)
JoyPl

armeniacum Album
Kerer

armeniacum Barbara
BayBl, Kerer, NewlR

armeniacum Blue Spike
DaffA, NewlR, VanEe

armeniacum Cantab
NewlR

armeniacum Early Giant
CottP, DaffA, Kayd

aucheri was tubergenianum
DaffA

aucheri Iceberg
Kerer

azureum
Kerer, NewlR

azureum Album
DaffA, Parva

blue
Altrf

botryoides
Kerer

botryoides Album
BayBl, CottP, DaffA, JoyPl, NewlR, Parva

Cambridge
DaffA

chalusicum now pseudomuscari
NewlR

commuttaum
Kerer

comosum (Tassle Hyacinth)
Kerer

comosum Plumosum (Feather/Tassel Hyacinth)
Kerer

grandiflorum
Kerer

latifolium
VanEe

neglectum
CottP, JoyPl, Kerer, MaraN, NewlR

pseudomuscari was chalusicum
NewlR

**sp like chalusicum but
erect lvs**
> RosPl

**tubergenianum now
aucheri**
> Kerer

turkewiczii
> DaffA

Musseanda

erythophylla Rosea
> LakeN

frondosa
> LakeN

Myoporum

debile
> Matwh, Orati

**decumbens (Off-shore
Ngaio)**
> Orati

insulare (Boobialla)
> Ford

laetum (Ngaio)
> Chedd, Ford, Gordn,
> Matwh, Morgn, Mtato,
> NZtr #, Orati, Pionr, Reic
> #, Seasd, Terra

**laetum Purpureum (Purple
Ngaio)**
> Mtato, Orati

**parvifolium (Creeping
Boobialla)**
> Mtato

parvifolium purpureum
> Butlr, Mtato

Myosotidium

varieties
> Roswd

**hortensia (Chatham Is
Forget-me-not)**
> AynDa, Denes, Dream,
> Egmon, Herew, Kayd,
> Mtato, Nikau, Orati,
> Parva, Reic #, Terra,
> Trans, TRidg, Wahpa

hortensia Alba
> AynDa, Herew, Kayd,
> Peak, TRidg

Myosotis

**alpestris Blue (Forget-me-
not)**
> King #

alpestris Rose
> King #

alpestris Ruth Fischer
> BayBl, CottP, NewlR

alpestris Ultramarine
> King #

alpestris White
> King #, Vall #

colensoi
> CottP, Gordn, Orati,
> Wahpa

explanata
> Peak

palustris   now scorpioides
> WaiMa, WilAq

petiolata pansa
> Orati

petiolata pottsiana
> Orati

saxosa
> NewlR

**scorpioides was palustris
(Water Forgetmenot)**
> Diack, WaiMa

scorpioides Pinkie
> TRidg

suavis
> Pgeon

Myricaria

cauliflora
> Frans

Myriophyllum

**aquaticum was brasiliense
(Parrot's Feather)**
> Diack

**propinquum (Water
Milfoil)**
> Diack, Orati, WaiMa,
> WilAq

robustum
> WaiMa

Myrrhis

odorata (Sweet Cicely)
> Della, MaraN, Sweet

umbelliferae
> Vall #

Myrsine

**australis (Red Matipo,
Mapou)**
> Gordn, Matai, Matwh,
> Morgn, Mtato, NZtr #,
> Orati, Ormon, Pionr,
> Terra, Wahpa

**divaricata (Weeping
Mapou)**
> Matai, NZtr #, Orati

salicina (Toro)
> Gordn, Mtato, Orati,
> Pionr, Wahpa

Myrtus

apiculata now Luma a.
> BlueM, Chedd, Denes

communis (Myrtle)
> BlueM, Denes, Orang,
> Ormon, Sweet

communis compacta
> TRidg

communis Nana
> Parva

communis variegata
> BlueM, Orang

**Glanleam Gold   now
Luma apiculata GG.**
> BlueM, Wahpa

luma now Luma apiculata
> Caves, Taunt

Native see Lophomyrtus
> Ref

ugni now Ugni molinae
> BlueM, Chedd, CottP,
> Denes, Mtato, Taunt,
> TreeC

Nandina

**domestica (Heavenly
Bamboo)**
> ZinoN

domestica Fire Power
> Denes, Frans, Wells

domestica Pygmaea
> BlueM, Matwh

domestica red
> Reic #

domestica Richmond
> Denes, Frans, Mtato

Narcissus

varietes mixed dwf & tall
> RosPl

Accent
> DaffA

Achduart
> DaffA

Acropolis
> DaffA

Actaea
> DaffA

Airmarshal
DaffA

April Cloud
DaffA

April Tears
DaffA

Ariel
DaffA

Arkle
DaffA

Ashanti
DaffA

asturiensis
NewlR

Auburn
DaffA

Audubon
DaffA

Aurelia
DaffA

Baby Moon
DaffA, Winga

Baccarat
DaffA

Bagatelle
Kerer

Ballade
VanEe

Bambi
CottP, DaffA, Kerer,
NewlR, RosPl

Bandit
DaffA

Bantam
DaffA

Bare None
DaffA

Barrett Browning
Winga

Beau Vite
DaffA

Beauvallon
DaffA

Bebop
DaffA, Kerer

Belcanto
DaffA

Bell Song
DaffA

Bellefleur
DaffA

Beryl
DaffA

Bob White
DaffA

Bobbysoxer
DaffA, Kerer, NewlR

Broadway Star
VanEe

**bulbocodium (Hoop
Petticoat Daffodil)**
Altrf, CottP, Kerer,
Mills, MJury, NewlR,
Oasis, Otepo, Trans,
TRidg

bulbocodium citrinus
MJury

bulbocodium Elfhorn
DaffA, Kerer

bulbocodium filifolius
DaffA, NewlR, RosPl

bulbocodium Jessamy
DaffA

bulbocodium Major
DaffA, RosPl

bulbocodium monophyllus
DaffA

bulbocodium nivalis
DaffA

bulbocodium obesus
DaffA, NewlR

bulbocodium Pandora
MJury

bulbocodium var citrinus
DaffA

**bulbocodium var
conspicuus**
Kerer

**bulbocodium var
tenuifolius**
RosPl

Buttercup
Kayd

Butterscotch
DaffA

calcicola
Kerer, NewlR

Camelot
DaffA

**canaliculatus now N.tazetta
lacticolor**
DaffA, Kerer, NewlR,
RosPl

Canasta
DaffA

Candida
DaffA

cantabricus
DaffA

cantabricus clusii
DaffA

**cantabricus foliosus (White
Hoop Petticoats)**
DaffA, JoyPl, Kerer,
NewlR

Cantata
DaffA

Cantatrice
DaffA

Canterbury Fair
DaffA

Carlton
Winga

Cassata
VanEe

Checkmate
DaffA

Cheerfulness
DaffA

Cherie
DaffA

Chit Chat
DaffA, NewlR

City Lights
DaffA

Clare
DaffA

Cloud Nine
DaffA

Colorama
DaffA

Coral Ribbon
DaffA

Coral Strand
DaffA

Countdown
DaffA

cyclamineus
DaffA, Herew

cyclamineus seedlings
DaffA

Cyclataz
DaffA

Dailmanach
DaffA

Dainty Miss
DaffA

Danger
DaffA

Danny
  DaffA

Daydream
  DaffA, VanEe, Winga

Dazzling
  Kayd

Dear Love
  DaffA

Debonair
  DaffA

Diane Joy
  DaffA

Dickcissel
  DaffA

Dinky Duffle
  DaffA

Dolly Mollinger
  DaffA

Donation
  DaffA

Double Gold
  DaffA

Double Yellow
  DaffA

Dresden
  DaffA

Dutch Master
  Winga

Dynasty
  DaffA

Early Mist
  DaffA

Easter Moon
  DaffA

Echo
  Altrf

Egmont Snow
  DaffA

Elf
  DaffA

Enterprise
  DaffA

Erlicheer
  Altrf, Kayd

Fairy Chimes
  DaffA

Falconet
  DaffA

Falstaff
  DaffA

Fanline
  DaffA

February Gold
  DaffA, Kerer, Winga

ferdinandesii
  DaffA, Kerer

filifolius see bulbocodium f.
  NewlR

First Frost
  DaffA

Flaming Jewel
  DaffA

Fleurimont
  Kayd

Fortune
  Winga

Gabriel Kleiberg
  DaffA

Galaxy Light
  DaffA

Galway
  DaffA

Garron
  Altrf

Gay Cavalier
  DaffA

Geranium
  DaffA, Kayd

Gipsy Queen
  DaffA

Glamour Girl
  DaffA

Glowing Red
  DaffA

Gold Charm
  DaffA

Gold Gem
  DaffA

Gold Shah
  DaffA

Gold Tan
  DaffA

Golden Aura
  DaffA

Golden Dawn
  DaffA

Golden Ducat
  DaffA

Golden Harvest
  Winga

Golden Orbit
  DaffA

Golden Rapture
  DaffA

Golden Torch
  Altrf

Golden Treasure
  Altrf

Golly
  DaffA

gracilis
  DaffA

Gweal
  DaffA

Harmony Bells
  DaffA

Hawera
  DaffA, JoyPl, MJury,
  Winga

henriquesu
  DaffA

High Note
  DaffA

Highfield Beauty
  DaffA

Highfire
  DaffA

Hillstar
  DaffA

Holiday Inn
  DaffA

Hollands Sensation
  VanEe

Homefires
  VanEe

Honey Bells
  DaffA

Honeybird
  DaffA

Hoopoe
  DaffA

Hotspur
  DaffA

Ice Follies
  Winga

Irish Minstrel
  DaffA

Irish Rover
  DaffA

Itzim
  DaffA

Jack Snipe
  DaffA, Winga

Janelle
  DaffA

Jet Fire
  DaffA, NewlR, Winga

jonquilia
DaffA, Herew, NewlR

Joyful
DaffA

Jumblie
DaffA

juncifolius now N.assoanus
DaffA

Kerak
DaffA

Kingsize
DaffA

Kissproof
VanEe

Lagura
Kayd

Larkwhistle
DaffA

Lemon Beauty
VanEe

Lemon Heart
DaffA

Liberty Bells
DaffA

Lilac Delight
DaffA

Lintie
DaffA

Little Emma
DaffA

Little Gentleman
DaffA

Little Jewel
DaffA

Lively Lady
DaffA

Louise
DaffA

Mabel Taylor
Kayd

Malvern City
Altrf, DaffA, Winga

March Sunshine
DaffA

Mary Plumstead
DaffA

Matakana
DaffA

Mayfair
DaffA

Merry King
DaffA

Metropolis
DaffA

Midget
DaffA

Minnow
DaffA, NewlR, RosPl,
VanEe, Winga

minor   was nanus
NewlR

Mirage
DaffA

Mistral
DaffA

Modulux
DaffA

Mondragon
DaffA

Monterrico
DaffA

Moondancer
DaffA

Mount Hood
VanEe

Mrs RO Backhouse
Winga

My Word
DaffA

nanus   now minor
Kerer, NewlR

New Hope
DaffA

Nylon
CottP, NewlR

Obelisk
DaffA

odorus Rugulosus
DaffA

Outward Bound
DaffA

Palette
DaffA

Panache
DaffA

Paole de Veronese
VanEe

Papua
DaffA

papyraceus (Paper Whites)
Altrf, Kayd

Parisienne
DaffA

Patrol
DaffA

Paula Cottell
DaffA

Peach Melba
DaffA

Pearl Shell
DaffA

Pencrebar syn Queen
Anne
DaffA, NewlR

Perimeter
DaffA

Petrel
DaffA

Philomath
DaffA

Pipit
DaffA

poeticus seedlings
DaffA

poeticus var recurvus
DaffA

Polar Imp
DaffA

Precedent
DaffA

Pretty Miss
DaffA

Professor Einstein
Winga

Pryda
DaffA

Purbeck
DaffA

Quail
DaffA, NewlR

Quasar
DaffA

Quirinus
Winga

Rainbow
DaffA

Rameses
DaffA

Rapture
DaffA

Recital
DaffA

Red Baron
DaffA

Red Cameo
DaffA

Red Ember
DaffA

Red Flame
    DaffA
Rhapsody
    DaffA
Richmond Gem
    DaffA
Riesling
    DaffA
Rimdance
    DaffA
Ringleader
    DaffA
Rippling Waters
    DaffA
Rival
    DaffA
Rock Gem
    RosPl
Romance
    DaffA
Romans
    Kayd
romieuxii
    DaffA, Marsh
romieuxii mesatlanticus
    DaffA
romieuxii Taffeta
    DaffA
romieuxii var Zianicus
    DaffA
Rondetto
    DaffA
Rosy Wonder
    VanEe
Royal Decree
    DaffA
Ruby Throat
    DaffA
Rufus
    DaffA
rupicola
    NewlR
Salome
    VanEe, Winga
Salute
    DaffA
Samantha
    DaffA
Santorin
    DaffA
Satellite
    DaffA

Seadream
    DaffA
serotinus
    DaffA
Shane
    DaffA
Shaz
    DaffA
Shrew
    MJury
Signal
    DaffA
Silken Sails
    DaffA
Silken Thomas
    DaffA
Silver Chimes
    DaffA
Silver Shell
    DaffA
Skylon
    DaffA
Sovereign
    DaffA
Split
    DaffA
Spring Fling
    DaffA
Springston Gem
    DaffA
St Issey
    Altrf
Stepforward
    DaffA
Stint
    DaffA
Stylish
    DaffA
Sundial
    DaffA, NewlR
Suzy
    DaffA
Sweet Luck
    DaffA
Sweet Pepper
    DaffA
Swell Time
    DaffA
Tahiti
    DaffA, VanEe
tananicus
    DaffA

Tangent
    DaffA
Tara Rose
    DaffA
tazetta italicus
    NewlR
tazetta lacticolor
    AynDa
Temple Bells
    DaffA
tenuifolius
    DaffA
tenuior
    DaffA
Tete a Tete
    Altrf, DaffA, VanEe,
    Winga
Thalia
    Winga
Tiritomba
    DaffA
Tonga
    DaffA
Top Hit
    DaffA
Travertine
    DaffA
triandrus capex
    DaffA
triandrus var albus now
triandrus var triandrus
    DaffA
Tripartite
    DaffA
Tropic Isle
    DaffA
Twinkle
    MJury
Unsurpassable
    Altrf, SoBul, Winga
Valdrome
    DaffA, VanEe
Vireo
    DaffA
Warne
    DaffA
Waxwing
    DaffA
Wee Bee
    NewlR
Wee Bee hybrid sdlgs
    NewlR

Welcome
DaffA
Whirlaway
DaffA
White Lion
DaffA
White Marvel
DaffA
Whitehouse
Altrf
Wybalena
DaffA
Xit
DaffA, NewlR
Yellow Cheerfulness
DaffA
Yimkin
Kerer

Nasturtium
officinale (Water Cress)
King #

Nectaroscordum
siculum was Allium s.
DaffA
siculum ssp bulgaricum
Kerer

Neillia
**thibetica was
longiracemosa**
Caves

Nemesia
varieties
Roswd
Bridal Pink
KeriP
Country Touch
Warwk
foetans now caerulea
BayBl, Kayd, Pgeon
foetans alba
Peak, Pgeon, Trans
foetans Arctic Blue
BayBl, KeriP, Warwk
foetans Blush
BayBl
foetans pink
Trans, Warwk
foetans Purpurea
KeriP
fruticans now caerulea
Ref

fruticulosa
Pgeon
**strumosa nana compacta
KLM**
King #
strumosa National Ensign
King #
strumosa Snow Princess
King #

Nemophila
atamaria Snowstorm
King #, Vall #
**maculata (Five Spot
Nemophila)**
King #
menziesii
King #
menziesii Penny Black
King #, Vall #

Neodypsis
decaryi (Triangle Palm)
PalmF, Reic #

Neolitsea
sericea was glauca
Caves

Neomarica
caerulea
JoyPi, MaraN, Parva

Neomyrtus
pedunculata (Rohutu)
Orati

Nepenthes
sp climbing (Pitcher Plant
AynDa

Nepeta
varieties
Roswd
camphorata
Dream, MaraN, Marsh,
MillH, Telfa
cataria (Catnip)
King #, Marsh, Mills,
Orang, Sweet, Trans
**cataria Citriodora (Lemon
Catnip)**
King #, MaraN, MillH,
Sweet

x faassenii (Catmint)
BayBl, CoFlo, CottP,
KeriP, King #, MaraN,
Marsh, Morgn, Orang,
Pgeon, Reic #, SelGr,
Telfa, Trans, TRidg,
Trolh
x faassenii alba
Oasis, Orang
glutinosa
MaraN
govaniana
Marsh, Peak
grandiflora
MaraN, Marsh, MillH
grandiflora Blue Beauty
BayBl, Marsh, Nikau,
Sweet
grandiflora Dawn to Dusk
BayBl
latifolia
Marsh
macrantha now sibirica
CottP
mussinii now racemosa
Mills, Pgeon
nepetella
Marsh, MillH
nervosa
Dream, Marsh, Parva,
Pgeon, SelGr
nervosa Blue Accents
CottP, Vall #
nervosa Forncett Select
BayBl
nuda
Marsh
parnassica
Marsh
Pukehou
KeriP, Peak, Warwk
racemosa was mussinii
Ashto, Marsh, Sweet
schugnanica
Marsh
sibirica was macrantha
BayBl, Marsh, Peak
sibirica Blue Beauty
CottP
**sibirica Souvenir d'Andre
Chaudron was Blue
Beauty**
Marsh, Trans

Six Hills Giant (Giant Catmint)
> BayBl, CoFlo, CottP, Egmon, KeriP, MaraN, Marsh, MillH, Mills, Nikau, Orang, Ormon, Parva, Peak, Pgeon, Pkrau, Seasd, SelGr, Sweet, Telfa, Trans

Snowflake
> BayBl, CottP, KeriP, Marsh, Nikau, Parva, Peak, Pgeon, Seasd, Telfa

sp C&Mc 835 blue purple 60 cm
> Marsh

sp deep lav/blue fl 40cm
> Marsh

subsessilis
> BayBl, Marsh, Parva

Superba
> Egmon, Nikau, Parva, Peak, Telfa, Warwk

tuberosa
> Marsh, Parva, Pgeon

Nephrolepsis

bornstedtiensis
> Reic #

coarse ladder fern tropical
> Manna

cordata comp. (cordifolia)
> Reic #

cordifolia plumosa
> Reic #

imbricata
> Reic #

maasii Boston   tropical
> Manna

sp (Native Ladder Fern)
> Orati

sp fine leaf indoor
> Manna

sp medium coarse leaf indoor
> Manna

Nerine

varieties
> SoBul

alta
> MJury

Aristocrat
> PukoG

Blushing Angel
> PukoG

Blushing Bride
> DaffA

bowdenii Alba
> CottP

bowdenii Fenwicks Variety
> NewlR

bowdenii pink
> Kayd

Bowdens Giant
> CottP

Cardinal
> PukoG

Carol Side
> PukoG

Cherry Ripe
> DaffA, PukoG

Clent Charm
> DaffA

Dame Alice Godman
> PukoG

Early Snow
> DaffA, PukoG

filifolia
> DaffA, NewlR

Fire Blaze
> PukoG

flexuosa Alba
> BayBl, Kayd, Ormon, Parva

fothergillii
> DaffA

fothergillii Major
> BayBl, Kayd

Frilly Lass
> DaffA

Grandeur
> PukoG

humilis
> JoyPl

Hybrid Pink
> Telfa

Inchmery Kate
> MJury

Lipstick
> DaffA

Lydia Harman
> PukoG

Magenta prince
> DaffA

Mansellii
> DaffA, MJury

masoniorum
> DaffA

Medallion
> PukoG

Meteor
> PukoG

Mrs Cooper
> PukoG

New Dawn
> BayBl

new hybrids mxd only
> JoyPl

Nicholas
> MJury

Peach Blush
> PukoG

Pearly Shells
> PukoG

Pink Brocade
> DaffA

Pink Distinction
> DaffA

Pink Fairy
> DaffA

Pink Parade
> PukoG

pudica
> JoyPl

Radiant Queen
> DaffA, PukoG

Rose Princess
> DaffA, PukoG

Royalty
> PukoG

Sacred Heart
> MJury

Salmon Queen
> DaffA

Salmon Supreme
> PukoG

sarniensis
> Backw

Smokey Queen
> MJury

Snow Maiden
> PukoG

sp white fl,wavy edge
> TRidg

Supreme
> DaffA

Thor
> MJury

undulata
> JoyPl

Virgo

DaffA

Nertera

depressa (Bead Plant)

Oasis, Orati

dichondrifolia

Orati

Nestegis

cunninghamii (Black Maire

Chedd, Mtato, Orati, Terra

lanceolata (White Maire)

Gordn, Orati

montana (Narrow-lvd Maire)

Mtato, Orati

Nicandra

physalodes (Shoo Fly Plant)

Della, Koan #, MTig #, Trolh

physalodes alba

TRidg

Nicotiana

alata alba

Orang, Trans

alata Lime Green

King #, Peak, TRidg

alata Pink

Peak, TRidg

alata Red

Peak, TRidg

alata Salmon pink

TRidg

alata White

King #, Peak, TRidg

langsdorffii (Huichol Tobacco)

Dream, King #, Peak, Telfa, Trans

Sensation mixed

King #

sylvestris

King #, MaraN, Trans, Vall #, Warwk

tabacum (Tobacco)

King #, Sweet, Vall #

Tinkerbells

King #

variegata

TRidg

Nierembergia

hippomanica now caerulea

Telfa

hippomanica Blue Cup (Blue Cup Flower)

Mtato

Mont Blanc

Reic #

repens was rivularis

MaraN, Oasis, Parva, Pgeon, Warwk

repens Violet Queen

Pgeon

rivularis now N.repens

BayBl, CottP, Della, KeriP, Parva, Peak, Telfa

violaceae

Denes

Nigella

10 varieties

King #

gardiella Summer Stars

King #

hispanica Curiosity

Della, King #

orientalis

TRidg

sativa

King #

Nolana

humifusa Little Bells

King #

paradoxa Blue Bird

King #

paradoxa Snowbird

King #

Nolina

recurvata now Beaucarnea r.

Ref

stricta glauca

JoyPl

Nomocharis

hybrids

Marsh

Nornambya

normanbyi

Reic #

Nothofagus

fusca (Tawhaimaunui, Red Beech)

BlueM, Chedd, Diack, EasyB, Hewsn, Matai, Morgn, Mtato, Orati, Pionr, Pukho, Terra, Wahpa

menziesii (Taehai, Silver beech)

BlueM, Burbk, Diack, Hewsn, Matai, Morgn, Mtato, Orati, Pionr, Terra

obliqua (Andean/Robel Beech)

Apple, Caves, Chedd, Diack, Dove, Ford, TopTr, Wensl

solandri var cliffortioides (Mountain Beech)

BlueM, Diack, Matai, Orati, Pionr, Terra

solandri var solandri (Tawhairauriki, Black Beech)

BlueM, Burbk, Denes, EasyB, Hewsn, Matai, Morgn, Mtato, Orati, Pukho

Notholirion

thompsonii

DaffA, JoyPl, TRidg

Nuytsia

floribunda (WA Christmas Tree)

NZtr #

Nymphaea (hardy)

Amabilis

WilAq, WriWa

Arc-En-Ciel

WilAq

Arethusa

WaiMa

Attraction

Waihi, WaiMa, WilAq, WriWa

Berit Strawn

WriWa

Candida

WilAq

Carnea

WaiMa, WriWa

Chromatella (Golden Cup)

Waihi, WaiMa, WriWa

Clarissa

WaiMa

Colonel AJ Welch
Waihi

Commanche
WaiMa, WilAq, WriWa

Commanche Orange
WriWa

Conqueror
Waihi, WaiMa, WilAq

Darwin (Hollandia)
WilAq

Escarboucle
WaiMa, WilAq, WriWa

Fabiola / Mrs Richmond
WriWa

Firecrest
Waihi, WaiMa, WilAq, WriWa

Formosa
WriWa

Galatea
WriWa

Gladstone
WilAq

Gloire deTemple Surlot
Waihi, WriWa

Gloriosa
Waihi, WriWa

Gonnere
Waihi, WaiMa, WilAq, WriWa

Hal Miller
WaiMa

Hermine
Waihi, WaiMa, WilAq, WriWa

Hollandia
WriWa

James Brydon
Waihi, WaiMa, WilAq, WriWa

James Hudson
WaiMa

Joey Tomocik
WriWa

Laydekeri Fulgens
WriWa

Louise
WriWa

Lucida
WaiMa, WriWa

Lustrous
WaiMa, WriWa

Marliac Chromatella
WilAq

Marliac Flammea
WilAq

Marliac Rosea
WilAq

Marliacea Carnea
Waihi, WilAq

Martha
WriWa

Mary
WriWa

Masaniello
WilAq, WriWa

Mayla
WriWa

Meteor
WaiMa

Mexicana
WaiMa

Mme Wilfron Gonnere
WaiMa

Moorei
WilAq, WriWa

Mrs Richmond
WriWa

Newton
WaiMa, WriWa

Norma Gedye
Waihi

Odorata Luciana
WriWa

Odorata W B Shaw
Waihi, WriWa

Paul Harriot
WaiMa

Pearl Of The Pool
WriWa

Peter Slocum
WilAq

Picciola
WaiMa, WriWa

Pink Peony
WriWa

Pink Sensation
Waihi, WaiMa

Princess Elizabeth
Waihi, WaiMa

Red Spider
WriWa

Rembrandt
WriWa

Rene Gerrard
WilAq

Richardsonii
Waihi

Rose Arey
Waihi, WaiMa, WilAq, WriWa

Roseanna Supreme
WriWa

Rosy Morn
WilAq

Sioux
Waihi, WaiMa, WriWa

Somptuosa
WriWa

Sulphura grandiflora yellow
WilAq

Sulphurea
WriWa

Sultan
WaiMa

Sunrise
WaiMa, WriWa

Superba
Waihi, WaiMa

Venusta
WriWa

Vesuve
Waihi, WriWa

Wilfron Gonnere
Waihi, WriWa

William Falconer
WaiMa, WilAq

Yuh Ling
WriWa

Nymphaea (mini)

Alba
WaiMa, WriWa

Andreana
WilAq

Aurora
Waihi, WriWa

Candida
WriWa

Carmine Laydekeri
WaiMa, WriWa

Clarissa
WriWa

Froebeli
Waihi

Helvola
Waihi

Indiana
Waihi, WaiMa, WilAq, WriWa

Joanne Pring
WaiMa, WriWa

Mary Patricia
Waihi, WaiMa, WilAq, WriWa

Phoebus
WaiMa

Pink Laydekeri
Waihi

Pink Opal
WriWa

Red Laydekeri
Waihi

Solfatare
WriWa

Walter Pagels
WilAq

White Laydekeri
Waihi, WaiMa, WriWa

Nymphaea (tropical)

A E Siebert
Waihi, WaiMa, WilAq

Albert Greenberg
WriWa

American Beauty
WriWa

Black prince
Waihi, WaiMa, WilAq, WriWa

Blue Beauty
WriWa

Col. Lindberg
WilAq, WriWa

Dauben
WriWa

HC Haarstick   night flwg
WriWa

Hilary
WilAq

Lilac Star
Waihi, WriWa

lotus cream
WriWa

lotus miniature pink
WriWa

lotus pink
WriWa

Mrs George H Pring
WaiMa, WriWa

Paula Louise
WriWa

Pink Star
WaiMa, WriWa

Rose Star
WaiMa, WriWa

St Louis Gold
WriWa

Stellata
Waihi, WaiMa, WilAq, WriWa

Trudy Slocum   night flwg
WriWa

WE Siebert
WriWa

White Delight
WriWa

Nyssa

aquatica (Water Tupelo)
Reic #

sinensis
Caves, Pukho, TopTr

sylvatica (Tupelo, Black Gum)
Apple, Caves, Chedd, Coatv, Denes, Diack, Dove, Mtato, Peele, Pionr, PuhaN, Pukho, Reic #, TopTr

sylvatica Autumn Cascades
Caves, Denes

sylvatica Pendula
TopTr

sylvatica Sheffield Park
Caves, Mtato, TopTr

Ochna

serrulata (Mickey Mouse Plant, Birds Eye Bush)
Reic #

Ocimum

basilicum (Sweet Basil)
Della, Kayd, King #, Orang, Sweet, Trans

basilicum Anise
King #

basilicum Bush Basil
King #, Orang, Sweet

basilicum Cinnamon Basil
Della, King #, Trans

basilicum cv citriodorum (Lemon Basil)
Kayd, King #, Sweet, Trans

basilicum Dark Opal
Della, King #, Orang, Sweet

basilicum Fino Verde
King #, Trans

basilicum Genovese
King #, Koan #, Sweet

basilicum Genovese Giant
King #

basilicum Greek Mini
King #

basilicum Green Ruffles
King #

basilicum Large Sweet
MTig #

basilicum Lettuce Leaf
King #

basilicum Liquorice
Della

basilicum Napolitano
King #

basilicum Purple Ruffles
Della, King #, Orang, Trans

basilicum Red Rubin
King #

basilicum Spicy Basil green lf flecked purple
Orang

basilicum Spicy Globe
King #

basilicum Thai
King #, Sweet

sanctum (Sacred/Temple Basil, Tulsi)
Della, King #, Orang, Sweet, Trans

Odontocidium

nishiyama Akire Onishi
AnnM

Odontoglossum

Golden Trident 'Waikanae Gold'
NormP

Odontonema

strictum
Denes

Odontospermum

maritimum Gold Coin (Canary Is Daisy)
Seasd

Oenanthe

javanica Flamingo
  BayBl, MillH, Taunt

Oenothera

varieties
  Roswd

acaulis
  Pgeon

acaulis Aurea
  MaraN

biennis
  Orang, Sweet, Trans

biennis pink
  CottP, Sweet

biennis white
  Sweet

caespitosa
  Della

depressus
  Ashto

fruticosa
  Ashto, Della

fruticosa Erica Robin
  BayBl

kunthiana
  Telfa

lamarckiana now glaziouana (Evening Primrose)
  Della, King #

lemon
  KeriP

Lemon Sunset
  AynDa, Warwk

longifolia
  MillH

mexicana now laciniata
  Vall #

mexicana Rosea now laciniata R
  Telfa

Mississippi Primrose
  Vall #

missouriensis now macrocarpa
  Ashto, AynDa, BlueM, Della, King #, MaraN, Pgeon, Reic #, Warwk

odorata
  Telfa

odorata Apricot
  Orang

odorata Sulphurea now O.stricta S
  Dream

pallida (Jasmine Primrose)
  AynDa, BayBl, Dream, King #

perennis
  NewlR

rosea Ballerina
  Wells

speciosa (Mexican Evening Primrose,Pink Rose of Mexico, Pink Petticoat)
  BayBl, Della, King #, MaraN, MillH, Mills, Orang, Pgeon, Trans, Trolh, Warwk

speciosa childsii now O.s. Rosea
  Trans

speciosa Pink Petticoats
  MillH, Ormon, Parva, Seasd

speciosa White Wonder
  Parva

speciosa Woodside White
  BayBl, Mills, Peak, Warwk

tetragona now fruticosa glauca
  BayBl, Della

tetragona Buttercup
  Parva

texensis
  MaraN

texensis Early Rise
  Dream

Yellow
  Ashto, Trolh, Vall #

Olea

africana
  Ether

europaea varieties
  Frans, TreeC

europaea Ascolano
  Chedd, Frans, MTig, Pukho

europaea Barnea
  Chedd, Frans, LanSc, SpecT, TopTr

europaea Carolea
  MarlO

europaea Chemlali
  MarlO

europaea El Greco
  Chedd, Denes

europaea Frantoio
  MarlO

europaea Hillsbrook
  Chedd

europaea Hojiblanca
  MarlO

europaea J2
  Frans

europaea J5
  Burbk, Chedd, Frans, Pukho

europaea Kadesh
  MarlO

europaea Kalamata
  MarlO

europaea Koroneiki
  Frans, MarlO

europaea Leccino
  MarlO

europaea Manzanillo
  Chedd, Frans, MTig

europaea Mission
  Chedd, Frans, MarlO

europaea Moraiolo
  MarlO

europaea Nabali Mouhasan
  Chedd, MarlO

europaea Picholine
  MarlO

europaea Picual
  MarlO

europaea Rakino
  Wells

europaea Sevillano
  Frans, MarlO

europaea Sourani
  MarlO

europaea Souri
  Chedd, Frans, MarlO

europaea Uovo di Piccione
  MarlO

europaea Verdale
  Chedd, Denes, Frans, LanSc, Wells

Olearia

varieties
  Coatv

albida (Tanguru)
  Gordn, Mtato, Orati, Ormon, Pionr, Terra

albida angulata

Mtato, Orati, Wahpa

allomi

Orati

angustifolia

Pkrau

arborescens (Forest Tree Daisy)

Matai, Orati, Terra, Wahpa

avicenniifolia (Tree Daisy, Akeake)

Diack, Ford, Matai, Morgn, NZtr #, Orati, Pkrau

Blue Gem

Mtato, ZinoN

chathamica (Tree Daisy)

Pionr

cheesmanii

Diack, Gordn, Matai, Mtato, Orati, Terra, Wahpa, Woodl

coriacea

Orati

furfuracea (Akepiro)

Matwh, Orati, Terra

gunniana now phlogopappa

SelGr

x haastii

Ford, Matai

x haastii x moschata

Matai

ilicifolia (Mountain/NZ Holly)

Matai, Orati, Wahpa

lacunosa

Orati

lineata (Twiggy Tree Daisy)

Morgn, Orati, SouWo

lineata Dartonii (Twiggy Tree Daisy)

BlueM, Diack, Matai, Ormon, Pkrau, Wahpa, Wensl

Lochiel

Pkrau

macrodonta (Mountain Holly)

Diack, Ford, Matai, Orati, Terra

macrodonta Minor

BlueM, Matai, Orati, Pkrau

nummulariifolia (Coin-lvd Olearia)

BlueM, Gordn, Matai, Mtato, Orati, Wahpa

paniculata (Akiraho, Golden Akeake)

BlueM, Chedd, Ford, Gordn, Matai, Morgn, Mtato, NZtr #, Orati, Ormon, Pionr, SelGr, Terra, Wahpa, Wensl

paniculata Forestii

Diack

phlogopappa Blue Gem

Denes, Diack, Nikau

phlogopappa Pink Gem

Diack, McKe, Nikau

phlogopappa White Gem (Dusty Daisy Bush)

Diack, Kayd, McKe, Nikau

solandri

Matai, Matwh, Orati, Pkrau, Terra

traversii (Chatham Is AkeAke, Silver AkeAke)

Chedd, Diack, Ford, Gordn, Hackf, Matai, Matwh, Morgn, Mtato, Orati, Ormon, Pionr, Pkrau, SelGr, SouWo, Terra, Wahpa, Wensl

traversii Tweedle Dee (v)

Pionr

traversii Variegata

Gordn, Matai

virgata

Ford, Orati

White Gem

Mtato, ZinoN

Olysnium

filifolium was Sysyrinchium f.

Pgeon

Omphaloides

cappadocia

BayBl, Egmon, Hackf, Marsh, NewlR, Parva, Pgeon, Pkrau, Taunt, Trans, TRidg

cappadocia Opal

Parva, Peak

linifolia (Navelwort, Greek Forget-me-not)

King #, Pgeon, Trans, TRidg, Warwk

verna

Pgeon

verna Alba

Taunt

Oncidium

anthroclus Everglades

AnnM

incurvum

AnnM

sphacelatum

AnnM

Onixotis

triquetra was Dipidax t.

JoyPl

Onobrychis

viciifolia (Sainfoin)

Sweet

Ononis

rotundifolia (Round-lvd Westharrow)

MillH

Onopordum

arabicum now nervosum (Onoporden, Cotton Thistles)

MillH

Ophiopogon

graminifolius now Liriope muscari

Caves

green

KeriP

japonicus (Mondo Plant, Snakes Beard)

BayBl, Diack, Hains, Parva, SelGr, Telfa, WaiMa

japonicus Compactus Nanus

NewlR

japonicus Minor

Parva

planiscapus (Green Mondo Grass)

Caves

planiscapus Nigrescens (Black Dragon, Black Mondo Grass)

BayBl, Caves, Denes, Diack, Frans, Hackf, Hains, Kayd, KeriP, Mtato, NewlR, Oasis, Parva, Pgeon, SelGr, TRidg, Vall #, WaiMa

Orchis

violet fl

Vall #

Origanum

Barbara Tingey

Parva, Peak

Buckland

Parva

dictamnus (Dittany of Crete)

Mills, Oasis, Pgeon, Trans, Trolh

Kent Beauty

Parva

laevigatum (Woolly Marjoram)

BayBl, Orang, Sweet, Telfa, Trans

laevigatum Album

Dream

laevigatum Herrenhausen

BayBl, CoFlo, Della, Hackf, Nikau, Oasis, Parva, Telfa, Trans

laevigatum Hopleys

Hackf, Marsh, Mills, Parva

majorana was hortensis (Sweet/Knotted Marjoram)

Della, King #, Mills, MTig #, Orang, Sweet, Telfa

onites (Pot Marjoram)

Mills, Sweet

onites Righanni (Righanni Marjoram)

Orang

onites Variegatum

Orang, Sweet

onites x Hopleys

Mills

Rosenkuppel

BayBl, Parva, Peak, Wells

rotundifolium

BayBl, Parva, Pgeon, Trans, Trolh

Santa Cruz

Parva

True Greek (Rigani)

CottP, Della, King #, Marsh, Mills, Sweet

vulgare (Oregano, Marjoram)

CottP, Della, King #, MillH, Mills, Orang, Sweet, Trans, Trolh

vulgare Aureum (Golden Marjoram)

CottP, Della, Looij, Marsh, Mills, Nikau, Orang, Pgeon, Sweet

vulgare Iden

Orang

Orlaya

grandiflora

Trans

Ornithogalum

arabicum (Black-eyed Susan)

JoyPl, Kayd, Kerer

arcuatum

Kerer

dubium

DaffA, JoyPl, Parva

montanum

DaffA, Kerer, NewlR

multifolium

DaffA

nova

JoyPl

nutans

Kerer, NewlR, TRidg, VanEe

saundersiae

DaffA

sibthorpii now sigmoideum

NewlR

sigmoideum was sibthorpii

NewlR

thyrsoides (Chincherinchee

Kayd, Telfa

umbellatum (Star of Bethlehem, Sea/Pregnant Onion)

Altrf, Ashto, CottP, Kayd, Kerer, Orang, Telfa

umbellatum double

DaffA

Orphium

frutescens

AynDa

Orthrosanthus

laxus

Peak

multiflorus

BayBl, Frans, Irida, NewlR, Otepo, Parva, WaiMa

Oryzopsis

lessoniana syn Anemanthele (Bamboo/Gossamer/Wind Grass)

Mtato, NZtr #, Seasd, Telfa, Terra

rigida

BlueM, Diack, Ford, Kayd

Osmanthus

x burkwoodii was Osmarea b.

BlueM

delavayi

Denes

x fortunei

Woodl

fragrans

Caves, Denes

fragrans Aurantiaca

Caves

heterophyllus Purpureus

BlueM, Denes

heterophyllus Variegatus (False Holly)

Butlr, Denes, Hackf, Woodl

ilicifolius now heterophyllus (Holly Olive)

Denes

yunnanensis

Woodl

Osmarea

burkwoodii now Osmanthus x b.

BlueM

Osmunda

regalis

Gordn

Osteomeles

schweriniae microphyllus
Woodl

Osteospermum
was Dimorphoteca
Ref

barbarae compacta now jucundum c.
Pgeon

Buttermilk
CottP, Hackf

deep purple
CottP

ecklonis
Seasd, Trans

ecklonis Starshine
Seasd

ecklonis Variegata
Seasd

pink
Della

Pinkie
Pgeon

Silver Sparkler (v)
AynDa

sinuata (African Daisy, Cape Marigold)
King #

Starry Eyes Blue
CottP

Starry Eyes Pink
CottP, MillH

Tawny
CottP

variegated
CottP

Whirligig
Della

white fl
CottP

Ostrya
carpinifolia (Hop Hornbeam)
Apple, Caves

Otanthus
maritimus
Ormon

Othonnopsis
cheirifolia now Othonna c.
Seasd

Ottelia

ovalifolia
WilAq

Ourisia
macrocarpa
Orati, Wahpa

macrophylla
Telfa

Oxalis
adenophylla
DaffA, NewlR

Alba
Telfa

bowiei
KeriP, MJury, Ormon, Parva

brasiliensis
CottP, DaffA

compressa
Kerer

compressa Flore Plena
Parva

deppei now tetraphylla
CottP, DaffA

deppei Iron Cross now tetraphylla I.C.
MJury

depressa
CottP, Otepo

ecklonii
DaffA

ecklonii var sonderi
JoyPl

Ecuador
JoyPl

enneaphylla
DaffA, Pgeon

enseyii
Telfa

fabaefolia
AynDa, BayBl, DaffA, JoyPl, KeriP, Parva

flava
Parva

flava pink fl
JoyPl

flava alba
DaffA, JoyPl

glabra
JoyPl

grandiflora
MJury

hirta
CottP, DaffA, JoyPl, Kerer, KeriP, MJury, Otepo, Parva, Pgeon, TRidg

kamiesbergensis
Parva

karrioca
DaffA

lactea Flore Pleno
CottP

leuteola
JoyPl, MJury

leuteola var mavulata
JoyPl

lobata
CottP, DaffA, Kerer, KeriP, Otepo, Parva

magellanica Flore Pleno
Parva

masonorum
JoyPl, MJury

massoniana
CottP, DaffA, JoyPl, Kerer, Parva

namaquana (Rabbits Ears Oxalis)
CottP, DaffA, Parva

obtusa
DaffA, Parva

pentaphylla
JoyPl, NewlR, Ormon

pes-caprae
JoyPl

polyphylla
Parva

polyphylla var pentaphylla
JoyPl

purpurea (pink fl)
DaffA, JoyPl, MJury, Telfa

purpurea Alba
BayBl, DaffA, JoyPl, KeriP, MJury

purpurea Ken Aslet
Parva

purpurea Nigrescens
BayBl, DaffA, KeriP, NewlR, Ormon, Parva, Pgeon

purpurea rosea
CottP, Kerer, Parva

purpurea rubra
JoyPl, Otepo

purpurea var purpurea
Trolh

sp bright pink fl, dp purple lvs
AynDa

species Sth Amer
JoyPl

teraphylla Iron Cross was deppei IC.
JoyPl, MJury

versicolor (Candy-striped Oxalis)
BayBl, CottP, DaffA, Kerer, MJury, NewlR, Parva, Telfa

Oxydendron

arboreum (Sorrel Tree)
Caves, MJury, Reic #

Oxypetalum

caeruleum now Tweedia c.
KeriP, Trans

Oxyria

digyna
MaraN, Vall #

Pachyrhizus

tuberosus (Jicama, Mexican Water Chestnut)
King #

Pachysandra

terminalis (Japanese Spurge)
BlueM, Looij, Parva, Peak, Pgeon, Pkrau, Telfa

terminalis Variegata
Parva

Pachystachys

coccinea
LakeN

Pachystegia

insignis (Marlborough/Rock Daisy)
Diack, Morgn, Mtato, NZtr #, Orati, Ormon, Seasd, Terra, Wahpa

Paeonia(herbaceous)

mixed
Kayd

Albert Crousse
Simm

albiflora now lactiflora
MPaeo

Allan 1
MPaeo

Allan 6
MPaeo

America
Simm

Angel Cheeks
MPaeo, PeoGa, Simm

Ann Cousins
MPaeo

Armistice
Craig, Simm

Asa Grey
Craig, MPaeo

Auguste Dessert
Craig, MPaeo, Simm

Autens 1816
Simm

Avalanche
MPaeo

B4
Simm

B55
Simm

B59
Simm

B60
Simm

Baroness Schroeder
MPaeo, Simm

Bev
Simm

Blush Queen
Simm

Bowl of Cream
MPaeo

Bright Knight
Simm

Buckeye Belle
MPaeo, PeoGa, Simm

Bunker Hill
Simm

Burma Ruby
PeoGa

Carol
Simm

Carrara
Simm

Charlie's White
MPaeo, Simm

Cheddar Cheese
PeoGa, Simm

Cheddar Supreme
Simm

Cheddar Surprise
PeoGa

Chiffon Parfait
Craig, MPaeo, PeoGa, Simm

Chippewa
MPaeo

Cincinnati
PeoGa, Simm

Claire de Lune
PeoGa

Constance Spry
PeoGa

Cora Stubbs
Simm

Coral 'n Gold
MPaeo, PeoGa, Simm

Coral Charm
Craig, MPaeo, PeoGa, Simm

Coral Fay
MPaeo, PeoGa, Simm

Coral Sunset
MPaeo, PeoGa, Simm

Coral Supreme
Craig, MPaeo, Simm

Cornelia Shaylor
Simm

Cytheria
PeoGa

David Harum
Simm

Do Tell
Craig, MPaeo, PeoGa, Simm

Dolorodell
Simm

Doreen
Simm

Duchess de Nemours
Simm

Dunstan Dream
PeoGa

Dutch Dwarf
PeoGa

Early Bird
MPaeo, PeoGa

Early Scout
MPaeo, PeoGa, Simm

Early Windflower
MPaeo, Simm

Edulis Superba
MPaeo, Simm, TRidg

Edulis Supreme
Simm

Ellen Cowley
Craig, MPaeo, PeoGa

Elsa Sass
MPaeo, PeoGa, Simm

emodi
Herew, MPaeo

Evelyn Tibbets
PeoGa

Eventide
MPaeo

Exquisite
Simm

Fairy Princess
MPaeo, PeoGa, Simm

Felix Crousse
Simm

Festiva Maxima
Simm

Flame
MPaeo, PeoGa, Simm

Florence Ellis
Craig, Simm

Garden Peace
Simm

Gardenia
MPaeo

Gay Paree
PeoGa, Simm

George W Peyton
MPaeo, Simm

Gilded Splendour
MPaeo

Gladys McArthur
Simm

Globe of Light
Simm

Gold Standard
PeoGa

Golden Glow
MPaeo

Hayes Glory
PeoGa

Hazel Lyons
MPaeo, Simm

Helen Sears
MPaeo

Hermoine
Craig, MPaeo, PeoGa

Hi-Mabel
Simm

Honey Gold
PeoGa, Simm

Illini Warrior
MPaeo, Simm

Isani Gudui
MPaeo

Itopa Shakuyaki
Simm

Ivory Jewel
MPaeo

Japan Shu Ikau
Simm

Jayhawker
Simm

Jean E Bockstoce
Simm

Johnny
PeoGa

Joseph Christie
PeoGa

K Bright Pink Double
Craig

Kamona Kerogana
PeoGa

Kansas
PeoGa, Simm

Karl Rosenfield
Craig, MPaeo, PeoGa, Simm

Kathryn Fonteyn
MPaeo

Kelways Glorious
MPaeo

Kelways Majestic
PeoGa

King of England
MPaeo

Krinkled White
Craig, PeoGa, Simm

La Lorraine
PeoGa, Simm

Lady Alexandra Duff
Craig, MPaeo, Simm

Lady Kate
Craig, Simm

Largo
Simm

Lavender
PeoGa

Lavender Angel
PeoGa

Le Cyne
Simm

Liebchen
PeoGa, Simm

Lois Arleen
Simm

Lord Kitchener
MPaeo

Lottie Dawson Rea
Craig, MPaeo, Simm

Ludovica
PeoGa

Lullabye
PeoGa

Madame Butterfly
Craig

Madylone
PeoGa

Maestro
PeoGa

Marie Fischer
PeoGa

Marietta Sisson
Simm

May Apple
Simm

Minnie Shaylor
Craig, MPaeo, PeoGa, Simm

Minuet
MPaeo, Simm

Miss America
Craig, MPaeo, PeoGa, Simm

Miss Mary
Simm

Mister Ed
Simm

mlokosewitschii
Herew, MPaeo, PeoGa

Mme Emile Debatene
Craig, Simm

Monsieur Jules Elie
MPaeo, Simm

Montezuma
Simm

Moon of Nippon
Simm

Moonstone
Simm

Mothers Choice
MPaeo, PeoGa

Mothers Day
Simm

Mountain Magic
PeoGa

Mrs Franklin D Roosevelt
MPaeo, PeoGa, Simm

My Pal Rudy
MPaeo, Simm

Myrtle Gentry
Simm

Nancy Nicholls
Simm

Nancy Nora
Simm

Nice Gal
PeoGa

Nick Shaylor
Craig, MPaeo, Simm

Norma Volz
Simm

O Shell Pink Bomb
Craig

officinalis Rosea Plena
MPaeo, PeoGa

officinalis Rubra Plena
MPaeo, PeoGa

Ottawa
Simm

Paddy's Red
MPaeo

Party Dress
MPaeo, PeoGa

Paul Bunyan
Simm

Paula Fay
Craig, MPaeo, PeoGa, Simm

Peach Delight
MPaeo, Simm

Peachy
PeoGa

Petticoat Flounce
Craig

Pillow Talk
PeoGa, Simm

Pink Formal
Simm

Pink Hawaiian Coral
Craig, MPaeo, PeoGa, Simm

Pink Lemonade
PeoGa

Pink Parfait
PeoGa

Plainsman
Simm

Plainsman Red
MPaeo

Port Royale
PeoGa

Postilion
Simm

Prairie King
Simm

Prairie Moon
PeoGa, Simm

President Taft
Simm

Purple
PeoGa

Quality Folk
PeoGa

Raspberry Pink
Craig

Raspberry Sundae
Simm

Red Beauty
MPaeo, PeoGa

Red Charm
MPaeo, PeoGa, Simm

Red Double
Simm

Requiem
PeoGa

Richard Carvel
Simm

Rosada
Simm

Rosedale
Simm

Roselettes Child
MPaeo, Simm

Rosemarie
MPaeo

Rubra Plena
Simm

Sarah Bernhardt
Craig, Simm

Sarah M Napier
Simm

Scarlet O'Hara
MPaeo, Simm

Seashell
MPaeo, PeoGa, Simm

Single Cream
MPaeo

Single Miniature Coral
MPaeo

Single Pink
MPaeo

Single Strong Pink
Simm

Soft Salmon Saucer
PeoGa

Sophie
MPaeo, PeoGa

Spellbinder
MPaeo

Spring Beauty
Craig, Simm

Star Dust
PeoGa

Susie Q
PeoGa

The Mighty Mo
Craig, MPaeo, Simm

Tom Eckhardt
PeoGa, Simm

Top Brass
Simm

Topeka Garnet
Simm

U / Glad Tidings
MPaeo

unnamed hybrids, imported from America
Waysi

Virginia Dare
Simm

Vivid Rose
Simm

Vodka
MPaeo

Wakatipu Wonder
PeoGa

Water Lily
Simm

Westerner
Simm

White Charm
Simm

White Hayes
PeoGa

White Innocence
PeoGa

William Sheraden
Simm

Wilmington
PeoGa

Wind Chimes
PeoGa

Yellow Canary
Simm

Zu Zu
MPaeo

Paeonia(tree)

mixed dk red & yellow
Vall #

Age of Gold
Craig, PeoGa

Alhambra
Craig

Banquet
Craig, PeoGa

Black Panther
PeoGa

Black Pirate
PeoGa

Boreas
PeoGa

Coral Glow
PeoGa

Cream Cracker
PeoGa

delavayi (Red Tree Peony)
BlueM, Caves, Hewsn,
JoyPl, MPaeo, Parva,
Peele, TRidg, Woodl

delavayi ludlowii was
P.lutea ludlowii (Yellow
Tree Peony)
BlueM, Craig, Hewsn,
JoyPl, MPaeo, Parva,
TopTr, Woodl

delavayi lutea was
P.lutea (Yellow Tree Peony)
Caves, Diack, Dove,
Peele, TRidg

Gauguin
PeoGa

Golden Bowl
MPaeo

Golden Hind
PeoGa

High Noon
PeoGa

Iphigenia
PeoGa

Jitsugetsu Nishiki
PeoGa

Joseph Rock (Rock's
Variety)
Craig, PeoGa

Julie D
PeoGa

Kate Stevens
PeoGa

Leda
Craig, PeoGa

x lemoinei Alice Harding
Craig, MPaeo, PeoGa

x lemoinei Souvenir de
Maxime Cornu
Craig

Lilac Time
PeoGa

pale pink
TRidg

Redon
PeoGa

suffruticosa syn arborea
(Mountain Tree Peony)
Reic #

suffruticosa Companion of
Serenity
Craig, MPaeo

suffruticosa Godaishu
Craig

suffruticosa Hana-kisoi
(Floral Rivalry)
Craig

suffruticosa Renkaku
(Flight of Cranes)
Craig

suffruticosa Yachiyo
Tsubaki
MPaeo

Summer Time
PeoGa

Themis
Craig

Tria
PeoGa

unnamed Chinese fr Lua
Yang
MPaeo

unnamed hybrids, imported
from America
Waysi

unnamed Japanese fr USA
MPaeo

Vesuvian
PeoGa

Zephyrus
PeoGa

Paesia

scaberula (Scented Fern)
Gordn, Orati

Pancratium

maritimum
MaraN

Pandorea

jasminoides
CouCl, Frans, Reic #

jasminoides Charisma
CouCl

jasminoides Deep Pink
Denes

jasminoides Lady Di
Denes

jasminoides Rosea Superba
Burbk, CouCl, Denes

pandorana (Wongawonga
Vine)
BlueM, CouCl, Denes

pandorana Alba
CouCl

pandorana Golden
Showers
CouCl

pandorana Ruby Heart
CouCl

Papaver

alpinum
Della

anomalum album
AynDa

bracteatum now orientale
b.
Pgeon

commutatum Red
Ladybird
King #

heldreichii now spicatum
MillH

Hen & Chickens
King #

lacinatum Fluffy Ruffles
mixed
King #

miyabeanum Pacino
KeriP

nudicaule Champagne
Bubbles (Iceland Poppies)
King #
nudicaule Pacino
Wells
orientale
Otepo, Pgeon, Warwk
orientale Allegro
BayBl
orientale Beauty of
Livermere
Ashto, Dream
orientale Blenary's Special
mixed
King #
orientale Brilliant
BayBl
orientale carneum
Ashto, BayBl, Peak
orientale Glowing Rose
Peak
orientale Perry's White
Peak
orientale Pizzicato
Ashto, King #, MillH
orientale Plena
Parva
orientale Princess Victoria
Louise
BayBl, CottP, King #,
Parva, Trans, Warwk
orientale Queen Alexandra
BayBl, MaraN
orientale Red Cardinal
Kayd
orientale Royal Wedding
Marsh, Parva
orientale Whirlwind
Kayd
orientale White
Mills
paeoniflorum Paeony series
King #
pilosum Orange Crepe
Double
King #
pilosum Orange Crepe
Single
King #
radicatum (Arctic Poppy)
Dream
radicatum Pink Form
Dream

rhaeticum (Alpine Poppy)
Pgeon
rhoeas Double mixed
(Shirley Poppy)
King #
rhoeas nana Angel Wings
mixed
King #
rhoeas Single mixed
King #
rupifragum
AynDa, KeriP, MaraN
spicatum was heldreichii
Marsh
ssp giganteum Maxi Pod
King #
ssp minimum Mini Pod
King #

Paphiopedalum
acmodontum
AnnM
arcus
AnnM
bennisianum
AnnM
callosum
AnnM
delenatii
AnnM
fowliei
AnnM
gratrixianum
AnnM

Paradisea
liliastrum (St Brunos Lily)
Telfa
lusitanica
TRidg

Parahebe
Blue Eyes
Pgeon
catarractae
BayBl, CottP, MillH,
Mtato, Nikau, Orati,
Ormon, Pgeon, Sweet,
Trans
catarractae Alba
Otepo
catarractae Delight
Otepo
catarractae purple
Sweet

catarractae Rosea
Otepo
catarractae Snow
Parva
decora
Nikau, Orati
hookeriana
CottP, Diack, Gordn,
Nikau
hookeriana Pink Parfait
Wells
hookeriana var olsenii
BlueM, Trans
Little Pinkii
Butlr
lyallii
BlueM, Butlr, Gordn,
Mtato, Orati, Pgeon,
Sweet
lyallii Baby Blue
Ashto, BayBl, BlueM,
CottP, Matwh, Nikau,
Pkrau, Trans
lyallii pink form
Pkrau
Mt Dalgety
BlueM, Matai
olsenii
BayBl, Nikau, Orati,
Pkrau
perfoliata was Veronica p.
Trans
perfoliata Oxford Blue was
Veronica p.OB.
Hackf
pink creeping
Sweet
Snowcap
Orati
White Snowcap
Matwh

Paranomus
reflexus
MatNu

Parasyringa
sempervirens now
Ligustrum
TopTr

Pardancanda
norrisii
MaraN

Parietaria

diffusa or officinalis now judaica (Pellitory of the Wall)

Mills, Sweet

Parnassia

palustris (Grass of Parnassus, Bog Star)

WaiMa

Parochetus

communis (Shamrock Pea, Himalayan Clover)

BayBl, MaraN, Nikau, Oasis, Peak, Roswd, Telfa, Trans

Parrotia

persica (Persian Ironwood, Persian Witchazel)

Apple, Burbk, Caves, Chedd, Denes, MJury, PuhaN, Pukho, Reic #, TopTr

persica Pendula

Caves

Parsonsia

capsularis (Native Jasmine)

CouCl, Orati

heterophylla (Kaiku, Kaiwhiria, NZ Jasmine)

CouCl, Gordn, NZtr #, Orati, Parva, Terra

Parthenocissus

henryana (Silver Vein Creeper)

CouCl, Denes, Woodl

himalayana

CouCl

quinquefolia (Virginia Creeper)

CouCl, Denes

quinquefolia var engelmannii

CouCl

tricuspidata (Boston Ivy)

BlueM, TopTr

tricuspidata Beverley Brook

CouCl

tricuspidata Lowii (Japanese Ivy)

CouCl, Denes

tricuspidata Veitchii

CouCl, Denes

tricuspidata Veitchii Minima

CouCl

Passiflora

adularia

CouCl

Amethyst

CouCl

ampullacea

CouCl

antioquiensis (Banana Passionfruit)

CouCl

caerulea

CouCl

coccinea

CouCl

edulis (Passionfruit(purple)

King #, Koan, MTig #, Reic #

edulis Giant Black

Diack

ligularis

Koan

manicata Kiss 'n' Run

CouCl

mixta

CouCl

mollissima (Banana Passionfruit)

Reic #

mollissima Sth. Is form

CouCl, Diack

Norfolk

Koan

pinnatistipula

CouCl

quadrangularis

CouCl

tetrandra was Tetrapathaea (NZ Passionfruit)

CouCl, Matwh, Orati, Pionr

Vanilla (banana p.)

Koan

Pastinaca

sativa (Parsnip)

Koan #, MTig #

Patrinia

triloba

MaraN

Paulownia

elongata (Princess/ Money/ Empress Tree)

Dove, Hewsn, NZtr #, Peele, PuhaN

fargesii

Burbk, Chedd, Peele, Pionr

fortunei

Peele

tomentosa (Princess/ Umbrella/ Empress Tree, Mountain Jacaranda)

Burbk, Chedd, Coatv, Denes, Mtato, NZtr #, Pionr, Pukho, Reic #

Pedilanthus

tithymaloides Nanus

LakeN

tithymaloides Variegatus (Zig Zag Plant)

LakeN

Pelargonium

Apple Blossom Rosebud

Parva, StMar

Balkon varieties

StMar

betulinum

Reic #

Bird's Egg Geranium varieties

StMar

Cactus Type Geranium varieties

StMar

capitatum

Reic #, Trans

capitatum Attar of Roses

Mills, Orang

Carlton Lace (Spicy)

CottP, StMar

Chocolate (Chocolate)

CottP, Orang, StMar

citriodorum (Lemon)

Orang

Claramar

Orang

Coconut

Sweet

crispum (Lemon)

Orang

crispum minor (Lemon)

Orang, Sweet

cucullatum
  Reic #
Deacon Type Geranium varieties
  StMar
Dwarf & Mini Geranium varieties
  StMar
filicifolium (Fernleaved Pelargonium)
  Orang
Flat varieties
  StMar
Formosum Type Geranium varieties
  StMar
x fragrans (Nutmeg)
  Orang
Gold & Bronze Leaved Geranium varieties
  StMar
graveolens (Rose)
  Sweet
graveolens Lady Plymouth (Rose)
  Orang
Harlequin varieties
  StMar
Hybrid Ivy Geranium varieties
  StMar
Hybrid Zonal Geranium varieties
  StMar
Irene Type Geranium varieties
  StMar
Ivy Geranium varieties
  StMar
Lemon Rose
  Sweet
lime scented
  Trans
Little Gem (Rose)
  CottP
Mabel Grey
  Orang, Trans
Madam Salleron (Geranium Dandy)
  KeriP
Miniature Ivy Geranium varieties
  StMar

Miniature Regal varieties
  StMar
nervosum (Lime)
  Orang
peltatum (Ivyleaved Geranium)
  Reic #
Plain Gold Leaf Geranium varieties
  StMar
Prince Rupert (lemon)
  Trolh
Prince Rupert variegated
  Trolh
quercifolium (Oakleaf Geranium)
  Orang, Reic #
quercifolium Royal Oak
  Orang, StMar, Trans
quercifolium Skeleta Oak
  Sweet
Regal varieties
  StMar
Rober's Rose
  Orang
rose scented
  Oasis
Rosebud Type Geranium varieties
  StMar
Silver & Green Leaved Geranium varieties
  StMar
sp (Rose)
  Orang
St Clements Bell
  Sweet
Star Series
  StMar
Stellar varieties
  StMar
tomentosum (Peppermint Geranium)
  CottP, King #, Orang, Sweet, Trans
tomentosum ssp (Peppermint)
  Orang
Tricolour Leaved Geranium varieties
  StMar
triste
  MaraN

Unusual Leaved Geranium varieties
  StMar
Variegated Ivy Geranium varieties
  StMar
Zonal Geranium varieties
  StMar

Pellaea
falcata
  Gordn, Orati, Reic #
hastata syn viridis
  Reic #
rotundifolia (Button Fern)
  Orati, Reic #

Peltiphyllum
peltatum see Darmera
  BayBl, KeriP, MaraN

Peltoboykinia
tellimoides
  Oasis
watanbei
  Titok

Pennantia
baylisiana
  Orati
corymbosa (Kaikomako)
  Gordn, Matai, Orati, Terra, Wahpa
corymbosa x baylisiana
  Orati

Pennisetum
setaceum was rueppellii (Fountain Grass)
  Hains, KeriP, Mtato
setaceum Rubrum (Rose Fountain Grass)
  KeriP, MillH

Penstemon
mixed
  Vall #
varieties
  Roswd
Alice Hindley
  BayBl, CottP, Egmon, KeriP, Nikau, Oasis, Ormon, Otepo, Parva, Peak, Shadi, Sweet, Trans, Trolh, Warwk
alpinus
  Hackf, Oasis

ambiguus
MaraN

angustifolius
Dream, MaraN, Pgeon

Apple Blossom
BayBl, KeriP, Peak,
Trans, Warwk

Barbara Barker
CottP, KeriP, Peak

barbatus
Ashto, BayBl, Dream,
Nikau, Otepo, Pgeon

barbatus Cambridge mixed
King #

barbatus Coccineus
MaraN, Ormon

barbatus praecox nanus
BlueM, Della, MaraN,
MillH

Beech Park
BayBl, KeriP, Parva

Betty's Red
Parva

Blackbird
CottP, KeriP, MaraN,
Marsh, MillH, Mills,
Oasis, Peak, Warwk

Blue of Zurich
Marsh

bridgesii   now rostriflorus
Otepo

Burgundy
BayBl, KeriP

cardwellii
TRidg

Charles Rudd
BayBl, CottP, Della,
KeriP, Shadi

cobaea
MaraN, Marsh

confertus
MaraN, MillH, NewlR,
Otepo

Countess of Dalkeith
Parva, Trans

cyaneus
Pgeon

Dainty Pink
Trans

deustus
MaraN

digitalis
AynDa, BlueM, Dream,
MaraN, Nikau, Ormon,
Pgeon, Trans

digitalis Huskers Red
BayBl, MillH, Parva,
Shadi, TRidg

Drinkstone
BayBl, CottP, Della,
Hackf, Marsh, Parva,
Trans

Evelyn
KeriP, Nikau, Otepo

Firebird
BayBl, CottP, Della,
KeriP, Marsh, MillH,
Pgeon

fruticosus
MaraN

Garnet
AynDa, BayBl, CottP,
Looij, Marsh, Mills,
Oasis, Pgeon

Garnet Spires
KeriP, Nikau

Gethsemane
Marsh

Gethsemane New Wine
Marsh

glaber
BlueM

Hackfalls
Hackf

hartwegii
Hackf, Telfa

hartwegii Betty's Red
Parva

heterophyllus (True Blue)
Ormon, Pgeon

heterophyllus Zuriblau
BayBl, MaraN, MillH,
Oasis, Parva, Trans

Hewell Pink
BayBl

Hidcote Pink
CottP, Hackf, KeriP,
Marsh, MillH, Nikau,
Shadi, Trans, Warwk

hirsutus
CottP, Dream, MaraN,
MillH

hirsutus pygmaeus
AynDa, BayBl, MaraN,
Otepo, Parva, Pgeon

hirsutus pygmaeus albus
Parva

humilis
BlueM

King George V
BayBl, Hackf, KeriP,
Marsh, Parva, Peak,
Trans, Warwk

**kunthii   now
campanulatus**
CottP, Hackf, KeriP,
MaraN, MillH

laevigatus digitalis
Telfa

leonensis
Marsh

lyallii
TRidg

Mother Of Pearl
BayBl, CottP, Della,
Egmon, KeriP, Marsh,
Mills, Nikau, Trans

newberryi
MaraN

ovatus
Dream, MaraN, TRidg

Pale Pink
Mills

Peace
BayBl, KeriP, Oasis,
Shadi, Sweet, Trolh

Pennington Gem
Peak, Pgeon

pinifolius
Della, MaraN, Marsh

pinifolius Mersea Yellow
Marsh

Pink Beauty
Marsh

Pink Clouds
BayBl, CottP, Hackf,
KeriP, Oasis, Shadi,
Telfa, Trolh

Pink Endurance
Ormon, Peak, Telfa,
Warwk

Pink Perfection
Wells

Port Wine
BayBl, KeriP, Shadi

procerus
MaraN, Otepo

pruinosus
Pgeon

Purple Passion
BayBl, CottP, Egmon,
Hackf, KeriP, MaraN,
Marsh, MillH, Oasis,
Ormon, Parva, Pgeon,
Trans, Trolh

Raven

BayBl, Della, Hackf,
KeriP, Marsh, Parva,
Sweet, Trans, Trolh,
Warwk

Redcoat

Shadi

Rich Ruby

CottP, Peak

rostriflorus

Otepo

Ruby

Peak

Ruby Jewel

KeriP

Salmon Mousse

KeriP

scouleri Alba

BlueM

secundiflorus

MaraN

Sentinel

MaraN

serrulatus

MaraN

Sissinghurst

KeriP, Peak, Shadi

smallii

MaraN, Telfa

Snowstorm

BayBl, CottP, Della,
Egmon, Hackf, KeriP,
MaraN, Marsh, Nikau,
Oasis, Ormon, Parva,
Peak, Pgeon, Shadi,
Trans, Warwk, Wells

Sour Grapes

Hackf, KeriP, MaraN,
MillH, Peak, Shadi,
Trans, Warwk

Stapleford Gem

CottP, Della, Egmon,
KeriP, Marsh, Oasis,
Parva, Peak, Shadi,
Telfa, Trans

Strawberry Ice

Shadi

strictus

Dream, MaraN, Telfa,
TopTr

Susan

BayBl, CottP, Della,
Hackf, KeriP, MaraN,
Nikau, Ormon, Shadi

Swan Lake

KeriP, MillH, Parva,
Sweet

The Cardinal

Sweet

Thorn

KeriP, Peak, Telfa, Trans

Tory

Parva

**True Blue now
heterophyllus**

CottP, Peak

utahensis Alba

MaraN

utahensis Utah Bugler

Hackf

venustus

MaraN

watsonii

MaraN

wilcoxii n.v.

Marsh

Pentapterygium

serpens now Agapetes s.

AynDa

Pentas

parviflora

Denes

Pentzia

grandiflora Gold Button

King #

Peperomia

urvilleana

Orati

Perilla

frutescens Green

King #

frutescens Purple

King #, Orang, Sweet

Pernettya

see Gaultheria

Ref

Perovskia

atriplicifolia (Russian Sage)

Dream

atriplicifolia Blue Spire

BayBl, Parva, Peak,
TopTr, Trans

Persea

Hass (Avocado)

Koan

Reed (Avocado)

Koan

Persicaria

**affinis Dimity now
a.Superba was Polygonum
a.D.**

BayBl, CottP, Otepo,
Wells

**affinis Donald Lowndes
was Polygonum a.DL.**

AynDa, Oasis

**bistorta Superba was
Polygonum**

CoFlo, JoyPl, Peak

**campanulata was
Polygonum c.**

CoFlo, CottP, Della

vacciniifolia

BayBl

**virginiana Painters Palette
was Tovaria**

Vall #

virginiana Variegata

BayBl

Petasites

**fragrans (Winter
Heliotrope, Butter-Burr)**

CottP, Mills, Sweet

Petrea

**volubilis (Purple Wreath,
Sandpaper Plant)**

CouCl, Denes, LakeN

Petroselinum

**crispum was hortense
(Parsley)**

Kayd, MTig #, Orang

crispum Curlina

King #

crispum Curly Parsley

Trans

crispum Dalmatian Parsley

Koan #, Trans

crispum Exotica

Della

crispum Genovese

King #

**crispum neapolitanum
(Italian Parsley)**

King #, Mills, Orang,
Trolh

**crispum neapolitanum
Gigante Italian**

Della, King #, Sweet

crispum Plain Leaf
King #

crispum Triple Curled
King #, Mills, Sweet, Trolh

crispum Unicurl
King #

crispum var tuberosum (Hamburg Parsley)
King #

Petunia

Double Heavenly Lavender
King #

Fantasy series
King #

Hush White
Parva

integrifolia var integrifolia
Parva

Jaspers Red
Parva

Lavender Lawn
Parva

Lilac Time
Parva

Loyalty Brick Red
Parva

Loyalty Melon Pink
Parva

Magenta Queen
Parva

Mauve Micro
Parva

Rose Taffeta
Parva

Storm series
King #

Super Cascade mixed
King #

Tigerlights
Parva

Phacelia

campanularia (Californian Bluebell)
King #

sp perennial, blue fl
Vall #

tanacetifolia (Aphid Plant, Tansy Phacelia)
Della, King #

Phaedranassa

cinera
DaffA

Phaiophleps

nigricans now Sisyrinchium stratum
AynDa, KeriP, Pgeon, Trans

Phalaenopsis

Amelie de Valec
NormP

Antarctic
NormP

Chamonix
NormP

Creme de Chantilly
NormP

Franck Fernandel
NormP

Miva Barbara x Terragone
NormP

Zermatt
NormP

Phalaris

arundinacea Picta (v)
Diack

Phaseolus

bean Burlotti - Stoppa (Climbing Bean)
Koan #

bean Butterbean (Bush Bean)
Koan #

bean coccineus Scarlet (Runner Bean)
MTig #

bean Dalmatian (Climbing Bean)
Koan #

bean Fin de Bagnols (Shoe String,Dwf French)
King #

bean Horticultural Bush (Bush Bean)
Koan #

bean King George (Climbing Bean)
Koan #

bean Purple Knight
MTig #

bean Purple Pod (Climbing Bean (heirloom))
Koan #

bean Roma II
King #

bean Romano Pole (Italian Pole)
King #

bean Top Crop
MTig #

caracalla now Vigna c.
AynDa, Denes, Reic #

Phebalium

billardieri
Hewsn

nudum (Mairehau)
Orati

squameum (Satin Wood)
BlueM, Diack, Ford, Morgn, Mtato, Pionr, SelGr, SouWo

squameum Illumination (v)
Denes, Hewsn, Morgn, Mtato

Phellodendron

amurense (Amur Cork Tree)
Apple, Caves, Diack, Dove, Peele, PuhaN, Wensl, YakuN

Philadelphus

Avalanche
Denes, TopTr, YakuN

Beauclerk
BlueM, Caves, Denes, Pukho, TopTr

Belle de Nancy
Denes

Belle Etoile
Caves, Denes, TopTr

Birchlands
Denes

Boule d'Argent
Denes

coronarius (Mock Orange)
Denes, Dove, TopTr

coulteri
Denes

delavayi calvescens now purpurascens
TopTr

Enchantment
Pukho

Frosty Morn
BlueM, Denes, Parva, TopTr

incanus
Caves

Innocence (v)
Denes

x lemoinei
Caves, Denes, TopTr

Manteau d'Hermine
BayBl, BlueM, Denes, Pukho

mexicanus
Denes, Hackf

Minnesota Snowflake
TopTr

Norma
TopTr

Snowflake
Denes

Sybille
BlueM, Denes, Parva, Pukho, TopTr

tomentosus
TopTr

Variegatus
BlueM

Virginal
BlueM, Chedd, Denes, Dove, Parva, Peele, Pukho, TopTr

Philodendron

Andersons Red
LakeN, Manna

bipinnatifidum
Reic #

cannifolium
LakeN

florida
LakeN

hastatum
Manna

Imbe
LakeN

lundii
Reic #

panduriforme now bipennifolium (Horses Head Foliage)
LakeN, Manna

scandens oxycardum
LakeN

selloum
Frans, Reic #

selloum Goldie
Manna

warmingii
LakeN

Phlomis

fruticosa
Hackf, MaraN, Mills, TopTr

italica
Hackf

lanata
Hackf

purpurea
Ormon

russeliana
CoFlo, Della, Looij, MaraN, Mills, Ormon, Otepo, Parva, Peak, Pgeon, Pkrau, Telfa, TopTr, TRidg

samia
BayBl, Dream, Parva

tuberosa
Dream

Phlox

adsurgens Wagon Wheels
CottP, NewlR, Parva

Aerial
WaiMa

amoena variegata
BayBl, CottP

Benita
NewlR

brittonii Rosea
Otepo, Telfa

carolina Bill Baker
BayBl, Marsh

carolina Miss Lingard
Egmon

Charles Ricardo
BayBl, Warwk

divaricata laphamii Chattahoochee
BayBl, CottP, Peak, Pgeon

divaricata May Breeze
BayBl

divaricata Perrys variety
BayBl, CottP, Parva, Peak, Telfa

douglasii Alba
Telfa

douglasii Apollo
Ashto

douglasii Betty
Ashto, NewlR, Nikau

douglasii Boothmans Variety
BayBl

douglasii Crackerjack
Ashto, NewlR, Pgeon

douglasii Iceberg
Otepo

douglasii Nelsonii
Ashto

douglasii Red Admiral
Pgeon

douglasii Violet Queen
NewlR, Telfa

douglasii Waterloo
Otepo

drummondii Pastel Shades (Phlox of Sheep)
King #

drummondii Twinkle mixed
King #

glaberrima
BayBl, CottP, Peak

grandiflora Alba
Parva, Warwk

hybrida compacta African Sunset
King #

hybrida Double Channel
King #

Kelly's Eye
Della

Lavender Beauty Rockery type
BayBl

Lisbeth
Warwk

Lord French
Parva

maculata Alpha
BayBl, BlueM, CottP, Egmon, Telfa, Warwk

maculata Omega
Ashto, BlueM, Egmon, Parva, Trans, Warwk

Moonlight
NewlR

Nelsonii
Della

paniculata alba
Mills, Trans

paniculata Alba Grandiflora
BayBl, Parva

paniculata Caroline Van Den Berg
BayBl

paniculata Cinderella
BayBl

paniculata Eva Cullum
BayBl

paniculata Franz Schubert
BayBl, CottP

paniculata Fujiyama
BayBl

paniculata Grandiflora
Peak

paniculata Lavender
Ashto, Peak

paniculata Le Mahdi
BayBl, Oasis

paniculata Pink
Ashto, CoFlo, Mills, Nikau, Telfa

paniculata Pinkie
Peak

paniculata Purple
Telfa

paniculata salmon pink
Trans

paniculata Sir John Falstaff
BayBl, CottP, Oasis

paniculata Snow Queen
MaraN

paniculata Starfire
CottP

paniculata White
Telfa

paniculata White Admiral
Peak

paniculata Win's Pink
MaraN

Pink Buttons
Otepo

Pink Gown
Parva

Pinkie
Parva

procumbens
MaraN

procumbens Variegata
Otepo

Serenity
Warwk

Snowman
Ashto, CottP, Parva, Warwk

x Spring Delight
BayBl, Parva

Starfire
Parva

stolonifera Ariane
BayBl, Peak, Pgeon, Telfa

stolonifera Blue Ridge
BayBl, CottP, NewlR, Parva, Pgeon, Trans, Wells

stolonifera Millstream
CottP

stolonifera Pink Ridge
BayBl, CottP, NewlR, Oasis, Parva, Peak, Pgeon, Trans

stolonifera Sherwood Purple
Parva

stolonifera Violet Vere
BayBl, CottP, Peak

subulata Alba
Telfa

subulata Camla
Della, Pgeon

subulata Daniel's Cushion
NewlR, Nikau, Oasis, Telfa

subulata Emerald Cushion
Oasis

subulata Greencourt Purple
MillH

subulata Greencourt Violet
BayBl, Oasis

subulata May Snow (Maischnee)
BayBl, Nikau, Oasis, Pgeon, Telfa

subulata Oakington Blue Eyes
NewlR, Nikau, Pgeon, Telfa

subulata Purple Beauty
CottP, Della

subulata Red Wings
CottP, Telfa

subulata Samson
CottP, Pgeon, Seasd, Telfa

subulata Scarlet Flame
BayBl, NewlR, Oasis, Otepo, Pgeon

subulata Temiscanning
BayBl, NewlR, Pgeon

subulata The Bride
CottP, NewlR

subulata var bright pink
KeriP, MillH

subulata White
Ashto

Vivid
CottP, NewlR

Phoenix

canariensis (Canary Is Date Palm)
Burbk, Coatv, Kayd, Lsendt, Manna, NZtr #, PalmF, Reic #

dactylifera
Reic #

reclinata (Senegal Date Palm)
Coatv, Frans, Lsendt, PalmF, SpecT

roebelenii (Dwarf Date Palm)
Coatv, Frans, Lsendt, PalmF, Reic #, SpecT

Phormium

Apricot Queen
NZFlax, Orati, Pionr

Bronze Baby
Chedd, Mtato

Co-ordination
Matai

cookianum was colensoi (Wharariki, Mountain Flax)
Burbk, Ford, Gordn, KeriP, Matwh, Morgn, Mtato, NZtr #, Orati, Pionr, Pkrau, Terra, Wahpa

cookianum Bronze
Burbk, Orati

cookianum Little Gem
Burbk

cookianum purpureum
Pionr, Wahpa

cookianum Tricolour
Reic #

Cream Delight
NZFlax, Pkrau

Crimson Devil
NZFlax

Dark Delight
Diack, NZFlax

Duet
NZFlax

Emerald Gem
Morgn

Emerald Green
Mtato

Evening Glow
NZFlax

Firebird
NZFlax

Green Dwarf
Orati

Guardsman
Orati

Jack Spratt
Mtato

Limelight
NZFlax

Maori MAiden
Diack

Maori Sunrise
Gordn

Misty
NZFlax

Pink Panther
Gordn, Matai, Orati

Pinkie
Mtato

Pizazz
NZFlax

Platts Black
Orati

Rainbow Hybrids
BlueM

Rainbow Maiden
NZFlax, Orati

Rainbow Queen
McKe, Mtato, NZFlax, Orati

Rainbow Sunrise
Mtato, NZFlax, Pionr

Stormy Dawn
NZFlax

Sundowner
Matai

Sunset
NZFlax

Surfer
NZFlax, Wahpa

Surfer Boy
Diack

tenax (Harakeke, Green Flax)
Chedd, Dove, Ford, Gordn, Matai, Matwh, McKe, Morgn, Mtato, NZtr #, Orati, Pionr, PuhaN, Reic #, SouWo, Terra, Wahpa

tenax Bronze
Mtato, Orati

tenax Purpureum
Gordn, Matai, McKe, Morgn, Mtato, NZtr #, Reic #, Terra, Wahpa

tenax red
PuhaN

tenax rubrum
Ford

tenax Variegated
Reic #

Thumbelina
Diack, Matai, Oasis

Tom Thumb
Mtato, NZFlax, Orati

Tricolour
McKe, NZFlax, Wahpa

Yellow Wave
Diack, Gordn, McKe, Mtato, Orati, Pionr, Pkrau, Wahpa

Photinia

beauverdiana
Caves

x fraseri Red Robin (Red Robin)
BlueM, Chedd, Diack, Ford, Hewsn, Kayd, Matai, Matwh, Morgn, Mtato, Pionr, Pkrau, SelGr, TopTr, Wells, Wensl, ZinoN

x fraseri Robusta
BlueM, Diack, Dove, Ford, Hewsn, ZinoN

villosa
Pukho

Phuopsis

stylosa
CottP, MaraN, MillH, Oasis, Pgeon

Phygelius

varieties
Roswd

aequalis
BayBl, MaraN, Marsh, Peak, Trans, Vall #, Warwk

aequalis dusky pink
Nikau

aequalis Yellow Trumpet
AynDa, Butlr, Egmon, KeriP, Marsh, Nikau, Trans

capensis
Dream, MaraN, Marsh

x erectus Moonraker
MaraN, Warwk

x erectus Salmon Leap
Kayd, KeriP, Wells

Lemon
Wells

Phyla

nodiflora was Lippia n.
CottP, Seasd, Wells

Phylica

gnidioides (Pink Tuft Bush)
Denes

plumosa (Feather/Flannel Flower/Head)
MatNu, Matth, Wells

pubescens (Flannel Bush)
Butlr, Denes, MatNu, Matth

Phyllocladus

asplenifolius var alpinus (Mountain Toatoa)
BlueM, Cedar, CPete, Gordn, Orati, Pionr, Terra

aspleniifolius var alpinus Blue Haze
Cedar

aspleniifolius var alpinus Cockayne's Blue
Cedar

aspleniifolius var alpinus Flamingo
Cedar

glaucus (Toatoa)
Cedar

trichomanoides (Tanekaha, Celery Pine)
BlueM, Cedar, Gordn, MJury, Mtato, Orati, Pionr, Terra

Phyllostachys

angusta
Isaac

aurea
Isaac

bambusoides
Isaac

banbusoides subvariegata
Isaac

bissetii
Isaac

boryana
Isaac

c. inversa variegata
Isaac

castillonis
Isaac

edulis (Moso Bamboo)
Caves, Isaac, Lsendt

edulis heterocycla Kikkou
Isaac

flexuosa
Isaac

makinoi
Isaac

marliacea
Isaac

meyeri
Isaac

mitis now sulphurea var viridis
Isaac

nigra
Isaac

nigra var henonis
Isaac

sulphurea
Isaac

viridis R Young
Isaac

vivax
Isaac

vivax Aureosulcata
Isaac

Phymatosorus

diversifolius (Hounds Tongue)
Orati

Physalis

alkekengi franchetii (Chinese Lantern)
BayBl, Kayd, King #, Reic #

alkekengi franchetii Gigantea
MaraN

ixocarpa Tomatillo
King #, Koan #

peruviana syn P. edulis (Cape Gooseberry, Goldenberry)
King #, Koan #, MTig #, Reic #

Physocarpus

opulifolius Luteus (Golden Ninebark)
Denes, Pukho

Physostegia

Snow White
CottP, Della

virginiana (Obedient Plant)
AynDa, MaraN, Trans, WaiMa

virginiana Alba
AynDa, BayBl, MaraN, MillH, Mills, Orang, Pgeon, Trans, Wells

virginiana Crown Of Snow
Egmon, KeriP

virginiana Driven Snow
WaiMa

virginiana pink form
CoFlo

virginiana Summer Snow
Telfa

virginiana Vivid
BayBl, CottP, Looij, Oasis, Pgeon

Phyteuma

betonicifolium
Della

humile
NewlR

nigrens
Della

orbiculare
MaraN, Vall #

scheuchzeri
Della, MaraN, Pgeon

spicatum
Della

Phytolacca

americana (Red-ink Plant, Pokeroot)
Oasis

Picea

abies (Romanian/Norway Spruce)
Apple, BlueM, Caves, Cedar, CPete, Ford, NZtr #, WakaC

abies Aurea (Golden Norway Spruce)
BlueM, Caves, Cedar, CPete, EasyB, WakaC

abies Compacta Globosa
Cedar, CPete

abies Decumbens
BlueM

abies dwarf forms
BlueM

abies Globosa Nana
Cedar, CPete

abies Humilis
Cedar, CPete

abies Inversa
Caves, CPete

abies Little Gem
Cedar, CPete, NewlR

abies Minima
Cedar, CPete

abies Nidiformis (Birds Nest Spruce)
Cedar, CPete

abies Ohlendorfii
Cedar

abies Procumbens
Cedar

abies Pumila
Cedar

abies Pumila Nigra
Cedar

abies Pygmaea
CPete

abies Pyramidalis
Cedar, CPete

abies Reflexa (Weeping Norway Spruce)
BlueM, Cedar

alba now P.glauca
Cedar

asperata (Chinese Dragon Spruce)
Cedar

bracytyla (North Sargent Spruce)
Cedar

breweriana (Brewers Weeping/Siskiyou Spruce)
BlueM, Cedar

chihuahuana (Chihuahua Spruce)
Cedar

engelmannii (Engelman Spruce)
Cedar, CPete, WakaC

glauca syn alba (White/Canadian Spruce)
Cedar, CPete

glauca Albertiana Conica was P.g.Conica (Dwarf Albert Spruce)
BlueM, Cedar, CPete, TopTr

glauca Densata (Black Hills White Spruce)
Cedar

glauca Echiniformis
BlueM, Cedar, CPete

glauca var albertiana (Albert White Spruce)
Cedar, WakaC

glauca var canadensis
Cedar

glehnii (Sakhalin Spruce)
Cedar

jesoensis (Yezo Spruce)
Cedar

jesoensis var hondoensis (Hondo Spruce)
Cedar, CPete

koraensis (Korean Spruce)
Cedar

koyamai (Koyama Spruce)
Cedar

likiangensis (Likiang Spruce)
Cedar, CPete

likiangensis var purpurea (Purple Likiang Spruce)
Cedar, CPete

lutzii (Little Lutz Spruce)
Cedar

mariana syn nigra (Black Spruce)
Cedar, CPete, WakaC

mexicana now P. engelmanii var mexicana
Caves, Cedar

meyerii (Kansu Spruce)
Apple, Cedar

omorika (Serbian Spruce)
Apple, BlueM, Caves, Cedar, Chedd, CPete, Diack, Ford, TopTr, WakaC

orientalis (Oriental/Eastern Spruce)
Apple, Cedar, CPete, WakaC

orientalis Nana
CPete

pungens (Colorado Spruce)
BlueM, WakaC

pungens Aurea
BlueM

pungens Glauca (Blue Colorado Spruce)
Apple, BlueM, Cedar, Chedd, CPete, Diack, Ford, Hewsn, Matwh, Mtato, NZtr #, TopTr, WakaC

pungens Glauca Pendula
BlueM

pungens Glauca Prostrata
CPete

pungens Koster (Kosters Blue Spruce)
BlueM, Caves, Cedar, CPete, Denes, EasyB

rubens was rubra (American Red Spruce)
Cedar, CPete

schrenkiana (Tian Shan Spruce)
Apple

sitchensis (Sitka/Alaskan Spruce)
Apple, Chedd, Coatv, CPete, Diack, Ford, Mtato, NZtr #, WakaC

smithiana was morinda (West Himalayan Spruce)
Cedar

spinulosa
Cedar

wilsonii (Wilson's Spruce)
Apple, Cedar, CPete, WakaC

Picrasma

quassioides was ailanthoides
Woodl

Pieris

Bert Chandler
BlueM

Brixton Bonfire
Denes

Flamingo
Denes

Forest Flame
Chedd, Denes

formosa forrestii Wakehurst (Chinese Pieris)
Denes

japonica Captain Blood
Denes

japonica Christmas Cheer
Matwh, Wells

japonica Coleman
Denes

japonica Compact Crimson
Ashto

japonica Dorothy Wyckoff
BlueM, Denes

japonica Mountain Fire
BlueM, Denes, Hewsn

japonica Pink Delight
Denes, Hewsn

japonica Purity
BlueM, Denes

japonica Spring Candy
Hewsn

japonica Taiwanensis
BlueM

japonica Tickled Pink
BlueM, Denes, Hewsn, MJury

japonica Valley Rose
Ashto

japonica Valley Valentine
Denes

japonica Variegata
Denes

japonica White Caps
Denes

japonica White Rim
BlueM

Miharo Delight
Denes

ryukuensis
Caves

ryukuensis Temple Bells
Butlr, Chedd, Denes, MJury, Wells

Pimelea

erecta glauca
Kayd, Mtato

ferruginea
Wells

ferruginea Bonne Petite
MatNu

longifolia (Taranga)
Orati

prostrata (Pinatoro, Anatoki, NZ Daphne)
BlueM, Butlr, CottP, Kayd, Looij, Matai, Mtato, Orati, Terra, Trans

prostrata Blue
Matwh, Orati, Wells

prostrata Blue Carpet
JoyPl

prostrata glauca
MatNu

rosea Snow Clouds
Wells

sericeovillosa
Matai

tomentosa
Matai, Orati

urvilleana
Orati

Pimpinella

anisum (Anise)
King #, Sweet, Trans

saxifraga (Lesser Burnet, Burnet Saxifrage, Moutain Balm)
Mills, Sweet

Pinanga

kuhlii
Reic #

Pinellia

tripartita
Caves

Pinus

albicaulis (Whitebark Pine)
Cedar

apulcensis was pseudostrobus a. (Apulco Pine)
Cedar

aristata (Bristlecone Pine)
BlueM, Cedar, CPete, WakaC

armandii (Armands Pine, Chinese White Pine)
Cedar, MJury, WakaC

attenuata (Knobcone Pine)
Apple, Cedar, Ford, WakaC

ayacahiute (Mexican White Pine)
Cedar, WakaC

banksiana (Jack Pine)
Cedar, CPete, NZtr #, WakaC

bungeana (Lacebark/Lead Pine)
Cedar, WakaC

canariensis (Canary Is Pine)
Cedar, Chedd, Ford, Ormon, WakaC

caribea (Caribean Pine)
Cedar

cembra (Swiss Stone/Arolla Pine)
Cedar, WakaC

cembroides (Mexican Pinyon Pine)
Cedar

cembroides var edulis now edulis
Cedar, CPete

cembroides var monophylla now monophylia
Cedar

chiapensis (Chiapas Pine)
Cedar

contorta var latifolia variegated form (Rocky Mountain Lodgepole Pine)
Cedar

coulteri (Big Cone Pine)
BlueM, Cedar, CPete, Diack, Ford, NZtr #, Pukho, WakaC

culminicola (Potosi Pinyon Pine)
Cedar

densata (Gaoshan Pine)
Cedar

densiflora (Japanese Red Pine)
Apple, Cedar, Diack

echinata (Short Leafed Pine)
Cedar, WakaC

edulis
Cedar, CPete

edulis var fallax
Cedar

eldarica
Cedar

elliotii (Slash Pine)
Apple, Cedar

engelmannii (Apache Pine. Arizona Longleaf Pine)
Cedar

flexilis (Limber Pine)

flexus var Reflexus
WakaC

gerardiana (Gerard's Pine)
WakaC

glabra (Spruce Pine)
Cedar, WakaC

greggii (Gregg Pine)
Cedar, CPete, WakaC

griffithii now wallichiana
Caves, Cedar, Diack, Pionr, WakaC, Wensl

halepensis (Aleppo Pine)
Cedar, Ford

halepensis Cedar's Lemon
Cedar

heldreichii var leucodermis was l. (Bosnian Pine)
Cedar, WakaC

herrerai (Herrera Pine)
Cedar

hwangshanensis (Hwangshan Pine)
Cedar

jeffreyi (Jeffrey's Pine)
Cedar

khaysa syn kesiya
Cedar

koraiensis (Korean Pine)
Cedar, Ford

lambertiana (Sugar Pine)
Cedar, WakaC

lawsonii (Lawsons Pine)
Cedar

leucodermis now heldrechii leucodermis
Cedar, WakaC

massoniana
WakaC

maximartinezii (Martinez Pinyon Pine)
Cedar

monophylla was P.cembroides m. (Single-lfd Pinyon)
Cedar

montezumae (Montezuma/Mexican Pine)
Cedar, Pionr

monticola (Western White Pine)
Cedar, WakaC

mugo (Dwarf Mountain Pine)
Cedar, CPete, Diack, Ford, Matwh, SpecT, WakaC

mugo Gnom (Swiss Mountain Pine)
BlueM, Cedar

mugo Mops
BlueM

mugo ssp uncinata
Cedar

mugo var pumilio (Dwarf Swiss Mountain Pine)
Cedar

mugo var rostrata now P.mugo uncinata
Cedar

muricata (Bishop Pine)
Cedar, Diack, TopTr

muricata blue strain
Apple, Cedar

nelsonii (Nelson Pine)
Cedar

nigra (Corsican/Austrian Black Pine)
BlueM, Cedar, Ford, Pionr, PuhaN, Wensl

nigra ssp pallasiana (Crimean Pine)
Apple, Cedar

nigra ssp pallasiana var pyramidata (Crimean Pine)
Cedar, WakaC

nigra ssp pallasiana var pyramidata Pinnacle
Cedar

oocarpa
Cedar

palustris (Long-leaf Pine)
Cedar, WakaC

parviflora (Japanese White Pine)
Cedar, WakaC

parviflora var pentaphylla
Cedar

patula (Mexican Weeping Pine, Jelecote Pine)
BlueM, Butlr, Cedar, Chedd, CPete, Ford, Ormon, Pionr, PuhaN, WakaC

peuce (Balkan/Macedonian Pine)
Cedar, WakaC

pinaster (Maritime Pine)
Apple, Cedar, Ford, TopTr

pinceana (Pince Pinyon Pine)
Cedar

pinea (Stone/Umbrella Pine, Pine Nut)
BlueM, Butlr, Cedar, Chedd, CPete, Diack, King #, Matai, Matwh, NZtr #, Ormon, Pionr, PuhaN, Sweet, WakaC

pityusa now brutia var pityusa
Cedar

ponderosa (Western Yellow Pine)
Cedar, Ford

pseudostrobus (False Weymouth / Smoothbark/White Bark Pine)
Cedar

pseudostrobus var apulcensis see P. apulcensis
Cedar

pungens (Hickory Pine, Table Mountain Pine)
Cedar

radiata (Monterey Pine)
Cedar, Diack, Ford, Matai, NZtr #

radiata Aurea
BlueM, Cedar

radiata GF 16
Pionr, SouWo, Wensl

radiata GF 16/17
Cedar, Ford, PuhaN

radiata GF 19
Morgn, Mtato, PuhaN, SouWo

radiata GF 28
Mtato, PuhaN, SouWo

radiata GFs 17, 19, 25, 27, 28etc
Ford

radiata Marshwood
Cedar, WakaC

resinosa (Norway/American Red Pine)
Cedar

rigida (Northern Pitch Pine
Cedar

roxburghii (Long Leafed Indian Pine)
Cedar, WakaC

rudis (Endlicher Pine)
Cedar

rzedowskii (Rzedowsk Pine
Cedar

sabineana (Digger Pine)
Cedar, WakaC

serotina (Pond Pine)
Cedar, WakaC

strobiformis (South Western White Pine)
Cedar

strobus (Weymouth Pine)
Cedar

sylvestris (Scots Pine)
Cedar, CPete, Diack, Ford, WakaC

sylvestris blue form/Gevaudan strain
Cedar

sylvestris var mongolica (Mongolian Scots Pine)
Cedar

sylvestris var rhodopaea (South Bulgarian Pine)
Cedar

tabulaeformis (Chinese Red Pine)
Cedar, CPete, WakaC

taeda (Loblolly Pine)
Cedar

thunbergii (Japanese Black Pine)
Caves, Cedar, CPete, Denes, SpecT, WakaC

virginiana (Scrub Pine)
Cedar, WakaC

wallichiana (was griffithi) (Bhutan Pine, Himalayan White Pine)
BlueM, Cedar, Chedd, Ormon, TopTr, WakaC

yunnanensis (Yunnan Pine)

    Cedar

Pisonia

brunoniana now umbrellifera (Parapara)

    Gordn, Orati

brunoniana Variegata

    Orati

variegata

    Manna

Pistacia

chinensis (Chinese Mastic Tree, Chinese Pistache)

    Caves, Chedd, Coatv, Denes, JoyPl, Ormon, PuhaN, Pukho, Reic #

vera (Pistachio Nut)

    Reic #

Pisum

Dalmatian Pea

    Koan #

sativa Snowflake (Snow Pea)

    King #

sativum Monty

    MTig #

sativum WF Massey (Pea)

    MTig #

Pittosporum

anomalum

    Orati, Terra

Argenteum

    Orati

colensoi (Rautawhiri, Black Mapou)

    Butlr, Mtato, NZtr #, SelGr, Terra

cornifolium (Tawhiri Karo)

    Orati

crassifolium (Karo)

    Chedd, Coatv, Dove, Gordn, Matai, Matwh, Morgn, Mtato, NZtr #, Orati, Pionr, Pukho, Reic #, SelGr, Terra, Wahpa, Wensl

dallii

    Orati

divaricatum

    Orati

ellipticum (Golden-lvd Kohuhu)

    Orati, Terra

eugenioides (Lemonwood, Tarata)

    BlueM, Burbk, Butlr, Chedd, Coatv, Diack, Dove, EasyB, Ford, Gordn, Hewsn, Matai, Matwh, Morgn, Mtato, NZtr #, Orati, Pionr, Pkrau, Pukho, SelGr, SouWo, Terra, TopTr, Wahpa, Wensl

eugenioides Mini Green

    Mtato

eugenioides var minima

    Butlr

eugenioides Variegatum (Variegated Lemonwood)

    BlueM, Chedd, Coatv, Gordn, Matai, Mtato, Orati, Pionr, Pukho, Wahpa, Wensl

French Lace

    Matai

Garnetti (v)

    Butlr

huttonianum

    Orati

kirkii

    Orati

obcordatum

    Ormon

pimelioides

    Burbk, Orati

ralphii (Ralph's Kohuhu)

    EasyB, Ford, Morgn, Mtato, NZtr #, Orati, Pukho, Terra

ralphii Green Globe

    Ormon

sandersii

    Burbk, Butlr

Silver Cloud

    Orati

Stirling Silver

    Orati

tenuifolium (Kohuhu, Black Matipo)

    BlueM, Burbk, Chedd, Coatv, Diack, Dove, Ford, Gordn, Hewsn, Matai, Matwh, Morgn, Mtato, NZtr #, Ormon, Pionr, Pkrau, Pukho, SelGr, SouWo, Terra, Wahpa, Wells, Wensl

tenuifolium Deborah

    BlueM, Butlr, Hewsn, Orati, Pionr, Wahpa

tenuifolium Gold Star

    Burbk, Diack, Matai, Orati, SelGr, Wahpa

tenuifolium Green Ripple

    Pionr, Wahpa

tenuifolium Irene Patterson

    BlueM, Butlr, Gordn, Orati, Wahpa

tenuifolium Jade

    Coatv

tenuifolium James Stirling

    Butlr, Matwh, Orati

tenuifolium Katie

    Butlr, Coatv, Pionr, Wahpa

tenuifolium Limelight

    BlueM, Coatv, Matai, Mtato, Orati

tenuifolium Marjorie Channon

    BlueM, Butlr, Matwh

tenuifolium Mellow Yellow

    Matwh, Wahpa

tenuifolium Moonlight

    BlueM

tenuifolium Mountain Green

    Chedd, Coatv, Matai, Mtato, Orati, Pionr, Pukho, Wahpa

tenuifolium Pixie

    BlueM, Butlr, Matai, Wahpa

tenuifolium Shirley

    Wahpa

tenuifolium Silver Magic

    Butlr, Coatv, Mtato

tenuifolium Silver Sheen

    Coatv, Matai, McKe, Orati, Ormon, SpecT, Wahpa

tenuifolium Stirling Gold

    Mtato

tenuifolium Sunburst

    BlueM, Gordn, McKe, Pionr

tenuifolium Tandarra Gold

    Burbk, Chedd, Matai, McKe, Pionr

tenuifolium Tiki

    Butlr, Gordn, Mtato

tenuifolium Tom Thumb

    BlueM, Mtato

tenuifolium Variegatum

BlueM, Butlr, Chedd, Coatv, Gordn, McKe, Mtato, Pionr, Pukho, Wahpa

tenuifolium Wai Iti

Wahpa

tenuifolium Waimea

Hewsn, SelGr

tenuifolium Warnham Gold

BlueM, Butlr

tenuifolium Wendell Channon

BlueM, Butlr Mtato, Wahpa

tenuifolium Yellow Wave

Butlr, Wahpa

tobira

Reic #

umbellatum (Haekaro)

Orati, Terra

undulatum (Sweet Pittosporum)

Reic #

Victoria

BlueM

Plagianthus

betulinus   now regius (Manatu, Ribbonwood)

Chedd, Coatv, Denes, EasyB, Ford, Gordn, Hewsn, Wahpa, Wells

divaricatus (Makaka, Swamp/Shore Ribbonwood)

Burbk, Matai, Matwh, NZtr #, Pkrau

maritimus (Coastal Ribbonwood)

Orati

regius   was betulinus (Ribbonwood)

Apple, Burbk, Diack, Ford, Matai, Mtato, NZtr #, Orati, Pionr, SouWo, Terra

regius x divaricatus

Orati

Planchonella

costata (Tawapou)

Gordn, Orati, Terra

Plantago

asiatica Variegata

Telfa

lanceolata purpurea (Purple Plantain)

Orang

major Atropurpurea (Purple Plantain)

BayBl, Diack, WaiMa

major Rubrum

Looij

major ssp bronze

Mills, Sweet

psyllium

Sweet

triandra

Orati

Platanus

x acerifolia   now x hispanica

Chedd, Coatv, Hewsn, NZtr #, PuhaN, Pukho

x acerifolia Pyramidalis

Pukho

x hispanica   was acerifolia (London Plane)

Burbk, Denes, Mtato, Peele, Pionr, PuhaN, TopTr

x hispanica Suttneri (v) (Variegated Plane Tree)

Burbk, Mtato, Pionr, Pukho

occidentalis (American Plane Tree, Buttonwood)

NZtr #

orientalis (Oriental Plane)

Chedd, EasyB, Mtato, NZtr #, Peele, PuhaN, TopTr

orientalis Autumn Glory

Coatv, Denes, Peele, Pukho

Platycarya

strobilacea

Denes

Platycerium

species (Staghorn Ferns)

LakeN

alcicorne now bifurcatum

Reic #

wilhelmina reginae

Reic #

Platycladus

orientalis   now Thuja o.

WakaC

Platycodon

grandiflorus (Balloon Flower)

BlueM, MaraN, Mills, Pgeon, Vall #

grandiflorus albus

Kayd, MaraN, Pgeon, Trans

grandiflorus Apoyama

MaraN, NewlR

grandiflorus Blue

Kayd, Trans

grandiflorus Double Blue

Pgeon

grandiflorus Florist Snow

MillH

grandiflorus Fuji Blue

Oasis

grandiflorus Fuji Pink

BayBl, BlueM, KeriP, Oasis

grandiflorus Halcone Blue

BlueM

grandiflorus Mother of Pearl

Pgeon

grandiflorus Parks Dble Blue

MillH, Oasis

grandiflorus Roseum

MaraN

grandiflorus Shell Pink

Oasis

pygmaea

Otepo

Plectranthus

amboinicus (All Herb, Five Seasons Herb)

Orang

argentatus

BayBl, Denes, JoyPi, Orang, Peak, Trans

ciliatus

Orang

ciliatus Drege

Orang

coleoides Marginatus now forsteri M.

Orang

coleoides variegated

KeriP

cylindracus

Orang

ecklonii (Blue Spur Flower)

Orang

251

fruticosus
Orang
fruticosus Behrii (Pink Spur Flower)
Orang
fruticosus James
Trans
grandis
KeriP, Orang
hadensis
Orang, Trans
hereoensis
Orang
mahonii
Woodl
oertendahlii
AynDa
ornatus was Coleus canina (Dogbane)
Orang, Sweet
saccatus
Orang
sp (Vicks Plant)
Orang

Pleioblastus

argenteostriata
Isaac
auricomus was Arundinaria viridistriata
Isaac
distichus
Isaac
fortunei now variegatus
Isaac
hindsii
Isaac
pumilus
Isaac
pygmaeus
Isaac
simonii
Isaac

Pleione

Alishan
BlueM
Alishan Foxhill
BlueM
Alishan Tui
BlueM
Blush Of Dawn
MJury

bulbcodioides Lapwing
BlueM
bulbocodioides Yunnan
BlueM
Colossus
MJury
El Pico Gold Crest
BlueM
El Pico Pheasant
BlueM
Etna Bullfinch
BlueM
formosana
BayBl
formosana seedlings
BlueM
formosana alba
BlueM
formosana Clare
BlueM
formosana Cutie
MJury
formosana Harberd's X
BlueM
formosana Lilac Beauty
Parva
formosana Lilac Splendour
BlueM
formosana Oriental Grace
Parva
formosana Oriental Splendour
BlueM
formosana Orwell Glory
BlueM
formosana Polar Sun
BlueM
formosana Serenity
Parva
formosana Silver Lining
BlueM
Hekla
BlueM
Irazu Mallard
BlueM
limprichtii
BayBl, Parva
Piton
BlueM
Rakata Shot Silk
BlueM
Shantung Apricot Brandy
BlueM

Shantung Miki
BayBl
Shantung Muriel Harberd
BlueM
Shantung Silver Wedding
BlueM
Soufriere
BlueM
Stromboli Fireball
BlueM
Tolima Moorhen
BlueM
Tolima Nightingale
BlueM
Tolima Waxwing
BlueM
Versailles seedlings
BlueM
Versailles Embers
BlueM
Versailles Heron
BlueM
Versailles Leopard AM
BlueM
Versailles Phoenix
BlueM
Versailles Puffin
BlueM
Versailles Tiger Fire
BlueM

Pleomele

angustifolia honoriae
LakeN
reflexa Song of India
LakeN

Plumbago

auriculata was capensis (Cape Plumbago/Leadwort)
Chedd, Denes, Reic #, Wells
auriculata alba
Denes
Royal Cape
Denes

Plumeria

acuminata (Frangipani)
Frans
hybrids (Frangipani)
LakeN

Poa

anceps
> Orati

caespitosa now cita
> Seasd

cita was laevis, caespitosa (Silver Tussock)
> Hains, Matai, NZtr #, Orati, Pkrau, Telfa, Terra

colensoi (Blue Tussock)
> Pkrau, Terra

Podalyria

calyptrata (Sweet Pea Bush)
> Reic #

calyptrata Alba
> Denes

calyptrata Compact Gem
> Denes

sericea (Satin Bush)
> Denes

Podocarpus

acutifolius (Needle-lvd Totara)
> Cedar, Orati

alpinus now lawrencei a.
> Cedar, CPete, Pkrau

andinus now Prumnopitys andina
> Cedar

dacrydioides now Dacrycarpus d.
> Cedar, Pukho

elatus
> Cedar

ferrugineus now Prumnopitis
> BlueM, Cedar, Coatv, Denes

gracilior (Fern Pine)
> Cedar, Coatv, Denes, Ether

hallii (Thin-barked/Halls Totara)
> Cedar, Mtato, Orati

henkelii -green new growth (Falcate Yellowwood)
> Woodl

henkelii -lemon new growth
> Cedar, SpecT

henkelii -pink new growth
> Cedar

imbricatus syn. P.papuanus & Dacrycarpus i. robusta
> Cedar

latifolius
> Cedar

lawrencei was alpinus (Mtn Plum Pine)
> BlueM, Cedar, Pkrau

lawrencei Purple King
> Cedar

macrophyllus (Yew podocarpus)
> Cedar, CPete, Denes, LanSc, Ormon

macrophyllus var maki (Shrubby Podocarpus)
> Cedar

nivalis (Alpine/Snow Totara)
> BlueM, Cedar, CPete, Gordn, Matai, MJury, Orati, Pkrau, SelGr, Terra

nivalis Bronze
> Cedar, Orati

nivalis Erecta
> Cedar

nivalis Jack's Pass
> Cedar

nivalis x
> Cedar

papuanus syn. P.imbricatus & Dacrycarpus i. robusta
> Cedar

salignus
> BlueM, Cedar

spicatus now Prumnopitys taxifolia
> Cedar

TH329 (possibly gracilior)
> Woodl

totara (Totara)
> Apple, BlueM, Burbk, Cedar, Chedd, Coatv, CPete, Ford, Gordn, Matai, Matwh, Morgn, Mtato, NZtr #, Orati, Pionr, SelGr, SouWo, Sweet, Terra, TopTr, Wahpa, Wensl

totara Aurea (Golden Totara)
> BlueM, Cedar, Chedd, Coatv, CPete, Denes, Gordn, Hewsn, Matai, Mtato, Orati, Pionr, SelGr, Wahpa, Wensl

totara Aurea Pendula
> Matai

totara Pendula
> Cedar, CPete, Frans

totara Pouakani
> Cedar

Podophyllum

emodi now hexandrum
> AynDa, TRidg

hexandrum (Himalayan May Apple)
> Otepo

Podranea

brycei
> CouCl

ricasoliana (Port St John Creeper)
> CouCl

Pogostemon

patchouli (Patchouli)
> Sweet

Polemonium

Blue Dove
> Parva

Blue Master
> Telfa

Blue Sapphire
> Nikau

brandegeei (Silver Jacobs Ladder)
> Della

caeruleum (Jacobs Ladder)
> AynDa, BayBl, BlueM, CottP, Della, Dream, KeriP, King #, MaraN, Marsh, MillH, Nikau, Orang, Pgeon, Sweet, Trans, Vall #

caeruleum album now P.c.lacteus
> AynDa, BayBl, CottP, KeriP, MaraN, Marsh, Nikau, Orang, Sweet, Vall #

caeruleum Blue Pearl
> Oasis

caeruleum ssp himalayanum
> Dream

caeruleum ssp himalayanum Album
> Dream

caeruleum White Pearl
> MillH

carneum
> MillH, Parva

carneum Apricot Delight
> KeriP, MaraN, Parva,
> Vall #, Wells

cashmerianum
> AynDa, CottP

foliosissimum lutea
> KeriP, MillH, Nikau

pauciflorum
> Dream, MaraN, Pgeon,
> Telfa

pulcherrimum
> MaraN

reptans
> CottP, Otepo

Sapphire
> Ashto, BayBl, Parva

Silver Leaf
> Wells

viscosum
> BlueM

Polianthes

tuberosa
> Telfa

Poliothyrsis

sinensis
> TopTr

Polygala

calcarea
> Pgeon

chamaebuxus Grandiflora
> NewlR, Pgeon

myrtifolia Grandiflora (Milkwort)
> Butlr, Mtato, Wells

Polygonatum

falcatum Variegatum
> JoyPl, Marsh

geminiflorum
> Titok

hookeri
> BayBl, Oasis

hybridum (Ladies Lockets, Solomons Seal)
> BayBl, Della, Trans,
> TRidg

multiflorum now x hybridum
> Ashto, CottP, Kayd,
> Mills, Orang, Parva,
> Pgeon

odoratum (Sweet-scented Solomons Seal)
> JoyPl

vaccinifolium
> Parva, Seasd

verticullatum (Whorled Solomons Seal)
> Titok

Polygonum

affine Donald Lowndes now Persicaria a. D L.
> Oasis

amplexicaule now Persicaria a.
> MaraN, MillH

bistorta Superbum now Persicaria b
> CoFlo, JoyPl, TRidg

campanulatum Persicaria c
> AynDa, CoFlo, CottP,
> Della, MaraN, MillH,
> Oasis, Pgeon

hydropiper fastigiatum (Water Pepper)
> King #

japonicum Compacta now Fallopia j.c.
> CoFlo

odoratum (Vietnamese Mint)
> CottP, Mills, Orang,
> Parva, Sweet

vaccinifolium (Knotweed)
> AynDa, Looij, NewlR,
> Oasis, Parva

Polymeria

calycina Prostrata
> Denes, Nikau

Polymnia

sonchifolia (Yacon)
> MTig, Sweet

Polypodium

glaucum
> Reic #

sp
> Lsendt

Polyscias

filicifolia
> LakeN

fruticosa
> LakeN

fulva
> Ether

guilfoylei
> LakeN

guilfoylei crispa
> LakeN

guilfoylei laciniata
> LakeN

paniculata
> LakeN

scutellaria
> LakeN

Polystichum

braunii
> Gordn, JoyPl

munitum
> Gordn

polyblepharum
> Gordn

proliferum
> Gordn

Rabbitsfoot tropical
> Manna

setiferum
> TRidg

vestitum (Prickly Shield Fern)
> Mtato, Orati

Polyxena

corymbosa
> DaffA

ensifolia
> JoyPl, Parva

Pomaderris

apetala (Tainui)
> Mtato, Orati, Pionr, Terra

edgerleyi
> Terra

edgerleyi prunifolia
> Orati

hamiltonii
> Orati, Terra

kumeraho (Kumarahou, Golden Tainui, Gumdiggers Soap)
> Denes, Gordn, Matwh,
> Orati, Pionr, Terra,
> Wahpa

phylicifolia ericifolia (Dwarf Pomaderris)
> Orati

phylicifolia polifolia
> Orati

prunifolia edgerleyii
> Orati

rugosa (Wrinkle-leaf Pomaderris)

Orati

Pontederia

cordata (Pickerel Rush, Pond Pickerel)

Diack, Mills, Nikau, Waihi, WaiMa, WilAq, WriWa

Populus

22,5

WakaC

22,6

WakaC

24,10

WakaC

83-11-15

WakaC

83-26-12

WakaC

87-110-6

WakaC

87-2-35

WakaC

alba f. pyramidalis

Ford

Androscoggin

Diack, Wensl

Argle

WakaC

Crows nest

Apple, Chedd, Diack, Ford, Matai, McKe, Mtato, Pionr, SouWo, TopTr, WakaC

Eridano

Apple, Ford, Mtato

Flevo

Diack, McKe, Mtato, Pionr

Hiltingbury Weeping

Pukho

Italian hybrids I 124

Ford

Kawa

Apple, Chedd, Diack, Ford, McKe, Mtato, Peele, Pionr, SouWo, WakaC

Lombardy Sunlight

Diack

luisa avanzo

Ford

Manawatu Gold

Burbk, Dove, TopTr

maximowicziana

Peele

nigra Italica (Lombardy/Italian Poplar)

Chedd, PuhaN

Pakai

Apple, WakaC

szechuanica (Szechuan Poplar)

PuhaN

szechuanica var. tibetica

TopTr

Tasman

Apple, Diack, Ford, Mtato, Pionr, PuhaN, SouWo, Wensl

Toa

Apple, Mtato, WakaC

tremuloides (Quaking/Trembling Aspen, American Aspen)

TopTr

trichocarpa

Ford

Veronese

Chedd, Diack, Ford, Matai, Mtato, Peele, SouWo, WakaC, Wensl

yunnanensis (Chinese Poplar)

Chedd, Ford, McKe, Mtato, Peele, Pionr, PuhaN, SouWo, TopTr

Potentilla

aff. cuneata Dhad 1416

Marsh

arbuscula now fruticosa a.

BlueM

argentea

MaraN

atrosanguinea

BayBl, CottP, MaraN, MillH, Oasis, Telfa, Vall #

atrosanguinea Chad 1384

Marsh

atrosanguinea var argyrophylla

Vall #

cinerea

NewlR

eriocarpa

NewlR

Etna

TRidg

Firedance

Pgeon, Telfa

Fireflame

BayBl

fruticosa

Ormon

fruticosa Day Dawn

Peak

fruticosa Elizabeth

BayBl

fruticosa Gold Finger

BlueM, Looij

fruticosa Lemon

Telfa

fruticosa Manchu

BlueM, Ormon

fruticosa Moana Rose

BayBl

fruticosa Mt Everest

BlueM, Looij

fruticosa Peaches and Cream

BayBl, BlueM, Telfa

fruticosa Princess

BayBl, Denes

fruticosa Red Ace

BlueM, Looij, Telfa

fruticosa Sunset

BlueM

fruticosa Tangerine

BayBl

fruticosa Wendonside

BlueM

Helen Jane

Peak

megalantha was fragiformis

Otepo

Melton Fire

AynDa, CottP, Oasis

myabei

NewlR

nepalensis

MaraN, Pgeon

nepaulensis Miss Wilmott

AynDa, BayBl, Dream, MillH, Mills, Nikau, Oasis, Peak, Pgeon, Reic #, Trans, TRidg, Vall #, Warwk, Wells

nepaulensis Roxana
BayBl, MaraN, Marsh,
Mills, Warwk

palustris (Marsh Cinquefoil)
WaiMa, WilAq

parvifolia (Cinquefoil)
Orang

peduncularis
MaraN

recta sulphurea now r. pallida
AynDa, KeriP, MaraN,
MillH, Mills, Telfa, Vall
#

recta Warrenii
Telfa, Trans

red
Telfa

rupestris
BayBl, Della, MaraN,
Pgeon

rupestris Cream
Nikau

rupestris white
Herew

salmon pink (form like Miss Wilmott)
Nikau

thurberi Monarch's Velvet
AynDa, Telfa

tormentilla now erecta (Tormentil)
Della, Sweet

verna nana now neumanniana nana (Cinquefoil)
NewlR, Otepo, Pgeon

White Queen
Telfa

Poterium

sanguisorba now Sanguisorba minor
Trans

Pouteria

obovata
Frans, Peak

Pratia

angulata (Panakanake)
CottP, Gordn, Mtato,
Oasis, Orati, Pgeon,
WaiMa, Wells

angulata Tim Rees
BayBl

macrodon
Orati

pedunculata
Looij, Peak

pedunculata County Park
Peak

puberula
BayBl, CottP, Mills,
Pgeon

puberula alba
Ashto

turberucca
CottP

Premna

maxima
Ether

Primula

varieties
Roswd

Alan Robb (dbl Barnhaven)
Parva

alpicola (Moonlight Primula)
Ashto, MaraN, TRidg

alpicola var violacea
BayBl, Peak, TRidg

anisodora
TRidg

auricula (mxd colour) (Auricula, Dusty Miller)
Ashto, CottP, Marsh,
Mills, Orang, Pgeon,
Telfa, TRidg

auricula sgle & dbl,scented
Herew

auricula Andrea Julie
CottP

auricula blood red,white eye
NewlR

auricula blue lavender,white centre
NewlR

auricula cerise/pink,cream centre
NewlR

auricula Clifton Blue
NewlR

auricula lavender double
NewlR

auricula mustard,sulphur ring
NewlR

auricula plum & cream
NewlR

auricula plum double
NewlR

auricula purple lge,lemon eye
NewlR

auricula Rabley Heath
CottP

auricula Show Yellow
NewlR

auricula ssp bauhinii
TRidg

auricula Woodpecker
Marsh, NewlR

auricula yellow double mostly
Della

auricula yellows
TRidg

beesiana (Candelabra P.)
Ashto, Nikau, Parva,
TRidg, WaiMa

Big Red Giant(dbl Barnhaven)
Parva

x bulleesiana (Candelabra P.)
Parva, WaiMa

bulleyana (Candelabra P.)
BayBl, Della, Nikau,
Otepo, Parva, WaiMa

burmanica
BayBl, Peak

capitata
Della, Herew, Otepo

capitata mooreana
TRidg

Captain Blood(dbl Barnhaven)
Parva

Cecily
MaraN, MillH

chionantha (Candelabra P.)
Della, Herew, Nikau,
Parva, Peak, TRidg

chungensis
Otepo

clarkeii
CottP

cockburniana
Otepo, TRidg

Corporal Baxter(dbl Bnhaven)
Parva

Dawn Ansell (dbl Barnhaven)
Parva

denticulata (Drumstick P.)
BayBl, Kayd, Pgeon, WaiMa

denticulata Alba
BayBl, CottP, Telfa, WaiMa

denticulata Blue
Ashto, CoFlo, TRidg

denticulata Cerise
CottP

denticulata mauve
CottP, Telfa

denticulata pompon purple fl
Della

denticulata pompon white fl
Della

denticulata Rose
CoFlo, Marsh

denticulata Rubin
BayBl

denticulata Ruby
MillH, TRidg

denticulata Snowball
Pgeon, TRidg

denticulata White
Ashto, CoFlo

Diane
Della

elatior (Oxlip)
Dream, MaraN

elatior Hose in Hose
Parva

elatior pallasii
TRidg

elliptica (CH490)
MaraN

farinosa
NewlR

firmipes
Parva

florindae (Giant Cowslip)
Ashto, BayBl, Della, Herew, MaraN, Otepo, Peak, Pkrau, TRidg, WaiMa

florindae Butterscotch Mix
Marsh

florindae Keilour Hybrid
WaiMa

florindae Rote Hybrid
WaiMa

frondosa
Marsh

gabbeana
Parva

Garryarde Guinivere
CottP, Pkrau

garryarde The Grail
CottP

glaucescens
TRidg

glomerata
MaraN

Harlow Carr Hybrids sdlg apricot orange parent
TRidg

Harlow Carr Hybrids sdlg scarlet pink
TRidg

helodoxa (Candelabra P.)
AynDa, BayBl, Herew, MaraN, Mills, Nikau, Parva, Telfa, TRidg, Vall #, WaiMa

Inshriach hybrids (Candelabra)
Marsh, Parva

integrifolia
TRidg

involucrata (C&Mc374)
MaraN

ioessa
Herew, NewlR

japonica mixed (Candelabra)
Ashto, BlueM, Nikau, Pgeon

japonica alba
Parva

japonica Millers Crimson
Parva, Peak

japonica Postford White
MillH, Parva, Pkrau, TRidg

japonica Rosea
CottP

Jill
Ashto, BayBl, Della

Joan Groves
MaraN

juliae
CottP

juliana Ideal
CottP

juliana Jill
CottP

Ken Dearman(dbl Barnhaven)
Parva

kewensis
Otepo

Lady Greer
Marsh

Lilian Harvey
Parva

luteola
TRidg

marginata
BayBl, CottP, NewlR, Parva

marginata Linda Pope
BayBl

Marie Crousse(dbl Barnhaven)
Parva

megaesifolia
Marsh

minima
TRidg

Miss Indigo (dbl Barnhaven)
Parva

mollis
TRidg

Olive Wyatt (dbl Barnhaven)
Parva

x polyanthus Gold Lace
MaraN, Mills, Trans

x polyanthus Interlace
Parva

x polyanthus red/maroon
Mills

x polyanthus Silver Star
Parva

x polyanthus Simple Touch
Parva

x polyanthus Velvet Glow
Parva

x pubescens Gigantea
TRidg

x pubescens Mrs JH Wilson
NewlR

pulveralenta (Candelabra P.)

Ashto, AynDa, BayBl, Della, MaraN, Mills, Nikau, Parva, TRidg, Vall #, WaiMa

Quakers Bonnet

Parva

rockii

NewlR

rosea Gigas (Bog Primula)

WaiMa

rosea Grandiflora (Bog Primula)

WaiMa

Roy Cope

Parva

secundiflora

Otepo

sibthorpii

NewlR

sieboldii (Star Primula)

Herew, Parva

sieboldii alba

NewlR

sieboldii Blue

Parva

sieboldii lavender form

NewlR

sieboldii Pink

Parva

sieboldii White

Parva

sieboldii white backed pink

Parva

sikkimensis

Peak, TRidg

sinopurpurea

Marsh

smithiana

TRidg

Snow White

NewlR

sp lemon w orange eye

NewlR

Sue Jervis (dbl Barnhaven)

Parva

Sunshine Suzie(dbl Bnhaven)

Parva

Titoki Pink (candelabra)

Parva

Val Horncastle(dbl Barnhaven)

Parva

veris (Cowslip, Hose in Hose, Fairy Bells, Fairy Cups, Peter's Keys,Golden Drops)

BlueM, CottP, Della, KeriP, King #, MaraN, Mills, Orang, Pgeon, Sweet, Telfa, TRidg

veris Firecracker

Pgeon

veris seedlgs red/orange

Mills

vialli (Bog Primula)

Ashto, AynDa, BayBl, MaraN, Parva, TRidg, WaiMa

vulgaris (Primrose)

MaraN, MillH, Mills, Parva, Pgeon, Telfa

vulgaris double

Mills, TRidg

vulgaris sibthorpii

CottP

Wanda

Ashto, Pgeon, Telfa

warshenewskiana

NewlR

yellow candelabra sdlgs

Mills

Pritchardia

pacifica

Reic #

thurstonii

Reic #

Prostanthera

species (Australian Mint Bush)

KeriP

aspalathoides (Scarlet Mint Bush)

BlueM

cuneata (Alpine Mint Bush)

BlueM, KeriP, Matwh

cuneata Alpine Gold

BlueM

cuneata Variegata

BlueM

Eddington Blue

Denes

incisa Rosea

BlueM

Kandos Dam

Denes

nivea

Denes

Poorinda Ballerina

BlueM, Denes, Kayd, KeriP, Mtato

rhombea

Butlr

rhombea Pink Surprise

Denes, KeriP, MillH

rotundifolia

BlueM

rotundifolia rosea

KeriP, MillH

saxicola var montana

BlueM

westringia

Butlr

Protea

aristata

Reic #

aurea Goodwood Red (Shuttlecock Protea)

MatNu, Matth

burchellii (pulchra)

Reic #

Clark's Red

Denes, MatNu, Matth

Coleman's Hybrid

MatNu

coronata (macrocephala)

Reic #

cynaroides (King Protea)

MatNu, Matth

eximea Duchess of Perth

MatNu, Matth

Franciscan Hybrid

Denes, MatNu, Matth

Frosted Fire

MatNu, Matth

grandiceps (Princess/Peach Protea)

MatNu, Matth

laurifolia Peach Sheen

MatNu

laurifolia Rosa Mink

MatNu, Matth

longifolia

MatNu, Matth

magnifica Snow Queen (was alba) (Queen Protea)

MatNu

mundii

MatNu

nana syn. P rosaceae (Mtn Rose)

MatNu, Matth

neriifolia

Reic #

neriifolia alba

Chedd, Denes, MatNu, Matth

neriifolia Green Ice (syn Moonshine)

MatNu, Matth

neriifolia Limelight

MatNu

neriifolia Margaret Watling

MatNu, Matth

neriifolia Ruby

MatNu, Matth

neriifolia Silvertips

MatNu, Matth

neriifolia Snowcrest

MatNu, Matth

obtusifolia

Reic #

Pacific Queen

MatNu

Pink Ice (syn Silvan Pink)

MatNu, Matth

repens

Reic #

repens alba (Sugar Bush)

MatNu

repens Guerna (Sugar Bush)

MatNu

scolymocephala

Denes, MatNu, Matth, Reic #

Sparkling Burgundy

MatNu, Matth

speciosa

MatNu

Sylvan Pink

Chedd, Wells

venusta (Swartberg Protea)

MatNu, Matth

Prumnopitys

andina was Podocarpus a.

Cedar

ferruginea was Podocarpus f. (Miro, Brown Pine)

Cedar, Chedd, Coatv, CPete, Denes, Gordn, Matwh, Mtato, NZtr #, Orati, Terra, Wahpa

taxifolia was Podocarpus spicatus (Matai, Black Pine

Apple, Cedar, Chedd, Gordn, Mtato, NZtr #, Orati, Pionr, Terra, Wahpa

Prunella

grandiflora

Mills, Oasis, Pgeon, Vall #

grandiflora rosea

CottP

grandiflora white

Mills

grandiflora White Loveliness

CottP

magnifica

AynDa

sp cone-like, rosepurple fl

Wells

vulgaris (Selfheal, Heart Of The Earth)

Della, MaraN, Sweet

vulgaris Grandiflora

Looij

Prunus

almond dulcis 402

Chedd

almond dulcis 403 (mariana rootstk-semidwarf)

Harri

almond dulcis Burbank

Coatv

almond dulcis Fabrin

Mtato

almond dulcis Fabrin (mariana rootstk-semidwarf)

Harri

almond dulcis Fabrin/403 double worked

Mtato

almond dulcis IXL

Chedd

almond dulcis Mona Vale

Coatv, Pionr

almond dulcis Mona Vale (mariana rootstk-semidwarf)

Harri

almond flwg glandulosa

Hackf

almond flwg glandulosa Alba Plena

Denes, Pukho

almond flwg glandulosa Flora Plena

Mtato

almond flwg glandulosa Rosea Plena

Denes, Hackf, Pukho

almond flwg x amygdalo-persica Pollardii

Denes, Pukho

apricot varieties

Coatv, TreeC

apricot dualgrafted: Sundrop,Trevatt (StJulian rootstk-semidwarf)

Harri

apricot Judge Turner

Mtanu

apricot Katy Cot

Diack

apricot Moorpark

Diack

apricot Newcastle Early Seedling

Chedd, Koan S

apricot Sundrop

Chedd, Diack, Pionr

apricot Sundrop (StJulian rootstk-semidwarf)

Harri

apricot Trevatt

Denes, Pionr, TopTr

apricot Trevatt (StJulian rootstk-semidwarf)

Harri

apricot Waipapakauri

Mtanu

apricot flwg armeniaca Dawn

Denes, Pukho

apricot flwg mume

Chedd

apricot flwg mume Peggy Clarke

Denes

apricot flwg mume
Spendons
Pukho

apricot flwg mume The
Geisha
Chedd, Denes, Peele,
Pukho

cherry   varieties
TreeC

cherry Compact Stella
Harri, Pionr

cherry Stella
Chedd

cherry Tangshe
Chedd, Coatv, Harri,
Pionr

cherry flwg Accolade
Burbk, Coatv, Denes,
Dove, EasyB, Hewsn,
MJury, Mtato, Peele,
Pukho, TopTr

cherry flwg Amanogawa
Burbk, Denes, Dove,
MJury, Mtato, Peele,
Pukho, TopTr

cherry flwg Asano
TopTr

cherry flwg autumnalis
Southern Gem
Hewsn

cherry flwg avium
(Mazzard Cherry, Sweet
Cherry)
Apple, Burbk, Diack,
NZtr #, PuhaN

cherry flwg Awanui see x
yeodensis A
Ref

cherry flwg campanulata
(Taiwan Cherry)
Burbk, Chedd, Peele,
TopTr

cherry flwg campanulata
Superba
Burbk, Coatv, Denes,
Dove, Mtato, SpecT

cherry flwg capuli syn
salicifolia (Capuli Cherry)
MTig

cherry flwg cerasus Rhexii
Denes, Pukho

cherry flwg cistena (Sand
Cherry)
Pukho

cherry flwg Felix Jury
Burbk, Coatv, Denes,
Dove, MJury

cherry flwg Fugenzo
Denes, TopTr

cherry flwg Golden Jewel
Mtato, TopTr

cherry flwg hillieri Spire
Denes, Mtato, Pukho,
TopTr

cherry flwg Hokusai
Denes, Peele

cherry flwg Ichiyo
Pukho

cherry flwg incisa (Fuji
Cherry)
BlueM, Diack

cherry flwg Ivensii
weepg
Dove

cherry flwg jamasakura
(Yamasakura Cherry)
Diack

cherry flwg Kanzan
Burbk, Chedd, Coatv,
Denes, Dove, Hewsn,
Mtato, Peele, Pionr,
Pukho, TopTr

cherry flwg Kiku-shidare-
zakura (Cheals Weeping
Cherry)
Burbk, Chedd, Coatv,
Denes, Dove, EasyB,
Mtato, Peele, Pionr,
Pukho, TopTr

cherry flwg Ko Fugen
EasyB, Pukho, TopTr

cherry flwg maackii
YakuN

cherry flwg mahaleb (St
Lucie Cherry)
Apple, PuhaN

cherry flwg Mimosa
MJury

cherry flwg Ojochin
Denes

cherry flwg Okame
(Okame Cherry)
Burbk, Chedd, Denes,
Peele, Pukho, TopTr

cherry flwg padus
(European Bird Cherry)
Burbk, Diack, PuhaN,
Pukho

cherry flwg Pearly
Shadows
Burbk, MJury

cherry flwg Peggy Wilson
EasyB

cherry flwg Petite Pink
Denes, MJury

cherry flwg Pink Cloud
Burbk, MJury, Mtato,
Pukho

cherry flwg Pink
Perfection
Burbk, Denes, Dove,
Hewsn, MJury, Mtato,
Peele, Pionr, Pukho

cherry flwg Red Veil
Pukho

cherry flwg sargentii
Peele, Pukho, TopTr

cherry flwg Seaview
Beauty
MJury

cherry flwg serotina
(Black Cherry)
Apple, Chedd, Diack,
Peele, PuhaN, Pukho

cherry flwg serrula (Birch
Bark Cherry)
Hewsn, MJury, Mtato,
Pukho, TopTr

cherry flwg serrulata (Hill
Cherry)
Apple, Diack, Mtato,
Peele, PuhaN

cherry flwg serrulata
pubescens (Korean Hill
Cherry)
MJury

cherry flwg Shimidsu
zakura now Okumiyako
(Asahibotan Cherry)
Burbk, Chedd, Coatv,
Denes, Dove, Hewsn,
MJury, Mtato, Peele,
Pionr, Pukho, TopTr

cherry flwg Shirofugen
Pukho, TopTr

cherry flwg Shirotae (Mt
Fuji Cherry)
Burbk, Chedd, Coatv,
Denes, Dove, Hewsn,
MJury, Mtato, Peele,
Pionr, Pukho, TopTr

cherry flwg subhirtella
(Rosebud Cherry, Japanese
Higan Cherry)
Diack, Mtato

cherry flwg subhirtella
Autumnalis
MJury, Pukho

cherry flwg subhirtella
Autumnalis Rosea
Denes

cherry flwg subhirtella
Autumnalis Southern Gem

Pukho

cherry flwg subhirtella
Falling Snow

Burbk, Coatv, Denes,
MJury, Mtato, Pionr,
Pukho, TopTr

cherry flwg subhirtella
Flore Pleno

Denes, Hewsn, Pukho

cherry flwg subhirtella
Fukubana

Denes, Mtato, Pukho,
TopTr

cherry flwg subhirtella
pendula

Chedd

cherry flwg subhirtella
Pendula Rosea

Burbk, Coatv, Denes,
Hewsn, MJury, Pionr,
Pukho, TopTr

cherry flwg subhirtella var.
ascendens now pendula
v.a.

Pukho, TopTr

cherry flwg Taihaku
(Great White Cherry)

Burbk, Chedd, Coatv,
Denes, Dove, Mtato,
Peele, Pionr, Pukho,
TopTr

cherry flwg Takasago

Denes, MJury, Pukho

cherry flwg Ukon

Chedd, Coatv, Denes,
Hewsn, Peele, Pionr,
Pukho, TopTr

cherry flwg x wrightii
(almond-cherry x)
(Almond-Cherry Hybrid)

TopTr

cherry flwg x yeodensis
(Yoshino Cherry)

EasyB, Hewsn, Pukho,
TopTr

cherry flwg x yeodensis
Awanui

Burbk, Chedd, Coatv,
Denes, MJury, Mtato,
Peele, Pionr, Pukho,
SpecT, TopTr

cherry flwg x yeodensis
Ivensii

MJury

cherry flwg x yeodensis
Perpendens

Burbk, Chedd, Coatv,
Denes, Dove, Hewsn,
Mtato, Peele, Pionr,
Pukho, TopTr

cherry flwg x yeodensis
Pink

Dove

cherry flwg x yeodensis Te
Mara

Burbk

laurocerasus (Cherry
Laurel)

Apple, Morgn, NZtr #,
SelGr

lusitanica (Portugese
Laurel)

Apple, Denes, Ford,
LanSc, SelGr, SpecT,
TopTr

nectarine varieties

TreeC

nectarine Armking

Coatv

nectarine Fantasia

Coatv, TopTr

nectarine Goldking

Coatv

nectarine Goldmine

Harri, Mtanu

nectarine Queen Giant

Chedd

nectarine Snow Queen

TopTr

nectarine Sth Is Goldmine

Mtanu

nectarine Whakapirau

Koan S

peach varieties

TreeC

peach Apricot Queen

Koan S

peach Belle of Georgia

Mtanu

peach Ben Hurst

Diack, Harri

peach Black Boy

Chedd, Coatv, Harri,
Koan S, Pionr, TopTr

peach Christina

Koan S

peach Elegant Lady

Chedd

peach Fayette

Coatv

peach Glohaven

TopTr

peach Golden Queen

Chedd, Coatv, Diack,
Harri, Koan S, TopTr

peach Gordon Glory

Diack, Harri

peach Grey's Seedling

Koan S

peach Ham's Special

Koan S

peach Karamu

Koan S

peach Maori

Koan S

peach Orion

Koan S

peach Red Haven

Harri

peach Reefton

Harri

peach River

Koan S, Mtanu

peach seedling

Chedd

peach Springcrest

Coatv, Koan S

peach Springtime

Chedd

peach Tamahere

Koan S

peach Tara

Koan S

peach Wiggins

Koan S, Mtanu

peach flwg Iceberg

Burbk, Denes, Mtato

peacherine

Koan S

plum Angelina Burdett

Koan S

plum Aue

Koan S

plum Billington's Early

Chedd

plum Billingtons

Coatv, Diack, Pionr

plum Black Amber

Harri, TreeC

plum Black Doris
(Japanese)

Chedd, Coatv, Diack,
Harri, Koan S, Pionr,
TopTr, TreeC

plum Black Prince
(Japanese)

Koan S

plum Burbank (Japanese)

Diack, Koan S, Mtanu,
Pionr

plum Christmas plum

Koan S, Mtanu

plum Coes Golden Drop

TopTr, TreeC

plum Damson

Diack, Harri, Koan S,
Mtanu, TopTr

plum Dan's Delight
(Japanese)

Koan S

plum Dan's Early
(Japanese)

Koan S, Mtanu

plum Doris

TreeC

plum Duffs Early Jewell
(J)

Mtanu, TopTr, TreeC

plum Elephant Heart (J)

Diack, Koan S, Mtanu,
TreeC

plum English Greengage

Diack, TopTr, TreeC

plum Friar

TreeC

plum Fruzuetsche

Koan S

plum Golden Drop

Koan S

plum Marabella
(Japanese)

Koan S, Mtanu

plum Meribel

Koan S

plum Omega

Harri, Pionr, TopTr,
TreeC

plum Princess (Japanese)

Koan S

plum Puhoi Plum

Koan S

plum Purple King
(Japanese)

Koan S, TreeC

plum Queen Rosa

TreeC

plum Reine Claude de
Bavy

TreeC

plum Reine Claude Gage

Koan S

plum Santa Rosa
(Japanese)

Diack, Harri, Koan S,
Mtanu, TreeC

plum Satsuma

Chedd, Coatv, Diack,
Harri, Koan S, TreeC

plum Scarletina (Japanese)

Koan S

plum Sharpes Early

Diack, Koan S

plum Shiro (Japanese)

TreeC

plum Sultan

Chedd, Coatv, Diack,
Harri, TreeC

plum Tamaki Special (J)

Koan S, Mtanu

plum Torwick

TreeC

plum Transparent Gage

Koan S

plum Transparent Gage
(Myrobalan rootstk)

Mtanu

plum Victoria

Koan S, Mtanu

plum Waimana

Chedd

plum Whakapirau Gold
(Japanese)

Koan S

plum Wilsons Early

Coatv, TreeC

plum dualgrafted:
Satsuma,Burbank

Harri

plum flwg Blireana

Chedd, Denes, Dove,
Pukho

plum flwg cerasifera
Elvins

Denes, Pukho

plum flwg cerasifera Nigra

Burbk, Coatv, Dove,
Pukho

plum flwg cerasifera
Thundercloud

Denes, Mtato, Peele

plum flwg cerasifera
Wrightii

Pukho

plumcot

Diack

prune Cacak early

Chedd

prune Cacak Late

Chedd

prune Italian

Mtanu

prune Marahemo

Koan S

prune Stanley

Mtanu, TreeC

prune Sugar Prune

Koan S, Mtanu

prune Tragedy

Koan S

Pseudocydonia

sinensis (Chinese False
Quince)

Caves, Denes, Dove,
Hackf, MTig, Ormon,
PuhaN

Pseudolarix

amabilis was kaempferi
(Golden Larch)

Cedar, CPete

Pseudopanax

varieties

Coatv, Wahpa

adiantifolius

Denes, Mtato

anomalus

Orati

arboreus (Five Finger,
Whauwhaupaku, Puahou)

BlueM, Gordn, Matai,
Matwh, Morgn, NZtr #,
Orati, Pionr, Pkrau, Reic
#, Terra, Wahpa

colensoi (Mountain Five
Finger, Three Finger)

Matai, Orati, Terra

crassifolius (Horoeka, Lancewood)

BlueM, Burbk, Chedd, Ford, Gordn, Hewsn, Matai, Matwh, Morgn, Mtato, NZtr #, Orati, Ormon, Pionr, Reic #, Terra, Wahpa

Cyril Watson

Denes, Mtato, Orati

discolor

Matai, Orati

edgerleyi (Raukawa)

Terra

ferox (Toothed/Savage Lancewood)

Gordn, Matai, MatNu, Mtato, NZtr #, Orati, Ormon, Pionr, Terra, Wahpa

laetus (Five Finger)

Burbk, Butlr, Gordn, Kayd, Matwh, Mtato, NZtr #, Orati, Pionr, Terra, Wahpa

lessonii (Houpara)

Matwh, Mtato, Orati, Pionr, Terra, Wahpa

lessonii hybrids

Burbk, Gordn, Matai, Reic #

lessonii Gold Splash

Denes, Matwh, Mtato, Orati, Pionr, Wells

lessonii Nigra

Denes

lessonii purpurea

Chedd, Ford, Matai, Mtato, Orati, Pionr

linearifolius

Mtato

MacIntyrei

Gordn, Orati

Rangitira

Mtato

Sabre

Denes, Mtato

simples (Haumakaroa)

NZtr #

Toru

Denes

Pseudoranthemum

reticulatum

LakeN

Pseudosasa

japonica

Isaac

Pseudotsuga

macrocarpa

CPete

menziesii (Douglas Fir)

Apple, Cedar, Chedd, CPete, Diack, Dove, Ford, Matai, Morgn, Mtato, NZtr #, Pionr, PuhaN, SelGr, SouWo, Terra, WakaC, Wensl

menziesii var glauca

Cedar, WakaC

wilsoniana (Taiwan Douglas Fir)

Cedar, WakaC

Pseudowintera

axillaris (Horopito, Pepper Tree)

Orati, Terra

colorata (Horopito, Pepper Tree)

BlueM, Coatv, Denes, Gordn, Mtato, NZtr #, Orati, Pionr, Terra, Wahpa, Wells

colorata Red Glow

Denes

colorata Red Leopard

Woodl

Psidium

cattleyanum (Red Guava)

Chedd, MTig #, Reic #

cattleyanum lucidum (Yellow Guava)

Koan, MTig #

pyrifolium (Yellow Guava)

Chedd, Reic #

seedlings (Guava)

MTig

tropical guava large pink

Koan

Psoralea

pinnata (Blue Pea)

Butlr, Ether

pinnata Blue Broom

Kayd

Pteridium

aquilinum var esculentum (Rarauhe, Bracken)

Orati, Sweet

Pteris

argyraea

Reic #

argyraea Variegata indoor

Manna

comans

Gordn, Orati

cretica (Cretan Fern)

Denes, Gordn

cretica albolineata

Reic #

cretica Major

Reic #

cretica Parkeri

Reic #

cretica Rowei

Reic #

cretica Wimsettii

Reic #

ensiformis

Reic #

longifolia

Reic #

macilenta

Orati

serrulata

Reic #

tremula

Orati

umbrosa Berliner

Reic #

Pterocarya

stenoptera (Chinese Wingnut)

Dove, TopTr

Pterocephalus

parnassi now P.perennis p.

Pgeon

Pterostyrax

corymbosa (Epaulette Tree

Caves

hispida (Fragrant Epaulette Tree)

Caves, Denes, Dove, Peele

Ptychosperma

elegans

Reic #

macarthuri

Reic #

microcarpum

Reic #

Pulmonaria

varieties

Roswd

angustifolia (Blue Lungwort)

CoFlo, Mills, Pgeon

angustifolia ssp azurea

CottP, JoyPl, Marsh, MillH, Telfa

Barfield Pink

Parva, Peak

Excalibur

BayBl, MillH, Parva, Peak, Taunt

Highdown now Lewis Palmer

Parva

Lavender Joy

Peak

Lewis Palmer was Highdown

Peak

Little Star

BayBl, Parva, Taunt

longifolia

MaraN, Nikau, Taunt, Telfa

longifolia Bertram Anderson

JoyPl

mollissima

Telfa

Mournful Purple

Peak

officinalis (Polka Dot Plant, Lungwort, Spotted Dog, Soldiers & Sailors)

Ashto, CottP, Della, Mills, Parva, Sweet, Telfa

officinalis Blue

Telfa

Pierres Pure Pink

Parva

Regal Ruffles

Parva

Roy Davidson

Peak

rubra

MillH, Mills, Telfa

rubra David Ward (v)

Parva, Peak

rubra Redstart

JoyPl

saccharata

JoyPl, Pgeon

Sissinghurst White

Hackf, JoyPl, MaraN, MillH, Mills, Nikau, Parva, Peak, Telfa

Spilt Milk

BayBl, Parva, Peak, Taunt

White Wings

Parva

Pulsatilla

ambigua

Della

halleri

MaraN

pratensis

Della

rubra

Della

vernalis

MaraN

vulgaris (Pasque/Wind Flower)

Ashto, CottP, Della, Hackf, MaraN, Marsh, Mills, Oasis, Parva, Reic #, Telfa

vulgaris alba

AynDa, Della, MaraN, MillH, Parva, TRidg

vulgaris Papageno

Parva

vulgaris red

BlueM, Parva, TRidg

Punica

granatum (Pomegranate)

Caves, Chedd, Denes, MTig

granatum nana

Reic #

Puschkinia

scilloides

JoyPl

scilloides libanotica

VanEe, Winga

scilloides libanotica Alba

Winga

Puya

berteroniana

Ormon

coerulea

TRidg

Pycnanthemum

flexuosum syn P.tenufolium (Horse Mint)

MillH

Pycnostachys

urticifolia

JoyPl

Pyracantha

Brilliant (Firethorn, Fireberry)

Kayd

Harlequin (v)

Butlr

Orange Glow

BlueM

Shawnee

Kayd, Mtato

Pyrethropsis

gayanum now Rhodanthemum g.

Marsh

Pyrethrum

roseum now Tanacetum coccineum

CoFlo

roseum Robinsons Crimson now Tanacetum coccineum RC.

Ashto

roseum Robinsons Rose Pink now Tanacetum

Ashto

Silver Lace now Tanacetum vulgare Silver Lace

KeriP, Wells

Pyrostegia

venusta (Flame Vine)

CouCl, Denes

Pyrrosia

serpens

Orati

Pyrus

calleryana (Chinese Pear - ornamental)

Apple, Chedd, Coatv, Diack, Ormon, Peele

communis (Pear, common)

Peele, PuhaN

communis dualgrafted:
Bn.Chrtn., BBosc
Diack

communis dualgrafted:
Bn.Chrtn., Confce
Diack

communis dualgrafted:
Bn.Chrtn., Win.Cole
Diack

communis dualgrafted:
Pkhms.Tri, Lou.Bon Jsy.
Harri

communis triplegrafted:
Bn.Chrtn., Win.Cole,
Pkham.
Diack

communis triplegrafted:
Rd Bartlt,Starks
Crim,Confce (quince
rootstk-dwarf)
Harri

communis Bartlett seedlg
Apple

communis Beurre bosc
Chedd, TreeC

communis Beurre Dale
(Asian pear rootstk)
Mtanu

communis Beurre Hardy
TopTr

communis Bon Cretian
Chedd

communis Clergou (Asian
pear rootstk)
Mtanu

communis Conference
Pionr

communis Conference
(quince rootstk-dwf)
Harri

communis Doyenne du
Comice
Pionr, TopTr, TreeC

communis Doyenne du
Comice (quince rtstk/dwf)
Diack, Harri

communis Kefer (Asian
pear rootstk)
Mtanu

communis Louis Bon
Jersey
TreeC

communis Packham's
Triumph
Chedd, TreeC

communis Princess (Asian
pear rootstk)
Mtanu

communis Red Bartlett
Diack, Pionr, TreeC

communis Red Bartlett
(quince rootstk-dwarf)
Harri

communis Seccles Honey
(Asian pear rootstk)
Mtanu

communis Stark's Crimson
Diack, TreeC

communis Triumph de
Vienna (Asian pear
rootstk)
Mtanu

communis William Bon
Chretien
Diack, Pionr, TreeC

communis William Bon
Chretien (Asian pear
rootstk)
Mtanu

communis William Bon
Chretien (quince rootstk-
dwf)
Harri

communis Winter Cole
Chedd, TreeC

communis Winter Cole
(Asian pear rootstk)
Mtanu

communis Winter Nells
Chedd, TreeC

salicifolia Pendula
(Weeping Silver Pear)
Chedd, Coatv, Denes,
Hewsn, Peele, Pionr,
Pukho, SpecT, TopTr

salicifolia Pendula Dwarf
Mtato

serotina (Nashi, Asian Pear
TreeC

serotina Hosui (Nashi)
Chedd, Pionr

serotina Kosui (Nashi)
Chedd

serotina Matapouri (Nashi)
Mtanu

ussuriensis (Chinese Eating
Pear)
Hackf

ussuriensis Hwahong
Diack

ussuriensis Tsu Li
Chedd

Quercus

afares (North African Oak)
PuhaN

alpestris
PuhaN

bicolor (White Swamp Oak
PuhaN

canariensis (Algerian Oak)
Apple, Diack, Ford,
Ormon, Pionr, PuhaN

canariensis x robur
Apple, Ormon, PuhaN,
Wensl

castaneifolia (Chestnut
Leafed Oak)
PuhaN

cerris (Turkey/Mossy-cup
Oak)
Apple, Chedd, Diack,
Dove, EasyB, Hewsn,
Matwh, MJury, Morgn,
Mtato, NZtr #, Ormon,
Peele, PuhaN, Pukho,
Wensl

coccinea (Scarlet Oak)
Apple, Burbk, Chedd,
Coatv, Denes, Diack,
Dove, Ford, Hewsn,
Mtato, Ormon, Peele,
Pionr, PuhaN, Pukho,
Terra, TopTr, Wensl

ellipsoidalis (Northern Pin
Oak)
Apple, BlueM, Chedd,
Diack, Ormon, YakuN

faginea (Portugese Oak)
Apple, Diack, Ormon,
TopTr

garryana (Oregon Oak)
Peele

x hispanica (cerris x suber
hyb) now x lucombeana
Matwh

x hispanica Lucombeana
now x lucombeana William
Lucombe (Lucombe Oak)
PuhaN

ilex (Holm/Evergreen/Holly
Oak)
Apple, Coatv, Denes,
Dove, Ford, Hewsn,
Matwh, NZtr #, Ormon

imbricaria (Shingle Oak)
PuhaN

x ludoviciana
TopTr

mongolica (Mongolian Oak
Apple, Ormon, PuhaN

palustris (Pin/Spanish Oak)
Apple, Burbk, Chedd,
Coatv, Denes, Diack,
Dove, EasyB, Ford,
Hewsn, Morgn, Mtato,
NZtr #, Peele, Pionr,
PuhaN, Pukho, SouWo,
TopTr, Wensl, YakuN

petraea (Sessile/Durmast Oak)
NZtr #

petraea Mespilifolia
Apple

prinus (Chestnut Oak)
Chedd, TopTr

pubescens var palensis (Pyrenean Oak)
Apple

robur (European, English Oak)
Apple, Burbk, Chedd,
Denes, Diack, Dove,
EasyB, Ford, Hewsn,
Mtato, NZtr #, Ormon,
Peele, Pionr, PuhaN,
Pukho, SouWo, Terra,
TopTr, Wensl

robur Cristata (Curly Leaf Oak)
Diack

robur fastigiata (Upright Oak)
Apple, Chedd, Denes,
Diack, Matai, PuhaN,
Pukho, Wensl

robur filicifolia syn.r.pectinata
TopTr

rubra (Red Oak)
Apple, Burbk, Chedd,
Coatv, Denes, Diack,
Dove, EasyB, Ford,
Hewsn, MJury, Mtato,
Ormon, Peele, Pionr,
PuhaN, Terra, Wensl

rubra Maxima
Denes, Pukho

suber (Cork Oak)
Chedd, Matwh, Morgn

variabilis (Chinese Cork Oak)
Chedd, Denes, PuhaN,
TopTr

Quintinia

acutifolia (Westland Quintinia)
Terra, Wahpa

serrata (Tawherowhero)
Burbk, Orati, Terra

Radermachera

frondosa
Reic #

sinica (Canton Lace, China Doll)
Burbk, Frans, Manna,
Reic #

Ranunculus

mixed
Kayd

aconitifolius
MaraN

acris Flore Pleno
BayBl

amphitrichus (Waioriki, Water Buttercup)
Diack, WaiMa

asiaticus Tecolote mixed
Altrf

cortusifolius
Parva

ficaria
Kerer, MaraN

ficaria albus
MaraN

ficaria aurantiaca
MaraN

ficaria Cupreus (Lesser Celandine)
CottP

ficaria EA Bowles
NewlR

ficaria Flore Pleno (Double Celandine)
CottP

ficaria Moonlight
CottP, Pgeon

gramineus
MaraN, NewlR, Parva

insignis
Vall #

lingua (Water Buttercup)
WaiMa

lyallii
Ashto

millefoliatus
NewlR

montanus
NewlR

Raoulia

australis
NewlR

hookeri
Orati, Seasd

hookeri var makara
CottP, Orati, Pgeon

tenuicaulis
Matai, NewlR, Orati

Rapanea

yunnanensis
Woodl

Raphanus

sativus Icicle (Radish)
MTig #

sativus Sparkler (Radish)
MTig #

Ratibida

columnifera (Mexican Hat)
KeriP, Pgeon

Rauvolfia

serpentina (Rauwolfia)
Sweet

Ravenala

madagascariensis (Travellers Palm)
Reic #

Ravenea

rivularis (Madagascar/Majestic Palm
PalmF, Reic #

Rehmannia

angulata   now elata
Hackf, Peak, Pgeon,
TopTr, Warwk

angulata Grace
JoyPl

elata was angulata (Chinese Foxglove)
BayBl, MaraN, Ormon,
Telfa, Trans

Reseda

alba (Wild Mignonette)
Dream, King #

lutea
Dream

luteola (Weld, Dyers Rocket)

Della, Orang, Sweet

odorata (Mignonette)

Della, KeriP, King #, MillH, Sweet, Trans, Vall #

Restio

tetraphyllus (Plume Rush)

Denes, Hains, KeriP, Telfa

Rhabdothamnus

solandri (Taurepo, NZ Gloxinia)

Gordn, Orati

Rhamnus

alaternus Argenteovariegata (Italian Buckthorn)

BlueM

californica (Cascara Bush, Coffee Berry)

Ormon

Rhaphithamnus

spinosus was cyanocarpus

Denes

Rhapis

excelsa (China/Lady Palm)

Caves, PalmF

Rheum

Ace of Hearts

Peak

australe was emodi (Himalayan Rhubarb, Red-veined Pie Plant)

MaraN, Marsh, TRidg, WaiMa

moorcroftianum (C&Mc813)

MaraN

palmatum (Ornamental Rhubarb) ;

CoFlo, Marsh, WilAq

palmatum var tangticum (Chinese/Turkish Rhubarb)

Sweet, WaiMa

palmatum var tanguticum Red Selection

TRidg

rhabarbarum (Rhubarb, common)

TreeC

rhaponticum

Marsh, TRidg

spiciforme (C&Mc418)

MaraN

tibeticum

MaraN

Rhodanthemum

gayanum was Chrysanth. mawii, Pyrethropsis

KeriP, Marsh, Oasis, Otepo, Seasd

hosmariense was Leucanthemum h.

BayBl, Oasis, Pgeon, Seasd

Rhodochiton

atrosanguineum was R.volubilis

Hackf, King #, MaraN, MillH, Reic #, Vall #

Rhododendron

varieties

Coatv, Kayd

Abigail Jury

MJury

Aladdin

Jordn

Albatross(Loderi x discolor)

Jordn

Alcesta

Brown

Alec Holmes

Jordn, Pukho, YakuN

Alice

Ashto, BlueM, Cross, Denes, Hewsn, Pukho, YakuN

Alison Johnstone

BlueM, Hewsn, Jordn, ZinoN

Allen's Surprise

Denes, Pukho, YakuN

Alpine Meadow

BlueM, Hewsn, Jordn, Taunt

Ambergris

Cross

Amity

Jordn

Amor

BlueM

Anah Krushke

BlueM, Mtato, Pukho, YakuN

Angelo

BlueM, Jordn, YakuN

Anna

BlueM, Jordn, MJury, YakuN

Anna Baldsiefen

BlueM, Jordn

Anna H Hall

YakuN

Anna Rose Whitney

Ashto, BlueM, Chedd, Cross, Denes, Hewsn, Mtato, Pukho, YakuN

Anne Teese

Woodl, YakuN

Anton Van Wheelie

BlueM

Anuschka

Cross

Apricot Fantasy

Pukho, Taunt, YakuN

Apricot Nectar

Denes, Mtato

Apricot Road

BlueM, Taunt

Apricot Sherbet

Jordn

April Glow

BlueM, Denes, YakuN

arboreum Alba

Jordn

arboreum Mt Victoria

Cross

arboreum Pink Perfection

YakuN

Arctic Tern

Jordn

argyrophyllum Chinese Silver

YakuN

Armatine

BlueM

Arthur Bedford

Ashto, BlueM, Hewsn, YakuN

Augfast

MJury

August Moon

BlueM, YakuN

augustinii
BlueM, Hewsn, MJury, ZinoN

augustinii Chasmanthum
Cross, YakuN

augustinii Glenfalloch
Cross, YakuN

augustinii Lem's Light Blue
YakuN

Augustinii Medlicott
BlueM, MJury, Woodl

augustinii Tower Court
Jordn

augustinii Wisley Seedling
BlueM

Aunt Martha
Cross, YakuN

auriculatum
Jordn

auritum
Hewsn

Autumn Gold
Ashto, BlueM, Cross, YakuN

Avalanche
BlueM, ZinoN

Award
Jordn, Pukho

Azurro
YakuN

Babylon
Jordn

Backer's Gold
BlueM

Baden Baden
BlueM, Hewsn, Mtato

Bambi
BlueM, Jordn

Bambino
Jordn

Barbara Jury
MJury, Woodl, YakuN

Barmstedt
Cross, Jordn

Baron Phillipe de Rothschild
BlueM

Bashful
BlueM, Hewsn

Beau Brummel
BlueM, Cross

Beauty Of Littleworth
BlueM, Hewsn, YakuN

Beefeater
Jordn

Belle Heller
BlueM, Cross, Hewsn, MJury

Bergie Larsen
YakuN

Bernard Shaw
BlueM

Bernice
Brown, MJury, Pukho, YakuN

Bernie Holland
Brown

Bernstein (Amber Stone)
Cross

Betsie Balcom
BlueM

Betty Wormald
BlueM, Hewsn

Beveley Tasker
BlueM, Jordn

Bibiani
Cross, Denes, Jordn, YakuN

Billy Budd
BlueM, Mtato

Black Magic
Cross, Denes, Jordn

Black Sport
BlueM, Cross, Jordn

Blancmange
Jordn, YakuN

Blaney's Blue
Cross

Blewbury
BlueM

Blue Bird
Hewsn, Jordn

Blue Boy
Cross, Taunt

Blue Danube
Cross

Blue Diamond
Ashto, BlueM, Cross, Denes, Hewsn, Jordn, Pukho, Woodl, YakuN, ZinoN

Blue Ensign
BlueM

Blue Gem
Cross

Blue Jay
BlueM, MJury, YakuN

Blue Lagoon
Cross

Blue Mist
Taunt, Wells, Woodl

Blue Pacific
BlueM, Cross, MJury

Blue Peter
BlueM, Brown, Cross, Denes, Jordn, Mtato

Blue Rhapsody
Cross

Blue River
BlueM, Brown, Cross, Pukho

Blue Tit
Cross, Jordn

Bluestone
YakuN

Blurettia
Cross

Bob Bovee x Red Cloud
Cross

Boddaertianum
Cross

Bonito
YakuN

Bonnie Doon
Chedd, Jordn, Mtato

Bow Bells
Cross

brachysiphon
YakuN

Bremen
BlueM

Brendon King
Cross

Bric-a-Brac
Hewsn

Brickdust
BlueM, YakuN

Brigadoon
Cross

Brigitte
Cross, YakuN

Brilliant
Jordn

Britannia
BlueM, YakuN

Brocade
YakuN

Broderie Anglais
Taunt

Bronze Wing
Jordn, YakuN

Broxon 7
Jordn

Bruce Brechtbill
Ashto, BlueM, Cross, Denes, Hewsn, Jordn, Mtato, Taunt, Woodl, YakuN

Bud Flanagan
BlueM, Cross, YakuN

bullatum
Jordn

Bullatum edgeworthii
Taunt

Bumble Bee
BlueM, Denes, Hewsn, Jordn, MJury, Pukho, YakuN

Burgandy
YakuN

burmanicum
Hewsn, Pukho

Burning Bush
BlueM

Butter Brickle
Denes, Jordn, YakuN

Butterfly Cream
Taunt

Buttermint
Ashto, BlueM, Cross, Jordn, MJury, Taunt

calastrotum Gigha
Hewsn

callimorphum
YakuN

calophytum
Caves

calostrotum
BlueM, Jordn, YakuN

calostrotum keleticum
YakuN

Calstocker
Jordn

Camembert
Taunt

Cameo Frost
Taunt

Cameo Pearl
Taunt

Camp Visey
Cross

campylogynum
Jordn

campylogynum Claret
BlueM, Jordn

campylogynum Pink
BlueM

campylogynum Yellow
BlueM, Jordn

Canadian Sunset
BlueM, Jordn, YakuN

Captain Jack
BlueM, Jordn, MJury, YakuN

Carex
Hewsn

Carita Reuthes Buff
YakuN

Carlene
Jordn

Carmen
Ashto, BlueM, YakuN

Caroline Allbrook
Jordn, MJury, Mtato

Caroline Grace
BlueM

Carousel
YakuN

Cary Ann
BlueM, Jordn, Mtato, YakuN

Castonets
Taunt

Centennial Celbration
Jordn

chameunum
Jordn, YakuN

Chapeau (Brittania x Purple Splendour)
Jordn

Chapmanii Wonder
BlueM, Hewsn, Mtato

Charisma
Brown, Woodl

Charles Lawson
BlueM

Charlotte De Rothschild
Jordn, YakuN

Cheer
BlueM, Mtato, YakuN

Cherry Custard
BlueM, Denes, Jordn, YakuN

Cherry Float
Jordn

Chevalier Felix de Sauvage
BlueM

Chiff Chaff
BlueM, Jordn

Chikor
BlueM, Hewsn, Jordn

Chionoides
BlueM, Mtato

Choremia
YakuN

Christmas Cheer
BlueM, Brown, Cross, Denes, Hewsn, Jordn, Mtato, Pukho, YakuN

Chrysomanicum
BlueM, Brown, Denes, Hewsn, Mtato, Pukho

ciliatum
MJury

ciliicalyx var Charisma
MJury, YakuN

Cilpinense
Hewsn, Mtato

Cincrass
Jordn

Circus
Cross

CIS.
BlueM, Jordn, MJury, Pukho

Clementine Le Maire
Jordn

Coconut Ice
MJury, Pukho, YakuN

Coker's Cream
Cross

College Pink
BlueM, Jordn, Mtato, YakuN

Colonel Coen
BlueM, Cross

concinnum var pseudoyanthinum
MJury, YakuN

Constance
YakuN

Copper Kettles
Cross

Coral Queen
BlueM, Cross, Jordn

Coral Velvet
BlueM, YakuN

Coralee
YakuN

Cornish Cross
BlueM, Jordn

Cornubia
Ashto, BlueM, Denes,
Mtato, Pukho, YakuN,
ZinoN

Coronation Day
Cross, Jordn, YakuN

Corry Koster
Jordn

COS.
Pukho

Cotton Candy
BlueM, Pukho, YakuN

Countess of Athlone
YakuN

Countess of Derby
BlueM

Countess of Haddington
Cross, Denes, Mtato,
Pukho, ZinoN

County Of York
BlueM, Jordn

Cowslip
BlueM, Cross

CP Raffill
YakuN

crassum
Cross

crassum (pink form)
YakuN

Crassum White
Woodl

Crater Lake
Ashto, BlueM, Denes,
Hewsn, YakuN

Cream Crest
BlueM, Hewsn, Jordn,
Mtato

Cream Glory
Cross

Creamy Chiffon
BlueM, Cross, Jordn,
Mtato, Pukho, YakuN

Cremastum Bodnant Red
BlueM

Crest
BlueM, Cross, Jordn

Crimson Pippin
Cross, Jordn, YakuN

Crossbill
Jordn

Crossroads
BlueM

cubitti
Hewsn, MJury

Cunningham's White
BlueM, Cross, Denes,
Hewsn, Mtato

Cupcake
Jordn, YakuN

Curlew
BlueM, Jordn

Cynthia
Hewsn

Dainty KB
BlueM

Dainty Lass
BlueM

Dainty Maiden
YakuN

Dairymaid
BlueM, Jordn, ZinoN

**dalhousiae x nuttallii x
lindleyi sdlg**
Cross

Dalkeith
BlueM, Hewsn, Jordn,
MJury

Dame Nellie Melba
BlueM, Denes, YakuN

Danella
Cross

Daphnoides
YakuN

davidsonianum Ruth Lyons
BlueM

Dawns Delight
BlueM

**Dayan (cinnabarinum
hybrid)**
Jordn

Debbie
BlueM

decorum
Jordn, Pukho

**delavayi v. albotom
(arboreum ssp. delavayi
v.a.)**
YakuN

Denali
YakuN

dendricola
Hewsn, Pukho

Denise
Mtato

desquamatum
MJury

Diane Titcomb
BlueM, Cross

dichroanthum
BlueM

Dido
BlueM, Jordn

discolor
Caves

Dixy Lee Ray
Cross

Doc
BlueM, Cross, Jordn,
MJury, Mtato, YakuN

Dopey
Ashto, BlueM, Cross,
Jordn

Dora Amateis
Ashto, BlueM, Cross,
Hewsn, Jordn, MJury,
YakuN

Dorinthia
BlueM

Dorothy Amateis
Cross

Double Date
BlueM, Jordn

Double Eagle
Taunt

Douglas R Stephens
Cross

Dr A. Block
YakuN

Dr Arnold W Entz
BlueM

Drum Major
YakuN

**drumonium now
telmateium**
Jordn

edgeworthii
BlueM, Jordn, YakuN

Edith Boulter
BlueM

Edwin O Weber
Cross, Jordn, YakuN

Eider
Jordn

El Camino
BlueM, Jordn, Mtato

Elaine Rowe
Jordn

Elegans
YakuN

Elizabeth
BlueM, ZinoN

Elizabeth Red Foliage
Cross

Elizabeth de Rothschild
YakuN

Elizabeth Hobbie
Ashto, BlueM, Hewsn, YakuN

Elizabeth Titcomb
BlueM, MJury, YakuN

elliotii
Denes, YakuN

Elsa Crisp
BlueM

Else Fry
BlueM, Cross, Denes, MJury

Emanuela
Cross

Enticement
Jordn, YakuN

Erebus
BlueM

Eric's Surprise
Cross

Eternity
Taunt

Ethel's Apricot
Cross

Etta Burrows
YakuN

Evening Glow
BlueM, Hewsn

Exbury Cornish Cross
Cross

Eyestopper
MJury

Fabia
YakuN

Fabia Romney Pottery
BlueM

Faggeters Favourite
BlueM, YakuN

Fairy Light
BlueM, Chedd

fastigiatum
BlueM, Jordn, Taunt, YakuN

Fastuosum Flore Pleno
Ashto, BlueM, Mtato, Pukho, YakuN

Fastuosum Plenum Flena
Hewsn

Fayetta
MJury

FC Puddle
BlueM

Felicity Fair
Cross, MJury, Pukho

fictolacteum
Jordn

Firedance
BlueM, Jordn

Fireman Jeff
BlueM, Mtato

fletcherianum
BlueM

Flirt
Cross, Jordn

Flora Markeeter
Jordn

Flora's Boy
Ashto, BlueM, Hewsn, Jordn, MJury, YakuN

Floral Dance
BlueM, Denes, Jordn, MJury

Floral Sun
MJury

Florence
BlueM

Forever Young
Taunt

formosum
Hewsn, YakuN

Formosum Early
Woodl

Formosum hybrid
Cross, Pukho

Fragrantem
Taunt

Fragrantissimum
Brown, Chedd, Hewsn, Mtato

Fragrantissimum Caerhays form
Woodl, YakuN

Fred Hamilton
Jordn, YakuN

Fred Robbins
Cross

Fred Rose
BlueM, Jordn

Freeman R Stevenson
BlueM

French Lady
YakuN

French Lady (Ex Lofthouse)
Cross, Jordn

Fresh Cream
Taunt

Frilled Petticoats
Jordn

Frontier
Jordn

Frosted Ice
Jordn

Furnivall's Daughter
BlueM, Cross, Denes, Jordn, MJury, YakuN

Fusilier
Cross

Gary Wally
Ashto

Georges Delight
Jordn

Gertrud Schale
BlueM

Ghenghis Khan
BlueM

Gibraltar
BlueM, Jordn

Gill's Crimson
YakuN

Ginger Rogers
Taunt

Ginny Gee
BlueM, Chedd, Cross, Denes, Hewsn, Jordn, Taunt, YakuN

glaucophyllum
BlueM

Glenfallock Blue
Pukho, Taunt

Glenfiddick
BlueM

Gloriana
BlueM

Goblin
BlueM

Goblin Orange
BlueM

Gold Finger
BlueM, Jordn, YakuN

Gold Mohur
BlueM

Goldbug
BlueM

Goldbukett
Cross

Golden Anniversary
Cross

Golden Belle
BlueM, Cross

Golden Cockerel
MJury, YakuN

Golden Dawn
Jordn

Golden Gate
Cross, YakuN

Golden Horn
YakuN

Golden Pheasant
BlueM

Golden Star
YakuN

Golden Torch
BlueM, Cross, Jordn, MJury, YakuN

Golden Witt
Cross, Jordn, YakuN

Goldsworth Crimson
BlueM

Goldsworth Red
ZinoN

Golfer
Pukho

Gomer Waterer
BlueM, YakuN

Good News
BlueM, YakuN

Goosander
BlueM

Gordon Valley Surprise
BlueM, MJury

Grace Seabrook
Ashto, BlueM, Cross, Jordn, MJury, YakuN

Graham
BlueM, Hewsn

Grand Marquis
Jordn

Grand Slam
Cross, Jordn, YakuN

Grande
Taunt

Great Scott
Denes, Jordn

Greer's Cream Delight
Cross

Grenadier
Hewsn

Grierpoint
Hewsn

griersonianum x yakushimanum
YakuN

griffithianum
Jordn

Grumpy
BlueM, Jordn

Gwen
BlueM

Gwen Grant
BlueM

Gwynneth Masters
MJury, YakuN

Hachmann's Brasilia
Cross

Hachmann's Constanze
Cross

Hachmann's Feuerschein (Firelight)
Cross

Hachmann's Rosarka
Cross, Jordn

haematodes
YakuN

Halfdan Lem
Ashto, BlueM, Denes, Jordn, MJury, YakuN

Hallelujah
BlueM, YakuN

hanceanum
Jordn

hanceanum nanum
BlueM, MJury

hanceanum Pink
BlueM

handcockii
Caves

Hanzel
Jordn

Hardijzer's Beauty
Cross

Harry Tagg
Denes, Hewsn, Mtato, Woodl, YakuN

Haru Ichiban
BlueM

Harvest Moon
BlueM, YakuN

Havelock
Hewsn

Hazel
BlueM

Hearts Delight
BlueM, Denes, Jordn, YakuN

Helen Dreucker
Jordn

Helen Webster
Jordn

Helene Schiffner
Cross, MJury, YakuN

High Society
MJury

hippophaeoides
BlueM, Hewsn, Jordn, YakuN

hirsutum double sp
Jordn

Ho Ho
YakuN

Hobbie X
BlueM

Holmslea Diamond
BlueM

Holy Moses
BlueM, Denes

Honeymoon
Ashto, BlueM, Cross, Jordn, Wells, Woodl

Hoppy
BlueM, Cross, Hewsn, Jordn, Mtato

Horizon Monarch
Pukho

Hotei
BlueM, Jordn

Humboldt Sunrise
Woodl

Hurricane
BlueM

Hussar
BlueM

Hydon Dawn
BlueM, Cross, Jordn, YakuN

Hydon Hunter
BlueM, Cross, Denes, Jordn, Mtato, YakuN

Hydon Magic
Denes

hyperythrum
YakuN

hyperythrum RV 9808
YakuN

Idealist
BlueM

Ilam Cerise
BlueM, Jordn

Ilam Cornubia
BlueM, Jordn

Ilam Cream
Cross

Ilam Cream Loderi
Jordn

Ilam Dark Red
YakuN

Ilam Fragrance
Brown

Ilam Pearl
YakuN

Ilam Red Glow
Cross

Ilam Violet
BlueM, ZinoN

Impeanum
BlueM

impeditum
BlueM, Denes

Impi
BlueM, Cross, Jordn

Ina Hair
Jordn, Pukho, YakuN

Inca Gold
Jordn

Indiana
BlueM

Inequale
Pukho, Woodl

Intrifast
Jordn

Irene Bain
BlueM, Jordn, YakuN

Irresistible Impulse
Cross, Jordn

irroratum
Caves, Jordn

irroratum Polka Dot
Jordn

Isaac Newton
BlueM

Isabel Pierce
BlueM

Ivan D Wood
BlueM, Pukho, YakuN

Ivanhoe
Cross

Ivery's Scarlet
YakuN

Jaded Lady
YakuN

Jalisco x Fawn
Jordn

James Burchett
BlueM, YakuN

Jan Bee
YakuN

Jan Dekens
BlueM, MJury

Jan Marchant
Woodl

Jane Rogers
Ashto, BlueM

Janet Blair
Ashto, BlueM

Jean
BlueM

Jean Marie de Montague
BlueM, Denes, Jordn, Mtato

Jeanne Church
Jordn, YakuN

Jedda
Taunt

Jennie Dosser
Cross

JG Millais
BlueM

Jibuti
BlueM

Jingle Bells
BlueM, Jordn, Mtato, YakuN

Jock Bonny Bells
BlueM, Hewsn

John Bull
Brown, Cross, Denes, Pukho, Woodl, YakuN

John Waterer
BlueM

Johnny Bender
BlueM, Cross, Jordn, YakuN

johnstoneanum
Hewsn, Mtato, Pukho, ZinoN

johnstoneanum Double
Jordn

johnstoneanum Double Diamond
BlueM, Cross

johnstoneanum Ken Burns
BlueM, Brown, Cross, Denes, Woodl, YakuN

Joy Jury
Jordn

JP Lade
Hewsn

Julia Tasker
Jordn

Jungfrau
BlueM, Jordn, MJury, YakuN

Jury # 910608 Crest hyb
YakuN

Jury # 910609 Decorum hyb
YakuN

Jury No 9
BlueM

Kaka
Cross, Denes, Mtato

Kalimna
Brown, Jordn, YakuN

Kalinka
Cross

Kaponga
Ashto, BlueM, Brown, Cross, Denes, Jordn, MJury, Mtato, Pukho, YakuN

Kapunatiki
BlueM

Karen Triplett
Jordn, Pukho, YakuN

Kathryn Fortesque
Jordn

Katie
MJury

Katrina
Jordn

Keay Slocock
YakuN

keiskei Yaku Fairy
MJury

keleticum see R.calostrotum keleticum
MJury, YakuN

Kevin
YakuN

Kew Pearl
BlueM

Kilimanjaro
Cross, MJury

273

Kim
Jordn

Kimbeth
Hewsn, Jordn

King Of Shrubs
Cross, Jordn

King Solomon
Cross

King's Buff
BlueM

Kings Milkmaid
Chedd, Cross, YakuN

Kings Mystery
YakuN

Kings Pink Glow
Ashto, BlueM

Kirsty Yates
YakuN

kiusianum
BlueM, YakuN

kiusianum Komo Kulsan
Jordn, YakuN

kiusianum White
Cross

Kiwi Magic
Jordn, Pukho

Kluis Sensation
BlueM

Koenig Carola
YakuN

Kokardia
Cross, Jordn, YakuN

Kotuku
Woodl

Kubla Khan
BlueM, Cross

kuisianum Album
BlueM

Kyla King
YakuN

Lady Bessborough Roberte
BlueM

Lady C. Mitford
Chedd

Lady Chamberlain Gleam
BlueM

Lady Chamberlain Salmon Trout
BlueM

Lady De Rothschild
Jordn

Lady Dorothy Ella
Jordn

Lady Hillington
BlueM

Lady of Spain
Cross

Lady Rosebury
Hewsn, ZinoN

Ladybird
BlueM

Lalique
BlueM, Jordn, Taunt, Woodl

Lamplighter
BlueM

Lascaux
BlueM

Late Love
Denes

Laurago
YakuN

Lavender Girl
BlueM, Jordn, YakuN

Leigton Tasker
Jordn

Lem's 121
Jordn

Lem's 49
Pukho

Lem's Cameo
BlueM, Cross, Jordn, Taunt, YakuN

Lem's Cameo x Tropicana
BlueM, Jordn, YakuN

Lem's Monarch
BlueM, Denes, Jordn, YakuN

Lem's Stormcloud
BlueM, Cross, Jordn, Taunt

Lemon Honey
Taunt

Lemon Ice
Cross, Pukho, YakuN

Lemon Lime
Taunt

Lemon Lodge
BlueM, Brown, Cross, Jordn, MJury, Pukho, Taunt, YakuN

Lemon Mist
BlueM, Chedd, YakuN

Leo
BlueM, Jordn, YakuN

Leonardslee Giles
Cross

leophyllum   (buxifolium)
BlueM

Letty Edwards
BlueM

Letty Edwards FCC
YakuN

Lila Pedigo
Jordn

Lily
Chedd

Lily No 7
Jordn

lindleyi
Cross, MJury

Lionel de Rothschild
ZinoN

Little Jack Horner
YakuN

Lodauric
Jordn

Loder's White
BlueM, Jordn

Loderi Fairyland
BlueM, Jordn, YakuN

Loderi Horsham
BlueM, YakuN

Loderi I M S
BlueM

Loderi Ilam Cream
BlueM

Loderi Irene Stead
Cross, Jordn, YakuN

Loderi Julie
BlueM

Loderi King George
BlueM, Jordn, YakuN

Loderi Patience
BlueM, Jordn

Loderi Pink Diamond
BlueM, Jordn, YakuN

Loderi Sir Edmund
BlueM, Jordn

Loderi Sir Joseph Hooker
BlueM, Jordn

Loderi The Dream
Jordn

Loderi Titan
Jordn

Loderi Venus
BlueM, Cross, Jordn, YakuN

Lodestar
Cross

Lollipop Time
BlueM

Lord Roberts
BlueM

Lori Eichelser
Jordn

Louis Pasteur
BlueM

Lucy Strike
BlueM

lutescens
Hewsn

Lydia
Cross, YakuN

macabeanum
BlueM, Hewsn, Jordn

macabeanum x Avalanche
Jordn

macebeanum Joybells
BlueM

Madah Jean
YakuN

maddenii
BlueM, Cross, Denes,
Hewsn, Pukho

maddenii L&S form
YakuN

maddenii var Virginalis
Brown, Cross, Denes,
Hewsn, Jordn, MJury,
Pukho

maddenii white
MJury, YakuN

Mai Tai
Jordn

**makinoi see
yakushimanum makinoi**
YakuN

Manda Sue
Cross

Mandalay
Ashto, BlueM

Mandarin
YakuN

**Marchioness of
Landsdowne**
BlueM, Hewsn

Marinus Koster
YakuN

Marion Street
Jordn, YakuN

Markeeta's Flame
Cross

Markeeta's Prize
BlueM, Jordn, MJury,
YakuN

Marquis of Lothian
BlueM

Mars
BlueM

Martha Wright
Cross

Mary Belle
YakuN

Mary Fleming
BlueM, YakuN

Mary Tasker
Jordn

Maryke
Jordn

Matador
Hewsn

Maurice Skipworth
Denes, YakuN

Mayday
BlueM

Medusa
ZinoN

megeratum
Jordn

Meryke
BlueM

Mi Amor
Cross, MJury

Michael Waterer
BlueM

Michael's Pride
BlueM, Brown, Cross,
Denes, MJury, Pukho

**microleucum now
orthocladum m.**
BlueM

microleucum alba
Jordn

microleucum Lilac
BlueM

Midnight
Jordn, YakuN

Midsummer
YakuN

Milkmaid
BlueM, Pukho

Mission Bells
BlueM, YakuN

Misty Moonlight
Jordn

Moerheim
BlueM, YakuN

Mollie Coker
BlueM

Mollies Gift
Woodl

Molly Ann
YakuN

Molly Miller
BlueM, Jordn

**Montroseanum
(Mollyanum)**
Taunt

Moon Orchid
Brown, MJury, Taunt,
YakuN

Moonstone
BlueM

Moonwax
Jordn

Morgenrot (Morning Red)
Cross, Jordn, YakuN

Morning Cloud
BlueM, Jordn, Mtato,
YakuN

Morning Magic
BlueM

Morning Song
BlueM

Moth
BlueM

Mother Bear
YakuN

Mother of Pearl
BlueM

Motherlode
Jordn

Mount Everest
BlueM, Cross, Denes,
Jordn, MJury, Mtato,
Pukho

moupinense pink form
YakuN

Mrs AT de la Mare
BlueM, MJury

Mrs Bernice Baker
Jordn

Mrs Betty Robertson
BlueM, Jordn, YakuN

Mrs CB van Ness
BlueM

Mrs CE Pearson
YakuN

Mrs Davies Evans
BlueM

Mrs George Huthnance
Cross, Jordn

Mrs GW Leak
Ashto, BlueM, Denes,
Hewsn, Jordn, Pukho

Mrs John Millais
Cross, Jordn

Mrs JP Lade
Woodl

Mrs Lamont Copeland
Jordn

Mrs Mary Ashley
BlueM, YakuN

Mrs PD Williams
Jordn

Mrs Tom Lowinsky
BlueM, Jordn

Mundai
Jordn

My Lady
Cross

Mystique
Taunt

Nancy Borthwick
BlueM, Jordn

Nancy Evans
BlueM, Jordn, MJury

Naomi Ann
BlueM

Naomi Exbury
_ Jordn

Naomi G8
BlueM

Naomi Honey
BlueM

Naomi Nautilus
BlueM, Jordn

Naomi Stella Maris
BlueM

Nestucca
Jordn

New Moon
Denes, Pukho, YakuN

Nicholas
YakuN

Norrie King
Mtato, YakuN

Northern Lights
Jordn

Noyo Brave
Jordn, YakuN

Noyo Chief
BlueM, Jordn, Mtato,
Pukho

nuttallii
Cross, Denes, Woodl

nuttallii x lindleyi Steads Best
MJury, YakuN

O'Canada
Jordn

Odee Wright
Ashto, BlueM, Jordn

Oklahoma
Cross

Old Copper
BlueM, Hewsn, Jordn,
Mtato, Pukho

Old Port
Cross, Jordn

oldhamii
Hewsn

Olin O Dobbs
Ashto, BlueM, Jordn,
MJury, Woodl, YakuN

Olive
BlueM

Olympic Knight
YakuN

Olympic Lady
BlueM

One Thousand Butterflies
Denes, Jordn, Taunt,
Woodl

Ooh Gina
Ashto, Denes, Jordn,
YakuN

Ooh La La
Cross

Ooh Too
Jordn

Opal Dawn
Pukho

Opal Fawcett
BlueM

Oratorium
Cross

Orchard Gold
BlueM

Orchard Road
BlueM

oreotrephes
BlueM, Hewsn

orthocladum microleucum alba
Jordn

Ostbo's Low Yellow
BlueM, Jordn, MJury,
Mtato, YakuN

Ostbo's Red Elizabeth
Ashto, BlueM

Oudijkes Sensation
Mtato

pachypodum
Caves

pachysanthum
Cross, Jordn

Pacific Queen
BlueM

Painted Star
YakuN

Paprika Spiced
Cross, Jordn, Taunt,
Woodl, YakuN

Parisienne
Brown, Hewsn, Mtato,
YakuN

Party Dress
Jordn

Pastel Pearl
Denes, Hewsn

Patty Bee
BlueM, Cross, Jordn,
MJury, Taunt, YakuN

Pawhuska
BlueM, Cross, YakuN

Pazzazz
Taunt

Peach Perfection
Taunt

Peggy Yates
BlueM

Pelican
Taunt

pemakoense
BlueM

pendulum
Titok

Percy Wiseman
Ashto, BlueM, Brown,
Cross, Denes, Jordn,
MJury, Mtato, Pukho,
Taunt, Woodl, YakuN

periclymenoides
YakuN

Persian Lady
BlueM, Pukho

Persimmon Golden Horn
BlueM

Peter Koster
BlueM

Petticoat Lane
Taunt

Phalarope
Hewsn

Phyllis Korn
Jordn

Picotee
Jordn, YakuN

Pineapple Delight
Jordn

pingianum
Caves

Pink Cherub
BlueM, Jordn, YakuN

Pink Cushion
Denes, Jordn, YakuN

Pink Drift
BlueM

Pink Pearl
BlueM, Brown, Chedd,
Denes, Mtato, Pukho,
Woodl, YakuN

Pink Porcelain
Jordn

Pink Sherbert
YakuN

Pink Twins
BlueM, Mtato, YakuN

Pink Walloper
BlueM, MJury

Pirouette
Jordn

PJM Regal
YakuN

Platinum Pearl
Mtato

Point Defiance
BlueM

Polar Bear
Denes, Jordn, Pukho,
Taunt

Polaris
Jordn

polyandrum cream form
Brown, MJury, Pukho,
Woodl

polycladum
Hewsn

ponticum
BlueM

ponticum Silver Edge
Hewsn, YakuN

Pony Tail
Jordn, YakuN

Popeye
Cross

Posy
BlueM

Prelude
BlueM

President Roosevelt (v)
BlueM, Brown, Cross,
Denes, Mtato, YakuN

Preston Rose
BlueM

Pretty Jessica
Taunt

Princess Alice
BlueM, Brown, Cross,
Denes, Jordn, Mtato,
Pukho, YakuN

Prue White
Woodl

pseudochrysanthum
Jordn

**pseudochrysanthum
Komokulshan form**
Pukho

**pseudochrysanthum
Taiwan form**
Cross

Ptarmigan
BlueM, Cross

pubescens
Hewsn

Puget Sound
BlueM, Jordn, MJury,
Pukho, YakuN

Purple Beauty
Cross

Purple Gem
Hewsn, Mtato

Purple Heart
YakuN

Purple Lace
BlueM, Cross, Jordn

Purple Splendour
BlueM, Chedd, Cross,
Jordn, Mtato

Quaver
Hewsn

Queen Elizabeth
Jordn

Queen Souriya
Jordn

racemosum
BlueM

racemosum Rock Rose
MJury, YakuN

Rachael
Cross

Racil
Hewsn

radicans
MJury

Radium
BlueM

Rainbow
BlueM, Hewsn, YakuN

Ramapo
Cross, Jordn

recurvoides
Cross

Red Cap Townshill
BlueM

Red Cloud
Jordn

Red Eye
Cross, Mtato

Red Glow
Jordn

Red Head
BlueM, Jordn

Red Imp
Hewsn, Jordn, YakuN

Red King
BlueM

Red Leaf Elizabeth
Jordn

Red Olympia
BlueM, Jordn, MJury,
Woodl, YakuN

Red Velvet
BlueM, Hewsn, YakuN

Red Walloper
BlueM, YakuN

Red Wonder
YakuN

Regal Lace
Taunt

Reina
Jordn, YakuN

Renoir
BlueM, Cross, Jordn,
YakuN

reticulatum
YakuN

reticulatum Nora
YakuN

Reve Rose
BlueM, Cross

Revlon
BlueM, Jordn

Rigidum
Taunt, YakuN

Ring of Fire
Ashto, BlueM, Cross, Jordn, Mtato, Taunt, YakuN

Riplet
Jordn

Rising Sun
Taunt

Rita
Woodl

Robert Balch
BlueM

Robinette
YakuN

Romany Chai
Brown

Ron Coker
Taunt

Rose Elf
BlueM, Hewsn, Taunt

Rosenkavalier
BlueM

Roseum Elegans
Hewsn

roxieanum
Jordn

Royal Pink
BlueM, Hewsn

Roza Stevenson
Jordn

Rubicon
BlueM, Brown, Cross, Denes, Jordn, MJury, Mtato, Pukho, Woodl, YakuN

Rubina
BlueM

Ruby Bowman
BlueM, Chedd, Jordn, Woodl

Ruby Hart
BlueM, Cross, Jordn, MJury, YakuN

Rudolph's Orange
YakuN

rupicola
Hewsn

rupicola Jack Drake
BlueM

russatum KB
BlueM, Hewsn

russatum Roseum (Rosebird)
BlueM, Hewsn, Jordn

RW Rye
YakuN

Saffron Queen
BlueM, Chedd, Denes, Hewsn, MJury, Mtato

Sammetglut (Velvet Glow)
Cross

Sapphire
BlueM, Cross

Sappho
BlueM, Cross, Denes, Jordn

sargentianum Maricee
BlueM

Sarita Loder
BlueM

Sarled
BlueM, Jordn

Satin Cloud
Woodl

Sauve
BlueM

Scarlet King
BlueM

Scarlet Wonder
BlueM, Cross, Hewsn, Jordn, MJury

schippenbachii
Caves

Schneewolke (Snowcloud)
Cross

Scintillation
BlueM, Jordn

Sea-Tac
YakuN

Seattle Gold
BlueM

Senora Meldon
Hewsn, Pukho, YakuN

Senorita Chere
Jordn, YakuN

September Snow
BlueM, Brown, Chedd, Hewsn, Wells, Woodl

Seta
BlueM, Cross, Denes, Hewsn, Jordn, Mtato, ZinoN

Seven Stars
BlueM, Jordn

Shamrock
Ashto, BlueM, Denes, Hewsn, YakuN

Shooting Star
Hewsn

Shrimp Girl
Jordn

Sierra Sunset
YakuN

Silberwolke (Silver Cloud)
Cross

Silent Shadows
Denes, MJury

Silver Edge (ponticum SS)
BlueM, Mtato

Silver Sixpence
YakuN

Simona
Cross

sino nuttallii -pink
MJury

sino nuttallii x nuttallii
MJury

sino-nuttalii
YakuN

sinogrande
YakuN

Sir Charles Lemon
BlueM, Jordn

Sir Frederick Shifner
BlueM

Sir Robert Peel
Brown, Denes, Pukho

Siren
BlueM

Sleepy
BlueM, Brown, Cross

Smarty Pants
Taunt

Smoked Salmon
Taunt

Smokey #9
Cross

Sneezy
Jordn, YakuN

Snipe
BlueM, Hewsn

Snow Crown
Taunt

Snow Lady
BlueM, Brown, Cross,
Hewsn, Mtato, Pukho,
YakuN

Snow Queen
MJury

So Sweet
Jordn

Sonatina
Cross

Songbird
Cross, Hewsn

Souvenir of WC Slocock
BlueM

Spiced Honey
Taunt, Woodl

spiciferum
BlueM, Hewsn, MJury,
YakuN

spiciferum sp
Jordn

Spicil
Brown, Jordn, YakuN

spinuliferum
BlueM, YakuN

Spring Dance
Cross, Hewsn, Pukho

Spring Girl
Taunt

Spring Magic
MJury

St Breward
BlueM, Hewsn, Woodl

St Tudy
Cross

Star Ship One
YakuN

Stead's Best Seedlings
BlueM

Stephanie
Cross

Stoneycroft (macabeanum hybrid)
Jordn

Strawberry Float
YakuN

Streatley
Cross

Suave
Hewsn, Jordn

Success
BlueM

Sugar Pink
BlueM, Jordn, YakuN

Summer Cloud
BlueM, Taunt

Sunday Gloves
Taunt

Sunrise Serenade
Jordn

Sunset Gold
Jordn

Sunset Queen
Pukho

Sunspray
Jordn

Sunup-Sundown
BlueM, Cross, Jordn,
Woodl

Superman
Jordn, Taunt

Surrey Heath
BlueM, Denes, Jordn,
Mtato, Pukho, YakuN

Susan
BlueM, Cross, Hewsn,
Jordn, YakuN

Swamp Beauty
BlueM, Jordn, YakuN

Sweet Sue
YakuN

Taggianum
Pukho

Tally Ho
YakuN

Tanyosho
Jordn, YakuN

taroense
YakuN

Tatjana
Cross

Taunton Ruffles
Taunt

Taunton Sunrise
Taunt

Taurus
BlueM, Jordn, Mtato,
Pukho, Woodl, YakuN

Ted's Orchid Sunset
BlueM, Denes

telmateium was drumonium
Jordn

Tensing
BlueM

The General
Cross

The President
Mtato

Thor
BlueM

Tidbit
BlueM

Tiffany
Hewsn, MJury

Titian Beauty
BlueM, Jordn

Too Bee
Jordn, YakuN

Top Banana
BlueM, Jordn, MJury

Topswort Pearl
MJury

Tortoiseshell Wonder
Cross

Touchstone
Jordn

Trail Blazer
Taunt

Treasure
BlueM

Tressa McMurry
YakuN

Trewithen Orange
BlueM, Jordn

trichostomum sp pink
Jordn

trichostomum sp white
Jordn

Trilby
YakuN

Trude Webster
BlueM, Brown, Denes,
Jordn, MJury, Mtato,
Pukho, YakuN

Tupare
Cross

Tyermannii
Brown, Jordn

Unique
BlueM, Brown, Cross,
Denes, Jordn, Mtato,
Pukho, YakuN, ZinoN

Unknown Warrior
BlueM, Cross

Ursula Sienes
BlueM

Valaspis
Hewsn
Valley Sunrise
Jordn
Van Dec
BlueM, YakuN
Van Nes Sensation
BlueM, Brown, Denes,
Jordn, Mtato, Pukho
Vanessa
BlueM, Hewsn
Vanessa Pastel
BlueM, Jordn
veitchianum
MJury
Venator hybrid
Hewsn
Vibrant Violet
Jordn, YakuN
Vicki Reine
Cross
Victorian Ruffles
Taunt
Victorianum
MJury
Viennese Waltz
Cross
vilmorinianum
YakuN
virgatum
Hewsn
Virginia Richards
BlueM, Brown, Hewsn,
Jordn, MJury, Mtato,
Pukho, YakuN
Virginia Teedham
Cross
Vivian Ward
BlueM
Vulcan
BlueM
Vulcans Flame
Chedd, Denes, Jordn,
Mtato
W. F. H.
YakuN
Walloper
BlueM
wardii BB pink
BlueM, Hewsn
wardii Meadow Pond
BlueM
Warlock
YakuN

Wee Bee
Jordn, YakuN
Wee Willie Winkie
YakuN
Werei
YakuN
weyrichii
YakuN
Whispering Rose
BlueM, Jordn
White Doves
Brown, Denes, MJury,
Taunt
White Gold
BlueM, Cross, MJury,
YakuN
White Ice
Jordn
White Linen
Taunt
White Pearl
BlueM, Brown, Cross,
Denes, Hewsn, Jordn,
Mtato
White Petticoats
Taunt
White Sails
BlueM, Jordn
Whitney Orange
Cross, Jordn, YakuN
Whitney's Late Orange
BlueM, YakuN
Whitney's Purple
BlueM
Wild Affair
Cross, Jordn
Wilgens Ruby
YakuN
William Downing
BlueM, YakuN
William King
YakuN
williamsianum Album
Titok
Winsome
BlueM, Brown, Cross,
Hewsn, MJury, Mtato,
Pukho, YakuN
Wissahickon
YakuN
Witchery
Cross
Woody Peach
YakuN

Yak Dainty Lass
Jordn
Yak Elliotii
BlueM
Yak No 6
Jordn
Yak Truly Fair
Jordn
Yak White Wedding
Jordn
Yak x Britannia
Jordn
Yak x Crest x Prelude
Jordn
Yak Yellow Hybrid
Jordn
Yakday
BlueM
Yakday x Elizabeth
BlueM
Yaku Angel
Jordn, YakuN
Yaku Fairy
BlueM
Yaku Incense
YakuN
Yaku Prince
YakuN
Yaku Princess
YakuN
Yaku Sunrise
Pukho, YakuN
yakushimanum
Cross
yakushimanum College Form
BlueM, Jordn, YakuN
yakushimanum Exbury
YakuN
yakushimanum F.C.C.
Jordn, MJury, Taunt,
ZinoN
yakushimanum Ken Janeck
Cross, Jordn, YakuN
yakushimanum Kochiro Wada
BlueM, YakuN
yakushimanum makinoi
YakuN
yakushimanum x bureaui
YakuN

yakushimanum x Dido
'Yates Second Best'
>YakuN

yakushimanum x elliotii
>YakuN

yakushimanum x Ilam
Orange
>YakuN

yakushimanum x Jean
Marie de Montagne
>Cross

yakushimanum x Jock
'Yock'
>YakuN

yakushimanum x Mayday
>MJury

yakushimanum x Noyo
Chief
>Cross

Yellow Creek x Jalisco
>Jordn

Yellow Hammer
>BlueM, Hewsn

Yellow Moon
>BlueM, Jordn

Yellow Petticoats
>BlueM, Cross, Jordn,
>Taunt, YakuN

Yellow Rolls Royce
>Jordn

yunnanense
>BlueM, YakuN

Yvonne Opaline
>Jordn

Yvonne Scott
>MJury

zaloucum TH834
>Caves

Rhododendron Azale

mollis seedlings
>Chedd

varieties decid. unnamed
>BlueM

Alaska
>Denes

Almond Icing
>Denes, MJury

Anthony Koster
>BlueM

Apple Blossom
>Denes, MJury

Ballerina
>BlueM

Barbecue
>Cross

Ben Morrison
>Cross

Berry Rose
>BlueM, Jordn

Betty Ann Voss
>Cross

Blaaws Pink
>Cross

Blue Danube
>Cross

Brides Bouquet
>Cross, Denes

Bullfinch
>BlueM

Butterfly
>Denes

Carmen
>BlueM

Cecile
>BlueM, Cross, MJury

Charley
>Wells

Chelsea Reach
>Denes, Pukho

Cherry Blossom
>Denes

Chiara
>Cross

Chinzan
>Cross

Christina
>Cross

Clarissa
>Cross

Cliff's Choice
>Denes

Cocade
>Denes

Cockade
>Cross

Cockatoo
>BlueM, Jordn

Collin Kendrick
>BlueM

Comte de Keretone
>Denes

Copper Frills
>Denes

Cream Bun
>Denes, MJury, Pukho

Creamy Yellow
>BlueM

Crimson Delight
>Cross

Cross Hills #16
>Cross

Crown Supreme
>Cross

Dancer
>Cross

Daphne
>Denes

De Waele's Favourite
>Cross

Debonaire
>Cross

Deep Gold
>Jordn

delicatissimum
>BlueM

Delicious
>Cross

Deutsche Perle
>Denes

Dorothy Corston
>BlueM, Jordn

Double Beauty
>Cross

Double Damask
>BlueM

Dr Glaser
>Denes

Dragoon
>Pukho

Dreadnought
>Cross

Dream Clouds
>Denes

Eikan
>Cross

Ellie Harris
>Cross

Else Kaegar
>Chedd, Denes

Elsie Lee
>Cross, Denes

Eureka
>Denes

Exquisitum
>BlueM

Fascination
>Cross

Fielders White
Cross, Denes

Florida
Cross

Forest Fire
MJury

Frosted Orange
Cross

Fruit Salad
MJury

Gardenia Supreme
Denes

Gay Paree
Cross, Denes

Georgia Grant
Cross

Ghent Cream
Cross

Ghent Yellow
Cross

Giant Orange
Cross

Girard's Crimson
Cross

Glacier
Cross

Glow
Cross

Goyet
Cross

Great Expectations
Cross

Greenwood Orange
Cross

Gumpo Pink
Denes

Gumpo Salmon
Cross

Gumpo White
Cross, Denes

Happy Days
Cross, Denes

Hardy Gardenia
Cross

Harwell
BlueM, Jordn

Homebush
BlueM, Denes, Jordn

Ilam Carmen
Cross, Denes

Ilam Hybrids
BlueM

Ilam Louie Williams
Denes, Pukho

Ilam Martie
Denes

Ilam Melford Flame
Cross

Ilam Melford Lemon
Denes

Ilam Ming
Cross, Denes, Pukho

Ilam Mountain Mist
Denes

Ilam Persian Rose
Denes

Ilam Pink Frills
Denes

Ilam Tangerine Pom Pom
Pukho

Ilam Yellow Ball
Pukho

Ilam Yellow Beauty
Cross

Ilam Yellow Giant
Cross

Impala
BlueM, Jordn

Issho-No-Haru
Cross

Ivan Anderson
Denes

James Belton
Denes

Jeanne Weeks
Cross

Joan Garrett
Cross

Johanna
Cross

Kathleen
BlueM

Kathy
Cross

Kirin
Chedd, Denes

Klondyke
Pukho

Lapwing
BlueM, Jordn

Lemonade
Pukho

Little Beauty
Cross

Little Girl
Wells

Lorna
Cross

Lucie
Denes

Mardi Gras
Cross

Marian Lee
Denes

Melford Flame
BlueM, Jordn, Woodl

Michael Hill
YakuN

Midas Touch
Jordn, Woodl

Mimosa
MJury, Pukho

Mollie
BlueM, Jordn

Mountain Mist
Jordn

Mrs Alfred Sanders
Cross

Mrs Kint
Denes

Mystique
Denes

Nancy of Robin Hill
Cross

Niagara
YakuN

occidentale Delicatissima
Cross, Denes, Pukho

occidentale Stagecoach
Cross

occidentalis Paramount
Denes

Osawa
Denes

Pacific Twilight
Denes

Paradise Coconut Ice
Kayd, Wells

Paradise Elfin
Kayd, Wells

Paradise Jennifer Anne
Kayd

Paradise Pixie
Kayd

Paradise Romance
Wells

Paramount
BlueM, Jordn

Pavlova
BlueM

Pax
Denes, Wells

Peach Kirin
Denes, Wells

Peaches & Cream
Denes

Pearl Bradford Sport
Brown, YakuN

Persian Rose
Pukho

Phil Schaeme
Cross

Pink Cloud
Cross

Pink Ice
Denes

Pink Thrills
BlueM

Princess Juliana
Cross

Princess Sonya
Denes

Purple Splendour
Cross

Raspberry Aid
BlueM

Raspberry Ripples
Pukho

Red Fountain
Cross

Red Light
Denes

Red Wings
Cross

Ripples
Cross

Rise and Shine
Taunt

Road Runner
Denes

Rosella
BlueM

Royal Robe
Cross

Sadie Kirk
Denes

Saint James
Cross

Salmonea
Denes

Scarlet Prince
Chedd, Denes

schlippenbachii
AynDa

Sherwood Red
Denes

Silver Anniversary
Denes, Wells

Silver Dollar
Cross

Silver Glow
Cross

Snow
Denes

Southern Aurora
Denes

Star Trek
Cross

Starburst
Denes

Strawberry Ice
BlueM

Sunburst
Denes

Sunray
BlueM

Sweet Surprise
Taunt

Taunton Apricot
Taunt

Taunton Blush
Taunt

Taunton Colour Glory
Taunt

Taunton Glow
Taunt

Taunton Ice
Taunt

Taunton Lace
Taunt

Taunton Pearl
Taunt

Tender Heart
Cross

The Teacher
Denes

Tico Tico
Denes

Val's choice
MJury

Vespers
Cross

Vibrant
Denes

Violacea multiflora
Chedd, Cross, Denes, Wells

Waeles Beauty
Denes

Waeles Elegance
Denes

Waeles Favourite
Denes

Wards Ruby
Chedd, Denes

White Moon
YakuN

Wryneck
BlueM, Jordn, Woodl

Rhododendron vireya

Apricot Charm
Brown

Bellendon Coral
Brown

Birat Red
Brown

Brightly
Brown

Buttermaid
Brown, Denes, MJury

Cameo Spice
Brown, Woodl

Candy
Kayd

Carillon Bells
Brown, JoyPl

carringtoniae
Brown

Cherry Pie
Brown, Denes, MJury, Woodl

Christianae Hybrid
Brown

christii
MJury

christii small-lvd form
MJury

commonae coral pink
Brown

commonae red
Brown

Coral Chance
Brown, Woodl

Coral Fare
  Brown
crassifolium
  MJury
Cristo Rey
  Brown, Woodl
Cyprian
  Brown, MJury
Dawn Chorus
  Brown
Felicitas
  MJury
Flamenco Dancer
  Brown
Gilded Sunrise
  Brown, Kayd, MJury
Golden Charm
  Brown, JoyPl, Kayd,
  MJury, Woodl, YakuN
goodenoughii
  MJury
Great Scentsation
  JoyPl, Woodl
Haloed Gold
  Brown
hellwigii
  Brown, Woodl
Hot Gossip
  Brown, MJury, Woodl
Hot Tropic x saxifragoides
  Brown
Hugh Redgrove
  Brown, Woodl
**jasminiflorùm var
punctatum**
  MJury
Java Light
  Brown, MJury
javanicum
  Brown
Kisses
  MJury
konorii
  MJury
Lemon Minuet
  MJury
leptanthum
  MJury
Lipstick
  MJury
Littlest Angel
  Brown, JoyPl, Kayd,
  MJury

lochae
  Brown
lochae x javanicum
  Brown
lochiae
  MJury
loranthiflorum
  MJury
Lulu
  Brown, MJury, Woodl
Luraluensis
  MJury
macgregoriae orange
  Brown
macgregoriae yellow
  Brown
Ne-Plus-Ultra
  Brown, Woodl
Nuigini Firebird
  Brown
Orange Maid
  MJury
Pendance
  Woodl
Pindi Pearl
  Brown
Pink Delight
  Brown, Woodl
pneumanathum
  MJury
polyanthemum
  MJury
Popcorn
  Brown, MJury
pratervissum
  Brown
Queen Of Diamonds
  MJury
Red Rover
  Brown, MJury
Rob's Favourite
  Brown, Woodl
robinsonii
  MJury
Rosy Chimes
  Brown, MJury
Salmon Star
  Brown
Satans Gift
  Brown, Denes, MJury
Saxon Blush
  JoyPl, Woodl

Saxon Glow
  JoyPl
Scarlet Beauty
  Brown
Silken Shimmer
  Brown, MJury
Silver Thimbles
  Brown, MJury
Simbu Sunset
  Brown, Denes, MJury
**Solar Flare (Konori x Dr
Sleumer) x Iochae**
  Brown
Souv de J H Mangles
  Brown
St Valentine
  Brown, MJury
Star Posy
  Brown
stenophyllum
  MJury
stevensianum hybrid
  Brown
suaveolens
  MJury
sumatranum
  Brown
Sunny
  Brown
Sunny Splendour
  Brown
Sweet Wendy
  Woodl
Tiffany Rose
  Brown
Tom Thumb
  Brown, JoyPl
Tropic Glow
  Brown
Tropic Glow x saxifrgoides
  MJury
Tropic Tango
  Brown, Woodl
tuba
  Brown, MJury, Woodl

Rhodohypoxis

Albrighton
  BayBl, CottP, DaffA,
  MJury, Parva
baurii
  Ashto, BayBl, CottP,
  Pgeon, TRidg

baurii bright pink
   TRidg

baurii deep rose
   MaraN

baurii pale pink
   MaraN, NewlR, TRidg

baurii Red
   BayBl

baurii very lge pale pink
   NewlR

baurii white
   NewlR, TRidg

Bright Eyes
   CottP

Dawn
   BayBl, Haslf, Parva

Fred Broome
   BayBl, CottP, DaffA, Hackf, Parva

Garnett
   BayBl

Great Scott
   BayBl, NewlR

Knockdolian
   DaffA

Knockdolian Red
   BayBl, CottP

Margaret Rose
   BayBl

Morning Star
   Parva

Picta
   BayBl, CottP, Pgeon

platypetala
   CottP, DaffA

Ruth
   BayBl, CottP, DaffA, MJury, NewlR

Stella
   Ashto, Parva

Susan
   MJury

Rhodophiala

bifida
   DaffA

bifida red form
   MJury

Rhodotypos

scandens was kerrioides
   Denes

Rhoeo

discolor now Tradescantia (Moses in the Cradle)
   LakeN

discolor dwarf form now Tradescantia
   LakeN

Rhopalostylis

baueri (Norfolk Is Nikau)
   Coatv, Lsendt, PalmF

sapida (Nikau)
   Chedd, Coatv, Gordn, Lsendt, Mtato, NZtr #, Orati, PalmF, Reic #, Terra, TRidg, Wahpa

sapida Chatham Is
   Lsendt, Orati

sapida Gt Barrier
   Orati

Rhus

glabra Laciniata
   Caves

potaninii
   Apple

succedeana (Sumach, Wax Tree)
   Burbk, Chedd, Frans, PuhaN, Reic #

typhina Laciniata
   Caves

Ribes

nigrum (Black Currant)
   Chedd, Sweet

nigrum Ben Rua
   TreeC

nigrum Magnus
   Harri, Pionr, TreeC

odoratum (Clove/Buffalo Currant)
   Denes, TopTr

rubrum (Red Currant)
   TreeC

rubrum Amgot
   Harri, Pionr

rubrum La Versailles
   TreeC

rubrum White Currant
   Chedd, TreeC

sanguineum (Pink Flowering Currant)
   Butlr, Diack, Dove, TopTr

sanguineum King Edward VII
   Denes, Pukho

uva-crispa (Gooseberry)
   Mills, Sweet

uva-crispa varieties
   TreeC

uva-crispa Invicta
   Chedd, Denes, Harri, TopTr, TreeC

Worcester Berry (black curr x Gooseberry)
   TreeC

Ripogonum

scandens (Supplejack)
   NZtr #, Orati

Robinia

x ambigua (Pink Robinia)
   Chedd, Peele

x ambigua decaisneana (Pink Wisteria Tree)
   Burbk, Denes, Dove, Mtato, Pukho, TopTr

pseudoacacia (Black Locust, Thorny/False Acacia)
   Apple, Chedd, Dove, McKe, NZtr #, Peele, Pionr, PuhaN

pseudoacacia Bessoniana
   Mtato, Peele, TopTr

pseudoacacia Casque Rouge now x margaretta C.R.
   Burbk, Chedd, Coatv, Denes, Dove, Mtato, Peele, TopTr

pseudoacacia Frisia
   Burbk, Chedd, Coatv, Denes, Dove, Hewsn, Mtato, Peele, Pionr, Pukho, TopTr

pseudoacacia Inermis syn umbraculifera (MopTop)
   Dove

pseudoacacia Lace Lady
   Denes, Pukho

pseudoacacia Nyirsezi
   Dove

pseudoacacia Rozynskyana
   Coatv, Denes, Mtato, Peele, TopTr

pseudoacacia Shipmast
   Chedd

pseudoacacia Ulloy

Dove

pseudoacacia Umbraculifera (MopHead Acacia)

Burbk, Coatv, Denes, Mtato, Peele, Pukho, TopTr

pseudoacacia Unifoliola

TopTr

pseudoacacia VATI 46

Dove

x slavinii Hillierii

Burbk, Denes, Dove, Pionr, Pukho, SpecT, TopTr

Rochea

coccinea now Crassula

Trans

Rodgersia

aesculifolia

Denes, MaraN, MJury, TRidg

henrici

MaraN, WaiMa

henrici hybrids

Parva

nepalense

Titok

pinnata

Looij, MaraN, Vall #, WaiMa

pinnata Purpurea

BlueM

pinnata Superba

AynDa, TRidg, Vall #

sambucifolia

MaraN, TRidg, WaiMa

tabularis now Astilboides tabularis

MaraN, Parva, TRidg, WilAq

Romanzoffia

sitchensis

Della

tracyi

Della

Romneya

Butterfly

Denes

coulteri (Californian Tree Poppy)

Denes, MaraN

coulteri trichocalyx

Denes

coulteri White Cloud

Denes

Romulea

atranda

AynDa

bulbocodium

DaffA, Irida, NewlR

bulbocodium alba

DaffA

bulbocodium leitchliniana

NewlR

bulbocodium var clusiana

DaffA, NewlR

citrina

DaffA

crocea

NewlR

flava

DaffA

flava alba

DaffA

grandiscapa

Irida

hantamensis

DaffA

hartumgii

DaffA

hirta

DaffA

leipoldii

DaffA

macowanii

Della

ramiflora

Della

rosea

BayBl, CottP, DaffA, Della, Irida, Kayd, NewlR, Telfa, Trans

rosea Alba

Irida, KeriP, Nikau, Ormon, Parva, Trans

sabulosa

JoyPl, MJury, Parva

tabularis

KeriP, Nikau

Rondeletia

amoena (Mexican Viburnum)

Denes

Rosa

A Longs Pedoncules

Kauri

Abbotswood

Waire

Abraham Darby (Eng)

AmFu, BayBl, DBoer, Denes, DSNur, Egmon, Kauri, Mason, Meado, Pukho, Trini, Waire, ZinoN

Academy

SouX

Ace Of Hearts (HT)

DBoer

Ada Perry

SouX

Adam (Cl)

Denes, DSNur, Kauri, Pukho, Waire

Adam Rackles

Kauri, Waire

Adelaide d'Orleans (Cl)

BayBl, DBoer, DSNur, Mason, Meado, Pukho, Trini, Waire

Agatha Incarnata (Old F)

Mason, Waire

Aglaia (Cl)

Trini

Agnes (Old F)

DBoer, DSNur, Kauri, Mason, Nikau, Parva, Pukho, Trini, Waire

Aimee Vibert (Cl)

DSNur, Egmon, Mason, Meado, Pukho, Trini, Waire

Akashi

SouX

Alain Blanchard

Kauri, Waire

alba (Old F)

Meado

alba Maxima

Nikau

alba semi plena (White Rose Of York)

Kauri, Trini

Alberic Barbier (Cl)

BayBl, DBoer, DSNur, Egmon, Mason, Meado, Nikau, Parva, Pukho, Trini, Waire, ZinoN

Albertine (Cl)

   AmFu, BayBl, Butlr,
   DBoer, Denes, DSNur,
   Egmon, Mason, Meado,
   MJury, Nikau, Parva,
   Pukho, SouX, Trini,
   Waire, ZinoN

Alchemist (Cl)

   AmFu, Denes, DSNur,
   Egmon, Kauri, Meado,
   Parva, Pukho, Trini,
   Waire, ZinoN

Alec's Red (HT)

   Egmon, Mason, Meado,
   Pukho, Rhine

Alexander (HT)

   AmFu, DBoer, DSNur,
   Egmon, Mason, Pukho,
   Rhine, Waire

Alfred de Dalmas (Old F)

   Egmon

Alister Stella Gray (Cl)

   DSNur, Egmon, Meado,
   Pukho, SouX, Trini,
   Waire, ZinoN

All Aglow (HT)

   Mason

Allgold climber (Cl)

   Mason, Rhine

Allgold (Fl)

   Rhine

Aloha (Cl)

   Denes, DSNur, Egmon,
   Kauri, Meado, Pukho,
   Waire

Altissimo (Cl)

   Meado, Waire

Amanda

   SouX

Amazing Grace (HT)

   Egmon, Pukho

Amazon (Fl)

   DBoer, Egmon, Pukho,
   Rhine, Waire

Amber Queen (Fl)

   DBoer, Egmon, Mason,
   Pukho, Rhine, Waire

Amberlight (HT)

   AmFu, DBoer, Denes,
   Egmon, LanSc, Mason,
   Meado, Pukho, Rhine,
   Waire, ZinoN

Ambridge Rose (Eng)

   AmFu, BayBl, Denes,
   DSNur, Egmon, Kauri,
   Meado, Pukho, Waire

America (Cl)

   DBoer, Egmon, Pukho,
   Waire

American Beauty

   Mtato, Waire

American Pillar (Cl)

   BayBl, DBoer, DSNur,
   Kauri, Pukho, SouX,
   Waire, ZinoN

Amethyste (Cl)

   Trini

Anais Segalas (Old F)

   BayBl, Kauri, Mason,
   Meado, Nikau, Trini,
   Waire

Andrea

   SouX

Anemone Rose (Old F)

   Trini

anemonoides

   Waire

anemonoides Ramona (Old F)

   Mason

Angel Darling

   SouX

Angel Dust

   SouX

Angel Face (Fl)

   Kauri, Pukho, Waire

Angel Pink

   SouX

Angela Rippon (Patio)

   Egmon, SouX

Angelita (Gc)

   Egmon, Mason, SouX

Anisley Dickson (Fl)

   Egmon

Anita Charles (Mini)

   Mason, SouX

Ann Endt (Old F)

   Kauri, Pukho, Trini

Ann Moore

   SouX

Anna Olivier

   Kauri, Waire

Anna Pavlova (HT)

   DSNur, Egmon, Kauri

Anna Wheatcroft (Fl)

   Rhine

Anna Zinkeisen (Old F)

   DSNur, Mason, Meado,
   Pukho, Waire

Anna-Marie de Montravel (Old F)

   BayBl, DSNur, Kauri,
   Pukho, Trini, Waire,
   ZinoN

Annan's Orchard (Otago Goldfields)

   Trini

Anne Harkness (Fl)

   DBoer, Mason, Rhine,
   Waire

Antique Rose

   SouX, Waire

Antonia d'Ormois

   Waire

Anytime

   SouX

Aoraki

   SouX

Aotearoa - NZ (HT)

   AmFu, DBoer, Denes,
   DSNur, Mason, Meado,
   Pukho, Rhine, Waire,
   ZinoN

Apothecary's Rose (R.gallica officinalis) (Old F)

   Kauri, Trini

Apple Blossom (Cl)

   SouX, ZinoN

Applejack

   DSNur, Pukho, Waire,
   ZinoN

Apricot Honey (Mini)

   Wells

Apricot Ice (Fl)

   Meado, Pukho

Apricot Mist

   SouX

Apricot Nectar (Fl)

   Rhine, Waire

Apricot Prince (Fl)

   Egmon, Meado

Apricot Queen (Old F)

   ZinoN

Archiduc Joseph (Old F)

   DSNur, Kauri, Meado,
   Pukho, Trini

Ard's Rover (Old F)

   Mason

Arethusa (Old F)

   Kauri, Trini, Waire

Arrowtown (Cl)

   DBoer, Denes, DSNur,
   Egmon, Mason, Meado,
   Waire

Arthur Bell (Fl)

   DBoer

Arthur Hillier

   Kauri, Waire

Ash Wednesday (Old F)
DSNur, Mason, Meado, Trini, Waire

Assemblages Des Beautes (Old F)
Mason

Auckland Metro (HT)
AmFu, DBoer, Denes, DSNur, Egmon, Kauri, Mason, Meado, Parva, Pukho, Rhine, Waire, ZinoN

Audrey Wilcox (HT)
Egmon

Aurora (Mod)
Meado

Ausonius (Old F)
Trini

Austragold (HT)
DBoer, Waire

Autumn Damask
Kauri, Waire

Autumn Delight (Old F)
BayBl, DSNur, Kauri, Mason, Meado, Pukho, Trini, Waire, ZinoN

Autumn Leaves (Eng)
Pukho, Trini, Waire

Autumn Sunlight (Cl)
DBoer

Avalanche (Fl)
DBoer, Denes, DSNur, Egmon, Kauri, Mason, Meado, Pukho, Rhine, Waire, ZinoN

Avandel
SouX

Avenue Red (Mod)
DBoer, Meado

Aviateur Bleriot (Cl)
Mason, Trini

Awakening (Cl)
BayBl, Denes, DSNur, Egmon, Kauri, Meado, Waire

Ayrlies Rose
Kauri, Waire

Azure Sea (HT)
Rhine

Baby Betsy McCall
SouX

Baby Darling
SouX

Baby Face
SouX

Baby Faraux (Old F)
Parva, Trini

Baby Katie
SouX

Baby Masquerade
SouX

Baby Rambler (Patio Cl)
Egmon

Ballerina (Hyb Musk,Old F
BayBl, DBoer, Denes, DSNur, Egmon, Kauri, Mason, Nikau, Pukho, SouX, Trini, Waire, ZinoN

Balmain
BayBl

Balmain Climber
Kauri, Waire

Bambino
SouX

banksiae "Lutescens" (Cl)
CouCl, Kauri

banksiae alba (Cl)
Denes, Egmon, Hewsn, Kauri, KeriP, Mason, Meado, Pukho, Trini

banksiae alba Plena (Cl)
CouCl, Waire, ZinoN

banksiae Lutea (Cl)
AmFu, BayBl, Butlr, CouCl, Denes, Egmon, Hewsn, Kauri, Mason, Meado, MJury, Parva, Pukho, Trini, Waire, ZinoN

banksiae The Pearl (Cl)
BayBl, CouCl, Kauri

Banksiae The Purezza (Cl)
Mason, ZinoN

Bantry Bay (Cl)
AmFu, BayBl, DBoer, Denes, DSNur, Egmon, Kauri, Mason, Meado, Parva, Pukho, Rhine, Trini, Waire, ZinoN

Barkarole (HT)
AmFu, DBoer, DSNur, Egmon, Mason, Meado, Pukho, Rhine, Waire

Baron Girod de l'Ain (Old F)
Egmon, Kauri, Trini, Waire

Baroness Rothschild (Old F)
DSNur, Kauri, Meado, Rhine, Trini, Waire

Baronne De Rothschild (HT)
Egmon

Baronne Henriette De Snoy
Kauri

Baronne Prevost (Old F)
DSNur, Egmon, Kauri, Mason, Meado, Pukho, Trini, Waire

Bay Glow
SouX

Beachcomber (Mod)
Meado

Beaute
Waire

Beautiful Doll
SouX

Beauty Secret (Mini)
Mason, SouX

Beauty Star (HT)
Egmon

Belle Amour
Kauri, Waire

Belle De Crecy (Old F)
Kauri, Pukho, Waire

Belle Isis
Kauri

Belle Poitevine (Old F)
DSNur, Egmon, Kauri, Parva, Pukho, Trini, Waire

Belle Story (Eng)
AmFu, BayBl, DSNur, Kauri, Meado, Pukho, Trini, Waire

Benson & Hedges Gold (HT)
DBoer, Egmon

Berkeley Beauty
SouX

Berlin (Old F)
DSNur, Pukho, Waire, ZinoN

Berolina (HT)
DBoer, Egmon, Meado, Waire

Beryl Bach (HT)
Mason, Waire

Bettina (HT)
Waire

Betty Uprichard
Waire

Biddy
SouX

Big Daddy (HT)
DBoer, Egmon, Mason, Pukho, Rhine

Big Purple (HT)
AmFu, DBoer, DSNur, Egmon, Meado, Pukho, Rhine, Waire

Billie And Lew
Kauri

Birthday Present (Cl)
DBoer, Denes, DSNur, Meado, Pukho, Waire

Bishop Darlington
Kauri

Black Beauty (Fl)
Egmon, Meado, Waire

Black Boy (Old F)
DSNur, Mason, Pukho, Waire

Black Jade (Patio)
Egmon, Mason, Meado, SouX, Waire

Black Velvet (HT)
Waire

Blairi No2 (Cl)
BayBl, DSNur, Egmon, Kauri, Mason, Pukho, Waire

Blanc De Vibert
Kauri

Blanc Double de Coubert (Muslin Rose)
DBoer, Denes, DSNur, Egmon, Kauri, Mason, Meado, MJury, Parva, Pukho, Trini, Waire

Blanc Moreau (Old F)
Pukho

Bleu Magenta (Cl)
DBoer, DSNur, Mason, Pukho, Waire

Bloomfield Abundance (Old F)
BayBl, DSNur, Kauri, Mason, Meado, Trini, Waire, ZinoN

Bloomfield Courage (Cl)
BayBl, DBoer, DSNur, Kauri, Mason, Nikau, Pukho, Trini, Waire, ZinoN

Bloomfield Dainty (Old F)
Trini

Blossomtime (Old F)
Kauri, Meado, Waire

Blue Moon (HT)
DBoer, Egmon, Meado, Waire

Blue Nile (HT)
Egmon

Blue Peter (Patio)
Egmon, Meado, SouX, Waire

Blue River (HT)
Mason, Waire

Blue Sky (HT)
DBoer, Egmon, Pukho, Waire

Blueblood
SouX

Blush China
Waire

Blush Noisette (Old F)
DSNur, Egmon, Kauri, Meado, Pukho, Trini, Waire

Blush Rambler (Cl)
BayBl, DBoer, Denes, DSNur, Kauri, Meado, Pukho, Trini, Waire

Blushing Lucy (Cl)
Denes, Kauri, Trini, Waire

Bobbie Charlton (HT)
DBoer

Bobby James (Cl)
DSNur, Mason, Pukho, Trini, Waire

Bon Silene
Kauri, Waire

Bonica (Old F)
DSNur, Meado, Pukho, SouX

Bonica 82 (Cott)
Egmon, Meado

Bonn (Old F)
Mason

Bonnie Scotland (HT)
DBoer, Egmon

Born Free
Kayd

Botzaris (Old F)
DBoer, Kauri, Meado, Pukho, Trini, Waire

Boule de Neige (Old F)
AmFu, Denes, DSNur, Egmon, Kauri, Meado, Waire

Bourbon Queen (Old F)
Mason, Trini, Waire

Bow Bells (Eng)
BayBl, DSNur, Egmon, Kauri, Mason, Waire

Bracteata (Macartney Rose) (Cl)
BayBl, Kauri, Trini

Brandy (HT)
DBoer, Denes, DSNur, Egmon, Mason, Meado, Pukho, Rhine, Waire

Breath Of Life (Cl)
AmFu, DBoer, DSNur, Egmon, Mason, Meado, Pukho, Waire

Bredon (Eng)
AmFu, DSNur, Kauri, Meado, Pukho, Trini, Waire

Breezy
SouX

Bridal Pink (Fl)
DBoer, Mason, Meado, Waire

Bronze Baby (Patio)
Egmon

Brother Cadfael (Eng)
BayBl, DSNur, Egmon, Kauri, Meado, Pukho, Waire

brunonii (Himalayan Musk Rose)
Kauri, Trini, Waire

Buff Beauty (Old F)
AmFu, BayBl, Butlr, DBoer, Denes, DSNur, Egmon, Kauri, Mason, Meado, Parva, Pukho, Trini, Waire, ZinoN

Bull's Red (HT)
DBoer, Egmon, Mason, Meado, Pukho, Rhine, Waire

Bullata (Lettuce Leaf Rose)
Kauri

Burgund (HT)
DBoer, Egmon, Rhine

Butterflies (Gc)
Egmon

Café (Fl)
DSNur, Meado, Waire

Calico Doll
SouX

Calocarpa (Old F)
Mason, Trini

Calumet
SouX

Cameo (Old F)
DSNur, Waire, ZinoN

Cameo Cream (HT)
AmFu, DBoer, Egmon, Rhine, Waire

Canary (HT)
DBoer, Rhine

Canary Bird (Xanthina C.B.)
DSNur, Egmon, Kauri, Meado, Parva, Waire

Cancan (HT)
Egmon

Candella (HT)
AmFu, DBoer, Denes, DSNur, Egmon, Mason, Meado, Pukho, Rhine, Waire

Candy Cane
SouX

canina (Dogrose)
Sweet

Cantabrigiensis
Kauri

Canterbury (Eng)
BayBl, DSNur, Kauri, Pukho, Waire

Caporusso
Kauri, Trini

Captain Christy
Kauri

Captain Cook (Fl)
DBoer

Carabella
BayBl, Waire

Cardinal Hume (Mod Shr)
DBoer, Egmon, Kauri, Meado, Pukho, Waire, ZinoN

Cardinal Richelieu (Old F)
DSNur, Egmon, Mason, Meado, Pukho, Trini, Waire, ZinoN

Careless Moment
SouX

Carmen (Old F)
DBoer

Carolyn (HT)
AmFu, DBoer, Denes, DSNur, Egmon, Mason, Meado, Pukho, Rhine, Waire

Casino
AmFu, Denes, DSNur, Egmon, Mason, Meado, Parva, Pukho, Trini, Waire

Catherine Deneuve (HT)
DBoer, Egmon, Meado, Waire

Catherine Mermet (Old F)
Mason

Cecile Brunner (Sweetheart Rose)
AmFu, BayBl, DSNur, Egmon, Kauri, Kayd, Mason, Meado, MJury, Nikau, Parva, Pukho, Waire, ZinoN

Cecile Brunner Climbing (Cl)
BayBl, CouCl, DBoer, DSNur, Egmon, Kauri, Meado, MJury, Mtato, Parva, Pukho, SouX, Trini, Waire, ZinoN

Cecile Brunner White (Old F)
DSNur, Meado, Parva, Waire, ZinoN

Cecile Lens
SouX

Celeste
Waire

Celestial (Old F)
Egmon, Kauri, Pukho, Trini

Celine Forestier (Cl)
DBoer, DSNur, Egmon, Kauri, Mason, Meado, Pukho, Trini, Waire, ZinoN

Celsiana (Old F)
Egmon, Kauri, Mason, Waire

centifolia muscosa (Common Moss) (Old F)
Trini

centifolia muscosa alba (White Bath) (Old F)
Mason

centifolia Variegata (La Rubanee, Village Maid)
Kauri

Centre Gold
SouX

Cerise Bouquet (Old F)
Egmon

Champagne (HT)
Egmon, Meado, Pukho

Champion Of The World
Kauri, Waire

Champneys Pink Cluster
Kauri

Chanelle (Old F)
Meado, Waire

Chapeau de Napoleon (Old F)
DBoer, Kauri, Mason, Trini, Waire

Chaplin's Pink Climber (Cl
Trini

Charisma (Fl)
DBoer

Charles Albanel (rugosa)
Mason, Pukho, Trini, Waire

Charles Austin (Eng)
AmFu, BayBl, DSNur, Egmon, Kauri, Meado, Pukho, Trini, Waire

Charles de Mills (Old F)
AmFu, DSNur, Egmon, Kauri, Mason, Meado, Nikau, Pukho, Trini, Waire

Charles Dickens (Fl)
DBoer

Charles Rennie MacKintosh (Eng)
AmFu, BayBl, DSNur, Egmon, Kauri, Meado, Pukho, Waire

Charlotte (Eng)
DBoer, DSNur, Egmon, Kauri, Pukho, Waire

Charlotte Kemp
BayBl

Charmglo
Kayd, SouX

Charmian (Eng)
AmFu, BayBl, DSNur, Kauri, Pukho, Trini, Waire

Charming Bells (Gc)
Mason, Pukho

Chasin' Rainbows
SouX

Chateau De Clos Vougeot
Kauri, Waire

Chaucer (Eng)
AmFu, BayBl, DSNur, Egmon, Kauri, Meado, Pukho, Waire

Cheer Up
SouX

Cheers
SouX

Chelsea
SouX

Cherish (Fl)
Egmon, Pukho

Cherokee (Cl)
Mason, Trini

Cherry
Waire

Cherry Magic
SouX

Chianti (Eng)
AmFu, BayBl, DBoer,
DSNur, Kauri, Mason,
Meado, Parva, Pukho,
Trini, Waire, ZinoN

Chicago Peace (HT)
Denes, Egmon, Mason,
Meado, Rhine, Waire

Chick-A-Dee
SouX

Chimo
Waire

Chinatown (Mod Shr)
DBoer

Chinatown Moss (Otago Goldfields)
Trini

chinensis
Kauri, Reic #

chinensis viridiflora (Green Rose) (Old F)
Mason

Chipper
SouX

Chiquita
SouX

Chivalry (HT)
DBoer, Rhine

Chloris (Old F)
Kauri, Trini, Waire

Choo Choo Centennial
SouX

Christingle (HT)
Mason, Waire

Christopher Stone (Old F)
Trini

Chrysler Imperial
Waire

Chrysler Imperial Climber
Kauri

Cider Cup (Patio)
Egmon, Pukho

ciliata (Old F)
Mason

Cinderella
SouX

City of Auckland (HT)
DBoer, Egmon, Mason,
Meado, Parva, Pukho,
Rhine, Waire

City of Belfast (Mod Shr)
Rhine, ZinoN

City of Christchurch (HT)
DBoer, Rhine

City of Leeds (Fl)
Rhine

City of London (Cl)
AmFu, DBoer, Denes,
DSNur, Egmon, Mason,
Meado, Parva, Pukho,
Waire

City of York (Cl)
DSNur, Pukho, Waire,
ZinoN

Clair Matin (Cl)
BayBl, DBoer, DSNur,
Egmon, Kauri, Mason,
Meado, Parva, Pukho,
Trini, Waire, ZinoN

Claire Jacquier (Cl)
BayBl, DBoer, DSNur,
Kauri, Meado, Parva,
Pukho, Trini, Waire

Claire Rose (Eng)
AmFu, BayBl, DSNur,
Egmon, Kauri, Pukho,
Trini, Waire

Clarissa (Patio)
Egmon, Pukho, SouX

Class Act (Fl)
DBoer, DSNur, Egmon,
Mason, Meado, Pukho,
Rhine, Waire, ZinoN

Classy
Kayd

Climbing Jackie (Cl)
DSNur, Kayd, SouX,
Waire

Cloth Of Gold (Cl)
DSNur, Kauri, Mason,
Pukho, Trini, Waire

Clytemnestra (Old F)
Trini

Cocktail (Shr/Cl)
Pukho, Waire

Colibri 79
SouX

Colibri'73 (Mini)
Mason

Colourbreak (Fl)
AmFu, DBoer, Denes,
DSNur, Egmon, Kauri,
Mason, Meado, Pukho,
Rhine, Waire

Commandant Beaurepaire (Old F)
Kauri, Trini, Waire

Common Moss (R centifolia muscosa (Old F)
Kauri, Trini

Compassion (Cl)
AmFu, BayBl, DBoer,
Denes, DSNur, Egmon,
Kauri, Mason, Meado,
Parva, Pukho, Trini,
Waire

Complicata (Old F)
DBoer, DSNur, Egmon,
Kauri, Meado, Nikau,
Orang, Ormon, Pukho,
SouX, Trini, Waire,
ZinoN

Comte de Chambord (Old F)
DBoer, DSNur, Egmon,
Kauri, Meado, Pukho,
Waire

Comtesse du Cayla (Old F)
ZinoN

Conditorum (Old F)
Kauri, Mason

Congratulations (HT)
Egmon

Constance Spry (Eng)
BayBl, DBoer, DSNur,
Egmon, Kauri, Mason,
Meado, Parva, Pukho,
Rhine, Trini, Waire

Constanze (HT)
Rhine

Coppa Nob (HT)
Mason, Waire

Copper Glow (Cl)
BayBl, Kauri

Copy Cat
SouX

Coral Reef
SouX

Cornelia (Old F)
BayBl, DBoer, DSNur,
Egmon, Kauri, Mason,
Meado, Parva, Pukho,
SouX, Trini, Waire,
ZinoN

Cornsilk
SouX

Corso (HT)
Egmon

Corylus (Shr)
DBoer, Kauri, Mason,
Trini, Waire

291

Cottage Dream (Cott)
Denes, Egmon, Pukho

Cottage Garden (Cott)
Egmon, Meado, Pukho

Cottage Maid (Cott)
Egmon, Meado, Pukho

Cottage Rose (Eng)
Pukho

Cotton Candy (HT)
DBoer, Rhine, Waire

Coup de Foudre (Fl)
Rhine

Coupe d'Hebe (Old F)
Mason, Trini

Courvoisier
Kauri, Waire

Coventry Cathedral (Fl)
DBoer, Egmon, Mason, Rhine, Waire

Crackerjack (Fl)
DBoer, Egmon, Rhine

Cramoisi Picotee
Kauri

Cream Delight (HT)
DBoer, DSNur, Egmon, Meado, Pukho, Rhine, Waire

Cream Gold
SouX

Crepuscle (Cl)
AmFu, BayBl, DSNur, Egmon, Kauri, Meado, Pukho, Trini, Waire, ZinoN

Cressida (Eng)
AmFu, DSNur, Kauri, Trini, Waire, ZinoN

Crested Jewel
Kauri

Cricket
SouX

Crimson Glory
Pukho, Waire

Cromwell Rose (Otago Goldfields)
Trini

Cromwell School (Otago Goldfields)
Trini

Crystal Palace (Fl)
Egmon

Cuddles
SouX

Cup Final (HT)
Mason

Cupcake
SouX

Cupid (Old F)
DSNur, Kauri, Meado, Waire

Cymbeline (Eng)
AmFu, BayBl, DSNur, Egmon, Kauri, Meado, Pukho, Waire

D'Aguesseau
Kauri

Dainty Bess (HT)
BayBl, DBoer, DSNur, Kauri, Mason, Meado, Pukho, SouX, Trini, Waire, ZinoN

Dainty Bess Climber
DSNur, Kauri, Pukho, Waire

Dainty Dinah (Patio)
Mason, SouX

damascena bifera (Quatre Saisons) (Old F)
Trini

Dame Prudence (Eng)
AmFu, DSNur, Kauri, Pukho, Waire

Danae (Old F)
Kauri, Meado, Pukho, Trini, Waire

Danny Boy (Cl)
Meado

Daphne (Old F)
Mason

Dapple Dawn (Eng)
BayBl, DSNur, Kauri, Mason, Meado, Parva, Pukho, Trini, Waire

David Dot
SouX

David Thompson (Old F)
Mason

Dawning (Cl)
DSNur, Kauri

Daybreak
Waire

Dearest (Fl)
Egmon, Kauri

Debutante (Cl)
Egmon, ZinoN

Deep Secret (HT)
AmFu, DBoer, Denes, DSNur, Egmon, Mason, Meado, Pukho, Rhine, Waire, ZinoN

Deep Velvet
SouX

Deirdre
Waire

Delicata (Old F)
Trini, ZinoN

Delightful Lady (HT)
DBoer, DSNur, Egmon, Waire

Desprez a Fleur Jaune (Cl)
BayBl, DSNur, Egmon, Kauri, Mason, Meado, Pukho, Trini, Waire

Deuil de Paul Fontaine (Old F)
Pukho, Waire

Devoniensis (Magnolia Rose)
DSNur, Mason, Meado, Waire, ZinoN

Devoniensis Climber
DSNur, Kauri, Pukho

Diadem (Fl)
DBoer, Waire

Diamond Jubilee (HT)
Egmon, Kauri, Mason, Meado, Waire

Dimples (Fl)
DBoer, Denes, DSNur, Kauri, Meado, Waire

Dior Essence
Waire

Disco Dancer (Fl)
DBoer, Egmon, Pukho

Doctor Dick (HT)
Egmon

Dolce Vita (HT)
DBoer

Donna Maria (Cl)
DBoer, Trini

Doris Ryker
BayBl, Kauri, Waire

Doris Tysterman (HT)
DBoer, Egmon, Mason, Meado, Waire

Dorola (Patio)
AmFu, Egmon, SouX

Dorothy Perkins (Cl)
BayBl, DSNur, Kauri, Parva, Pgeon, Pukho, Trini, Waire

Dortmund (Cl)
DBoer, Kauri, Waire, ZinoN

Double Delight (HT)

AmFu, DBoer, Denes, DSNur, Egmon, Mason, Pukho, Rhine, Waire

Dove (Eng)

AmFu, DSNur, Kauri, Meado, Trini, Waire, ZinoN

Dr Grill (Old F)

Trini

Dr Huey

Waire

Dr Jackson (Eng)

DSNur, Kauri, Pukho, Waire

Dr W Van Fleet (Cl)

DBoer

Dream Glo (Mini)

Kayd, Mason, SouX

Dreaming (HT)

DBoer, Egmon, Mason

Dresden Gold

SouX

Dublin Bay (Cl)

AmFu, BayBl, DBoer, Denes, DSNur, Egmon, Kauri, Mason, Meado, Mtato, Parva, Pukho, Rhine, Waire, ZinoN

Duc De Cambridge

Kauri

Duc de Guiche

Waire

Duchess de Brabant (Old F

DSNur, Kauri, Meado, Nikau, Ormon, Parva, Pukho, Trini, Waire

Duchesse d'Angouleme (Old F)

Kauri, Trini

Duchesse de Montebello (Old F)

DBoer, DSNur, Kauri, Pukho, Trini, Waire

Duke Of Edinburgh (Old F

Mason, Waire

Dundee Rambler (Cl)

Mason, Trini, Waire

Dupontii (Old F)

DSNur, Kauri, Pukho, Trini, Waire, ZinoN

Dusky Dancer (Patio Cl)

Egmon

Dusterlohe (Old F)

Mason

Dutch Gold (HT)

Egmon, Mason, Waire

Dwarfking

SouX

Easleas Golden Rambler (Cl)

DSNur, Egmon, Mason, Meado, SouX

Easter Morning (Mini)

Mason, SouX

Eden Rose

Waire

Eglantine

Waire

Eiffel Tower (HT)

DBoer, Egmon

Eldorado (Fl)

AmFu, DBoer, DSNur, Egmon, Mason, Meado, Pukho, Rhine, Waire

Elina (HT)

AmFu, DBoer, Egmon, Mason, Meado, Pukho, Waire, ZinoN

Elite

Waire

Ellen (Eng)

AmFu, BayBl, DSNur, Kauri, Meado, Pukho, Waire

Ellen Wilmott (Old F)

DSNur, Kauri, Meado, Trini, Waire

Elmshorn (Old F)

DSNur, Kauri, Mason, Meado, Trini, Waire

Emanuel (Eng)

AmFu, BayBl, DSNur, Egmon, Kauri, Meado, Pukho, Trini, Waire

Emily Gray (Cl)

Egmon, Kauri, Trini

Emily Louise (Fl)

DSNur, Mason, Pukho

Empress Josephine

Kauri, Waire

Ena Harkness

Pukho, Waire

Enchantment (Fl)

AmFu, DBoer, Denes, DSNur, Egmon, Kauri, Mason, Meado, Pukho, Waire

English Elegance (Eng)

AmFu, BayBl, DSNur, Kauri, Meado, Pukho, Waire, ZinoN

English Garden (Eng)

AmFu, BayBl, DBoer, DSNur, Egmon, Kauri, Meado, Pukho, Waire, ZinoN

English Miss (Fl)

Egmon, Kauri, Pukho, Rhine, Waire

English Wedding Day

ZinoN

Erfurt (Old F)

DSNur, Kauri, Trini, Waire

Erotica (HT)

DBoer, Egmon, Pukho, Waire

Escapade

SouX

Esmeralda (HT)

DBoer, Egmon, Pukho, Rhine, Waire

Etoile de Hollande (Old F)

DSNur, Kauri, Mason, Meado, Waire

Etoile de Hollande Climber

DSNur, Kauri, Pukho, Waire

Eugenie Guinosseau (Old F

Kauri, Trini

Euphrosyne

Kauri

Europeana (Fl)

DBoer, Egmon, Mason, Rhine

Eva (Shr)

DBoer, Kauri, ZinoN

Evangeline (Cl)

ZinoN

Evelyn (Eng)

AmFu, DBoer, DSNur, Egmon, Meado, Waire

Evening Star (HT)

Rhine

Everest Double Fragrance (Fl)

Kauri, Pukho, Rhine, Waire

Everglow (Fl)

DBoer

Excelsa (Cl)

BayBl, DBoer, Trini, Waire

Eyeopener (Cott)

Denes, Egmon, Kauri, Mason, Meado, Pukho, SouX, Waire

293

Eyepaint (Mod Shr)

DBoer, DSNur, Egmon, Pukho, SouX, Waire

Fabvier

Waire

Fair Bianca (Eng)

AmFu, BayBl, DSNur, Egmon, Kauri, Mason, Meado, Pukho, Waire

Fairlane

SouX

Fairy Changeling (Gc)

Egmon

Fairy Dancers (Fl)

DBoer, DSNur, Egmon, Mason, Meado, Pukho, Rhine, Waire

Fairy Moon (Cott)

Egmon, Meado, Pukho, SouX

Fairy Moss

SouX

Fairy Princess (Fl)

Rhine

Fairyland (Old F)

DSNur, Mason

Falkland (Shr)

DBoer, Waire

Fantasy

SouX

Fantin Latour (Old F)

BayBl, DSNur, Egmon, Kauri, Mason, Meado, Pukho, Trini, Waire

Felicia (Old F)

AmFu, BayBl, DBoer, DSNur, Egmon, Kauri, Mason, Meado, Parva, Pukho, Trini, Waire, ZinoN

Felicite et perpetue (Cl)

AmFu, BayBl, DBoer, DSNur, Egmon, Kauri, Mason, Meado, Pukho, SouX, Trini, Waire

Felicite Parmentier (Old F)

DSNur, Egmon, Kauri, Meado, Trini, Waire

Fellemberg (Old F)

Mason, Waire

Fellowship (Fl)

DBoer, DSNur, Egmon, Mason, Rhine, Waire

Ferdinand Pichard (Old F)

AmFu, Pukho, Waire

Ferdy (Gc)

Pukho, SouX

Ferris Wheel (Patio)

Egmon

Fiesta Gold

SouX

Figurine

SouX

Filipes Kiftsgate (Cl)

BayBl, DSNur, Kauri, Meado, Pukho, Trini, Waire

Fimbriata (Phoebes Frilled Pink)

DSNur, Kauri, Pukho, Waire

Financial Times Centenary (Eng)

AmFu, BayBl, DSNur, Kauri, Pukho, Waire

Fire Side (HT)

Rhine

Firelight (Fl)

DBoer

First Lady (HT)

DBoer, Rhine

First Love (HT)

DBoer, Denes, DSNur, Egmon, Mason, Meado, Pukho, Rhine, Waire, ZinoN

Fisherman's Friend (Eng)

DSNur, Egmon, Pukho

FJ Grootendorst (Shr)

DBoer, Kauri, Mason, Pukho, Waire

Flamboyance (HT)

Egmon

Flamingo (HT)

DBoer, Denes, Egmon, Mason, Meado, Rhine, Waire

Flower Carpet Appleblossom (Cott)

Parva, Pukho

Flower Carpet Pink (Cott)

Egmon, Parva, Pukho

Flower Carpet White (Cott

Egmon, Parva, Pukho

foetida bicolor (Old F)

Egmon

foetida Lawrence Johnstone

Waire

foliolosa Anne Endt

Waire

Forgotten Dreams (HT)

Egmon

Fortune's Double Yellow (Cl)

BayBl, Kauri, Trini

Fortuneana

Kauri

Fosters Wellington Cup (HT)

DBoer, DSNur, Egmon, Mason, Pukho, Waire

Fountain (Mod Shr)

DBoer, Egmon

Fragrant Cloud (HT)

AmFu, DBoer, Denes, DSNur, Egmon, Mason, Meado, Pukho, Rhine, Waire

Fragrant Delight (Fl)

Egmon

Fragrant Dream (HT)

Egmon

Fragrant Gold (HT)

Egmon, Pukho

Fragrant Hour (HT)

Denes, Rhine, Waire

Francesca (Old F)

DSNur, Kauri, Meado, Parva, Waire, ZinoN

Francine Austin

BayBl, DSNur, Kauri, Waire

Francis Dubreuil (Old F)

AmFu, DSNur, Kauri, Meado, Pukho, Trini, Waire

Francis E Lester (Cl)

DSNur, Kauri, Pukho, Waire

Francis Phoebe (HT)

DBoer, DSNur, Egmon, Waire

Francois Juranville (Cl)

AmFu, BayBl, DBoer, Egmon, Kauri, Trini, Waire

Francois Poisson (Cl)

Trini

Frau Dagmar Hastrupp (Old F)

DBoer, DSNur, Egmon, Kauri, Mason, Meado, Pukho, Trini, Waire

Frau Karl Druschki (Old F

DSNur, Egmon, Kauri, Mason, Trini, Waire

Freegold

SouX

French Lace (Fl)
AmFu, DBoer, Denes, DSNur, Egmon, Kauri, Mason, Meado, Pukho, Rhine, Waire

Frensham (Fl)
BayBl, DSNur, Kauri, Meado, Pukho, Trini, Waire

Fresh Pink
SouX

Freude (HT)
DBoer

Friesia (Fl)
AmFu, DBoer, Denes, DSNur, Egmon, Mason, Meado, Parva, Pukho, Rhine, Waire, ZinoN

Fritz Nobis (Old F)
DBoer, DSNur, Egmon, Kauri, Mason, Meado, Pukho, Trini, Waire, ZinoN

Fruhlingsanfang (Shr)
DBoer, Waire

Fruhlingsduft (Shr)
DBoer, Waire

Fruhlingsgold (Old F)
DSNur, Egmon, Kauri, Meado, Waire, ZinoN

Fruhlingsmorgen (Old F)
DBoer, DSNur, Egmon, Kauri, Pukho, Waire, ZinoN

Fulton Mackay (HT)
Egmon

Gabrielle Noyelle (Old F)
Kauri, Mason

gallica officionalis (Apothecary) (Old F)
Kauri, Trini, Waire

gallica versicolor (Rosa Mundi) (Old F)
Kauri, Mason

Galway Bay (Cl)
DBoer, DSNur, Egmon, Meado, Pukho

Garden Party (HT)
DBoer, Egmon, Rhine, Waire

Gardenia (Cl)
DSNur, Kauri, Trini, Waire

Gee Gee
SouX

General Gallieni (Old F)
DSNur, Kauri, Mason, Meado, Trini, Waire

General Jacqueminot
Kauri

General Kleber (Old F)
Trini

General Schablikine (Old F
DSNur, Kauri, Meado, Trini, Waire

Gentle Clown (Patio)
Mason

Gentle Kiss (Patio)
Mason, SouX

Gentle Maid (Patio)
Kauri, Mason, Meado, SouX

Gentle Touch (Patio)
Egmon

George Will
Kauri, Waire

Georgette
SouX

Georgie Anderson (Fl)
DBoer, Waire

Georgie Girl (Fl)
DBoer, DSNur, Egmon, Pukho, ZinoN

Geraldine (Fl)
DBoer, Egmon, Rhine

Geranium (Old F)
Egmon, Meado, Pukho

Gerbe Rose (Cl)
BayBl, DSNur, Kauri, Mason, Waire

Gertrud Schweitzer (HT)
DBoer, DSNur

Gertrude Jekyll (Eng)
AmFu, BayBl, DBoer, DSNur, Kauri, Mason, Meado, Pukho, Trini, Waire

Ghislaine de la Feligonde (Old F)
AmFu, BayBl, DSNur, Egmon, Kauri, Meado, Pukho, Trini, Waire, ZinoN

gigantea cooperi now R.laevigata Cooperi (Coopers Burmese Rose)
Kauri, Waire

Gilt Edged (Patio Cl)
Egmon

Ginger Rogers (HT)
DBoer

Glad Tidings (Fl)
Egmon

Glamis Castle 1997
AmFu

glauca syn rubrifolia
Pukho

Glenfiddich (Fl)
Egmon

Glengarry (Fl)
DBoer

Gloire de Dijon (Old F)
AmFu, DSNur, Kauri, Meado, Waire

Gloire de Ducher (Old F)
Mason

Gloire de Guilan (Old F)
Kauri, Trini, Waire

Gloire Lyonnaise (Old F)
DSNur, Kauri, Trini, Waire

Glowing Cushion
Egmon, Pukho

Goethe (Old F)
Trini

Gold Bunny (Fl)
DBoer, Kauri, Meado, Waire

Gold Medal (HT)
AmFu, DBoer, DSNur, Egmon, Mason, Meado, Pukho, Waire, ZinoN

Golden Angel
SouX

Golden Chersonese (Mod Shr)
DBoer, Waire

Golden Gardens
SouX

Golden Jubilee (HT)
Egmon, Waire

Golden Moss
Kauri

Golden Ophelia (Old F)
DSNur, Kauri, Mason, Waire

Golden Queen (HT)
DBoer

Golden Rosamini (Mini)
Mason

Golden Salmon
Waire

Golden Showers (Cl)
Denes, DSNur, Egmon, Kauri, Meado, Pukho, Trini, Waire, ZinoN

Golden Song (Cl)
Kayd, SouX

Golden Wings (Old F)

AmFu, BayBl, DSNur,
Egmon, Kauri, Mason,
Meado, Pukho, Waire,
ZinoN

Goldfinch (Cl)

BayBl, DBoer, DSNur,
Kauri, Meado, Parva,
Trini, Waire

Good As Gold (Patio Cl)

Egmon, Pukho

Grace Darling

Kauri, Waire

Graham Thomas (Eng)

AmFu, BayBl, DBoer,
DSNur, Egmon, Kauri,
Mason, Meado, Parva,
Pukho, Rhine, Trini,
Waire, ZinoN

Grand Hotel (Cl)

DBoer, Denes, Egmon,
Meado, Waire

Grand Masterpiece (HT)

DBoer, Egmon

Grandchild

Pukho, Waire

Grande Duchesse Charlotte

Waire

Grandpa Dickson (HT)

DBoer, Egmon, Meado,
Waire

Great Maiden's Blush

Waire

Great Rise 'N Shine

SouX

Great Western (Old F)

Kauri, Mason, Waire

Green Diamond

SouX

Green Ice (Patio)

DSNur, Meado, Pukho,
SouX, Waire

Greensleeves (Old F)

AmFu, DSNur, Kauri,
Meado, Parva, Pukho,
Waire

Grouse (Gc)

Egmon, Meado, SouX,
Waire

Gruss An Aachen (Fl)

AmFu, DSNur, Egmon,
Kauri, Mason, Meado,
Pukho, Rhine, Trini,
Waire, ZinoN

Gruss An Coburg

DSNur, Kauri, Waire

Gruss An Teplitz

DSNur, Kauri, Waire

Gruss An Zabern

Kauri, Waire

Guinee (Cl)

AmFu, DSNur, Egmon,
Kauri, Waire

Gustav Grunnerwald (Old F)

Kauri, Trini, Waire

Gypsy Moth (Fl)

DBoer, DSNur, Rhine,
Waire

Hamburg

Waire

Handel (Cl)

AmFu, DBoer, Denes,
DSNur, Egmon, Kauri,
Meado, Pukho, Waire

Hannah Hansen

Kauri

Hans Christian Anderson (Fl)

DBoer, Egmon, Rhine,
Waire

Hansa (Old F)

DSNur, Kauri, Pukho,
Trini, Waire

Happy Days (HT)

DBoer, Mason, Rhine

Happy Daze

SouX

Happy Go Lucky (Fl)

DBoer, Denes, Mason

Happy Hour

SouX

Harmonie (HT)

DBoer, Egmon, Rhine,
Waire

Harriet Sheppard

Kauri

Harry Wheatcroft (HT)

Egmon, Waire

Hauraki (Patio)

Egmon, Pukho

Heart 'N Soul

SouX

Heart Of Gold (HT)

DBoer, DSNur, Egmon,
Mason, Pukho, Waire

Heart Throb (HT)

AmFu, DBoer, Egmon,
Mason, Meado, Rhine,
Waire

Hebe's Lip (Old F)

Kauri, Trini, Waire

Heideroslein (Old F)

Trini, ZinoN

Heidi (Patio)

Egmon

Helen Traubel (HT)

DBoer, Waire

Henri Martin

Waire

Henrietta

Waire

Henry Hudson (Old F)

DSNur, Egmon, Mason,
Pukho, Trini, Waire

Heritage (Eng)

AmFu, BayBl, DBoer,
DSNur, Egmon, Kauri,
Mason, Meado, Parva,
Pukho, Waire

Hermosa (Old F)

DSNur, Kauri, Waire

Hero (Eng)

DSNur, Kauri, Pukho,
Trini, Waire

Hi De Hi

Parva

High Hopes (Cl)

Denes, DSNur, Egmon,
Mason, Waire

High Spirits

SouX

High Stepper (Cl)

Kayd, SouX

Hilda Murrell (Eng)

DSNur, Kauri, Waire

Hilltop

Waire

Hippolyte (Old F)

BayBl, Kauri, Mason,
Parva, Trini, Waire

Holiday Time

SouX

Hombre

SouX

Honey Bunch

SouX

Honey Dew (Mod)

Meado

Honor (HT)

DBoer, Egmon, Meado,
Rhine, Waire

Honorine de Brabant (Old F)

BayBl, Egmon, Kauri,
Mason, Meado, Trini,
Waire

Horstmann's Rosenresli
Kauri

Hot Chocolate (Fl)
DBoer, Denes, DSNur, Egmon, Kauri, Meado, Pukho, Rhine, Waire, ZinoN

Hot Gossip (Patio)
Egmon

Hotline
SouX

Hugonis (Old F)
Trini

Hula Girl
SouX

Humdinger
SouX

Hurdy Gurdy
SouX

Ice Angel (Patio)
Egmon

Ice Fairy
BayBl

Ice Princess
SouX

Ice White (Fl)
Rhine

Iceberg (Fl)
AmFu, BayBl, DBoer, Denes, DSNur, Egmon, Kauri, Mason, Meado, Mtato, Parva, Pukho, Rhine, SouX, Trini, Waire, ZinoN

Iceberg Climber (Cl)
AmFu, BayBl, DBoer, Denes, DSNur, Egmon, Kauri, Mason, Meado, Parva, Pukho, SouX, Waire, ZinoN

Iced Ginger (Fl)
DSNur, Egmon, Meado, Pukho, Waire

Immortal Juno (Eng)
AmFu, BayBl, DSNur, Kauri, Meado, Mtato, Pukho, Trini, Waire

Impatient (Fl)
DBoer

Indian Summer (Patio Cl)
DSNur, Mason, Pukho, SouX, Waire

indica major (Cl)
BayBl, Kauri, Parva, Trini

Ingrid Bergman (HT)
AmFu, DBoer, Egmon, Mason, Meado, Parva, Pukho, Rhine, Waire

Innocence
Kauri

Integrity (HT)
AmFu, DBoer, Egmon, Mason, Waire

Irene Jane
Kauri

Irish Fireflame (Old F)
DSNur, Mason, Waire

Irresistible
SouX

Ispahan (Old F)
AmFu, DBoer, DSNur, Egmon, Kauri, Mason, Meado, Pukho, Trini, Waire

Jacaranda (HT)
DBoer, Denes, DSNur, Egmon, Meado, Pukho, Waire

Jackie (Patio Cl)
Pukho

Jacqueline Du Pre (Mod Shr)
DSNur, Egmon, Pukho, Waire

Jacquenetta (Eng)
DSNur, Kauri, Meado, Waire

Jacques Cartier (Old F)
DBoer, DSNur, Egmon, Kauri, Mason, Meado, Parva, Pukho, Trini, Waire

Jadis (HT)
DBoer

James Mason (Old F)
Kauri, Mason, Waire

Janice
SouX

Jayne Austin (Eng)
AmFu, BayBl, DBoer, DSNur, Egmon, Kauri, Mason, Meado, Pukho, Trini, Waire

Jean Ducher (Old F)
DSNur, Kauri, Meado, Parva, Pukho, Trini, Waire

Jean Kenneally (Patio)
Egmon, Mason, SouX

Jeanne d'Arc (Old F)
Kauri, Trini

Jeanne de Montfort
Waire

Jeanne Lajoie (Patio Cl)
BayBl, Egmon, Kayd, Mason, Pukho, SouX, Waire

Jennifer
SouX

Jenny Duval (Old F)
Kauri, Trini, Waire

Jens Monk (rugosa)
Mason, Trini, Waire

Jet Trail
SouX

Jewel Box (Mini)
Mason, SouX

Jim Dandy
SouX

John Cabot (Old F)
Mason

John Franklin (Old F)
Mason

John Waterer (HT)
DBoer

John Wickcliffe (Cl)
Trini

Jolene
SouX

Josephine Bruce (HT)
DSNur, Egmon, Kauri, Meado, Pukho, Waire

Josephine Bruce Climber
DSNur, Kauri, Waire

Josephs Coat (Mod Shr)
DSNur, Egmon, Meado, Pukho, Waire

Joycie
SouX

Jubilee Celebration (Fl)
Egmon

Judy Fischer
SouX, Waire

Julias Rose (HT)
AmFu, DBoer, DSNur, Kauri, Mason, Meado, Pukho, Rhine, Waire

Julie Ann
SouX

Julischka (Fl)
DBoer, Egmon, Mason, Meado, Pukho, Waire

June Time
SouX

Just Joey (HT)
AmFu, DBoer, Denes, DSNur, Egmon, Mason, Meado, Pukho, Waire

Kaikoura (Patio)
AmFu, Egmon, SouX, Waire

Kapiti (Cott)
DSNur, Egmon, Pukho, SouX, Waire

Karl Forster (Old F)
DSNur, Kauri

Karma (HT)
DBoer

Kate Sheppard (Fl)
Egmon, Pukho

Katharina Zeimet
Kauri, Waire

Katherine Mansfield (HT)
DBoer, Denes, Egmon, Meado, Pukho, Rhine

Kathleen (Old F)
DSNur, Kauri, Waire

Kathleen Harrop (Old F)
DSNur, Kauri, Meado, Pukho, Waire

Kathryn McGredy (HT)
Egmon

Kathryn Morley (Eng)
BayBl, DBoer, DSNur, Egmon, Kauri, Mason, Meado, Pukho, Trini, Waire

Kathy Reid (Old F)
Mason

Kathy Robinson
SouX

Katrina
Kauri

Kazanlik (Old F)
Trini, Waire

Kent
Waire

Kerryman (Fl)
DBoer, Denes, DSNur, Egmon, Mason, Waire

Kew Rambler (Cl)
BayBl, Trini, ZinoN

Kia Ora (HT)
DBoer, DSNur, Egmon, Mason

King's Ransom (HT)
DBoer, Rhine

Kiri (Mod)
DBoer, DSNur, Mason, Meado, Waire

Ko's Yellow (Patio)
Egmon, Meado, SouX

Koenigin Von Danemark
Kauri, Waire

Kordes Robusta (Mod Shr)
DSNur, Egmon

Korona (Fl)
DBoer

Kronenbourg (HT)
AmFu, Egmon, Meado, Pukho, Rhine, Waire

La Belle Distinguee (Old F)
Mason, Waire

La Belle Sultan (R Violacea)
Kauri

La France (Old F)
Kauri, Trini, Waire, ZinoN

La Marsellaise (HT)
Egmon

La Noblesse
Kauri, Waire

La Reine
Kauri, Waire

La Reine Victoria (Old F)
DSNur, Egmon, Kauri, Mason, Meado, Parva, Pukho, Trini, Waire

La Rubanee (R.Centifolia Variegata)
Kauri, Waire

La Ville de Bruxelles (Old F)
Kauri, Trini

Lady Alice Stanley
Kauri, Waire

Lady Barbara (Cl)
AmFu, DBoer, Denes, Egmon, Mason, Meado, Pukho, Waire

Lady Curzon (Old F)
Mason, Trini

Lady Gay (Cl)
Trini

Lady Glencora (Fl)
DBoer

Lady Hillingdon (Old F)
DSNur, Kauri, Meado, Trini, Waire

Lady Hillingdon Climbing (Cl)
Pukho, Waire

Lady Mary Fitzwilliam (Old F)
Kauri, Trini, Waire

Lady Of The Dawn (Mod Shr)
Egmon, Pukho

Lady Roberts (HT)
DBoer

Lady Rose (HT)
AmFu, DBoer, Egmon, Waire

Lady Waterloo (Cl)
DSNur, Kauri, Waire

Lady Waterloo Climber
Waire

Lady X (HT)
DBoer

laevigata (Cherokee Rose)
Kauri, Meado, Waire

laevigata alba
BayBl

Lamarque (Cl)
AmFu, BayBl, DSNur, Egmon, Kauri, Meado, Pukho, Trini, Waire

Landora (HT)
AmFu, DBoer, Denes, Egmon, Meado, Rhine, Waire, ZinoN

Lantern (HT)
Egmon

Laura Ford (Patio Cl)
Denes, Egmon, Mason, Pukho, SouX, Waire

Laure Davoust (Cl)
BayBl, Kauri, Mason, Trini, Waire

Lavender Dream (Cott)
BayBl, DSNur, Egmon, Kauri, Meado, Parva, Pukho, SouX, Waire, ZinoN

Lavender Jade
SouX

Lavender Jewel (Patio)
Egmon, Mason, SouX, Waire

Lavender Lassie (Old F)
AmFu, BayBl, DBoer, DSNur, Egmon, Kauri, Mason, Meado, Mtato, Parva, Pukho, SouX, Trini, Waire, ZinoN

Lavender Pinnochio (Fl)
AmFu, DSNur, Meado, Pukho, Trini, Waire

298

Lawrence Johnston (Cl)
DSNur, Kauri, Pukho

LD Braithwaite (Eng)
AmFu, BayBl, DSNur,
Egmon, Kauri, Mason,
Meado, Pukho, Trini,
Waire

Leander (Eng)
AmFu, BayBl, DSNur,
Egmon, Kauri, Mason,
Meado, Parva, Pukho,
Trini, Waire

Leaping Salmon (Cl)
DBoer, Egmon, Meado,
Pukho, Rhine, Waire

Leda (Old F)
AmFu, Kauri, Pukho,
Trini, Waire

Lemon Delight (Mini)
Mason

Lemon Honey
DBoer, Egmon, Meado,
Pukho, Rhine

Lemon Twist
SouX

Leonie Lamesch (Old F)
Kauri, Trini

Leontine Gervais (Cl)
Trini, ZinoN

Leverkusen
DSNur, Kauri, Pukho,
Waire

Libby
SouX

Lilac Charm (Fl)
Pukho

Lilac Rose (Eng)
AmFu, BayBl, DSNur,
Kauri, Pukho, Waire

Lili Marlene (Fl)
Egmon, Meado

Lilian Austin (Eng)
AmFu, BayBl, DSNur,
Egmon, Kauri, Meado,
Parva, Pukho, Trini,
Waire, ZinoN

Linda Campbell
Kauri, SouX

Little Bo-Peep (Gc)
Egmon, Meado, Pukho

Little Darling (Fl)
DBoer

Little Gem
Kauri, Waire

Little Girl (Patio Cl)
Egmon, Kayd, Pukho,
SouX, Waire

Little Jackie (Patio)
Egmon, Kayd, SouX

Little Linda
SouX

Little Miss Muffet (Gc)
Egmon

Little Nugget (Patio)
AmFu, Egmon, Mason,
Pukho, SouX, Waire

Little Opal (Patio)
DSNur, Egmon, Pukho,
Waire

Little Prince (Patio)
Mason, SouX

Little Sapphire (Patio)
Mason

Little Scotch (Mini)
Mason, SouX

Little Showoff
SouX

Little White Pet (Old F)
BayBl, DSNur, Kauri,
Meado, Pgeon, Waire

Liverpool Echo (Mod Shr)
DBoer, DSNur, Egmon,
Mason, Pukho, Rhine,
Waire

Lolita (HT)
DBoer, Waire

**longiscupis (White Rose of
Sissinghurst)**
Trini, ZinoN

Lordly Oberon (Eng)
DSNur, Kauri, Meado,
Trini, Waire

Lorraine Lee (Old F)
DSNur, Kauri, Meado,
Pukho, Trini, Waire

Lorraine Lee Climber (Cl)
DSNur, Kauri, Pukho,
Trini, Waire

Louis XIV (Old F)
DSNur, Kauri, Pukho,
Trini, Waire

Louise Gardner (HT)
Egmon, Rhine

Louise Odier (Old F)
DSNur, Egmon, Kauri,
Meado, Pukho, Waire

Love (HT)
DBoer, Rhine

Lovely Fairy (Cott Fl)
DBoer, DSNur, Egmon,
Mason, Rhine, Waire

Lovely Lady (HT)
DBoer, DSNur, Egmon,
Waire

Loving Memory (HT)
AmFu, DBoer, DSNur,
Egmon, Mason, Meado,
Parva, Pukho, Rhine,
Waire, ZinoN

Loving Touch (Patio)
AmFu, Egmon, Meado,
Pukho, SouX, Waire

**Lowburn Rose (Otago
Goldfields)**
Trini

Lucetta (Eng)
AmFu, BayBl, DSNur,
Kauri, Mason, Meado,
Pukho, Trini, Waire

Lucky Me (Patio)
AmFu, Mason, SouX,
Waire

Luis Brinas
Waire

Luis Desamero
SouX

Lulu (HT)
DBoer

Lynn Ann
SouX

Mabella (HT)
DBoer

macrantha (Old F)
DBoer, Kauri, Mason

Madam President (Fl)
AmFu, DBoer, Denes,
DSNur, Egmon, Kauri,
Mason, Meado, Pukho,
Waire

Maestro (HT)
Egmon, Meado, Rhine

Magenta (Old F)
Kauri, Meado

Maggie Barry (HT)
DBoer, DSNur, Egmon,
Mason, Pukho, Rhine,
Waire, ZinoN

Magic Carousel (Mini)
Kayd, Mason, SouX

Magic Dragon (Patio Cl)
Egmon, Kayd, Pukho,
SouX, Waire

Magic Moments (HT)
DBoer, Egmon, Rhine

Magnifica (Old F)
Trini

Maidens Blush (Old F)
DBoer, DSNur, Egmon,
Kauri, Pukho, Trini,
Waire

Maigold (Old F)
DSNur, Kauri, Pukho,
Waire, ZinoN

Make Believe
SouX

Malaga (Cl)
DBoer, Egmon, Meado

Maleica (Fl)
DBoer, Mason, Pukho

Maman Cochet
Waire

Manaia (HT)
Egmon

Manapouri (Patio)
Egmon

Many Happy Returns (Fl)
DSNur, Egmon

Marechal Niel (Cl)
Mason, Trini

Margaret Merril (Fl)
AmFu, DBoer, Denes,
DSNur, Egmon, Kauri,
Mason, Meado, Parva,
Pukho, Rhine, Trini,
Waire, ZinoN

Marguerite Hilling (Old F)
DBoer, Trini

Mari Dot
Waire

Maria Callas (HT Climber)
Pukho, Rhine

Marie de Blois (Old F)
Kauri, Trini, Waire

Marie Louise (Old F)
Kauri, Mason, Trini

Marie Parvie (Old F)
DSNur, Meado, Pukho,
Waire

Marie Van Houte
Waire

Marijke Koopman (HT)
DBoer, Egmon, Waire

Marjorie Fair (hyb. musk)
Kauri, Mason, Pukho,
SouX, Trini

Martin Frobisher (Old F)
BayBl, DBoer, DSNur,
Kauri, Meado, Pukho,
Trini, Waire, ZinoN

Marty's Triumph
SouX

Mary Adair
SouX

Mary Anna Bumby
Kauri

Mary Marshall (Mini)
Mason, SouX

Mary Rose (Eng)
AmFu, BayBl, DBoer,
DSNur, Egmon, Kauri,
Mason, Meado, Parva,
Pukho, Trini, Waire

Mary Webb (Eng)
BayBl, DSNur, Kauri,
Pukho, Waire

Masquerade (Cl)
DSNur, Rhine, Trini

Matangi (Fl)
DBoer, Egmon, Mason,
Rhine, Waire

Max Graf (Old F)
Mason

May Queen (Cl)
BayBl, DBoer, DSNur,
Kauri, Pukho, Trini,
Waire, Wells, ZinoN

McGredy's Yellow (HT)
Waire

Meg (Old F)
DSNur, Kauri, Mason,
Meado, Pukho, Trini,
Waire, ZinoN

Meg Merrilees (Old F)
Egmon, Waire

Meillandina (Mini)
Mason

Melina (HT)
DBoer, Egmon

Melissa
SouX

**Melmore Terracew (Otago
Goldfields)**
Trini

Melody Marshall
SouX

Menja
DBoer, Trini

Mermaid (Cl)
BayBl, Kauri, Mason,
Meado, Pukho, Trini,
Waire, ZinoN

Merry Widow (HT)
Rhine

Mev GA van Rossem
Waire

Michelangelo (Fl)
DBoer, Egmon, Mason,
Rhine, Waire

Michele Meilland (HT)
Rhine, Waire

**Michelle Meilland climber
(Cl)**
DSNur, Meado, Pukho

micrugosa (Old F)
Mason

Mignonette
BayBl, Kauri, Waire

Milky Way (HT)
DBoer, DSNur, Egmon,
Mason, Pukho, Rhine

Millie Walters
SouX

**Miners Cottage (Otago
Goldfields)**
Trini

Minnehaha (Cl)
DBoer

Minnie Pearl (Mini)
Mason, SouX

Minuetto (Mini)
Mason, SouX

Mirage (HT)
DBoer, Rhine

Mirato (HT)
DBoer, Waire

Miriam (Fl)
DBoer, Egmon, Meado,
Rhine

Mirza
Waire

Miss Harp (HT)
DBoer

Mission Bells
Waire

Mister Lincoln (HT)
Meado, Pukho

Misty Dawn
SouX

Mlle Franziska Kruger
Kauri

Mme Alfred Carriere (Cl)
AmFu, BayBl, DSNur,
Egmon, Kauri, Meado,
Pukho, Trini, Waire,
ZinoN

Mme Alice Garnier (Cl)
DSNur, Trini

Mme Berard
Kauri

Mme Berkeley
Kauri, Waire

Mme Bravy
Kauri

Mme Butterfly (Old F)
DSNur, Kauri, Mason, Meado, Waire

Mme Caroline Testout (Old F)
DSNur, Kauri, Trini, Waire

Mme Caroline Testout Climber
Kauri, Waire

Mme Charles
Kauri, Waire

Mme Ernst Calvat (Old F)
DSNur, Egmon, Kauri, Mason, Meado, Pukho, Trini, Waire

Mme Falcot (Old F)
DSNur, Kauri, Waire

Mme Georges Bruant (Old F)
Kauri, Trini, Waire

Mme Gregoire Staechelin (Cl)
DSNur, Egmon, Kauri, Meado, Pukho, Trini, Waire

Mme Hardy (Old F)
DBoer, DSNur, Egmon, Kauri, Mason, Meado, Nikau, Orang, Pukho, Waire

Mme Isaac Pereire (Old F)
AmFu, DSNur, Egmon, Kauri, Meado, Pukho, Trini, Waire

Mme Jules Gravereaux (Old F)
Kauri, Trini, Waire

Mme Laurette Messimy (Old F)
BayBl, DSNur, Kauri, Meado, Trini, Waire

Mme Lauriol de Barny (Old F)
DSNur, Egmon, Kauri, Pukho

Mme Legras de St Germaine (Old F)
Egmon, Kauri, Trini, Waire

Mme Lombard (Old F)
Kauri, Meado

Mme Louis Leveque (Old F)
DSNur, Meado

Mme Pierre Oger (Old F)
DSNur, Egmon, Kauri, Mason, Meado, Pukho, Trini, Waire

Mme Plantier (Old F)
BayBl, DBoer, DSNur, Egmon, Kauri, Meado, Pukho, Trini, Waire

Mme PS Du Pont
Waire

Mme Sancy de Parabere (Old F)
Mason

Mme Zoetmans (Old F)
DBoer

Modern Art (HT)
DBoer, Mason

Moje Hammarberg (Shr)
DBoer

Molly McGredy (Fl)
DBoer, Rhine

Mon Cheri (HT)
DBoer, Denes, Egmon, Mason, Meado, Waire

Monica (HT)
DBoer, Waire

Monsieur Tillier (Old F)
AmFu, BayBl, Kauri, Meado, Parva, Waire, ZinoN

Montezuma
Waire

Monthly Rambler syn Ruby Alison
Kauri, Waire

Moody Blues (Fl)
AmFu, DBoer, DSNur, Egmon, Mason, Meado, Pukho, Rhine, Waire

Moody Dream (Fl)
Egmon

Moon River (Patio)
DSNur, SouX, Waire

Moonbeam (Eng)
BayBl, DSNur, Kauri, Meado, Pukho, Trini, Waire

Moonlight (Old F)
BayBl, DBoer, DSNur, Egmon, Kauri, Meado, Mtato, Pgeon, Pukho, Trini, Waire, ZinoN

Moonlight Lady (Mini)
Mason, SouX

Moonraker (Fl)
DBoer

Morgengruss (Shr/Cl)
Pukho

Morning Light (Cl)
DBoer, DSNur, Mason, Meado

moschata nastarana now R.Nastarana
Kauri, Waire

Mothers Love
SouX

Mountbatten (Mod Fl)
DSNur, Egmon, Mason, Meado, Pukho, Waire

Mountie (Mini)
Mason, SouX

moyesii
Kauri, Waire

moyesii-geranium (Old F)
Mason

moyesii-highdownensis (Old F)
Mason

moyesii-sealingwax (Old F)
Mason

Mrs Anthony Waterer (Old F)
Kauri, Mason, Pukho

Mrs B.R.Cant
Kauri, Waire

Mrs Bosanquet
Kauri, Waire

Mrs Herbert Stevens (Old F)
DSNur, Kauri, Meado, Trini, Waire

Mrs Herbert Stevens Climber (Cl)
AmFu

Mrs John Laing (Old F)
DBoer, DSNur, Egmon, Kauri, Waire

Mrs Merrilees
BayBl

Mrs Oakley Fisher (Old F)
DSNur, Kauri, Trini, Waire

Mrs OG Orpen (Old F)
Mason, Trini, Waire

Mrs RM Finch (Old F)
BayBl, DSNur, Kauri, Meado, Pukho, Trini, Waire

Mrs Sam McGredy (Cl)
Mason, Waire

Mullard Jubilee (HT)
Mason, Rhine

multiflora
Ormon

Multiflora de la Grifferaie
BayBl, Kauri, Parva

multiflora Grevillei was Platyphylla, Seven Sisters
Kauri

multiflora nana (Old F)
Trini

multiflora Platyphylla now R.m.Grevillei
Kauri

Mutabilis was Tipo Ideale (Old F)
BayBl, DSNur, Egmon, Kauri, Mason, Meado, Nikau, Parva, Peak, Pukho, SouX, TRidg, Trini, Waire, ZinoN

My Sunshine
SouX

My Valentine
SouX

Nancy Haywood (Cl)
DSNur, Kauri, Mason, Meado, Pukho, SouX, Waire, ZinoN

Nancy Steen (Fl)
AmFu, DBoer, Denes, DSNur, Egmon, Kauri, Mason, Meado, Mtato, Pukho, Rhine, Waire, ZinoN

Narrow Water (Cl)
Kauri, ZinoN

Nastarana was moschata n. (Persian Musk Rose)
Kauri, Waire

National Trust (HT)
DBoer

Nevada (Old F)
DSNur, Mason, Meado, Pukho, Trini, Waire

Nevis Moss (Otago Goldfields)
Trini

New Dawn (Cl)
AmFu, BayBl, CottP, DBoer, DSNur, Egmon, Kauri, Mason, Meado, Nikau, Parva, Pukho, Trini, Waire, ZinoN

New Year (HT)
DBoer, Egmon, Mason, Rhine, Waire

New Zealand (HT)
Egmon

News (Fl)
Rhine, Waire

Nickelodeon
SouX

nitida (Old F)
Mason, Trini

Nitouche (Fl/HT)
DSNur, Meado, Pukho, Waire

Nobilo's Chardonnay (HT)
AmFu, Egmon, Meado, Pukho, Waire

Noelle Marie
SouX

Northland (Fl)
DBoer, Egmon, Pukho, Waire

Norwich Castle
Waire

Nozomi (Old F)
CottP, DSNur, Mason, SouX, ZinoN

Nuits de Young (Old F)
DSNur, Egmon

Nur Mahal (Old F)
Trini, Waire

Nypels Perfection (Old F)
Pukho

Old Blush syn China Monthly (Old F)
BayBl, DSNur, Kauri, Meado, Pukho, Waire

Old Blush Climbing
Kauri, Parva, Pukho, Trini

Old Flame (HT)
Rhine

Old Master (Fl)
DBoer, Pukho

Old Port (Fl)
AmFu, DBoer, DSNur, Egmon, Kauri, Mason, Meado, Pukho, Rhine, Waire

Old Red (Otago Goldfields)
Trini

Old Stone School (Otago Goldfields)
Trini

Olympiad (HT)
Egmon, Rhine

Olympic Gold (Cl)
DBoer, Egmon, Mason, Meado, Pukho, Trini, Waire

Olympic Torch (HT)
DBoer, Mason

Omar Khayyam (Old F)
Kauri, Trini

omeiensis pteracantha see R sericea o.p.
Kauri, SouX, Waire

Onekaha Rose
Waire

Ontario Celebration
SouX

Ophelia (Old F)
DSNur, Kauri, Mason, Pukho, Waire

Orange Honey (Patio)
Kayd, Matwh, SouX

Orange Moss
SouX

Oranges And Lemons (Fl)
DBoer, DSNur, Egmon, Mason, Pukho, Rhine, Waire

Oratia Maid
Parva

Orchid Lace (Patio)
Denes, DSNur, Egmon, SouX

Othello (Eng)
AmFu, BayBl, DSNur, Egmon, Kauri, Meado, Mtato, Pukho, Trini, Waire, ZinoN

Over The Rainbow (Mini)
Kayd, Mason

Pacesetter
SouX

Paddy Stephens (HT)
DBoer, Egmon, Mason, Parva, Waire, ZinoN

Paintbrush Moss
Trini

Painted Doll
SouX

Panache
SouX

Pandemonium (Patio)
Egmon, SouX

Pania (HT)
DBoer

Paola (HT)
Egmon, Pukho, Rhine, Waire

Papa Gontier (Old F)
Kauri, Meado, Trini

Papa Meilland (HT)
DSNur, Meado, Pukho

Parabon (Mini)
Mason

Parade (Old F)
DSNur, Kauri, Meado, Pukho, Waire

Paradise (HT)
AmFu, DBoer, Denes, Egmon, Rhine, Waire

Paree Red (Old F)
DSNur, Mtato, Waire

Paree Roses (Old F)
Meado

Paree Salmon (Old F)
Waire

Paree White (Old F)
Waire

Parfum de l'Hay (Rose a Parfum...)
DSNur, Kauri, Waire

Parkdirektor Riggers (Cl)
DSNur, Egmon, Mason, Pukho, Trini, Waire, ZinoN

Partridge (Gc)
Egmon, Waire

Party Girl
SouX

Pascall (HT)
DBoer, Egmon, Mason, Meado, Rhine, Trini, Waire

Patio Charm (Patio Cl)
Egmon, Waire

Patio Cloud (Patio)
Egmon, Pukho, Walre

Patio Flame
SouX

Patio Gem
AmFu, Waire

Patio Honey (Patio Cl)
Egmon, Pukho

Patio Jewel (Patio)
AmFu, Egmon, Pukho, Waire

Patio Pearl (Cott)
Egmon, Kauri, SouX, Waire

Patio Prince (Patio)
Egmon, Kauri, Pukho, SouX

Patio Princess (Patio Cl)
Egmon, Pukho, SouX, Waire

Patio Queen (Patio Cl)
Egmon, Pukho, SouX, Waire

Paul Lede (Cl)
DSNur, Egmon, Pukho

Paul Ricault (Old F)
Kauri, Mason, Trini, Waire

Paul Transon (Cl)
BayBl, DSNur, Egmon, Kauri, Meado, Pukho, Trini, Waire, ZinoN

Paul's Himalayan Musk (Cl)
Egmon, SouX, Trini

Paul's Lemon Pillar (Cl)
BayBl, DSNur, Kauri, Trini, Waire

Paul's Scarlet (Old F)
DSNur, Meado, Waire

paulii (Old F)
Kauri, Mason, Waire

Pax (Old F)
DSNur, Kauri, Waire

Peace (HT)
DBoer, Denes, DSNur, Egmon, Kauri, Mason, Meado, Rhine, Trini, Waire

Peace Climber (Cl)
Kauri, Pukho, Trini, Waire

Peach Blossom (Eng)
BayBl, DSNur, Kauri, Meado, Pukho, Waire

Peach Surprise (HT)
DBoer, Egmon, Mason, Waire

Peaches 'N Cream
SouX

Peachy Keen
SouX

Peachy White
SouX

Pearl d'Or
Nikau, Pgeon

Pearl Drift (Fl)
DSNur, Egmon, Kauri, Meado, Waire

Peek A'Boo (Patio)
Egmon, Mason, SouX

Peep O'Day (HT)
DBoer

Peer Gynt (HT)
Rhine

Penelope (Old F)
AmFu, BayBl, DBoer, DSNur, Egmon, Kauri, Mason, Meado, Parva, Pukho, SouX, Trini, Waire, ZinoN

Perdita (Eng)
AmFu, BayBl, DSNur, Egmon, Kauri, Mason, Meado, Pukho, Trini, Waire, ZinoN

Perfect Moment (HT)
DBoer, Egmon, Pukho

Perfume Delight (HT)
DBoer, Denes, Egmon

Parle d'Or (Old F)
DSNur, Kauri, Mason, Pukho, Waire, ZinoN

Peter Frankenfeldt (HT)
DBoer, Egmon, Mason

Petite Folie
SouX

Petite Penny
SouX, Waire

Petticoat Lane
SouX

Phantom (Cott)
DSNur, Egmon, Mason, Pukho, Waire

Pharein (Fl)
Rhine

Phyllis Bide (Cl)
BayBl, DSNur, Kauri, Meado, Pukho, SouX, Trini, Waire, ZinoN

Phyllis Shackleford (Mini)
DSNur, Pukho, SouX

Picture (Cl)
DSNur, Meado, Pukho, Waire

Pierre S du Pont
Parva

Pierrine
SouX

Pink Bells (Cott Gc)
DSNur, Egmon, Mason, SouX, Waire

Pink Cameo (Patio Cl)
Kayd, SouX, Waire

Pink Cherub
Kayd, SouX

Pink Delight
SouX

Pink Grootendorst (Old F)
DBoer, DSNur, Egmon, Kauri, Mason, Pukho, Waire

Pink Gruss An Aachen (Eng)
DSNur, Kauri, Pukho, Waire

Pink Leda (Old F)
Kauri, Trini

Pink Mandy
SouX

Pink Mermaid
Kauri, Waire

Pink Panther (HT)
Egmon, Rhine

Pink Parfait (Fl)
DBoer, Rhine

Pink Perpetue (Cl)
DBoer, DSNur, Egmon

Pink Petticoat (Mini)
Kayd, Mason, SouX

Pink Porcelain
SouX

Pink Prosperity (Old F)
DSNur, Kauri, Trini, Waire

Pink Silk (HT)
DBoer

Pink Triumph
SouX

Pinkie
Kauri, Pgeon

Pinkie Bush
Waire

Pinkie Climber
DSNur, Kauri, Waire

Playboy (Fl)
DBoer, Egmon, Pukho, Waire

Plum Duffy
SouX

Poker Chip
SouX

polyantha Grandiflora (Cl)
Kauri, Pukho, Waire, ZinoN

Polygold
Waire

pomifera Duplex now R.Wolley-Dod
Kauri

Pompom De Paris
Kauri, Waire

Pompon de Bourgogne
SouX

Popcorn
SouX

Portland Rose (R.Portlandica)
Kauri, Waire

Pot O' Gold (HT)
DBoer, Egmon, Pukho, Rhine

Potter & Moore (Eng)
AmFu, BayBl, DSNur, Kauri, Mtato, Waire, ZinoN

Poulsen's Delight
Waire

Poulsen's Park Rose (Old F
Kauri, Mason, Waire

Pour Toi
SouX

Precious Platinum (HT)
DBoer, Denes, Egmon, Mason, Meado, Rhine, Waire

President de Seze
Kauri

Pretty Jessica (Eng)
AmFu, BayBl, DSNur, Egmon, Kauri, Mason, Meado, Pukho, Waire, ZinoN

Pretty Polly (Patio)
AmFu, DSNur, Egmon, Mason, Pukho, SouX, Waire

Pride Of Hurst
BayBl, Kauri, SouX

Prima Ballerina (HT)
Egmon, Rhine, Waire

Primevere
Kauri

Prince Camille de Rohan (Old F)
Kauri, Trini, Waire

Prince Charles (Old F)
Mason, Waire

Prince Napoleon
Waire

Princess de Monaco (HT)
DBoer, Egmon, Mason

Princess Michael Of Kent (HT)
Mason

Priscilla Burton (Fl)
AmFu, Egmon

Pristine (HT)
Denes, DSNur, Egmon, Pukho, Rhine, Waire

Prominent (Fl)
DBoer

Prosperity (Old F)
AmFu, BayBl, DBoer, DSNur, Egmon, Kauri, Mason, Nikau, Parva, Pukho, Trini, Waire, ZinoN

Prospero (Eng)
AmFu, BayBl, DSNur, Egmon, Kauri, Meado, Pukho, Waire

Proud Titania (Eng)
AmFu, BayBl, DBoer, DSNur, Kauri, Mason, Meado, Parva, Trini, Waire

Pure Bliss (HT)
DSNur, Mason, Waire

Purple Beauty (HT)
Egmon, Waire

Purple Splendour (Mod)
Meado

Quatre Saisons (R. damascena bifera) (Old F)
Trini

Queen Elizabeth (HT)
DBoer, DSNur, Egmon, Meado, Pukho, Waire

Queen Elizabeth climber (HT)
Pukho

Queen Mother (Cott)
Egmon

Queen Nefertiti (Eng)
DBoer, DSNur, Kauri, Mason, Mtato, Pukho, Trini, Waire, ZinoN

Queen Of The Musk
Kauri

Radiant
SouX

Radox Bouquet (Old F,Fl)
DSNur, Mason, Pukho

Radway Sunrise (Old F)
Kauri, Trini

Ragtime (Mini)
Kauri, Mason, SouX, Waire

Rainbow's End (Mini)
Mason, SouX

Ralph's Creeper (Gc)
Egmon, SouX

Rambling Rector (Cl)
BayBl, DBoer, DSNur,
Kauri, Pukho, SouX,
Trini, Waire, ZinoN

Raspberry Ice (Fl)
AmFu, DBoer, Denes,
Egmon, Mason, Pukho,
Rhine, Waire

Raubritter (Old F)
BayBl, DBoer, DSNur,
Egmon, Kauri, Meado,
Trini, Waire

Red Ace (Mini)
Mason, SouX

Red Beauty
SouX

Red Bells (Cott)
Egmon, Mason, SouX,
Waire

Red Blanket (Old F)
DSNur, Mason, SouX,
Waire, ZinoN

Red Flush
SouX

Red Lion (HT)
DBoer

Red Max Graf
Waire

Red Mini
Kayd

Red Planet (HT)
DBoer, Rhine

Red Wagon
SouX

Red Wand (Patio Cl)
Kayd, SouX

Redcoat (Eng)
DSNur, Kauri, Mason,
Meado, Trini, Waire,
ZinoN

Redoute (Eng)
BayBl, Pukho, Trini

Regensberg (Patio,Fl)
DSNur, Egmon, Mason,
Meado, Pukho

Reine des Violettes (Old F)
DSNur, Egmon, Kauri,
Meado, Parva, Pukho,
Waire

Reine Marie Henriette
Kauri, Waire

Remember Me (HT)
AmFu, DBoer, Denes,
Egmon, Mason, Meado,
Pukho, Rhine, Waire

Remuera (Fl)
DBoer, Egmon, Kauri,
Mason, Meado, Waire

Reve d'Or (Old F)
Kauri, Meado, Trini,
Waire

Rexy's Baby (Patio)
Denes, DSNur, Egmon,
Mason, Pukho, SouX,
Waire

Rima (HT)
Rhine

Ring Of Fire
SouX

Ripples (Fl)
AmFu, DBoer, Denes,
DSNur, Egmon Kauri,
Meado, Parva, Pukho,
Rhine, Waire

Rise 'n' Shine (Patio)
AmFu, Egmon, Mason,
Pukho, SouX, Waire

Rob Roy (Fl)
DBoer

Robert le Diable (Old F)
Mason

Robin Hood (Old F)
SouX, Trini

Robin Redbreast (Cott)
Egmon, Mason, Meado,
SouX

Robusta (Shr)
DBoer

Rock 'n Roll (Fl)
DBoer, Egmon, Rhine

Romeo (HT)
DBoer, DSNur, Egmon,
Mason, Meado, Pukho,
Rhine, Waire

Rosa Cooperi
Waire

Rosa Mundi syn gallica versicolor (Old F)
DSNur, Egmon, Kauri,
Meado, Parva, Trini,
Waire

Rosa Rouletti
SouX

Rosabell (Patio)
Mason

Rosamunde (Fl)
DBoer

Rosarama (HT)
DBoer, Egmon

Rose a Parfum de l'Hay
Kauri

Rose Bracteata
Waire

Rose de Rescht (Old F)
DBoer, Egmon, Kauri,
Waire

Rose Du Maitre d'Ecole
Kauri

Rose Du Roi A Fleurs Pourpres
Kauri

Rose Gilardi
SouX

Rose Hills Red
SouX

Rose Marie Viaud
BayBl

Rosemary Harkness (Mod)
Mason, Meado, ZinoN

Rosemary Rose (Old F)
DSNur, Kauri, Waire

Rosenthal (HT)
Mason, Meado, Pukho,
Rhine

Roseraie de l'Hay (Old F)
DBoer, DSNur, Egmon,
Kauri, Mason, Meado,
Nikau, Pukho, Waire,
ZinoN

Rosette Delizy (Old F)
DSNur, Kauri, Waire

Rosie
SouX

Rosy Cushion (Old F)
DBoer, DSNur, Egmon,
Kauri, Mason, Pukho,
SouX, Waire, ZinoN

Rosy Dawn
SouX

Rosy Mantle (Cl)
DBoer, DSNur, Egmon,
Kauri, Mason

Rote Max Graf
SouX, Trini

Roulettii
Parva

Roundelay
Kauri, Waire

roxburghii Plena (Old F)
BayBl, Kauri, Mason,
Nikau, Trini, Waire

Royal Dane (HT)
DBoer, Egmon, Meado,
Rhine, Waire

Royal Lavender (Cl)
DBoer, DSNur

Royal Romance (HT)
DBoer, Egmon

Royal William (HT)
AmFu, DBoer, Egmon,
Rhine, Waire

Ruatara
Kauri

rubrifolia syn glauca
Waire

rubrifolia Carminetta (Old F)
Mason

Ruby Allison syn Monthly Rambler
BayBl, Kauri

Ruby Wedding (HT)
DBoer

rugosa alba (Old F)
DSNur, Kauri, Mason,
Meado, Nikau, Pukho,
Trini, Waire

rugosa scabrosa (Old F)
ZinoN

Ruskin
Pukho, Waire

Rustica (HT)
DBoer

Sachet
SouX

Sadler
SouX

Sadlers Wells (Old F)
DSNur, Kauri, Pukho,
Trini, Waire

Safrano
Kauri, Waire

Sally Holmes (Mod Shr)
BayBl, DBoer, DSNur,
Egmon, Kauri, Mason,
Meado, Pukho, SouX,
Trini, Waire, ZinoN

Salmon Paree
Kauri

Samaritan (HT)
Egmon

San Jose Sunshine
SouX

Sancta
Waire

Sanders White (Cl)
BayBl, DBoer, DSNur,
Kauri, Meado, Nikau,
Trini, Waire, ZinoN

Santana (Cl)
DSNur, Egmon, Mason,
Meado, Pukho, Waire

Sarah Jayne
SouX

Sarah Van Fleet (Old F)
DSNur, Egmon, Kauri,
Waire

Satchmo (Fl)
DBoer, Egmon, Mason,
Meado, Rhine, Waire

Scabrosa (Old F)
DSNur, Egmon, Kauri,
Mason, Meado, Trini,
Waire, ZinoN

Scarlet Fire Scharlachgut (Old F)
Kauri, Mason, ZinoN

Scarlet Meillandina (Mini)
Mason

Scarlet Moss
SouX

Scarlet Runner (real name unknown)
Orang

Scentasia (Patio)
AmFu, Pukho

Schneelicht
Kauri

Schneeswerg (Old F)
DSNur, Egmon, Mason,
Pukho, Trini, Waire

Schoener's Nutkana (Old F
Mason

Schoolgirl (Cl)
AmFu, DBoer, DSNur,
Egmon, Meado, Pukho,
Trini, Waire

Scintillation
Kauri, SouX, Waire

Sea Foam (Cott)
AmFu, BayBl, CottP,
DSNur, Egmon, Kauri,
Mason, Meado, Nikau,
Ormon, Pukho, SouX,
Waire, ZinoN

Seabreeze
SouX

Seagull (Cl)
DSNur, Kauri, Pukho,
Trini, Waire

Semperflorens (Slaters Crimson China)
Kauri, Waire

Sensass (Cl)
DBoer, Egmon, Rhine,
Waire

Sequoia Gold
SouX, Waire

Sericea omiensis pteracantha (Old F)
Kauri, Mason

setigera (Cl)
Mason, Trini

setipoda
Kauri

Seven Sisters see R.Multiflora Grevillei
Kauri

Sexy Rexy (Fl)
AmFu, DBoer, Denes,
DSNur, Egmon, Mason,
Meado, Parva, Pukho,
Rhine, Waire, ZinoN

Shakespeare Festival
SouX

Sharifa Asma (Eng)
AmFu, BayBl, DBoer,
DSNur, Egmon, Kauri,
Mason, Meado, Pukho,
Rhine, Trini, Waire,
ZinoN

Sheer Bliss (HT)
AmFu, DBoer, DSNur,
Egmon, Meado, Pukho,
Rhine, Waire

Sheer Elegance (HT)
Egmon

Sheila's Perfume (HT)
Egmon, Pukho

Shiner (Gc)
Egmon, Mason

Shocking Blue (Fl)
Egmon, Meado, Pukho,
Waire

Shot Silk (Mod)
DSNur, Egmon, Meado,
Pukho, Rhine, Trini,
Waire

Shower of Gold
BayBl, Kauri, Waire

Shropshire Lass (Eng)
BayBl, DSNur, Kauri,
Meado, Trini, Waire,
ZinoN

Si
Parva, SouX

Sierra Glow
Denes

Sierra Sunrise
SouX

Silent Night (HT)
DBoer

Silky Mist (HT)
DBoer, Denes, Egmon,
Meado

Silver
SouX

Silver Jubilee (HT)
DBoer, Egmon, Mason, Meado, Waire

Silver Lining (HT)
DBoer, Waire

Silver Moon (Cl)
BayBl, DSNur, Kauri, Trini, Waire, ZinoN

Silver Wedding (HT)
DBoer

Simplicity (Mod Shr)
Egmon, SouX

Sir Clough (Eng)
DSNur, Kauri Meado, Waire

Sir Walter Raleigh (Eng)
BayBl, DSNur, Egmon, Kauri, Meado, Pukho, Waire

Sissinghurst Castle (Old F)
DBoer, Pukho, Trini, Waire

Slater's Crimson China (Old F)
Trini

Snow Carpet (Gc)
BayBl, Egmon, Mason, SouX, TRidg, Wells

Snow Twinkle
SouX, Waire

Snow Waltz (Cl)
DBoer, DSNur, Mason, Pukho, Rhine, Waire, ZinoN

Soft Lights
SouX

Softly Softly (Fl/HT)
DBoer, DSNur, Egmon, Mason, Meado, Pukho, Rhine, Waire

Soldier Boy (Old F)
ZinoN

Soleil d'Or (Old F)
DSNur, Mason, Waire

Solfaterre (Old F)
Mason, Meado

Solitaire (HT)
DBoer, Egmon, Meado, Rhine, Waire

Sombreuil (Cl)
AmFu, DSNur, Egmon, Kauri, Meado, Pukho, Trini, Waire, ZinoN

Sonia (HT)
DBoer, Meado, Waire

Sophie's Perpetual (Shr/Cl)
Waire

soulieana
Parva

Southern Alps
SouX

Souvenir d'un Ami (Old F)
DSNur, Kauri, Mason, Meado, Pukho, Trini, Waire

Souvenir de la Malmaison (Old F)
DSNur, Egmon, Kauri, Mason, Meado, Pukho, Trini, Waire

Souvenir de la Malmaison Climber
AmFu, DSNur, Egmon, Kauri, Mason, Meado, Parva, Pukho, Trini, Waire

Souvenir de Mme Boullet (Old F)
Mason

Souvenir de Mme Leonie Viennot (Cl)
AmFu, BayBl, DSNur, Kauri, Mason, Meado, Parva, Pukho, Trini, Waire

Souvenir de Philemon Cochet (Old F)
DSNur, Kauri, Pukho, Waire

Souvenir de St Anne's (Old F)
DSNur, Kauri, Pukho, Trini, Waire, ZinoN

Souvenir du Docteur Jamain (Old F)
DSNur, Egmon, Kauri, Pukho, Waire

Sparkler (Cott)
Denes, Egmon, Kauri, Mason, Meado, Pukho, SouX, Waire

Sparrieshoop (Mod Shr)
DSNur, Egmon, Kauri, Mason, Meado, Pukho, Trini, Waire, ZinoN

Spek's Centennial (Fl)
AmFu, DBoer, DSNur, Egmon, Mason, Meado, Parva, Pukho, Rhine, Waire

Spek's Yellow (Cl)
Trini

Spice Drop
SouX

Spiced Coffee (HT)
AmFu, DBoer, DSNur, Egmon, Mason, Meado, Pukho, Rhine, Waire

spinosissima single cherry (Old F)
Mason

spinossima Double Blush (Old F)
DSNur, ZinoN

spinossima Double Cream (Old F)
ZinoN

Sprinter (HT)
DBoer, Denes, DSNur, Egmon, Mason, Meado, Pukho, Waire

St Cecilia (Eng)
AmFu, BayBl, DBoer, DSNur, Egmon, Kauri, Mason, Meado, Pukho, Trini, Waire

St Swithun (Eng)
DBoer, DSNur, Egmon, Kauri, Pukho, Waire

Stacey Sue
SouX

Stanwell Perpetual (Old F)
DBoer, DSNur, Egmon, Kauri, Mason, Meado, Pukho, Trini, Waire

Star Delight
SouX

Stargazer (Fl)
DSNur, Mason, Pukho

Starglo
SouX

Starina
SouX

Starlight (HT)
DBoer, Egmon, Mason, Meado, Rhine, Waire

Stars 'n' Stripes (Mini)
Mason

Stella Polaris
Trini

Strawberry Ice (Fl)
DBoer, Egmon, Mason, Meado, Pukho, Waire

Sugar 'N Spice
SouX

Suma
Mason, SouX

Summer Dream (Fl)
Egmon

Summer Fashion (Fl)
DBoer, Egmon, Meado, Rhine, Waire

Sun King (HT)
DBoer, Meado, Rhine

Sun Princess
SouX

Sunbright (HT)
DBoer, Egmon, Rhine

Sunflare (Fl)
DBoer, Egmon, Rhine

Sunmaid (Mini)
Mason, SouX

Sunny Honey (Mod)
Kauri, Meado, Rhine, Waire, ZinoN

Sunny June (Old F)
DSNur, Mason, Pukho

Sunny South (Old F)
Trini

Sunnyside (Gc)
DSNur, Egmon, Mason

Sunrose (Fl)
DBoer, Mason, Waire

Sunsplash (Patio)
Egmon

Super Bowl (HT)
Egmon

Super Star (HT)
DBoer, DSNur, Egmon, Rhine

Susan Devoy (HT)
AmFu, DBoer, DSNur, Egmon, Mason, Pukho, Waire

Susan Hampshire (HT)
Egmon

Sutters Gold (HT)
DBoer, Egmon, Meado, Pukho, Trini, Waire

Sutters Gold climbing
Pukho, Waire

Suzanne (Old F)
DSNur, Pukho, Trini, Waire

Swan (Eng)
BayBl, DSNur, Egmon, Kauri, Meado, Trini, Waire

Swan Lake (Cl)
AmFu, DBoer, DSNur, Egmon, Mason, Meado, Pukho, Trini, Waire

Swany (Old F)
DSNur, Egmon, Meado, Waire

Swedish Doll
SouX

Sweet Chariot (Mini)
DSNur, Pukho, SouX

Sweet Dream (Patio)
Egmon, Pukho

Sweet Juliet (Eng)
AmFu, BayBl, DBoer, DSNur, Egmon, Kauri, Mason, Meado, Pukho, Waire

Sweet Magic
SouX

Sweet Perfume (Fl)
Denes, Egmon, Meado, Pukho, Waire

Sweet Raspberry
SouX

Sweet Repose (Fl)
DBoer

Sweetheart (HT)
Mason

Swinger
SouX

Sylvia (HT)
AmFu, DBoer, DSNur, Egmon, Mason, Meado, Pukho, Rhine, Waire

Sympathie (Cl)
AmFu, Egmon, Mason, Meado, Pukho, Rhine, Trini, Waire

Symphony (Eng)
DSNur, Egmon, Kauri, Meado, Pukho, Waire

Taffeta (Patio Cl)
Egmon

Taihape Sunset (HT)
DBoer, Egmon, Mason

Tamora (Eng)
AmFu, BayBl, DSNur, Kauri, Meado, Pukho, Trini, Waire

Taupo (Fl)
Pukho

Tausendschon (Cl)
BayBl, DBoer, DSNur, Kauri, Mason, SouX, Trini, Waire, ZinoN

Te Kawanata Hou
Kauri

Tea Rambler (Cl)
BayBl, DSNur, Kauri, Mason, Trini, Waire

Teddy (Mod)
Meado

Tempo (Cl)
DBoer

Tequila (Fl)
DBoer

Tequila Sunrise (HT)
AmFu, DBoer, Denes, Egmon, Mason, Meado, Waire

Teresa (HT)
Egmon, Waire

Thalia (Cl)
Trini

The Bishop (Centifolia)
BayBl, Kauri, Mason, Meado, Waire

The Bride
Kauri, Waire

The Countryman (Eng)
DSNur, Egmon, Kauri, Pukho, Waire

The Dark Lady (Eng)
AmFu, BayBl, DSNur, Kauri, Pukho, Waire

The Fairy (Old F)
BayBl, CottP, Denes, DSNur, Egmon, Kauri, Kayd, Mason, Meado, Nikau, Orang, Parva, Pgeon, Pukho, SouX, Trini, Waire

The Friar (Eng)
AmFu, DSNur, Kauri, Meado, Waire

The Garland (Cl)
BayBl, DSNur, Kauri, Mason, Meado, SouX, Trini, ZinoN

The Herbalist (Eng)
BayBl, DSNur, Kauri, Meado, Waire

The Knight
BayBl, Kauri, Waire

The Lady (HT)
Egmon

The Miller (Eng)
AmFu, BayBl, DSNur, Kauri, Meado, Parva, Trini, Waire

The Moth (Eng)
Pukho, Waire

The Naseby Rose (Otago Goldfields)
Trini

The Nun (Eng)

BayBl, DSNur, Kauri, Meado, Trini, Waire, ZinoN

The Pilgrim (Eng)

AmFu, BayBl, DBoer, DSNur, Egmon, Kauri, Mason, Meado, Pukho, Trini, Waire

The Prince (Eng)

AmFu, BayBl, DSNur, Egmon, Kauri, Meado, Pukho, Waire

The Prioress (Eng)

AmFu, DSNur, Kauri, Meado, Trini, Waire, ZinoN

The Reeve (Eng)

AmFu, DSNur, Kauri, Meado, Trini, Waire

The Squire (Eng)

AmFu, BayBl, DSNur, Kauri, Meado, Trini, Waire, ZinoN

The World (HT)

DBoer, Egmon, Waire

The Yeoman (Eng)

AmFu, BayBl, DSNur, Egmon, Meado, Pukho, Trini, Waire

Therese Bugnet

Kauri, Trini

Thisbe (Old F)

DSNur, Meado, Trini

Thornfree Wonder

Kauri

Thusnelda (Old F)

DBoer

Tiffie

SouX

Tiger (HT)

DBoer, Waire

Tiki (Fl)

DBoer

Tinkerbell (Patio)

Egmon, Mason, Meado

Tinwell Moss

Kauri

Tom Brown (Fl)

Pukho

Tony Jacklin (Fl)

DBoer, Rhine

Top Marks (Patio)

Denes, Egmon, Pukho

Topaz Jewel (Old F)

DSNur, Egmon, Kauri, Pukho, SouX, Trini, Waire

Touch Of Class (HT)

DBoer, DSNur, Egmon, Waire

Tour de Malakoff

Kauri, Waire

Tracey Wickham

SouX

Tradescant (Eng)

AmFu, DBoer, DSNur, Egmon, Kauri, Pukho, Waire

Tranquility (HT)

DBoer

Traumland (Fl)

Rhine

Treasure Trove (HT)

Pukho, Waire

Tricolore De Flandre (Old F)

Mason

Trier (Old F)

BayBl, DSNur, Kauri, Nikau, Trini, Waire, ZinoN

Trigintipetala (Old F)

DBoer, Kauri

Trinity (Cott HT)

DBoer, DSNur, Egmon, Mason, Meado, Pukho

Triomphe de l'Exposition (Old F)

Trini

Troillus (Eng)

AmFu, BayBl, DSNur, Kauri, Meado, Pukho, Waire

Tropical Skies (HT)

Egmon

True Love (HT)

DBoer, Egmon, Waire

Trumpeter (Fl)

DBoer, DSNur, Egmon, Meado, Rhine, Waire

Tuscany (Old Velvet Rose)

Kauri, Mason, Waire

Tuscany Superb (Old F)

DSNur, Egmon, Kauri, Waire

Typhoo Tea (HT)

DBoer, Waire

Typhoon (HT)

DBoer

Ueterson (Cl)

AmFu, Denes, DSNur, Egmon, Kauri, Mason, Meado, Pukho, Trini, Waire, ZinoN

Ulrich Brunner (Old F)

Trini

Uncle Walter (Mod Shr HT)

DBoer, DSNur, Egmon, Rhine, Waire

Urlich Brunner fils

Waire

Valentine Heart (Fl)

DBoer, Mason, Pukho

Valerie Jeanne (Mini)

Mason, SouX

Vanity (Shr)

BayBl, DBoer, Kauri, Parva, Trini, Waire

Variegata di Boulogna (Old F)

DSNur, Egmon, Pukho, Trini

Veilchenblau (Cl)

AmFu, BayBl, DBoer, DSNur, Kauri, Mason, Meado, Nikau, Parva, Pukho, SouX, Trini, Waire, ZinoN

Velvet Fragrance (HT)

DBoer, Denes, DSNur, Egmon, Mason, Pukho, Waire

Velvet Lustre (HT)

DBoer, Egmon, Rhine, Waire

Velveteen (HT)

Egmon

Veronica (HT)

Rhine

Vesper (Fl)

DBoer, DSNur, Kauri, Meado, Pukho, Rhine, Trini, Waire

Victor Borge (HT)

DBoer, DSNur, Egmon, Mason, Meado, Pukho, Rhine, Waire

Victor Verdier (Old F)

Trini

Vienna Woods (HT)

DBoer, Meado, Rhine

Village Lass

SouX

Village Maid (R.Centifolia Variegata)

Kauri

Violacea (La Belle Sultan)
Kauri, Waire

Violette (Cl)
BayBl, Mason, Nikau

virginiana
Kauri

Virgo (HT)
DBoer, DSNur, Meado, Waire

viridiflora (Green Rose)
AmFu, BayBl, DSNur, Kauri, Meado, Pukho, Waire

Vol De Nuit (HT)
DBoer

Voodoo (HT)
Egmon

Waikato (HT)
AmFu, DBoer, Egmon, Meado, Rhine, Waire

Wanaka (Patio)
Egmon, Meado, Waire

Warm Welcome (Patio Cl)
Egmon, Pukho, SouX, Waire

Warm Wishes (HT)
Denes, Egmon, Meado, Pukho

Warrior (Fl)
DBoer, Mason, Pukho

Warwick Castle (Pukho)
AmFu, BayBl, DSNur, Egmon, Kauri, Mtato, Trini, Waire

Water Colour (Mini)
Mason

Wedding Bells (Patio Cl)
Pukho

Wedding Day (Cl)
AmFu, BayBl, DBoer, DSNur, Kauri, Mason, Meado, Orang, Parva, Pukho, Rhine, Trini, Waire, ZinoN

Wee Jock (Patio)
Egmon, Mason, SouX

Weisse New Dawn (Cl)
DSNur, Kauri, Waire

Wendy (Patio)
AmFu, DSNur, Egmon

Wenlock (Eng)
BayBl, DSNur, Egmon, Kauri, Meado, Mtato, Parva, Waire

West Coast (HT)
DBoer, Egmon, Meado, Parva, Pukho, Waire

Westerland (Cl)
AmFu, DBoer, Denes, DSNur, Egmon, Kauri, Mason, Meado, Pukho, Trini, Waire, ZinoN

Western Sun (HT)
DBoer, Rhine

Westfalenpark (Cl)
DBoer, Denes, DSNur, Egmon, Mason, Meado, Waire

Whiskey (Mod)
Mason, Meado, Rhine, Waire, ZinoN

Whiskey Mac see Whiskey (Mod)
AmFu, DBoer, Denes, DSNur, Egmon, Meado, Pukho

Whisky Gill (HT)
Egmon

White Bells (Cott)
DSNur, Egmon, Mason, SouX, Waire

White Cecile Brunner (Old F)
DSNur, Kauri, SouX, Trini, ZinoN

White Cockade (Cl)
Mason, Waire, ZinoN

White Dream (Patio)
DSNur, Egmon, Mason, Meado, Pukho, SouX

White Duchess de Brabant (Old F)
Kauri, Meado, Waire

White Flight (Cl)
Trini, ZinoN

White Grootendorst
Kauri, Waire

White Knights (Cl)
Egmon, Meado, Pukho, Waire

White Lightnin' (HT)
DBoer, Denes, Egmon, Rhine

White Mini
Kayd

White New Dawn
Waire

White Out (Patio)
AmFu, Egmon, Kauri, SouX, Waire

White Paree
Kauri

White Sparrieshoop (Mod Shr)
DSNur, Egmon, Kauri, Parva, Pukho, Trini, Waire

White Spray (Fl)
DBoer, Denes, Waire, ZinoN

White Tausendschon (Cl)
DSNur, Kauri, Waire

White Wings (Old F)
DSNur, Kauri, Pukho, Trini, Waire

Why Not (Mini)
Mason, SouX

Wichmoss
Kauri

Wife of Bath (Eng)
AmFu, BayBl, DSNur, Egmon, Kauri, Meado, Pukho, Waire

Wild 'N Rare
SouX

Wild Flower (Eng)
BayBl, DSNur, Kauri, Meado, Pukho, Waire

Wilhelm (Shr)
DBoer, Mason, Trini, Waire

William & Mary (Old F)
Kauri, Mason, Waire

William Lobb (Old Velvet Moss) (Old F)
DSNur, Egmon, Kauri, Mason, Trini, Waire

William Shakespeare (Eng)
DSNur, Egmon, Kauri, Pukho, Waire

Wimi (HT)
DBoer, Egmon

Winchester Cathedral (Eng
AmFu, BayBl, DBoer, DSNur, Egmon, Mason, Meado, Pukho, Waire, ZinoN

Wind Chimes
Kauri

Windrush (Eng)
BayBl, DSNur, Kauri, Meado, Parva, Pukho, Trini, Waire

Winsome
SouX

Winter Magic (Mini)
Denes, DSNur, Mason, SouX

Wise Portia (Eng)
AmFu, BayBl, DSNur,
Egmon, Kauri, Meado,
Pukho, Waire

Wizard (Patio)
Egmon

Wolley-Dod was pomifera Duplex
Kauri

Work Of Art
SouX

Xanthina Canary Bird
Kauri

Yabadabadoo (HT)
DBoer, Egmon, Waire

Yellow Dutton (Eng)
AmFu, BayBl, DSNur,
Kauri, Meado, Pukho,
Waire

Yellow Charles Austin (Eng)
AmFu, BayBl, DSNur,
Kauri, Meado, Pukho,
Trini, Waire, ZinoN

Yellow Doll
SouX

Yesterday (Old F)
DSNur, Mason, Pukho,
Waire

York & Lancaster (Old F)
Kauri, Trini, Waire

Young Quin (HT)
Rhine

Zephirin Drouhin (Cl)
AmFu, BayBl, DBoer,
DSNur, Egmon, Kauri,
Mason, Meado, Pukho,
Waire

Zinger
SouX

Zonta Rose (HT)
Mason

Roscoea

alpina
Della

procera now R.purpurea
Parva

purpurea
Vall #

purpurea procera now R.purpurea
MaraN

Rosmarinus

lavandulaceus(prostrate)
CottP, Mtato

officinalis (Rosemary)
Della, King #, Mills,
Morgn, Orang, Ploug,
SelGr, Sweet, Telfa,
Trans, Trolh

officinalis Benenden Blue
BayBl, BlueM, Ploug

officinalis Blue Lagoon
Butlr, KeriP, Mills,
Mtato, Ormon, Pgeon,
Ploug, Trans

officinalis Collingwood Ingram
Ploug, Seasd

officinalis Genges Gold
BlueM, Hackf, KeriP,
Mtato

officinalis Lockwood
Hackf

officinalis Lockwood De Forest
BayBl, BlueM, Butlr,
Denes, KeriP, Mtato,
Ormon, Ploug, Telfa,
TopTr

officinalis Majorca Pink
KeriP, Marsh, MillH,
Mtato, Ploug, Telfa,
Wells

officinalis Miss Jessop's Upright
Denes, Marsh, Ploug,
TopTr

officinalis Prostratus (Weeping Rosemary)
CottP, Mills, Morgn,
Mtato, Orang, Ploug,
Seasd, SelGr, Sweet,
Trolh

officinalis Roseus
Denes, Orang, Ploug,
Sweet

officinalis Tuscan Blue
BlueM, Butlr, MillH,
Mtato, Ormon, Pgeon,
Ploug, Seasd, SelGr,
TopTr, Trans

officinalis Variegatus
Orang, Sweet

Pink Remembrance
KeriP, Trolh

semi-prostrate form
Sweet

Rosularia

pallida
Seasd

Rotala

indica
WaiMa

macrantha
Diack, WaiMa

wallichi
WilAq

Rothmannia

capensis
Reic #

globosa
Reic #, Woodl

Roystonea

oleracea
Reic #

regia
Reic #

Rubia

tinctorum (Madder)
Orang, Sweet

Rubus

australis
Orati

x barkeri
Orati

Benenden
Hackf

blackberry laciniatus Thornless
Kayd

boysenberry
Kayd, TreeC

boysenberry Kotata
TreeC

cissoides (Tataramoa/ Bush Lawyer)
NZtr #, Orati

fockeanus now pentalobus
Hackf

loganberry Waimate
TreeC

nepaulensis
Oasis, Parva, Peak

parvus
JoyPl, Orati

raspberry Autumn Bliss
TreeC

raspberry Fairview
Kayd

raspberry Glen Moy
TreeC

raspberry Glen Prosen
TreeC
raspberry Heritage
Kayd
raspberry idaeus red
Sweet
raspberry Marcy
TreeC
squarrosa
Orati
Tayberry (blackberry x raspberry)
TreeC
Tridel Benenden see Benenden
Ref

Rudbeckia

fulgida (Black-eyed Susan)
CottP, Mills
fulgida speciosa was newmanii
BayBl, Reic #
fulgida sullivantii Goldsturm (Coneflower, Black-eyed Susan)
BlueM, Looij, MillH, Reic #, Trans
Herbstsonne (Autumn Sun)
Peak, Telfa
hirta Becky mixed
King #
hirta Indian Summer
King #
hirta Irish Eyes syn R.h.Green Eyes
MillH
laciniata
CottP
laciniata Golden Glow
BayBl
maxima
Warwk
nitida
BayBl
occidentalis Green Wizard
Parva, Reic #
speciosa
MaraN

Ruellia

ciliosa
Trans

humilis
Pgeon
macrantha
AynDa, Trans, Woodl
squarrossa
LakeN
wherryi (Water Bluebell)
WilAq

Rumex

acetosa (Garden/Broad Leaf Sorrel)
Della, King #, Orang
acetosella (Sheeps Sorrel)
Sweet
crispus (Yellow Dock)
Sweet
scutatus (French Sorrel)
Mills, Orang, Sweet

Rumohra

adiantiformis
Reic #

Ruscus

aculeatus (Butchers Broom
Orang

Russelia

equisetiformis was juncea
Frans

Ruta

graveolens (Rue, Herb of Grace)
Della, King #, Orang, Sweet, Trans
graveolens Jackmans Blue
AynDa, BayBl

Sabal

mexicana
Reic #
minor
PalmF, Reic #
palmetto (Palmetto Palm)
Caves, Frans, Lsendt, Reic #
princeps
Reic #

Saccharum

officinarum (Sugarcane)
Koan, LakeN

Sagina

glabra Aurea now subulata A.
TRidg
subulata was glabra
Diack, NewlR
subulata Aurea (Irish Moss
Ashto, Diack, Telfa

Sagittaria

montevidensis (Arrowhead)
WaiMa
sagittifolia (Old World Arrowhead)
WaiMa, WilAq

Salix

alba Pendula (Weeping White Willow)
PuhaN
alba vitellina (Golden Willow)
Chedd, Diack
alba vitellina Pendula now S.alba Tristis (Golden Weeping Willow)
Burbk, Chedd, Dove, Hewsn, Peele, Pionr, Pukho, TopTr
babylonica (Weeping Willow)
Chedd, Peele, PuhaN
caprea (Pussy Willow)
Chedd, Diack
caprea Kilmarnock syn male caprea pendula (Kilmarnock Willow)
EasyB, Pukho, TopTr
caprea pendula
Denes
caprea x cinerea (Pussy Willow)
PuhaN
daphnoides (Violet Willow)
Diack, TopTr
discolor (Pussy Willow)
Mtato, Pionr
furcata now fruticulosa
Hackf
hastata Wehrhahnii
TopTr
kinuyanagi (Japanese Fodder Willow)
Apple, Chedd, Diack, Mtato, Peele, Pionr, PuhaN, TopTr

magnifica
Denes, TopTr

magnifica Female
MJury

magnifica Male
MJury

matsudana (Peking Willow)
Chedd, Mtato

**matsudana Pendula
(Weeping Matsudana
Willow)**
Burbk, Mtato, Pionr,
Pukho

matsudana Purpurea
Diack

**matsudana Tortuosa
(Twisted Willow)**
Diack, Dove, Hewsn,
Mtato, Pionr, PuhaN

**matsudana xAlba 1040
(Willow Tangoio)**
Diack, Ford, Mtato,
Pionr, Wensl

**matsudana xAlba 1184
(Willow Moutere)**
Diack, Ford, Mtato,
Pionr, SouWo, Wensl

medemii (Bee Willow)
Chedd

**Melanostachys
(gracilistyla M.)**
Diack

x moorei   v dwf
Seasd

myrsinifolia
Hackf

myrsinites
YakuN

opaca
TopTr

pentandra (Bay Willow)
PuhaN

purpurea Booth
Mtato

purpurea eugenei
Peele

**purpurea Green Dicks
Basket Willow**
Chedd

**purpurea nana Basket
Willow**
Chedd

**purpurea pendula
(Weeping Purple Willow)**
Denes, Dove, Pukho

repens var argentea
Denes

**seringeana (Grey-lvd
Willow)**
Peele, Seasd

**triandra Black Maul Basket
Willow**
Chedd

udensis Sekka
Diack

**viminalis Gigantea basket
willow**
Chedd

Salpiglossis

**sinuata Casino mixed
(Painted Tongue Velvet,
Trumpet Flower)**
King #

sinuata Gloomy Rival
King #

Salvia

varieties
Roswd

**aethiopis
(Mediterraneum/African
Sage)**
MaraN, Marsh, MillH

africana
Orang, Sweet

**africana lutea   was aurea
(Golden Salvia)**
KeriP, MaraN, MillH,
Orang

africana-caerulea
Trans

**Alan's Maroon (Burning
Embers)**
Trans

amplexicaulis
Marsh

apiana (White Sage)
King #, MillH, Sweet,
Trans

argentea (Silver Sage)
Della, Dream, MaraN,
MillH, Parva, TRidg

Argentine Skies
Peak, Warwk

arizonica
Marsh

austriaca
MaraN

azurea
BayBl, CottP, Dream,
KeriP, Marsh, Peak,
Pgeon, Telfa, Warwk

Bernies Red
MaraN

Blue Ribbon
Peak, Warwk

Bluebird
Egmon, KeriP

buchananii
BayBl, Otepo, Telfa

bulleyana
MaraN, Marsh, Parva

**bulleyana hybrids not
yellow**
Marsh

canariensis
MaraN

candelabrum
Marsh

castanea
Marsh

**chamaedryoides Blue
Ribbon**
BayBl, Peak

clevelandii (Fragrant Sage)
Della, Dream, King #,
MillH, Sweet

coccinea Cherry Blossom
Dream, King #

coccinea Coral Nymph
King #, Nikau

coccinea Snow Nymph
King #

**coccinea Starry Eyed
mixed**
King #

confertiflora
Hackf, Parva, TopTr,
Trans

crisata
Ashto

deserta now x sylvestris
KeriP, MaraN

dichroa
MaraN

dolomitica
Reic #

dumetorum
Marsh

Edward Bowles
Nikau

elegans Scarlet Pineapple (Pineapple Sage)
CottP, Della, Marsh, Mills, MTig, MTig #, Nikau, Trolh

farinacea Argent White
King #

farinacea Blue Bedder
King #

farinacea Strata
Dream, King #

forsskaolii
Dream, Looij, MaraN, Marsh, Mills, Vall #

fulgens (Red Sage)
Orang

glutinosa (Jupiters Distaff)
KeriP, Marsh

grahamii
Della, Orang, Ormon

greggii
MaraN

greggii Alba
Parva, Peak

guaranitica
Marsh, TRidg

guaranitica Black Knight
BayBl, CottP, Hackf, KeriP, MaraN, Sweet, Trans

guaranitica Blue Enigma
Peak, Warwk

guaranitica Blue Ensign
Parva

haematodes
BayBl, Pgeon, Sweet

hians
MaraN, TRidg

hormium (Red Topped/Painted Sage)
Della, King #

hormium Blue Monday
King #, Sweet

hormium Pink Sunday
King #

hormium White Swan
King #, Sweet

Indigo spires
CottP, Peak

involucrata
Pgeon

involucrata Bethelii
Hackf, KeriP, MaraN, Marsh, Orang, Parva, Sweet, Wells

jurisicii
MaraN, Pgeon

leucantha (Mexican Bush Sage, Chenille Plant)
BayBl, MaraN, Oasis, Orang, Pgeon

lyrata
Orang

macrosiphon
MaraN

madrensis
KeriP, Parva, Trans

mellifera (Black Sage)
Della, King #, Sweet

mexicana (Mexican Sage)
Dream, Hackf, KeriP, MaraN, Orang, Parva, Sweet, Telfa, Trans

mexicana alba
KeriP, Parva

microphylla Purple
Marsh

microphylla var neurepia
Marsh, Pgeon

microphylla var wislizenii was lemmonii
Marsh

moellerii
Marsh

moorcroftiana
MaraN

multicaulis was acetabulosa
Marsh

nemorosa
Marsh

nemorosa Amethyst
BayBl

nemorosa Blue Hills
Parva

nemorosa Ostfriesland (East Friesland)
BayBl, Egmon, KeriP, Marsh, MillH, Parva, Pgeon, Warwk

nemorosa Rosewein
KeriP

nubicola
MaraN

nubicola   mixed col.
AynDa

officinalis (Kitchen Sage)
Della, Dream, Kayd, King #, Mills, Orang, Sweet, Trans

officinalis Aurea (Golden Sage)
Orang, Trolh

officinalis Broad Leaf
Della

officinalis deep pink form
Orang

officinalis Grandiflora
Marsh

officinalis Icterina (v)
Marsh, Sweet

officinalis Lincoln Green
Marsh

officinalis Purpurascens (Purple/Red Sage)
Della, Looij, Marsh, MillH, Mills, Nikau, Orang, Peak, Pgeon, Pkrau, Seasd, SelGr, Sweet, Trans, Trolh

officinalis Rosea
Marsh

officinalis Tricolor (v)
Looij, Orang, Sweet

patens
Della, KeriP, MaraN, Marsh, Pgeon, Warwk

patens Alba
Marsh

patens Cambridge Blue
Marsh, Pgeon, Trans

patens Chilcombe
Marsh, Parva, Telfa

patens White Trophy
Peak, Warwk

Pink Beauty
Hackf

pratensis (Meadow Sage, Meadow Clary)
Marsh, Peak, Sweet, Telfa

pratensis Haematodes
Dream, MaraN

pratensis Haematodes Indigo
MaraN

przewalskii
MaraN, Marsh

puberula
Marsh

puberula El Butano
Marsh

Purple Knight
Trolh

recognita
Marsh

Red Dragon
Marsh, Pgeon

regeliana
Marsh

regla
Marsh

repens
Marsh

reptans
MaraN

rutilans now elegans Scarlet Pineapple
Della, Orang, Sweet

scabiosifolia
Sweet

scabra
Marsh

sclarea (Clary Sage)
King #, Koan #, Marsh, Mills

sclarea v turkestanica (Clary Sage)
Della, Dream, MaraN, Marsh, Peak, Sweet, Warwk

soulieli now brevilabra
Marsh

splendens Salsa series
King #

x superba (Blue Sage)
CottP, Mills

x sylvestris was S.deserta
KeriP, MaraN

x sylvestris Blauhugel (Blue Hills)
BayBl, Marsh

x sylvestris Blue Queen
Dream, MaraN, Marsh, Oasis, Warwk

x sylvestris Indigo Spires
BayBl

x sylvestris Rose Queen
CoFlo, MaraN, Marsh, MillH, Oasis, Warwk

uliginosa (Bog Sage)
BayBl, CottP, Diack, Egmon, KeriP, Marsh, Mills, Orang, Parva, Pgeon, Pkrau, Sweet, Telfa, Trans, WaiMa

Velvet Slipper
KeriP

verbenaca (Wild Clary, Vervain Sage)
AynDa, MaraN, Orang, Sweet

verticillata
KeriP, MaraN, Marsh, MillH, Mills

verticillata Alba
Marsh

virgata
Marsh

viscosa
Marsh

Sambucus

Adam
Koan C

caerulea (glauca)
TopTr

nigra (Elderberry)
Chedd, Dove, Orang, Sweet, TreeC

nigra Aurea (Golden Elderberry)
Burbk, Chedd, Dove, Orang, Sweet, TopTr

nigra Guincho Purple
Titok, TopTr

nigra laciniata (Fern-lvd Elderberry)
TopTr

nigra Variegata
Orang

racemosa Plumosa Aurea
Caves, Denes, Pukho

williamsii
TopTr

Samolus

repens (Maakoako)
Seasd

valerandii (Water Pimpernel, Green Water Rose)
WaiMa

Sandersonia

aurantiaca (Golden Lily of the Valley)
DaffA, Kayd, Otepo, Vall #

Sanguinaria

canadensis
MaraN

canadensis Plena
NewlR, Peak

Sanguisorba

minor was Poterium sang. (Salad Burnet)
Della, King #, Mills, MTig #, Orang, Seasd, Sweet, Trans, Trolh

obtusa
CoFlo, Della

Santolina

Bowles Lemon
BayBl, KeriP, MillH, Parva, Peak

chamaecyparissus (Lavender Cotton, Cotton Lavender)
CottP, Della, KeriP, Looij, Marsh, MillH, Mtato, Nikau, Orang, Ormon, Parva, Pkrau, Ploug, Seasd, SelGr, Sweet, Telfa

chamaecyparissus Weston
Marsh

Lemon Fizz
Ploug, TopTr

Lemon Gem
KeriP, Seasd

Lime Fizz
KeriP, MillH, Parva, Ploug, TopTr

pinnata ssp neopolitana
Marsh, Orang, Ploug

rosmarinifolia
Orang, Parva, Ploug, Sweet

rosmarinifolia Holy Flax
Marsh

rosmarinifolia Primrose Gem
KeriP, Peak

rosmarinifolia spp
rosmarinifolia was viridis
Marsh, Orang, Sweet

virens now S.rosmarinifolia spp rosmarinifolia
Ploug, Seasd, Sweet

viridis now S.rosmarinifolia spp rosmarinifolia
Orang, Ploug

Sapindus

Mukorossi
Apple

Sapium

japonicum
Caves

sebiferum (Chinese Tallow Tree)
Chedd, Reic #, TopTr

Saponaria

caespitosa
Otepo

x lempergii Max Frei
BayBl

ocymoides (Rock Soapwort
BayBl, Della, King #,
Looij, MaraN, Sweet

ocymoides Alba
Della

officinalis (Soapwort, Bouncing Bet)
CottP, Della, King #,
MaraN, Mills, Orang,
Seasd, Sweet, Wells

officinalis Alba Plena
BayBl

officinalis Rosea Plena
BayBl, CottP, KeriP,
Nikau

x olivana
BayBl, NewlR, Otepo

Rose Dream
Egmon, MillH, Parva

Sarcochilus

Fitzhart
AnnM

hartmannii
NormP

Melba
AnnM

Sarcococca

confusa
Caves

hookeriana
Woodl

ruscifolia (Christmas Box, Sweet Box)
BlueM, Denes, TopTr

ruscifolia chinensis
Caves

Sasa

amabilis
Isaac

chrysantha
Isaac

palmata nebulosa
Isaac

senanensis
Isaac

tsuboiana
Isaac

Sassafras

tzumu
Caves

Satureja

hortensis (Summer Savoury)
Della, King #, Sweet

montana (Winter Savoury)
Della, King #, MillH,
MTig #, NewlR, Sweet

repanda   now spicigera (Creeping Savoury)
BayBl, Mills, Orang,
Sweet

Sauromatum

guttatum   now venosum (Voodoo Lily)
Caves

Saururus

cernuus (Mouses Ear, Lizards Tail, Swamp Lily)
Diack, WaiMa, WilAq

Saxifraga

aizoon   now paniculata
AynDa

apiculata alba
NewlR

borisii
NewlR

burseriana sulphurea
NewlR

cochlearis
NewlR

cotyledon
CottP

cotyledon Caterhamensis
NewlR

cuneifolia (White London Pride)
CottP, Oasis

ferdinandi-coburgi
NewlR

fortunei
Hackf, Parva

Gold Dust
NewlR

granulata
MaraN

hostii
NewlR, Pgeon

hypnoides (Dovedale Moss)
Pgeon

juniperifolia sancta
NewlR

lingulata   now callosa
Ashto

moschata
MaraN, Pgeon

moschata Cream
Pgeon

Mossy Pink
Ashto

paniculata   was aizoon
NewlR

paniculata baldensis
Pgeon

paniculata orientalis
NewlR

Peter Pan
BayBl

primuloides Elliot's Variety
BayBl, Parva

Rosie
BayBl, CottP

rotundifolia
TRidg

stolonifera
Telfa

Stormont's Variety
CottP

Sulphur Queen
BayBl

Triumph
BayBl, CottP

umbrosa (London Pride)
Ashto, MaraN, NewlR,
Nikau, Parva, Telfa,
Trans, TRidg

umbrosa Elliots Variety
CottP

x urbium (London Pride)
Mills, Pgeon

White Hills
CottP, Oasis

x zimmetri
Pgeon

Scabiosa

varieties
Roswd

alba now Cephalaria a.
Ashto

alpina
NewlR, Nikau, Telfa

Butterfly Blue
Telfa

caucasica (Pincushion Flower)
CottP, MaraN, Marsh, Pgeon, Trans

caucasica alba
BayBl, Parva

caucasica Fama
TRidg

caucasica Lavender Blue
Nikau

caucasica Perfecta
BayBl, Parva

caucasica Perfecta Alba
Parva, TRidg

caucasica Perfecta Lilac
Egmon

caucasica Summer Snow
Pgeon

columbaria
BayBl, CottP, KeriP, MaraN, Pgeon, Trans

columbaria Nana
Parva, Pgeon

columbaria Pink Lace
BayBl, Pgeon, Trans

farinosa
CottP, KeriP, MaraN, Nikau, Pgeon, Seasd, Trans

graminifolia
Ashto, BayBl, Parva

lucida (Shining Scabious)
BayBl, Oasis

Midnight
BayBl, Nikau, Parva

minoana
MaraN

ochroleuca now columbaria o.
MillH, Parva, Trans

Pink Lace
CottP, Egmon, KeriP, Parva, Taunt

purple
MillH

rumelica now Knautia macedonia
Ref

stellata Starball
King #

triandra
Telfa

Scadoxus

multiflorus ssp katherinae was Haemanthus k. (Blood Lily)
BayBl, DaffA, JoyPl, MJury, Parva

puniceus was Haemanthus nataliense
MJury

Scandia

rosaefolia (Native Angelica)
Orati, Parva

Schefflera

actinophylla (Queensland Umbrella Tree)
Coatv, Frans, Manna, PalmF, Reic #

arboracola Compacta
Manna

arboricola (Dwarf Umbrella Tree, Hawaiian Elf Schefflera)
LakeN, Manna, Reic #

digitata (Pate, Seven Finger)
Coatv, Gordn, NZtr #, Orati, Reic #, Terra

HongKong Bicolour (v)
LakeN

renata
PalmF

Schima

argentea GWC 110
Woodl

khasiana
Denes, MJury

Schinus

molle (Pepper/Peruvian Mastic Tree)
Burbk, Denes, Mtato, NZtr #, Pionr, Reic #

terebinthifolius (Brazilian Pepper Tree)
Burbk, Coatv, Reic #

Schisandra

chinensis
CouCl

grandiflora
CouCl

sphenanthera (Magnolia Vine)
Denes

Schizocentron

elegans now Heterocentron
BayBl

Schizolobium

paraphyllum (Brazilian Fern Tree)
Manna

Schizophragma

hydrangeoides
BlueM, Caves, CouCl, Denes, Hackf, Parva, Taunt, Woodl

integrifolium
CouCl

integrifolium faurei
Woodl

pink
MJury

Schizostylis

coccinea (Kaffir Lily)
BayBl, Brown, Kayd, Ormon, Pgeon, Telfa, Trans, Vall #, WaiMa, Wells

coccinea alba
Ashto, BayBl, CottP, Diack, KeriP, NewlR, Ormon, Pgeon, Telfa, Trans, WaiMa

coccinea Blush syn Lady Anne
Hackf, JoyPl, MaraN

coccinea Major
BayBl

coccinea Mrs Hegarty
NewlR

coccinea Pink
Ashto, Diack, Ormon, Trans, WaiMa

coccinea Red
Ashto, Diack, MillH, NewlR

coccinea Rosea
Telfa

coccinea Sunrise
Hackf, KeriP

Schoenoplectus

validus (Club Rush)
Orati, Terra, WaiMa

Schotia

brachypetala (Weeping Boer-bean)
Ether, Reic #

Schreba

alata
Manna

Sciadopitys

verticillata (Japanese Umbrella Pine)
BlueM, Cedar, CPete, Denes, MJury

Scilla

adamsii
KeriP

autumnalis (Autumn Squill
Kerer

bifolia (Alpine Squill)
Kerer

bifolia Rosea
Kerer, Winga

campanulata Rose Queen now Hyacinthoides hispanica
Kerer

campanulatus see Hyacinthoides hispanica
NewlR

campanulatus Excelsior
VanEe

greilhuberi
Kerer

hispanica
JoyPl

hohenackeri
CottP, JoyPl

King of the Blues (Woodland Hyacinth)
BayBl, Kayd

litardierei was pratensis (Fairy Scilla, Woodland Hyacinth)
BayBl, Kerer

litardierei hoogiana
NewlR

mischtschenkoana
Kerer

monophyllos (One-lvd Squill)
Kerer

natalensis
JoyPl

non scripta now Hyacinthoides n.s.
JoyPl, Kerer, Mills

persica
NewlR

peruviana
Pgeon

pratensis now litardierei
Parva, RosPl

ramburei
NewlR

Rosenia
Kayd

siberica
NewlR, Winga

siberica Alba
Winga

The Rose (Woodld Hyacinth)
BayBl

turbergeniana
CottP, Parva, Winga

verna
Kerer

White City (Woodld Hyacinth)
BayBl

White Palace
Kayd

Scindapsus

aureus now Epipremnum a.
LakeN

pictus argyraeus
LakeN

Sciodoptys

verticillata (Japanese Umbrella Pine)
Taunt

Scirpus

americanus (Triangle-stemmed Sedge)
NZtr #

atrovirens
Diack, WaiMa

cernuus now Isolepsis c. (Fibre Optics Grass)
KeriP, NewlR

isolepsis (Fairy Grass)
WaiMa

sylvaticus (Wood Club Rush)
Diack, WaiMa

Scleranthus

biflorus (Twin Flower Knawel)
Matai, MillH, NewlR, Orati, Trans, Wahpa

uniflorus
CottP, Diack, KeriP, Matai, Orati, Pgeon, Seasd, Terra, Trolh

Scorzonera

hispanica
King #

Scrophularia

aquatica Variegata now auriculata V.
Diack, Marsh, WaiMa

nodosa (Figwort)
Mills, Orang, Sweet

Scutellaria

alpina
BayBl, MaraN, Pgeon, Telfa

baicalensis (Helmet Flower, Baikal Scullcap)
Parva, Sweet, Trans, Vall #

Cerise
Parva

formosana (Helmet Plant)
BayBl, Nikau

indica japonica now i.parvifolia
BayBl, Pgeon

indica Snowdrift
BayBl, Trans

laterifolia (Scullcap)
MTig #, Orang, Sweet

laterifolia Virginian Skullcap
Marsh

orientalis
Parva

orientalis var. pinnatifida
MaraN

pontica
BayBl, Parva
reptans
KeriP
salvifolia
Pgeon
scordiifolia (Helmet plant,
Scullcap)
KeriP, MillH, Orang
Snowdrift
Parva

Sedum

varieties
Roswd
acre
MillH
Autumn Joy syn
Herbstfreude
BayBl, CoFlo, CottP,
Egmon, KeriP, MaraN,
MillH, Mills, Oasis,
Ormon, Parva, Telfa,
Trans
Bertam Anderson
BayBl, CottP, Parva,
Peak, Trans
caeruleum
Parva
caespitosum syn rubrum
Otepo
cauticola Lidakense
Peak
floriferum Variegatum
now kamtschaticum V
BayBl, Telfa, Trans
Gold Form
Parva
kamtschaticum
Loolj, MaraN, Telfa
kamtschaticum
Variegatum
CottP, Peak
kirilovii
Pgeon
maximum Atropurpureum
BayBl
morganianum (Burrow's
Tail)
LakeN
reflexum now rupestre
(Reflexed Stonecrop)
CottP
reflexum cristatum
Seasd

Ruby Glow
BayBl, CottP, Egmon,
Peak, Trans
spathulifolium
Mills, Seasd
spathulifolium Cape
Blanco
CottP, Otepo, Pgeon,
Seasd
spathulifolium Purpureum
CottP
spathulifolium variegatum
Flore Pleno
Mills
spectabile
Della, Seasd, Trans
spectabile Brilliant
BayBl, Kayd, Mills,
Parva, Pgeon, Telfa
spectabile Carmen
Della
spectabile Stardust
BayBl, CottP, Parva, Peak
spectabile Variegatum
Oasis, Parva
spurium
KeriP, Seasd
spurium Coccineum
MaraN, Oasis, Pgeon
spurium Fuldaglut
BayBl, CottP, Marsh,
Otepo, Peak
spurium Ruby Mantle
BayBl, CottP, L'ooij,
Marsh, Parva
spurium Tricolour
Parva
Stewed Rhubarb Mountain
Peak
telephium Borderi
BayBl
telephium Munstead Dark
Red
BayBl, Peak
variegata
Nikau, Ormon, Parva
Vera Jamieson
BayBl, Hackf, Peak,
Pgeon, Telfa, Warwk
Weihenstephaner Gold
Telfa

Selaginella

kraussiana
NewlR

Selago

alba
Butlr
densiflora
KeriP
densifolius
Butlr

Selliera

radicans (Remuremu)
Orati, Seasd

Semiaquilegia

double ruby-purple
Orang
ecalcarata was
S.simulatrix
Herew, MaraN, Parva,
Telfa, TRidg, Vall #
ecalcarata double maroon
Trans

Semiarundinaria

fastuosa
Isaac

Sempervivum

calcareum Sir William
Lawrence
CottP
Centennial
Peak
Climax
Peak
Crimsonette
Peak
dolomiticum
Parva
Grey lady
Peak
hausenmannii
Parva
Hookeri
Pgeon
hybrids green & purple
Oasis
kindingeri
CottP
Old Rose
Peak
Pacific Red
CottP
Pacific Red Rose
Peak

Pekinese
Parva, Seasd

Sampler
Peak

tectorum
Mills, Trans

tectorum calcareum
Parva

Triste
Parva, Seasd

Unicorn
Peak

x widderi
Parva, Seasd

Senecio

articulatus (Candle Plant)
Ormon

cineraria (Dusty Miller)
MillH

cineraria Silverdust
Dowde, MaraN

Desdemona now Ligularia
Ashto

greyii see Brachyglottis g.
Ref

pectinatus
Ashto

rowleyanus (String of Pearls)
LakeN

scorpiodes
Marsh

viravira
BayBl, Denes

Sequoia

sempervirens (Californian Redwood)
Apple, BlueM, Burbk,
Cedar, Chedd, Coatv,
CPete, Dove, Ford,
McKe, Mtato, NZtr #,
Pionr, PuhaN, Terra,
TopTr, WakaC

sempervirens Adpressa
Cedar, CPete, Denes

sempervirens Dolomore
BlueM

sempervirens Filoli
Cedar

sempervirens Los Altos
Cedar

sempervirens Prostrata
Cedar

sempervirens Soquel
Cedar

Sequoiadendron

giganteum (Wellingtonia, Sierra Redwood, Giant Redwood)
BlueM, Caves, Cedar,
CPete, EasyB, Ford,
Matai, Mtato, NZtr #,
Pionr, PuhaN, WakaC

Serenoa

repens
Reic #

Seriphidium

canum was Artemesia c. (Silver Sagebrush)
Sweet

maritimum was Artemisia m. (Beach Wormwood, Old Woman)
Orang

Serissa

foetida Flora Plena now japonica FP.
Denes

Serratula

shawii now seoanei
NewlR, Telfa

Serruria

barbigera (Silky Serruria)
MatNu, Matth

florida (Blushing Bride)
MatNu, Matth

pedunculata (Grey Serruria)
MatNu, Matth

rosea (Bridesmaid)
Matth

Setaria

palmifolia
Telfa

Shibataea

kumasasa
Isaac, Peak

Sibbaldia

cuneata
Pgeon, Telfa

procumbens
MaraN

Sidalcea

candida
Pgeon, Vall #

candida Bianca
Nikau, Parva, Peak,
Telfa, Warwk

hybrida (Prairie Mallow)
Marsh, Orang

Jimmy Whittet
AynDa

Party Girl
CottP, Della, Dream,
KeriP, King #, MaraN,
Nikau, Parva, Pgeon

Purpuretta
Parva, Warwk

Rosaly
Warwk

Rosanna
Parva

Silene

acaulis
NewlR, Pgeon

alpestris
AynDa, MaraN, Nikau,
Pgeon

asterias
MaraN, Telfa

Backyard (loose sprays pink fls)
Vall #

californica
MaraN, Vall #

caroliniana
Della

caucasica
Della

conica Balletje
King #

dioica
Dream, KeriP, Nikau,
Trans

dioica Richmond
Telfa

elizabethae
Della

maritima now uniflora (Sea Campion)
Ashto, Looij, MaraN,
Trans, Trolh, Vall #

maritima Flore Pleno now S.uniflora Robin Whitebreast
Della

maritima prostrate
Vall #

maritima Rosea now uniflora R.
Della, Trans

pendula Peach Blossom
Ashto, King #, TRidg

pendula Snowball
Ashto, King #

regia
BayBl

Rose Parasol
Ashto

saxifraga
Della

schafta Catch fly
BayBl, Della, Looij

Swan Lake
Ashto, BayBl, Ormon, Parva, Pgeon

uniflora Druetts Variegated
BayBl

venose
KeriP

vulgaris (Bladder Campion
Della, Dream, King #

vulgaris pink
Nikau

vulgaris prostrata
Della

vulgaris white
Nikau

x Windrest
Parva

zawadskii
CottP, NewlR

Sisymbrium

luteum was Hesperis lutea
Marsh

Sisyrinchium

varieties
Roswd

angustifolium (Blue Eyed Grass)
Ormon, Pgeon

angustifolium album
Telfa

bermudianum
BayBl, CottP, Della, MaraN

brachypas now californicum b.
Looij

Californian Skies
Egmon

californicum (Golden-eyed Grass)
Della, Looij, Nikau, Pgeon, Trans

ecklonii
Kayd

filifolium now Olysnium f.
Pgeon

graminifolium (Dwarf Satin Iris)
Diack, WaiMa

idahoense was bellum (Californian Blue-eyed Grass)
AynDa, BayBl, Diack, Dream, KeriP, King #, Nikau, Oasis, Pgeon, Trans, WaiMa

idahoense Album
MaraN, Trans

macounii alba now idahoense Album
BayBl, CottP, Della, Diack, KeriP, Mills, NewlR, Nikau, Ormon, Pgeon, Telfa, Trans

macrocarpon
CottP

Mrs Spivey
CottP, JoyPl

striatum was Phaiophleps nigricans
BayBl, Della, Irida, KeriP, MaraN, MillH, Mills, Nikau, Ormon, Pgeon, Telfa, Trans, TRidg, Vall #

Sium

sisarum (Skirret)
Sweet

Skimmia

japonica
SelGr

japonica female
BlueM, Caves, Denes

japonica male
BlueM, Caves, Denes

japonica ssp reevesiana (Dwarf Skimmia)
Caves, Denes

Smilacina

racemosa
Hackf, Vall #

yesoensis
Titok

Smyrnium

olusatrum (Alexanders Herb)
Mills, Orang, Sweet, Titok

Solandra

grandiflora (Chalice Vine)
CouCl

longiflora
CouCl

Solanum

aviculare (Poroporo)
Gordn, NZtr #, Terra

crispum Glasnevin
ZinoN

dulcamara (Bittersweet)
Sweet

grandiflora
ZinoN

jasminoides (White Potato Vine)
CouCl, Denes, Kayd

jasminoides Grandiflora
Mtato

jasminoides variegata
CouCl

laciniatum (Poroporo)
Orati

muricatum (Pepino)
Koan, MTig

Naranjilla
Koan

potato mixed sp many colours
Koan #

potato Rainbow mixed
Koan #

rantonnetti
Butlr, Denes

seaforthianum (Brazilian Nightshade)
Denes

wendlandii (Blue Potato Vine)
Denes

Soldanella

carpatica

BayBl

montana (Fringe Flower)

Pgeon

pindicola

BayBl, Della, Parva

pusilla (Dwarf Snowbell)

Della, MaraN

villosa

BayBl, NewlR

Soleirolia

soleirolii was Helxine s. (Babies Tears)

Sweet, WaiMa

Solidago

Baby Gold

Della, KeriP, Looij, Oasis

canadensis

Della, KeriP, Mills, Orang, Pgeon, Sweet

Golden Baby

Ashto

Golden Shower

Telfa

Golden Thumb now Queenie

NewlR

x hybrida Colin

MaraN, MillH

Rockery Miniature

Ashto

sp dwarf

Mills, Orang

virgaurea

Ashto

Solidaster

luteus

BayBl, Coult, Pgeon, Telfa

luteus Lemore

BayBl, Parva

Sollya

heterophylla was fusiformis (Blue Bell Creeper, Australian Bluebell)

CouCl, Denes, Parva, Reic #, YakuN

heterophylla Rosea

CouCl, Denes

heterophylla White

CouCl, Reic #

Sophora

Dragons Gold

Coatv, Diack, Frans, Gordn, Kayd, Matai, Mtato, Orati

japonica (Japanese Pagoda tree)

Apple, Burbk, Chedd, Denes, Diack, Dove, EasyB, NZtr #, Peele, Pionr, PuhaN, Reic #, TopTr

japonica Pendula

Caves, Denes

microphylla (SI Kowhai)

Apple, Coatv, Diack, Gordn, Hewsn, Matai, Matwh, Morgn, Mtato, NZtr #, Orati, Pionr, Pukho, Reic #, SouWo, Terra, Wahpa, Wells, Wensl

microphylla longicarinata

BlueM, EasyB, Matai, Matwh, Orati

microphylla var fulvida

Orati

microphylla weeping form

Matai

mollis

Dove

prostrata

Matwh, Morgn, NZtr #, Orati

prostrata Little Baby

BlueM

tetraptera (NI Kowhai)

Apple, AynDa, Chedd, Coatv, Diack, EasyB, Ford, Gordn, Hackf, Hewsn, Matai, Matwh, Morgn, Mtato, NZtr #, Orati, Pionr, Pukho, Reic #, Terra, Wahpa, Wensl

tetraptera Gnome

Orati

tetraptera Grandiflora

BlueM

tetraptera Otari Gnome

BlueM, Matai, Pionr

Sorbaria

tomentosa

Hackf

Sorbus

americana (American Rowan)

Apple

aria (Whitebeam)

BlueM

aria Lutescens (Golden Whitebeam)

Denes, Mtato, Pukho, TopTr

aucuparia (Mountain Ash, Rowan)

Apple, BlueM, Chedd, Diack, Dove, Ford, Hewsn, Mtato, NZtr #, Pionr, PuhaN, Pukho, Wensl

aucuparia Edulis

Hewsn

aucuparia Red Marbles

Hewsn

aucuparia Roy

Pukho

aucuparia Xanthocarpa (Yellowfruited Rowan)

Apple, Dove, Hewsn

caloneura (Whitebeam(Chinese))

Caves

cashmiriana

BlueM, Denes, Diack, Hewsn

Chinese Lace

Pukho

commixta var rufoferruginea

TopTr

decora

Apple, Diack, Dove, Hewsn

devoniensis Devon form S. aria

Apple, Dove

discolor (Chinese rowan)

Denes, Pukho

esserteauana

BlueM

forrestii

Hackf

forrestii Forest

EasyB

gracilis

Hewsn

hibernica

BlueM

hupehensis (Hupeh Mtn Ash, Chinese Rowan)

Apple, Diack, Dove, EasyB, Ford, PuhaN, Pukho, TopTr

x hybrida
TopTr
Joseph Rock seedling
TopTr
Kirsten Pink
Denes, Hewsn, Pukho
koehneana
Burbk, Diack
pohuashanensis (Chinese Rowan)
Apple, Diack, Hewsn
reducta (Dwarf Rowan)
Apple, BlueM, Hackf, TRidg
Scarlet King
Burbk
vilmorinii
BlueM

Sorghum

Mennonite sorghum
Koan #

Sparaxis

mixed hybrids
Altrf, JoyPl, Kayd
new named hybrids
Irida
see also Synottia
Ref
tricolours mixed
Kayd
Blue Bird
Kerer
Golden Glory
Della
Purple Gem
DaffA
Scarlet Glory
CottP, DaffA

Sparganium

erectum
WaiMa

Sparrmannia

africana (Cape Stock-rose)
Ether, Hackf
ricinocarpa
AynDa

Spathiphyllum

species
LakeN

Spathodea

campanulata (Tulip Tree, tropical)
Reic #

Sphaeralcea

fendleri venusta
Dream
munroana pale pink
Trans
Priscilla Pink
Butlr, Denes, Mtato, Ormon

Spiloxene

alba
Brown, JoyPl, Trans
aquatica
DaffA
canaliculata
DaffA
capensis
DaffA
capensis mixed colours
Irida

Spiraea

Arguta (Bridal Wreath)
BlueM, PuhaN
betulifolia
Ormon
bumalda Anthony Waterer now S.japonica A.W.
Denes
canescens
Nikau
cantoniensis
BlueM
cantoniensis Flore Pleno
BayBl, Denes
cantoniensis Lanceata (Reeves Spiraea)
BlueM, Ormon
x Cristata
BlueM
douglasii
Nikau
fritschiana
TopTr
japonica
Dove
japonica albiflora
Ormon
japonica Alpina now j.Nana
BlueM

japonica Anthony Waterer was bumalda AW. (Red Spiraea)
Dove, Kayd, Nikau, Pgeon, Wells, YakuN
japonica Bullata
Ashto, BayBl, BlueM
japonica Crispa
Denes
japonica Gold Flame
BlueM
japonica Gold Mound
BlueM, Hackf
japonica Pink Ice
BayBl, TopTr
nipponica
Ormon
nipponica Snowmound
Ashto, BlueM, Denes, YakuN
Nyewoods Pink
Denes
Pink Lace
Ashto
prunifolia
BlueM
prunifolia Plena
Ashto, BlueM, Denes
salicifolia
Denes
thunbergii (Bridal Wreath)
BlueM, Looij, ZinoN

Sporodanthus

traversii (Giant NZ Restiad
Orati, Terra

Sprekelia

formosissima (Jacobean/Aztec Lily)
DaffA, Kayd, Mills

Stachys

byzantina was lanata (Lambs Ear)
Ashto, AynDa, CoFlo, CottP, Della, KeriP, Looij, MaraN, MillH, Mills, Nikau, Orang, Ormon, Pkrau, SelGr, Sweet, Telfa, Trans, Wells
byzantina Big Ears
Peak, Warwk
byzantina Cotton Boll
Telfa

byzantina giant form
BayBl

byzantina Limelight
MillH, Orang, Telfa, Trans, Wells

byzantina Medium
Peak

byzantina Primrose Heron
Peak

byzantina Sheila McQueen now b.Cotton Boll
Marsh

byzantina Silver Carpet
Marsh, Orang, Peak, Pgeon, Telfa

discolor was S.nivea (White Betony)
Marsh

lanata see S.byzantina
Ref

macrantha
Marsh, Vall #

macrantha Robusta
Peak

monieri
Marsh, Pgeon

nivea now discolor
CottP, Marsh, NewlR, Orang, Otepo

nivea alba
Telfa

nivea pink
Telfa

nivea plum
Telfa

officinalis (Betony, Bishopwort)
Della, Mills, Nikau, Orang, Sweet

officinalis Rosea Superba
Parva, Peak

sieboldii (Chinese Artichoke)
Mills

sylvatica (Hedge Woundwort)
Sweet

Stachyurus

praecox (Spiketail Bush, Early Spiketail)
Denes, Peele, Pukho

Staphylea

bumalda (Bladder Nut, Hokkaido Bladder Nut)
Dove, Ormon

x elegans (Bladder Nut)
TopTr

Stauntonia

hexaphylla (Japanese Staunton Vine)
BlueM, CouCl, Denes

Stenocarpus

sinuatus (Fire Whee! Tree)
Burbk, Chedd, Coatv, Denes, Matth, Reic #

Stenomesson

pearcei
JoyPl

Stephanotis

floribunda (Madagascar Jasmine)
CouCl, Denes, LakeN

Sternbergia

lutea (Autumn Crocus)
Irida, NewlR, Ormon, Parva

Stevia

rebaudiana (Stevia)
Orang

Stewartia

malacodendron
Caves

pseudocamellia (Japanese Stewartia)
Denes

pteropetiolata
Woodl

sinensis
Denes, Pukho

Stipa

gigantea
Titok

tenuifolia
Egmon

tenuissima
Telfa

teretifolia
Orati

Stokesia

laevis (Stoke's Aster)
BayBl, MaraN, Oasis, Telfa, Trans

laevis Alba
BayBl, MaraN

laevis Mary Gregory
Parva

laevis Silver Moon
Parva

Streblus

banksii (Banks Milk Tree)
Orati

heterophyllus (Milk Tree)
Orati

smithii (Smiths Milk Tree)
Burbk, Orati

Strelitizia

nicollai (Giant Bird Of Paradise)
Frans, JoyPl, Lsendt, PalmF, Reic #, SpecT

reginae (Bird Of Paradise)
Coatv, Denes, JoyPl, Lsendt, Reic #

Streptocarpus

capensis hybrids
Backw

Kim
Parva

Lynne
Parva

Ruby
Parva

Streptosolen

jamesonii (Orange Browallia, Marmalade Bush)
Denes

Strobilanthes

anisophyllus (Goldfussia)
Woodl

dyerianus
LakeN

purple fl ex Beth Chatto
Vall #

purple lvs & fl
KeriP

Strumaria

rubella
JoyPl

truncata
JoyPl

Stylophorum

diphyllum (Celandine Poppy)

BayBl

lasiocarpum

AynDa, Della, Vall #

Styrax

hemsleyanus (Chinese Snowbell Tree)

Apple, Caves, Denes, TopTr

japonicus (Japanese Snowbell Tree)

Apple, Caves, Chedd, Denes, Diack, Dove, Mtato, Peele, PuhaN, Pukho, TopTr, YakuN

obassia (Fragrant Snowbell Tree)

Apple, Diack, Peele, PuhaN, TopTr

Sutera

cordata

Pgeon, Wells

cordata Snowflake

CottP, Otepo

Sutherlandia

frutescens

Ether, Reic #

Swertia

perennis (Marsh Felwort)

WaiMa

Syagrus

romanzoffiana was Arecastrum r. (Queen/Cocos Palm)

Frans, LakeN, Lsendt, PalmF, SpecT

Symphoricarpos

albus (Snowberry, Waxberry)

BlueM, Chedd

x doorenbosii Mother of Pearl (Snowberry)

Denes

Symphyandra

hofmannii

Looij, Vall #

zanzegura

Oasis

Symphytum

caucasicum Eminence

BayBl, Parva, Peak

Goldsmith (v)

CottP, Parva, Peak

grandiflorum now ibericum

BayBl, KeriP, Looij, Seasd, Sweet, Trans

Hidcote Pink

Peak

ibericum was grandiflorum

BayBl, CottP, KeriP, Marsh, Orang, Peak

ibericum Hidcote

Marsh

ibericum Wisley Blue

Peak, Warwk

officinale

CottP, Koan #, MaraN, Mills, MTig, MTig #, Orang, Sweet

sp dwarf

Mills

tuberosum

Telfa

x uplandicum

Della

variegata

Telfa

Synadenium

grantii

LakeN

grantii rubra (Red Milk Bush)

LakeN

Syncarpia

glomulifera (Turpentine Tree)

NZtr #, Reic #

Syngonium

Infrared

LakeN

macrophyllum

LakeN

podophyllus

Manna

podophyllus Variegatum

Manna

White Butterfly

LakeN

xanthophyllum Green Gold

LakeN

Synottia

now Sparaxis

DaffA

bicolor

DaffA

parviflora

DaffA

variegata var metelerkampiae

DaffA

variegata var variegata

JoyPl

villosa

AynDa, JoyPl, Trans

Synthyris

missurica

Denes

Syringa

afghanica now protolaciniata (Miniature Lilac)

BayBl, BlueM, Denes

Alice Eastwood

Pukho

Clarke's Giant

Pukho

General Pershing

Pukho

x hyacinthiflora Esther Staley

Pionr, Pukho

x josiflexa Bellicent (Bellicent Lilac)

BlueM, Chedd, Denes, Dove, Pukho

josikaea (Hungarian Lilac)

Dove, MJury, Mtato

Madame Fracisque Morel

Pukho

meyeri Palibin (Korean Lilac)

Denes

microphylla Superba

Denes, Hackf, Parva

missimo

Denes

oblata

Caves, MJury

Olivier de Serres

Denes, Hewsn

palibiniana now meyeri Palibin (Korean Lilac)

MJury

patula maybe S.meyeri
Palibin (Korean Lilac)
   Butlr
x persica
   Denes, Herew
Princess Clementine
   Denes
vulgaris Belle de Nancy
   Hewsn, Pukho
vulgaris Charles Joly
   Denes, Pionr, Pukho
vulgaris Katherine
Havemeyer
   Denes, Pionr
vulgaris Mme Lemoine
   Denes, Hewsn, Pionr,
   Pukho
vulgaris Mrs Edward
Harding
   Pukho
vulgaris President Grevy
   Denes, Pukho
vulgaris Sensation
   Denes, Pionr, Pukho
vulgaris Souvenir de Louis
Spaeth
   Denes, Pukho

Syzygium

australe was Eugenia,
Acmena (Australian Rose
Apple, Bush Cherry)
   Burbk, Kayd
maire (Swamp Maire)
   Gordn, Orati, Pionr

Tabebuia

chrysantha
   Frans, Reic #

Tagetes

French Vanilla
   King #
lemmonii (Mexican
Marigold)
   AynDa, Della, King #,
   Trolh
lucida (Cloud Plant, Sweet
Marigold, Anisillo -
Pericon, Winter Tarragon)
   King #, Mills, Orang,
   Sweet
lunulata (Himalayan
Marigold)
   King #

patula (French Marigold)
   Sweet
patula Harmony (French
Marigold)
   King #
patula Striped Marvel
   King #
tenuifolia Lemon Gem
   King #
tenuifolia Starfire mixed
   King #
tenuifolia Tangerine Gem
   King #, Koan #, Sweet

Taiwania

cryptomerioides
   Cedar
cryptomerioides not blue,
finer foliage
   Cedar

Tamarindus

indica (Tamarind)
   Reic #

Tamarix

juniperina (Juniper
Tamarix)
   BlueM
pentandra Rubra now
ramosissima R. (Salt Cedar
   Pukho
ramosissima Pink Cascade
   Denes, Pukho

Tanacetum

balsamita was
Chrysanthemum b.
(Camphor)
   CottP, MillH, Sweet
balsamita ssp balsamita
(Costmary, Bible leaf,
Alecost)
   CottP, Orang, Sweet
balsamita tomentosum
was Balsamita major var t.
(Camphor Plant)
   Marsh
cinerarifolium was
Chrysanthemum c.
(Pyrethrum, Silver Feathers
   Della, King #, MillH,
   Seasd, Sweet
niveum (Silver Tansy)
   MillH

parthenium was
Chrysanthemum (Feverfew
   CottP, Della, Orang,
   Trans
parthenium aureum
(Golden Feverfew)
   CottP, Della, Orang
parthenium double (Double
Feverfew)
   Della, Sweet
ptarmiciflorum
(Pyrethrum)
   Marsh, Oasis
sp a giant feverfew 2m
   Marsh
sp C&M 1062
   Marsh
tibeticum
   MaraN
vulgare (Tansy)
   CottP, Della, King #,
   Mills, Orang, Sweet,
   Telfa
vulgare Goldsticks
   Della
vulgare Silver Lace (v)
   KeriP

Taxodium

ascendens now distichum
imbricatum
   Apple, Cedar, Pukho
ascendens Nutans now
d.i.N. (Pond Cypress)
   Denes, MJury
distichum (Swamp/Bald
Cypress)
   Apple, Butlr, Cedar,
   Chedd, Coatv, CPete,
   Denes, Dove, McKe,
   MJury, Mtato, NZtr #,
   Peele, Pionr, PuhaN,
   TopTr, WakaC
mucronatum (Mexican
Swamp Cypress,
Montezuma Cypress)
   Cedar, Diack, MJury,
   PuhaN, TopTr, WakaC
mucronatum pendulum
(Weeping Swamp Cypress)
   Caves, CPete

Taxus

baccata (Yew)
   BlueM, Cedar, Chedd,
   Denes, Ford, SelGr,
   ZinoN

baccata Amersfoort
Cedar
baccata Aurea Prostrata
BlueM
baccata Cavendishii
(Cavendish Yew)
Cedar
baccata Dovastoniana
Cedar
baccata Dovastonii
Aurea(v)
Cedar
baccata Fastigiata (Irish
Yew)
BlueM, Cedar, CPete,
Danu, Howen, Ormon
baccata Fastigiata Aurea
Cedar, CPete
baccata Fastigiata
Aureomarginata
BlueM, Cedar
baccata Fastigiata Silver
Spire now T.b. S.S.
Cedar
baccata Overeynderi
BlueM, Cedar, CPete
baccata Repandens
Cedar
baccata Semperaurea
Cedar
baccata Silver Spire (v)
Cedar
baccata Standishii
Cedar
baccata upright form
Cedar
cuspidata
Cedar
cuspidata Capitata
Cedar
wallichiana (Himalayan
Yew)
Cedar

Tecoma

alata
Frans
capensis (Cape
Honeysuckle)
Butlr
garrocha
Frans
smithii
Denes

stans
Frans, Woodl

Tecomanthe

hillii
CouCl, JoyPl, Wells
montana
CouCl, JoyPl, MJury
speciosa
CouCl, Denes, Frans,
Gordn, JoyPl, Matwh,
MJury, Orati, Pionr,
Wells
venusta
CouCl, JoyPl

Tecomaria

see Tecoma
Ref

Tecophilaea

cyanocrocus (Chilean Blue
Crocus)
DaffA, Parva
cyanocrocus Leichtlinii
DaffA, JoyPl

Telekia

speciosa
Marsh

Tellima

grandiflora (Fringecups)
Ashto, AynDa, Della,
Looij, MaraN, MillH,
Mills, Nikau, Peak, Trans
grandiflora Purpurea
Telfa
grandiflora Rubra
Peak

Telopea

Burgundy syn hybrida
Denes, MatNu, Matth
hybrida
Diack
oreades (Victorian
Waratah)
Apple, BlueM, Chedd
speciosissima (NSW
Waratah)
Denes, MatNu, Matth,
Reic #
speciosissima Dawn Fire
Denes, MatNu, Matth

Tetracentron

sinense
Caves, MJury

Tetragonacalmus

quadrulangularis
Isaac

Tetragonia

expansa (NZ Spinach)
King #

Tetragonolobus

purpurea now Lotus
(Asparagus Pea)
King #, Vall #

Tetrapanax

papyriferus (Rice Paper
Plant)
Denes

Tetrapathea

tetandra now Passiflora t.
Orati, Reic #, Terra

Tetrastigma

serrulatum
CouCl

Teucridium

parviflorum
Orati

Teucrium

chamaedrys (Wall
Germander)
Della, Looij, Nikau,
Orang, Seasd, SelGr,
Sweet
chamaedrys small form
Sweet
flavum
Marsh
fruticans (Silver
Germander)
BlueM, Butlr, Denes,
Ford, Morgn, Mtato,
Nikau, Pionr, SelGr,
TopTr, ZinoN
fruticans Azureum
Denes
hircanicum
Marsh, Warwk
x lucidrys
Marsh
massiliense (Sweet
Germander)
Della, Marsh
polium
NewlR

Royal Robe

Parva

scorodonia (Sage-leaf Germander, Wood Sage)

Orang, Sweet, Warwk

scorodonia Crispum

AynDa, BayBl, Hackf, Marsh, Ormon, Peak, Pgeon, Telfa, Trans, Vall #

sp pink fl catmint-like lvs

Marsh

Thalictrum

aquilegiifolium

AynDa, BayBl, BlueM, MaraN, Oasis, Parva, Pgeon, Telfa, TRidg

aquilegiifolium Purpureum

MaraN

aquilegiifolium var album

CoFlo, MaraN, Parva

coreanum now ichangense

NewlR

delavayi was dipterocarpum

AynDa, BayBl, Dream, MaraN, Mills, Parva, Pgeon, Trans

delavayi Album

AynDa, BayBl, KeriP, MaraN, Parva, Peak, Vall #, Warwk

delavayi Hewitts Double

BayBl, BlueM, Hackf, Kayd, Mills, Oasis, Peak, Taunt, TRidg

dipterocarpum now delavayi

Ashto, Dream, Kayd, MaraN, Trans

flavum var glaucum was speciosissimum

BayBl, Marsh, Otepo, Parva, Trans, Vall #, Warwk

glabra (Meadowrue)

Orang, Sweet

ichangense was coreanum

NewlR

javanicum

TRidg

kuisianum

Parva, Titok

minus

Ashto, Kayd, TRidg

minus adiantifolium

Pgeon

rochebruneanum

Caves, KeriP, MaraN, Parva, TRidg, Vall #

sp tiny pink/lavender fl, 90 cm

Vall #

speciosissimum now flavum glaucum

MaraN, MillH

Thamnocalamus

anceps

Isaac

microphyllus

Isaac

murielae

Isaac

nitida

Isaac

Thermopsis

lanceolata

MaraN, MillH, Warwk

Thlaspi

alpinum was Hutchinsia

Della

nevadensis

Della

rotundifolium

Della

Thryptomene

calycina Parry's Pink

Denes, Matth

calycina Pratt's Pink

KeriP, Nikau

calycina Taylors White

Denes, MatNu

denticulata

Denes, MatNu, Matth

saxicola Rosea (Rock Heath Myrtle)

Mtato

sp pink fl, tiny form

Parva

Thuja

koraiensis (Korean Arborvitae)

BlueM, Cedar

occidentalis (American Arborvitae, White Cedar)

BlueM, Cedar, PuhaN

occidentalis Aurea

BlueM

occidentalis Caespitosa

BlueM, Cedar

occidentalis Columbia

Cedar

occidentalis Danica

Cedar

occidentalis Ericoides (Heath Arborvitae)

Cedar, CPete, Kayd

occidentalis Filiformis

Cedar

occidentalis Globosa

Cedar

occidentalis Holmstrup

Cedar

occidentalis Little Gem

CPete

occidentalis Lutea

Cedar, CPete

occidentalis Ohlendorfii

Cedar

occidentalis Pendula

Cedar

occidentalis Pumilio Sudworthii

BlueM, Cedar

occidentalis Pyramidalis

BlueM, Cedar, Coatv, CPete, Diack, EasyB, Pionr, SpecT

occidentalis Rheingold

BlueM, Cedar, CPete, Hewsn, Matai, Mtato

occidentalis Spiralis

BlueM, Cedar

occidentalis Sunkist

Cedar

occidentalis Variegata

BlueM

occidentalis Vervaeneana now T. plicata Zebrina

Cedar

occidentalis Wansdyke Silver

BlueM, Cedar

occidentalis Wareana

BlueM

occidentalis Wareana Lutescens

Cedar, CPete

occidentalis Woodwardii

BlueM, Cedar, CPete

orientalis (Chinese Arborvitae, Northern White Cedar)
Cedar, NZtr #, WakaC

orientalis Aurea
Cedar

orientalis Aurea Nana
CPete

orientalis Aureovariegata
Cedar

orientalis Beverleyensis
Cedar

orientalis Blackman's Blue
BlueM, Cedar

orientalis Blue Cone
Cedar, CPete

orientalis Collen's Gold
Cedar

orientalis Filiformis Erecta
Cedar

orientalis Golden Ball
Cedar, CPete

orientalis Green Cone
BlueM, Cedar, CPete

orientalis Juniperoides
Cedar, CPete

orientalis Meldensis
BlueM, Cedar, CPete

orientalis Pyramidalis
Chedd

orientalis Rosedalis
Cedar, CPete

orientalis Sanderii
BlueM, Cedar, CPete

orientalis Sieboldii
Cedar

orientalis Spire
Cedar

orientalis Wainui Petite
Cedar

orientalis Westmont
BlueM, Cedar, CPete

plicata (Western Red Cedar)
Apple, BlueM, Cedar, Chedd, CPete, Diack, Dove, EasyB, Ford, Matai, Morgn, Mtato, NZtr #, Pionr, PuhaN, TopTr, WakaC, Wensl

plicata Aurea
BlueM

plicata Can Can
BlueM, Cedar, CPete, EasyB, Kayd, TopTr

plicata Gold King (Golden Cedar)
Pionr

plicata Old Gold
BlueM, Cedar, Coatv, Diack, EasyB, Kayd, Mtato, WakaC

plicata Rogersii
BlueM, Cedar

plicata Stoneham Gold
BlueM, Cedar

plicata Zebrina
BlueM, Cedar, EasyB, Hewsn, Matai

standishii
Cedar

Thujopsis

dolabrata (Deer Horn Thuja)
Cedar

dolabrata Nana
BlueM, Cedar, CPete

dolabrata Variegata
Cedar

Thunbergia

alata Suzie mixed (Blackeyed Susan)
King #

coccinea (Scarlet Clock Vine)
CouCl

gibsonii
CouCl

grandiflora (Sky Flower, Bengal Clock Vine)
CouCl, Frans

grandiflora Alba
CouCl

lutea
CouCl

mysorensis (Lady's Slipper
CouCl, Frans, LakeN

natalensis
BayBl

Thymbra

spicata (Zatar)
Trolh

Thymophylla

tenuiloba (Dahlberg Daisy, Shooting Star, Golden Fleece)
King #

Thymus

alba
Mills

Andersons Gold
Della, KeriP, Nikau, Sweet, Trolh

Aurea sp
CottP

Aureus
Della, Pgeon

Bergamot
CottP, KeriP, Parva, Seasd

billiardii
Telfa

Dressingham Pink
Della

carneus (Golden Thyme)
BayBl, Della, NewlR

Caspian
CottP, Della, Marsh, Seasd

cilicicus
MaraN

x citriodorus (Lemon Thyme)
CottP, Della, KeriP, Nikau, Orang, Trans

x citriodorus Argenteus (Silver Posie Thyme)
CottP, Marsh, Nikau

x citriodorus Aurea (Golden Lemon Thyme)
BayBl, CottP, Della, Marsh, MillH, Mills, Orang, Parva

x citriodorus Bertram Anderson
Marsh, Orang

x citriodorus Carol Ann
KeriP

x citriodorus Golden Carpet
Della, Parva

x citriodorus Lemon Spreader
Della, Mills, Parva

x citriodorus Silver Queen
Nikau

coccinea
BayBl, Marsh

doefleri
NewlR

Doone Valley (v)

CottP, Della, KeriP,
Mills, Nikau, Orang,
Parva, Seasd, Telfa

**drucei albus now
T.polytrichus britannicus
albus**

Seasd

drucei coccineus

NewlR

**drucei Minor now
T.polytrichus britannicus
minus**

Della, Telfa

**fragrantissimus (Orange
Thyme)**

CottP, Della, KeriP,
Marsh, Mills, Nikau,
Orang, Trans, Trolh

Golden Carpet

BayBl, Orang

Golden Spreader

Della

Goldstream

Della, Orang

Grey Smoke Thyme

CottP, Della

**Herba Barona (Caraway
Thyme)**

CottP, Della, KeriP,
Mills, Orang, Parva,
Sweet

lanuginosus

BayBl, Parva, Telfa

Lavender Spreader

Della

Lemon Carpet

KeriP

nitidus (Elfin Thyme)

Seasd

**nummularis
(Pizza/Oregano Thyme)**

CottP, Della, KeriP,
Marsh, Mills, Nikau,
Orang, Parva, Pgeon,
Sweet, Telfa, Trolh

**odoratissimus (Bergamot
Thyme)**

Della

Pink Chintz

CottP, Della

polytrichus

Della

polytrichus Porlock

BayBl, CottP, Della,
Marsh

**praecox Albus now
polytrichus a.**

Della

**praecox articus now
T.polytrichus britannicus**

Ref

praecox articus Coccineus

Marsh

**praecox articus Rainbow
Falls**

Marsh

**pseudolanuginosus (Woolly
Thyme)**

Orang, Parva, Seasd,
Trans

pulegoides

Della, Orang

serpyllum (Wild Thyme)

King #, Oasis, Orang

serpyllum albus

BayBl, Marsh, Parva,
Pgeon, Telfa

serpyllum Annie Hall

Della, Pgeon

serpyllum Bergamot

Mills, Orang

serpyllum carneus

CottP, Della

serpyllum coccineus

BayBl, CottP, Della,
Parva, Pgeon

serpyllum coccineus majus

Orang

serpyllum Elfin

CottP, Della, NewlR,
Parva

serpyllum Integer

CottP, Della, NewlR,
Orang, Pgeon, Seasd

**serpyllum lanuginosus
now pseudolanuginosus**

CottP, Della, Pgeon,
Trans

serpyllum Lemon Curd

Della, Seasd

serpyllum Minor

Orang

serpyllum Purple Robe

Della, Orang

serpyllum Rainbow Falls

Della, Mills, Nikau,
Parva, Seasd

Silver Queen

KeriP, MillH

Silver Strike

Parva

transylvanicus

Della

vulgaris (Thyme)

Della, Kayd, Mills,
Orang, Pgeon, Sweet,
Trolh

**vulgaris English Winter
(German/Winter Thyme)**

Della, King #, MTig #

**vulgaris French (French
Thyme)**

Orang

vulgaris French Summer

Della, MillH

vulgaris Silver Posy

Della, Orang, Sweet

**Westmoreland (Chicken
Thyme)**

Della, Marsh

White Carpet sp

CottP

Thysanotus

multiflorus (Fringe Lily)

BayBl

multiflorus alba

BayBl

Tiarella

varieties

Roswd

**cordifolia (Foam Flower,
Coolwort)**

Della, Mills, NewlR,
Peak, Pgeon, Sweet, Telfa

Filigree Lace

CottP, Parva, Peak

Pinwheel

Parva

polyphylla

TRidg

Tiger Stripe

Parva

wherryi (Foam Flower)

AynDa, BayBl, Looij,
MaraN, Telfa, Trans

wherryi Dark Eyes

Parva, Peak

wherryi Oak Leaf

Titok

Tibouchina

Alstonville

Frans

granulosa
Frans

organensis Grandiflora
Chedd

organensis Moonstruck
Denes, Parva

sp. small version 1m
Trans

urvilleana Grandiflora
Denes

Tigridia

hybrids (Jockey Caps)
AynDa, Irida, Kayd, KeriP, Vall #

pavonia alba
Nikau, Telfa, TRidg

pavonia golden
Telfa

pavonia maroon
Telfa

pavonia pink
Nikau, TRidg

pavonia red
Dream, Nikau

Tilia

americana (American Linden, Basswood)
Reic #

amurensis (Amur Linden)
Apple, Diack, PuhaN, Wensl

cordata (Small-lvd lime)
Apple, BlueM, Chedd, Diack, Dove, NZtr #, Peele, Pionr, PuhaN, Pukho, Reic #, TopTr, Wensl

dasystyla (Caucasian Linden)
Apple

x europaea (Linden, Lime)
Diack, EasyB, PuhaN

henryana (Henry's Lime)
TopTr

japonica
Dove

x Moltkei
TopTr

mongolica
TopTr

oliveri
Apple, TopTr

Petiolaris
Peele, TopTr

platyphyllos (Broad-lvd/Big-lvd Lime)
Apple, BlueM, Chedd, Dove, Mtato, NZtr #, Peele, Pionr, PuhaN, Reic #, TopTr

tomentosa (Silver Linden/Lime)
Apple, Denes, Dove, Peele, PuhaN, Reic #, TopTr

Tillandsia

aeranthos x bergeri var minor
NormP

aeranthos x stricta
NormP

baileyi
NormP

bergeri var major
NormP

bergeri var minor
NormP

butzii
NormP

floribunda
NormP

geminiflora
NormP

ixioades x montana
NormP

lindenii
NormP

seleriana
NormP

tenuifolia
NormP

usneoides (Old Mans Beard)
LakeN

Tipuana

tipu (Pride of Bolivia, Rosewood)
Coatv, Frans

Tithonia

speciosa Goldfinger (Mexican Sunflower)
King #, Vall #

Todea

barbara
Orati

Tofieldia

calyculata (Alpine Asphodel)
MaraN

Tolmiea

menziesii (Piggyback Plant, Mother of Thousands)
MillH

menziesii Variegata now m.Taff's Gold
Oasis

Tolpis

barbata Black Eyes
King #

Toona

sinensis was Cedrela s. (Chinese Toon)
Chedd, KeriP, Peele, Wells

Toronia

toru (Toru)
Burbk, Orati

Torreya

nucifera
Cedar

Trachelium

caeruleum (Blue Throatwort)
Dream, MaraN, MillH, Ormon

Trachelospermum

asiaticum
CouCl

jasminoides (Star Jasmine)
BlueM, CouCl, Denes, LanSc

jasminoides Variegatum
CouCl, Denes

Trachycarpus

fortunei (Chinese Windmill Palm)
Burbk, Chedd, Coatv, Kayd, Lsendt, NZtr #, PalmF, Reic #

martianus
Frans

Tradescantia

species also see Rhoeo
LakeN

x andersoniana (Spider Lily, Spiderwort)
CoFlo

x andersoniana Blue Danube
BayBl

x andersoniana Innocence
Dream

x andersoniana Iris Pritchard
BayBl

x andersoniana JC Weguelin
Pgeon

x andersoniana Osprey
BayBl

x andersoniana Pink
BayBl

x andersoniana Purity
BayBl

x andersoniana Purple Dome
BayBl, Pgeon, WaiMa

cerise pink
Telfa

pale blue
Telfa

Wilmot Rose
Pgeon

Tragopogon

porrifolius (Salsify, Vegetable Oyster)
King #, Koan #, Orang

Trevesia

palmata (Snowflake Tree)
Frans

sundaica
MJury

Tricyrtis

formosana
Telfa

formosana Stolonifera
Mills

hirta (Toad Lily)
AynDa, BayBl, Dream, Kayd, MaraN, Oasis, Pgeon, Telfa

hirta alba
BayBl, Telfa

hirta dwarf form
AynDa, KeriP

hirta hybrid mauve-white
Trans

hirta hybrid purple
Trans

hirta Nigra
MaraN

hirta Togen
Parva

macrantha
JoyPl, MJury, Parva

macropoda
Parva

ohsumiensis
MJury, Parva

T & M hybrids
Vall #

Trifolium

nigra (Black Shamrock)
Della

sp limegreen lvs w black edge
AynDa

Trigonella

foenum-graecum (Fenugreek)
King #, Sweet

Trillium

mixed
Parva

cernuum
Taunt

chloropetalum
TRidg, Vall #

ovatum
RosPl, Taunt

ozarkianum
Taunt

rivale
RosPl, Taunt

sessile alba
Kerer, Taunt

sessile red
Kerer, MJury, Taunt

viride
Titok

Tripterygium

regelii
CouCl

wilfordii
CouCl

Tristania

conferta now Lophostemon
Burbk, NZtr #, Reic #

Tristaniopsis

laurina was tristania (Water Gum, Kanooka)
Coatv, Reic #

Triteleia

hyacintha syn lactea
Kerer

laxa was Brodiaea l
Kerer, MaraN

laxa minima
AynDa, NewlR

laxa Queen Fabiola
Kerer

peduncularis
Kerer

Tritonia

mixed
Altrf, Kayd

Baby Doll
DaffA

Bridal Veil
Altrf

crocata (Montbretia)
DaffA

deusta ssp deusta
DaffA

deusta ssp miniata
DaffA

flabellifolia
DaffA

lineata
Irida

Pink Sensation
Altrf, DaffA

Salmon
Parva

securigera
DaffA

Serendipity
Altrf

squalida
DaffA

Trochodendron

aralioides
Caves

Trollius

europaeus Superbus
MaraN

ledebourii Golden Queen now chinensis GQ
  Della, MaraN
pumilus
  Della

Tropaeolum

majus Alaska mixed
  King #
majus Empress of India
  King #
majus Hermine Grashoff
  Parva
majus Moonlight
  King #
majus Peach Melba syn Strawberry & Cream
  King #
majus Salmon Baby
  King #
majus Top Flowering colours
  King #
majus Whirlybird Mix
  King #
pentaphyllum climbing (Flame Creeper)
  JoyPl
peregrinum (Canary Creeper)
  King #
tricolorum
  MJury, Peak
tuberosum (Mashua, anu)
  Hackf, Mills, MTig

Tsuga

canadensis (Eastern/Canadian Hemlock)
  Apple, Chedd, CPete, WakaC
canadensis Cole's Prostrate
  Cedar
canadensis Golden Seedling
  Cedar, CPete
canadensis Jeddeloh
  Cedar
canadensis Pendula (Weeping Hemlock)
  Cedar, CPete
canadensis Verkade Recurved
  Cedar

canadensis Yellow seedling form
  Cedar
chinensis (Chinese Hemlock)
  Apple
diversifolia (North Japanese Hemlock)
  Cedar
dumosa (Himalayan Hemlock)
  Cedar
heterophylla (Western Hemlock)
  Apple, BlueM, Cedar, Chedd, Dove, EasyB, Ford, Flom, PuhaN, WakaC
mertensiana (Mountain Black Hemlock)
  BlueM, Cedar, CPete, WakaC
sieboldii (Southern Japanese Hemlock)
  Cedar, CPete

Tuberaria

lignosa (Rockrose)
  Ashto

Tuberosa

polianthes
  JoyPl, Kayd

Tulbaghia

fragrans
  BayBl, Kayd, TRidg
fragrans alba
  BayBl
John Rider
  Telfa
violacea (Society Garlic)
  Hackf, Mills, Orang, Sweet, TRidg
violacea Silver Lace (v)
  BayBl, KeriP

Tulipa

Abba (double)
  VanEe
Abu Hassan (Single)
  VanEe
Ad Rem (Darwin hybrid)
  VanEe
Advance (Darwin hybrid)
  VanEe

Allegretto (double)
  VanEe
Apeldoorn
  Kayd, VanEe, Winga
Apricot Beauty (Single)
  VanEe
Artist (Fringed)
  VanEe
bakeri now saxatilis bakeri
  Parva
bakeri Lilac Wonder
  Parva
Ballade (Lily)
  VanEe
batalinii
  Parva
batalinii Bright Gem
  Parva
batalinii Bronze Charm
  Kerer, Parva
Beppy
  Kayd
Black Diamond (Single)
  VanEe
Black Parrot (Parrot)
  VanEe
Boccherini (Single)
  VanEe
Boutada (Dwarf)
  VanEe
Burning Heart (Darwin hybrid)
  VanEe
Cashmir (Single)
  VanEe
celsiana
  RosPl
Christmas Dream
  Kayd
Christmas Marvel (Single)
  VanEe
Clara Carder (double)
  VanEe
clusiana Cynthia
  Parva, VanEe
clusiana var chrysantha
  Kerer, Parva
Creme Jewel (Darwin hyb)
  VanEe
Crystal Beauty (Fringed)
  VanEe

Daydream (Darwin hybrid)
 VanEe
Debutante (Single)
 VanEe
Dillenburg
 Kayd
Don Quichotte (Single)
 VanEe
Donna Bella (Dwarf)
 VanEe
Doorman (Parrot)
 VanEe
Dreamboat (Dwarf)
 VanEe
Dreamland (Single)
 VanEe
Dutch Fair (Darwin hybrid)
 VanEe
Elite (double)
 VanEe
Elsi Eloff (Single)
 VanEe
Fancy Frills (Fringed)
 VanEe
Flaming Parrot (Parrot)
 VanEe
fosteriana
 Kerer
fosteriana Honorose
 NewlR
fosteriana Orange Emperor
 VanEe
fosteriana Princeps
 VanEe
fosteriana Princess Royale
 VanEe
fosteriana Purissima
 VanEe
fosteriana Red Emperor
 Kerer
Francois (Single)
 VanEe
Fringed Elegance (Fringed)
 VanEe
Fritz Kriesler (Dwarf)
 VanEe
Gaiety (Dwarf)
 VanEe

gesneriana lutea
 Kayd
Goldcoin (Dwarf)
 VanEe
Golden Age
 Kayd
Golden Day (Dwarf)
 VanEe
Golden Parade (Darwin hyb)
 VanEe
Greenland (Fringed)
 VanEe
greigii
 Kerer
Gudoshnik (Darwin hybrid)
 VanEe
hageri
 Parva
Hermione (double)
 VanEe
High Society (Single)
 VanEe
Hocus Pocus (Single)
 VanEe
humilis
 Parva
humilis Persian Pearl
 VanEe
Ile de France (Single)
 VanEe
Inglescomb Yellow
 Kayd
Inzell (Single)
 VanEe
Isolda
 Kayd
Jewel of Spring (Darwin hyb)
 VanEe
Karen Pratt
 Kayd
Kees Nelis (Single)
 VanEe
Klara Park (Parrot)
 VanEe
Leen van der Mark (Single)
 VanEe
Lilac Perfection (double)
 VanEe

Lilac Time (Lily)
 VanEe
Lily Schreyer (Single)
 VanEe
London (Darwin hybrid)
 VanEe
Madam de la Mar (Single)
 VanEe
marjoletii
 Kerer
Maytime (Lily)
 VanEe
Monsella (double)
 VanEe
Monte Carlo (double)
 VanEe
Moonshine (Lily)
 VanEe
Mount Tacomba (double)
 VanEe
ocutis
 Parva
Orange Toronto (Dwarf)
 VanEe
Orange Wonder (Single)
 VanEe
Oxford Elite (Darwin hyb)
 VanEe
persica
 Parva
Pink Diamond (Single)
 VanEe
Pink Impression (Darwin hyb)
 VanEe
Plaisir (Dwarf)
 VanEe
Purple Prince (Single)
 VanEe
Queen of Sheba (Lily)
 VanEe
Red Riding Hood (Dwarf)
 VanEe
saxatilis
 Kerer, NewlR, Parva
saxatilis Lilac Wonder
 VanEe
saxatilis var bakeri
 Parva
Shirley (Single)
 VanEe

Silverstream (Darwin hyb)
VanEe

Splendour
Kayd

sprengeri
Kerer

Spring Green (Fringed)
VanEe

stellata
Parva

Sunkist (Single)
VanEe

Sweet Lady (Dwarf)
VanEe

sylvestris
Kerer, Parva

tarda
Kerer, VanEe

Temples Favourite (Single)
VanEe

turkestanica
Kerer, Parva, VanEe

Vulcano (Darwin hybrid)
VanEe

Vvedenskyi
Parva

White Dream (Dwarf)
VanEe

Tunica

saxifraga now Petrorhagia
MaraN, Pgeon

saxifraga Alba Plena
Pgeon

saxifraga Rosette
BayBl, Parva

Tupidanthus

calyptrata (Burmese Umbrella Tree)
Frans, PalmF, Reic #

Tutcheria

spectabilis
Caves

Tweedia

caerulea (Tweedia)
Dream, KeriP, Orang, Reic #, Sweet, Trans, Vall #, Wells

Typha

angustifolia (Lesser Bullrush, Narrow-lvd Reed Mace, Soft Flag)
Diack, WaiMa

latifolia (Cats Tail, Bullrush, Nail Rod)
Diack, WaiMa

muelleri (Bullrush, Reed Mace, Cats Tail)
Diack, WaiMa

orientalis (Raupo)
Orati, Sweet

shuttleworthii (Bullrush, Reed Mace, Cats Tail)
WaiMa

Ugni

molinae was Myrtus ugni (Cranberry, Chilean Guava, Murtilla)
Chedd, Mtato, MTig, TreeC

Ulmus

carpinifolia Variegata (Variegated Elm)
Burbk, Chedd, Denes, Dove, Pukho, TopTr

elegantissima Jacqueline Hillier
MJury

glabra
EasyB

glabra Camperdownii (Camperdown Weeping Elm)
Pukho

glabra Horizontalis
Burbk, Denes, Diack, EasyB, Pukho

glabra Lutescens (Golden Elm)
Burbk, Chedd, Coatv, Mtato, Peele, Pionr, Pukho, TopTr

glabra Pendula (Weeping Elm)
Burbk, Chedd, Coatv, Denes, Mtato

x hollandia Groeneveld disease resist cv
Apple, Peele

x hollandica Lobel disease resist cv
Pukho

parvifolia (Chinese Elm)
Apple, Chedd, Denes, Diack, Dove, Mtato, Peele, Pionr, PuhaN, Pukho, TopTr

parvifolia Frosty (v)
Pukho

procera Argenteovariegata
Burbk

procera Louis Van Houtte (Golden Elm)
BlueM, Burbk, Denes, Diack, Dove, EasyB, Hewsn, Mtato

procera Variegata (Variegated Elm)
Peele

pumila disease resistt (Siberian Elm)
Denes, TopTr

pumila De Haag disease resistt
Diack, Peele

sarniensis purpurea
TopTr

Umbellularia

californica
Apple

Uncinia

egmontiana (Egmont Hook Sedge, Mt Egmont Tussock)
BlueM, Diack, Orati

rubra (Red Hook Sedge)
Diack, Gordn, Hains, KeriP, Matai, NZtr #, Orati, Telfa, Terra

uncinata (Watau, Dense Sedge, Hook Grass)
Hains, Nikau, NZtr #, Terra

Urtica

dioica (Nettle)
Sweet

ferox (Ongaonga)
Orati

Uvularia

grandiflora
NewlR

Vaccinium

corymbosum Bluecrop
MTig

corymbosum Darrow
MTig

corymbosum Dixie
MTig
corymbosum Eliot
TreeC
corymbosum Pacific Blue
TreeC
corymbosum Powder Blue
TreeC
cranberry
Orang, Pionr, TreeC
delavayi
Ashto, BlueM
moupinense
BlueM

Valeriana

montana (Mountain Valerian)
Mills
officinalis (Valerian)
CoFlo, CottP, Della, King #, MaraN, Marsh, MillH, Mills, Orang, Sweet
phu
Marsh

Valerianella

locusta (Corn Salad, Lambs lettuce)
King #, Koan #, Mills, MTig #

Vallea

stipularis
Hackf

Vallota

speciosa now Cyrtanthus elatus
AynDa, DaffA, MaraN
speciosa delicata
DaffA, Parva

Vancouveria

hexandra
BayBl, Hackf, Parva, Pgeon, TRidg

Veitchia

johannis
Reic #
merrillii
Reic #

Veltheimia

bracteata Rosealba
MJury

capensis
DaffA, JoyPl, KeriP, MJury, TRidg
viridifolia
MaraN

Venidium

fastuosum Zulu Prince (Monarch of the Veldt)
Della

Verbascum

adzharicum (Mullein)
Dream
blattaria albiflorum (White Moth Mullein)
Dream, Mills
blattaria Yellow Form
Vall #
bombyciferum
KeriP, MaraN, Sweet
Bridal
KeriP, Nikau
chiaxii
MaraN, Telfa, Vall #, Warwk
chiaxii Album
Della, Dream, King #, MaraN, Marsh, Oasis, Parva, Pgeon, Sweet, TRidg, Vall #
chiaxii Gainsborough
Parva
chiaxii Pink Domino
Parva, Peak
chiaxii yellow & white mixed
Mills
creticum
MaraN
Helen Johnson
BayBl, Parva, Peak
Jackie
BayBl, Parva, Peak
Letitia
BayBl, Parva, Peak
lychnitis (White Mullein)
MaraN, TRidg
nigrum (Black Mullein)
MaraN, MillH, Mills, Sweet
nigrum var album
MillH
olympicum
MaraN

olympicum Arctic Summer
MillH
olympicum Polarsummer
Trans, Warwk
phoeniceum
BayBl, Della, MaraN, Mills, Parva, Pgeon, Telfa, Trans
phoeniceum Album
Pgeon
phoeniceum Flush Of White
AynDa, BayBl, Della, King #, Peak, Sweet, Trans, Warwk
phoeniceum mixed hybrids
Dream, Kayd
phoenicium hybrid yellow fl w mauve eye
Looij
pyramidatum
MaraN
sp pale-pink fl, 2m (Moth Mullein)
Orang
Spica
BayBl, Marsh
thapsus (Mullein)
Della, Sweet
weidemannianum
AynDa, Della, Dream, King #, Mills, Nikau, Pgeon, Sweet, Trans, Warwk, Wells
yellow fl,green foliage
Nikau

Verbena

Blue Lagoon
King #
bonariensis was patagonica
Ashto, AynDa, Della, MaraN, MillH, Mills, Nikau, Otepo, Parva, Telfa
Boysenberry Cream
CottP
Bridal Pink
BayBl
Candy Stripe
BayBl, CottP, Nikau, Parva
Carenage Crimson
CottP
Crimson Queen
CottP, MillH

Cyclamen
CottP
Driven Snow
BayBl, CottP, MillH,
Parva
Garnet Red
BayBl
hastata
MaraN, Nikau
hastata Alba
MillH
Imagination
BayBl, Dream
Jester
BayBl, CottP
Lavender
CottP, Parva
Lavender Blue
Nikau
Lavender Mist
BayBl
Mauve Queen
Pgeon
Mulberry
CottP
nervosa Rigida Polaris
AynDa
**officinalis (Simplers Joy,
Vervain)**
Della, King #, MillH,
Orang, Sweet
Pale Pink
Pgeon
Panache
BayBl, Nikau
Peppermint
Pgeon
**peruviana was
chamaedrifolia**
CottP, Pgeon
Pink Delight
Parva
Pink Favourite
Nikau
Pink Parfait
BayBl, CottP, Pgeon
Purple King
Nikau
Red Carpet
Parva
rigida was venosa
Della, King #

rigida Lilacina
Trans
rigida Polaris
Della, King #, Nikau
rigida vernosa
CottP
Rose Queen
Pgeon
Scarlet Queen
Pgeon
Seaview
CottP
Sissinghurst
BayBl, CottP, Nikau
tenera was pulchella
Nikau
tenera Mahonetti
CottP
tenuisecta
MaraN, Oasis

Veronica
varieties
Roswd
alba
CottP
alpina Alba
Peak
Angels Eyes
Telfa
austriaca
CottP
austriaca ssp teucrium
AynDa, Oasis
**austriaca ssp teucrium
Bluebird**
NewlR
**austriaca ssp teucrium
Crater Lake Blue**
CottP, Peak, Trans,
Warwk
**austriaca ssp teucrium
Kings Blue**
BayBl
**austriaca ssp teucrium
Shirley Blue (Speedwell)**
Looij, Telfa
beccabunga (Brookline)
WaiMa, WilAq
chamaedrys
NewlR
cinerea
BayBl, NewlR, Otepo

filiformis (Speedwell)
Looij
fruticans (Speedwell)
MaraN
**gentianoides (Speedwell,
Birdseye)**
AynDa, BayBl, CoFlo,
CottP, MaraN, MillH,
Telfa, Trans, TRidg,
WaiMa
Goodness Grows
Egmon, Peak
incana
Ashto, MaraN, Telfa
kellereri
NewlR
Lila Karine
Peak
longifolia
CoFlo, CottP, MillH,
Warwk
longifolia Rosea
Pgeon
longifolia Snow Giant
BayBl, Peak
oltensis
Pgeon
Parvane
KeriP
pectinata
BayBl, CottP, Pgeon
pectinata Rosea
NewlR, Pgeon
peduncularis
Hackf, Telfa
peduncularis Georgia Blue
BayBl, CottP, Peak,
Sweet, Warwk
pink
Sweet
Pink Spires
MillH
prostrata
NewlR
prostrata Mrs Holt
BayBl, Pgeon
prostrata Trehane
BayBl, MillH, Pgeon,
Telfa
**selleri now
V.wormskjoldii**
Pgeon

spicata (Spike Speedwell)

AynDa, Della, King #,
Pgeon, Pkrau, Sweet,
Telfa, Vall #, Warwk

spicata Alba

MaraN, Marsh

spicata Blauest Spielarten

Marsh

spicata Blue Spire

Pgeon

spicata pink form

AynDa, Nikau, Vall #,
Warwk

spicata Rosy

MaraN

spicata Rote Spielarten

Marsh

spicata Sightseeing

Ashto

spicata ssp spicata

Nikau

spicata var incana

Nikau, Peak, Warwk

subsessilis hyb Blau Pyramide (Speedwell, Birdseye)

Marsh, WaiMa, Warwk

The Shirley

Marsh

thessalica

Telfa

virginica now Veronicastrum

MillH, Mills

Waterperry Blue

Nikau

Veronicastrum

virginicum (Culver's Root, Bowmen's Root)

MillH

virginicum album

Peak

Vestia

foetida was lycioides

Marsh, Vall #

Viburnum

betulifolium

Apple

x bodnantense Dawn

BlueM, Denes, Pukho,
Woodl

x burkwoodii

BlueM, Butlr, Chedd,
Denes, Diack, Hackf,
Hewsn, TopTr, ZinoN

x burkwoodii Anne Russell

BlueM, Pukho

x burkwoodii Fulbrook

BlueM, Ford, Pukho

x carlcephalum (Fragrant Snowball)

Denes, Pukho

carlesii Aurora

Denes, Hackf, Pukho

Chesapeake

Woodl

cylindricum

TopTr

davidii

BlueM, Diack, ZinoN

davidii female

Denes, TopTr

davidii male

Denes

erubescens

TopTr

Eskimo

Denes

farreri

BlueM, TopTr

x globosum Jermyn's Globe

TopTr, Woodl

japonicum (Japanese Viburnum)

BlueM, Hackf, Mtato

x juddii

Pukho

lantana Versicolor

BlueM

macrocephalum (Giant Chinese Snowball)

Denes, Pukho

odoratissimum (Sweet Viburnum)

Woodl

odoratissimum Emerald Lustre

Butlr, Denes, TopTr

opulus Compactum

BlueM, Denes

opulus Nanum (Dwarf Guelder Rose)

Caves, Denes, TopTr

opulus Sterile now V.o.Roseum (Snowball Tree)

BlueM, Butlr, Denes,
Dove, Mtato, Pionr,
Pukho, TopTr

opulus Xanthocarpum (Lacecap Viburnum)

BlueM, Caves, Dove,
Pukho

plicatum

BlueM

plicatum Lanarth

BlueM, Caves, Chedd,
Denes, Pukho, TopTr,
Wells, Woodl

plicatum Mariesii

Ashto, BlueM, Caves,
Denes, MJury, Pukho,
TopTr

plicatum Pink Beauty

BlueM, Caves, Denes,
Dove

plicatum Roseace

Denes, Pukho, TopTr,
TRidg

plicatum Summer Snowflake

BlueM, Caves, Woodl

plicatum tomentosum

Denes, MJury

plicatum tomentosum Roseum

Denes

rhytidophyllum

Apple

setigerum (Upright Viburnum)

Apple, BlueM, Denes,
Dove, TopTr

sieboldii

TopTr

tinus (Laurustinus)

Diack, Ford, Morgn,
Ormon, Pkrau, TopTr

tinus Bewleys Variegated

BlueM, Kayd, Matwh,
Mtato, Wells

tinus Eve Price

BlueM, Denes

tinus laurustinus

Mtato, SelGr

tinus Lucidum

Denes, Mtato, Pionr,
TopTr

tinus Variegatum

SelGr

tomentosum now plicatum
  Butlr, ZinoN
tomentosum Lanarth now plicatum L.
  TopTr
trilobum (American Cranberry Viburnum)
  BlueM, Butlr, Pukho

Vicia

cracca
  Vall #
fabia (Broad Bean)
  MTig #

Vigna

caracalla was Phaseolus c. (Snail Flower Creeper)
  CouCl, Parva
Yard Long Bean (Dow Gauk Bean, Asparagus Bean, Long Black Seeded)
  King #

Vinca

Golden Wanderer
  BayBl
minor (Lesser Periwinkle)
  MillH
minor Argenteovariegata
  Pgeon
minor Atropurpurea
  Mtato
minor Azurea Flore Pleno
  BlueM
minor Double Blue
  CottP
minor Double Plum
  CottP
minor Funky Purple
  CottP
minor Gertrude Jekyll
  BayBl, BlueM, CottP, Seasd
minor Multiplex
  BlueM
minor Variegata
  MillH
minor Wine
  CottP

Viola

Andross Gem
  Marsh, Nikau

arenaria rosea now rupestris rosea
  TRidg
arvensis (Field Pansy)
  Orang
Bowles Black
  NewlR, TRidg
Butter Yellow
  Ashto
Clear Crystals Black (Black Pansy)
  King #
Coeur d'Alsace
  Pgeon
confusa hagasakiensis
  Parva, TRidg
Cornetto
  Nikau
cornuta alba
  CottP, Otepo, Peak, Pgeon, TRidg, Trolh
cornuta Apricot Ripple
  Parva
cornuta Bambini mixed
  King #
cornuta Belmont Blue
  BayBl, Marsh
cornuta Boughton Blue
  Peak
cornuta Chantreyland
  MillH, Parva
cornuta Cream Princess
  Della
cornuta Gustav Wermig
  Dream
cornuta Lilacina
  Marsh, Peak
cornuta minor
  TRidg
cornuta Moonlight
  Peak
cornuta Penny Azure Wing
  King #
cornuta Penny mixed
  King #
cornuta Princess mixed
  King #
cornuta Sorbet Blueberry Cream
  Della, King #
cornuta Sorbet Lavender Ice
  Della, King #

cornuta Sorbet Lemon Chiffon
  Della, King #
cornuta Sorbet Purple Duet
  Della, King #
cornuta Sorbet Yellow Frost
  Della, King #
cornuta White Perfection
  Dream
cornuta Yellow Perfection
  Dream
cucullata striata Alba
  Dream
cunninghamii
  Mills
Dairymaid
  Marsh
elatior
  MaraN, TRidg
Haslemere
  CottP, Nikau, Peak, Pgeon
hederacea (Pixie Viola, Australian Violet)
  CottP, MaraN, Mills, NewlR, Nikau, Oasis, Pgeon, Seasd, TRidg
hederacea alba
  Oasis, Parva
Irish Molly
  BayBl, CottP, Marsh, Parva
Jack-a-Napes
  Marsh
Jeans Blue
  Marsh
Jersey Gem
  Marsh
jooi
  MaraN, TRidg
Karmen
  Ashto
koreana (Cyclamen Violet)
  Parva
labradorica
  Oasis, Telfa
labradorica purpurea
  Mills
Maggie Mott
  MaraN, Marsh, NewlR, Nikau, Peak
Maggie Nott purple M.Mott
  Peak

Major Primrose
 Parva
Marie Louise
 Pgeon
Martin
 BayBl
Mayfair
 Trolh
Milkmaid
 Marsh
Molly Sanderson
 Peak
Moonlight
 MaraN, Marsh, Parva
Nellie Britten
 Marsh
oblique
 Della
odorata
 CottP, Della, Telfa
odorata Flamingo
 TRidg
odorata Gothic
 TRidg
odorata Irish Elegance
 Marsh, Parva
odorata Mrs R Barton
 Marsh
odorata Princess de Galles(Princess Of Wales)
 BlueM, Marsh, TRidg
odorata Queen Charlotte
 TRidg
odorata rosea
 Marsh
odorata Sulphurea (Apricot Viola)
 Pgeon, TRidg
odorata var pink
 MillH
parma Blue
 BlueM
parma Doubles mauve or lavender
 Ashto, Mills
parma Doubles White
 Ashto, Mills
Pat Kavanagh
 Parva, Peak
pedatifida
 NewlR
Pixie Blue
 Nikau

Prince Of Wales
 Ashto, Kayd, Mills, Pgeon
Princess May
 Marsh
Purple Wood
 Trolh
Rebecca
 BayBl, Parva
Rodney Davey (v)
 Parva, TRidg
Romeo And Juliet
 Della
rupestris rosea was arenaria r.
 TRidg
selkirkii
 TRidg
septentrionalis
 CottP
setelica
 TRidg
Sidborough Poppet
 Parva
sororia alba
 TRidg
sororia Freckles
 Ashto, AynDa, CoFlo, CottP, Della, Dream, Mills, NewlR, Pgeon, Telfa
sororia rubra
 TRidg
Susannah
 Parva, Peak
Swanley White
 Pgeon
tricolour (mixed) (Heartsease)
 Orang, Trolh
tricolour King Henry (Heartsease)
 King #
tricolour Miss Helen Mount (Heartsease)
 King #
williamsii Velour colours
 King #
wittrockiana Baby Franjo
 Dream
wittrockiana Baby Lucia
 Della, MillH
wittrockiana Chalon mixed
 King #

wittrockiana Jolly Joker
 Della, King #
wittrockiana Jolly Joker Light Blue
 King #
wittrockiana Padparadja
 Della, King #
wittrockiana Romeo & Juliet
 King #
yedoensis
 Della, TRidg

Virgilia
divaricata (Keurboom)
 Chedd, Coatv, Denes, Mtato, Pionr, Reic #
oroboides syn. capensis
 Burbk, Hewsn, Morgn, Mtato, TopTr

Viscaria
oculata mixed
 King #
oculata candida White
 King #
oculata Cherry Blossom
 King #
oculata nana Blue Angel
 King #
oculata nana Rose Angel
 King #

Vitaliana
primuliflora
 NewlR

Vitex
agnus-castus (Chaste Tree)
 Denes, Orang, Sweet
keniensis (Meru Oak)
 Ether
lucens (Puriri)
 Burbk, Chedd, Coatv, Denes, Frans, Gordn, Matwh, Mtato, Orati, Pionr, Pukho, Terra

Vitis
amurensis (Amur Vine)
 CouCl, Denes, TopTr
coignetiae
 CouCl, ZinoN
grape Albany Surprise
 Koan C
grape Black Dalmatian
 Koan C

grape Cardinal
  Harri

grape Chassela's d'Or de Versailles
  Harri

grape Diamond
  Harri

grape Flame
  Harri

grape Interlaken
  Harri

grape Ngunguru Red/Ngunguru White
  Mtanu

grape Niagra
  Koun O

grape Pinot Meunier
  Harri

grape Purpurea
  CouCl, Denes

grape Schuyler
  Harri

Wachendorfia

brachyandra
  AynDa

paniculata
  JoyPl, Vall #

parvifolia
  AynDa

thrysiflora
  Backw, MaraN, Telfa, WaiMa

Wahlenbergia

albomarginata (NZ Bluebell)
  Oasis

sp sm rosettes/pale blue fl
  Pgeon

Waldsteinia

fragarioides
  NewlR

Warrea

tricolour x Zygopetalum blackyi x Zygo Helen Ku
  NormP

Washingtonia

filifera (Cotton/Petticoat Palm)
  Coatv, NZtr #, Reic #

robusta (Mexican Fan/ American Cotton / Washingtonia Palm)
  Burbk, Chedd, Coatv, Frans, Lsendt, PalmF, Reic #, SpecT

Waterhousea

floribunda   syn Eugenia ventenati
  Pukho, SpecT

Watsonia

mixed colours dwarf hybrids
  DaffA, JoyPl, MJury

mixed colours lge hybs
  Kayd

aletroides
  AynDa, DaffA

aletroides hybrid
  JoyPl

brevifolia   now laccata
  AynDa, Irida, Parva

Dwarf Hybrid -pink shades
  BayBl

green buds/cream fls
  KeriP, Parva

latifolia
  Parva

marginata
  AynDa, Della

marginata var minor
  DaffA

meriana
  Irida

pillansii
  AynDa

Pink Fairy
  BayBl

tabularis
  AynDa

viridiflorus
  DaffA

Wattakaka

sinensis   now Dregea s.
  Denes

Weigela

Bristol Ruby
  Chedd

decora (Mountain Weigela)
  Dove

Eva Rathke
  BlueM

Evita
  Chedd, Denes

florida Foliis Purpureis
  BlueM

florida Variegata (Apple Blossom)
  BlueM, Chedd, Pionr, PuhaN, Wells

Grace Warden
  Denes

Looymansii Aurea
  BayBl

Minuet
  Denes

Newport Red
  BlueM, Denes, PuhaN

Praecox Variegata
  Ormon

Rosabella
  BlueM

Snowflake
  BlueM, Denes, Dove

subsessilis
  Hackf, TopTr

Weinmannia

Kiwi Red
  Orati

racemosa (Kamahi)
  Gordn, Hewsn, Matai, Morgn, Mtato, NZtr #, Orati, Pionr, Terra

silvicola (Towai, Tawhero)
  Mtato, Orati, Terra

Westringia

brevifolia (Australian Rosemary)
  Butlr, Denes, Mtato

brevifolia Highlight
  Kayd, Mtato

fruticosa (Coast Rosemary)
  Kayd, Seasd

fruticosa Silverlight (v)
  Seasd

fruticosa Variegata   was rosmariniformis V.
  BlueM

Widdringtonia

nodiflora   was cupressoides, whytei (Sapree-Wood)
  Cedar

Wisteria

floribunda (Japanese Wisteria)
  Coatv, CouCl
floribunda alba
  CouCl, Denes
floribunda Black Dragon
  Caves, Parva, Pukho
floribunda Blue
  CouCl, LanSc
floribunda carnea
  CouCl
floribunda Cascade
  CouCl
floribunda Domino
  CouCl, Parva
floribunda Geisha
  CouCl
floribunda Harlequin
  CouCl
floribunda Lavender Lace
  CouCl, Parva
floribunda Lipstick
  CouCl, Parva
floribunda longissima
  CouCl
floribunda longissima alba
  CouCl
floribunda Macrobotrys
  Caves, Pukho
floribunda Magenta
  CouCl
floribunda Peaches & Cream
  CouCl
floribunda Pink Ice
  CouCl, Pukho, TopTr
floribunda Purple Patches
  CouCl
floribunda Rosea (Pink Flowered Wisteria)
  Caves
floribunda Royal Purple
  Pukho
floribunda Snow Showers
  Denes, Parva, Pukho
floribunda violaceae plena
  CouCl, Denes, TopTr
sinensis (Chinese Wisteria)
  Coatv, CouCl, Mtato, Pkrau, Pukho
sinensis Amethyst
  CouCl, Denes, Parva

sinensis Blue Sapphire
  Denes
sinensis Caroline
  Chedd, CouCl, Denes, Parva, TopTr
sinensis Flora Plena
  Denes
sinensis Prematura Alba
  Pukho
sinensis Reindeer
  CouCl
venusta (Silky Wisteria)
  CouCl, Parva, TopTr
venusta White Silk
  Denes

Wodyeti
bifurcata
  Reic #

Worsleya
raineri (Empress of Brazil)
  JoyPl

Wulfenia
carinthiaca
  MaraN

Xanthoceras
sorbifolium
  Apple, Ormon

Xanthorrhoea
australis (Black Boy, Australian Grass Tree)
  JoyPl, LakeN

Xanthosoma
jacquinii lineatum
  LakeN
sagittiifolium
  LakeN
sp violet lvs
  Frans

Xeranthemum
annuum Lumina
  King #
annuum White
  King #

Xeronema
callistemon (Rapo-taranga, Poor Knights Lily)
  Denes, Gordn, JoyPl, KeriP, Matwh, Orati, Parva, Terra

Yucca

elata
  MaraN
filamentosa (Adam's Needle)
  Pgeon
Garland's Gold
  Kayd, MJury
glauca (Small Soapweed)
  TopTr
glauca elata radiosa
  JoyPl
whipplei (Our Lord's Candle)
  Caves, JoyPl

Zaluzianskya
capensis Midnight Candy (Night Phlox)
  King #

Zamia
species
  Reic #
furfuracea (Cardboard Plant Cycad)
  PalmF

Zantedeschia
mixed
  Kayd, Reic #
aethiopica (Arum Lily)
  CottP, Reic #
aethiopica Childsiana
  BayBl
aethiopica Chromatella
  MillH, WilAq
aethiopica Green Goddess
  AynDa, BayBl, CottP, Diack, Herit, Reic #
aethiopica Little Child
  WilAq
aethiopica Little Gem
  Diack, WaiMa
Angelique
  Eyrew, Parva
Best Gold
  Eyrew
Black Eyed Beauty
  Eyrew
Black Magic
  Eyrew, Parva
Bridal Blush
  Eyrew
Butterscotch
  Parva

Cameo
  Eyrew
Chianti
  Eyrew
Cleopatra
  Parva
Cream
  Parva
Dominique
  Eyrew, Parva
Eldorado
  Eyrew
Elliotiana
  Eyrew
Fandango
  Eyrew
Fantasy
  Parva
Harvest Moon
  Eyrew
Hazel Marie
  Eyrew
Lady Luck
  Eyrew
Moonlight
  Eyrew
Morning Mist
  Eyrew
Mystique
  Eyrew
Pacific Pink
  Eyrew
palaestinum
  Telfa
Peachy Pink
  Parva
Pink Opal
  Eyrew
Pink Pearl
  Eyrew
Pink Persuasion
  Eyrew
Rose Queen
  Eyrew
Rosy Dawn
  MillH
Sensation
  Eyrew
Treasure
  Eyrew, Parva

Zauschneria

californica garettii
  NewlR

Zea

Early Gem
  Koan #
gracillima Strawberry Corn (ornamental)
  King #
japonica (Indian Ornamental Corn)
  King #
japonica Mini
  King #
Maori Corn (for Kaanga Pirau)
  Koan #
mays Hawaiian (Sweetcorn
  MTig #
mays Indian Rainbow
  MTig #
Silver Platinum
  Koan #

Zelkova

carpinifolia (Caucasian/Elm Zelkova)
  Apple, Caves, PuhaN, TopTr
serrata (Japanese Zelkova, Japanese Keaki)
  Apple, BlueM, Denes, Diack, EasyB, Ormon, Peele, Pionr, PuhaN, Pukho, Wensl
sinica (Chinese Zelkova)
  Diack, Dove, Ormon, TopTr, Wensl

Zenobia

pulverulenta
  Titok

Zephyranthes

ajax
  DaffA
alba
  TRidg
candida (Flower of the West Wind)
  AynDa, CottP, Kerer, NewlR, Telfa
longifolia
  DaffA
tubespathus
  DaffA

Verunda
  Kerer

Zieria

Pink Crystals
  Parva

Zigadenus

nuttallii
  TRidg

Zingiber

Mioga (ginger but not root, cold tolerant)
  Koan, Mills, Parva

Zinnia

elegans Envy
  King #
linearis Trailing Classic
  Della, King #
linearis Trailing Classic White Star
  Della, King #

Zygopetalum

b.g. White Jumbo
  AnnM
crinitum
  AnnM
intermedium
  AnnM
mackayii
  AnnM

Zyzyphus

jujuba (Jujube, Chinese Date)
  MTig #, NZtr #, Reic #

Common Names Index

Apricot ..... see Prunus

Apricot Viola ..... Viola odorata Sulphurea

Apulco Pine ..... Pinus apulcensis was P pseudostrobus var a.

Araluen Gum ..... Eucalyptus kartzoffiana

Arctic Poppy ..... Papaver radicatum

Argentine Pea ..... Lathyrus pubescens

Argyle Apple ..... Eucalyptus cinerea

Arizona Ash ..... Fraxinus velutina

Arizona Cypress ..... Cupressus arizonica

Arizona Longleaf Pine ..... Pinus engelmannii

Armands Pine ..... Pinus armandii

Armenian Grape Hyacinth ..... Muscari armeniacum

Arnica ..... Arnica montana

Arolla Pine ..... Pinus cembra

Arrowhead ..... Sagitteria montevidensis

Arrowroot ..... Canna edulis

Arrowroot ..... Maranta arundinacea

Arthritis Herb ..... Centella asiatica

Artichoke, Jerusalem ..... Helianthus tuberosus

Arugula ..... Eruca sativa

Arum Lily ..... Zantedeschia aethiopica

Asahibotan Cherry ..... Prunus (cherry flwg) shimidsu zakura (Okumiyako)

Ashes ..... Fraxinus species

Asparagus Pea ..... Tetragonolobus purpurea

Aspen ..... Populus tremula

Atherton Palm ..... Laccospadix australasica

Atlantic White Cedar ..... Chamaecyparis thyoides

Atlas Cedar ..... Cedrus atlantica

Auricula ..... Primula auricula

Australian Bean Flower ..... Kennedia vine

Australian Bluebell ..... Sollya heterophylla was fusiformis

Australian Cabbage Tree ..... Livistonia australis

Australian Cypresses ..... Callitris species

Australian Frangipani ..... Hymenosporum flavum

Australian Fuchsia ..... Correa species

Australian Hoop Pine ..... Araucaria cunninghamii

Australian Mint Bush ..... Prostanthera species

Australian Pencil Orchid ..... Dendrobium Aussie Cascade x striolatum

Australian Rose Apple ..... Syzygium australe was Eugenia, Acmena

Australian Rosemary ..... Westringia brevifolia

Australian Violet ..... Viola hederacea

Austrian Black Pine ..... Pinus nigra

Autumn Crocus ..... Colchicum speciosum

Autumn Crocus ..... Sternbergia lutea

Autumn Fern ..... Dryopteris erythrosora

Autumn Snowflake ..... Leucojum autumnalis was Acis a.

Autumn Squill ..... Scilla autumnalis

Avens ..... Geum urbanum

Avocado ..... Persea varieties

Aztec Lily ..... Sprekelia formosissima

Babaco ..... Carica pentagona

Babies Tears ..... Bacopa caroliniana

Babies Tears ..... Soleirolia soleirolii was Helxine s.

Baboon Flower ..... Babiana species

Baby Blue Eyes ..... Nemophila menziesii

Baby's Breath ..... Gypsophila species

Bachelor's Button ..... Kerria japonica Pleniflora

Baeuerlens Gum ..... Eucalyptus baeuerlenii

Baikal Scullcap ..... Scutellaria baicalensis

Balearic Is Box ..... Buxus balearica

Balkan Pine ..... Pinus peuce

Balloon Flowers ..... Platycodon grandiflorus

Balm of Ecuador ..... Azorella trifurcata

Balm of Gilead ..... Cedronella canariensis was triphylla

Balsam Fir ..... Abies balsamea

Balsam Pear ..... Momordica charantia

Bamboo ..... Arundinaria species

Bamboo ..... Bambusa species

Bamboo ..... Chaminobambusa species

Bamboo ..... Dendrocalamus species

Bamboo ..... Gigantachloa species

Bamboo ..... Phyllostachys species

Bamboo ..... Pleioblastus species

Bamboo ..... Pseudosasa species

Bamboo ..... Sasa species

Bamboo ..... Semiarundinaria species

Bamboo ..... Shibataea species

Bamboo ..... Tetragonacalamus species

Bamboo ..... Thamnocalamus species

Bamboo Grass ..... Anemanthele lessoniana syn Oryzopsis l.

Bamboo Palm ..... Chamaedorea seifrizii

Banana ..... Musa species

Banana (ornamental) ..... see Ensete

Banana Passionfruit ..... Passiflora antioquiensis

Banana Passionfruit ..... Passiflora mollissima

Bangalay ..... Eucalyptus botryoides

Bangalow palm ..... Archontophoenix cunninghamia

Banks Milk Tree ..... Streblus banksii

Barberry ..... Berberis species

Barbers Gum ..... Eucalyptus barberi

Barren Mountain Mallee ..... Eucalyptus approximans

Barronwort ..... Epimedium species

Basil ..... Ocimum basilicum

Basil Mint ..... Mentha x piperita citrata Basil

Bats in the Belfry ..... Campanula trachelium

Bay Tree ..... Laurus nobilis

Bay Willow ..... Salix pentandra

Beach Wormwood ..... Artemisia stelleriana

Beach Wormwood ..... Seriphidium maritimum was Artemisia m.

Bead Plant ..... Nertera depressa

Bead tree ..... Melia azederach

Bean ..... Phaseolus species

Bean, Asparagus ..... Vigna Yard Long (sesquipedalis)

Bean, Broad ..... Vicia fabia

Bean, Long Black Seeded ..... Vigna Yard Long (sesquipedalis)

Bear Berry ..... Arctostaphylos uva-ursi Woods Red

Bears Breeches ..... Acanthus species

Beautiful Little Red Girl ..... Acer palmatum Beni-komachi

Beautiful Magnolia ..... Magnolia amoena

Beauty Berry ..... Callicarpa bodinieri Profusion

Beauty Bush ..... Kolkwitzia amabilis

Bee Balm ..... Monarda species

Bee Willow ..... Salix medemii

Beeches ..... Fagus species

Beetroot ..... Beta species

Beetroot (aquatic) ..... Alternanthera Sessilis Rubra

Belladonna Lily ..... Amaryllis species

Bellflowers ..... Campanula species

Bellicent Lilac ..... Syringa x josiflexa Bellicent

Bells of Ireland ..... Moluccella laevis

Bergamot ..... Monarda species

Bergamot Mint ..... Mentha citrata

Bergamot Thyme ..... Thymus odoratissimus

Bermuda Juniper ..... Juniperus bermudiana

Betchels Crab ..... Malus crabapple ioensis plena

Betony ..... Stachys officinalis

Bhutan Cypress ..... Cupressus torulosa

Bhutan Pine ..... Pinus wallichiana (was griffithi)

Bible leaf ..... Tanacetum balsamita ssp balsamita was Chrysanthemum b.tanacetoides

Big Badja Gum ..... Eucalyptus badjensis

Big Cone Pine ..... Pinus coulteri

Big Elephant Ears ..... Colocasia esculenta

Big Leaf Magnolia .,... Magnolia macrophylla

Big Leaf Maple ..... Acer macrophyllum

Billy Buttons ..... Craspedia globosa

Birch Trees ..... Betula species

Bird Of Paradise ..... Strelitizia reginae

Birds Nest Banksia ..... Banksia baxteri

Birds Nest Fern ..... Asplenium nidus

Birds Nest Spruce ..... Picea abies Nidiformis

Birdseye ..... Veronica species

Bishop Pine ..... Pinus muricata

Bishops Flower ..... Ammi majus

Bishopwort ..... Stachys officinalis

Bitter Melon ..... Momordica charantia

Bittersweet ..... Solanum dulcamara

Blaauw's Juniper ..... Juniperus chinensis Blaauw

Black Alder ..... Alnus glutinosa

Black Banana ..... Musa ethiopian

Black Beech ..... Nothofagus solandri var solandri

Black Birch ..... Betula nigra

Black Box ..... Eucalyptus largiflorens

Black Boy ..... Xanthorrhoea australis

Black Butt Gum ..... Eucalyptus pilularis

Black Cherry ..... Prunus (cherry flwg) serotina

Black Chokeberry ..... Aronia meloncarpa

Black Coral Pea ..... Kennedia nigricans

Black Currant ..... Ribes nigrum

Black Dragon ..... Ophiopogon planiscapus Nigrescens

Black Fritillary ..... Fritillaria camschatsensis

Black Gum ..... Eucalyptus aggregata

Black Hills White Spruce ..... Picea glauca Densa

Black Hollyhock ..... Alcea rosea var. nigra

Black Horehound ..... Ballota nigra

Black Juniper ..... Juniperus wallichiana

Black Locust ..... Robinia pseudoacacia

Black Maire ..... Nestegis cunninghamii

Black Mamaku ..... Cyathea medullaris

Black Mapou ..... Pittosporum colensoi

Black Matipo ..... Pittosporum tenuifolium

Black Mondo Grass ..... Ophiopogon planiscapus Nigrescens

Black Mullein ..... Verbascum nigrum

Black Peppermint ..... Eucalyptus amygdalina

Black Peppermint ..... Mentha piperita nigra

Black Pine ..... Prumnopitys taxifolia

Black Ponga ..... Cyathea medullaris

Black Sage ..... Salvia mellifera

Black Sally ..... Eucalyptus stellulata

Black Sarana ..... Fritillaria camschatsensis

Black Sassafras ..... Atherosperma moschatum

Black Shamrock ..... Trifolium nigra

Black Sheoak ..... Casuarina littoralis now Allocasuarina l.

Black Spruce ..... Picea mariana syn nigra

Black Stemmed Taro ..... Colocasia esculenta Fontanesii

Black Taro ..... Colocasia esculenta Black

Black Walnut ..... Juglans nigra

Black Wattle ..... Acacia mearnsii. syn. A. mollissima

Black-eyed Susan ..... Ornithogalum arabicum

Black-eyed Susan ..... Rudbeckia fulgida

Blackberry ..... Rubus species

Bladder Campion ..... Silene vulgaris

Bladder Nut ..... Staphylea bumalda

Blakely's Red Gum ..... Eucalyptus blakeleyi

Blanket Flower ..... Gaillardia pulchella

Blaxland Stringybark ..... Eucalyptus blaxlandii

Blazing Star ..... Liatris spicata

Bleeding Heart ..... Clerodendron thomsonae

Blessed Thistle ..... Cnicus benedictus

Blood Leaf ..... Iresine herbstii

Blood Lily ..... Haemanthus coccineus

Blood Lily ..... Scadoxus multiflorus ssp katherinae

Bloodflower ..... Asclepias curassavica

Bloody Cranesbill ..... Geranium sanguineum

Blue Atlas Cedar ..... Cedrus atlantica Glauca

Blue Brilliant ..... Aristea thyrsiflorus

Blue Bugle ..... Ajuga reptans

Blue Carpet Juniper ..... Juniperus horizontalis Bar Harbour

Blue Clover ..... Parochetus communis

Blue Colorado Spruce ..... Picea pungens Glauca

Blue Cup Flower ..... Nierembergia hippomanica Blue Cup now caerulea BC

Blue Dragonhead ..... Dracocephalum moldavicum

Blue Eyed Grass ..... Sisyrinchium angustifolium

Blue Fescue ..... Festuca ovina glauca

Blue Flag Iris ..... Iris versicolor

Blue Ginger ..... Alpinia caerulea

Blue Ginger ..... Dichorisandra thyrsiflora

Blue Grama ..... Bouteloua gracilis

Blue Grass ..... Agropyron scabrum

Blue Grass (Oat) ..... Helictotrichon sempervirens

Blue Grass (Wheat) ..... Elymus solandri (E. rectisetus, Agropyron scabrum)

Blue Grass, Chatham Is ..... Festuca ovina coxii

Blue Grass, Kentucky ..... Festuca glauca

Blue Harebells ..... Campanula chamissonis was pilosa

Blue Hygrophila ..... Hygrophila augustifolia

Blue Lungwort ..... Pulmonaria angustifolia

Blue Marguerite ..... Felicia amelloides

Blue Mountain Ash ..... Eucalyptus oreades

Blue Mountains Mahogany ..... Eucalyptus notabilis

Blue Mountains Mallee Ash ..... Eucalyptus stricta

Blue Noble Fir ..... Abies procera Glauca

Blue Pea ..... Psoralea pinnata

Blue Pimpernel ..... Anagallis arvensis ssp coerulea

Blue Sage ..... Salvia x superba

Blue Sausage Bush ..... Decaisnea fargesii

Blue Sedge Grass ..... Carex montana

Blue Smoke Statice ..... Limonium perezzii

Blue Spanish Fir ..... Abies pinsapo Glauca

Blue Spiraea ..... Caryopteris x clandonensis

Blue Spur Flower ..... Plectranthus ecklonii

Blue Spurge ..... Euphorbia myrsinites

Blue Strawflower ..... Catananche caerulea

Blue Throatwort ..... Trachelium caeruleum

Blue Tussock ..... Poa colensoi

Blue Woodruff ..... Asperula azurea-setosa

Blue-lvd Stringybark ..... Eucalyptus agglomerata

Bluebeard ..... Caryopteris x clandonensis

Bluebell Creeper ..... Sollya heterophylla was fusiformis

Bluebell, Common ..... Hyacinthoides non scripta was Scilla n.s. & Endymion

Bluebell, Spanish ..... Hyacinthoides hispanica was Scilla campanulata

Blueberry ..... Vaccinium x corymbosum

Blueberry (native) ..... Dianella nigra

Blunt Greenhood ..... Pterostylis curta

Blushing Bride ..... Serruria florida

Boerbean ..... see Schotia

Bog Gum ..... Eucalyptus kitsoniana

Bog Lily ..... Bulbinella hookeri

Bog Pine ..... Halocarpus bidwillii was Dacrydium b.

Bog Primula ..... Primula species

Bog Sage ..... Salvia uliginosa

Bog Star ..... Parnassia palustris

Boneset ..... Eupatorium perfoliatium

Boobialla ..... Myoporum insulare

Borage ..... Borago officinalis

Bosnian Pine ..... Pinus heldreichii var leucodermis was P leucodermis

Boston Ivy ..... Parthenocissus tricuspidata

Bottlebrush ..... Callistemon species

Bouncing Bet ..... Saponaria officinalis

Bowles Golden Grass ..... Milium effusum Aureum

Bowmen's Root ..... Veronicastrum virginicum

Box ..... Buxus sempervirens

Box Elder ..... Acer negundo

Bracelet Honey Myrtle ..... Melaleuca armillaris

Bracken ..... Pteridium aquilinum esculentum

Brass Buttons ..... Cotula coronopifolia

Brazilian Fern Tree ..... Schizolobion paraphyllum

Brazilian Nightshade ..... Solanum seaforthianum

Brazilian Pepper Tree ..... Schinus terebinthifolius

Brazilian Plume Flower ..... Justicia carnea

Breath of Heaven ..... Coleonema species

Breath of Heaven ..... Diosma ericoides

Brewers Weeping Spruce ..... Picea breweriana

Bridal Veil Broom ..... Genista monosperma

Bridal Wreath ..... Francoa ramosa

Bridal Wreath ..... Francoa sonchifolia

Bridal Wreath ..... Spiraea arguta

Bridal Wreath ..... Spiraea thunbergii

Bridesmaid ..... Serruria rosea

Bristle Scirpus ..... Isolepsis setacea   was Scirpus s.

Bristlecone Fir ..... Abies bracteata

Bristlecone Pine ..... Pinus aristata

Brit.Columbian Mtn Maple ..... Acer glabrum var douglasii

Brittle Gum ..... Eucalyptus mannifera

Broad Leaf ..... Griselina littoralis

Broad-lvd Peppermint ..... Eucalyptus dives

Broad-lvd Red Ironbark ..... Eucalyptus fibrosa

Broad-lvd Snow Tussock ..... Chionochloa flavescens

Broad-lvd Stringybark ..... Eucalyptus calignosa

Broadleaf Maple ..... Acer amplum

Broadleaf Sorrel ..... Rumex acetosa

Broccoli ..... see Brassica

Bronze Fennel ..... Foeniculum vulgare purpureum

Brookers Gum ..... Eucalyptus brookeriana

Brookline ..... Veronica beccabunga

Brooms ..... see Genista, Cytisus, Carmichaelia, Chordospartium

Brown Barrel Gum ..... Eucalyptus fastigata

Brown Boronia ..... Boronia megastigma

Brown Pine ..... Prumnopitys ferruginea

Brush Box ..... Lophostemon confertus was Tristania

Brussel Sprouts ..... see Brassica

Buckthorn ..... Cryptandra scortechinii

Buckthorn ..... Rhamnus species

Buckwheat ..... Fagopyrum esculentum

Budawang Ash ..... Eucalyptus dendromorpha

Buffalo Currant ..... Ribes odoratum

Bull Banksia ..... Banksia grandis

Bullrush ..... Typha species

Bunya-Bunya ..... Araucaria bidwillii

Burdock ..... Arctium lappa

Burmese Umbrella Tree ..... Tupidanthus calyptrata

Burnet Saxifrage ..... Pimpinella saxifrage ·

Burning Bush ..... Euonymus alatus

Burning Bush ..... Kochia trichophylla

Burr Oak ..... Quercus macrocarpa

Burrow's Tail ..... Sedum morganianum

Bush Balm ..... Melissa altissima

Bush Cherry ..... Syzygium australe

Bush Flax ..... Astelia grandis

Bush Lawyer ..... Rubus cissoides

Bush Lily ..... Astelia fragrans

Bush Rice Grass ..... Microlaena avenacea

Butchers Broom ..... Ruscus aculeatus

Butter-Burr ..... Petasites fragrans

Buttercup ..... Ranunculus species

Buttercup Tree ..... Cassia corymbosa John Ball

Butterfly Bush ..... Buddleia davidii

Butterfly Plant ..... Gaura lindheimeri

Butterknife Bush ..... Cunonia capensis

Butternut ..... Juglans cinerea

Button Bush ..... Berzelia lanuginosa

Button Bush ..... Cephalanthus occidentalis

Button Fern ..... Pellaea rotundifolia

Button Snakewort ..... Liatris spicata syn.L. callilepsis

Buttonwood ..... Platanus occidentalis

Buxton Silver Gum ..... Eucalyptus crenulata

Cabbage ..... see Brassica varieties

Cabbage Gum ..... Eucalyptus amplifolia

Cabbage Tree ..... Cordyline species

Cabbage Tree ..... Cussonia species

Calamint ..... Calamintha species

Calamus root ..... Acorus calamus

Calathian Violet ..... Gentiana pneumonanthe

Calico Aster ..... Aster lateriflorus Horizontale

Calico Bush ..... Kalmia species

California Fire Cracker ..... Brodiaea ida maia

Californian Blue-eyed Grass ..... Sisyrinchium idahoense (bellum)

Californian Buckwheat ..... Eriogonum fasciculatum

Californian Firecracker ..... Dichelostemma ida-maia

Californian Lilac ..... Ceanothus species

Californian Poppy ..... Eschscholtzia species

Californian Redwood ..... Sequoia sempervirens

Californian State Flower ..... Eschscholtzia californica orange

Californian Tree Poppy ..... Romneya coulteri

Callas ..... Zantedeschia species

Cambridge Cranesbill ..... Geranium x cantabrigiense

Camden White Gum ..... Eucalyptus benthamii

Camden Woollybutt ..... Eucalyptus macarthurii

Camphor Laurel/Tree ..... Cinnamomum camphora

Camphor Plant ..... Tanacetum balsamita was Chrysanthemum b.

Campion ..... Lychnis species

Canadian Hemlock ..... Tsuga canadensis

Canadian Maple ..... Acer rubrum

Canadian Redbud ..... Cercis canadensis

Canadian Spruce ..... Picea glauca syn alba

Canary Creeper ..... Tropaeolum peregrinum

Canary Is Daisy ..... Odontospermum maritimum Gold Coin

Canary Is Date Palm ..... Phoenix canariensis

Canary Is Holly ..... Ilex perado platyphylla

Canary Is Ivy ..... Hedera canariensis

Canary Is Pine ..... Pinus canariensis

Canary Island Lavender ..... Lavandula canariensis

Candelabra Primula ..... Primula species

Candelabra Tree ..... Araucaria angustifolia

Candle Bark ..... Eucalyptus rubida

Candle Plant ..... Senecio articulatus

Candy-striped Oxalis ..... Oxalis versicolor

Candytuft ..... Iberis species

Canterbury Bells ..... Campanula medium

Canton Lace ..... Radermachera sinica

Canton Water Pine ,,,,, Glyptostrobus pencilis was lineatus

Cape Chestnut ..... Calodendron capense

Cape Forget-me-not ..... Anchusa capensis

Cape Gooseberry ..... Physalis peruviana syn P.edulis

Cape Hyacinth ..... Galtonia candicans

Cape Leadwort ..... Plumbago auriculata was capensis

Cape Stock-rose ..... Sparrmannia africana

Cape Wattle ..... Albizia lophantha now Paraserianthes

Capuli Cherry ..... Prunus (cherry flwg) capuli (P. salicifolia)

Caraway ..... Carum carvi

Caraway Thyme ..... Thymus Herba Barona

Cardboard Plant Cycad ..... Zamia furfuracea

Cardinal Flower ..... Lobelia cardinalis

Cardinal Flower ..... Lobelia fulgens

Cardoon ..... Cynara cardunculus

Caribean Pine ..... Pinus caribea

Carmel Creeper ..... Ceanothus griseus horizontalis Yankee Point

Carob ..... Ceratonia siliqua

Carolina Allspice ..... Calycanthus floridus

Carolina Jessamine ..... Gelsemium sempervirens

Carpathian Harebell ..... Campanula carpatica

Carpentaria Palm ..... C. acuminata

Carrot ..... Daucus carota var sativus

Casana ..... Cyphomandra cajanumensis

Cascara Bush ..... Rhamnus californica

Cashew Nut ..... Anacardium occidentale

Cat Claw Vine ..... Macfadyena unguis-cati was Doxantha

Catkin Bush ..... Garrya elliptica

Catmint ..... Nepeta x faassenii

Catnip ..... Nepeta cataria

Cats Tail ..... Typha species

Catsfoot ..... Antennaria dioica

Caucasian Fir ..... Abies nordmanniana

Caucasian Linden ..... Tilia dasystyla

Caucasian Maple ..... Acer cappadocium

Caucasian Zelkova ..... Zelkova carpinifolia

Cauliflower ..... see Brassica

Cavendish Yew ..... Taxus baccata Cavendishii

Cedar ..... Cedrus & Thuja species

Cedar of Lebanon ..... Cedrus libani

Cedar Wattle ..... Acacia elata

Celandine Poppy ..... Stylophorum diphyllum

Celandine, Double ..... Ranunculus ficaria Flore Pleno

Celandine, Greater ..... Chelidonium majus

Celeriac ..... Apium graveolens

Celery ..... Apium graveolens var dulce

Celery Pine ..... Phyllocladus trichomanoides

Celery-rooted Turnip ..... Apium graveolens

Celtuce ..... Lactuca sativa var asparagina

Centaury ..... Centaurea erythraea

Century Plant ..... Agave americana

Ceylon Gooseberry ..... Dovyalis hebecarpa

Chalice Vine ..... Solandra grandiflora

Chamomile, Double ..... Chamaemelum nobile flore pleno

Chard ..... Beta species

Chaste Tree ..... Vitex agnus-castus

Chatham Is AkeAke ..... Olearia traversii

Chatham Is Forget-me-not ..... Myosotidium hortensia

Chatham Is Geranium ..... Geranium traversii

Chatham Is Korokio ..... Corokia macrocarpa

Chatham Is Nikau ..... Rhopalostylis sapida
Chatham Is

Cheals Weeping Cherry ..... Prunus (cherry flwg) Kiku-shidare-zakura

Cheng Cypress ..... Cupressus chengiana

Chenille Plant ..... Salvia leucantha

Chenille Plants ..... Acalypha varieties

Cherimoya ..... Annona cherimola

Cherokee Rose ..... Rosa laevigata

Cherry ..... see Prunus

Cherry Laurel ..... Prunus laurocerasus

Cherry Pie ..... Heliotropium arborescens

Cherry Plum ..... Prunus (plum flwg) cerasifera

Cherrystone Juniper ..... Juniperus monosperma

Chervil ..... Anthriscus cerefolium

Chestnut ..... Castanea sativa

Chestnut Leafed Oak ..... Quercus castaneifolia

Chestnut Oak ..... Quercus prinus

Chiapas Pine ..... Pinus chiapensis

Chicken Thyme ..... Thymus Westmoreland

Chicory ..... Cichorium intybus

Chihuahua Spruce ..... Picea chihuahuana

Chilacayote ..... Cucurbita ficifolia

Chilean Bellflower ..... Lapageria rosea

Chilean Blue Crocus ..... Tecophilaea cyanocrocus

Chilean Cedar ..... Austrocedrus chilensis

Chilean Cranberry ..... Ugni molinae   was Myrtus ugni

Chilean Fire Bush ..... Embothrium coccineum Longifolium

Chilean Giant Rhubarb ..... Gunnera tinctoria   was chilensis

Chilean Glory Flower ..... Eccremocarpus scaber

Chilean Guava ..... Ugni molinae   was Myrtus ugni

Chilean Lantern Tree ..... Crinodendron hookerianu

Chilean Mayten ..... Maytenus boaria

Chilli ..... Capsicum species

Chimney Bellflower ..... Campanula pyramidalis

China Aster ..... Callistephus chinensis

China Doll ..... Radermachera sinica

China Flower ..... Adenandra uniflora

China Palm ..... Rhapis excelsa

Chinaman's Cap ..... Holmskioldia sanguinea Aurea

Chincherinchee ..... Ornithogalum thyrsoides

Chinese Arborvitae ..... Thuja orientalis

Chinese Artichoke ..... Stachys sieboldii

Chinese Ash ..... Fraxinus chinensis

Chinese Beauty Berry ..... Callicarpa dichotoma

Chinese Bush Cherry ..... Prunus glandulosa

Chinese Bush Clover ..... Lespedeza bicolor

Chinese Cabbage ..... Brassica Pak Choi

Chinese Celery ..... Apium graveolens C.C.

Chinese Coffin Tree ..... Cunninghamia lanceolata

Chinese Cork Oak ..... Quercus variabilis

Chinese Cypress ..... Cupressus duclouxiana

Chinese Daphne ..... D. genkwa

Chinese Date ..... Zyzyphus jujuba

Chinese Dogwood ..... Cornus kousa chinensis

Chinese Dragon Spruce ..... Picea asperata

Chinese Edible Chysanthemum ..... C. coronarium

Chinese Elm ..... Ulmus parvifolia

Chinese Fan Palm ..... Livistonia chinensis

Chinese Fir ..... Cunninghamia lanceolata

Chinese Forget-me-not ..... Cynoglossum amabile

Chinese Foxglove ..... Rehmannia elata   was angulata

Chinese Fringe Tree ..... Chionanthus retusus

Chinese Hemlock ..... Tsuga chinensis

Chinese Holly ..... Ilex cornuta

Chinese Holly Grape ..... Mahonia lomariifolia

Chinese Indigo ..... Indigodera decora

Chinese Juniper ..... Juniperus chinensis

Chinese Lace Flower ..... Filipendula rubra

Chinese Lantern ..... Abutilon x hybridum

Chinese Lantern ..... Physalis franchetii

Chinese Leek ..... Allium odorum

Chinese Lettuce ..... Brassica mizuna

Chinese Loosestrife ..... Lysimachia clethroides

Chinese Mastic Tree ..... Pistachia chinensis

Chinese Mugwort ..... Artemisia verlotorum

Chinese Pear (Eating) ..... Pyrus ussuriensis

Chinese Pear(ornamental) ..... Pyrus calleryana

Chinese Pistache ..... Pistachia chinensis

Chinese Plum Yew ..... Cephalotaxus fortunei

Chinese Poplar ..... Populus yunnanensis

Chinese Preserving Melon ..... Benincasa hispada Chinese Winter

Chinese Red Pine ..... Pinus tabulaeformis

Chinese Redbud ..... Cercis chinensis

Chinese Rhubarb ..... Rheum palmatum var tangticum

Chinese Rowan ..... Sorbus species

Chinese Snowbell Tree ..... Styrax hemsleyanus

Chinese Spinach ..... Amaranthus gangeticum

Chinese Swamp Cypress ..... Glyptostrobus pencilis   was lineatus

Chinese Sweet Gum ..... Liquidambar formosana

Chinese Toon ..... Toona sinensis   was Cedrela s.

Chinese Tree of Heaven ..... Ailanthus altissima

Chinese Trumpet Flower ..... Incarvillea delavayi

Chinese Weeping Cypress ..... Chamaecyparis funebris was Cupressus f.

Chinese White Pine ..... Pinus armandii

Chinese Windmill Palm ..... Trachycarpus fortunei

Chinese Wingnut ..... Pterocarya stenoptera

Chinese Winter Melon ..... Benincasa hispada Chinese Winter

Chinese Wisteria ..... Wisteria sinensis

Chinese Witch Hazel ..... Hamamelis mollis

Chinese Wonder Tree ..... Idesia polycarpa

Chinese Zelkova ..... Zelkova sinica

Chives ..... Allium schoenoprasum

Chocolate Cosmos ..... Cosmos atro-sanguineum

Chocolate Vine ..... Akebia quinata

Christmas Bells ..... Blanfordia punicea

Christmas Box ..... Sarcococca ruscifolia

Christmas Lily ..... Lilium longiflorum

Christmas Lily ..... Lilium regale

Christmas Rose ..... Helleborus foetidus

Christmas Rose ..... Helleborus niger

Chrysanthemum, Florists ..... Dendranthema varieties

Cicatrice Tree Fern ..... Cyathea cooperi

Cickabiddy ..... Asarina procumbens

Cider Gum (blue form) ..... Eucalyptus gunnii

Cigar Plant ..... Cuphea species

Cilantro ..... Coriandrum sativum

Cilician Fir ..... Abies cilicica

Cinnamon Myrtle ..... Luma apiculata   was Myrtus a.

Cinquefoil ..... Potentilla species

Claret Ash ..... Fraxinus oxycarpa Raywood   now angustifolia Raywood

Clary Sage ..... Salvia sclarea

Clary Sage ..... Salvia sclarea v turkestanica

Claw Aster ..... Aster sp

Claybush Wattle ..... Acacia glaucoptera

Clematis, Anemone ..... C. montana

Clematis, Fern-lvd ..... C. cirrhosa balearica

Clematis, Golden ..... C. tangutica

Clematis, Leafless ..... C. afoliata

Clematis, Orange Peel ..... C. orientalis

Clematis, Scented ..... C. foetida

Cliff Mallee Ash ..... Eucalyptus rupicola

Climbing Alstroemeria ..... Bomarea species

Climbing Hydrangea ..... Hydrangea anomala petiolaris

Climbing Hydrangea ..... Hydrangea serratifolia

Clock Vine, Bengal ..... Thunbergia grandiflora

Clock Vine, Scarlet ..... Thunbergia coccinea

Cloud Plant ..... Tagetes lucida

Clove Currant ..... Ribes odoratum

Clove Pinks ..... Dianthus caryophyllus

Clustered Bellflower ..... Campanula glomerata

Coahuilan Fir ..... Abies durangensis var. coahuilensis

Coast Banksia ..... Banksia integrifolia & attenuata

Coast Grey Gum ..... Eucalyptus bosistoana

Coast Rosemary ..... Westringia fruticosa

Coast She Oak ..... Allocasuarina stricta   was Casuarina s.0

Coastal Ribbonwood ..... Plagianthus maritimus

Coastal Spleenwort ..... Asplenium flaccidum haurakiense

Coastal Tea Tree ..... Leptospermum laevigatum

Coastal Tussock ..... Chionochloa bromoides

Coastal Wattle ..... Acacia sophorae

Cobra Lilies ..... Arisaema species

Cockscomb ..... Celosia species

Cockspur Coral Tree ..... Erythrina crista-galli

Cocos Palm ..... Syagrus romanzoffiana was Arecastrum r.

Coffee Berry ..... Rhamnus californica

Coffin Juniper ..... Juniperus recurva var coxii

Coliseum Maple ..... Acer cappadocium

Colorado Spruce ..... Picea pungens

Colorado White Fir ..... Abies concolor

Columbine ..... Aquilegia species

Columnar White Cedar ..... Thuja occidentalis Fastigiata

Comfrey ..... Symphytum species

Common Juniper ..... Juniperus communis

Coneflowers ..... Echinacea species

Coneflowers ..... Isopogon anethifolius

Coneflowers ..... Rudbeckia species

Confetti Bush ..... Coleonema pulchrum

Cooba Wattle ..... Acacia salicina

Cook's Scurvy Grass ..... Lepidium oleraceum

Coolwort ..... Tiarella cordifolia

Coopers Burmese Rose ..... Rosa gigantea cooperi now R.laevigata Cooperi

Cootamundra Wattle ..... Acacia baileyana

Copper Beech ..... Fagus sylvatica Purpurea

Coral Bark Maple ..... Acer palmatum Senkaki

Coral Bells ..... Heuchera species

Coral Bush ..... Russelia equisetifolia   was juncea

Coral Gum ..... Eucalyptus torquata

Coral Pea Climber ..... Hardenbergia species

Coral Trees ..... Erythrina species

Coral Vine ..... Berberidopsis corallina

Coriander ..... Coriandrum sativum

Cork Oak ..... Quercus suber

Corkscrew Hazel ..... Corylus avellana Contorta

Corn ..... Zea species

Corn Cockle ..... Agrostemma githgo

Corn Lettuce ..... Cichorium intybus

Corn Lily ..... Ixia species

Corn Salad ..... Valerianella locusta

Cornelian Cherry ..... Cornus mas

Cornflowers ..... Centaurea species

Corsican Black Pine ..... Pinus nigra

Corsican Mint ..... Mentha requienii

Costmary ..... Tanacetum balsamita ssp balsamita was Chrysanthemum b.tanacetoides

Cottage Pinks ..... Dianthus pulmarius mixed

Cotton Daisy ..... Celmisia spectabilis

Cotton Lavender ..... Santolina chamaecyparissus

Cotton Palm ..... Washingtonia filifera

Cotton Plant ..... Celmisia semicordata

Cotton Thistles ..... Onopordum arabicum

Cow Parsley ..... Anthriscus sylvestris

Cow's Tail Pine ..... Cephalotaxus harringtonia va drupacea

Cowslip ..... Primula veris

Coyote Brush ..... Baccharis halimifolia Twin Pea

Crabapples ..... Malus species

Cranberry ..... Vaccinium cranberry

Cranberry,Chilean ..... Ugni molinae was Myrtu ugni

Cranesbills ..... Geranium species

Creek Fern ..... Blechnum fluviatile

Creeping Bellflower ..... Campanula rapunculoide

Creeping Boobialla ..... Myoporum parvifolium

Creeping Fig ..... Ficus pumila Minima

Creeping Fuchsia ..... Fuchsia procumbens

Creeping Gloxinia ..... Lophospermum erubescer was Asarina e.

Creeping Jenny ..... Lysimachia nummularia

Crepe Camellia ..... Gordonia axillaris

Crepe Myrtles ..... Lagerstroemia species

Cretan Fern ..... Pteris cretica

Crimean Pine ..... Pinus nigra ssp pallasiana

Crimson Bottlebrush ..... Callistemon citrinus

Crimson Mallee ..... Eucalyptus lansdowneana

Crocus, Dutch ..... Crocus chrysanthus

Cross-lvd Heath ..... Erica tetralix Alba Mollis

Crotons ..... Codiaeum hybrids

Crow Garlic ..... Allium vineale

Crown Fern ..... Blechnum discolor

Crown Imperial ..... Fritillaria imperialis

Crown Vetch ..... Coronilla varia Penngift

Cruel Plant (pest up north) ..... Araujia sericifera

Cuckoo Flower ..... Cardamine pratensis

Cuckoo Flower ..... Lychnis flos cuculi

Cucumber ..... Cucumis (sativus)

Cucumber Tree ..... Magnolia acuminata

Cucumber-leaf Sunflower ..... Helianthus debilis

Culver's Root ..... Veronicastrum virginicum

Cumin ..... Cuminum cyminum

Cup & Saucer Vine ..... Cobaea scandens

Cup Gum ..... Eucalyptus cosmophylla

Cup of Gold ..... Solandra maxima

Cupid's Dart ..... Catananche caerulea

Curly Leaf Oak ..... Quercus robur cristata

Currants, black,white,red ..... Ribes species

Curry Plant ..... Helichrysum italicum serotinum

Curved Leaf Grass ..... Dracophyllum recurvum

Cushion Sandwort ..... Arenaria tetraquetra

Cushion Spurge ..... Euphorbia polychroma

Custard Banana ..... Asimina triloba

Custard Pawpaw ..... Asimina triloba

Cutleaf Birch ..... Betula pendula dalecarlica

Cutleaf Japanese Maple ..... Acer palmatum Dissectum

Cutleaf Norway Maple ..... Acer platanoides Dissectum

Cycad ..... Cycas species

Cyclamen Violet ..... Viola koreana

Cypress Spurge ..... Euphorbia cyparissias

Cypresses ..... Cupressus species

Cyprus Cedar ..... Cedrus brevifolia

Daffodil ..... Narcissus species

Daffodil Bush ..... Coronilla valentina glauca Variegata

Dahlberg Daisy ..... Thymophylla tenuiloba

Dahurian Buckthorn ..... Rhamnus davurica

Daisy Bush ..... Argyranthemum varieties

Daisy, Marlborough Rock ..... Pachystegia insignis now Olearia

Dancing Lady ..... Onicidium flexuosum

Darley Dale Heath ..... Erica darleyensis

Davids Maple ..... Acer davidii

Dawn Redwood ..... Metasequioa glyptostroboides

Day Lilies ..... Hemerocallis species

Deer Horn Thuja ..... Thujopsis dolabrata

Dense Sedge ..... Uncinia unciniata

Desert Ash ..... Fraxinus oxycarpa now angustifolia

Desert Banksia ..... Banksia ornata

Desert Marigold ..... Baileyana multiradiata

Desert Pony Tail ..... Beaucarnea stricta

Devils Walking Stick ..... Aralia spinosa

Diamond Lilies ..... Nerine species

Diehard Stringybark ..... Eucalyptus cameronii

Digger Pine ..... Pinus sabineana

Dill ..... Anethum graveolens

Dittany of Crete ..... Origanum dictamnus

Doddering Dillies ..... Briza media

Dogbane ..... Plectranthus ornatus was Coleus canina

Dogrose ..... Rosa canina

Dogs Tooth Violets ..... Erythronium species

Dogwoods ..... Cornus species

Douglas Fir ..... Pseudotsuga menziesii

Dove Tree ..... Davidia involucrata

Dovedale Moss ..... Saxifraga hypnoides

Dow Gauk Bean ..... Vigna Yard Long (sesquipedalis)

Downy Birch ..... Betula pubescens

Downy Serviceberry ..... Amelanchier arborea

Dragon Tree ..... Cordyline terminalis tricolour

Dragon Tree ..... Dracaena draco

Drooping Sedge ..... Carex pendula

Drooping Sheoak ..... Allocasuarina stricta was Casuarina s.O.

Dropwort ..... Filipendula vulgaris was hexapetala

Drumstick Primrose ..... Primula denticulata

Drumsticks ..... Isopogon anethifolius

Duckweed ..... Lemna minor

Dune Cypress Pine ..... Callitris rhomboidea syn cupressiformis

Dunns White Gum ..... Eucalyptus dunnii

Durango Fir ..... Abies durangensis

Durmast Oak ..... Quercus petraea

Dusty Daisy Bush ..... Olearia phlogopappa

Dusty Miller ..... Primula auricula (mxd colour)

Dusty Miller ..... Senecio cineraria

Dutch Savin Juniper ..... Juniperus sabina Erecta

Dutchmans Pipe ..... Aristolochia elegans

Dwarf Albert Spruce ..... Picea glauca Albertiana Conica was P.g.Conica

Dwarf Balsam Fir of Canada ..... Abies balsamea f. hudsonia

Dwarf Box ..... Buxus sempervirens suffruticosa

Dwarf Cabbage Tree ..... Cordyline pumilio

Dwarf Chinese Lace Flower ..... Filipendula palmata nana was digitata n.

Dwarf Cobra Lily ..... Arisaema praecox

Dwarf Coral Tree ..... Erythrina humeana

Dwarf Date Palm ..... Phoenix roebelinii

Dwarf Lebanon Cedar ..... Cedrus libani Nana

Dwarf Mountain Pine ..... Pinus mugo

Dwarf Oak ..... Casuarina nana

Dwarf Rowan ..... Sorbus reducta

Dwarf Satin Iris ..... Sisyrinchium graminifolium

Dwarf Snowbell ..... Soldanella pusilla

Dwarf Sweet Flag ..... Acorus gramineus Variegatus

Dwarf Swiss Mountain Pine ..... Pinus mugo var pumilio

Dwarf Toetoe ..... Chionochloa flavicans

Dyer's Broom ..... Genista tinctoria

Dyer's Chamomile ..... Anthemis tinctoria

Dyer's Coreopsis ..... Coreopsis tinctoria

Dyer's Rocket ..... Reseda luteola

Eagle Claw Maple ..... Acer palmatum Dissectum Palmatifidum

Early Black Wattle ..... Acacia decurrens

Early Spiketail ..... Stachyurus praecox

Earth Chestnut ..... Bunium bulbocastanum

Eastern American Redbud ..... Cercis canadensis

Eastern Hemlock ..... Tsuga canadensis

Eastern Red Cedar ..... Juniperus virginiana

Eastern Spruce ..... Picea orientalis

Eau de Cologne Mint ..... Mentha citrata

Edelweiss ..... Leontopodium alpinum

Edible Chrysanthemum ..... Chrysanthemum coronarium

Eggplant ..... Solanum melongena (var esculentum)

Egmont Daisy ..... Celmisia major

Egmont Hook Sedge ..... Uncinia egmontiana

Egyptian Papyrus ..... Cyperus papyrus

Egyptian Tree Onion ..... Allium cepa varieties

Elderberry ..... Sambucus nigra

Elecampagne ..... Inula helenium

Elephant Foot Tree ..... Beaucarnea recurvata

Elephant Garlic(a leek) ..... Allium ampeloprasum

Elephants Ear ..... Bergenia cordifolia

Elephants Ears ..... Alocasia species

Elephants Ears ..... Haemanthus coccineus

Elfin Herb ..... Cuphea hyssopifolia

Elfin Thyme ..... Thymus nitidus

Elm Zelkova ..... Zelkova carpinifolia

Elms ..... Ulmus species

Empress of Brazil ..... Worsleya raineri

Empress Trees ..... Paulownia species

Endive ..... Cichorium endiva

Endlicher Pine ..... Pinus rudis

Engelman Spruce ..... Picea engelmannii

English Bluebell (true) ..... Hyacinthoides non-scriptus was Endymion n.s.,Scilla n.s.

English Holly ..... Ilex aquifolium

English Iris ..... Iris latifolia

Epaulette Trees ..... Pterostyrax species

Epazote ..... Chenopodium ambrosioides

Ethiopian Banana ..... Ensete ventricosum

Ettrema Mallee ..... Eucalyptus sturgissiana

Eumong River Cooba ..... Acacia stenophylla

European Alder ..... Alnus glutinosa

European Ash ..... Fraxinus excelsior

European Beech ..... Fagus sylvatica

European Bird Cherry ..... Prunus (cherry flwg) padus

European Dogwood ..... Cornus sanguinea

European Fan Palm ..... Chamaerops humilis

European Larch ..... Larix decidua

European Oak ..... Quercus robur

European Silver Fir ..... Abies alba

European Snowy Mespilus ..... Amelanchier ovalis

Evening Primrose ..... Oenothera species

Evergreen Alder ..... Alnus jorullensis

Evergreen Japanese Dogwood ..... Cornus kousa angustata

Evergreen Magnolia ..... Magnolia grandiflora

Evergreen Oak ..... Quercus ilex

Evergreen Silk Tree ..... Albizia lophantha now Paraserianthes

Fairy Bamboo ..... Bambusa gracilis

Fairy Bells/Cups ..... Primula veris

Fairy Foxglove ..... Erinus alpinus

Fairy Grass ..... Scirpus isolepsis

Fairy Scilla ..... Scilla litardierei was pratensis

Fairy Thimbles ..... Campanula cochlearifolia was pusilla

Falcate Yellowwood ..... Podocarpus henkelii

False Chamomile ..... Anthemis punctata ssp cupianiana

False Maire ..... Mida salicifolia

False Mallow ..... Malvastrum lateritum

False Spaniard ..... Celmisia lyallii

False Starwart ..... Boltonia asteroides

False Weymouth Pine ..... Pinus pseudostrobus

Fan palm ..... Livistonia australis

Farewell to Spring ..... Godetia amoena

Farges Catalpa ..... Catalpa fargesii

Feather Flower/Head ..... Phylica plumosa

Feather Hyacinth ..... Muscari comosum plumosum

Federation Daisies ..... Argyranthemum species

Feijoa ..... Acca sellowiana

Fenugreek ..... Trigonella foenum-graecum

Fern Pine ..... Podocarpus gracilior

Fern-lvd Beech ..... Fagus sylvatica Laciniata

Fern-lvd Elderberry ..... Sambucus nigra laciniata

Fern-lvd Pelargonium ..... Pelargonium filicifolium

Fernleaf Dill ..... Anethum graveolens Fernleaf

Feverfew ..... Tanacetum parthenium

Fibre Optics Grass ..... Scirpus cernuus now Isolepsis c.

Field Maple ..... Acer campestre

Field Pansy ..... Viola arvensis

Field Scabiosa ..... Knautia arvensis

Fig ..... Ficus species

Fig, edible ..... Ficus carica

Figwort ..... Scrophularia nodosa

Fire Bush ..... Embothrium coccineum

Fire Wheel Tree ..... Stenocarpus sinuatus

Firecracker Plant ..... Cuphea ignea

Firethorn ..... Pyracantha species

Firewheels ..... Gaillardia pulchella

Firs ..... see Abies, Pseudotsuga, Cunninghamia

Fish Tail Hoya ..... Hoya polyneura

Five Finger ..... Pseudopanax arboreus

Five Finger ..... Pseudopanax laetus

Five Seasons Herb ..... Plectranthus amboinicus

Flame Creeper ..... Tropaeolum pentaphyllum

Flame Vine ..... Pyrostegia venusta

Flamingo Flowers ..... Anthurium andreanum

Flamingo Plant ..... Justicia carnea

Flannel Flower/Bush ..... Phylica pubescens

Flax, Linen ..... Linum species

Flax, NZ ..... Phormium species

Fleabane ..... Erigeron karvinskianus was mucronatus

Fletcher's Cypress ..... Chamaecyparis lawsoniana Fletcheri

Flinders Range Wattle ..... Acacia iteaphylla

Floating Fern ..... Azola fairy moss

Florence Fennel ..... Foeniculum vulgare var dulce

Floss Silk Tree ..... Chorisia speciosa

Flower of Jove ..... Lychnis flos-jovis

Flower of the West Wind ..... Zephyranthes candida

Flowering Ash ..... Fraxinus ornus

Flowering Dogwood ..... Cornus florida

Foam Flower ..... Tiarella species

Foo Gwa ..... Momordica charantia

Forest Cabbage Tree ..... Cordyline banksii

Forest Pansy ..... Cercis canadensis Forest Pansy

Forest Tree Daisy ..... Olearia arborescens

Forest Velvet Allophyllus ..... Allophyllus abyssinicus

Forget-me-not ..... Anchusa species

Forget-me-not ..... Myosotis species

Forget-me-not, Cape ..... Anchusa capensis

Forget-me-not, Chinese ..... Cynoglossum amabile

Forget-me-not, Greek ..... Omphaloides linifolia

Formosan Cypress ..... Chamaecyparis formosensis

Fortnightly Iris ..... Dietes grandiflora

Fountain Grass ..... Pennisetum setaceum (P.rupellii)

Four O'clock Plant ..... Mirabilis jalapa

Foxgloves ..... Digitalis species

Fragrant Epaulette Tree ..... Pterostyrax hispida

Fragrant Hellebore ..... Helleborus odorus

Fragrant Sage ..... Salvia clevelandii

Fragrant Snowball ..... Viburnum x carlcephalum

Fragrant Snowbell Tree ..... Styrax obassia

Frangipani ..... Plumeria acuminata & hybrids

Fraser River Birch ..... Betula papyrifera commutata

Fraser's Fir ..... Abies fraserii

French Cranesbill ..... Geranium endressii Wargrave Pink

French Marigold ..... Tagetes patula

French Sorrel ..... Rumex scutatus

French Thyme ..... Thymus vulgaris French

Fried Egg Tree ..... Gordonia axillaris

Fried Eggs ..... Limnanthes douglasii
Fringe Flower ..... Loropetalum chinense
Fringe Flower ..... Soldanella montana
Fringe Lily ..... Thysanotus multiflorus
Fringecups ..... Tellima grandiflora
Fringed Wattle ..... Acacia fimbriata
Fruit Salad Plant ..... Monstera deliciosa
Fruiting Coprosma ..... Coprosma brunnea
Fuji Cherry ..... Prunus (cherry flwg) incisa
Full Moon Maple ..... Acer japonicum
Fuzzy Box ..... Eucalyptus conica
Fuzzy Deutzia ..... D. scabra
Gaoshan Pine ..... Pinus densata
Garden Gnome ..... Anacyclus depressus
Garden Sorrel ..... Rumex acetosa
Garland Flower ..... Daphne cneorum
Garlic ..... Allium sativum
Garlic Chives ..... Allium tuberosum
Gay Feather ..... Liatris spicata
Geranium, Ivyleaved ..... Pelargonium peltatum
Geranium, Oakleaf ..... Pelargonium quercifolium
Geranium, Peppermint ..... Pelargonium tomentosum
Gerard's Pine ..... Pinus gerardiana
German Chamomile ..... Matricaria chamomilla now recutita
German Thyme ..... Thymus vulgaris English Winter
Germander ..... Teucrium species
Ghost Bush ..... Calocephalus brownii
Ghost Tree ..... Davidia involucrata
Giant Angelica ..... Angelica gigas
Giant Bird Of Paradise ..... Strelitizia nicollii
Giant Catmint ..... Nepeta Six Hills Giant
Giant Cowslip ..... Primula florindae
Giant Lily ..... Cardiocrinum giganteum
Giant Mexican Hyssop ..... Agastache mexicana
Giant NZ Restiad ..... Sporodanthus traversii
Giant Pennywort ..... Hydrocotyle bonariensis
Giant Redwood ..... Sequoiadendron giganteum
Giant Scabiosa ..... Cephalaria gigantea
Gimlet ..... Eucalyptus salubris
Ginger ..... Hedychium, Heliconia, Zingiber species
Ginger Mint ..... Mentha suaveolens variegata
Ginger Mint ..... Mentha x gracilis Variegata
Ginger(not root), cold tolerant ..... Zingiber Mioga
Glaucus Piripiri ..... Acaena caesiiglauca

Globe Artichoke ..... Cynara scolymus
Globe Centaury ..... Centaurea macrocephala
Globe Thistle ..... Echinops ritro
Glory Of The Snow ..... Chionodoxa species
Glory of the Sun ..... Leucocoryne species
Glossy Abelia ..... Abelia x grandiflora
Goat's Beard ..... Aruncus dioicus was sylvester
Goats Rue ..... Galega officinalis
Gold Box Honeysuckle ..... Lonicera nitida aurea
Gold Coast Juniper ..... Juniperus x media Gold Coast
Gold Dust ..... Alyssum saxatile
Gold Dust Wattle ..... Acacia acinacea
Gold Moneywort ..... Lysimachia nummularia Aurea
Gold Sawara Cypress ..... Chamaecyparis pisifera Filifera Aurea
Golden Abelia ..... Abelia x grandiflora Francis Mason
Golden Akeake ..... Olearia paniculata
Golden Ash ..... Fraxinus excelsior Aurea
Golden Ash ..... Fraxinus excelsior Jaspidea
Golden Atlas Cedar ..... Cedrus atlantica Aurea
Golden Beech ..... Fagus sylvatica Zlatia
Golden Box Elder ..... Acer negundo Elegans
Golden Cedar ..... Thuja plicata Gold King
Golden Chain Tree ..... Laburnum anagyroides
Golden Chain Tree ..... Laburnum x watereri vossii
Golden Chalice Vine ..... Solandra maxima
Golden Chinese Juniper ..... Juniperus chinensis Aurea
Golden Corn Plant ..... Dracaena fragrans Massangeana
Golden Creeping Jenny ..... Lysimachia nummularia Aurea
Golden Drops ..... Primula veris
Golden Elderberry ..... Sambucus nigra aurea
Golden Elm ..... Ulmus glabra Lutescens
Golden Elm ..... Ulmus Louis Van Houtte
Golden Everlasting ..... Helichrysum bracteatum
Golden Feverfew ..... Tanacetum parthenium aureum was Chrysanthemum p.a.
Golden Fleece ..... Thymophylla tenuiloba
Golden Garlic ..... Allium moly
Golden Guinea Everlasting ..... Helichrysum argyrophyllum
Golden Hair ..... Chrysocoma coma-aurea
Golden Himalayan Cedar ..... Cedrus deodara Aurea

Golden Hinoki cypress ..... Chamaecyparis obtusa Crippsii

Golden Irish Moss ..... Arenaria caespitosa aurea now Minuartia verna c.

Golden Larch ..... Pseudolarix amabilis

Golden Lily of the Valley ..... Sandersonia aurantica

Golden Marjoram ..... Origanum vulgare Aureum

Golden Norway Spruce ..... Picea abies Aurea

Golden Privet ..... Ligustrum ovalifolium Aureum was Aureomarginatum

Golden Rain Tree ..... Koelreuteria paniculata

Golden Rod ..... Solidago species

Golden Ruin Wattle ..... Acacia prominens

Golden Sage ..... Salvia officinalis Aurea

Golden Salvia ..... S. africana-lutea

Golden Shower Tree ..... Cassia fistula

Golden Spaniard ..... Aciphylla aurea

Golden Spear Grass ..... Aciphylla aurea

Golden Stemmed Red Alder ..... Alnus rubra aurea

Golden Tainui ..... Pomaderris kumeraho

Golden Thyme ..... Thymus carneus

Golden Torch Flowering Ginger ..... Heliconia psittacorum

Golden Totara ..... Podocarpus totara Aurea

Golden Wattle ..... Acacia pycnantha

Golden Weeping Willow ..... Salix alba vitellina Pendula now S.alba Tristis

Golden Whitebeam ..... Sorbus aria lutescens

Golden Willow ..... Salix alba vitellina

Golden Wreath Wattle ..... Acacia saligna syn cyanophylla

Golden-eyed Grass ..... Sisyrinchium californicum

Golden-lvd Kohuhu ..... Pittosporum ellipticum

Goldenberry ..... Physalis peruviana syn P.edulis

Goldflower, Prostrate ..... Hypericum cerastioides

Goldfussia ..... Strobilanthes anisophyllus

Goldilocks ..... Chrysocoma coma-aurea

Good King Henry ..... Chenopodium bonus-henricus

Goose Foot Maple ..... Acer pensylvanica

Gooseberry (edible) ..... Ribes uva-crispa varieties

Gooseberry (ornamental) ..... Ribes speciosum

Gooseneck ..... Lysimachia clethroides

Gosford Wattle ..... Acacia prominens

Gossamer Grass ..... Anemanthele lessoniana syn Oryzopsis l.

Gossamer Wattle ..... Acacia baileyana

Gossamer Wattle ..... Acacia floribunda

Gotu Cola ..... Centella asiatica   was Hydrocotyle a.

Gourd ..... Laganeria siceraria

Gourd ..... see Cucurbita

Gourd, White/Wax ..... Benincasa hispada Chinese Winter

Graceful Boronia ..... Boronia crenulata

Graceful Wattle ..... Acacia decora

Grampian Gum ..... Eucalyptus alpina

Grand Fir ..... Abies grandis

Granny's Bonnet ..... Aquilegia vulgaris

Granny's Ringlets ..... Cryptomeria japonica spiralis

Grape ..... Vitis species

Grape Hyacinths ..... Muscari species

Grapefruit ..... see Citrus

Grass of Parnassus ..... Parnassia palustris

Grass Tree, Australian ..... Xanthorrhoea australis

Grass Trees NZ ..... Dracophyllum species

Gravel Bottlebrush ..... Beaufortia sparsa

Great Bellflower ..... Campanula latifolia var macrantha

Great White Cherry ..... Prunus (cherry flwg) Taihaku

Grecian Fir ..... Abies cephalonica

Grecian Foxglove ..... Digitalis lanata

Green Ash ..... Fraxinus pennsylvanica

Green Flax ..... Phormium tenax

Green Lavender ..... Lavandula viridis

Green Rose ..... Rosa viridiflora

Green Taro ..... Colocasia esculenta

Green Water Rose ..... Samolus valerandii

Green Wattle ..... Acacia decurrens

Gregg Pine ..... Pinus greggii

Grey Alder ..... Alnus incana

Grey Guinea Flower ..... Hibbertia obtusifolia

Grey Haired Euryops ..... Euryops pectinatus

Grey Serruria ..... Serruria pedunculata

Grey-budded Snakebark ..... Acer rufinerve

Grey-lvd Willow ..... Salix seringeana

Gromwell ..... Lithospermum officinalis

Grosser's Maple ..... Acer grosseri

Ground Ivy ..... Glechoma hederacea

Ground Orchid ..... Dactylorhiza maculata

Guadalupe Cypress ..... Cupressus guadalupensis

Guadalupe Palm ..... Brahea edulis

Guava, Chilean ..... Ugni molinae

Guavas ..... Psidium species

Guelder Rose, Dwarf ..... Viburnum opulus Nanum

Guinea Gold Vine ..... Hibbertia scandens

Gully Fern ..... Pneumatopteris pennigera

Gully Gum ..... Eucalyptus smithii

Gum Cistus ..... Cistus ladanifer

Gum Trees ..... see Eucalyptus

Gumdiggers Soap ..... Pomaderris kumeraho

Gumplant ..... Grindelia robusta

Gypsywort ..... Lycopus europaeus

Haekaro ..... Pittosporum umbellatum

Hair Grass ..... Eleocharis acicularis

Halls Totara ..... Podocarpus hallii

Hamburg Parsley ..... Petroselinum crispum var tuberosum

Handkerchief Tree ..... Davidia involucrata

Hangehange ..... Geniostoma rupestre

Harakeke ..... Phormium tenax

Hardy Gloxinia ..... Incarvillea delavayi

Harebell ..... Campanula rotundifolia

Harlequin Glorybower ..... Clerodendron trichotonum fargesii

Harry Lauder's Walking Stick ..... Corylus avellana Contorta

Haumakaroa ..... Pseudopanax simples

Hawaiian Elf Schefflera ..... S. arboricola

Hawk's Beard ..... Crepis species

Hawkweed ..... Hieracium auranticum

Hawthorn ..... Crataegus species

Hazelnut ..... Corylus avellana

Hazels ..... Corylus species

Heart Of The Earth ..... Prunella vulgaris

Heart-lvd Silver Gum ..... Eucalyptus cordata

Heartsease ..... Viola tricolour

Heath Arborvitae ..... Thuja occidentalis Ericoides

Heath Myrtle, Grampians ..... Thryptomene calycina

Heath Myrtle, Rock ..... Thryptomene saxicola Rosea

Heath, Bell ..... Erica cinerea

Heath, Bridal ..... Erica bauera

Heath, Colombian ..... Cavendisha acuminata

Heath, Common ..... Epacris impressa

Heath, Cornish ..... Erica vagans Alba

Heath, Flame ..... Agapetes serpens

Heath, Hairy ..... Erica cerinthoides

Heath, Hairy-flowered ..... Erica hirtiflora

Heath, Irish ..... Erica erigena

Heath, Kaffir ..... Erica caffra

Heath, Knobby ..... Erica conica

Heath, Pink Garland ..... Erica persoluta

Heath, Spanish ..... Erica australis

Heath, St Daboec's ..... Daboecia cantabrica

Heath, Velvet ..... Erica peziza

Heath, Wax ..... Erica ventricosa Globosa

Heath, Winter ..... Erica darleyensis

Heath-lvd Banksia ..... Banksia ericifolia

Heather ..... Erica species

Heather, False ..... Cuphea hyssopifolia

Heather, Scotch ..... Calluna species

Heavenly Bamboo ..... Nandina domestica

Hedge Maple ..... Acer campestre

Hedge Woundwort ..... Stachys sylvatica

Helmet Plant/Flower ..... Scutellaria species

Hemlocks ..... Tsuga species

Hemp Agrimony ..... Eupatorium cannabinum

Hen & Chickens Fern ..... Asplenium bulbiferum

Hen & Chickens Marigold ..... Calendula officinal prolifera

Henna ..... Lawsonia species

Henry's Lime ..... Tilia henryana

Herb Bennet ..... Geum urbanum

Herb of Grace ..... Ruta graveolens

Herb Twopence ..... Lysimachia nummularia

Herrera Pine ..... Pinus herrerai

Hers Snakebark Maple ..... Acer grosseri hersii -

Hickory Pine ..... Pinus pungens

Hickory Wattle ..... Acacia falciformis

Hickory Wattle ..... Acacia penninervis

Hidcote Gold ..... Hypericum Hidcote

Hill Cherry ..... Prunus (cherry flwg) serrulata

Hillgrove Gum ..... Eucalyptus michaeliana

Himalayan Alder ..... Alnus nitida

Himalayan Birch ..... Betula utilis jacquemontii

Himalayan Cedar ..... Cedrus deodara

Himalayan Clover ..... Parochetus communis

Himalayan Cypress ..... Cupressus torulosa

Himalayan Daphne ..... D. bholua

Himalayan Daphne ..... D. longilobata

Himalayan Evergreen Spindle ..... Euonymus ting

Himalayan Fir ..... Abies spectabilis

Himalayan Giant Lily ..... Cardiocrinum gigranteur

Himalayan Hemlock ..... Tsuga dumosa

Himalayan Marigold ..... Tagetes lunulata

Himalayan May Apple ..... Podophyllum hexandrum

Himalayan Musk Rose ..... Rosa brunonii

Himalayan Pine ..... Pinus wallichiana was P.griffithii

Himalayan Poppy ..... Meconopsis betonicifolia was baileyi

Himalayan Rhubarb ..... Rheum australe was emodi

Himalayan White Pine ..... Pinus wallichiana was griffithi

Himalayan Yew ..... Taxus wallichiana

Hime-Kan-Suge ..... Carex oonica

Hin Choy ..... Amaranthus gangeticum

Hinau ..... Elaeocarpus dentatus

Hinds Walnut ..... Juglans hindsii

Hinoki Cypress ..... Chamaecyparis obtusa

Hokkaido Bladder Nut ..... Staphylea bumalda

Hokkaido Mountain Alder ..... Alnus maximowiczii

Hokotaka ..... Corokia macrocarpa

Holly ..... Ilex species

Holly Oak ..... Quercus ilex

Holly Olive ..... Osmanthus heterophyllus was ilicifolius

Holly, False ..... Osmanthus heterophyllus Variegatus

Hollyhocks ..... Alcea species

Hollyleaf Sweetspine ..... Itea ilicifolia

Hollywood Cherry ..... Prunus (cherry flwg) ilicifolia

Hollywood Juniper ..... Juniperus chinensis Kaizuka

Holm Oak ..... Quercus ilex

Holy Grass ..... Hierochloe redolens

Hondo Spruce ..... Picea jesoensis var hondoensis

Honesty ..... Lunaria annua

Honey Locust ..... Gleditsia triacanthos

Honeysuckle ..... Lonicera species

Honeysuckle, Box ..... Lonicera nitida

Honeysuckle, Bush ..... Diervilla x splendens

Honeysuckle, Cape ..... Tecoma capensis

Honeysuckle, French ..... Hedysarum coronarium

Honeysuckle, NZ ..... Knightia excelsa

Honeysuckle, Red ..... Banksia serrata

Honeywort ..... Cerinthe major

Hoop Petticoat Daffodil ..... Narcissus bulbocodium

Hoop Pine ..... Araucaria cunninghamii

Hop Bush ..... Dodonea viscosa

Hop Hornbeam ..... Ostrya carpinifolia

Hop Wattle ..... Acacia stricta

Hops ..... Humulus lupulus

Horehound ..... Marrubium vulgare

Hornbeams ..... Carpinus species

Horned Poppy ..... Glaucium species

Horoeka ..... Pseudopanax crassifolius

Horokaka ..... Disphyma australe

Horopito .....: Pseudowintera species

Horse Chestnut ..... Aesculus species

Horse Mint ..... Monarda didyma

Horse Mint ..... Pycnanthemum flexuosum syn P.tenufolium

Horse Tail Oak ..... Casuarina equisetifolia

Horseradish ..... Armoracia rusticana was Cochlearia arm.

Horses Head Foliage ..... Philodendron panduriforme now bipennifolium

Horsetail ..... Equisetum arvense

Hose in Hose ..... Primula veris

Hose in Hose Primula ..... Primula elatior Hose in Hose

Houhere ..... Hoheria populnea

Hounds Tongue ..... Cynoglossum officinale

Hounds Tongue ..... Phymatosorus diversifolius

Houpara ..... Pseudopanax lessonii

Houseleeks ..... Sempervivum species

Huichol Tobacco ..... Nicotiana langsdorfii

Hunangamoho ..... Chionochloa conspicua

Hungarian Lilac ..... Syringa josikaea

Hungarian Oak ..... Quercus frainetto

Huon Pine ..... Lagarostrobos franklinii was Dacrydium f

Hupeh Mountain Ash ..... Sorbus hupehensis

Hutu ..... Ascarina lucida

Hwangshan Pine ..... Pinus hwangshanensis

Hyacinth Orchid ..... Bletilla striata

Hyssop ..... Hyssopus officinalis

Ice Plants ..... Lampranthus (was Mesembryanthemum) species

Iceland Poppy ..... Papaver nudicaulis

Illawara Pine ..... Callitris muelleri

Illawarra Flame Tree ..... Brachychiton acerifolius

Incense Cedar ..... Calocedrus decurrens

Incense Plant ..... Olearia moschata

Indian Bean Tree ..... Catalpa bignonioides

Indian Cedar ..... Cedrus deodara

Indian Hawthorn ..... Raphiolepsis species

Indian Horse Chestnut ..... Aesculus indica

Indian Lilac ..... Melia azederach

Indian Rope ..... Hoya carnosa compacta moan loa

Indian Strawberry ..... Duchesnea indica

Indigo ..... Indigofera species

Indigo ..... Indigofera tinctoria

Indigo (false) ..... Baptisia australis

Irises, NZ ..... Libertia species

Irish Flax ..... Linum perenne

Irish Heath ..... Daboecia species

Irish Juniper ..... Juniperus communis Hibernica

Irish Moss ..... Sagina subulata Aurea

Irish Spurge ..... Euphorbia hyberna

Irish Yew ..... Taxus baccata Fastigiata

Italian Alder ..... Alnus cordata

Italian Maple ..... Acer opalus

Italian Parsley ..... Petroselinum hortense

Italian Pencil Cypress ..... Cupressus sempervirens stricta

Ivy ..... Hedera species

Ivy-lvd Toad Flax ..... Cymbalaria muralis

Jack Pine ..... Pinus banksiana

Jack-in-the-Pulpit ..... Arisaema triphyllum

Jacob's Ladder ..... Polemonium species

Jacobean Lily ..... Sprekelia formosissima

Japanese Alder ..... Alnus firma

Japanese Angelica ..... Angelica acutiloba

Japanese Aralia ..... Fatsia japonica

Japanese Black Pine ..... Pinus thunbergii

Japanese Blood Grass ..... Imperata cylindrica rubra (Red Baron)

Japanese Cedar ..... Cryptomeria japonica

Japanese Chestnut ..... Castanea crenata

Japanese Crabapple ..... Malus crabapple floribunda

Japanese Dogwood ..... Cornus kousa

Japanese Fan Columbine ..... Aquilegia flabellata

Japanese Flowering Quince ..... Chaenomeles japonica

Japanese Fodder Willow ..... Salix kinuyanagi

Japanese Garden Juniper ..... Juniperus procumbens

Japanese Greens ..... Brassica mizuna

Japanese Ground Orchid ..... Bletilla striata

Japanese Higan Cherry ..... Prunus (cherry flwg) subhirtella

Japanese Holly ..... Ilex crenata

Japanese Hornbeam ..... Carpinus japonica

Japanese Horse Chestnut ..... Aesculus turbinata

Japanese Hydrangea ..... Hydrangea paniculata

Japanese Ivy ..... Parthenocissus tricuspidata Lowii

Japanese Keaki ..... Zelkova serrata

Japanese Larch ..... Larix kaempferi

Japanese Laurel ..... Aucuba japonica

Japanese Laurel ..... Euonymus japonicus

Japanese Maple ..... Acer palmatum

Japanese Menthol Mint ..... Mentha arvensis peper

Japanese Millet ..... Echinochloa frumentacea Japanese

Japanese Pagoda tree ..... Sophora japonica

Japanese Plum Yew ..... Cephalotaxus harringtonia Fastigiata

Japanese Privet ..... Ligustrum japonicum Rotundifolium

Japanese Quince ..... Chaenomeles speciosa

Japanese Raisin Tree ..... Hovenia dulcis

Japanese Red Pine ..... Pinus densiflora

Japanese Rose ..... Kerria japonica

Japanese Sedge Grass ..... Carex hachijoensis Evergold

Japanese Silver Birch ..... Betula ermanii

Japanese Snowbell Tree ..... Styrax japonicus

Japanese Spicebush ..... Lindera obtusiloba

Japanese Spindle ..... Euonymus sieboldianus

Japanese Spurge ..... Pachysandra terminalis

Japanese Staunton Vine ..... Stauntonia hexaphylla

Japanese Stewartia ..... Stewartia pseudocamelia

Japanese Twisted Bamboo ..... Bambusa Wong Tsai

Japanese Umbrella Pine ..... Sciadopitys verticillata

Japanese Viburnum ..... Viburnum japonicum

Japanese Walnut ..... Juglans ailantifolia

Japanese White Birch ..... Betula platyphylla japonica

Japanese White Pine ..... Pinus parviflora

Japanese Windflower ..... Anemone x hybrida was japonica

Japanese Wisteria ..... Wisteria floribunda

Japanese Witch Hazel ..... Hamamelis japonica

Japanese Zelkova ..... Zelkova serrata

Japonica ..... Chaenomeles japonica

Jarrah ..... Eucalyptus marginata

Jasmine Primrose ..... Oenothera pallida

Jasmine, Azores ..... Jasminum azoricum

Jasmine, Chilean ..... Mandevillea laxa was suavelolens

Jasmine, Madagascar ..... Stephanotis floribunda

Jasmine, Primrose ..... Jasminum mesnyi

Jasmine, Rock ..... Androsace lanuginosa

Jasmine, Spring ..... Jasminum polyanthum

Jasmine, Star ..... Trachelospermum jasminoides

Jasmine, Winter ..... Jasminum nudiflorum

Java Shower Tree ..... Cassia javanica

Jeffrey's Pine ..... Pinus jeffreyii

Jelecote Pine ..... Pinus palustris

Jelly palm ..... Butia capitata

Jellybeans ..... Disphyma clavellatum

Jerusalem Cross ..... Lychnis chalcedonia

Jerusalem Sages ..... Phlomis species

Jew's Mallow ..... Kerria japonica

Jewel Mint ..... Mentha requienii

Jicama ..... Pachyrhizus tuberosus

Jillaga Ash ..... Eucalyptus stenostoma

Job's Tears ..... Coix lacryma-jobi

Jockey Caps ..... Tigridia species

Joe Pye Weed ..... Eupatorium purpureum

Joe Pye Weed ..... Eupatorium purpureum maculatum Atropurpureum

Jointed Gourd ..... Benincasa hispada Fuzzy

Josephs Coat ..... Amaranthus tricolour

Jounama Snow Gum ..... Eucalyptus pauciflora var debeuzevillei

Judas Tree ..... Cercis siliquastrum

Jujube ..... Zyzyphus jujuba

Juniper Myrtle ..... Agonis juniperina

Juniper Tamarisk ..... Tamarix juniperina

Jupiters Distaff ..... Salvia glutinosa

Kaffir Lily ..... Clivia miniata

Kaffir Lily ..... Schizostylis coccinea

Kaffir Plum ..... Harpephyllum caffrum

Kahakaha ..... Collospermum hastatum

Kahikatea ..... Dacrycarpus dacrydioides

Kahikatoa ..... Leptospermum scoparium

Kaikawaka ..... Libocedrus bidwillii

Kaikomako ..... Pennantia corymbosa

Kaiku ..... Parsonsia heterophylla

Kaiwhiria ..... Parsonsia heterophylla

Kakabeak ..... Clianthus puniceus

Kakaha ..... Astelia fragrans

Kakaho ..... Cortaderia fulvida

Kale ..... see Brassica

Kamahi ..... Weinmannia racemosa

Kangaroo Paws ..... Anigozanthos species

Kanono ..... Coprosma australis

Kanono ..... Coprosma grandifolia

Kanooka ..... Tristaniopsis laurina

Kansas Gayfeather ..... Liatris pychnostachya

Kansu Spruce ..... Picea meyerii

Kanuka ..... Kunzea ericoides   was Leptospermum e.

Kapuka ..... Griselina littoralis

Karaka ..... Corynocarpus laevigatus

Karamu ..... Coprosma robusta

Karo ..... Pittosporum crassifolium

Karri Gum ..... Eucalyptus diversicolor

Kashmir Cypress ..... Cupressus cashmeriana

Katsura Tree ..... Cercidiphyllum japonicum

Kauri ..... Agathis australis

Kauri Grass ..... Astelia trinervia

Kawaka ..... Libocedrus plumosa

Kawakawa ..... Macropiper excelsum

Kei Apple ..... Dovyalis caffra

Kenilworth Ivy ..... Cymbalaria muralis

Kentia Palm ..... Howea species

Kentucky Coffee Tree ..... Gymnocladus dioicus

Kermadec Is kiokio ..... Blechnum sp Kermadec Is

Kermadec Is Pohutukawa ..... Metrosideros kermadecensis

Kermadec Is Pohutukawa ..... Metrosideros Lewis Nicholls

Keurboom ..... Virgilia species

Kidney Vetch ..... Anthyllis vulneraria

Killarney Strawberry Tree ..... Arbutus unedo

Kilmarnock Willow ..... Salix caprea Kilmarnock

King Cup ..... Caltha palustris

King Fern ..... Marattia fraxinea

King Fern ..... Marattia salicina

King Palm ..... Archontophoenix alexandrae

King Protea ..... Protea cynaroides

King William Pine ..... Athrotaxus selaginoides

Kingfisher Daisies ..... Felicia species

Kings Spear ..... Asphodeline lutea

Kiokio ..... Blechnum Green Bay

Kiokio ..... Blechnum sp 1

Kiss-me-quick Shrub ..... Brunsfelsia calycina

Kiwakiwa ..... Blechnum fluviatile

Kiwifuit ..... Actinidia chinensis

Knapweed, Greater ..... Centaurea scabiosa

Knife-leaf Wattle ..... Acacia cultriformis

Knobcone Pine ..... Pinus attenuata

Knotted Marjoram ..... Origanum majorana (hortensis)

Knotweed ..... Polygonum vaccinifolium

Kobus Magnolia ..... Magnolia kobus

Kohe Kohe ..... Dysoxylum spectabile

Koheriki ..... Gingidia montana

Kohlrabi ..... see Brassica

Kohuhu ..... Pittosporum tenuifolium

Kokomuka ..... Hebe elliptica

Korean Arborvitae ..... Thuja koraiensis

Korean Fir ..... Abies koreana

Korean Hill Cherry ..... Prunus (cherry flwg) serrulata pubescens

Korean Lilac ..... Syringa palibiniana   now meyeri Palibin

Korean Lilac ..... Syringa patula

Korean Mint ..... Agastache rugosa

Korean Pine ..... Pinus koraiensis

Korean Spruce ..... Picea koraensis

Korokio ..... Corokia cotoneaster

Korokio taranga ..... Corokia buddleioides

Koromiko ..... Hebe salicifolia

Koromiko ..... Hebe stricta

Koromiko-taranga ..... Hebe parviflora

Kosters Blue Spruce ..... Picea pungens Koster

Kotukutuku ..... Fuchsia excorticata

Kowhais ..... Sophora species

Kowharawhara ..... Astelia solandri

Koyama Spruce ..... Picea koyamai

Kumarahou ..... Pomaderris kumeraho

Kumikumi ..... Cucumis species

Kumquat ..... Fortunella margarita

Kunn Choi ..... Apium graveolens Chinese Celery

Kurikuri ..... Aciphylla squarrosa

Kybean Mallee Ash ..... Eucalyptus kybeanensis

Lacebark Pine ..... Pinus bungeana

Lacebarks ..... Hoheria species

Lacecap Viburnum ..... Viburnum opulus xanthocarpum

Laceflower ..... Didiscus species

Lad's Love ..... Artemisia abrotanum

Ladder Ferns ..... Nephrolepsis species

Ladies Lockets ..... Polygonatum multiflorum

Ladies Mantle ..... Alchemilla mollis

Lady Palm ..... Rhapis excelsa

Lady's Bedstraw ..... Galium verum

Lady's Fingers ..... Anthyllis vulneraria

Lady's Locket ..... Dicentra spectabilis

Lady's Slipper ..... Thunbergia mysorensis

Lady's Smock ..... Cardamine pratensis

Lady's Wand ..... Dierama pulcherrimum

Ladybell ..... Adenophora confusa

Lambs Ear ..... Stachys byzantina   was lanata

Lambs Lettuce ..... Valerianella locusta

Lancewoods ..... Pseudopanax species

Landcress ..... Barbarea verna

Larch common ..... Larix decidua

Large Flower Broom ..... Carmichaelia williamsii

Large-lvd Mahoe ..... Melicytus macrophyllus

Larkspur ..... Consolida species

Laurel Magnolia ..... Magnolia grandiflora

Laurustinus ..... Viburnum tinus

Lavender Cotton ..... Santolina chamaecyparissus

Lavender Trails ..... Drosanthemum floribundum

Lavender, English ..... Lavandula angustifolia

Lavender, French ..... Lavandula stoechas

Lavender, Spike ..... Lavandula latifolia

Lawn Chamomile ..... Chamaemelum nobilis Treneague

Lawson Cypress ..... Chamaecyparis lawsoniana

Lawsons Pine ..... Pinus lawsonii

Lead Pine ..... Pinus bungeana

Leaf Celery ..... Apium graveolens secalinum

Leatherwood ..... Eucryphia lucida

Leek ..... Allium ampeloprasum

Leek, Round-headed ..... Allium sphaerocephalon

Lemon ..... see Citrus

Lemon Balm ..... Melissa officinalis

Lemon Basil ..... Ocimum basilicum cv citriodorum

Lemon Bergamot ..... Monarda citriodora

Lemon Catnip ..... Nepeta cataria Citriodora

Lemon Grass ..... Cymbopogon citratus

Lemon Scented Gum ..... Eucalyptus citriodora

Lemon Scented Myrtle ..... Backhousia citriodora

Lemon Tea Tree ..... Leptospermum petersenii wa citratum

Lemon Thyme ..... Thymus x citriodorus

Lemon Verbena ..... Aloysia triphylla was Lippia citriodora

Lemonwood ..... Pittosporum eugenioides

Lenten Rose ..... Helleborus orientalis

Leopard Lily ..... Belamcanda sp

Leopard Tree ..... Caesalpina ferrea

Leopards Bane ..... Doronicum species

Lesser Bullrush ..... Typha angustifolia

Lesser Burnet ..... Pimpinella saxifrage

Lesser Calamint ..... Calamintha nepeta

Lesser Celandine ..... Ranunculus ficaria cupreus

Lesser Periwinkle ..... Vinca minor

Lettuce ..... Lactuca sativa

Lettuce Leaf Rose ..... Rosa Bullata

Leyland Cypress ..... Cupressocyparis leylandii

Lightwood ..... Acacia implexa

Likiang Spruce ..:... Picea likiangensis

Lilac ..... Syringa species

LillyPilly ..... Eugenia species

Lily Magnolia ..... Magnolia liliflora

Lily of the Valley ..... Convallaria majalis

Lily of the Valley Bush ..... Pieris japonica

Lily of the Valley Shrub ..... Leucothoe fontanesiana   now walteri

Lily of the Valley Tree ..... Clethra arborea

Limber Pine ..... Pinus flexilis

Lime (fruit) ..... see Citrus

Lime Trees ..... Tilia species

Linden ..... Tilia species

Linseed ..... Linum ultratissimum

Lions Ear/Tail ..... Leonotis leonurus   now ocymifolia

Lipstick Plant ..... Bixa orellana

Liquorice ..... Glycyrrhiza glabra

Little Lutz Spruce ..... Picea lutzii

Little Robin Cranesbill ..... Geranium purpureum

Livingstone Daisy ..... Mesembryanthemum oriniflorum

Lizards Tail ..... Saururus cernuus

Loblolly Pine ..... Pinus taeda

Lobster Claw ..... Clianthus puniceus

Lombardy Poplar ..... Populus nigra Italica

London Plane ..... Platanus x hispanica   was acerifolia

London Pride ..... Saxifraga umbrosa

London Pride ..... Saxifraga x urbium

Long Leafed Indian Pine ..... Pinus roxburghii

Long-leaf Pine ..... Pinus palustris

Long-lvd Box ..... Eucalyptus goniocalyx

Loosestrife ..... Lysimachia species

Loosestrife ..... Lythrum virgatum

Loquat ..... Eriobotrya japonica

Lord Anson's Blue Pea ..... Lathyrus nervosus

Lord Howe Wedding Lily ..... Dietes robinsoniana

Lords and Ladies ..... Arum maculatum

Louisiana Sage ..... Artemisia ludoviciana

Lovage ..... Levisticum officinale

Love in a Mist ..... Nigella species

Love Lies Bleeding ..... Amaranthus caudatus

Lucombe Oak ..... Quercus x hispanica
Lucombeana   now x lucombeana William Lucombe

Luffa ..... Luffa aegyptica

Lungworts ..... Pulmonaria species

Lupin ..... Lupinus species

Maakoako   Samolus repens

Mace Yarrow ..... Achillea ageratum   was decolorans

Macedonian Pine ..... Pinus peuce

MacNab's Cypress ..... Cupressus macnabiana

Madagascar Palm ..... Ravenea rivularis

Madder ..... Rubia tinctorum

Maggi Herb ..... Levisticum officinale

Magic Flower ..... Cantua buxifolia

Magnolia Rose ..... Rosa Devoniensis

Magnolia Vine ..... Schisandra sphenanthera

Mahoe ..... Melicytus ramiflorus

Mahoewao ..... Melicytus lanceolatus

Mahogany Gum ..... Eucalyptus botryoides

Maidenhair Ferns ..... Adiantum species

Maidenhair Tree ..... Gingko biloba

Maidens Gum ..... Eucalyptus maidenii

Maidens Wreath ..... Francoa ramosa

Maire ..... Nestegis species

Mairehau ..... Phebalium nudum

Majestic Palm ..... Ravenea rivularis

Makaka ..... Plagianthus divaricatus

Makamaka ..... Caldcluvia rosaefolia   was Ackama r.

Makomako ..... Aristotelia serrata

Malabar Spinach ..... Basella rubra

Mallow, Black ..... Alcea rosea var. nigra

Mallow, Common ..... Malva sylvestris

Maltese Cross ..... Lychnis chalcedonia

Mamangi ..... Coprosma arborea

Mana Gum ..... Eucalyptus viminalis

Manatu ..... Plagianthus regius

Manchurian Birch ..... Betula platyphylla

Manchurian Snakebark Maple ..... Acer tegmentosum

Mandarin ..... see Citrus

Mangeao ..... Litsea calicaris

Manna Ash ..... Fraxinus ornus

Manuka ..... Leptospermum scoparium

Mao Gwa ..... Benincasa hispada Fuzzy

Maori Anise ..... Gingidia montana

Maori Onion ..... Bulbinella hookeri, angustifolia

Mapere ..... Gahnia setifolia

Maples ..... Acer species

Mapou ..... Myrsine australis

Marbleleaf ..... Carpodetus serratus

Marguerite Daisies ..... Argyranthemum species

Marigold ..... Calendula officinalis

Maritime Pine ..... Pinus pinaster

Marjoram ..... Origanum vulgare

Marlborough Daisy ..... Pachystegia insignis now Olearia

Marlborough Lilac ..... Heliohebe hulkeana was Hebe h.

Marmalade Bush ..... Streptosolen jamesonii

Maroonhood ..... Pterostylis pedunculata

Marsh Cinquefoil ..... Potentilla palustris

Marsh Felwort ..... Swertia perennis

Marsh Gentian ..... Gentiana pneumonanthe

Marsh Marigold ..... Caltha palustris

Marshmallow(true) ..... Althaea officinalis

Martinez Pinyon Pine ..... Pinus maximartinezii

Maruba Santo ..... Brassica Santo

Marvel of Peru ..... Mirabilis jalapa

Mashua (anu) ..... Tropaeolum tuberosum

Mask Flower ..... Alonsoa species

Masterwort ..... Astrantia major

Matagouri ..... Discaria toumatou

Matai ..... Prumnopitys taxifolia   was Podocarpus spicatus

Maudlin ..... Achillea ageratum   was decolorans

Maukoro ..... Carmichaelia odorata

Mayten Tree ..... Maytenus boaria

Mazanita ..... Arctostaphylus mazanita

Mazzard Cherry ..... Prunus (cherry flwg) avium

McKies Stringybark ..... Eucalyptus mckieana

Meadow Clary ..... Salvia pratensis

Meadow Cranesbill ..... Geranium ibericum

Meadow Cranesbill ..... Geranium pratense

Meadow Sage ..... Salvia pratensis

Meadowfoam ..... Limnanthes douglasii

Meadowrue ..... Thalictrum glabra

Meadowsweet ..... Filipendula ulmaria

Mealy Stringybark ..... Eucalyptus cephalocarpa

Mediterranean Cypress ..... Cupressus sempervirens

Mediterranean Hackberry ..... Celtis australis

Mediterraneum Sage ..... Salvia aethiopis

Medlar ..... Mespilus germanica

Melilot ..... Melilotus officinalis

Melon ..... Cucumis species

Melon, Water ..... see Citrullus

Mendocina Cypress ..... Cupressus goveniana var pygmaea

Menemene ..... Eugenia uniflora

Meru Oak ..... Vitex keniensis

Messmate Stringybark ..... Eucalyptus obliqua

Mexican Alder ..... Alnus jorullensis

Mexican Blood Flower ..... Distictis buccinatoria was Phaedranthus b.

Mexican Bush Sage ..... Salvia leucantha

Mexican Crepe Poppy ..... Argemone varieties

Mexican Cypress ..... Cupressus lusitanica

Mexican Evening Primrose ..... Oenothera speciosa

Mexican Fan Palm ..... Washingtonia robusta

Mexican Fire Plant ..... Euphorbia heterophylla

Mexican Hat ..... Ratabida columnifera

Mexican Hyssop ..... Agastache mexicana Champagne

Mexican Marigold ..... Tagetes lemmonii

Mexican Orange Blossom ..... Choisya ternata

Mexican Pine ..... Pinus montezuma

Mexican Pinyon Pine ..... Pinus cembroides

Mexican Sage ..... Salvia mexicana

Mexican Sunflower ..... Tithonia speciosa

Mexican Swamp Cypress ..... Taxodium mucronatum

Mexican Tea ..... Chenopodium ambrisioides

Mexican Tree Dahlia ..... Dahlia tenuicaulis

Mexican Water Chestnut ..... Pachyrhizus tuberosus

Mexican Weeping Juniper ..... Juniperus flaccida

Mexican Weeping Pine ..... Pinus patula

Mexican White Pine ..... Pinus ayacahiute

Mibuna ..... see Brassica

Michaelmas Daisies ..... Aster novi-belgii

Mickey Mouse Plant ..... Ochna serrulata

Mid-west Sugar Maple ..... Acer saccharum ssp nigrum

Midsummer Aster ..... Erigeron karvinskianus was mucronatus

Mignonette ..... Reseda odorata

Mikoikoi ..... Libertia grandiflora

Milk Tree ..... Streblus heterophyllus

Milkwort ..... Polygala myrtifolia Grandiflora

Miner's Lettuce ..... Claytonia perfoliata

Mingimingi ..... Coprosma propinqua

Mingimingi ..... Leucopogon fasciculata

Mint Bush, Australian ..... Prostanthera species

Mint, Common ..... Mentha spicata

Miro ,,,,, Prumnopitys ferruginea was Podocarpus f.

Misome ..... Brassica misome

Miss Wilmott's Ghost ..... Eryngium giganteum

Mission Bells ..... Fritillaria biflora

Mitsuba ..... Cryptotaenia japonica

Mizuna ..... Brassica mizuna(juncea var japonica)

Mock Cypress ..... Kochia trichophylla

Mock Oranges ..... Philadelphus species

Moldavian Balm ..... Dracocephalum moldavicum

Momi Fir ..... Abies firma

Monarch Birch ..... Betula maximowicziana

Monarch of the Veldt ..... Venidium fastuosum

Mondo Grass ..... Ophiopogon species

Money Tree ..... Paulownia elongata

Moneywort ..... Lysimachia nummularia

Mongolian Oak ..... Quercus mongolica

Mongolian Scots Pine ..... Pinus sylvestris var mongolica

Monkey Apple ..... Eugenia smithii syn acmena

Monkey Musk(common large) ..... Mimulus guttatus

Monkey Puzzle ..... Araucaria araucana

Monkshood ..... Aconitum species

Montbretia ..... Crocosmia masoniorum

Montbretia ..... Tritonia crocata

Monterey Cypress ..... Cupressus macrocarpa

Monterey Pine ..... Pinus radiata

Montezuma Cypress ..... Taxodium mucronatum

Montezuma Pine ..... Pinus montezumae

Montpellier Maple ..... Acer monspessulanum

Moon Climber ..... Ipomoea alba

Moonflower ..... Ipomoea species

Moonlight Holly ..... Ilex aquifolium Flavescens

Moonlight Primula ..... Primula alpicola

MopTop/MopHead Acacia ..... Robinia pseudoacacia Umbraculifera syn Inermis

Moreton Bay Fig ..... Ficus macrophylla

Moreton Bay Pine ..... Araucaria cunninghamii

Morning Glory ..... Ipomoea species

Morning Glory, Ground ..... Convolvulus sabatius

Morocco Broom ..... Cytisus battandieri

Morrisby's Gum ..... Eucalyptus morrisbyi

Moses in the Cradle ..... Rhoeo discolor now Tradescantia

Moso Bamboo ..... Phyllostachys edulis

Mosquito Grass ..... Bouteloua gracilis

Mossy-cup Oak ..... Quercus cerris

Moth Mullein ..... Verbascum sp pale-pink

Mother of Herbs ..... Artemisia vulgaris

Mother of Thousands ..... Tolmiea menziesii

Mother-in Law's Tongue ..... Sanseveria trifasciata Laurentii

Motherwort ..... Leonurus cardiaca

Mountain Ash ..... Eucalyptus regnans

Mountain Ash ..... Sorbus aucuparia

Mountain Astelia ..... Astelia nervosa

Mountain Avens ..... Dryas octapetala

Mountain Balm ..... Pimpinella saxifrage

Mountain Beech ..... Nothofagus solandri var. Cliffortioides

Mountain Black Hemlock ..... Tsuga mertensiana

Mountain Bluet ..... Centaurea montana

Mountain Cabbage Tree ..... Cordyline indivisa

Mountain Cedar ..... Libocedrus bidwillii

Mountain Cornflower ..... Centaurea montana

Mountain Cottonwood ..... Cassinia leptophylla vauvilliersii

Mountain Cushion Daisy ..... Celmisia sessiflora

Mountain Dogwood ..... Cornus nuttalli

Mountain Five Finger ..... Pseudopanax colensoi

Mountain Flax ..... Phormium cookianum

Mountain Grey Gum ..... Eucalyptus cypellocarpa

Mountain Gum ..... Eucalyptus dalrympleana

Mountain Holly ..... Olearia ilicifolia

Mountain Holly ..... Olearia macrodonta

Mountain Jacaranda ..... Paulownia tomentosa

Mountain Lacebark ..... Hoheria lyallii

Mountain Laurel ..... Kalmia latifolia

Mountain Pawpaw ..... Carica pubescens

Mountain Phlox ..... Linanthus grandiflorus

Mountain Plum Pine ..... Podocarpus lawrencei was alpinus

Mountain Rimu ..... Lepidothamnus laxifolius was Dacrydium

Mountain Sandwort ..... Arenaria montana

Mountain Silverbell ..... Halesia monticola

Mountain Spinach ..... Atriplex hortensis

Mountain Swamp Gum ..... Eucalyptus camphora

Mountain Toatoa ..... Phyllocladus aspleniifolius var alpinus

Mountain Tobacco ..... Arnica montana

Mountain Valerian ..... Valerian montana

Mountain Weigela ..... Weigela decora

Mountain Wineberry ..... Aristotelia fruticosa

Mountain Yellow Gum ..... Eucalyptus subcrenulata

Mourning Widow ..... Geranium phaeum

Mourning Widow Iris ..... Hermodactylus tuberosus

Mouse Plant ..... Arisarum proboscideum

Mouses Ear ..... Saururus cernuus

Mt Atlas Daisy ..... Anacyclus depressus

Mt Buffalo Sally ..... Eucalyptus mitchelliana

Mt Egmont Tussock ..... Uncinia egmontiana

Mt Etna Broom ..... Genista aetnensis

Mt Fuji Cherry ..... Prunus (cherry flwg) Shirotae

Mudgee Wattle ..... Acacia spectabilis

Mugga Ironbark ..... Eucalyptus sideroxylon

Mugwort ..... Artemisia vulgaris

Mulberry, Black ..... Morus nigra

Mullein ..... Verbascum species

Murtilla ..... Ugni molinae was Myrtus ugni

Musk Mallow ..... Malva moschata

Muskmelon ..... Cucumis melon musk(melo var reticulatus)

Muslin Rose ..... Rosa Blanc Double de Coubert

Mustard ..... see Brassica

Mustard Spinach ..... see Brassica

Mutton Bird Sedge ..... Carex trifida

Myrtle ..... Myrtus communis

Myrtle Wattle ..... Acacia myrtifolia

Nail Rod ..... Typha latifolia

Naked Lady ..... Amaryllis species

Naples Garlic ..... Allium neapolitanum

Napuka ..... Hebe speciosa

Naranjilla ..... Solanum species?

Nardoo Plant ..... Marsilea quadrifolia

Narrow Leaved Sally ..... Eucalyptus moorei

Narrow-lvd Ash ..... Fraxinus angustifolia was oxycarpa

Narrow-lvd Ironbark ..... Eucalyptus crebra

Narrow-lvd Lacebark ..... Hoheria angustifolia

Narrow-lvd Maire ..... Nestegis montana

Narrow-lvd Mallee Ash ..... Eucalyptus apiculata

Narrow-lvd Peppermint ..... Eucalyptus radiata

Narrow-lvd Reed Mace ..... Typha angustifolia

Narrow-lvd Snow Tussock ..... Chionochloa rigida

Narrow-lvd Stringybark ..... Eucalyptus oblonga

Narrowlvd Black Peppermint Gum ..... Eucalyptus nicholii

Nashi ..... Pyrus serotina

Nasturtium ..... Tropaeolum majus

Natal Bottlebrush ..... Greyia radlkoferi

Natal Plum ..... Carissa grandiflora

Navelwort ..... Omphaloides linifolia

Nectarine ..... see Prunus

Needle Juniper ..... Juniperus rigida

Needle-lvd Totara ..... Podocarpus acutifolius

Neinei ..... Dracophyllum latifolia

Nelson Pine ..... Pinus nelsonii

Nettle ..... Urtica dioica

Nettle-lvd Bellflower ..... Campanula trachelium

New England Blackbutt ..... Eucalyptus andrewsii

New England Peppermint ..... Eucalyptus nova-anglica

Ngaio ..... Myoporum laetum

Night Phlox ..... Zalusianskya capensis

Night-scented Jessamine ..... Cestrum nocturnum

Night-scented Stock ..... Mathiola bicormis

Nikau ..... Rhopalostylis sapida

Nikko Fir ..... Abies homolepis

Ninebark, Golden ..... Physocarpus opulifolius Luteus

Noah's Ark Juniper ..... Juniperus communis Compressa

Noble Fir ..... Abies procera

Nootka Cypress ..... Chamaecyparis nootkatensis

Norfolk Is Hibiscus ..... Lagunaria pattersonii

Norfolk Is Nikau/Palm ..... Rhopalostylis baueri

Norfolk Is Pine ..... Araucaria heterophylla

North African Oak ..... Quercus afares

North American Hackberry ..... Celtis occidentalis

North Cape Hibiscus ..... Hibiscus diversifolius

North Chinese Black Birch ..... Betula davurica

North Chinese Mtn Birch ..... Betula costata

North Is Broom ..... Carmichaelia aligera

North Japanese Hemlock ..... Tsuga diversifolia

North Sargent Spruce ..... Picea bracytyla

Northern Pin Oak ..... Quercus ellipsoidalis

Northern Pitch Pine ..... Pinus rigida

Northern White Cedar ..... Thuja orientalis

Norway Maple ..... Acer platanoides

Norway Pine ..... Pinus resinosa

Norway Spruce ..... Picea abies

NSW Christmas Bells ..... Blanfordia grandiflora

NSW Cycad ..... Macrozamia communis

NSW Waratah ..... Telopea speciosissima

NZ Angelica ..... Gingidia montana

NZ Angelica ..... Scandia rosaefolia

NZ Begonia ..... Elatostema rugosum

NZ Bluebell ..... Wahlenbergia albomarginata

NZ Calceolaria ..... Jovellana sinclairii

NZ Daphne ..... Pimelea prostrata

NZ Gloxinia ..... Rhabdothamnus solandri

NZ Holly ..... Olearia ilicifolia

NZ Iceplant ..... Disphyma australe

NZ Irises ..... Libertia species

NZ Jasmine ..... Parsonsia capsularis

NZ Jasmine ..... Parsonsia heterophylla

NZ Ladder Fern ..... Nephrolepis sp

NZ Laurel ..... Corynocarpus laevigatus

NZ Lilac Hebe ..... Heliohebe hulkeana   was Hebe h.

NZ Linen Flax ..... Linum monogynum

NZ Mint ..... Mentha cunninghamii

NZ Passionfruit ..... Passiflora tetrandra was Tetrapathea

NZ Spinach ..... Tetragonia expansa

NZ White Daisy ..... Celmisia incana

NZ Woodrush ..... Luzula ulophylla

Oak Leafed Hydrangea ..... Hydrangea quercifolia

Oaks ..... Quercus species

Obedient Plant ..... Physostegia virginiana

Oioi, Jointed Wirerush ..... Leptocarpus similis

Okra, Chinese ..... Luffa acutangula

Old Lace Pinks ..... Dianthus plumarius

Old Man ..... Artemisia abrotanum

Old Mans Beard ..... Chionanthus virginicus

Old Mans Beard -Air Plant ..... Tillandsia usneoides

Old Velvet Rose ..... Rosa Tuscany

Old Woman ..... Seriphidium maritimum was Artemisia m.

Old World Arrowhead ..... Sagitteria sagittifolia

Olives ..... Olea species

Ombu ..... Phytolacca dioica

Omeo Gum ..... Eucalyptus neglecta

One Stone Juniper ..... Juniperus monosperma

One-lvd Squill ..... Scilla monophyllus

Ongaonga ..... Urtica ferox

Onion ..... Allium cepa

Onopordon ..... Onopordum arabicum

Orach ..... Atriplex hortensis

Orange ..... see Citrus

Orange Ball Tree ..... Buddleia globosa

Orange Browallia ..... Streptosolen jamesonii

Orange Jessamine ..... Murraya paniculata

Orange Mint ..... Mentha citrata

Orange Peel Clematis ..... Clematis vernayi

Orange Thyme ..... Thymus fragrantissimus

Orchid Tree ..... Bauhinia species

Oregano ..... Origanum vulgare

Oregano Thyme ..... Thymus nummularis

Oregon Alder ..... Alnus rubra

Oregon Ash ..... Fraxinus latifolia

Oregon Oak ..... Quercus garryana

Oriental Plane ..... Platanus orientalis

Oriental Spruce ..... Picea orientalis

Ornamental Quince ..... Chaenomeles cathayensis

Ornamental Rhubarb ..... Rheum palmatum

Orris Root ..... Iris germanica var florentina

Orris Root ..... Iris pallida

Ostrich Fern ..... Matteuccia struthiopteris

Oswego Tea ..... Monarda species

Our Lord's Candle ..... Yucca whipplei

Ovens Wattle ..... Acacia pravissima

Oxlip ..... Primula elatior

Oxygen Weed ..... Elodea canadensis

Oyama Magnolia ..... Magnolia sieboldii

Pacific Dogwood ..... Cornus nuttalli

Pagoda Dogwood ..... Cornus alternifolia

Pahautea ..... Libocedrus bidwillii

Painted Ladies ..... Gladiolus nana

Painted Maple ..... Acer mono

Painted Maple ..... Acer truncatum mayrii

Painted Sage ..... Salvia hormium

Painted Tongue Velvet ..... Salpiglossis sinuata

Painted Trumpet ..... Clytostoma callistegioides

Pak Choi ..... see Brassica

Pale Vanilla Lily ..... Arthropodium milleflorum

Palmetto Palm ..... Sabal palmetto

Pampas ..... Cortaderia selloana

Panakanake ..... Pratia angulata

Pansy ..... Viola species

Papauma ..... Griselina littoralis

Paper Birch ..... Betula papyrifera

Paper Bush ..... Edgeworthia papyrifera now chrysantha

Paper Mulberry ..... Broussonetia papyrifera

Paper Whites ..... Narcissus papyraceus

Paperbark Maple ..... Acer griseum

Papyrus ..... Cyperus species

Par-Cel ..... Apium graveolens Par-Cel

Parapara ..... Pisonia brunoniana now umbrellifera

Parasol Tree ..... Firmiana platanifolia

Parataniwha ..... Elatostema rugosum

Paris Daisy ..... Euryops species

Parlour Palm ..... Chamaedorea elegans

Parrot Beak ..... Clianthus puniceus

Parrots Beak ..... Alstroemeria psittacinus

Parrots Feather ..... Myriophyllum aquaticum was braziliense

Parsley ..... Petroselinum crispum

Parsnip ..... Pastinaca sativa

Pasque Flower ..... Pulsatilla vulgaris

Passion Flower Tree ..... Passiflora lindeniana

Passionfruit ..... Passiflora edulis

Patchouli ..... Pogostemon patchouli

Pate ..... Schefflera digitata

Paw Aster ..... Aster species

Pawpaw ..... Asimina species

Pea ..... Pisum sativum

Peach ..... see Prunus

Peach Protea ..... Protea grandiceps

Peach-lvd Bellflower ..... Campanula persicifolia

Peacock Camelia ..... Camellia Hakuhan Kujaku   japonica

Peacock Flower ..... Delonix regia

Peacock Irises ..... Moraea species

Pear ..... Pyrus communis

Pearl Berry ..... Margyricarpus pinnatus

Pearl Bush ..... Exochorda species

Pecan ..... Carya illinoensis

Pee Gee Hydrangea ..... Hydrangea paniculata Grandiflora

Peking Willow ..... Salix matsudana

Pellitory of the Wall ..... Parietaria diffusa or officinalis   now judaica

Pennyroyal ..... Mentha pulegium

Pennywort ..... Cardamine lyrata

Pennywort ..... Hydrocotyle leucocephala

Pepino ..... Solanum muricatum

Pepper ..... Capsicum annum

Pepper Tree ..... Macropiper excelsum

Pepper Tree ..... Pseudowintera species

Pepper Tree ..... Schinus molle

Peppermint ..... Mentha piperita

Peppermint Willow ..... Agonis flexuosa

Perching Lily ..... Collospermum hastatum

Perfume Wattle ..... Acacia farnesiana

Persian Everlasting Pea ..... Lathyrus rotundifolius

Persian Ironwood ..... Parrotia persica

Persian Musk Rose ..... Rosa Nastarana

Persian Silk Tree ..... Albizia julibrisin

Persian Witch Hazel ..... Parrotia persica

Persimmon ..... Diospyros kaki varieties

Peruvian Lilies ..... Alstroemeria species

Peruvian Mastic Tree ..... Schinus molle

Peter's Keys ..... Primula veris

Petticoat Palm ..... Washingtonia filifera

Pfitzer Juniper ..... Juniperus x media Pfitzeriana

Phoebes Frilled Pink ..... Rosa Fimbriata

Pigeon House Ash ..... Eucalyptus triflora

Pigeonwood ..... Hedycarya arborea

Piggyback Plant ..... Tolmiea menziesii

Pin Oak ..... Quercus palustris

Pin Oak Ivy ..... Hedera helix Pin Oak

Pinatoro ..... Pimelea prostrata

Pince Pinyon Pine ..... Pinus pinceana

Pincushion Bush ..... Hakea species

Pincushion Flower ..... Hakea laurina

Pincushion Flower ..... Scabiosa species

Pine Nut ..... Pinus pinea

Pineapple Broom ..... Cytisus battandieri

Pineapple Flower ..... Eucomis species

Pineapple Guava ..... Feijoa sellowiana

Pineapple Lily ..... Eucomis comosa

Pineapple Mint ..... Mentha suaveolens variegata
Pineapple Sage ..... Salvia elegans Scarlet Pineapple
Pingao ..... Desmoschoenus spiralis
Pink Cedar ..... Acrocarpus fraxinifolius
Pink Coral Pea ..... Hardenbergia monophylla Rosea
Pink Diosma ..... Coleonema pulchrum
Pink Felicia ..... Felicia petiolata
Pink Flowering Currant ..... Ribes sanguineum
Pink Mallow ..... Anisodontea scabrosa
Pink Mimosa ..... Albizia julibrisin
Pink Petticoat ..... Oenothera speciosa
Pink Rice Flower ..... Pimelea rosea
Pink Robinia ,,,,, Robinia x ambigua
Pink Rose of Mexico ..... Oenothera speciosa
Pink Shower Tree ..... Cassia grandis
Pink Spur Flower ..... Plectranthus fruticosus Behrii
Pink Tuft Bush ..... Phylica gnidioides
Pink Tulip Tree ..... Magnolia campbellii
Pink Wisteria Tree ..... Robinia x ambigua decaisneana
Pinks ..... Dianthus species
Pinkwood ..... Eucryphia moorei
Piripiri ..... Acaena species
Pistachio Nut ..... Pistachia vera
Pitcher Plant ..... Nepenthes sp climbing
Pitt Is Toetoe ..... Cortaderia tubaria
Piupiu ..... Blechnum discolor
Pixie Viola ..... Viola hederacea
Pizza Thyme ..... Thymus nummularis
Plane Trees ..... Platanus species
Plantain ..... Plantago species
Plum ..... see Prunus
Plumbago, Cape ..... Plumbago auriculata was capensis
Plumbago, Chinese ..... Ceratostigma species
Plume Albizia ..... A. lophantha now Paraserianthes l.
Plume Cedar ..... Cryptomeria japonica Elegans
Plume Incense Cedar ..... Libocedrus plumosa
Plume Poppy ..... Macleaya cordata
Plumed Tussock Grass ..... Chionochloa conspicua
Poataniwha ..... Melicope simplex
Pohuehue ..... Muehlenbeckia complexa
Pohutukawa ..... Metrosideros excelsus & varieties
Poinciana ..... Caesalpinia gilliesii
Poinsettia ..... Euphorbia pulcherrimum

Pokaka ..... Elaeocarpus hookerianus
Pokeroot ..... Phytolacca americana
Polka Dot Plant ..... Pulmonaria officinalis
Polyanthus ..... Primula x polyanthus
Pomegranate ..... Punica granatum
Pompon Tree ..... Dais cotonifolia
Pond Cypress ..... Taxodium ascendens Nutans (distichum imbricatum Nutans)
Pond Pickerel ..... Pontederia cordata
Pond Pine ..... Pinus serotina
Ponytail Palm ..... Beaucarnea recurvata was Nolina r.
Poor Knights Lily ..... Xeronema callistemon
Poor-man's Hosta ,,,,, Plantago species
Popcorn Bush ..... Callistemon didymobotrya
Poplars ..... Populus species
Poppy ..... Papaver species
Poppy Pacino ..... zz Genus unknown Poppy Pacino
Porokaiwhiri ..... Hedycarya arborea
Poroporo ..... Solanum aviculare
Poroporo ..... Solanum laciniatum
Port Jackson Mallee ..... Eucalyptus obtusiflora
Port St John Creeper ..... Podranea ricasoliana
Port Wine Magnolia ..... Michelia figo
Portugese Laurel ..... Prunus lusitanica
Portugese Oak ..... Quercus faginea
Pot Marjoram ..... Origanum onites
Pot Marjoram variegated ..... Origanum onites variegatum
Potato ..... Solanum potato (tuberosum)
Potato Vine (white) ..... Solanum jasminoides
Potato Vine, Blue ..... Solanum wendlandii
Potosi Pinyon Pine ..... Pinus culminicola
Powdered Gum ..... Eucalyptus pulverulenta
Prairie Blazing Star ..... Liatris pychnostachya
Prairie Mallow ..... Sidalcea species
Pregnant Onion ..... Ornithogalum umbellatum
Prickly Moses ..... Acacia verticillata
Prickly Moses ..... Acacia verticillata Rewa
Prickly Moses, Western ..... Acacia pulchella
Prickly Shield Fern ..... Polystichum vestitum
Pride Of Barbados ..... Caesalpina species
Pride of Bolivia ..... Tipuana tipu
Pride of Gibraltar ..... Cerinthe major
Pride of India ..... Koelreuteria paniculata

Pride Of Madeira ..... Echium candicans was fatuosum

Pride of Teneriffe ..... Echium pininana

Primrose ..... Primula vulgaris

Prince Albert's Yew ..... Saxegothea conspicua

Princess Flower ..... Tibouchina organensis

Princess Protea ..... Protea grandiceps

Princess Tree ..... Paulownia species

Privet ..... Ligustrum ovalifolium

Privet-lvd Stringybark ..... Eucalyptus lingustrina

Prune ..... see Prunus

Puarangi ..... Hibiscus trionum

Puataua ..... Clematis forsteri

Puawhananga ..... Clematis paniculata

Puhou ..... Pseudopanax arboreus

Puka ..... Griselina lucida

Puka ..... Meryta sinclairii

Puketia ..... Laurelia novae zelandiae

Pukio ..... Carex secta

Pumpkin ..... see Cucurbita

Puriri ..... Vitex lucens

Purple Barberry ..... Berberis thunbergii Atropurpurea

Purple Leaf Wattle ..... Acacia baileyana purpurea

Purple Likiang Spruce ..... Picea likiangensis var purpurea

Purple Loosestrife ..... Lythrum salicaria

Purple Ngaio ..... Myoporum laetum Purpureum

Purple Norway Maple ..... Acer platanoides Nigrum

Purple Perilla ..... Perilla frutescens

Purple Piripiri ..... Acaena inermis Purpurea

Purple Plantain ..... Plantago lanceolata purpurea

Purple Plantain ..... Plantago major Atropurpurea

Purple Sage ..... Salvia officinalis purpurascens

Purple Saucer Magnolia ..... Magnolia soulangeana

Purple Stalked Daisy ..... Celmisia petiolata

Purple Sycamore ..... Acer pseudoplatanus Purpureum

Purple Wreath ..... Petraea volubilis

Purple-leaf Choke Cherry ..... Prunus (cherry flwg) virginiana schubert

Purple-lvd Hazel ..... Corylus maxima purpurea

Pussy Toes ..... Antennaria dioica

Pussy Willow ..... Salix caprea

Pussy Willow ..... Salix caprea x cinerea

Pussy Willow ..... Salix discolor

Putaputaweta ..... Carpodetus serratus

Pygmy Pine ..... Lepidothamnus laxifolius was Dacrydium l.

Pyrenean Oak ..... Quercus pubescens v palensis

Pyrethrum ..... Tanacetum cinerarifolium

Pyrethrum ..... Tanacetum ptarmiciflorum

Quaking Aspen ..... Populus tremuloides

Quaking Grass ..... Briza species

Queen Anne's Lace ..... Ammi Majus

Queen Anne's Thimbles ..... Gilia capitata

Queen of the Meadows ..... Filipendula ulmaria

Queen of the Prairie ..... Filipendula rubra

Queen Palm ..... Syagrus romanzoffiana was Arecastrum r.

Queensland Bottle Tree ..... Brachychiton rupestri

Queensland Box ..... Lophostemon conferta was Tristania c.

Queensland Silver Wattle ..... Acacia podalyriifoli

Queensland Umbrella Tree ..... Schefflera actinaphylla

Quince ..... Cydonia oblonga

Quince, Chinese False ..... Pseudocydonia sinensi

Quinoa ..... Chenopodium quinoa

Rabbits Ears Oxalis ..... Oxalis namaquana

Rabbits Foot Fern ..... Davallia fejeesis

Raddichio ..... Cichorium intybus

Radish ..... Raphanus sativus

Ragged Robin ..... Lychnis flos cuculi

Rainbow Chard ..... Beta vulgaris Five Colour

Rainbow Tree ..... Dracaena marginata tricolour

Ralph's Kohuhu ..... Pittosporum ralphii

Ramarama ..... Lophomyrtus bullata

Rangiora ..... Brachyglottis repanda

Rapo-taranga ..... Xeronema callistemon

Rarauhe ..... Pteridium acuilinum var esculentum

Raspberries ..... Rubus species

Raspberry Jam Wattle ..... Acacia acuminata

Rata ..... Metrosideros species

Rauhuia ..... Linum monogynum

Raukawa ..... Pseudopanax edgerleyi

Raukumara ..... Brachyglottis peridicoides

Raupo ..... Typha orientalis

Rautawhiri ..... Pittosporum colensoi

Rauwolfia ..... Rauvolfia serpentina

Red Alder ..... Alnus rubra

Red Ash ..... Fraxinus pennsylvanica

Red Bear Berry ..... Arctostaphylos uva-ursi

Red Beech ..... Nothofagus fusca

Red Beet ..... Beta vulgaris Early Wonder

Red Boronia ..... Boronia heterophylla

Red Box ..... Eucalyptus polyanthemos

Red Broom ..... Cytisus Burkwoodii

Red Buckeye ..... Aesculus pavia

Red Campion ..... Melandrium rubrum (now Silene)

Red Canna ..... Canna edulis

Red Cedar ..... Toona sinensis

Red Chicory ..... Cichorium intybus Verona

Red Chinese Birch ..... Betula albo-sinensis

Red Chokeberry ,..... Aronia arbutifolia

Red Crown Shaft Palm ..,.. Geonoma undata

Red Currant ..... Ribes rubrum

Red Fir ..... Abies amabilis

Red Fir ..... Abies magnifica

Red Flowered Ironbark ..... Eucalyptus sideroxylon Rosea

Red Flowering Gum ..... Eucalyptus ficifolia

Red Ginger ..... Alpinia purpurata

Red Ginger ..... Hedychium greenii

Red Hook Sedge ..... Uncinia rubra

Red Horse Chestnut ..... Aesculus carnea

Red Hygrophila ..... Hygrophila roseafolia

Red Ink Plant ..... Phytolacca americana

Red Matipo ..... Myrsine australis

Red Milk Bush ..... Synadenium grantii rubra

Red Oak ..... Quercus rubra

Red Ornamental Banana ..... Ensete Maurelli

Red Osier Dogwood ..... Cornus stolnifera Kelseyi

Red River Gum ..... Eucalyptus camaldulensis

Red Robin ..... Photinia x fraseri Red Robin

Red Ruby Pony Tail ..... Beaucarnea guatemalensis

Red Sage ..... Salvia fulgens

Red Sage ..... Salvia officinalis purpurascens

Red Snakebark Maple ..... Acer capillipes

Red Stem Dogwood ..... Cornus stolonifera Baileyi

Red Stemmed Wattle ..... Acacia rubida

Red Stringybark ..... Eucalyptus macrolyncha

Red Swamp Banksia ..... Banksia hookerana occidentalis

Red Topped Sage ..... Salvia hormium

Red Tree Peony ..... Paeonia(tree) delavayi

Red Tussock ..... Chionochloa rubra

Red Valerian ..... Centranthus ruber

Red Vein Bell Flower ..... Enkianthus campanulatus

Red Veined Pie Plant ..... Rheum australe was emodi

Red Yarrow ..... Achillea millefolium Roseum

Red Yucca ..... Hesperaloe parviflora

Redbarked Dogwood ..... Cornus alba

Reed Mace ..... Typha muelleri

Reed Mace ..... Typha shuttleworthii

Reeves Spiraea ..... S. cantoniensis Lanceata

Reflexed Stonecrop ..... Sedum reflexum now rupestre

Regal Lily ..... Lilium regale

Reinga Lily ..... Arthropodium cirratum

Remuremu ,..... Selliera radicans

Rengarenga lily ..... Arthropodium cirratum

Resurrection Lily ..... Kaempferia rotunda

Reticulatum Maple ..... Acer palmatum Shigitatsu-sawa

Rewarewa ..... Knightia excelsa

Rhubarb (common) ..... Rheum rhabarbarum

Rhubarb, Turkish ..... Rheum palmatum var tangticum

Ribbonwood ..... Plagianthus regius

Rice Paper Plant ..... Tetrapanax papyriferus

Rigani ..... Origanum True Greek

Righanni Marjoram ..... Origanum onites Righanni

Rimu, Red Pine ..... Dacrydium cupressinum

Risdon Peppermint ..... Eucalyptus risdonii

River (Dog) Rose ..... Bauera rubioides

River Birch ..... Betula nigra

River Peppermint ..... Eucalyptus elata

River Sheoak ..... Casuarina cunninghamiana

River's Copper beech ..... Fagus sylvatica Riversii

Robel Beech ..... Nothofagus obliqua

Robin Redbreast Bush ..... Melaleuca laterita

Rocambole ..... Allium sativum Ophioscorodon

Rock Bells ..... Aquilegia canadensis

Rock Daisy ..... Brachyscome multifida

Rock Gypsophila ..... Gypsophila repens Alba

Rock Harlequin ..... Corydalis sempervirens

Rock Rose ..... Cistus species

Rock Rose ..... Helianthemum species

Rock Rose ..... Tuberaria lignosa

Rock Soapwort ..... Saponaria ocymoides

Rocket ..... Eruca sativa

Rockmelon ..... see Cucumis

Rockspray Cotoneaster ..... Cotoneaster microphyllus

Rocky Mountain Garland ..... Clarkia unguiculata

Rocky Mountain Juniper ..... Juniperus scopulorum

Rocky Mountain Lodgepole Pine ..... Pinus contorta var latifolia (variegated form)

Rohutu ..... Lophomyrtus obcordata

Rohutu ..... Neomyrtus pedunculata

Romaine lettuce ..... Lactuca sativa Cos

Roman Chamomile ..... Chamaemelum nobile

Roman Wormwood ..... Artemisia pontica

Romanian Spruce ..... Picea abies

Roquette ..... Eruca sativa

Rose Campion ..... Lychnis coronaria

Rose Gum ..... Eucalyptus grandis

Rose of Sharon ..... Hibiscus syriacus

Rose of the West ..... Eucalyptus macrocarpa

Rose Sheoak ..... Allocasuarina torulosa was Cauarina t.

Rosebud Cherry ..... Prunus (cherry flwg) subhirtella

Rosemary ..... Rosmarinus officinalis

Rosewood ..... Tipuana tipu

Rough Tree Fern ..... Cyathea australis

Rough Tree Fern ..... Dicksonia squarrossa

Round-leaf Wattle ..... Acacia uncinata syn. A undifolia

Round-lvd Gum ..... Eucalyptus deanei

Round-lvd Shad Bush ..... Amelanchier alnifolia

Round-lvd Westharrow ..... Ononis rotundifolia

Rowan ..... Sorbus aucuparia

Royal Flamboyant ..... Delonix regia

Royal Poinciana ..... Delonix regia

Rubber Plant ..... Ficus elastica decora

Rudbeckia ..... Echinacea purpurea

Rudbeckia ..... Rudbeckia species

Rue ..... Ruta graveolens

Rupture Wort ..... Herniaria glabra

Rush ..... see also Typha & Leptocarpus

Rush, Club ..... Schoenoplectus validus

Rush, Corkscrew ..... Juncus effusus Spiralis

Rush, Hard ..... Juncus inflexus (glaucus)

Rush, Japanese ..... Acorus gramineus Variegatus

Rush, Jointed Twig ..... Baumea articulata

Rush, Knobby Club ..... Isolepsis nodosus

Rush, Pakihi ..... Baumea teretifolia

Rush, Pickerel ..... Pontederia cordata

Rush, Plume ..... Restio tetraphyllus

Rush, Sea ..... Juncus maritimis

Rush, Tall Spike ..... Eleocharis sphacelata

Rush, Wood Club ..... Scirpus sylvaticus

Russian Mulberry ..... Morus alba tartarica

Russian Olive ..... Elaeagnus angustifolia

Russian Sage ..... Perovskia atriplicifolia

Rustfree Mint/Spearmint ..... Mentha x smithiana

Rusty Foxglove ..... Digitalis ferruginea

Rusty Stars ..... Cooperia pendunculata

Rutabaga ..... Brassica rutabaga (napus)

Rzedowsk Pine ..... Pinus rzedowskii

Sacred Basil ..... Ocimum sanctum

Sacred Fir ..... Abies religiosa

Sacred Flower of the Incas ..... Cantua buxifolia

Saffron Crocus ..... Crocus sativus

Sage ..... Salvia species

Sage (kitchen) ..... Salvia officinalis

Sage-leaf Germander ..... Teucrium scorodonia

Sago Palm ..... Cycas revoluta

Sainfoin ..... Onobrychis viciifolia

Sakhalin Fir ..... Abies sachalinensis

Sakhalin Spruce ..... Picea glehnii

Salad Burnet ..... Sanguisorba minor was Poterium s.

Sallow/Sally Wattle ..... Acacia floribunda

Salsify ..... Tragopogon porrifolius

Salt Bush ..... Atriplex halimus

Salt Cedar ..... Tamarix pentandra

Sand Dune Coprosma ..... Coprosma acerosa

Sand Gunnera ..... Gunnera arenaria

Sand Juniper ..... Juniperus conferta

Sand Sedge ..... Carex pumila

Sandpaper Plant ..... Petraea volubilis

Santo ..... see Brassica

Sapote, Black ..... Diospyros dignya

Sapote, White ..... Casimiroa edulis

Sapree-Wood ..... Widdringtonia nodiflora wasW.cupressoides,W.whytei

Sargent Cypress ..... Cupressus sargentii

Satin Bush ..... Podalyria sericea

Satin Leaf ..... Heuchera hispida

Satin Poppy ..... Meconopsis napaulensis

Satin Wood ..... Phebalium squameum

Savoury, Creeping ..... Satureja repanda now spicigera

Savoury, Summer ..... Satureja hortensis

Savoury, Thyme-lvd ..... Micromeria thymifolia

Savoury, Winter ..... Satureja montana

Saw Banksia ..... B. serrata

Sawtooth Camelia ..... Camellia Nokogiri-Ba japonica

Scarborough Lily ..... Cyrtanthus elatus was Vallota speciosa

Scarlet Banksia ..... Banksia coccinea

Scarlet Oak ..... Quercus coccinea

Scarlet Pimpernel ..... Anagallis arvensis ssp arvensis

Scarlet Piripiri ..... Acaena microphylla

Scarlet Wisteria Tree ..... Daubentonia tripetii syn Sesbania t.

Scent Bark ..... Eucalyptus aromaphloia

Scented Broom ..... Carmichaelia odorata

Scented Fern ..... Paesia scaberula

Scented Taro ..... Alocasia odora

Scotch Broom ..... Cytisus scoparius

Scots Pine ..... Pinus sylvestris

Scottish Viola ..... V. cornuta

Scrambling Broom ..... Carmichaelia kirkii

Scribbly Gum ..... Eucalyptus rossii

Scribby Gum ..... Eucalyptus haemastoma

Scrub Pine ..... Pinus virginiana

Scullcaps ..... Scutellaria species

Scurvy Grass ..... Cochlearia officinalis

Sea Campion ..... Silene maritima now uniflora

Sea Daffodil ..... Chlidanthus fragrans

Sea Heath ..... Frankenia laevis

Sea Hollies ..... Eryngium species

Sea Lavender ..... Limonium latifolia

Sea Onion ..... Ornithogalum umbellatum

Sea Pink/Thrift ..... Armeria maritima

Sea Urchin ..... Hakea laurina

Seaforthia Palm ..... Archontophoenix cunninghamia

Seaside Daisy ..... Erigeron karvinskianus was mucronatus

Sedge Grass ..... Carex coriacea & remota

Sedge, Bamboo Spike ..... Eleocharis sphacelata

Sedge, Golden Sand ..... Desmoschoenus spiralis

Sedge, Sharp Spike ..... Eleocharis acuta

Sedge, Triangle-stemmed ..... Scirpus americanus

Sedges ..... Carex, Uncinia species

Selfheal ..... Prunella vulgaris

Senegal Date Palm ..... Phoenix reclinata

Senposai ..... Brassica senposai

Sensitive Plant ..... Mimosa pudica

Sentry Palm ..... Howea belmoreana

Serbian Spruce ..... Picea omorika

Serviceberry ..... Amelanchier lamarkii

Sessile Oak ..... Quercus petraea

Seven Finger ..... Schefflera digitata

Seven Son Flower of Zhejiang ..... Heptacodium jasminoides

Shad Bush ..... Amelanchier canadensis

Shades of Pink Plant ..... Breynia nivosa Roseo Picta

Shagbark Hickory ..... Carya ovata

Shamrock Pea ..... Parochetus communis

Shantung Maple ..... Acer truncatum

Shasta Daisy ..... Leucanthemum maximum (also see L x superbum)

Sheeps Bit/Scabious ..... Jasione laevis was J.perennis

Sheeps Sorrel ..... Rumex acetosella

Shell Ginger ..... Alpinia zerumbet

Sheoak, Swamp ..... Casuarina species

Sheoaks ..... see Allocasuarina

Shepherd's Purse ..... Capsella bursa-pastoris

Shien ..... Amaranthus gangeticum

Shingle Oak ..... Quercus imbricaria

Shining Gum ..... Eucalyptus nitens

Shining Karamu ..... Coprosma lucida

Shining Scabious ..... Scabiosa lucida

Shining Spleenwort ..... Asplenium oblongifolium

Shirley Poppy ..... Papaver rhoeas

Shoo Fly Plant ..... Nicandra physalodes

Shooting Star ..... Dodecatheon maedia

Shooting Star ..... Thymophylla tenuiloba

Shore Astelia ..... Astelia banksii

Shore Fuchsia ..... Fuchsia procumbens

Shore Juniper ..... Juniperus conferta

Shore Ribbonwood ..... Plagianthus divaricatus

Short Leafed Pine ..... Pinus echinata

Showy Banksia ..... Banksia speciosa

Shrimp Plant ..... Justicia brandegeeana was Beleperone guttata

Shungiku ..... Chrysanthemum coronarium

Shuttlecock Protea ..... P. aurea Goodwood Red

Siam Lily ..... Curcuma roscoeana

Siberian Dogwood ..... Cornus alba sibirica

Siberian Eidelwess ..... Anaphalis margaritacea

Siberian Elm ..... Ulmus pumila

Siberian Fir ..... Abies sibirica

Siberian Motherwort ..... Leonurus sibericus

Sierra Redwood ..... Sequoiadendron giganteum

Silk Tree ..... Albizia julibrissin

Silky Oak ..... Grevillea robusta

Silky Serruria ..... Serruria barbigera

Silky Wisteria ..... Wisteria venusta

Silver AkeAke ..... Olearia traversii

Silver Banksia ..... Banksia marginata

Silver Beech ..... Nothofagus menziesii

Silver Birch ..... Betula pendula

Silver Box Elder ..... Acer negundo Variegatum

Silver Bush ..... Convolvulus cneorum

Silver Dollar Gum ..... Eucalyptus cinerea

Silver Feathers ..... Tanacetum cinerarifolium

Silver Fern ..... Cyathea dealbata

Silver Geranium ..... Geranium incanum

Silver Germander ..... Teucrium fruticans

Silver Ghost ..... Calocephalus brownii

Silver Jacob's Ladder ..... Polemonium brandegeei

Silver Lime ..... Tilia tomentosa

Silver Linden ..... Tilia tomentosa

Silver Maple ..... Acer saccharinum

Silver Mound ..... Artemisia schmiditiana Nana

Silver Peppermint ..... Eucalyptus tenuiramis

Silver Posie Thyme ..... Thymus x citriodorus Argenteus

Silver Sage ..... Salvia argentea

Silver Sagebrush ..... Seriphidium canum was Artemesia c.

Silver Tansy ..... Tanacetum niveum

Silver Tassel ..... Garrya elliptica

Silver Top Gum ..... Eucalyptus nitens

Silver Tree ..... Leucadendron argenteum

Silver Tussock ..... Poa cita was P. laevis, P. caespitosa

Silver Vein Creeper ..... Parthenocissus henryana

Silver Wattle ..... Acacia dealbata

Silver Wormwood ..... Artemisia arborescens

Silver-lvd Mountain Gum ..... Eucalyptus pulverulenta

Silverbeet ..... see Beta

Silverbell Tree ..... Halesia carolina

Silvertop Ash ..... Eucalyptus sieberi

Silvertop Stringybark ..... Eucalyptus laevopinea

Simplers Joy ..... Verbena officinalis

Single-leafed Pinyon ..... Pinus monophylla was P.cembroides m.

Siskiyou Spruce ..... Picea breweriana

Sitka Spruce ..... Picea sitchensis

Skeleton Bush ..... Calocephalus brownii

Skirret ..... Sium sisarum

Sky Flower ..... Thunbergia grandiflora

Skyrocket ..... Ipomopsis rubra

Slash Pine ..... Pinus elliotii

Slaters Crimson China ..... Rosa Semperflorens

Sleeping Beauty ..... Commelina coelestis

Small leaved Gum ..... Eucalyptus parvifolia

Small Soapweed ..... Yucca glauca

Small Yellow Onion ..... Allium flavum

Smiths Milk Tree ..... Streblus smithii

Smithton Peppermint ..... Eucalyptus nitida

Smoke Bush ..... Cotinus coggygria

Smooth Bark Pine ..... Pinus pseudostrobus

Smooth Grevillea ..... Grevillea glabrata

Smooth Stem Pineapple ..... Ananas cosmosus

Smooth Tasmanian Cedar ..... Athrotaxus cupressoides

Snail Flower Creeper ..... Vigna caracalla

Snake Plant ..... Sanseveria laurantii

Snake Vine ..... Hibbertia scandens

Snakebark Maple ..... see Acer

Snakes Beard ..... Ophiopogon japonicus

Snakeshead Fritillary ..... Fritillaria meleagris

Snakeshead Iris ..... Hermodactylus tuberosus

Snapdragons ..... Antirrhinum species

Sneezewort ..... Achillea ptarmica

Snow Gum ..... Eucalyptus coccifera

Snow Gum ..... Eucalyptus pauciflora

Snow in Summer ..... Cerastium tomentosum

Snow in Summer ..... Melaleuca linarifolia

Snow Myrtle ..... Calytrix alpestris

Snow on the Mountain ..... Euphorbia marginata

Snow Totara ..... Podocarpus nivalis

Snow Tussock ..... Chionochloa flavicans

Snow Tussock, Mid-ribbed ..... Chionochloa pallin

Snowball Tree ..... Viburnum opulus Sterile now V.o.Roseum

Snowbell Trees ..... Styrax species

Snowberry ..... Symphoricarpos species

Snowberry, NZ ..... Gaultheria antipoda

Snowdrop (English) ..... Galanthus nivalis

Snowdrop Tree ..... Halesia carolina

Snowdrop Windflower ..... Anemone sylvestris

Snowflake Acacia ..... Calliandra portoricensis

Snowflake Tree ..... Trevesia palmata

Soapwort ..... Saponaria officinalis

Society Garlic ..... Tulbaghia violacea

Soft Flag ..... Typha angustifolia

Soldiers & Sailors ..... Pulmonaria officinalis

Soldiers Buttons ..... Cotula coronopifolia

Solomons Seal ..... Polygonatum hybridum

Solomons Seal ..... Polygonatum multiflorum

Sorrel Tree ..... Oxydendron arboreum

South African Sage Wood ..... Buddleia salvifolia

South African Veldt Flowers ..... Osteospermum species

South Bulgarian Pine ..... Pinus sylvestris var rhodopaea

South Western White Pine ..... Pinus strobiformis

Southern Balsam Fir ..... Abies fraseri

Southern Blue Gum ..... Eucalyptus bicostata

Southern Japanese Hemlock ..... Tsuga sieboldii

Southern Mahogany Gum ..... Eucalyptus botryoides

Southernwood ..... Artemisia abrotanum

Spanish Chestnut ..... Castanea sativa

Spanish Fir ..... Abies pinsapo

Spanish Foxglove ..... Isoplexis canariensis

Spanish Juniper ..... Juniperus thurifera

Spanish Juniper ..... Juniperus utahensis syn J.osteosperma

Spanish Oak ..... Quercus palustris

Spanish Sage ..... Salvia lavandulifolia

Spanish Shawl ..... Heterocentron elegans was Schizocentron, Heeria

Spaths Ash ..... Fraxinus spaethiana

Spear Grass ..... Aciphylla species

Spearmint ..... Mentha species

Speedwell ..... Veronica species

Spice Bush ..... Calycanthus occidentalis

Spider Flower ..... Cleome species

Spider Flower ..... Grevillea species

Spider Lily ..... Tradescantia species

Spiderwort ..... Tradescantia species

Spike Gay Feather ..... Liatris spicata syn.L. callilepsis

Spike Speedwell ..... Veronica spicata

Spiked Winter Hazel ..... Corylopsis spicata

Spiketail bush ..... Stachyurus praecox

Spinach ..... Beta species

Spinach ..... Spinacea species

Spindle ..... Euonymus species

Spinning Gum ..... Eucalyptus perriniana

Spleenwort, Hanging ..... Asplenium flaccidum

Spleenwort, Mother ..... Asplenium bulbiferum

Spotted Dog ..... Pulmonaria officinalis

Spotted Emu-bush ..... Eremophila maculata Red

Spotted Gum ..... Eucalyptus maculata

Spring Snowflake ..... Leucojum Gravetye Giant

Spring Star Flower ..... Ipheion uniflorum

Spruce Pine ..... Pinus glabra

Spruces ..... Picea species

Spur-wing Wattle ..... Acacia triptera

Spurge ..... Euphorbia species

Squash ..... see Cucurbita

Squills ..... Scilla species

St Bernards Lily ..... Anthericum liliago

St Brunos Lily ..... Paradisea liliastrum

St Johns Wort ..... Hypericum species

St Lucie Cherry ..... Prunus (cherry flwg) mahaleb

Staghorn Ferns ..... Platycerium species

Standing Cypress ..... Ipomopsis rubra

Star Anise ..... Illicium anisatum

Star Hydrangea ..... H. aspera

Star Lily ..... Arthropodium candidum

Star Magnolia ..... Magnolia stellata

Star of Bethlehem ..... Ornithogalum umbellatum

Star of the Veldts ..... Osteospermum species

Star Primula ..... Primula sieboldii

Starfruit ..... Averrhoa carambola

Statice ..... Limonium & Goniolinum species

Statice, Tartarian ..... Goniolimon tartaricum

Stem Turnip ..... Brassica kohlrabi

Stevia ..... Stevia rebaudiana

Sticky Wattle ..... Acacia howittii

Stinkwood ..... Coprosma foetidissima

Stocks ..... Matthiola incarna varieties

Stoke's Aster ..... Stokesia laevis

Stone Pine ..... Pinus pinea

Stonecrops ..... Sedum species

Storksbill ..... Erodium reichardii alba

Strawberry ..... Fragaria species

Strawberry Tree, Himalayan ..... Cornus capitata

Strawberry Tree, Irish ..... Arbutus unedo
Strawflower ..... Helichrysum bracteatum
String of Pearls ..... Senecio rowleyanus
Sturt's Desert Pea ..... Clianthus formosus
Subalpine Fir ..... Abies lasiocarpa
Sugar Maple ..... Acer saccharum
Sugar Bush ..... Protea repens
Sugar Gum ..... Eucalyptus cladocalyx
Sugar Pine ..... Pinus lambertiana
Sugarcane ..... Saccharum officinarum
Sugi Cedar ..... Cryptomeria japonica
Sumach ..... Rhus succedeana
Summer Cypress ..... Kochia trichophylla
Summer Hyacinth ..... Galtonia viridiflora
Summer Lilac ..... Buddleia davidii
Summer Poinsettia ..... Amaranthus tricolour
Sun Rose ..... Cistus species
Sun Rose ..... Helianthemum species
Sunflower (perennial) ..... Heliopsis Summer Sun
Sunflowers ..... Helianthus species
Sunshine Wattle ..... Acacia botrycephala
Supplejack ..... Ripogonum scandens
Swainsons Pea ..... Swainsonia galegifolia alba
Swamp Astelia ..... Astelia grandis
Swamp Banksia ..... Banksia robur
Swamp Brush Myrtle ..... Beaufortia sparsa
Swamp Cypress ..... Taxodium distichum
Swamp Daisy ..... Actinodium cunninghamia
Swamp Gum ..... Eucalyptus ovata
Swamp Kiokio ..... Blechnum minus
Swamp Lily ..... Saururus cernuus
Swamp Mahogany ..... Eucalyptus robusta
Swamp Maire ..... Syzygium maire
Swamp Mallet ..... Eucalyptus spathulata
Swamp Musk ..... Mazus radicans
Swamp Paperbark ..... Melaleuca leucadendron
Swamp Peppermint ..... Eucalyptus rodwayii
Swamp Ribbonwood ..... Plagianthus divaricatus
Swamp Rose Mallow ..... Hibiscus mosheutus
Swamp Sheoak ..... Casuarina species
Swamp Wattle ..... Acacia retinoides
Swamp Yate ..... Eucalyptus occidentalis
Swan Plant ..... Asclepias physocarpa
Swan River Cypress ..... Actinostrobus pyramidalis
Swan River Daisy ..... Brachyscome iberidifolia

Swan River Myrtle ..... Calytrix alpestris   was Lhotskya a.
Swede ..... see Brassica
Swedish Birch ..... Betula pendula dalecarlica
Swedish Turnip ..... see Brassica
Sweet Alyssum ..... Alyssum saxatile
Sweet Angelica ..... Angelica archangelica
Sweet Annie ..... Artemisia annua
Sweet Basil ..... Ocimum basilicum
Sweet Bay ..... Laurus nobilis
Sweet Bay ..... Magnolia virginiana
Sweet Box ..... Sarcococca ruscifolia
Sweet Buckeye ..... Aesculus flava
Sweet Chestnut ..... Castanea sativa
Sweet Cicely ..... Myrrhis odorata
Sweet Flag ..... Acorus calamus
Sweet Germander ..... Teucrium massiliense
Sweet Gum ..... Liquidambar styraciflua
Sweet Marigold ..... Tagetes lucida
Sweet Marjoram ..... Origanum majorana (horten
Sweet Milfoil ..... Achillea ageratum   was decolorans
Sweet Nancy ..... Achillea aurea Grandiflora   no A.chrysocoma G
Sweet Pea ..... Lathyrus odoratus
Sweet Pea Bush ..... Podalyria calyptrata
Sweet Pepper ..... Capsicum annuum
Sweet Pittosporum ..... P. undulatum
Sweet Rocket ..... Hesperis matrionalis
Sweet Sultan ..... Centaurea moschata
Sweet Verbena Tree ..... Backhousia citriodora
Sweet William ..... Dianthus barbatus mixed
Sweet Woodruff ..... Galium odoratum   was Asperula o.
Sweet Wormwood ..... Artemisia annua
Sweet-scented Solomons Seal ..... Polygonatum odoratum
Sweet-scented Wattle ..... Acacia suaveolens
Sweetcorn ..... Zea varieties
Sweetheart Rose ..... Rosa Cecile Brunner
Sweetpepper Bush ..... Clethra alnifolia
Swiss Mountain Pine ..... Pinus mugo Gnom
Swiss Stone Pine ..... Pinus cembra
Sword Plant ..... Sanseveria laurantii
Sycamore ..... Acer pseudoplatanus
Sydney Blue Gum ..... Eucalyptus saligna

Sydney Golden Wattle ..... Acacia longifolia

Sydney Peppermint ..... Eucalyptus piperita

Sydney Red Gum ..... Angophora costata

Syrian Ash ..... Fraxinus angustifolia syrica

Syrian Rose ..... Hibiscus syriacus

Szechuan Poplar ..... Populus szechuanica

Table Dogwood ..... Cornus controversa

Table Mountain Pine ..... Pinus pungens

Taehai ..... Nothofagus menziesii

Tagasaste ..... Chamaecytisus palmensis

Taginaste Roja ..... Echium wildpretti

Tahoata ..... Carex dipsacea

Tainui ,,,,, Pomaderris apetala

Taiwan Alder ..... Alnus formosana

Taiwan Cherry ..... Prunus (cherry flwg) campanulata

Taiwan Douglas Fir ..... Pseudotsuga wilsoniana

Taiwan Fir ..... Abies kawakamii

Taiwanese Snakebark Maple ..... Acer caudatifolium   was A. kawakamii, A.morrisonense

Takinogawa ..... Arctium lappa

Tala ..... Celtis spinosa

Tallow Tree, Chinese ..... Sapium sebiferum

Tallowwood ..... Eucalyptus microcorys

Tamarillo ..... Cyphomandra betacea varieties

Tamarind ..... Tamarindus indica

Tamingi ..... Epacris pauciflora

Tanekaha ..... Phyllocladus trichomanoides

Tanguru ..... Olearia albida

Tansy ..... Tanacetum vulgare

Tansy Phacelia ..... P. tanacetifolia

Taraire ..... Beilschmiedia tarairi

Taranga ..... Pimelea longifolia

Tarata ..... Pittosporum eugenioides

Taro ..... Colocasia species

Taro edible ..... Alocasia species

Tarragon, French ..... Artemisia dracunculus

Tarragon, Russian ..... Artemisia dracunculus dracunculoides

Tarragon, Winter ..... Tagetes lucida

Tasman Blue Gum ..... Eucalyptus globulus

Tasmanian Blackwood ..... Acacia melanoxylon

Tasmanian Cedar ..... Athrotaxus laxifolia

Tasmanian Cypress Pine ..... Callitris oblonga

Tasmanian Heath ..... Bauera rubioides Alba

Tasmanian Laurel ..... Anopterus glandulosus

Tasmanian Manuka ..... Leptospermum Green Ice

Tasmanian Olearia ..... Olearis phlogopappa

Tasmanian Snow Gum ..... Eucalyptus coccifera

Tasmanian Waratah ..... Telopea truncata

Tassle Hyacinth ..... Muscari comosum

Tataki ..... Carex trifida

Tataramoa ..... Rubus cissoides

Tauhinu ..... Cassinia leptophylla

Taupata ..... Coprosma repens

Taurepo ..... Rhabdothamnus solandri

Tawa ..... Beilschmiedia tawa

Tawapou ..... Planchonella costata

Tawari ..... Ixerba brexioides

Tawhaimaunui ..... Nothofagus fusca

Tawhairauriki ..... Nothofagus solandri var solandri

Tawhero ..... Weinmannia silvicola

Tawherowhreo ..... Quintinia serrata

Tawhiri Karo ..... Pittosporum cornifolium

Tayberry ..... Rubus Tayberry (blackberry x raspberry)

Tea ..... Camellia sinensis

Tea Tree (NZ) ..... Leptospermum scoparium

Tea Tree, Shiny ..... Leptospermum nitidum Copper Sheen

Teasel (true hooked) ..... Dipsacus fullonum

Temple Basil ..... Ocimum sanctum

Temple Plant ..... Hygrophila corymbosa

Texas Lupin ,,,,, Lupinus texensis

Texas Plume ..... Ipomopsis rubra

Thatch Palm ..... Howea fosteriana

The Bride ..... Exochorda x macrantha The Bride

Thick-lvd Porcupine Plant ..... Melicytus crassifolius

Thin-barked Totara ..... Podocarpus hallii

Thin-lvd Stringybark ..... Eucalyptus eugenoides

Thornless Honey Locust ..... Gleditsia triacanthos f. inermis

Thorny Acacia ..... Robinia pseudoacacia

Three Birds Flying ..... Linaria triornithophora

Three Finger ..... Pseudopanax colensoi

Three Kings Kawakawa ..... Macropiper melchior

Thrift ..... Armeria species

Thyme ..... Thymus vulgaris

Ti Kouka ..... Cordyline australis

Ti-ngahere ..... Cordyline banksii

Tian Shan Spruce ..... Picea schrenkiana

Tickseed ..... Coreopsis grandiflora

Tingiringi Gum ..... Eucalyptus glaucescens
Titirangi ..... Hebe speciosa
Titoki ..... Alectryon excelsus
Toad Flaxes ..... Linaria species
Toad Lilies ..... Tricyrtis species
Toatoa ..... Hallogurus erecta Wellington Bronze
Toatoa ..... Phyllocladus glaucus
Tobacco ..... Nicotiana tabacum
Tobacco Plants ..... Nicotiana species
Toetoe ..... Cortaderia species
Toi ..... Cordyline indivisa
Tokyo Bekana ..... Brassica Santo
Tomatillo ..... Physalis ixocarpa
Tomato ..... Lycopersicon species
Tong Gwa ..... Benincasa hispada Chinese Winter
Toothed Boronia ..... Boronia denticulata
Toothed Lancewood ..... Pseudopanax ferox
Tormentil ..... Potentilla tormentilla
Toro ..... Myrsine salicina
Toronchi Pawpaw ..... Carica stipulata
Toropapa ..... Alseuosmia macrophylla
Toru ..... Toronia toru
Totara ..... Podocarpus totara
Towai ..... Weinmannia silvicola
Toyon, The ..... Heteromeles arbutifolia
Transvaal Bottlebrush ..... Greyia radlkoferi
Travellers Joy ..... Clematis brachiata
Travellers Palm ..... Ravenala madagascariensis
Tree Anemone ..... Carpenteria californica
Tree Bignonia ..... Catalpa bignonioides
Tree Dahlia ..... Dahlia imperialis
Tree Daisy ..... Olearia avicenniaefolia
Tree Daisy ..... Olearia chathamica
Tree Ferns ..... Cyathea species
Tree Ferns ..... Dicksonia species
Tree Fuchsia ..... Halleria lucida
Tree Fuchsia (Mexican) ..... Fuchsia arborescens
Tree Fuchsia (Native) ..... Fuchsia excorticata
Tree Hazel ..... Corylus colurna
Tree Heath ..... Erica arborea
Tree Lucerne ..... Chamaecytisus palmensis
Tree Peony ..... Paeonia (tree)
Tree Spinach ..... Atriplex hortensis
Tree Wisteria ..... Bolusanthus speciosus
Tree wormwood ..... Artemisia arborescens

Trembling Aspen ..... Populus tremuloides
Triangle Palm ..... Neodypsis decaryi
Tricolour Maple ..... Acer palmatum Roseomarginatum
Trident Maple ..... Acer buergerianum
Trojan Fir ..... Abies equi-trojani
Trout Lilies ..... Erythronium species
Trumpet Flower ..... Salpiglossis sinuata
Tseet Gwa ..... Benincasa hispada Fuzzy
Tuart ..... Eucalyptus gomphoecphala
Tuckeroo ..... Cupaniopsis anarcardioides
Tufted Hair Grass ..... Deschampsia caespitosa
Tukauki ..... Libertia ixioides
Tulip Magnolia ..... Magnolia soulangeana
Tulip Tree ..... Liriodendron tulipifera
Tulip Tree (tropical) ..... Spathodea campanulata
Tulipwood ..... Harpullia pendula
Tulsi ..... Ocimum sanctum
Tumbledown Red Gum ..... Eucalyptus dealbata
Tupelo ..... Nyssa sylvatica
Turf Lily ..... Liriope muscari
Turk's Cap Lily ..... Lilium martagon
Turkey Fir ..... Abies bornmuelleriana
Turkey Oak ..... Quercus cerris
Turkish Balm ..... Melissa altissima
Turkish Filbert ..... Corylus colurna
Turpentine ..... Syncarpia glomulifera
Turtlehead ..... Chelone obliqua
Turutu ..... Dianella species
Tussock, Hard ..... Festuca novae zelandiae
Tutu ..... Coriaria arborea
Tweedia ..... Tweedia caerulea was Oxypetalum
Twelve Apostles ..... Campanula glomerata
Twiggy Tree Daisy ..... Olearia virgata var lineata
Twin Flower Knawel ..... Scleranthus biflorus
Twining Snapdragon ..... Maurandya barclayana was Asarina b.
Twinspur ..... Diascia cordata
Twisted Willow ..... Salix matsudana Tortuosa
Umbrella Grass ..... Cyperus alternifolius now involucrata
Umbrella Pine ..... Pinus pinea
Umbrella Tree ..... Melia azedarach
Umbrella Tree ..... Paulownia tomentosa
Umbrella Tree ..... Schefflera species
Upland Cress ..... Barbarea verna

Upright Daphne ..... D. odora Leucanthe

Upright Oak ..... Quercus robur fastigiata

Urn Gum ..... Eucalyptus urnigera

Utah Juniper ..... Juniperus osteosperma syn J.utahensis

Utah Sugar Maple ..... Acer saccharum ssp grandidentatum

Valerian ..... Valeriana officinalis

Valerian (False) ..... Centranthus species

Vanilla Tree ..... Azara microphylla

Variegated Apple Mint ..... Mentha suaveolens variegata

Variegated Broad leaf ..... Griselina littoralis variegata

Variegated Coral Tree ..... Erythrina indica picta

Variegated Elm ..... Ulmus carpinifolia variegata

Variegated Elm ..... Ulmus procera Variegata

Variegated Ground Ivy ..... Glechoma hederacea variegata

Variegated Japanese Laurel ..... Euonymus japonicus variegatum

Variegated Lemon Balm ..... Melissa officinalis Aurea

Variegated Lemonwood ..... Pittosporum eugenioides Variegatum

Variegated Myrtle ..... Myrtus communis variegata

Variegated Pukanui ..... Meryta Moonlight

Variegated Upland Cress ..... Barbarea verna variegata

Varnish Tree ..... Koelreuteria paniculata

Varnish Wattle ..... Acacia verniciflua

Vegar Fir ..... Abies vejarii

Vegetable Oyster ..... Tragopogon porrifolius

Vegetable Sponge ..... Luffa aegyptica

Veitch Fir ..... Abies veitchii

Veldt Flowers ..... Osteospermum species

Velvet Ash ..... Fraxinus velutina

Velvet Cassia ..... C. renigera

Velvet Plant ..... Gynura aurantica

Venetian Sumach ..... Cotinus coggygria

Veronica Brill Blue ..... Hebe gautheriana Blue Brill

Vervain ..... Verbena officinalis

Vervain Sage ..... Salvia verbenaca

Viburnum ..... see Viburnum

Viburnum, Mexican ..... Rondeletia amoena

Vicks Plant ..... Plectranthus sp (Vicks Plant)

Victorian Silver Gum ..... Eucalyptus crenulata

Victorian Waratah ..... Telopea oreades

Vietnamese Mint ..... Polygonum odoratum

Vine Maple ..... Acer circinatum

Violet Willow ..... Salix daphnoides

Virginia Creeper ..... Parthenocissus quinquefolia

Virginia Stock ..... Malcomia maritima

Virginian Cowslip ..... Mertensia virginica

Voodoo Plant ..... Hydrosme rivieri

WA Christmas Tree ..... Nuytsia floribunda

WA Coral Pea ..... Hardenbergia comptoniana

WA Weeping Wattle ..... Acacia saligna

Wadbilliga Ash ..... Eucalyptus paliformis

Waioriki ..... Ranunculus amphitrichus

Walking Stick Palm ..... Linospadix monostachya

Wall Germander ..... Teucrium chamaedrys

Wall Germander ..... Teucrium lucidum

Wallangara White Gum ..... Eucalyptus scoparia

Wallich Juniper ..... Juniperus wallichiana

Walnut ..... Juglans regia

Wampee/Wampi ..... Clausina lansium

Wand Flowers ..... Dierama species

Waratah Banksia ..... B. coccinea

Warminster Broom ..... Cytisus x praecox Warminster

Washingtonia Palm ..... Washingtonia robusta

Watau ..... Uncinia uncinata

Water Avens ..... Geum rivale

Water Bluebell ..... Ruellia wherryi

Water Bush ..... Banksia occidentalis

Water Buttercup ..... Ranunculus amphitrichus & lingua

Water Clover ..... Marsilea quadrifolia

Water Fern ..... Histiopteris incisa

Water Forgetmenot ..... Myosotis palustris now scorpioides

Water Gum ..... Tristaniopsis laurina was tristania

Water Hawthorn ..... Aponogeton distachyus

Water Hyssop ..... Bacopa caroliniana

Water Lily ..... Nymphaea varieties

Water Milfoil ..... Myriophyllum propinquum

Water Mint ..... Mentha aquatica

Water Pepper ..... Polygonum hydropiper

Water Pimpernel ..... Samolus valerandii

Water Plantain ..... Alisma plantago-aquatica

Water Spinach ..... Ipomoea aquatica

Water Tulepo ..... Nyssa aquatica

Water Wisteria ..... Hygrophila difformis

Watermelon ..... see Citrullus

Wattle-lvd Peppermint ..... Eucalyptus acaciaformis

Wattles ..... Acacia species

Wax Flower ..... Eriostemon myoporoides

Wax Flower ..... Stephanotis floribunda

Wax Mallow ..... Malvaviscus arboreus

Wax Tree ..... Rhus succedeana

Waxberry ..... Symphoricarpos albus

Wedding Bells ..... Deutzia gracilis

Wedding Cake Dogwood ..... Cornus controversa

Weeping Alder ..... Alnus incana Pendula

Weeping Blue Cedar ..... Cedrus atlantica Glauca Pendula

Weeping Boer-bean ..... Schotia brachypetala

Weeping Bottle Brush ..... Callistemon viminalis

Weeping Broom ..... Chordospartium stevensonii

Weeping Elm ..... Ulmus glabra Pendula

Weeping Fig ..... Ficus benjamina

Weeping Golden Ash ..... Fraxinus excelsior Aurea Pendula

Weeping Gum ..... Eucalyptus caesia

Weeping Hemlock ..... Tsuga canadensis Pendula

Weeping Lebanon Cedat ..... Cedrus libani Sargentii

Weeping Lillypilly ..... Eugenia ventenati

Weeping Mapou ..... Myrsine divaricata

Weeping Mazzard Cherry ..... Prunus (cherry flwg) avium pendula

Weeping Myall ..... Acacia pendula

Weeping Norway Spruce ..... Picea abies Reflexa syn P.a.Inversa

Weeping Rosemary ..... Rosmarinus officinalis prostratus

Weeping Silver Pear ..... Pyrus salicifolia Pendula

Weeping Swamp Cypress ..... Taxodium mucronatum pendulum

Weeping White Mulberry ..... Morus alba pendula

Weeping Willow ..... Salix babylonica

Weeping Willow, Matsudana ..... Salix matsudana Pendula

Weeping Willow, Purple ..... Salix purpurea pendula

Weeping Willow, White ..... Salix alba Pendula

Weld ..... Reseda luteola

Wellingtonia ..... Sequoiadendron giganteum

Welsh Onions ..... Allium sp Welsh Onions

Welsh Poppy ..... Meconopsis cambrica

Werilda Wattle ..... Acacia retinoides

West Himalayan Fir ..... Abies pindrow

West Himalayan Spruce ..... Picea smithiana was morinda

Western Catalpa ..... Catalpa speciosa

Western Hemlock ..... Tsuga heterophylla

Western Juniper ..... Juniperus occidentalis

Western Red Cedar ..... Thuja plicata

Western White Pine ..... Pinus monticola

Western Yellow Pine ..... Pinus ponderosa

Westland Pine ..... Lagarostrobos colensoi was Dacrydium c.

Westland Quintinia ..... Quintinia acutifolia

Westonbirt Dogwood ..... Cornus alba sibirica

Weymouth Pine ..... Pinus strobus

Whakataka ..... Corokia macrocarpa

Wharangi ..... Melicope ternata

Wharariki ..... Phormium cookianum

Wharawhara ..... Astelia banksii

Whau ..... Entelea arborescens

Whauwhaupaku ..... Pseudopanax arboreus

Whe ..... Cyathea smithii

Wheki ..... Dicksonia squarrossa

Wheki Ponga ..... Dicksonia fibrosa

White Ash ..... Fraxinus americana

White Ash Gum ..... Eucalyptus fraxinoides

White Bark Pine ..... Pinus pseudostrobus

White Betony ..... Stachys discolor was nivea

White Birch ..... Betula pubescens

White Bush Daisy ..... Brachyscome multifida

White Cedar ..... Thuja occidentalis

White Crepe Myrtle ..... Lagerstroemia subcostata

White Cupids Dart ..... Catananche caerulea bicolor

White Fairy Thimbles ..... Campanula cochleariifoli var. alba

White False Valerian ..... Centranthus ruber Albus

White Ginger ..... Hedychium coronarium

White Gum ..... Eucalyptus viminalis

White Honeysukle ..... Banksia integrifolia

White Hoop Petticoats ..... Narcissus cantabricus ss cantabrius var foliosus

White London Pride ..... Saxifraga cuneifolia

White Loosestrife ..... Lysimachia ephemerum

White Maire ..... Nestegis lanceolata

White Melilot ..... Melilotus Alba

White Moth Mullein ..... Verbascum blattaria albiflorum

White Mugwort ..... Artemisia lactiflora

White Mulberry ..... Morus alba

White Mullein ..... Verbascum lychnitis

White Penny Royal ..... Mentha pulegium alba

White Peppermint ..... Eucalyptus pulchella

White Pine, Kahikatea ..... Dacrycarpus dacrydioides

White Protea ..... Protea neriifolia alba

White Rose of Sissinghurst ..... Rosa longiscupis

White Rose Of York ..... Rosa alba semi plena

White Sage ..... Salvia apiana

White Snakeroot ..... Eupatorium ruginosa

White Spindle ..... Euonymus europaeus Albus

White Spruce ..... Picea glauca syn alba

White Stringybark   Eucalyptus globoidea

White Swamp Oak ..... Quercus bicolor

White Tea Tree ..... Kunzea ericoides was
Leptospermum e.

White Topped Box ..... Eucalyptus quadrangulata

White variegated Lacebark ..... Hoheria populnea
alba variegata

White Yarrow ..... Achillea millefolium white

White-fruited Spindle ..... Euonymus hamiltonia
maackia

Whitebark Pine ..... Pinus albicaulis

Whitebeam ..... Sorbus aria

Whitebeam, Chinese ..... Sorbus caloneura

Whiteywood ..... Melicytus ramiflorus

Whitloof ..... Cichorium intybus Verona

Whorl Flower ..... Morina longifolia

Whorled Solomons Seal ..... Polygonatum
verticulatum

Wild Basil ..... Calamintha clinopodium

Wild Basil ..... Clinopodium vulgare

Wild Bergamot ..... Monarda fistulosa

Wild Clary ..... Salvia verbenaca

Wild Dagga ..... Leonotis leonurus alba

Wild Gaillardia ..... Gaillardia pulchella

Wild Godetia ..... Godetia amoena

Wild Iris ..... Dietes grandiflora

Wild Lasiandra ..... Dissotis canescens

Wild Lemon Balm ..... Melissa altissima

Wild Service Tree ..... Sorbus torminalis

Wild Thyme ..... Thymus serpyllum

Willmotts Winter Hazel ..... Corylopsis willmottiae

Willow Gentian ..... Gentiana asclepiadea

Willow Herb ..... Epilobium parviflorum

Willow Moutere ..... Salix matsudana xAlba 1184

Willow Myrtle ..... Agonis flexuosa

Willow Tangoio ..... Salix matsudana xAlba 1040

Willow Wattle ..... Acacia salicina

Willow-lvd Mahoe ..... Melicytus lanceolatus

Willows ..... Salix species

Wilson's Maple ..... Acer wilsonii

Wilson's Spruce ..... Picea wilsonii

Wilton Carpet Juniper ..... Juniperus horizontalis
Wiltonii

Wind Flower ..... Pulsatilla vulgaris

Wind Grass ..... Oryzopsis lessoniana   was
Anemanthele l.

Windmill Palm ..... Trachycarpus fortunei

Wine Palm ..... Butia capitata

Winter Daphne ..... Daphne mezereum

Winter Heliotrope ..... Petasites fragrans

Winter Thyme ..... Thymus vulgaris English Winter

Winter's Bark ..... Drimys winterii

Winter-flowering Gladioli ..... Gladiolus psittacinus

Winter-flowering Gum ..... Eucalyptus leucoxylon

Winter-flowering Honeysuckle ..... Lonicera
fragrantissima

Wintersweet ..... Chimonanthus praecox

Wirenetting Bush ..... Corokia cotoneaster

Witch Hazel ..... Hamamelis species

Woad ..... Isatis tinctoria

Wolgan Snow Gum ..... Eucalyptus gregsoniana

Wolin Gum ..... Eucalyptus olsenii

Woman's Tongue ..... Albizia lebbek

Wongawonga Vine ..... Pandorea pandorana

Wood Cranesbill ..... Geranium sylvaticum

Wood Sage ..... Teucrium scorodonia

Woodland Anemone ..... Anemone nemorosa

Woodland Chervil ..... Anthriscus sylvestris

Woodland Hyacinth ..... Scilla species

Woolly Foxglove ..... Digitalis lanata

Woolly Lavender ..... Lavandula lanata

Woolly Marjoram ..... Origanum laevigatum

Woolly Thyme ..... Thymus pseudolanuginosus

Woolly Yarrow ..... Achillea tomentosa

Worcester Berry ..... Ribes Worcester Berry (black
curr x Gooseberry)

Wormwood ..... Artemisia absinthum

Wrinkled Coprosma ..... Coprosma rugosa

Wyalong Wattle ..... Acacia cardiophylla

Yacon ..... Polymnia sonchifolia

Yamasakura Cherry ..... Prunus (cherry flwg) jamasakura

Yarra Gum ..... Eucalyptus yarraensis

Yarran ..... Acacia homalophylla

Yarrows ..... Achillea species

Yedo Spindle ..... Euonymus yedoensis

Yellow Avens ..... Geum macrophyllum

Yellow Bellflower ..... Campanula thyrsoides

Yellow Birch ..... Betula alleghaniensis

Yellow Box ..... Eucalyptus melliodora

Yellow Buckeye ..... Aesculus flava was octandra

Yellow Buttons ..... Cotula coronopifolia

Yellow Centaury ..... Centaurea macrocephala

Yellow Daphne ..... Edgeworthia papyrifera (now chrysantha)

Yellow Dock ..... Rumex crispus

Yellow Flag Iris ..... Iris pseudacorus

Yellow Foxglove ..... Digitalis lutea

Yellow Giant Hyssop ..... Agastache nepetoides

Yellow Gum ..... Eucalyptus johnstonii

Yellow Gum ..... Eucalyptus leucoxylon

Yellow Hardhead ..... Centaurea macrocephala

Yellow Lobelia ..... Monopsis lutea

Yellow Loosestrife ..... Lysimachia punctata

Yellow Loosestrife ..... Lysimachia vulgaris

Yellow Onion ..... Allium moly

Yellow Ox-eye ..... Buphthalmum species

Yellow Pine ..... Halocarpus biformis was Dacrydium biforme

Yellow Poplar ..... Liriodendron tulipifera

Yellow Silver Pine ..... Lepidothamnus intermedius   was Dacrydium I.

Yellow Stringybark ..... Eucalyptus muellerana

Yellow Tree Peony ..... Paeonia(tree) delavayi ludlowii   was P.lutea ludlowii

Yellow Tree Peony ..... Paeonia(tree) delavayi lutea   was P.lutea

Yellow Trout Lily ..... Erythronium tuolumnense

Yellow Turk's Cap Lily ..... Lilium pyrenaicum

Yellow Yarrow ..... Achillea filipendulina

Yellow/green variegated Lacebark ..... Hoheria populnea (aurea) variegata

Yellowfruited Holly ..... Ilex aquifolium Bacciflava was Fructu Luteo

Yellowfruited Rowan ..... Sorbus aucuparia Xanthocarpa

Yellowwood ..... Cladastris lutea

Yesterday,Today,Tomorrow Bush ..... Brunfelsia calycina Eximea & latifolia

Yew ..... Taxus baccata

Yew Podocarpus ..... P. macrophyllus

Yezo Spruce ..... Picea jesoensis

Yoshino Cherry ..... Prunus x yeodensis

Youmans Stringybark ..... Eucalyptus youmanii

Young's Weeping Birch ..... Betula pendula Youngii

Yukon Paper Birch(Neoalaskan) ..... Betula papyrifera humilis

Yulan Magnolia ..... Magnolia denudata

Yunnan Pine ..... Pinus yunnanensis

Zatar ..... Thymbra spicata

Zuchini ..... see Cucurbita

Nursery Directory

Altrf Altorf Spring Bulbs Ltd,
Freepost 759, Taha Rd,
Waimauku
Contact: Joan & Peter
Phone: 09 411 8747
Fax: 09 411 7579
Mail order hotline 0800 103 747
Catalogue free.
Specialist: Bulbs

AmFu Amberelle Fuchsias, 156
Pickering Rd, RD1, Cambridge
Contact: Jill Morrison
Phone: 07 827 4375
Open: Sep - Apr , Wed - Sun, 9-
5pm.
Mail order catalogues: F $2, R
$1.
Specialist: Fuchsias, Roses

AnnM Ann Marie Orchids, PO Box
489, Whangarei,
Contact: Syd Wray
Phone: 09 436 0515
Mail order lists of all different
orchid genera free.
Specialist: Orchids

Apple Appletons' Tree Nursery, Main
Rd South, Wakefield 7181,
Contact: Eric & Robert Appleton
Phone: 03 541 8309
Fax: 03 541 8007
Ahr/Mobile: 03 541 8546
Mail order catalogue free-stock
sold in multiples of 10 or 25.
Specialist: Trees

Ashto Ashton Glen, Estate Rd,
Wairuna, RD Clinton, Otago
Contact: Ross & Ruth Mitchell
Phone: 03 415 7687
Open: most days, closed Sundays.
Mail order catalogue $5
refundable w. 1st order, no
minimum order.
Specialist: Perennials

Aynda Ayndara Nurseries, PO Box 30,
Taupo,
Contact: Peter & Clare Jensen
Phone: 07 333 2258
Ahr/Mobile: 025 757 663
Open: daily except Mon & Tue.
Mail order catalogue.
Specialist: Plants of Distinction

Backw Backwater Plants, 779
Portobello Rd, Dunedin,
Contact: Gill & Tudor Caradoc-
Davies
Phone: 03 478 0080
Fax: 03 478 0080
Ahr/Mobile: 025 337 041
Open: Weekends Dec to Feb.
Mail order.
Specialist: Disa uniflora & S
African wild veldt flower species

BayBl Bay Bloom Nurseries, PO Box
502, Tauranga,
Contact: Grant Iles, Terry Shuker
Phone: 07 578 9902
Fax: 07 577 9752
Open: 7 days 9am-5pm.
Mail order catalogue $5.
Specialist: Perennials.bulbs,roses

BeauB Beautiful Begonias, Rocklands
Rd, Clifton, Takaka
Contact: Graham & Robyn
Hardwick
Phone: 03 525 9058
Open: gardens daily 10 - 6pm,
Dec - May.
Mail order catalogue.
Specialist: Begonias

383

BlueM Blue Mountain Nurseries, 99 Bushy Hill St, Tapanui,
Contact: Denis & Margaret Hughes
Phone: 03 204 8250
Fax: 03 204 8278
Open: daily excl Sun.
Mail order catalogues.
Specialist: Rhododendron & Decid. Azaleas, Conifers

Brown Browns Nursery, 79 Vernon Rd, RD1, Tauranga
Contact: David & Pauline Brown
Phone: 07 552 4966
Fax: 07 552 4966
Open: by appointment only.
Mail order catalogue free but send SAE.
Specialist: Vireya Rhododendrons

Burbk Burbank Goldfish & Tree Farm, 7 Bullens Rd, Ardmore, RD2, Papakura
Contact: Phil Collis
Phone: 09 296 2256
Fax: 09 298 4810
Ahr/Mobile: 09 298 4810
Open: 7 days.
Stock list available.
Specialist: BIG Trees, shrub lines

Butlr Butlers Nurseries, East Bank Rd, Thornton RD3, Whakatane
Contact: Stephen & Elizabeth Butler
Phone: 07 304 9869
Fax: 07 304 9869
Mail order- Min: 5 plants/variety, 80 plants total.
Specialist: Shrubs

CameH Camellia Haven, PO Box 537, Papakura,
Contact: Neville Haydon
Phone: 09 298 7392
Fax: 09 298 7392
Open:Nursery & Gardens 1st March-31st October 8.30am-4.30pm 80 Manuroa Rd,Takanini.
Mail order catalogue.
Specialist: Camelias

Caves Cave's Tree Nursery, Pukeroro, RD3, Hamilton
Contact: Peter Cave
Phone: 07 827 6601
Fax: 07 827 6601
Garden open to only groups by arrangement.
Mail order catalogue free, min order $50.
Specialist: Trees & shrubs

Cedar Cedar Lodge Conifers, 63 Egmont Rd, RD2, New Plymouth
Contact: David & Noeline Sampson
Phone: 06 755 0369
Fax: 06 755 0369
Open:7 days except Jan-Mar:closed Sunday.
Mail order catalogue, send 80c stamp.
Specialist: Conifers

Chedd Cheddar Valley Trees, Wainui Rd, RD2, Opotiki
Contact: Nick & Pauline Nelson-Parker
Phone: 07 312 4639
Fax: 07 312 4638
Open: Mon - Sat.
Mail order catalogue
Specialist: Trees, Shrubs, Fruit trees

Coatv Coatesville Tree Nurseries, Main Rd Coatesville, RD3, Albany
Contact: Jim Maxwell
Phone: 09 415 9983
Fax: 09 415 9983
Ahr/Mobile: 09 415 8818
Open: daily.
Mail order catalogue.
Specialist: Trees, Shrubs, Fruit trees

CoFlo Cottage Flower Plants, Tramway Rd West, Seaward Downs, Edendale
Contact: Alison Caldwell
Phone: 03 206 6558
Ahr/Mobile: 03 206 6558
Open: most Saturdays or by appointment.
Mail order catalogue.
Specialist: Perennials

Corom Coromandel Fuchsias, Papa Aroha, RD4, Coromandel
Contact: June & Rex Brett
Phone: 07 866 8331
Ahr/Mobile: 07 866 8331
Open: most days,phone first.
Mail order.
Specialist: Fuchsias

CottP Cottage Plants, Petit Cavenage Bay, RD2, Akaroa
Contact: Robyn & Peter Dimmock
Phone: 03 304 5882
Fax: 03 304 5882
Ahr/Mobile: 03 304 5882
Open: daily but closed June,July,August.
Mail order catalogue $5 (year's sub).
Specialist: Cottage Plants

CouCl Courier Climbers, PO Box 2458, Tauranga,
Contact: John & Christine Nicholls
Phone: 025 815 157bus hours
Not open to public.
Mail order list, send 4 x 40c stamps.
Specialist: Climbers

Coult Coulter's Nursery, 183 Weston Rd, PO Box 5288, Papanui, Christchurch
Contact: Michael & Susan Coulter
Phone: 03 355 4656
Open: Nov-Oct. Flower viewing: 8,9 March only.
Mail order catalogue free.
Specialist: Chrysanthemums

CPete Conifer Pete's Nursery, Pakowhai, RD3, Napier
Contact: Peter & Marilyn Collinge
Phone: 06 878 2917
Fax: 06 878 2487
Ahr/Mobile: 025 442 714
Open: 7 days, please phone first.
Mail order ontalogue free.
Specialist: Conifers

Craig Craigmore Peonies Partnership, Craigmore, RD2, Timaru
Contact: Kathryn Hill
Phone: 03 612 9840
Fax: 03 612 9890
Ahr/Mobile: 025 393 961
Open: one open day only.
Mail order catalogue free (SAE appreciated).
Specialist: Peonies

Cross   Crosshills Gardens, RD54,
Kimbolton 5600,
Contact: Rodney & Faith Wilson
Phone: 06 328 5797
Fax: 06 328 5773
Open: nursery sales Jun-Nov,
Display Gardens Sep-May.
Mail order catalogue $5.
Specialist: Rhododendrons

DaffA   Daffodil Acre, Box 834,
Tauranga,
Contact: Bill & Willy Dijk
Phone: 07 552 5383
Fax: 07 552 5383
Ahr/Mobile: 07 552 5383
Not open to public.
Mail order list free.
Specialist: Bulbs

DBoer   De Boer Roses, PO Box 15,
Edendale, Southland
Contact: Gerrit & Riet De Boer
Phone: 03 206 6026
Fax: 03 206 6026
Open: 9-5pm, Closed Sun, Mon
& public hols.
Mail order catalogue.
Specialist: Roses

Della   Dellawood Herbs, Lynne Marie
Tuhou, RD2 Owaka, Sth Otago
Contact: Lynne Marie Tuhou
Phone: 03 415 8579
Open: daily August to April.
Mail order catalogue $3.
Specialist: Herbs, Alpines,
Perennials

Denes   Dene's Garden Way, St Hill
LAne, PO Box 8019, Havelock
North
Contact: Dene Thomas, Jenny
Speedy
Phone: 06 877 7162
Fax: 06 877 7162
Open: Mon - Sat 9-5pm, Sun
9.30-4.30pm.
Mail order catalogues.
Specialist: Shrubs, Trees, Roses,
Clematis

Diack   Diack's Nurseries Ltd, PO Box
181, Cnr Tweed & Inglewood
Rd, Invercargill
Contact: Ray Diack
Phone: 03 216 8265
Fax: 03 216 8089
Ahr/Mobile: 025 322 417
Open: daily.
Retail price list.
Specialist: Trees, Shrubs

Dove   Dove Nurseries, Dovedale, RD2,
Wakefield
Contact: Steve & Sue Johnson
Phone: 03 543 3856
Fax: 03 543 3856
Mail order catalogue.
Specialist: Trees, Shrubs

Dowde   Dowdeswell Delphiniums, 18
Henderson Ave, Tuakau,
Contact: Terry & Janice
Dowdeswell
Phone: 09 236 8475
Fax: 09 236 8884
Not open to public except by
prior arrangement.
Mail order catalogue -spring
dispatch.
Specialist: Delphiniums

Dream Dream Plants, Orere, RD5, Papakura
Contact: Sandra van der Hoff
Phone: 09 292 2623
Open: Thu - Sat.
Mail order catalogue $2.
Specialist: Perennials

DSNur D & S Nurseries, PO Box 21, Onga Onga, Central Hawkes Bay
Contact: Doug & Sue Pacey
Phone: 06 856 6858
Fax: 06 856 6523
Open: Wed-Sun 25 Jun to end Oct, then daily to 14 Dec.
Mail order catalogue, bareroot only.
Specialist: Roses

EasyB Easy Big Trees, 241 North Rd, Invercargill,
Contact: Chris Harrison
Phone: 03 215 8899
Mail order list.
Specialist: BIG Specimen Trees

Egmon Egmont Roses, Box 3162, New Plymouth,
Contact: John Martin
Phone: 06 753 4283
Fax: 06 753 3762
Open:for rose viewing 7 days Jan-Apr,Winter dispatch.
Mail order catalogue.
Specialist: Roses (High Health)

Ether Etherington's Nursery Ltd, 95 Clover St East, Hope, PO Box 3046, Richmond 7031
Contact: Geoff Etherington
Phone: 03 542 3036
Fax: 03 542 3036
Ahr/Mobile: 03 542 3736
Gardens Of The World entry $4.
Mail order list, send 2 x 40c stamps.
Specialist: African Trees

Eyrew Eyrewell Gardens, 534 Downs Rd, West Eyretown, Rangiora
Contact: MD & CB Stewart
Phone: 03 312 5009
Mail order catalogue.
Specialist: Lilies

Ford Ford's Nurseries Ltd, Ferry Rd, 1KRD, Oamaru
Contact: Adrian, Elaine & Antony Ford
Phone: 03 431 3626
Fax: 03 431 3624
Ahr/Mobile: or 0800 421 444
Mail order catalogue.
Specialist: Trees:forest,amenity,native

Frans Russell Fransham Subtropicals, RD3, Matapouri Bay, Whangarei
Contact: Russell Fransham
Phone: 09 434 3980
Ahr/Mobile: 09 434 3980
Plant list available.
Specialist: Subtropicals

GMill Graham Milligan, PO Box 23, Dipton, Southland
Contact: Graham Milligan
Phone: 03 248 5147
Fax: 03 248 5053
Ahr/Mobile: 025 880 870
Open: 7 days but please contact first.
Mail order catalogues: $4 Trees; Seeds.
Specialist: Eucalyptus (cold tolerant) trees & seeds

Gordn Gordons Nurseries, 159a Scenic Drive, Titirangi, Auckland
Phone: 09 817 3498
Ahr/Mobile: 025 805 159
Open: daily.
No mail order, local delivery only.
Specialist: Natives

Hackf Hackfalls Arboretum Charitable
Trust Nursery, PO Box 3,
Tiniroto, Gisborne
Contact: Bob & Lady Anne Berry
Phone: 06 863 7091
Fax: 06 863 7083
Open: daily, entry fee.
Mail order.
Specialist: Trees, Shrubs

Hains Hains Horticulture, Simpson Rd,
RD4, Wanganui
Contact: P Hains
Phone: 06 345 2211
Open: Mon,Wed, Fri.
Mail order list free, no minimum.
Specialist: Grasses

Harri Harrisons Trees, RD1,
Palmerston North,
Contact: J Vernon Harrison
Phone: 06 357 0054
Fax: 06 3568938
Not open to public.
Mail order only.
Specialist: Fruit trees

Herew Hereweka Garden & Nursery,
Hereweka St, Portobello, Dunedin
Contact: Anna Moore
Phone: 03 478 0880
Ahr/Mobile: 03 478 0165
Catalogue available.
Specialist: Perennials, Cottage
Garden Plants

Herit Heritage Horticulture, Woolrich
Rd, RD8, Te Kowhai
Contact: Ian & Helen Gear
Phone: 07 829 7607
Fax: 07 829 7607
Ahr/Mobile: 025 868 131
Mail order catalogue $6.
Specialist: Iris, Hemerocallis

Hewsn Hewson's Nurseries, Rocky
Hundreds Rd, RD2, Timaru
Contact: David Hewson
Phone: 03 684 4402
Fax: 03 688 1002
Ahr/Mobile: 025 357 404
Open: Mar - Dec, Fri - Mon, 10-
4.30 or by arrangement.
Mail order catalogue.
Specialist: Trees & Shrubs

HostG Hosta Garden, Glencoe, No2RD,
Invercargill
Contact: Gaynor & Chris Miller
Phone: 03 230 6144
Fax: 03 230 6144
Open Oct 1 - Mar 31 Wed -Sat,
Display Garden Oct - Dec.
Mail order catalogue. Dispatch
dates Oct -Mar.
Specialist: Hostas, Hemerocallis

Irida Iridaceae, Chris Duval Smith,
Kaiaua via Pokeno, South
Auckland
Contact: Chris Duval Smith
Phone: 09 232 2856
Visitors please ring first.
Mail order catalogue: send long
SAE, no minimum.
Specialist: Iridaceae

Isaac Isaachsens Bamboo Nursery,
833 West Coast Rd, Oratia,
Auckland
Contact:
Phone: 09 814 9847
Mail order list.
Specialist: Bamboo

Jordn Jordan's Nursery, 6 Melcombe
St, Tinwald, Ashburton
Contact: Ken & Jenny Jordan
Phone: 03 308 7253
Fax: 03 308 2342
Nursery & Display Gardens open
Mon-Fri 9am-5.30pm , Sat 10-
4pm , Sun (Sep-Oct) 10-4pm.
Mail order catalogue.
Specialist: Rhododendrons,
Camellias

JoyPl Joy Plants, Pukekohe East, RD2,
Pukekohe
Contact: Terry,Pam, Lindsay
Hatch
Phone: 09 238 9129
Open: Mon-Sat 9am-5pm.
Mail order:lists available- no
minimum.
Specialist: Bulbs, Rare
Perennials, Shrubs, Trees

Kauri Kauri Creek Nursery, RD1,
Katikati,
Contact: Norman & Joanne
Knight
Phone: 07 549 1104
Fax: 07 549 1104
Mail order catalogue.
Specialist: Old Time Roses

Kayd Kaydees Gardens, 54 Pyes Pa
Rd, PO Box 2050, Tauranga
Contact: David Tait
Phone: 07 552 4443
Fax: 07 552 4371
Open seasonally.
Mail order catalogue.
Specialist: Cottage Plants

Kerer Kereru Bulbs, Bachelors Rd,
Little River 8162, Banks
Peninsula
Contact: Maevis & David Watson
Phone: 021 812 354
Fax: 03 325 1003
Mail order list.
Specialist: Bulbs

KeriP Keri Perennials, Box 355,
Kerikeri,
Contact: Jamie Edgecombe
Phone: 09 407 5020
Fax: 09 407 5020
Not open to public.
Mail order catalogue-send 6 x
40c stamps.
Specialist: Perennials

King # Kings Seeds, 1660 Gt North Rd,
PO Box 19 084, Avondale,
Auckland
Contact: Ross King
Phone: 09 828 7588
Fax: 09 828 7588
Open: Herb & seed shop 9 - 5pm
Mon-Fri.
Mail order catalogue $6.
Specialist: Seeds

Koan Koanga Gardens, RD2,
Maungatoroto, Northland
Contact: Kay & Bob Baxter
Phone: 09 431 2145
Fax: 09 341 2901
Open : by appointment or on
specific Open Days.
Mail order catalogue.
Specialist: Seeds, Subtropicals,
Fruit Scionwood

Kopua Koputaroa Iris Gardens, 178
Paiaka Rd, RD5, Levin
Contact: Dawn & Bob Wright
Phone: 06 368 4997
Fax: 06 368 4997
Open.
Mail order catalogues - send 40c
stamp.
Specialist: Irises, Hemerocalis

LakeN   Lake Ngatu Plantations, Sweetwater Rd, Awanui, Box 493, Kaitaia

Contact: Peter & Pauline Endicott

Phone: 09 406 7570

Fax: 09 406 7570

Ahr/Mobile: 025 826 519

Open: Mon-Sat 8.00-5.00.

Mail order catalogue free.

Specialist: Subtropicals

LanSc   Landscape Nursery, PatulloRd, Patumahoe, RD4, Pukekohe

Contact: Paul & Jenny Lagerstadt

Phone: 09 236 3072

Fax: 09 236 3084

Open: phone first.

Mail order list.

Specialist: Topiary, Standards, Hedging

LeFab   Le Faber Dahlia Cultures, Waitangi Falls Rd, RD1, Waiuku

Contact: Trudy & Willem Lefeber

Phone: 09 235 3710

Fax: 09 235 3710

Open: by appointment only.

Mail order catalogue, no minimum.

Specialist: Dahlia

LiliB   Lilies In Bloom, Tukurua, RD2, Takaka, Golden Bay

Contact: Gordon & Bess Hampson

Phone: 03 525 8353

Fax: 03 525 8353

Open: Mon - Sat, flowering season Nov - Apr, picnic, beach.

Mail order catalogue.

Specialist: Lilies

Lilyf   Lily Fields Mt Somers, No1RD, Ashburton,

Contact: David & Wendy Millichamp

Phone: 03 303 9743

Mail order colour catalogue $5 refundable w 1st order.

Specialist: Lilies

Liman   The Lilyman, 33 Esperance St, Christchurch 5,

Contact: Kevin & Mary Dolan

Phone: 03 355 3410

Fax: 03 355 4710

Mail order list.

Specialist: Lilies

Looij   Looij , Thomas, 17 Panapa Rd, RD2, Hastings

Contact:

Phone: 06 878 7025

Mail order: minimum order 5 plants.

Specialist: Perennials,Herbs, Groundcovers

Lsendt   Landsendt Exotic Plants, 108 Parker Rd, Oratia, Auckland

Contact: Dick Endt

Phone: 09 818 6914

Fax: 09 818 6391

Ahr/Mobile: 025 538 078

Open.

Catalogue available.

Specialist: Subtropicals

Manna   Manna Gardens, 81 Pukaki Rd, Mangere, Auckland

Contact:

Phone: 09 275 8556

Open: 7 days but completely closed in winter.

Mail order list, plants supplied bare-rooted.

Specialist: Tropical Plants,all sizes

MaraN	Mara Nurseries, Allen Rd, RD12, Hawera
Contact: Roger & Margaret Springett
Phone: 06 272 2806
Fax: 06 272 2033
Ahr/Mobile: 06 272 2879
Open: Mon - Sat 9-4.30pm, Sun 1-4.30pm.
Mail order catalogue $4.
Specialist: Perennials

Margu	Margueritas Agapanthus, Box 103, Cambridge,
Contact: Marguerita McBeath
Phone: 07 827 7190
Fax: 07 827 5038
Mail order list.
Specialist: Agapanthus

MarlO	Marlborough Olives, PO Box 876, Blenheim,
Contact: Hamish MacFarlane
Phone: 03 577 8834
Ahr/Mobile: 03 577 8834
Mail order list.
Specialist: Olives

Marsh	Marshwood Garden & Nursery, Leonard Rd, West Plains RD4, Invercargill
Contact: Geoff & Adair Genge
Phone: 03 215 7672
Fax: 03 215 7672
Open: Wed - Sat 10 - 5pm, Sun 1 - 5pm, entry private garden $2.
Mail order catalogue.
Specialist: Perennials, Shrubs

Mason	Frank Mason & Son Ltd, Sandon Rd, PO Box 155, Feilding
Contact: Tony Migo
Phone: 06 323 5226
Fax: 06 323 5226
Open: 8am-4.30pm Mon-Fri, 9.30-2pm Sat, closed Sun & Stat hols.
Mail order catalogue.
Specialist: Roses, Fuchsias

Matai	Matai Nurseries, 52 Harris St, Waimate,
Contact: Lester Davey
Phone: 03 689 8928
Ahr/Mobile: 03 689 8235
Open: daily except Fridays (or please ring), 8am - 5.30pm.
Mail order catalogue.
Specialist: Trees, Natives

MatNu	Matthews' Nursery, French Farm Valley Rd, RD2, Akaroa 8161
Contact: Lew & Kaye Matthews
Phone: 03 304 5849
Fax: 03 304 5849
Open: 7 days 9am-5pm.
Mail order : minimum 6 plants(except Chch).
Specialist: Protea Family

Matth	Matthews' Nursery (Anderson & Sanson), Box 21, Manakau, Horowhenua
Contact: Jim Anderson & Peggy Sanson
Phone: 06 362 6827
Open: daily except Mondays.
Mail order : minimum 6 plants.
Specialist: Protea Family,Camelias(not by mail)

Matwh	Matawhero Nursery, RD1, Gisborne,
Contact:
Phone: 06 868 4483
Fax: 06 868 4458
Ahr/Mobile: 0800Matawhero
Open: Mon-Fri 8am-4.30pm (& Saturdays in winter).
Mail order: Minimum $35 excl freight.
Specialist: Natives,Eucalypts,Camelias,Trees & Shrubs

McKe   McKechnie Nurseries, Robinson Rd, Coatesville, RD3, Albany

Contact: Grant & Julie McKechnie

Phone: 09 415 8806

Fax: 09 415 8806

Open: 9-5pm, May-Sep: 7 days, Summer: week days.

Mail order list.

Specialist: Trees, Natives

Meado   Meadowbank Florist & GardenCentre, 20 St Johns Rd, Meadowbank, Auckland

Contact: Deborah Fox & Rebecca Butts

Phone: 09 521 2010

Open: 7 days.

Mail order catalogue free.

Specialist: Roses all types including standards

MillH   Mill House Nursery, Cnr Seftons/Boleyns Rds, Okains Bay, RD3, Akaroa

Contact:

Phone: 03 304 7744

Fax: 03 304 7744

Open: 1 Nov - 1 Apr, Tue & Wed 9am-5pm, Sat 9am-1pm.

Mail order catalogue $3.

Specialist: Perennials

Mills   Millstream Gardens, Pukehou, Private Bag, Napier

Contact: Jan Holman & Geoff Speeder

Phone: 06 878 1511 $2

Fax:

Ahr/Mobile: 025 538 895

Open: 9-5pm, closed Tue,Wed.

Mail order catalogue send $2 in stamps.

Specialist: Herbs,Bulk Comfrey,Pond Plants

Mjury   Mark Jury Nursery, Tikorangi, 591 Otaraoa Rd, RD43, Waitara

Contact: Mark & Abbie Jury

Phone: 06 754 8577

Fax: 06 754 6671

Open: Mon-Sat. Garden open 1 Sep-mid Nov.

Mail order: Minimum $35 excl freight. Dispatch May to early Nov.

Specialist: Rhododendrons, Camelias, Bulbs, Magnolias

Morgn   Morgans Road Nursery Ltd, Morgans Rd, RD3, Blenheim

Contact: Lee Gilbert

Phone: 03 578 1412

Fax: 03 578 1412

Open: daily.

Mail order list.

Specialist: Trees, Shrubs, Natives

MPaeo   Marsal Paeonies, Old South Rd, RD Dunsandel, Canterbury

Contact: Julie & John Allan

Phone: 03 325 4003

Fax: 03 325 4003

Open to view flowers: 3rd & 4th weekends Nov, 1st one Dec.

Mail order colour catalogue $5.

Specialist: Paeonies

Mtanu   Matanui Nurseries, Box 10107, Te Mai, Whangarei

Contact: Dona Shiell

Phone: 09 438 1966

Fax: 09 438 1966

Mail order catalogue free.

Specialist: Fruit Trees (uncommon)

Mtato Matatoa Trees & Shrubs, Engles Rd, PO Box 31, Shannon
Contact: Jeanine Hathaway
Phone: 06 362 7477
Fax: 06 362 7472
Ahr/Mobile: 06 362 7399
Open: 7 days Apr-Nov, 5 days Dec-Mar.
Mail order catalogue free.
Specialist: Trees, Shrubs,small-large grades

MTig Mt Tiger Gardens, RD1, Oncrahi, Whangarei
Contact: Waltraud Mittman
Open.
Mail order catalogues: Subtropicals,Cacti etc.
Specialist: Sutropicals

NewlR Newlands Rock Gardens, Clandeboye, RD26 Temuka, Sth Canterbury
Contact: Bev % Peter Davidson
Phone: 03 615 9828
Open: 7 days but please ring first.
Mail order catalogue free, no minimum order.
Specialist: Rock gardening,Bulbs

Nikau Nikau Hill Cottage Garden Plants, RD3, Dannevirke,
Contact: Doreen Higginson
Phone: 06 374 1569
Open: please ring first.
Mail order catalogue, also seed list.
Specialist: Cottage plants and seeds

NormP Norm Porter Orchids, 23 Parata St, Waikanae,
Contact: Norm Porter
Phone: 04 293 6977
Fax: 04 293 6977
Open: Tue - Sat 9-5 pm.
Mail order catalogue.
Specialist: Orchids

NZFlax NZ Flax Hybridisers, Box 3028, Tauranga,
Contact:
Not open.
Mail order: send SAE for list.
Specialist: Flax

NZtr # New Zealand Tree Seeds, PO Box 435, Rangiora, Nth Canterbury
Contact: Fred Howard
Phone: 03 312 4635
Fax: 03 312 4833
Mail order catalogue $3.
Specialist: Seeds (of trees & shrubs)

Oasis Oasis Plants, 75 Vogel St, Woodville,
Contact: Gilliaqn McIlraith & Chris Daish
Phone: 06 376 5455
Fax: 06 376 5455
Open: 9am -5pm daily except Wednesday.
Mail order catalogue free.
Specialist: Perennials

Orang Oranga Plants, 60 Port St East, Feilding,
Contact: Marilyn & Ian Wightman
Phone: 06 323 4233
Fax: 06 323 4233
Open: 7 days nursery & display gardens.
Mail order catalogue, send 7 x 40c stamps, no minimum.
Specialist: Herbs

Orati Oratia Native Plant Nursery, 66 Parker Rd, Oratia, Auckland 7
Contact: Geoffrey Davidson
Phone: 09 818 6467
Fax: 09 818 6457
Open: Mon-Sat 9am - 4.30pm.
Will courier plants.
Specialist: Natives plus offshore island plants

Ormon Ormonds Garden & Nursery, RD14, Havelock North, Hawkes Bay
Contact: Peter & Elizabeth Ormond
Phone: 06 874 7820
Fax: 06 874 7660
Open: Sep-Mar: Wed-Sun 9-5pm, Apr-Aug: Fri-Sun Or by appointment.
Mail order catalogue - send SAE.
Specialist: Plants for dry/difficult areas

Otara O'tara Birch Gardens, Waitohi Rd, Box 81, Rongotea
Contact: Eddie Johns & Adrian Ballinger
Phone: 06 324 8490
Fax: 06 324 8490
Open: daily 10 - 5pm. Garden: late Oct - Easter.
Mail order catalogue.
Specialist: Dahlias, Irises

Otepo Otepopo Garden Nursery, 8 Troup St, Herbert, North Otago
Contact: Gwenda Harris
Phone: 03 439 5514
Open: Wed - Sun, 10 - 5pm or by arrangement.
Mail order catalogues $2.
Specialist: Perennials, Natives

PalmF The Palm Farm, 119 Walmsley Rd, Mangere, Auckland
Contact:
Phone: 09 275 5454
Fax: 09 275 5454
Open: Mon-Fri 8am to 4pm Sat/Sun 10am to 3pm.
Mail order catalogue.
Specialist: Palms

Parva Parva Plants, Box 2503, Tauranga,
Contact: Ian & Barbara Duncalf
Phone: 07 552 4902
Fax: 07 552 4902
Not open to public.
Mail order catalogue $5 refunded w 1st order.
Specialist: Perennials, Collectors plants

Peak Peak Perennials, 23 Toop St, Havelock North,
Contact: Gillian Blackmore & Alice Thrum
Phone: 06 877 6051
Fax: 06 877 6067
Open: Thu, Fri, or strictly by arrangement.
Mail order catalogue $3.
Specialist: Perennials

Peele Peeles Plant Propagation, Waihou, RD3, Te Aroha
Contact: Jim & Coralie Peele
Phone: 07 884 9963
Fax: 07 884 9963
Open: please phone first.
Mail order catalogue, no minimum but 10% surcharge under $50.
Specialist: Trees

PeoGa The Peony Gardens, Lake Hayes, No1RD, Queenstown
Contact: Dorothy & Bruce Hamilton
Phone: 03 442 1210
Fax: 03 442 1210
Open: daily for 6 weeks from Nov 4, 9 -5pm, delivery autumn.
Mail Order catalogue.
Specialist: Paeonies

Pgeon	Pigeon Valley Nursery, Pigeon Valley Rd South, RD 2, Wakefield
Contact: Carl Christiansen
Fax: 03 541 8856 eveng
Ahr/Mobile: 03 541 8856
Open: please phone first.
Mail order catalogue.
Specialist: Perennials

Pionr	Pioneer Nursery, Taonui Rd, Colyton RD5, Feilding
Contact: David & Jo Belcher
Phone: 06 328 7803
Fax: 06 328 7803
Open: Mon - Sat 8.30-5pm, Sun 10 -4pm.
Mail order catalogue free.
Specialist: Trees, Shrubs, Fruit

Pkrau	Pukerau Nursery, RD2, Gore,
Contact: Arne & Jenny Cleland
Phone: 03 205 3801
Fax: 03 205 3703
Open: Mon-Fri 9am-5pm, Sat by arrangement.
Mail order catalogue,send SAE.
Specialist: Groundcovers, Ornumental Grasses

Ploug	The Ploughman's Garden And Nursery, Duff Rd, RD2, Waiuku
Contact: Peter Carter
Phone: 09 235 9739
Fax: 09 235 2659
Open: Wed-Sun 10am-5pm or by appointment, 3 acre Display garden $3 entry.
No mail order.
Specialist: Lavender Collection, Rosemary

Podgo	Podgora Gardens, Shoemaker Rd, PO Box 46, Waipu
Contact: Paul & Sonja Mrsich
Phone: 09 432 0202
Visitors Welcome.
Mail order catalogue.
Specialist: Cannas

PuhaN	Puha Nursery, RD4, Te Karaka, Gisborne
Contact: Graeme Falloon, Gary Hope
Phone: 06 862 3819
Fax: 06 862 3065
Ahr/Mobile: 0800 808 733
Open: Mid May to Mid Sep, Mon-Fri 7.30-5.30pm.
Mail order catalogue, minimum order 10 trees (of any mix).
Specialist: Trees

Puket	Puketapu Iris Gardens, 226 Corbett Rd, No3RD, New Plymouth
Contact: Dorothy Wood
Phone: 06 755 2900
Fax: 06 755 2900
Open: daily Oct-Mar.
Mail order catalogue, send 40c stampSpecific delivery times.
Specialist: Irises,Daylilies (Hemerocallis)

Pukho	Pukehou Nurseries, Main Highway, Manakau, RD31, Levin
Contact: Mary & Deane Robertson
Phone: 06 362 6869
Fax: 06 362 6865
Open: 7 days.
Mail order catalogues free.
Specialist: Trees, Shrubs, Rhododendrons, Roses, BIG Trees

PukoG	Pukeko Gardens, RD3, Hunterville,
Contact: David & Anna Husbands
Phone: 06 328 6855
Open: please phone first.
Mail order catalogue, send SAE.
Specialist: Nerines

Ranch   Ranch North, Clements Rd, RD3, Whangarei
Contact: Sandra Gaskell & John Holdsworth
Not open to public.
Mail order catalogue
Specialist: Louisiana Irises

Reic #   Reichenbach Seeds, PO Box 759, Gisborne,
Contact: Kathy Reichenbach
Phone: 06 862 6398
Fax: 06 867 0496
Mail order catalogue.
Specialist: Seeds

Rhine   Rhinelander Roses, 22 Koromiko St, Christchurch 8002,
Contact: Rosemarie Tonk
Phone: 03 332 1616
Fax: 03 332 1601
Not open to public.
Mail order catalogue.
Specialist: Roses

Richm   Richmond Iris Garden, 376 Hill St, Richmond, Nelson
Contact: Alison & David Nicoll
Phone: 03 544 6513
Open: Display Garden mid-Sep to mid-Nov, Tue-Sat, 9am-12noon.
Mail order catalogue $3, refunded w order.
Specialist: Irises

RosPl   Roslyn Plains, Roslyn Bush, RD2, Invercargill
Contact: Nola & Murray Calvert
Phone: 03 230 4780
Fax: 03 230 4780
Visit only by prior arrangement.
Mail order- dispatch Jan-Mar.
Specialist: Irises

Roswd   Rosewood Nursery, Murphy's Rd, RD1 Pauatahanui, Wellington
Contact: Sue Rowe
Phone: 04 235 5583
Ahr/Mobile: 025 315 533
Open: Wed noon - 5pm, Weekends 9 - 5.30pm.
No mail order.
Specialist: Perennials

Seasd   Seaside Plants, PO Box 18 857, Christchurch,
Contact: Lee Osborn
Phone: 03 388 7099evengs
Visit only by prior arrangement.
Mail order catalogue, send 2 x 40c stamps, min order 12 plants.
Specialist: Coastal Plants

SelGr   Selwyn Grove, Brookside, RD Leeston, Canterbury
Contact: Jenny Chater & Rob Parker
Phone: 03 329 1823
Fax: 03 329 1881
Ahr/Mobile: 025 713 843
Open: phone first.
Mail order catalogue, send 40c stamp.
Specialist: Hedging

Shadi   Shadie Stables, 1 Jamieson Rd, Buckland, RD2, Pukekohe
Contact: Barbara & Katrina Rotherham
Phone: 09 238 8275
Open: 7 Days, 9.30 - 5pm.
Mail order catalogue.
Specialist: Fuschia, Penstemon

Sherl   Sherlock Dahlias, Atkins Rd, RD1, Otaki
Contact:
Phone: 06 362 6698
Open: Thu - Sun, 10 - 4 pm.
Mail order catalogue.
Specialist: Dahlias, Begonias

Simm   Simmons Paeonies, 16 Rountree
St, Ilam, Christchurch 8004
Contact: Paul & Esther Simmons
Phone: 03 348 0777
Fax: 03 348 0777
Mail order catalogue free,send
SAE,or with coloured brochure
$4.
Specialist: Peonies

SoBul   Southern Bulbs, Edendale
Wyndham Rd, Edendale,
Southland
Contact: Rudy & Glenda
Dykgraaf
Phone: 03 206 4940
Fax: 03 206 4940
Specialist: Bulbs

SouWo   Southern Woods Tree Nursery,
PO Box 16 148, Christchurch,
Contact: Murray Manall
Phone: 03 347 9221
Fax: 03 347 9223
Ahr/Mobile: 0800 800 352
Open: Mon -Fri 8.30-5pm, Sat 9-
12noon(April-Nov only).
Mail order catalogue.
Specialist: Trees

SouX   Southern Cross Nurseries, 566
Trents Rd, Prebbleton,
Christchurch
Contact: Dawn, Barry & Andrew
Eagle
Phone: 03 349 3051
Fax: 03 349 9640
Open: Mon-Fri :summer 9-5pm,
winter 10-4pm, Sat Sun 10-
4.30pm, Min order $20 excl p&p.
Mail order catalogue $5.
Specialist: Roses,patio &
miniature

SpecT   The Specimen Tree Co, 180
Princes St East,Otahuhu, PO Box
22 606, Auckland 6
Contact: Shane Potter, Maureen
O'Higgins
Phone: 09 276 1041
Fax: 09 276 1042
Open: daily except Sun.
List available.
Specialist: BIG Trees

StMar   St Martins Geranium Nursery
Ltd, 13A St Martins Rd,
Christchurch 2,
Contact: B.E.R Jones
Phone: 03 332 1872
Ahr/Mobile: 03 332 1872
Open: Oct - Easter daily.
Mail order catalogue $3.
Specialist: Pelargoniums,
Geraniums

SumG   SummerGarden, PO Box 890,
Whangarei,
Contact: Jeffrey Griggs, Vicki
Sampson, Kerry Goodison
Ahr/Mobile: 09 435 1759
Open: please ring first. "Open
weekends" -1st 3 wkds of Dec.
Mail order catalogue $3 in coins
& 80c stamp.
Specialist: Hemerocallis

Sweet   Sweet Cicely Nurseries,
Bulltown Rd, Waihi,
Contact: Thom Tasman &
Wellemyn Pruyt
Phone: 07 863 6322
Open: Tue - Sat 8.30-4.30pm,
Sun 1.30-4.30pm.
Mail order- send large SAE for
catalogue.
Specialist: Herbs (organic BD)

| Taunt | Taunton Gardens, Allandale, RD1, Lyttleton | TopTr | Top Trees Nursery, Ferry Rd, Clive, Hawkes Bay |

Taunt   Taunton Gardens, Allandale, RD1, Lyttleton
Contact: Lyn & Barry Sligh
Phone: 03 329 9746
Fax: 03 329 9746
Open: May-Aug :Fri,Sat,Sun, Sep-Apr 6 days, closed Mon, Display Garden $5.
Mail order catalogue $5, Min order $35, Dispatch Jun-Sep.
Specialist: Rhododendrons, Hostas,Special Plants

Telfa   Telfars Nursery, Beaconsfield Rd, RD24, Stratford 4700
Contact: Bruce & Carmel Telfar
Phone: 06 762 8726
Open: 7 Days.
No mail order but will courier, catalogue available.
Specialist: Perennials, Natives

Terra   Terra Firma,Taupo Native Plant Nursery, 155 Centennial Drive, PO Box 437, Taupo
Contact: Philip Smith
Phone: 07 378 5450
Fax: 07 378 6038
Open: Daily except Sunday.
Mail order catalogue.
Specialist: Natives

Titok   Titoki Point Garden & Nursery, Koukoupo Rd, RD1, Taihape
Contact: Gordon, Annette & Meredith Collier
Phone: 06 388 0085
Fax: 06 388 0085
Open season starts 1st Oct.
Mail order-min 6 plants.
Specialist:
Hosta,Trillium,Woodland & Bog Plants

TopTr   Top Trees Nursery, Ferry Rd, Clive, Hawkes Bay
Contact: Tim Barker,Linda & Chris Ryan
Phone: 06 870 0082
Fax: 06 870 0082
Open: Mon - Fri.
Mail order catalogue, send 6 x 40c stamps.
Specialist: Trees, Shrubs, Fruit Trees

Trans   Trans Plant Nurseries, PO Box 11 217, Ellerslie, Auckland
Contact: Anne Mercer
Phone: 09 579 0780
Fax: 09 579 0780
Not open to public.
Mail order catalogue $2.
Specialist: Perennials,herbs

TreeC   The Tree Centre, 30 Whitcombe Tce, Box 80, Hokitika
Contact: Michael Orchard
Phone: 03 755 7310
Fax: 03 755 7310
Open.
Mail order catalogue, specific seasonal ordering times and dispatch.
Specialist: Fruit Trees, Berryfruit, Books

TRidg   The Ridges, SHW 1, RD1, Marton
Contact: Sally Marshall
Phone: 06 327 8484
Fax: 06 327 8279
Open: daily 10-4.30 pm 20 Sep-30 Nov & 20 Mar - 30 April (not Easter) or by Appointment.
Mail order catalogue $2.
Specialist: Perennials, clematis

Trini Trinity Farm, Waitohu Valley
Rd, Box 50, Otaki Railway, Otaki
Contact: Ann & Lloyd Chapman
Phone: 06 364 6193
Fax: 06 364 6193
Open: 7 days but phone first.
Mail order catalogue.
Specialist: Roses

Trolh Trollheimen Nursery, 32 Sefton
Ave, Grey Lynn, Akl
Contact: Ruth Bookman
Phone: 09 378 4749
Open: ring to arrange time.
Mail order catalogue, send $2.50
in stamps.
Specialist: Lavender

Vall # Vallenders Seeds, c/- Anne
Dodd, 202 Regan St, Stratford
Contact: Anne Dodd
Phone: 06
Mail order only.
Catalogue available.
Specialist: Seeds

VanEe Van Eeden Tulips, West Plains,
4RD, Invercargill
Contact: Philip van Eeden
Phone: 03 215 7836
Fax: 03 215 7821
Open: for display 3 weekends
starting Labour wkd usually.
Mail order catalogue.
Specialist: Bulbs

Wahpa Waihapa Native Plants, Bird Rd,
RD23, Stratford
Contact: Neil & Denise Phillips
Phone: 06 762 2773
Fax: 06 762 2973
Open: only by arrangement.
Mail order catalogue, send SAE.
Specialist: Natives

Waihi Waihi Waterlilies, Pukekauri
Rd, RD2, Waihi
Contact: Laurie & Liz Ball
Phone: 07 863 8267
Open all year, gardens open Nov-
Apr daily.
Mail order catalogue.
Specialist: Water Lilies

WaiMa Waimara, PO Box 374,
Warkworth,
Contact: Ian & Ruth Henderson
Phone: 09 425 9262
Fax: 09 425 9383
Not open, mail order only.
Mail order catalogue $5.
Specialist: Water Gardening

Waire Wairere Nursery, Gordonton Rd,
RD1, Hamilton
Contact:
Phone: 07 824 3430
Open: daily.
Mail order catalogue.
Specialist: Roses

WakaC Wakanui Conifers, Don & Viv
Tantrum, RD1, Taihape
Contact: Don & Viv Tantrum
Phone: 06 388 0635
Fax: 06 388 0635
Open: May - Sep, Ring First
Please.
Mail order catalogue. Dispatch
Winter,Early Spring.
Specialist: Conifers,Timber
Trees,Dwarf Conifers(Not listed)

Warwk Warwick Hills Perennial
Nursery, Falkner Rd, Rere,
Gisborne
Contact: Liz Lane
Phone: 06 867 0820
Fax: 06 867 2473
Open: by appointment.
No mail order , will courier.
Specialist: Perennials

Waysi Wayside Gardens, PO Box 2152, Timaru,
Contact: Derek Irvine
Phone: 03 684 4899
Fax: 03 688 2206
Open by appointment only.
Catalogue not yet available.
Specialist: Paeonia

Wells Wellsford Wholesale Plants Ltd, PO Box 215, Wellsford,
Contact:
Phone: 09 423 8882
Fax: 09 423 8882
Open: most weekends, some weekdays, ring first.
Mail order catalogue.
Specialist: Perennials. Shrubs

Wensl Wensley Forest Nursery, Thomsons Crossing West, 1RD, Winton
Contact: LW Malcolm & Sons
Phone: 0800 521 010
Open: Mon-Fri 8-5pm.
Price list available.
Specialist: Trees

WHazl Wairata Hazels, Wairata Forest Farm, Bag 1070, Opotiki
Contact: Murray Redpath
Phone: 07 315 7763
Mail order list.
Specialist: Hazels

WilAq Wilsons Aquatic Nursery, 190 Lindsay Rd, RD9, Hamilton
Contact: Ian Wilson
Phone: 07 849 5035
Fax: 07 849 5035
Open.
Mail order catalogue $5.
Specialist: Water Lilies, Water Plants

Winga Wingatu Bulbs, 62 Wingatui Rd, Mosgiel,
Contact: Peter & Els McIntosh,Ray Parker,Sharon Corcoran
Phone: 03 489 8557
Ahr/Mobile: 03 473 8103
Mail order only.
Catalogue, dispatch Feb-Apr.
Specialist: Bulbs

Woodl Woodleigh Nursery, 1403 South Rd, RD4, New Plymouth
Contact: Glyn & Gail Church
Phone: 06 7527 597
Fax: 06 7527 657
Mail order only.
Catalogue.
Specialist: Shrubs

Wpuna Waipuna Bamboo Nursery, SH 1, Pakaraka RD2, Kaikohe
Contact: Rex & Debra Shand
Phone: 09 405 9645
Ahr/Mobile: 09 405 9614
Mail order list.
Specialist: Bamboo

WriWa Wrights Water Gardens, RD3, Mauku Rd, Pukekohe
Contact: Malcolm & Dael Wright
Phone: 09 236 3642
Fax: 09 236 3642
Mail order catalogue.
Specialist: Water Lilies, Water Plants

YakuN   Yaku Nursery The
Rhododendron People,
Tikorangi Rd, RD43, Waitara
4656

Contact: Per & Merry Sorenson

Phone: 06 754 4500

Fax: 06 754 4500

Open: Sep-Nov & Mar-May on
Saturdays & Rhodo Festival
Week 9.30-5pm Or by
appointment.

Mail order catalogue $3.50, min
order $35 excl freight.

Specialist: Rhododendrons

ZinoN   Zino Nurseries, PO Box 6,
Hawarden, Nth Canterbury

Contact: Penny Zino, Max
Walker, Leonie Church

Phone: 03 314 4412

Fax: 03 314 4493

Ahr/Mobile: 03 314 4950

Open: 7 days.

Mail order catalogue.

Specialist: Roses